TRUE OR FALSE POPE?

Refuting Sedevacantism
and other Modern Errors

TRUE OR FALSE POPE?

Refuting Sedevacantism
and other Modern Errors

JOHN SALZA
ROBERT SISCOE

Foreword by
HIS EXCELLENCY
BERNARD FELLAY

STAS
EDITIONS

TRUE OR FALSE POPE? -
Refuting Sedevacantism
and other Modern Errors

Published by:
STAS Editions
St. Thomas Aquinas Seminary
21077 Quarry Hill Road
Winona, Minnesota 55987
www.stas.org

ISBN: 978-1-4951-8142-9

Printed and Published in the United States of America
First Edition, First Printing
10 9 8 7 6 5 4 3 2 1

Cover Design: Josef Seno

All Scripture quotations are taken from the Douay-Rheims translation.

To order this book, go to www.trueorfalsepope.com.

Please also see the authors' websites:
www.johnsalza.com
www.robertsiscoe.com

John Salza

John Salza is a *cum laude* graduate of the University of Wisconsin Law School. A practicing attorney for over 20 years, Mr. Salza is also a widely acclaimed Catholic writer and speaker. He is the author of eleven books on the topics of Catholic doctrine, Scripture, Fatima and Freemasonry, including the popular *"The Biblical Basis for..."* apologetics series (*the Catholic Faith; Eucharist; Papacy; Purgatory; Tradition*) published by Our Sunday Visitor and St. Benedict's Press. His book *The Mystery of Predestination – According to Scripture, the Church and St. Thomas Aquinas* (TAN Books) is also considered one of the most important contributions to the field. He is a regular columnist for *Catholic Family News, The Remnant* newspaper, and *The Fatima Crusader* magazine. He has appeared on radio and television programs throughout the world, including the *Eternal Word Television Network* (EWTN), *The Discovery Channel*, and *Church Militant TV*, and has produced a daily Catholic apologetics series for *Fatima TV* called "Apologetics 101." For more information, including books, articles and videos, see www.johnsalza.com.

Robert Siscoe

Robert Siscoe was born and raised in Houston, Texas. He has enjoyed a successful business career, beginning at the age of 23 when he was the top producing trader for an international Forex trading firm. He has founded several successful companies, including a mortgage brokerage firm at the age of 25, and currently works for himself in the insurance and financial industry. Mr. Siscoe converted to the Catholic Church in his 20s and never lost his convert's zeal. He quickly became a fervent student of all things Catholic, with a special interest in theology and metaphysics. Mr. Siscoe is a widely published author. His articles have appeared in publications throughout America and Europe and he is a regular contributor to *The Remnant* and *Catholic Family News*, the two leading traditional Catholic publications in the U.S.A.

Dedication

We dedicate this book to our
Mother and Teacher (*"Mater et Magistra"*),

the One, Holy, Catholic and Apostolic Church,

and to all those who have remained faithful
to her during her mystical Passion.

In imitation of Our Lady's unwavering faith
during the Passion of Her Son,
may we also persevere in our fidelity to the Church,
over whom the gates of hell shall never prevail.

"As divine scripture clearly proclaims, 'Do not find fault before you investigate, and understand first and then find fault.' And does our law judge a person without first giving him a hearing and learning what he does? Consequently this holy and universal synod justly and fittingly declares and lays down that no lay person or monk or cleric should separate himself from communion with his own patriarch before a careful inquiry and judgment in synod. (…) If anyone shall be found defying this holy synod, he is to be debarred from all priestly functions and status if he is a bishop or cleric; if a monk or lay person, he must be excluded from all communion and meetings of the church [i.e., excommunicated] until he is converted by repentance and reconciled."

Fourth Ecumenical Council of Constantinople,
Canon 10 (869-870 A.D.)

"We must point out, besides, that the faithful can certainly distinguish a true prophet from a false one, by the rule that we have laid down, but for all that, if the pastor is a bishop, they cannot depose him and put another in his place. For Our Lord and the Apostles only lay down that false prophets are not to be listened to by the people, and not that they depose them. And it is certain that the practice of the Church has always been that heretical bishops be deposed by bishop's councils, or by the Sovereign Pontiff."

St. Robert Bellarmine (1542-1621 A.D.)

"Three things have been established with certainty, namely, 1) that the Pope, because he has become a heretic, is not deposed *ipso facto* by human or divine law; 2) that the Pope has no superior on earth; and 3) that if he deviates from the faith, he must be deposed…"

Cardinal Thomas Cajetan (1469-1534 A.D.)

"…a heretic should be avoided after two admonitions legally made and with the Church's authority, and not according to private judgment. For great confusion would follow in the Church if it would suffice that this warning could be made by a private individual, rather than by a declaration coming from the Church…Therefore, it is necessary that, just as the Church designates the man and proposes him to the faithful as being elected Pope, thus also the Church declares him a heretic and proposes him as one to be avoided."

John of St. Thomas (1589-1644 A.D.)

Praise for *TRUE OR FALSE POPE? - Refuting Sedevacantism and other Modern Errors*

"The most devastating prosecution of the Sedevacantist thesis in print. Any Sedevacantist who reads this book with an open mind can no longer hold his position in good faith."

-CHRISTOPHER FERRARA, J.D.
President, American Catholic Lawyers Association

"This book appears at a very opportune moment, when increasing numbers of serious Catholics are openly expressing profound disenchantment with the liberalizing direction of the current pontificate. One harmful response to this crisis is Sedevacantism, which claims that the conciliar Popes have not been Popes at all. This book by John Salza and Robert Siscoe is the most detailed and scholarly rebuttal of Sedevacantism yet to appear. They show that while classical theologians and canonists agree that a Pope might fall into formal heresy and so lose his office, these authorities would unanimously reject the modern Sedevacantist approach, which leaves the decision as to whether this has happened – and, if so, what to do about it – to the private judgment of individual Catholics. The last chapter, documenting Sedevacantists' bitter, pride-filled – and inevitable – internal divisions is particularly revealing. Salza and Siscoe are themselves avowed Traditionalists who sharply criticize the revised Roman liturgy and certain Vatican II teachings. But one does not necessarily have to share that stance in order to appreciate their valuable and timely effort to prevent further infliction of wounds on the Church's unity."

-FR. BRIAN HARRISON, O.S.
Emeritus Professor of Theology
Pontifical Catholic University of Puerto

"The most comprehensive, exhaustively documented, well-reasoned critique of Sedevacantism to date. A calm, objective treatment of what can often be an emotional topic. Outstanding work."

-JOHN VENNARI
Editor, Catholic Family News

"With an ever deepening crisis in the Church, Sedevacantism poses a real danger because it offers an apparent solution to a real problem. It does so at the expense of fidelity to the perennial Magisterium of the Church. This masterful tome provides a detailed, well-researched, and persuasive argument against the many varieties of the Sedevacantist position. Salza and Siscoe start at the beginning, presenting a firm grounding in immutable doctrine about the nature of the Church. They proceed to demonstrate how every form of Sedevacantism leads to the denial or distortion of traditional ecclesiology. The authors use prominent Sedevacantists' own words to refute their arguments. All of this vast material is written in an easy to read and understandable style. Anyone who is aware of the crisis in the Church must read this book, destined to become a classic."

-BRIAN MCCALL, J.D.
Associate Dean of Academics
University of Oklahoma College of Law

"I read every page of this book with great interest. It is a thorough treatment of the questions raised by Sedevacantism, grounded in solid Catholic theology, on the Fathers, Doctors and Popes. It will give light to all its readers and be an invaluable help to dispel the confusions caused by the present crisis of the Church. May our Lady, Mother of the Church, obtain these graces of light and love of the Church to all its readers!"

-FR. FRANÇOIS LAISNEY
Former U.S. District Superior
Society of St. Pius X

"This is the most thoroughly researched and articulately presented book of its kind. Whether you are a Sedevacantist, or researching the movement, this book is irreplaceable. Brilliant!"

-TIM STAPLES
Director of Apologetics and Evangelization
Catholic Answers

"For 50 years we at *The Remnant* have fought against the false conclusions of the Sedevacantist thesis. We have insisted that, despite the revolution, the Church is still ours - our castle, our home, our mother and we cannot abandon her. Taking their lead from St. Athanasius during the Arian crisis, John Salza and Robert Siscoe have elevated the discourse of this pivotal debate to an entirely new level that encourages Catholics to keep the old Faith and fight for our Church under siege. This book serves notice to the occupiers of the Catholic Church: Traditional Catholics are not going anywhere. We'll stay and we'll fight until all of 'our buildings' are in the hands of Catholics once again."

-MICHAEL MATT
Editor, The Remnant newspaper

"*True or False Pope?* is simply luminous. This highly readable work of ecclesiology draws from the perennial Magisterium and practice of the Church the light of truth necessary to lay bare the myriad errors of Sedevacantism. Salza and Siscoe expose the common opinions of the greatest theologians in a way accessible to all. This clear exposé of Catholic doctrine will nourish the Faith of all Catholics of good will, while rendering the Sedevacantist thesis untenable.

The authors moreover amply illustrate the principle of true Catholic obedience in today's crisis - "Recognize and Resist." This principle commands us to reverence the Vicar of Christ on Earth and obey him in all things lawful, but to refuse any of his directives at odds with the teaching of Christ as expressed in the constant and infallible Magisterium of the Church. Following the example of St. Peter, we are to obey God rather than man.

Such a calm and scholarly treatment of such an impassioned and tangled controversy is long overdue. Covering a vast territory with unique clarity, it surpasses every work of its kind. *True or False Pope?* is arguably one of the most important books written on the post-conciliar crisis. Serving as a sort of North Star, the book indicates the true path of fidelity to the Church during these disorienting times. May the Blessed Virgin Mary, Morning Star, obtain for its reader this grace of fidelity."

-FR. STEVEN REUTER
Professor, Natural Law Ethics
St. Thomas Aquinas Seminary, Winona

"At last, the English speaking world has in its hands a thoroughgoing refutation of the error of Sedevacantism. Salza and Siscoe did not leave a single stone face down in their seek and destroy mission, lopping off head after head of that hydra which tries in every which way to prove that the Church has no head. The exhaustive completeness of this book is alone sufficient to recommend it to traditionalists for a place on their shelves. With it in their possession, they will never be unprepared when encountering someone looking to shake their faith in Mother Church.

Moreover, in their desire to systematically skewer Sedevacantism, Salza and Siscoe communicate to their readers another great benefit: they patiently and clearly present the constant teaching of the Church on her own nature. Thus, readers are not just informed about the errors of sedes; they are also deepened considerably in their knowledge of the Catholic Faith, particularly in the area referred to as ecclesiology. And is it not precisely the lack of such knowledge that causes Sedevacantists themselves to fall into their despairing position?

As if these two advantages were not sufficient to recommend *True or False Pope?*, I must mention a third: a sobering example is presented in these pages of the grave danger of extreme reactions to the crisis in the Church. We are told by Our Lord to judge by fruits, and the fruits of Sedevacantism are laid out in detail for us to inspect. Its adherents are caught time and again in the act of anathematizing and ridiculing one another, deposing centuries of Popes, creating parallel hierarchies, home-aloneing it, twisting quotes, and arguing sophistically. The impression becomes overwhelming that Sedevacantism is not healthy for the soul, and that this alone is sufficient motive to set it aside.

Let the reader, then, take up this book, expecting to find within its pages a refutation of every Sedevacantist argument that has ever been put forward, a user-friendly presentation of fundamental theology on the Church, and a case study of the effects of Sedevacantism on the soul. *True or False Pope?* would be worth a perusal for possessing only one of these attributes; let all three, then, call out for its purchase and careful reading."

-FR. PAUL ROBINSON
Professor of Dogmatic Theology
Holy Cross Seminary, Australia

Acknowledgments

The authors are grateful to acknowledge the following people who played a role in helping us bring this book to fruition:

His Excellency Bernard Fellay, who graced us with his endorsement and Foreword to this book; Fr. Shannon Collins, Fr. Brian Harrison, Fr. Sean Kopczynski, Fr. François Laisney, Fr. Paul Robinson, Fr. Thomas Scott, Fr. Daniel Themann, Fr. Raymond Taouk, Fr. Stephen Zigrang, Br. Ansgar Santogrossi, and David Rodriguez, who critically reviewed chapters and provided valuable insights; Fr. Yves le Roux (Rector), Fr. Steven Reuter, and Rev. Mr. Reid Hennick of St. Thomas Aquinas Seminary, who provided helpful guidance and assistance; Fr. Paul Robinson, Fr. Brian Harrison, and Ryant Grant, who assisted with Latin translations of original texts; Professor Albert Doskey, who was kind enough to translate the entire treatise of John of St. Thomas on the loss of office for a heretical Pope; Mr. John Vennari, Editor of *Catholic Family News*, and Mr. Michael Matt, Editor of *The Remnant* newspaper, who first published our articles on Sedevacantism; Mr. Laurence Gonzaga, who manages our websites; and countless others who have provided prayers and encouragement over the years.

Table of Contents

Table of Contents - *continued*

Foreword

When we reflect on the crisis of faith in the Catholic Church, our heart cannot but ache for its countless victims, both lay and clerical. The victims who most readily come to mind are those of the "left." Through unwitting obedience to recent Popes, these now profess and practice a faith unrecognizable to our forefathers. Nevertheless, even if smaller in number, those of the "right" must not be overlooked. So scandalized by the deviations of recent Popes, these overreact by denying the papacy to such men. Left or right, both extremes result from the same error — an exaggerated notion of papal infallibility. Charity demands that we show both factions the errors and the dangers in their respective paths.

Concerning the left, the history of our Society bears witness to our constant effort to do just that. But until now — at least in the English-speaking world — only articles and booklets have been published against Sedevacantism and its related errors. A comprehensive and definitive refutation, firmly grounded in ecclesiology, has been sorely needed. We thus pray that *True or False Pope?* finds its way to many Catholics of good will, be they of perplexed mind at the moment. Mr. Salza and Mr. Siscoe's book will surely afford much clarity to the reader, but the underlying mystery will remain: today's crisis touches a mystery that can be confronted only by faith — the mystery of divine suffering.

As Pope Pius XII defined Her, the Catholic Church is the Mystical Body of Christ. At present She is re-living His Passion. Let us take the Blessed Virgin Mary, who stood faithful by her Son's Cross to the very end, as our model of fidelity. The Mother knew her Son to be God Almighty, but knew Him also to be the suffering servant. The suffering was real and not a fantasy as the Docetists taught. These ancient heretics renounced the Incarnation and the Humanity of Christ because of the scandal of the Cross. In like manner the Sedevacantists, succumbing to this same temptation, deny that the visible Church, during Her Passion, remains divine. Let us reassert our belief in the mystery of Her divine and human reality. The Catholic Church is One, Holy, Catholic, and Apostolic, yet composed of fragile members. She is founded on St. Peter and the gates of hell will not prevail against Her.

Our venerable founder, a true son of the Church, suffered very acutely at the sight of his Mother in such a pitiable state. The victims of Sedevacantism who failed to accept this great mystery of the divine suffering augmented his own. Yet, in spite of his suffering, even at the

i

hands of the men of the Church, he refused to abandon Her during Her Passion. It was in this spirit of fidelity that he had founded the Society; it is this spirit that we strive to keep. May Mary, the Mother of Christ and the Church, lead us through the narrow gate and the strait way that leads to life, erring neither to the left nor to the right.

+ Bernard Fellay

Superior General of the Society of Saint Pius X

Feast of All Saints, November 1, 2015

Preface

Since the closing of the Second Vatican Council (1962-1965), the Catholic Church has experienced one of her worst crises in history.[1] Millions of Catholics have defected from the Faith, including countless priests and religious. All aspects of Catholic life (e.g., parishes, schools, seminaries, vocations, baptisms, ordinations, etc.) have experienced rapid decline. According to some reports, the number of seminarians has dropped by more than 90 percent, seminaries by 65 percent, priests by 60 percent, nuns by almost 90 percent, and Catholic high schools by more than 50 percent.[2] What happened?

Honest Catholics would agree that the source of this crisis can be traced to Vatican II and the reforms that have been implemented since the council. However, from this group of people, two extreme camps have emerged. In one camp are the "conservative" Catholics who argue that the crisis has not been caused by Vatican II itself, but by a failure to properly understand the council's doctrines (e.g., ecumenism, religious liberty) and a failure to properly implement its reforms, (e.g., a New Mass, etc.). This position is based upon the Major Premise that whatever comes from or is approved by a true Pope must necessarily be true and good, because "the Pope is infallible." The Minor Premise is that the Vatican II teachings and reforms were ratified by, and therefore came from, the Pope. Therefore, the conservatives' conclusion is that the council's teachings and practices (approved and promoted by the conciliar Popes[3] from John XXIII to Francis) must necessarily be true and good *in themselves*, and consequently the problem can only be

---

[1] As learned Catholics well know, Our Lady warned of this crisis in her apparitions at Quito ("Masonry will enter the Church in the twentieth century"), La Salette ("Rome will lose the Faith and become the seat of the antichrist"), Fatima (the apostasy will begin at the top) and Akita ("the devil will infiltrate the Church").

[2] See, for example, Michael S. Rose, *Goodbye, Good Men* (Washington, D.C.: Regnery Publishing, Inc., 2002, pp. 1-12). See also Tim Unsworth, *The Last Priests in America* (New York: Crossroad Publishing Co., 1991) and John F. Quinn, "Priest Shortage Panic" in *Crisis Magazine*, October 1, 1996; Kenneth C. Jones, *Index of Leading Catholic Indicators: The Church since Vatican II* (Fort Collins, Colorado: Roman Catholic Books, 2003); A. W. Richard Sipe, *Celibacy in Crisis: A Secret World Revisited* (New York: Brunner-Routledge, 2003; and, Richard Schoenherr and Lawrence Young, *Full Pews and Empty Altars: Demographics of the Priest Shortage in United States Catholic Dioceses* (Madison, Wisconsin: University of Wisconsin Press, 1993).

[3] In this book, we use the term "conciliar" to describe something pertaining to the Second Vatican Council. The "conciliar" Popes are those Popes who have ruled the Church since the beginning of the council (John XXIII, Paul VI, John Paul I, John Paul II, Benedict XVI and Francis).

that the teachings and reforms are being misunderstood and improperly implemented.

Those in the other camp begin with the same Major Premise, namely, that whatever comes from or is approved by a true Pope must necessarily be true and good, because "the Pope is infallible." However, they have the opposite Minor Premise. They maintain that the current crisis can be traced to Vatican II's teachings and reforms *themselves*, not simply to a misunderstanding or incorrect implementation of them. This group ends by concluding that the Popes from Vatican II forward could not have been true Popes, but false Popes, since these purported Popes have approved, or at least embraced, the erroneous teachings and reforms of Vatican II. These people are referred to as "Sedevacantists" (from the Latin *sede vacante*, or empty chair), and they hold that we have not had a true Pope since the death of Pius XII in 1958, if not earlier. They claim that since that time, the papal chair has been vacant.[4]

The respective syllogisms,[5] which show the same Major Premise, and the opposite Minor Premise, leading to different Conclusions, are as follows:

The Syllogism of the "Conservatives"

Major Premise:
Whatever comes from or is approved by a Pope
must be true and good because "the Pope is infallible."

Minor Premise:
The conciliar teachings and practices
were approved by the Pope.

Conclusion:
Therefore, the conciliar teachings and practices
must be true and good in themselves (they are only being
misinterpreted and incorrectly applied).

The Syllogism of the Sedevacantists

Major Premise:
Whatever comes from or is approved by a Pope

---

[4] Some even maintain that there may be a secret Pope in hiding.
[5] A syllogism is an argument containing three propositions: two premises (a Major and a Minor) and a conclusion.

must be true and good because "the Pope is infallible."

Minor Premise:
Some of the conciliar teachings and practices
are erroneous and/or harmful.

Conclusion:
Therefore, the conciliar teachings and practices
could not have come from a true Pope.[6]

Both conclusions (of the conservatives and Sedevacantists) are overreactions to the crisis in the Church, resulting in two opposite errors against the Faith. The conservatives' Conclusion (the conciliar doctrines and practices must necessarily be true and good) is erroneous because Vatican II's novel doctrines (e.g., religious liberty, ecumenism) and post-Vatican II practices (e.g., female altar boys, interfaith prayer) are at odds with the pre-Vatican II Magisterium. The Sedevacantists' Conclusion (the conciliar Popes are not true Popes), which is based upon the same erroneous notion of infallibility, ends in a denial of essential doctrines and properties of the Church (e.g., indefectibility, apostolicity, and visibility), as we will further explain in this book.

Both errors are due to the same faulty and incomplete Major Premise, namely: Whatever comes from or is approved by a Pope must be true and good, because "the Pope is Infallible." As we have said, this error is rooted in an erroneous understanding of the dogma of papal infallibility, or, as we will see in Chapter 13, an erroneous understanding of the infallibility of the Ordinary and Universal Magisterium. As St. Thomas says, "a small error in the beginning results in a big error in the end," and this is the case with the Conclusions of both the "conservatives" and Sedevacantists, which is due to the error of their Major Premise (the "error in the beginning").

The correct Major Premise is actually the following: "A true Pope cannot give or approve evil[7] teachings and practices *when he invokes Christ's gift of infallibility*" (which is *not* an habitually active charism).[8]

---

[6] As we will see, Sedevacantists argue that either the Popes were public heretics before being elected (and thus were never validly elected to begin with) or became public heretics after their election (and consequently lost their office at that time). In either case, the Sedevacantists maintain that the evil did not come from true Popes at all, but from false Popes.

[7] The word evil here is being used in the philosophical sense of "a privation of a due good."

[8] A "charism" is a special grace of the Holy Ghost which is ordered to the benefit of the Church. *Cf.*, Catechism of the Catholic Church, para. 799.

After all, Christ granted St. Peter and his successors the *negative* protection of infallibility (immunity from error) only when they "bind or loose on earth" (*cf.* Mt 16:19). It follows that when a Pope does *not* invoke the charism of infallibility (he does *not* "bind" or "loose"), he *can* give evil teachings and practices to the Church (as history proves); but the teachings will *never* be definitively *imposed* upon the universal Church as a revealed truth that *must be believed with Divine and Catholic Faith;* nor will universal practices (disciplines) ever be imposed upon the universal Church which are directly contrary to a revealed truth.

Thus, the current crisis in the Church is not only a crisis of faith, but also *a crisis of infallibility,* and this is so for two reasons. First, the conciliar Popes over the last 50 years have failed to *exercise* their infallibility by defining doctrine and condemning error (indeed, the gift of infallibility does not *inspire* the Popes to teach truth or condemn heresy). Rather, these Popes have chosen to teach in a non-dogmatic and pastoral way, even admitting that Vatican II itself did not define any doctrines with a note of infallibility, nor did it *definitively impose* any erroneous teachings or practices upon the universal Church (which the Holy Ghost would have prevented).

Second, the faithful who have fallen into these errors have failed to understand the Church's definition of infallibility (that is, the scope and parameters of papal, conciliar and disciplinary infallibility), and this, ironically, is very much due to the novel nature of Vatican II. Never before had the Church convoked an ecumenical council (a gathering of the world's bishops in union with the Pope) that did not define any doctrines, nor definitively condemn errors, until Vatican II. Indeed, the Second Vatican Council is in a category of its own, and consequently Catholics have been trying to determine how to qualify its teachings (especially those of a novel character) ever since its last Session closed in 1965.

In so doing, those in the two extreme camps have committed the error of excess, by extending infallibility to all aspects of papal teaching and practice (including the novel Vatican II doctrines and practices) without distinction. This error has led them to conclude either that the novel Vatican II doctrines and practices cannot be considered evil, or that they did not come from true Popes. The cardinal virtue of prudence, enlightened by the true teaching of the Church, strikes at the mean between excess and defect,[9] and, as applied here, leads to the

---

[9] An error of *defect* (as opposed to an error of *excess*) is committed by those on the Liberal Left, who reject doctrines that were infallibly defined in the past, based upon the erroneous notion that truth evolves, or those who maintain that Catholics are only obliged to believe what has been solemnly defined by the Church.

conclusion that while some of Vatican II's teachings are ambiguous and even erroneous, they have not compromised the Church's infallibility. While the current crisis in the Church is, in some ways, unprecedented, the gates of hell have not prevailed against her, and consequently, the visible Church remains indefectible, according to the promise of Christ.

This book primarily critiques the error of Sedevacantism, while also addressing other modern errors which are an overreaction to opposite errors on the Liberal Left. While the Sedevacantist position is held by only an extreme minority of people (less than .001 percent of the Church), its plausibility is nevertheless a question in the minds of certain Catholics who are looking for a simple explanation for the crisis. This need has increased during the reign of Pope Francis, given the many statements he has made which undermine the Faith. Francis' opening the door to admitting sodomites and fornicators to Holy Communion has only added fuel to the fire. Added to this is the controversial resignation of Pope Benedict XVI, which left many publicly questioning if he was forced out, and if he truly intended to renounce the *munus petrinus* (the papal office).[10] Some have come forward publicly and argued that Benedict is still the Pope,[11] while many others secretly hold to this position. While some recognize this as a theoretical possibility, the thesis is problematic and ultimately would have to be decided by the Church.[12]

What cannot be denied is that what we have seen thus far from Pope Francis is extremely troubling. During his short reign, he has

---

[10] The questions surrounding Pope Benedict XVI's resignation have been publicly raised by some of the most prominent journalists in Rome, such as Stefano Violi (Professor of Canon Law at the Faculty of Theology in Bologna and Lugano) and Italy's esteemed writer Vittorio Messori, who hypothesize that Pope Benedict XVI did not intend to renounce the papal office but only the active exercise thereof. In his book *Non e' Francesco: La Chiesa Nella Grande Tempesta* (*It's Not Francis: The Church in a Great Tempest*), Antonio Socci also argues that Pope Benedict's resignation is invalid based, in part, on irregular canonical procedures that Bergoglio himself may have leaked to the public. In his book called *The Great Reformer*, Dr. Austen Ivereigh also questions the canonical validity of Pope Benedict's resignation given the formal conspiracy to get Bergoglio elected, which has also been acknowledged by Cardinal Godfried Danneels (who even admitted publicly that he was part of a secret club of Cardinals who opposed Benedict XVI and supported the election of Francis).

[11] This has been publicly argued by popular traditionalist priest Fr. Paul Kramer.

[12] As we will see in Chapter 12, when a Pope is universally and peaceably accepted by a moral unanimity of the Church, it is an infallible sign that he is a true Pope, and any canonical irregularities in the election are "healed in the root." Due to the controversy surrounding Pope Benedict's resignation and the election of Jorge Bergoglio, coupled with the public doubts being raised about Pope Francis' legitimacy, some have questioned if Pope Francis has, in fact, been peacefully and universally accepted by the Church.

publicly stated that there is no Catholic God; atheists go to Heaven; he doesn't judge sodomites; we shouldn't obsess about sins against nature; counting prayers is Pelagian; proselytism is solemn nonsense; Our Lady may have felt deceived during Her Son's Passion; the souls of the damned are annihilated; Catholics shouldn't breed "like rabbits"; and the greatest evils afflicting the Church are youth unemployment and the loneliness of the aged. Catholics are asking themselves, "Can a true Pope speak like this?" As Fr. Linus Clovis recently said, "There used to be a saying, rhetorical, 'Is the Pope Catholic?' That's no longer funny."[13] Indeed, it isn't funny, especially when such scandalous statements lead scandalized Catholics out of the Church and into one of the Sedevacantist sects.[14] But none of these scandalous statements were in any way contrary to the doctrine of infallibility, since papal infallibility is only engaged when a Pope defines a doctrine, which Pope Francis has never done.

Sedevacantism is a brand new error in the Church, dating back only to the mid-1970s (when the conciliar reforms were in full swing)[15] and no Sedevacantist has produced a detailed, systematic defense of the position to date. No such work will likely be produced, not only because the Sedevacantist thesis[16] is indefensible (and any Sedevacantist *apologia* will now have to answer the many critical objections set forth in this book), but also because Sedevacantists disagree amongst themselves about the most basic "tenets" of their own position. This is because Sedevacantism is founded upon the same root error as Protestantism – namely, private judgment, which inevitably ends in division.

Some Sedevacantists claim the conciliar Popes are not true Popes because they were heretics before their election, while others claim they

---

[13] http://the-american-catholic.com/2015/05/18/popewatch-francis-effect-4/.

[14] By "sect" we mean a Sedevacantist group, which stands in opposition to the Catholic Church by rejecting the conciliar Popes and most of the post-Vatican II hierarchy. The term "sect" is to be distinguished from individual Sedevacantists who have embraced the error out of ignorance.

[15] When we refer to Sedevacantism beginning in the mid-1970s, we mean the movement itself. Some credit Mexican Jesuit priest Fr. Joaquín Sáenz Arriaga (d. 1976) for being the first Sedevacantist. He advocated holding a Conclave to elect a new Pope. Others say Bishop Guérard des Lauriers (d. 1988) was the first actual Sedevacantist. He came up with the *materialiter/formaliter* (also called "Cassiciacum" or "sedeprivationist") thesis, which maintains that the conciliar Popes are legal/material designees to the papacy, but not actual/formal Popes because of their public heresies (discussed in Chapter 10). While Fr. Michael Collin (d. 1974) declared himself Pope in 1950 (during the reign of Pius XII), the Sedevacantist movement actually began in earnest toward the end of the reign of Paul VI.

[16] In this book we use the term "thesis" to mean the main point or claim of the Sedevacantists (that the conciliar Popes are not true Popes).

0 000 0000

were validly elected but fell from their office after the fact, due to public heresy. Some Sedevacantists claim a Pope automatically loses his office for the *sin* of heresy, others for the *crime* of heresy, while others believe a true Pope cannot fall into heresy at all. Some Sedevacantists (called "material-formalists") claim the conciliar Popes are only Popes materially (legal designees to the papacy), but not formally (in fact, or actually), while others say they are not Popes in any way (called "totalists"). Some claim Paul VI *imposed* the New Mass and other harmful disciplines upon the Church, while others say he did not. Some argue that the new rites of ordination of priests and episcopal consecration of bishops are invalid, while others disagree. Some Sedevacantists claim that Vatican II was an infallible act of the Extraordinary Magisterium, while others classify it as being infallible by virtue of the Ordinary and Universal Magisterium (and therefore, that Vatican II violated infallibility by teaching error). The disagreements go on and on. But what is common among them is their belief that the ultimate determination of who is a valid Pope and who is not *is a matter of the private judgment of individual Catholics*, and not the authority of the Catholic Church.

In fact, this ultimate judgment of who is a valid Pope and who is not perhaps best exemplifies the reflexive "Protestant" nature of Sedevacantism. While the majority of Sedevacantists believe the last true Pope was Pius XII, other Sedevacantists have different opinions. Some say the antipopes began with Leo XIII in 1878. Others say the antipopes started with Innocent II in 1130. There is no telling how far back their private judgment will eventually take them. Some Sedevacantists have even convened a "Conclave" and elected their own "Pope" (they are called "Conclavists"). There have been well over a dozen "Popes" elected by the Sedevacantist sects to date, with each purported Pope competing against the others for the office of Vicar of Christ.

For example, Mirko Fabris (d. 2012), a stand-up comedian from Croatia, was elected by a "Conclave" in 1978 and became "Pope" Krav (his stage name). David Bawden, a seminary drop-out who lives with his mother in a farmhouse in Kansas, was elected "Pope" Michael by six lay people including his parents in 1990. During his "reign," Bawden has had to compete with various other Sedevacantist groups who have elected their own "Popes" – namely, Linus II (in 1994), Pius XIII (in 1998), Leo XIV (in 2006), Innocent XIV (in 2007) and Alexander IX (in 2007). Still other Sedevacantists have simply declared themselves Pope without an election, even claiming their election came from Heaven itself, such as Gregory XVII (in 1968), Emmanuel (in 1973), another Gregory XVII (in 1978), Peter II (1980), Gregory XIV (in 1983), another Peter II (in 1995), yet another Peter II (in 2005), Gregory XVIII (in 2011), and John Paul III (in 2015), among others. And those Sedevacantist clerics who have not declared themselves Pope certainly act as *de facto* Popes over their Sedevacantist communities, such as Bishops Clarence Kelly, Donald Sanborn, Mark Pivarunas and Daniel Dolan, as well as Fr. Anthony Cekada, a flamboyant Sedevacantist priest and prolific defender of the sect, whose theories are critiqued in great detail throughout this book.

When you boil it down, people ultimately embrace the error of Sedevacantism, not because of sound theological arguments that favor the position (there are none, as this book demonstrates), but rather because of their inability to believe that God would permit His Church to suffer what the Church is undergoing in the current crisis. Such denial is anything but Catholic. In his 1882 book *The Relations of the Church to Society*, Fr. Edmund O'Reilly warned that we must be careful when it comes to putting limits on what God may permit His Church to undergo. He says:

> "The great schism of the West suggests to me a reflection which I take the liberty of expressing here. If this schism had not occurred, the hypothesis of such a thing happening would appear to many chimerical. They would say it could not be; God would not permit the Church to come into so unhappy a situation. Heresies might spring up and spread and last painfully long, through the fault and to the perdition of their authors and abettors, to the great distress too of the faithful, increased by actual persecution in many places where the heretics were dominant. (...) What I would infer is that we must not be too ready to pronounce on what God may permit. We know with absolute certainty that He will fulfil His promises; not allow anything to occur at variance with them; that He will sustain His Church and enable her to triumph over all enemies and difficulties; that He will give to each of the faithful those graces which are needed for each one's service of Him and attainment of salvation, as He did during the great schism we have been considering, and in all the sufferings and trials which the Church has passed through from the beginning. (...) But we, or our successors in future generations of Christians, shall perhaps see stranger evils than have yet been experienced, even before the immediate approach of that great winding up of all things on earth that will precede the day of judgment. I am not setting up for a prophet... All I mean to convey is that contingencies regarding the Church, not excluded by the Divine promises, cannot be regarded as

practically impossible, just because they would be terrible and distressing in a very high degree."[17]

By arguing that the "terrible and distressing" things which have occurred in the Church since 1958 exceed what God in His Divine Wisdom could possibly permit, Sedevacantists presume to know the limits of the permissive will of God. But what Sedevacantists (and the rest of us) have been experiencing during the last five decades is not the replacement of the true Pope with a false Pope and the true Church with a false Church, but rather the *Passion* of the true Mystical Body of Christ, quite similar to that which was endured by Christ Himself.

Like Our Lord during His Passion, the Church today is bloody, disfigured, and in many respects unrecognizable, but it is still the true visible Church – just as our disfigured Lord was true God as He hung dying upon the cross. Due to this unprecedented ecclesiastical trial that God has permitted, many have lost the Faith *in the Church*, just as the Apostles lost the Faith *in Christ* on Good Friday. During the Passion of Christ, the Apostles retained faith in God's Old Testament revelation (e.g., the promise of the Messiah), but they lost faith that Jesus Christ was the fulfillment of that revelation. In the same manner, during the Passion of the Church, some Catholics have retained faith in God's New Testament revelation (the Catholic Faith), but have lost faith *in the Church*, the Mystical Body of Christ and the divine repository of that revelation.

During the Passion of Christ, the Apostles could no longer discern His divinity, because Christ Himself willed that His divine nature be entirely hidden beneath his disfigured humanity. It is the same with the Passion of the Church today. Her divine *nature (the beauty of her teachings, her sacraments, etc.)* is hidden behind her disfigured human nature (her members) – disfigured in large part due to the action and inaction of the conciliar Popes who have failed to use their infallible teaching authority to define doctrine and condemn error, and instead chosen to conciliate the Church's enemies with the new, ecumenical, pastoral teachings according to "the Spirit of Vatican II." These actions, and lack thereof, have contributed to the disfiguring of the face of the Bride of Christ, changing her appearance while retaining her substance. And so, just as Christ Our Lord suffered at the hands of the High Priest Caiaphas and the leaders of the Old Covenant Church, so it is with the Mystical Body of Christ in our day, which is suffering at the hands of

---

[17] O'Reilly, *The Relations of the Church to Society: Theological Essays* (London: John Hodges, 1892), pp. 287-288. Also quoted in *The Dublin Review*, No. 27 (1874), pp. 249-250.

the conciliar Popes and bishops, the leaders of the New Covenant Church.

In the face of this tremendous crisis, and having lost faith in the Church, Sedevacantists vilify the Church with diabolical fervor. While the Liberals and Modernists attack the Church from within,[18] Sedevacantists attack the Church (their Mother) from without. They expose the wounds of the Church, not so they can be dressed and healed; but in order to mock, ridicule, and discredit the Church. Their criticisms (which in many cases are objectively justified) are not *medicinal* in nature, but poisonous. They end by becoming the enemies of the Church, just as the unbelieving Jews (who claimed to believe in the Old Testament revelation) were the enemies of Christ. "This cannot be the true Church!," the Sedevacantists proclaim. "God would simply not permit it. It is impossible!" And why is it impossible? They claim it is not possible because of the alleged violations of the Church's infallibility. But about this they are gravely mistaken, for nothing that God has permitted has violated any of His promises or the infallibility of His Church, as this book will aptly demonstrate.

The question of the Sedevacantist thesis appeared to weigh heavily on the mind and heart of Archbishop Lefebvre. His Excellency was particularly scandalized by the interreligious prayer meeting held by Pope John Paul II in Assisi in 1986, in which the Vicar of Christ invited members of assorted pagan religions and provided each with a special room where they could offer false worship to their "gods" (a mortal sin against the First Commandment) in the hope of attaining world peace. Even before the event occurred, Lefebvre publicly questioned whether a true Pope could engage in such a sinful and scandalous activity. Yet, Archbishop Lefebvre lived not only to see Assisi in 1986, but also John Paul II's continued and ongoing participation in pagan worship which took place in Kyoto (1987), Rome (1988), Warsaw (1989), Bari (1990) and Malta (1990), and the Archbishop still refrained from declaring the Pope a manifest heretic, which, in his words, would only "lead to interminable, theoretical discussions."

Being the prudent churchman that he was, Archbishop Lefebvre avoided the error of excess, preferring to leave this most serious question for the proper Church authorities. Archbishop Lefebvre's biographer, Bishop Tissier de Mallerais, explains that the Archbishop's preference was to avoid private judgment, even by those in positions of authority, and defer to the Church's authoritative judgment instead:

---

[18] St. Pius X said the Modernists "put their designs for her ruin into operation not from without *but from within*" (*Pascendi Dominici Gregis*, No. 3, September 8, 1907, emphasis added).

"But the wisdom of Archbishop Lefebvre made him feel, to the contrary, that the premises of this reasoning [regarding this question] were as shaky *as the authority that formulated it, be it that of a theologian or even a bishop.*"[19]

Tissier further recounts: "He [Lefebvre] said more than once about these popes – about Paul VI from 1976, and about John Paul II, after the prayer meeting of religions at Assisi in 1986 – that he did not exclude the possibility that these popes were not popes, that one day *the Church* will have to examine their situation, that *a future pope and his cardinals* might have to pronounce the finding that these men had not been popes."[20] For all of the brilliance, education, holiness and supernatural virtue of Archbishop Lefebvre, Bishop Tissier explains that, "But for himself, he preferred to consider them as popes. This supposes that he did not feel that he possessed *sufficient knowledge of the pertinent facts nor the necessary power for making such a judgment.* This is of critical importance to bear in mind."[21] Our years of research into this subject have only confirmed the prudence and sound judgment of this position. And the pernicious fruits of the Sedevacantist sect, which will be discussed throughout the book and especially in Chapter 21, are a further confirmation that the position of the Archbishop was correct, since a good tree does not produce such rotten fruits.

This book responds to the three general arguments used in defense of the Sedevacantist thesis:

1) That the recent Popes have been heretics *and therefore could not be true Popes;*

2) That the men who have been recognized as Pope since Vatican II have done things that a true Pope simply could not do (i.e., violated papal infallibility*), and therefore could not be true Popes;*

3) That the new rite of episcopal consecration, approved by Paul VI, is invalid, and consequently those consecrated

---

[19] *Fideliter*, 1988 (emphases added).
[20] Ibid., (emphasis added).
[21] Ibid., (emphasis added). Because Archbishop Lefebvre preferred to leave the public judgment of *sede vacante* to the Church, and because he believed public disagreement over the question could lead to schism, he suppressed those within the Society who publicly promoted the Sedevacantist position (he even dismissed Fr. Guerard des Lauriers in 1977 and Bernard Lucien in 1979 for their promotion of Sedevacantism; and refused to ordain members of Fr. Olivier De Blignieres' religious community who were openly Sedevacantist).

> bishops in this new rite (Benedict XVI and Francis) are not true bishops, *and therefore could not be true Popes* – since a non-bishop cannot be the Bishop of Rome.

The first and third arguments are based upon the *realm of being*: that is, either the Pope is a heretic (in the realm of being) or a non-bishop (in the realm of being), *and therefore cannot be a Pope.*

The second argument is based upon a conclusion arrived at by considering the *realm of action*: that is, the Pope has *done things* that are not possible for a Pope to do, *and therefore he cannot be a true Pope.*

Responding to all three modes of argumentation, this book is organized as follows. We begin (Chapters 1-2) by considering the Church and its qualities (marks and attributes). These first two chapters, in and of themselves, demonstrate that Sedevacantism is not tenable and, in fact, leads straight to heresy. Next (Chapters 3-4), we provide some very important foundational material on ecclesiology (including how the loss of faith affects membership in the Church, and the loss of ecclesiastical office), which will serve the reader in understanding later chapters, and then address the dogma of No Salvation Outside the Church (Chapter 4). We then address the distinction between heresy and lesser degrees of theological error (Chapters 6-7). Next, we address the issue of whether a Pope can fall into heresy, and, if so, how he would lose his office (Chapters 8-11). In these four chapters, we explore in depth the various theological opinions concerning a heretical Pope, respond to various Sedevacantist arguments and objections, and demonstrate the common agreement among the Doctors and theologians on the role that the Church must play in the determination and deposition of a heretical Pope.

After a transitional chapter discussing the issue of heresy *preventing* a Pope from being validly elected, and the peaceful and universal acceptance of an elected Pope (Chapter 12), we begin our consideration of the Sedevacantist arguments corresponding to the realm of acting (Chapters 13-17). These chapters directly address the alleged violations of infallibility (e.g., conciliar teachings and disciplines, the New Mass, canonizations), which Sedevacantists claim could not possibly have been approved, or even tolerated, by true Popes. We then undertake a detailed and thorough analysis of the new rites of episcopal consecration and ordination (Chapters 18-19). We conclude with material on the "Recognize & Resist" position and the unfortunate, bitter fruits of Sedevacantism (Chapters 20-21). The chapters proceed in an orderly and systematic fashion, with later chapters referring back to and building upon material covered in the earlier chapters.

Before closing this Preface, these authors wish to make it clear that this book is not a defense of the erroneous doctrines and novel practices of the conciliar Popes. To the contrary, our own personal bewilderment over these departures from Catholic teaching and *praxis* has led us to investigate and tackle head-on the question of Sedevacantism, with an open mind. To that end, we have spent the last ten years researching this topic, by studying all of the writings (to our knowledge) of the Church's greatest theologians on the question of a heretical Pope, and the arguments made by the world's leading Sedevacantist apologists. As you will see, our method is to let the Church's theologians and the Sedevacantists speak for themselves.

We have coordinated all this material into a systematic treatment of the major issues, which has resulted in this 700-page book. In the process, we have discovered an abundance of material that Sedevacantists have never addressed, at least publicly, and which proves fatal to their thesis. Our study into this subject has led us from wondering if perhaps the Sedevacantist position provided the answer to the current crisis, to the firm conclusion that it is an utterly erroneous thesis that cannot be defended or held.

We pray that this book will not only assist Catholics who are questioning the legitimacy of the conciliar Popes as they seek to make sense of this crisis, but also those Sedevacantists who have embraced their error in good faith, as an easy answer and simple solution to the crisis. A crisis of this magnitude will require a supernatural solution, and that will come from God alone. He has willed to permit this crisis, no doubt to sift the wheat from the chaff, and it will not last a second longer than He wills. In the meantime, let us recognize and follow the Pope in all things lawful, and resist him if he departs from Christ and the Faith. And to remain unshaken in our faith during this present crisis, let us heed the divinely inspired instruction of St. Paul who teaches us to *stand fast and hold to tradition* (2Thess. 2:14), which, as St. Vincent Lerins said, "can never be led astray by any lying novelty."

John F. Salza
Robert J. Siscoe
3 September A.D. 2015
Feast of Pope St. Pius X

Chapter 1

~ The Church and Its Attributes ~

The Sedevacantist thesis begins by affirming that there is no Pope, and ends in a rejection of the Church itself. Because of this, we will begin our treatment of Sedevacantism by considering what the Church is, how Our Lord Jesus Christ constituted His Church, and the *permanent qualities* with which He endowed it. We will see that these *permanent qualities* enable us to know not only that there *is* one true Church, but also *where* the Church is at all times - even in extraordinary times, such as the Modernist crisis and diabolical disorientation of our day.

In this first chapter, we will consider the Church's *attributes*; in Chapter 2 we will discuss the Church's *marks*. Although the material in the first two chapters is related and, in many ways, interconnected, we have chosen to discuss the marks and attributes separately, as far as possible. These first two chapters will demonstrate that the Sedevacantist thesis is not tenable and, in fact, leads directly to heresy. The chapters that follow will provide a systematic treatment and refutation of the erroneous arguments used to defend Sedevacantism, and which have been used to draw individuals into their sects. All of the arguments and objections presented in defense of Sedevacantism will be addressed *directly* and treated *thoroughly*.

At the outset, it is important to make a distinction between two different but related errors: First, there is the simple error that the post-Vatican II Popes have not been true Popes and that, consequently, the Papal See is vacant (*sede vacante*). The second error, which follows almost immediately, is that the entire Church over which the post-Vatican II Popes have reigned is a false Church. Virtually all who embrace the first error quickly fall into the second. Throughout the book, both of these errors are referred to under the name "Sedevacantism," which is not only a rejection of the recent Popes, but also a rejection of the visible Church founded by Christ, over which the recent Popes have reigned. As we will demonstrate, when one loses faith *in the Church* (the second error), he ends by adhering to a definition of the Church that is virtually identical to that professed by Protestantism, whose founders, coincidentally, also lost faith in the Church.

While most Sedevacantists claim to believe in the Catholic Church, and in the permanent qualities (the attributes and the marks) that constitute and identify the true Church, their refusal or inability to see them in the crucified Church of our day results in a practical denial of their existence (which results in a practical or explicit denial of several articles of Faith). Because the Sedevacantists cannot see these enduring qualities in the post-Vatican II Church (which they claim is a false Church), and further cannot point to a Church that does possess them, they end by reducing the meaning of "Church" to the Protestant concept of a scattered body of "true believers" (rather than a visible institution).

As we will demonstrate throughout this chapter and the next, the unavoidable consequence of their stated position is that "the gates of hell"[1] have indeed prevailed against the *visible Church* founded by Christ. We know, however, based on the promises of Christ, that this cannot be the case. No heresy – not even the "Synthesis of all Heresies"[2] - will ever destroy the Church or take away any of her essential and permanent qualities. Nor will the faithful have to question where she is, for as Our Lord said about the Church: "A city seated on a mountain cannot be hid" (Mt. 5:14).

This is not to say, however, that the human elements of the Church will never disfigure her, in the eyes of men, by their sin and errors. Just as Christ suffered and died in plain view on the mountain of Calvary (bloody and disfigured in His human nature), so too, the Church today, seated on the mountain of Christ, is suffering her own bitter Passion in plain view for all to see. And just as Jesus warned His Apostles, "all of you shall be scandalized in me this night" (Mt. 26:31), so too are many today scandalized as they witness the Church going through her own bitter Passion. And if the Apostles (three of whom having just witnessed the Transfiguration) lost the faith in Christ during His Passion, it should be no surprise that many today have lost the faith in the Church as she undergoes her Passion. But, as with Christ during His Passion, the Church's divine nature remains unchanged, and her marks and attributes are still intact, and recognizable by the faithful – that is, *not* by those who have been so scandalized that they fled, but by those who have remained in faith at the foot of her cross, believing that Christ will remain with His suffering Church "even to the consummation of the world" (Mt. 28:20).

---

[1] Pope Vigilius defined the "gates of hell" as the "death-dealing tongues of heretics" (Second Council of Constantinople, 553 A.D.) and Pope St. Leo IX similarly referred to them as "the disputations of heretics" (*In terra pax hominibus*, 1053 A.D.).
[2] This is the term Pope St. Pius X used to refer to the error of our times, known as Modernism (*Pascendi*, No. 39, September 8, 1907.)

We will now discuss what the Church is, and then consider the attributes that perfect her nature. Although some of the material that follows may seem basic for some, it is necessary to lay the foundation so that the errors that will be addressed at the end of the chapter and throughout the rest of the book will be more clearly understood. We will close the chapter by addressing what is known as the "Siri Theory."

What is the Church?

The Roman Catholic Church is the Mystical Body of Jesus Christ on Earth, the supernatural and supranational society founded by Our Lord for the salvation of mankind. The Church of Christ is not an invisible society of true believers known to God alone. It does not consist only of the just (as Luther taught) or only the predestined (as Calvin held). Nor does the Church exclude sinners, for it consists of both good seed and bad (Mt. 13:30). The Church was not established by a group of individuals who, professing belief in Christ as the Messiah, came together to form a community; nor was the Church *indirectly* founded by Christ through the agency of men with whom He entrusted the task.

Rather, the Church of Christ was instituted personally and directly by the Son of God, Our Lord Jesus Christ,[3] as a *visible hierarchical society*.[4] It was established upon the foundation of the Apostles and the prophets before them, with Our Lord as its cornerstone (Eph. 2:20-21) and St. Peter its visible head (Mt. 16:18-19). Blessed Peter, and his perpetual successors, serve as the principle of unity, and the visible foundation, in the Church.[5] As Vicar of Christ, the Pope receives his authority directly from Christ, and visibly represents Him, who is the true but *invisible* Head of the *visible* society.

Christ Establishes the Papacy

The divine institution of the papacy is revealed in the Gospel of St. Matthew, Chapter 16, when Christ declared to Simon:

---

[3] The Oath Against Modernism: "With unshaken faith I believe that the Church was immediately and directly established by the real and historical Christ Himself while he was living in our midst." (Denz., 2145).

[4] "Christ established the Church as a hierarchical society ... This thesis is historically certain, it is theologically *de fide*" (Tanquery, *Dogmatic Theology*, Vol I. p. 107).

[5] Vatican I: Dogmatic Constitution *Pastor Aeternus*, §1 (July 18, 1870).

"That Thou art Peter; and upon this rock I will build my Church, and the gates of hell shall not prevail against it. And I will give to thee the keys of the kingdom of heaven. And whatsoever thou shalt bind upon earth, it shall be bound also in heaven: and whatsoever thou shalt loose upon earth, it shall be loosed also in heaven." (Mt. 16:18)[6]

The primacy of St. Peter, as head of the universal Church, was a personal prerogative of St. Peter alone, insofar as it was not given to the other Apostles; but it was not a personal prerogative in the sense that it was to die with him. Just as Christ's Church was established to continue until Our Lord's Second Coming, so too was the office of Peter to continue perpetually through his successors. Consequently, the papacy is a permanent office that will be filled by the successors of St. Peter until the end of time. And, as history confirms, there has been a continuous succession of Popes occupying the Chair of St. Peter since the beginning.

In a letter written against the Donatist schism, St. Augustine provided a list of St. Peter's successors up to his day. He wrote:

"For if the lineal succession of bishops is to be taken into account, with how much more certainty and benefit to the Church do we reckon back till we reach Peter himself, to whom, as bearing in a figure the whole Church, the Lord said: 'Upon this rock will I build my Church, and the gates of hell shall not prevail against it!' Matthew 16:18. The successor of Peter was Linus, and his successors in unbroken continuity were these:— Clement, Anacletus, Evaristus, Alexander, Sixtus, Telesphorus, Iginus, Anicetus, Pius, Soter, Eleutherius, Victor, Zephirinus, Calixtus, Urbanus, Pontianus, Antherus, Fabianus, Cornelius, Lucius, Stephanus, Xystus, Dionysius, Felix, Eutychianus, Gaius, Marcellinus, Marcellus, Eusebius, Miltiades, Sylvester, Marcus, Julius, Liberius, Damasus, and Siricius, whose successor is the present Bishop Anastasius." (St. Augustine, Letters 53:1:2, A.D. 412)[7]

It is an article of Faith, defined by the First Vatican Council, that Blessed Peter will have a continuous line of successors:

---

[6] For further information, including extensive Scriptural and patristic testimony and analysis, see John Salza's *The Biblical Basis for the Papacy* (Huntington, Indiana: Our Sunday Visitor, 2007).
[7] Schaff, Philip, *A Select Library of the Nicene and Post-Nicene Fathers of the Christian Church*, vol. I (New York: Charles Scribner and Son's, 1907), p. 298.

"For no one can be in doubt, indeed it was known in every age that the holy and most blessed Peter, prince and head of the apostles, the pillar of faith and the foundation of the Catholic Church, received the keys of the kingdom from our lord Jesus Christ, the savior and redeemer of the human race, and that to this day and for ever he lives and presides and exercises judgment in his successors the bishops of the Holy Roman See, which he founded and consecrated with his blood. Therefore whoever succeeds to the chair of Peter obtains by the institution of Christ himself, the primacy of Peter over the whole Church. ...

Therefore, if anyone says that it is not by the institution of Christ the Lord Himself (that is to say, by divine law) that blessed Peter <u>should have perpetual successors (*perpetuos successores*) in the primacy over the whole Church</u>; **or** (*aut*) that the Roman Pontiff is not the successor of blessed Peter in this primacy: let him be anathema."[8]

Two articles of Faith must be affirmed according to the above teaching: 1) By Divine law, St. Peter will have *perpetual successors* in the primacy, and 2) the Roman Pontiff is the successor of St. Peter in this primacy. Notice that the two clauses in the above citation are separated by "or" (Latin, *aut*) to distinguish that St. Peter will have "perpetual successors in the primacy" from the dogma that the Roman Pontiff is the successor of St. Peter. The Vatican Council makes a clear distinction between the primacy of the papal office, which will continue until the end of time, and the individual Popes – the "perpetual successors" - who fill the office. Thus, they are each dogmas in their own right (the former refutes the errors of Protestantism and Eastern Orthodoxy while the latter refutes Sedevacantism). This means the Church will *always* be able to elect a new Pope to fill the chair of St. Peter after the death or resignation of the former Pope (of course, having a perpetual office does no good unless the Church is able to fill the office with a successor).

Now, because Sedevacantists claim we have not had a successor of St. Peter for the past six decades (or longer), some will attempt to *limit* the council's teaching to affirming that the *office* of Peter will continue until the end of time (i.e., that the primacy didn't die out when Peter died), but *not* that there will be "perpetual successors in the Primacy."

---

[8] First Vatican Council, Session IV, Ch. II, 1870 (emphasis added). The phrase "perpetual successors in the primacy" also confirms that those whom the Church elects to fill the vacancy *are legitimate successors to St. Peter*. Latin: "*Si quis ergo dixerit, non esse ex ipsius Christi Domini institutione seu iure divino, ut beatus Petrus in primatu super universam Ecclesiam habeat perpetuos successores:* <u>*aut*</u> *Romanum Pontificem non esse beati Petri in eodem primatu successorem: anathema sit.*" (Denz., 1825).

They will no doubt concede that those who are elected to serve in the "perpetual office" (and who they personally accept as being true Pope) are the successors of St. Peter in the same primacy, but again, their position requires them to deny the council's plain teaching that there will be a *perpetual line of successors* until the end.

In response to a questioner during one of his talks, the Sedevacantist preacher, Gerry Matatics, revealed how he and his colleagues are forced to deny the teaching of the First Vatican Council:

> "Questioner: 'Concerning an article in Vatican I. People against Sedevacantism state that in Vatican I, there is an anathema that says those who believe that there will not be a pope until the end of time, let him be anathema. So what do you say…?'
>
> Matatics: 'OK, very good … doesn't Vatican I exclude Sedevantism when it says that Peter will always have perpetual successors until the end of time, and anathematizes those who say otherwise? … Vatican I does not say that Peter will always have successors, in the sense that there will always be a pope at any given time… In the Latin it is in the present tense, it says 'Peter has successors,' <u>in other words, the office of Peter is not an office that died with him</u>. There are successors to it; <u>that's all that Vatican I is stating</u> – that the papacy is an office that does continue in the Church. It didn't die when Peter died.'"[9]

So, Mr. Matatics claims that Vatican I's reference to "perpetual successors in the primacy," *only* means that the *office* of the papacy will continue, and not that there will be a continuous line of successors who fill the office (as if the office could have any significance without a successor of St. Peter to fill it). In his answer, Mr. Matatics not only conveniently omitted the word "perpetual" from his quotation of the infallible Vatican I canon, but he also erred in claiming that the verb "has" is in the present tense ("Peter *has* successors"), meaning the present indicative. No, the Latin verb *habeat* is in the present subjunctive which means that the sentence expresses the idea of an efficacious purpose or intention, looking to the future (Christ established that St. Peter *would have* perpetual successors) rather than a simple statement of what currently happens to be the case (St. Peter *has* successors).

Mr. Matatics then referred to some unidentified theologians who, he claims, have held that an *office* can continue to exist for up to 100 years if it is not actually filled (which begs the question of why 100

---

[9] Matatics, Compact Disc ("CD") talk entitled, "Counterfeit Catholicism vs. Consistent Catholisism," Second Edition 2008 (Revised and Expanded), disc 4 of 6, track 15.

years and not something more or less?). He then asserted that, according to this teaching, the *office* of Peter would only cease to exist if it were vacant for more than 99 years. Unfortunately, in addition to his omission of "perpetual" and erroneous understanding of the Latin, Mr. Matatics does not quote a single authority to support his assertion that Vatican I's use of "perpetual successors in the primacy" means only that the *office* will continue, and not that there will be a *continuous line of successors* who fill the office. This is because Mr. Matatics' view directly contradicts what the Church's theologians teach regarding the matter.

During the same talk, Mr. Matatics said one of his "favorite authors is Fr. E. Sylvester Berry, professor of Scripture at Mt. St. Mary's Seminary... in the 1920s and 30s." He then referred to Fr. Berry's "wonderful book called *The Church of Christ*."[10] Since Mr. Matatics publicly praises this author and book, let's listen to what Fr. Berry himself teaches in the book about the unbroken line of successors to St. Peter. Commenting on the above teaching from the First Vatican Council, Fr. Berry explains that "the primacy with all its powers and privileges is transmitted to the successors of St. Peter, *who form an unbroken line of supreme pastors to rule the Church in its continued existence.*" A little later, he adds: *"the Church must ever have a custodian, a supreme law-giver and judge, if she is to continue as Christ founded her."*[11] So one of Mr. Matatics' "favorite authors" teaches that "the Church must ever have a custodian," whereas Mr. Matatics claims that the Church hasn't had a custodian for two or three generations.

Msgr. Van Noort teaches the same as Fr. Berry. He wrote: "it is a fact beyond question that *the Church can never fail to have a successor to Peter...*"[12] Commenting further on the same point, he wrote: "Since Christ decreed that Peter should have a *never-ending line of successors* in the primacy, there must always have been and there must still be someone in the Church who wields his primacy."[13]

Contrary to what Mr. Matatics claims, the First Vatican Council not only affirmed that the Pope holds the primacy of St. Peter (and that the *office* is perpetual), but *also* that St. Peter will always have perpetual successors to rule the Church.[14] Needless to say, this poses an

---

[10] Ibid., disc 4 track 9.
[11] Berry, *The Church of Christ*, (Eugene, Oregon: Wipf and Stock Publishers, 2009, previously published by Mount Saint Mary's Seminary, 1955), pp. 196-197 (emphasis added).
[12] Van Noort, *Christ's Church*, (Westminster, Maryland: Newman Press, 1961), p. 153 (emphasis added).
[13] Ibid., p. 75 (emphasis added).
[14] See also Ludwig Ott, *Fundamentals of Catholic Dogma*, (Rockford, Illinois: TAN Books and Publishers, Inc., 1974), p. 282.

insurmountable problem for Sedevacantists who claim that the Church has been unable to elect a Pope *for generations*. While it is true (as the Vatican Council Fathers were obviously aware) that there is a temporary vacancy during an interregnum (following the death of one Pope and the election of another), the Church has *never failed* to provide a successor to St. Peter.[15]

In the post-Vatican II era, the Church has not failed to provide a successor of St. Peter. Following the death (or resignation) of each Pope, a Conclave has been convened and a Pope elected. He may not have been a good Pope, but a Pope was nevertheless elected to fill the Chair of St. Peter.

The Church is Both Human and Divine

The Church is at once human and divine, natural and supernatural. Christ, her Divine Founder, is the true Head of the Church. The Church is a supernatural society in her origin, constitution and purpose, as well as in her authority and means of sanctification. But the Church is also a human society, insofar as it consists of human members. Pope Leo XIII wrote:

> "God indeed even made the Church a society far more perfect than any other. For the end for which the Church exists is as much higher than the end of other societies as divine grace is above nature, as immortal blessings are above the transitory things on the earth. Therefore the Church is a society divine in its origin, supernatural in its end and in means proximately adapted to the attainment of that end; but it is a human community, inasmuch as it is composed of men."[16]

As a divinely instituted society, the Church is also a "perfect society," which means it is complete in and of itself, and not dependent upon any other society for its existence or for the attainment of its end.[17] Yet, because the Church consists of human members subject to

---

[15] The *longest* interregnum was three and one-half years between the death of Pope St. Marcellinus (296-304 A.D.) and the election of Pope St. Marcellus (308-309 A.D).
[16] Pope Leo XIII, *Satis Cognitum* (No. 10, June 29, 1896).
[17] Both the Church and the State are perfect societies. The end or purpose of the State is the temporal good; the end or purpose of the Church is the spiritual good and salvation of man. While the two societies are distinct, they should not be altogether separated, but should work together for the good of the whole man (for both his natural and supernatural ends), with the temporal society reflecting the moral law of God in its laws, and looking to the Church for guidance. Pope Leo XIII brilliantly explicated these

sin and error, her divine nature can, at times, be obscured by her human nature. But even in those times in which her divine nature seems to be eclipsed by her weak and wavering human members, she will never disappear or be destroyed, and in her divine nature there will be "no change, nor shadow of alteration" (Jam. 1:17).

The Life of the Church

The life and existence of the Church Militant will reflect the earthly life of its Head. Just as Christ suffered, so too will the Church suffer. As Our Lord endured a Passion at the end of His life, so too will the Church undergo a Passion before the Second Coming. But, like Christ the King, she too will rise again. In the words of Pope Pius XII:

> "[T]he society established by the Redeemer of the human race resembles its divine Founder, who was persecuted, calumniated and tortured by those very men whom He had undertaken to save."[18]

Persecution (whether externally or internally) has been called a *quasi-mark* of the true Church. Fr. Sylvester Berry, in his book *The Church of Christ*, elaborated on this point. He wrote:

> "Persecution may serve as a quasi-mark of the Church ... Christ has foretold that His Church must suffer unrelenting hatred and persecution: 'If the world hates you, know that it hated me before you...As Christ was hated, despised, calumniated, and persecuted in His natural body, so also shall He be in His mystical body, the Church. Therefore a Church that is not thus despised and persecuted, can scarcely be the one which Christ had in mind when He uttered the words quoted above. It is always consoling to realize that those who calumniate the Church and stir up persecution against her, are fulfilling the prophecies of Christ and thus unwittingly prove her divine character. Thus does 'He that dwelleth in Heaven laugh at them; and the Lord derided them' (Psalm 2:4)."[19]

---

principles in such encyclicals as *Immortale Dei*, No. 10, November, 1885 and *Libertas*, No. 18, June 20, 1888.

[18] *Mystici Corporis Christi*, No. 3, June 29, 1943.

[19] Berry, *The Church of Christ*, p. 89.

The Church's Properties

The Church's properties are those qualities that flow from her very *essence* and which are necessarily a part of her *nature*. Although authors sometimes differ in their enumeration of these properties, the difference is primarily one of method and terminology rather than the subject matter itself. The properties of the Church can be aptly broken out into seven distinct qualities: four *marks* and three *attributes.*

The *marks* of the Church are distinctive characteristics that render the Church *recognizable* to all, and clearly distinguish it from every other religious society.[20] The four marks of the Church are, as we profess in the Nicene Creed, that she is "one, holy, catholic (universal), and apostolic."[21] (These *marks* will be treated separately in the next chapter.) The *attributes* are those inherent qualities of the Church that perfect her nature. The three attributes can be listed as perpetual-indefectibility, visibility, and infallibility.

In spite of all the trials that God may permit His Church to suffer throughout the course of her existence, she will *always* retain these properties, precisely because they are essential to her true nature.[22] There will not be a moment in time when the Church will lack a single one of them, for the Church's organic constitution is immutable.[23]

The Church is Visible

The Catholic Church was constituted by Christ as a visible society. For this reason, it is described in Scripture as a city seated on a mountain or hill:

> "[T]he Church, as a city seated on a mountain, shall ever be visible. 'Neither the sun nor the sun's light is so plain as the

---

[20] "The true Church of Christ was established by Divine authority, and is known by a fourfold mark, which we assert in the Creed must be believed; each one of these marks so cling to the others that it cannot be separated from them." (Letter of the Holy Office under Pius IX, September 18, 1864, Denz., 1686).

[21] In *Mystici Corporis Christi*, Pius XII adds a fifth mark: "If we would define and describe this true Church of Jesus Christ - which is the One, Holy, Catholic, Apostolic <u>and Roman Church</u>, we shall find nothing more noble, more sublime, or more divine than the expression 'the Mystical Body of Christ.'" (No. 13, June 29, 1943).

[22] "The Church can never lose a single one of them [her properties], nor fail in her existence. In other words, the Church founded by Christ must exist until the end of time without any essential change." (Berry, *The Church of Christ*, p. 31).

[23] In his encyclical *Lamentabili*, Pope St. Pius X condemned the proposition of the Modernists who held that "the organic constitution of the Church is not immutable." (Denz., 2053).

Church: for the house of the Lord is on top of the mountains,' says St. John Chrysostom. 'There is no safeguard of unity,' wrote St. Augustine, 'save from the Church made known by the promises of Christ – a Church which being seated on a hill, cannot be hid. Hence it is known to all parts of the world.'"[24]

Now, no one denies that the *members* of the Church are visible, but the visibility of its members alone is not what is meant by the *visible Church*. Protestants erroneously profess an *invisible* Church ("an invisible society of true believers known to God alone"), but they do not deny that the *members* of the Church are *visible*. As we will see, the Sedevacantists, having lost the faith in the Church, have come to profess the same Protestant error, which reduces the notion of the "visible Church" to "visible members" who profess the true Faith.

They both err by not realizing that the Church is a permanent *visible society* – a visible social unit – composed of a divinely instituted hierarchy[25] (a Pope, bishops, priests, deacons) and laity. This *visible society* will always exist, because it is the *visible society*, as such, to which the promises of Christ apply: "the gates of hell shall not prevail against it," and "I will be with you all days, even to the consummation of the world," etc. According to the promises of Christ, the visible society can never be substantially altered or transformed into a false Church; nor can it be reduced to an invisible society loosely composed of merely *visible members*.

Commenting on the visible character of the Church, Van Noort wrote:

> "That the Church is visible follows necessarily from the fact that it is a real society, for there can be no genuine society in the world of men unless it be visible. (...) No one denies that the Church's members are visible, for they are flesh and blood people; but some do question whether, by the institution of Christ Himself, these members are bound together by external bonds so as to form a society that can be perceived by the senses, a society of such a nature that one readily discerns who belongs to it and who does not."[26]

---

[24] *Publications of the Catholic Truth Society*, vol. 24, (London: Catholic Truth Society, 1895), pp. 8-9.
[25] "If anyone says that in the Catholic Church a hierarchy has not been instituted by divine ordinance, which consists of bishops, priests, and ministers, let him be anathema" (Council of Trent, Denz., 966).
[26] *Christ's Church*, p. 12.

25

In Chapter 3, we will discuss in detail the *internal* and *external bonds* that unite a person to the visible society. For now, it is important to emphasize, once again, that it is this *visible society* as such (and not individual "true believers") to which the promises of Christ apply. Van Noort[27] affirms:

> "Once one proves that the one and only Church which Christ founded is *visible from its very nature*, then it necessarily follows: (a) that an invisible Church such as that to which Protestants appeal is a pure fiction, and (b) that all the promises which Christ made to His Church refer to a visible Church."[28]

The Nature of Visibility

Visibility signifies two things: 1) that the thing can be seen; and 2) that it can be known for what it is. The *material aspect* of visibility is the object of the senses (what the senses perceive); the *formal aspect* of *visibility* is the object of the intellect (the *quiddity*[29] – or the "whatness" of the thing).

In his comprehensive book, *The Creed Explained* (1897), Fr. A. Devine explains the distinction between formal and material visibility:

> "*Material visibility* is that which we see in a thing, when we attend only to its corporeal aspect. In this sense a man, as to his body, is visible. *Formal visibility* is when the external signs, or that which is seen by the eye, conveys to the mind the invisible or interior qualities of a thing."[30]

The following example will help to illustrate this point:

A person may see an animal (a deer, for example) running through the woods, but be unable to tell what it is he sees. The senses perceive

---

[27] We are citing Van Noort extensively, primarily because he is so highly respected among most Sedevacantists. In fact, after posting a portion of Msgr. Van Noort's dogmatic manual on his website, the Sedevacantist apologist, John Lane, stated that no one is permitted to comment on the topic in question until they have read the material from Van Noort. He then added: "Nor is anybody permitted to disagree with Monsignor Van Noort unless they can quote another theologian doing so." Thus, we will demonstrate the error of Sedevacantism based upon the teaching of their own favorite authorities (Van Noort, Bellarmine, etc.). Citation from Mr. Lane found at http://www.strobertbellarmine.net/viewtopic.php?f=2&t=124).

[28] Ibid., p. 13 (emphasis added).

[29] The term *quiddity* is a philosophical term which means the inherent nature or essence of someone or something.

[30] Rev. A. Devine, *The Creed Explained, an Exposition of Catholic Doctrine*, 2nd ed. (New York, Cincinnati, Chicago: Benzinger, Bros., 1897), p. 265.

something running, but the intellect does not yet know *what* it is. If the animal runs into a clearing, the intellect will be able to judge what it is that the senses perceived. This example helps to illustrate the twofold visible character of material beings: the *material visibility,* which is the external visible qualities (what is perceived by the senses) and the *formal visibility,* which is the *quiddity* (what the thing is). The senses perceive *something,* but it is the job of the intellect to know *what* it is.

Now, a religious society also possesses a formal and material visibility. The material visibility is its members, its rites and ceremonies, the places where its members meet, etc. By perceiving (with the senses) the external characteristics, the intellect can apprehend that it is: 1) a religious society and, with further abstraction: 2) what particular religion it is. In other words, the intellect is not only able to apprehend that a particular group (Jews, Muslims, or Protestants) is some kind of religious society, but it can also deduce which religious society it happens to be. Let us listen to Fr. Devine:

> "A Society is said to be visible in a material sense, when it is made up of men assembled together in a congregation, without attending to the object or ends that binds them together in one body. ... The formal visibility of a society is that by which we regard it, not merely as an assembly of men, but an assembly of men united together for some specific object .... When we speak of the visibility of the Church, we have to understand that it is not only visible in the material sense, that is, a society of men who are visible to their fellow-creatures, but in a formal sense, that is, that she can be seen as the society of the faithful, and that she manifests conspicuously the characters of her divinity. ... The Church is visible in this two-fold sense."[31]

In light of the above explanation, we can better understand what is meant by the visible character of the Church. It does not merely refer to its *members* being visible; nor does its visibility simply imply that it can be known as a religious society. The *visibility* of the Catholic Church is such that it can be known to be *the true Church* established by Jesus Christ. What makes it possible for the Catholic Church to be known as the true Church are the four *marks* which she possesses, namely, she is *one, holy, catholic (universal)* and *apostolic.* Van Noort explains the visibility of the Church as follows:

---

[31] Ibid., pp. 265-266.

"The visible form of the Church, which is the subject of this present discussion, must not be confused with what is strictly its knowability. It is one thing to ask whether the Church which Christ founded is a public society, and quite another to ask whether that society can be recognized *as the true Church of Christ* by certain distinguishing *marks*. Its being formally recognizable presupposes its being [materially] visible, but the two are not identical."[32]

In his book, *The Church of Christ*, Fr. Berry wrote the following about the visible character of the Church:

"When we say that the Church of Christ is visible, we mean, primarily, that it is a society of men with external rites and ceremonies and all the external machinery of government by which it can easily be recognized as a true society. But we further maintain that the Church of Christ also has certain *marks* by which it may be recognized as the one true Church founded by Christ when He commissioned the apostles to convert all nations. In other words, we maintain that the Church of Christ is *formally visible*, not only as a society known as a Christian Church, but also as the one true Church of Christ."[33]

Elaborating further, he adds:

"The Church of Christ is *formally visible*, not only as a Church, but also as the true Church of Christ. This is an article of faith, having been defined by the [First] Vatican Council in the following words: 'God established a Church through His only begotten Son, and endowed it with manifest marks [material visibility] of its institution, that it might be <u>known</u> by all [formal visibility] as the guardian and teacher of the revealed word.'[34] This is a clear and comprehensive definition of formal visibility. The Church has certain evident marks by which it can be recognized as the true Church of Christ, the guardian and teacher of the revealed word."[35]

He continues:

"The thesis contains two propositions: (a) the Church is an external society that can be recognized as such by all, - and its formal visibility as a religious society or Church; (b) This society

---

[32] *Christ's Church*, p. 12 (emphasis added).
[33] *The Church of Christ*, p. 37 (emphasis added).
[34] Denz., 1793.
[35] *The Church of Christ*, pp. 39-40.

has certain *marks* by which it may be distinguished from all other churches and recognized as the true Church, - it is *formally* visible as the true Church... it has been amply proved that Christ established His Church under the form of an *external visible society*."[36]

In his book, *The Pillar and Ground of Truth*, published in 1900, Fr. Thomas E. Cox explained that "the Church which Christ established is a visible, tangible institution, capable of being known and pointed out."[37] He then added:

"The visibility of the Church follows of necessity if there exists an obligation to enter the Church. God could not command me to hear a Church that could not be known, nor to enter a Church that could not be found."[38]

We can see that the Catholic Church is an *external visible society* that can be *known*, by the light of reason alone, to be the true Church founded two millennia ago by Jesus Christ.[39] This is what is meant by the visibility of the Church.

Perpetual Indefectibility

The Church also possesses the inherent qualities of indefectibility and perpetuity, which are closely related to one another, and often combined into one single attribute. Fr. Berry defines *indefectibility* as "the inability to fail, to fall short, to perish." He continues: "Applied to the Church it means that she cannot be deprived of any essential power or quality, so long as she continues to exist."[40] In short, *indefectibility* guarantees that the Church will always possess the four marks and

---

[36] Ibid., p. 40 (emphasis added)

[37] Cox, T. E., *The Pillar and Ground of Truth, a Series of Lenten Lectures on the True Church, Its Marks and Attributes* (Chicago: J.S. Hyland and Co., 1900), p. 36.

[38] Ibid., p. 37.

[39] As Wernz and Vidal note in their commentary on canon law, arriving at the knowledge that the Catholic Church is, in fact, the true Church requires moral diligence. They wrote "the visibility of the Church consists in the fact that she possesses such signs and identifying marks that, when moral diligence is used, she can be recognized and discerned, especially on the part of her legitimate officers." (Wernz-Vidal, *Commentary on the Code of Canon Law. 454 Scholion.*) Even in the midst of our current ecclesiastical crisis, the formal visibility of the Church can be known, although it may require greater moral diligence to arrive at the conclusion. This is especially true if the Church is viewed in light of her current condition (as she suffers her Passion), rather than simply from a historical perspective.

[40] *The Church of Christ*, p. 29.

three attributes. *Perpetuity* means that the Church will continue to exist until the end of the world. Comparing these two qualities of the Church and their relation to one another, Fr. Berry wrote:

> "*Perpetuity* is indefectibility in existence. Strictly speaking, *indefectibility* pertains to the essential qualities of the Church, *perpetuity* to her existence. These two qualities, although distinct, are so closely related that it is difficult to treat them separately. ... the two attributes may be combined as *perpetual indefectibility*."[41]

When combined, these attributes tell us that the *visible society* founded by Christ must continue to exist until the end of time, exactly as He founded her, with all of her qualities – that is, with her *marks* and *attributes*. "If the Church is indefectible in her essential qualities and perpetual in her existence," wrote Fr. Berry, "she must be perpetually indefectible in all essential qualities."[42]

The Church may be persecuted from without, and Our Lord may even permit it to be infiltrated and persecuted from within for a time, but it will never be destroyed. St. Jerome said:

> "We know that the Church will be harassed by persecution until the end of the world, but it cannot be destroyed; it shall be tried, but not overcome, for such is the promise of an omnipotent God whose word is as a law of nature."[43]

Referring to the Church's perpetuity, Msgr. Van Noort wrote:

> "The present question has to do with the perpetuity of that Church which alone was founded by Christ, the *visible Church*. Any society can fail in either of two ways: it can simply cease to be, or it can become unfit for the carrying out of its avowed aim through a substantial corruption. The Church cannot fail in either way."[44]

Due to her promise of perpetual indefectibility, the *visible society* of the Church will continue to exist, with her hierarchical constitution established by Christ, until the end of the world. Even during those times in which God permits her to suffer through internal and external persecution, which disfigures her human nature and eclipses her

---

[41] Ibid., pp. 29-30.
[42] Ibid., p. 30.
[43] St. Jerome, 'In Isaiam,' iv, 6; P.L.,24,74, cited in Berry, *The Church of Christ*, p. 34.
[44] *Christ's Church*, p. 25.

divine nature, the Church will remain *"without any essential change."*[45] This is the divine promise of Jesus Christ.

Infallibility

The infallibility of the Church means that she teaches without error when she uses the fullness of her authority to define an article of faith. This charism can be exercised by the Pope personally, or by an ecumenical council. The charism of infallibility is not to be confused with *revelation* (the communication of some truth by God through means which are beyond the ordinary course of nature) or *inspiration* (the act by which God moves a human agent to write or speak what He wills). Nor is it to be confused with *impeccability*, which is the inability to sin.

Infallibility is merely a negative charism that prevents the Church from the possibility of erring *when the necessary conditions are present*. By saying "when the necessary conditions are present" is meant to show that the charism is not always active. It is engaged *only* when the conditions (as the Church has defined them) have been satisfied. We will address infallibility in detail in Chapters 8, 13 and 14, and thus only briefly mention it here. The reason it will be treated more thoroughly in subsequent chapters is because, as we noted in the Preface, a fundamental misunderstanding of infallibility is one of the principle causes of the Sedevacantist error.

An Introduction to Sedevacantist Errors

As was mentioned previously, the error of Sedevacantism (the belief that the recent Popes have not been true Popes)[46] quickly leads to a loss of faith in the Church itself. It ends by denying that the Catholic Church of today is, in fact, the same Catholic Church that existed before the election of John XXIII in 1958. Sedevacantists claim that the Church after 1958 not only lacks true Popes, but also lacks the *attributes* that the true Church will *always* possess – namely, visibility, indefectibility and infallibility. But if the Church from 1958 onward ("the Vatican II Church"[47]) does not possess these three *attributes*, then

---

[45] *The Church of Christ* (emphasis added), p. 31.
[46] The vast majority of Sedevacantists believe that the last six consecutive Popes (John XXIII, Paul VI, John Paul I, John Paul II, Benedict XVI and Francis) are false Popes, although others go further back beyond John XXIII.
[47] The Sedevacantists usually refer to the Church from 1958 forward as the "Vatican II Church," even though the Second Vatican Council began in 1962 and closed in 1965.

they must exist in *another* Church, since the true Church (which itself will always exist), will *always* possess them. But in what Church do they exist? In what visible social unit are they to be found? And where is that *visible* Church, exactly? That is the question the Sedevacantists cannot answer.

Because the Sedevacantist sects do not possess these *attributes,* they cannot be considered "the Church," as some of them imagine themselves to be. And if they cannot point to a *visible society* that does possess these *attributes* (and they can't), it means the Church, as founded by Christ, no longer exists - but this would mean that the indefectible Church has defected, which is not possible.

Donald Sanborn, a Sedevacantist bishop, recognized this difficulty with the Sedevacantist thesis. In his article "Resistance and Indefectibility," he correctly frames the issue when he writes: "At the root of nearly all of the disputes is the question of the Church. *Where is the Church?*"[48] After asking again, "where is the visible Church?," Sanborn responds by saying "It is realized in those who publicly adhere to the Catholic Faith, and who at the same time look forward to the election of a Roman Pontiff."[49]

Notice what the bishop just did. He reduced the Church to the Protestant concept of a loose association of individuals who profess the true faith, yet who are *not united under a divinely established hierarchy.* This is what he erroneously calls the "visible Church." This is essentially the same notion of the "visible Church" professed by Protestantism. For example, the Protestant Westminster Confession says:

> "The visible Church, which is also called Catholic or universal under the gospel, consists of all those throughout the world who profess the true religion, and their children."[50]

This false notion of the visible Church, as professed by Bishop Sanborn and the Westminster Confession, is most certainly not what is meant by the *visible Church.* As we have seen, the *visible Church* is not just individuals, but rather a *visible and hierarchical society.*

The Sedevacantist preacher, and ex-Protestant minister, Gerry Matatics, similarly reduces the "visible Church" to the visibility of her

---

[48] Sanborn, "Resistance and Indefectibility," http://www.traditionalmass.org/articles/article.php?id=21&catname=10 (emphasis in original).
[49] Ibid.
[50] *The British Mellinial Harbinger*, vol. VII, 3rd Series (London: A. Hall and Co., 1859), p. 349.

individual members (rather than a *visible society*). In his Compact Disc talk entitled, "Counterfeit Catholicism vs. Consistent Catholicism," he says:

"People will say 'Where is the Catholic Church in our day?' It's not that the Church is invisible. That is a Protestant heresy. The Church is always visible – it's made of <u>visible people</u>, people like you and me."[51]

Did you catch that? Like the Protestants, Matatics defines the visible Church as "visible people." This explanation, of course, is virtually identical to the definition of the Church in the Westminster Confession - a definition Mr. Matatics surely learned at the Westminster Theological Seminary where he studied. Perhaps realizing that what he just said would gladden the hearts of the most Modernist of Protestants, Mr. Matatics went on to add the words "One, Holy, Catholic and Apostolic," to his Protestant definition, no doubt in the hope of making it sound more Catholic. Unfortunately, it didn't help. In fact, his second attempt was even worse than his first. Matatics continues:

"The Church of Jesus Christ – the One, Holy, Catholic and Apostolic Church – is still here. It's <u>found in the hearts and minds</u> and the lives and in the families and the prayers of all those who believe what the Popes have taught us to believe."[52]

So Mr. Matatics would have us believe that the visible Church exists in the "hearts and minds" of the faithful. Clearly, Mr. Matatics' definition of the Church is a *denial* of the *attribute* of *visibility*, no matter how pious he wants to make his definition sound. The reason Mr. Matatics is forced to profess such errors about the visibility of the Church, is because he believes, and publicly states, that the hierarchy of the Church (the Magisterium) *no longer exists,* but is only a thing of the past (which would mean the Church defected). He asserts that "there is no living voice of the Magisterium. It doesn't mean we're lost; it doesn't mean we're abandoned, because we've got *the Magisterium of the past.*"[53]

As we will see in the next chapter, it is *de fide* (of the faith) that the Magisterium (composed of validly ordained bishops *with jurisdiction*) will always exist. This is one of the most essential *marks* of the Church -

---

[51] "Counterfeit Catholicism vs. Consistent Catholicism," disc 4 of 6, track 15.
[52] Ibid., track 16.
[53] Ibid., track 15.

the one that most clearly distinguishes the true Church from all the sects and false "churches." Unfortunately, by embracing the error of Sedevacantism, Mr. Matatics has reverted back to his erroneous Protestant view that the "visible Church" means only that she consists of *visible members*. The difference is that his current opinion affirms that there *was* a Magisterium from 33 A.D. to 1958 A.D, which he did not acknowledge while a Protestant. One can't help but see the irony of the Sedevacantists' rejection of the last six Popes, because they allegedly professed heresy, while the Sedevacantists, themselves, publicly profess the Protestant heresy of the invisible Church consisting of "visible members."

As we saw earlier, the promise of Christ that "the gates of hell shall not prevail" against the Church, applies to the *visible society*. It does not simply mean there will always exist in the world "true believers." But what does Mr. Matatics teach about this? In the same CD series, "Counterfeit Catholicism vs. Consistent Catholicism," he once again departs from "consistent Catholicism" by presenting the following "counterfeit" teaching. He says:

> "Our Lord promised that the gates of hell will not prevail against the Church, <u>that there would always be **true believers** until the end of time</u>."[54]

Compare the above teaching of Mr. Matatics with the following taken from the eighteenth century anti-Catholic book, *A Preservative Against Popery*, defending the English Reformation. See if you find any similarities between their explanation and that of Matatics. After denying the teaching of the "Roman Church" which insists that the promise of indefectibility applies to the visible society, the anti-Catholic books says:

> "Our Savior promised, 'That the Gates of Hell should not prevail against it.' A Promise... <u>that there should never want a Succession of **true Believers** in the World</u>, not to any particular organized Church. ... When Our Savior says, that the Gates of Hell shall not prevail against his Church, we may consider it either as a Promise, or a prophecy, or both, that <u>there always shall be found some orthodox Believers in the World</u>..."[55]

---

[54] Ibid., disc 3 of 6, track 10.
[55] Gibson, Edmund, *A Preservative Against Popery*, vol. I (London, 1738) ch. I, TIT. III, p. 42.

Notice that Mr. Matatics' definition of indefectibility is identical to that professed by the Protestants. The reason Mr. Matatics professes the Protestant notion of *indefectibility* is because he has embraced the Protestant notion of *"visibility."* Having lost faith in the Church (the visible society), Mr. Matatics has reduced the Church to the Protestant notion of "true believers."[56] If the visible Church is only "true believers," as Mr. Matatics erroneously believes, then the *indefectibility* of the Church must mean there will "always be true believers until the end of time," which is precisely what Matatics claims. Being that Mr. Matatics publicly professes such errors in the name of Catholicism, perhaps he should have shortened the title of his CD set to simply read *"Counterfeit Catholicism,"* as this would have more accurately described the content of his message.

The late Sedevacantist apologist, Rama Coomaraswamy, further demonstrates that the Sedevacantist apologists are unable to provide a cogent answer to the objection that their position is incompatible with the *indefectibility* of the *visible* Church. For example, in responding to the book *Sedevacantism: A False Solution to a Real Problem*, Mr. Coomaraswamy wrote:

> "The author holds that the sedevacantist denies the indefectibility of the Church. This is to put it mildly, nonsense. Anyone who is not as blind as the proverbial bat can see that 'the Pope and the Bishops in union with him' have defected from the true Church. ... It should be clear – indeed obvious – that it is not the Church which has defected for such is impossible. It is the new and post-Conciliar organization which has defected from the true

---

[56] There is an often-cited quotation attributed to St. Athanasius. The alleged quotation, which is directed to his flock, says: "Even if Catholics faithful to Tradition are reduced to a handful, they are the ones who are the true Church of Jesus Christ." Some Sedevacantists (such as Gerry Matatics) have quoted this as support for their position that the visible Church can be reduced to a tiny remnant of "true believers." The source cited for the alleged quotation is *"Coll. Selecta SS. Eccl. Patrum.* Caillu and Guillou, vol. 32, pp. 411-412." The complete title of the book is *Collectio Selecta Ss. Ecclesiae Patrum: Complectens Exquisitissima Opera Tum Dogmatica Et Moralia, Tum Apologetica Et Oratoria,* vol. XXXII (Paris: Ant. Poilleux, 1830), ed. by Armand-Benjamin Caillau and Guillou (the letter of Athanasius is on pp. 411-412). The book can be viewed online at http://www.archive.org/stream/operaath03atha#page /n7/ mode/2up. Not only does the alleged teaching of St. Athanasius violate the doctrine of moral Catholicity (and seemingly confuse Church membership with salvation) as we will see, but the quotation is a fabrication. A check of the book, which is in Latin, shows that this sentence is missing. Whoever first translated it evidently added that sentence at the end. A review of the same letter of St. Athanasius to his flock, as found in *The Nicean and Post Nicean Fathers* (1892) by Philip Schaff, (second ed. vol. IV, p. 551), again finds the sentence missing, thereby corroborating the conclusion that the alleged quotation is not authentic.

Church which still continues to exist and against which the Gates of Hell cannot not prevail."[57]

But this statement in no way helps Mr. Coomaraswamy's position, since he doesn't tell us where the true Church *is*; only where, in his opinion, it *is not*. He does the same in his book, *The Destruction of the Christian Tradition*. In the chapter dedicated to the marks of the Church, he goes on for several pages arguing why, in his opinion, the Catholic Church of today does not possess the marks, but then fails to tell us in what Church today they can be found. All he can say is, "the Church that teaches and worships in the manner that he (Christ) taught," and "has added or subtracted nothing from the original content... is, as the earliest of Creeds attest, the 'One, Holy, Catholic and Apostolic Church.'"[58] Mr. Coomaraswamy would have a difficult time finding an anti-Catholic Protestant who would disagree with his definition of the Church.

According to Coomaraswamy, the Vicar of Christ and his bishops (as well as 99.9 percent of the faithful) all became members of a New Church, without realizing it. But if this were the case, then the gates of hell would have prevailed over the *visible society* which is the Church. And if the "underground Church" is still visible, as Mr. Coomaraswamy claims,[59] then where is it? And why are Sedevacantists now forced to profess a Protestant definition of the visible Church to defend their position?

As we gather from the statements of Sanborn, Matatics, Coomaraswamy and others, the proponents of the Sedevacantist error not only claim there is no Pope, but also maintain that the *visible social unit* became a New Church.[60] The reason they hold this position is

---

[57] Coomaraswamy, "The Society of Pius X, A False Solution to a Real Problem" (2004), http://www.the-pope.com/socpxsed.html.
[58] Coomaraswamy, *The Destruction of the Christian Tradition* (Bloomberg, Indiana: World Wisdom, Inc. 2006), p. 410
[59] "That the true Church is in a certain sense 'underground,' but by no means 'invisible' is a fact of our days." Coomaraswamy, "The Society of Pius X, A False Solution to a Real Problem," 2004.
[60] The term "New Church" (or Conciliar Church) is sometimes used by traditional Catholics in a metaphorical sense, not to mean that the Catholic Church morphed into a new entity, but rather to describe either the "fifth column" within the Church (i.e., an organized body of men who have infiltrated the Church with the intent to subvert it); or to describe what has become of the Church (at least the Western Rite) over the past fifty years – that is, "the whole new orientation of the Church, which is no longer a Catholic orientation." (Archbishop Lefebvre, Spiritual conference at Ecône, 13 March 1978). The Modernist Archbishop Giovanni Benelli first used the term "Conciliar Church" in his June 25, 1976 correspondence with Archbishop Lefebvre (Lefebvre thereafter used the

because they erroneously believe that the Church after 1958 (after the election of Pope John XXIII) has done things that are contrary to the promise of infallibility. But because they know the true Church is infallible, they are forced to argue that the Church that allegedly violated infallibility is a <u>New Church</u>, and not the <u>true Church</u>. How can they possibly make this argument? Here's how: They say that in 1958, the true Church elected a false Pope and then *morphed* into a New Church. It is this New Church, they say, and not the True Church, that defected from the Faith, leaving the true Church behind and intact.

But if that's the case, then where did the true visible Church go? Wasn't the Church that existed on October 27, 1958 (during the Conclave) the same Church that elected and accepted John XXIII as Pope the next day? If not, then again, where did the true Church go? Up in smoke? Out to lunch? On vacation? How could the pre and post Conclave "Churches" be two different *visible societies*, particularly when their membership was identical, aside from a few deaths and baptisms during the time in which the Conclave was convened?

Again, Sedevacantists have no answer, other than to say, as Sanborn and Matatics do, that the true Church now exists "in the hearts and minds" of true Catholic believers, "those who publicly adhere to the Catholic Faith." But this explanation is not satisfactory, since, as we have shown, the promise of indefectibility pertains to the *visible society* itself, and not to individual believers. And the *visible society* that existed on October 27, 1958 is the same *visible society* that existed on October 28, 1958 and in the years and decades that followed.

That visible society includes the Cardinals who elected John XXIII and the rest of the Church who accepted him as Pope. Likewise, the visible society that existed in November of 1965 (before the documents of Vatican II were ratified), remained the same visible society that existed in January of 1966 (after the close of Vatican II). This means that a person cannot maintain, as many Sedevacantists do, that the "New Church" was *born* when Vatican II was ratified – that is, without necessarily denying the *indefectibility* of the Church, or reducing it, as Mr. Matatics has done, to the Protestant notion of "true believers" existing "until the end of time."

Others claim that the defection did not happen at one event (such as the election of John XXIII or ratification of Vatican II). They admit that it is untenable to maintain that an instant defection occurred. Instead, they insist that the defection happened gradually, as if this in

term in a metaphorical sense to describe "the whole new orientation of the Church," while rejecting the Sedevacantist thesis).

any way helps their case. For example, the Sedevacantist apologist, John Lane, wrote:

> "The Catholic Church didn't cease to exist, or to have a hierarchy, in an instant in, say, 1958 or 1965. Such a view would be not merely nutty, but manifestly unorthodox. It's sufficiently clear that what happened was a process of apostasy..."[61]

Someone should inform Mr. Lane that there is no essential difference between claiming the Church defected overnight, and claiming it happened gradually over a period of months, or perhaps years, since any defection of the Church (either overnight or by a "process") would violate its attribute of indefectibility. And Mr. Lane seems curiously aware of the difficulties that his position necessarily entails, since he concedes that reconciling it with the Catholic Faith is "an extraordinarily difficult task" - so much so, he concedes, that those who attempt it usually end "with some kind of unorthodoxy." This is what he says: "Explaining this process in terms properly orthodox is an extraordinarily difficult task. Most commentators won't even attempt to do so. Those who have tried, usually end with some kind of unorthodoxy or at least folly."[62]

In other words, Mr. Lane cannot explain how the Church defected (i.e., Sedevacantism), and yet he chooses to hold the position anyway. Of course, the reason Sedevacantists "usually" (read: "always") end in "unorthodoxy" in attempting to explain their position is because their position is false: they begin with an erroneous premise and then try to explain something that did not occur. The remedy for their unorthodoxy is to realize that the true Church did not morph into a New Church, either in an "instant" or by a "process of apostasy." Rather, the true Church has been infiltrated by Modernists who are attacking it from within, and, as a result, it is currently undergoing a Passion similar to that of Christ, while remaining the same institution, just as Christ remained the same Divine Person during His Passion.

Can the True Church Elect and Follow a False Pope?

The Sedevacantists cannot avoid the inescapable conclusion of their position, namely, that the true Church defected, simply by claiming that it was not a *true* Pope and the *true* Church that defected, but rather a false Pope who gave birth to a *New Church* that defected. The reason

---

[61] Taken from http://sedevacantist.com/viewtopic.php?f=2&t=1552 (emphasis added).
[62] Ibid.

this theory does not hold is because it requires that the *true Church* (not a false Church) elected and followed a false Pope. This, in and of itself, is contrary to the promise of perpetual indefectibility of the visible Church, *irrespective* of whether the alleged false Pope, who was elected, subsequently taught heresy.

Cardinal Billot explains that if the entire Church accepted a false Pope as the true Pope, it would mean the gates of hell had prevailed against the Church (the visible society). He wrote:

> "Finally, whatever you still think about the possibility or impossibility of the aforementioned hypothesis [of the Pope falling into heresy], at least one point must be considered absolutely incontrovertible and placed firmly above any doubt whatever: the adhesion of the universal Church will be always, in itself, an infallible *sign* of the legitimacy of a determined Pontiff, and therefore also of the existence of all the conditions required for legitimacy itself. It is not necessary to look far for the proof of this, but we find it immediately in the promise and the infallible providence of Christ: 'The gates of hell shall not prevail against it,' and 'Behold I shall be with you all days.' For the adhesion of the Church to a false Pontiff would be the same as its adhesion to a false rule of faith[63]... As will become even more clear by what we shall say later, God can permit that at times a vacancy in the Apostolic See be prolonged for a long time. He can also permit that doubt arise about the legitimacy of this or that election. He cannot however permit that the whole Church accept as Pontiff him who is not so truly and legitimately."[64]

Notice that the adhesion of the Church to a Pope is an *infallible* sign of his legitimacy. As we will discuss in more detail in Chapter 12, to claim that the entire Church adhered to a false Pope is itself to deny the Church's promise of infallibility as well. Hence, those who hold to the Sedevacantist thesis are forced to deny, not only the *visibility* and *indefectibility* of the Church, but also the Church's *infallibility* (all three attributes).

Like the Apostles who lost faith in Christ during His Passion (by witnessing first hand what Our Lord permitted His enemies to do to Him), so too, the Sedevacantists have lost faith in the Church (by

---

[63] We should note here that the personal opinions of a Pope do not constitute the rule of faith. The rule of faith consists of the definitive (infallible) teachings of the Church. "Since faith is Divine and infallible, the rule of faith must be also Divine and infallible." *Catholic Encyclopedia* (1913), vol. V, p. 766.
[64] Billot, *Tractatus de Ecclesia Christi*, vol. I, pp. 612-613 (emphasis added).

painfully living through what God is permitting His enemies to do to His Church). As a consequence of their loss of faith *in the Church*, they end by denying the attributes and are forced to profess the Protestant definition of the Church, as existing in the "hearts and minds" of those individuals "who publicly adhere to the Catholic Faith." What this shows is that, as we noted at the beginning of the chapter, the Sedevacantist thesis necessarily entails that the gates of hell have prevailed against the visible Church, something the Sedevacantists themselves don't realize, or else refuse to admit.

A former Sedevacantist apologist, who attended a Sedevacantist seminary, recently published a book demonstrating this very point. Based on the Sedevacantist errors he had embraced, he was forced to admit that what he had come to believe and professed "proved" that the Catholic Church defected. Although he is quite mistaken on this point, his Sedevacantism led him to conclude that the Catholic Church is *not* infallible nor indefectible, as she claims to be. He now publicly rejects these dogmas and, having lost the faith in the Church, ended by joining the schismatic Eastern Orthodox sect. The following are a few excerpts from his recently published book, entitled *The Sedevacantist Delusion*:

> "...all Sedevacantists deny the *possibility* of a defection of the Church, while simultaneously proving that a defection has occurred *in fact*. ... That's why the Sedevacantists had to base their argument upon a theory of two Churches: an apostate Church in Rome and themselves."[65]

> "An earnest search for an infallible and indefectible Catholic Church turns up contradictions on all sides. Today I have no doubt that the reason is that such a Church never existed."[66]

> "My objective in this work is to prove that Sedevacantism violates fundamental doctrines of the Church and is therefore a heretical theory. In addition, I will propose an alternative explanation to the doctrinal problems the Church has created that does not necessitate espousing contradictions ... This will entail entertaining the following *five premises about the Catholic Church that I hold* and upon which this work is based:

---

[65] Pontrello, John, *The Sedevacantist Delusion* (North Charleston, South Carolina: CreateSpace Independent Publishing Platform., 2015), pp. xx-xxi.
[66] Ibid., xviii.

1.) The Sedevacantists have successfully proven the defection of the Catholic Church at or subsequent to Vatican II.
2.) The Church can defect and remain the Church.
3.) The post-Vatican II Church is the real Catholic Church, and Francis is the real pope.
4.) Infallibility is a myth.
5.) The papacy is not the original foundation of the Roman Church..."[67]

"...the Sedevacantists have in fact proven the defection of the Catholic Church" which is "precisely why Sedevacantism is so devastating to Roman Catholicism and at the same time supportive of Eastern Orthodoxy."[68]

"Pope Francis is a true Catholic pope, but only because the Catholic Church can defect and still remain the same institution down through the ages."[69]

"I believe that the divine prerogatives of the Papacy are false..."[70]

The logical deductions of this author, albeit from very false premises, confirm exactly what we have said, namely, that the errors of Sedevacantism logically and necessarily lead to a denial of the attributes of the Church (at least indefectibility and infallibility), to a loss of faith in the Church itself, and finally, to heresy.

The Siri Theory

Before concluding this chapter, we will briefly address another theory that has been used to explain the current crisis in the Church. While this book examines the mainstream Sedevacantist thesis that the post-Vatican II Church has been deprived of having true Popes, some present another theory.[71] This theory maintains that Cardinal Giuseppe Siri (1906-1989), the former Archbishop of Genoa, was elected Pope in 1958 in the Conclave that eventually elected Cardinal Angelo Roncalli (John XXIII), but was forced to resign during the Conclave.[72] They

---

[67] Ibid., xli.
[68] Ibid., p. 101.
[69] Ibid., back cover.
[70] Ibid., p 103.
[71] In this book, we use the term "theory" in a non-scientific manner, to mean an unsubstantiated explanation to support a conclusion.
[72] Some claim that Siri was also elected in the 1963 and 1978 Conclaves as well.

maintain that the forced resignation was invalid and that Cardinal Siri (to whom they attribute the name Pope Gregory XVII) remained the true Pope until his death in 1989. Some go further by claiming that he has since been succeeded by hidden Popes. Thus, they "get to have their cake and eat it too": a true Pope was elected while a false Pope led the Church into heresy.

The Siri Theory does not hold for a number of obvious reasons: First, as we have seen and will further explain, it is not possible for the entire Church to follow a false Pope (in this case, John XXIII). Second, the claim that Siri was elected and forced to resign behind closed doors is pure speculation (by people who were not behind those closed doors). It has not been corroborated by any proven facts; nor is the theory even provable, given that the Cardinal electors are oath-bound not to reveal the confidential happenings of the Conclave under pain of excommunication. Would it not be extremely rash and contrary to the Catholic sense for us to have to base our faith, our eternal salvation for that matter, on speculation? Third, if Siri were the true Pope, he would not have been bound by the secret of the Conclave (since the Pope is not bound by positive ecclesiastical law), and therefore *could* have revealed the truth to the Church. Fourth, Siri not only gave no indication that he was the true Pope, but he himself publicly accepted John XXIII as Pope. Fifth (and most damaging to the theory), Siri remained a member of "the Vatican II Church," and went along with all of the changes that followed the council, which would mean he was part of the alleged mass defection.

Of course, if Siri's acquiescence, to the novelties of the past fifty years, could be excused for such reasons as threats, undue influence, or whatever other creative explanation Sedevacantists may come up with to explain how Siri could be a member of the "New Church" and still be Pope of the true Church, then the same mitigating reasons could also be applied to the conciliar Popes. For this reason, some have claimed that even if Siri were the true Pope for a time, he lost his office when he went along with the errors.

Needless to say, this theory raises the same objections concerning the disappearance of the visible Church. Furthermore, we have infallible certitude that Siri was not the true Pope due to the fact that John XXIII was universally and peaceably accepted as Pope by the entire Church. As Cardinal Billot explains, the acceptance of a Pope by the universal Church not only provides infallible certitude of his legitimacy, *but it also heals in the root any defect in the election.* This means that even if there was an irregularity during the Conclave (which may well have been the case), the acceptance of John XXIII, by the Church, removes any doubt about the validity of his election. Regarding this, Cardinal Billot wrote:

> "From the moment in which the Pope is accepted by the Church and united to her as the head to the body, it is no longer permitted to raise doubts about a possible vice of election or a possible lack of any condition whatsoever necessary for legitimacy. For the aforementioned adhesion of the Church <u>heals in the root all fault in the election and proves infallibly the existence of all the required conditions.</u>"[73]

In Chapter 12, we will see how the Sedevacantist bishop, Donald Sanborn, attempts to get around this teaching by claiming that the peaceful and universal acceptance only guarantees that the election was valid, and not that the Pope elected is a true Pope, when the *exact opposite* is true: universal acceptance *guarantees* we have a true Pope, even if there were irregularities in his election. With the information covered in the following chapters, by the time we get to Chapter 12, the bishop's error will be crystal clear.

In his Doctrinal Dissertation, "Supplied Jurisdiction According to Canon 209," Francis Miaskiewicz explained that even "if a Pope were invalidly elected, once he were regarded by the world as Pope all of his jurisdictional acts would be valid."[74] St. Alphonsus Liguori taught the same: "It is of no importance that in past centuries some Pontiff was illegitimately elected or took possession of the Pontificate by fraud; it is enough that he was accepted afterwards by the whole Church as Pope, since by such acceptance he would have become the true Pontiff."[75] The notion that the true Church elected *and peacefully accepted* a false Pope cannot be held without denying the infallibility and indefectibility of the visible Church – that is to say, without falling into heresy.

As noted, Chapter 12 is devoted entirely to explaining why the Church's universal and peaceful acceptance of a Pope is an infallible sign that he is the true Pope. For now, it suffices to close this introductory chapter by noting that the Sedevacantist thesis results in a practical denial of the three *attributes* of the Church: *perpetual-indefectibility, visibility* and *infallibility*. By claiming that the Church (the

---

[73] Billot, *Tractatus de Ecclesia Christi*, vol. I, pp. 612-613 (emphasis added).

[74] Miaskiewicz, "Supplied Jurisdiction According to Canon 209" (Washington, D.C.: The Catholic University of America, 1940), p. 26.

[75] St. Alphonsus Liguori, *Verita della Fede – Opera de S. Alfonso Maria de Liguori*, vol. VIII. (Torino: Marietti, 1887), p. 720, n. 9, http://www.intratext.com/IXT/ITASA0000/_P3BD.HTM.

visible society) morphed into a New Church, and then reducing the notion of the visible Church to "visible persons" who have the true faith in their "hearts and minds," the Sedevacantists have effectively embraced the Protestant heresy of the invisible Church. The inescapable conclusion of their position is that the *indefectible* Church defected, and consequently that the gates of hell have prevailed against the Church, which is contrary to the promise of Christ. In the next chapter, we will examine the four marks of the Church, and in so doing, further expose the errors of the Sedevacantist thesis.

Chapter 2

~ The Church and Its Marks ~

In Chapter 1, we saw that the Church is an indefectible *visible society*. We also saw that the Church has certain distinguishing *marks*, which enable it to be known, not only as a religious society, but as the true Church founded by Christ. In this chapter, we will consider each of these *marks* individually, and, in so doing, will see: 1) that the Sedevacantist sects lack these marks; and 2) the only Church that even claims to possess them is the Catholic Church – that is, the Church that everyone except the Sedevacantists recognizes as the Catholic Church. Because these *marks* must be with the true Church until the end of time, if the Catholic Church (the visible society) were to lose a single one of them (which the Sedevacantists claim to be the case), it would mean "the gates of hell" had prevailed against the Church, which is not possible (Mt. 16:19).

Although we will address all four marks in this chapter, we will succinctly treat the first three (one, holy, catholic), and focus special attention on the fourth mark, *apostolicity*, since this is acknowledged by the Church's theologians as being the most important of the four marks, in the sense that it is the one that most clearly distinguishes the true Church from false churches and heretical sects. At the end of the chapter, we will see the difficulty that *apostolicity* poses for the Sedevacantist apologists. We will close the chapter by briefly addressing some of the "end times" prophecies used by the Sedevacantist apologists to defend the Sedevacantist thesis.

The Marks of the Church

In Chapter 1, we discussed the material and formal visibility of the true Church, which is known by her four marks. The marks of the Church are her *unity, holiness, catholicity* and *apostolicity* (*"unam, sanctam, catholicam, apostolicam"*). Just as the error of Sedevacantism ends by denying the three *attributes* (as we saw in the last chapter), so too Sedevacantism effectively denies these four marks, since it cannot point to any Church today that possesses them. Because these marks are not found in the Sedevacantist sects (nor in the "hearts and minds" of "true believers"), the Sedevacantists are again forced to deny the visibility of the Church, since the *marks* are those things by which the *visible Church* can be *known*. Let us now examine each of these four marks.

The Church is One

The first mark of the Church is its oneness, or unity. The unity of the Church is found in its threefold unity of doctrine, worship and government. The unity of doctrine is professed in her Creed, and is found in her definitive teachings, which all Catholics are required to believe with the *assent of divine Faith*. The Church is also unified in her sacraments and worship; this aspect of unity is not compromised by the differences found in the various rites of the Church.[1] Lastly, the Church is one because it is united under one and the same hierarchy – the bishops and the Pope. According to the promise of Chist, the Church will always possess this threefold unity of doctrine, worship and government.

Material Divisions

Due to the imperfection of the human condition, it is possible for there to be *material* divisions within the Church in doctrine or government due to an error of fact. A material division in government occurred, for example, during the Great Western Schism (1378-1417), when there were two and eventually three claimants to the papal throne, and it was unclear which of the claimants was the true Pope. But as Van Noort explains, this material division within the membership of the visible society did not cause a rupture in *formal* unity. He explained that "at the time of the Western Schism, when for forty years two or three men claimed to be the sovereign pontiff," unity "was only materially, not formally, interrupted."[2]

Due to those extraordinary circumstances, in which it was difficult for the faithful to ascertain which of the alleged Popes was, in fact, the true Pope, "those who through no fault of their own gave allegiance to an illegitimate pope would no more be schismatics than a person would be a heretic who, desirous of following the preaching of the

---

[1] Van Noort qualifies the unity of worship by saying that it "is absolutely necessary to the extent that the worship was determined by Christ Himself" and the adds: "However, liturgical unity is already included in other unities: in unity of faith, since faith includes also the revealed doctrine on the sacrifice of the Mass and the sacraments; in unity of communion, since this involves the sharing in the same spiritual benefits. This is perhaps the reason that neither the Vatican Council nor Leo XIII in his encyclical on the unity of the Church make any specific mention of liturgical unity." (*Christ's Church*, p. 131).

[2] *Christ's Church*, p. 131.

Church, would admit a false doctrine because he was under the impression that it was taught by the Church."[3] Later in this chapter, we will address material division in *doctrine*, such as what occurred during the Arian crisis of the fourth century. We will see how there can be a *material* doctrinal division within the membership of the Church, during a time of doctrinal crisis, without there being a formal rupture in *doctrinal* unity.

The Church is Holy

Holiness consists in union with God, the Supreme Good and Source of all holiness. Strictly speaking, holiness can be applied to rational creatures alone. However, it can be predicated analogously of irrational things, such as Church buildings, altars, sacramentals, etc., inasmuch as they are set apart and used for the worship of God.

The Church is holy, firstly, because it was founded by Jesus Christ, who is All-Holy. It is holy because it is dedicated and set apart by God, and because of the mission it received from Christ, which is the glory of God and salvation of souls. It is holy in the doctrines that it teaches,[4] in its special gifts or charisms, and it is externally holy in many of its holy members. Commenting on the mark of holiness, Van Noort wrote:

> "Christ's Church is holy on several counts: e.g., because of its Founder and Head, who is the only-begotten Son of God; because of its purpose, which is the glory of God and the sanctification of mankind; about these there is no difficulty. Catholic teaching states in addition that the Church, by the institution of Christ and therefore necessarily and irrevocably, is adorned with a threefold external and visible holiness: that of its *means* of sanctification, that of its *members*, and that of its *charisms*."[5]

The *charisms* that the Church will always possess refer to the miraculous gifts and miracles that will always be found in the Church. While there will be more miracles in some ages than others, "in every age" the Church will "be enriched with certain miraculous gifts through which God manifest its holiness."[6]

---

[3] Ibid.

[4] As we will see later, the doctrines definitively taught by the Church are not to be confused with error professed by her members, even if those members are high-ranking prelates.

[5] *Christ's Church*, p. 135.

[6] Ibid., p. 139.

Regarding the holiness of its *members*, this does not exclude there being "chaff" mixed with the "wheat" in the field of the Church. The Church's members retain the effects of Original Sin and possess free will. Consequently, they are capable of living a life out of conformity with the Church's doctrines and moral precepts that they profess. The reason the chaff are "chaff," rather than "wheat," is precisely because they fail to live up to the teachings they profess. The holiness of its members is found in those who, by the help of grace, *do* sanctify themselves by partaking of the sacraments and living in conformity with the teaching of the Church. *Ordinary holiness* consists of living in the habitual state of sanctifying grace, which entails being free from mortal sin (very difficult without the sacraments, but very attainable with them); *outstanding holiness* is found in those members whose extraordinary interior sanctity manifests itself in a life of shining heroic virtue.

We also find the miraculous *charisms* in the post-Vatican II Church. Padre Pio, for example (who remained a member of the modern Church and accepted Paul VI as Pope until his death in 1968),[7] performed countless miracles throughout his life. He possessed the miraculous gift of reading hearts, which he did daily in the confessional. He also miraculously bore the wounds of Christ (the "*stigmata*") which he suffered until his death. This is just one example of the *charisms* present in the Church since Vatican II.

The Church is Catholic or Universal

The next *mark* of the Church is catholicity. Now, the Church has been called by the name *Catholic* since the earliest years of her existence. The Apostles' Creed says "I believe in … the Holy Catholic Church." The Nicene Creed says the same: "I believe in the One, Holy, *Catholic* and Apostolic Church." We also find the Church being called by the name *Catholic* in the writings of the earliest Church Fathers, such as the Bishop of Antioch and martyr, St. Ignatius, who is commonly

---

[7] It is a matter of public record that Padre Pio, shortly before his death, sent a letter to Pope Paul VI dated September 12, 1968, in which we read, in part: "Your Holiness: Availing myself of Your Holiness' meeting with the Capitular Fathers, I united myself in spirit with my Brothers, and in a spirit of faith, love and obedience to the greatness of Him whom you represent on earth, offer my respect homage to Your August Person, humbly kneeling at Your feet…I thank your Holiness for the clear and decisive words you have spoken in the recent encyclical '*Humane Vitae*,' and I reaffirm my own faith and my unconditional obedience to your inspired directives." https://www.ewtn.com/library/MARY/PIOPOPE.HTM (emphases added).

believed to have been ordained by St. Peter.[8] On his way to Rome where he was to be martyred, St. Ignatius wrote an epistle to the Smyrnaeans (in 107 A.D.) in which he said: "Wherever Jesus Christ is, there is the Catholic Church."[9] Since the first centuries, the name *Catholic* has been used as the proper name for the Church founded by Christ.

But the mark of "catholicity" does not refer to the *name* of the Church, but to its true *universality*. Universality means that the Church is not confined to one period of time,[10] or to one nation, but is spread throughout the entire world. The Catechism of the Council of Trent explains:

> "The third *mark* of the Church is that she is Catholic, that is, universal. And justly is she called Catholic, because, as St. Augustine says: 'She is diffused by the splendor of one faith from the rising to the setting sun.'[11] Unlike republics of human institution, or the sects of heretics, she is not confined to any one country or class of men, but embraces within the amplitude of her love all mankind, whether barbarians or Scythians, slaves or freemen, male or female. Therefore, it is written: 'Thou...hast redeemed us to God in thy blood, out of every tribe, and tongue, and people, and nation, and hast made us to our God, a kingdom' (Apoc. 5:9,10)."[12]

Moral Catholicity

The Church's theologians make a distinction between catholicity *by right*, and catholicity *in fact*. Catholicity *by right* means the Church "has the *aptitude* to spread over the whole world because there is nothing in

---

[8] For example, John Malalas (491-578), the Greek chronicler from Antioch, said: "St. Peter ordained St. Ignatius after the death of Evodius." The Dublin Review, vol. 123 (London: Burns & Oats, July – October, 1898), p. 283.

[9] The Epistle of St. Ignatius to the Smyrnaeans, Chapter VIII. St. Ignatius was the second successor of St. Peter as bishop of the Church at Antioch. Now, in the Acts of the Apostles, we learn that "at Antioch the disciples were first named Christians" (Acts 11:26). Perhaps at Antioch, Christians were also first called "Catholics" (the terms being synonymous at that time, unlike today), given the use of the name "Catholic Church" by St. Ignatius in this letter.

[10] The Church is universal in time because it includes all the faithful who have ever lived, "from Adam to the present day, or who shall exist." *The Catechism of the Council of Trent* (Rockford, Illinois: TAN Books and Publishers, Inc., 1982, p. 106).

[11] St. Augustine. serm. 131 & 181. de temp.

[12] *The Catechism of the Council of Trent*, p. 106.

its structural principles which bind it to one nation."[13] Catholicity *in fact* refers to,

> "the *actual* spread of the Church throughout the world. If the actual diffusion extends to all people, it is called *absolute* catholicity;[14] if it reaches only a great number of people, it is called *moral* catholicity."[15]

Van Noort explains that once the Church obtained *moral* catholicity *in fact* (which it did in the decades following its founding), this characteristic became a perpetual and necessary quality of the Church. He remarks:

> "The Church is endowed with moral catholicity: Christ's Church, after its beginning, should always be conspicuous for its morally universal diffusion. ...
> To satisfy the requirements of moral catholicity *in fact* – a quality belonging to Christ's Church perpetually and necessarily – we stated there was required: 'a great number of men from many *different nations.*' ... Such diffusion, obviously, cannot be had without a really large number of adherents."[16]

Because *moral catholicity* requires "a great number of people," the *visible society* will never be reduced to only a small remnant. There may come a time when the *internal virtue* of faith is only present in a small number of the members of the visible Church. But, as we will see in Chapter 3, the loss of interior faith alone does not, in and of itself, separate a man from the visible Church. Hence, the loss of faith in the end times, alluded to by Christ (Luke 18:8) and St. Paul (2 Thes. 2:3), does not contradict the teaching that the Church will always possess, as Van Noort said, "a great number of men from many different nations."

The Church is Apostolic

The final mark of the true Church is *apostolicity*. Apostolicity is the most important of the four marks, not only because it implicitly contains the others, but also because it most clearly distinguishes the

---

[13] *Christ's Church*, p. 144.
[14] It is commonly held that *absolute catholicity* will be attained before the Second Coming. This will likely occur during the period of peace promised by various prophets, including the Queen of Prophets, Our Lady of Fatima.
[15] *Christ's Church*, p. 144 (italics in original; underline added).
[16] Ibid., pp. 146-147.

true Church from false churches and heretical sects. The *Catholic Encyclopedia* explains:

> "Apostolicity is the *mark* by which the Church of today is recognized as identical with the Church founded by Jesus Christ upon the Apostles. It is of great importance because it is the surest indication of the true Church of Christ, it is most easily examined, and it virtually contains the other three *marks*, namely, Unity, Sanctity, and Catholicity."[17]

All of the non-Catholic "churches" and sects that profess to be Christian acknowledge the *mark* of apostolicity in some sense, but their definition always "misses the mark" (pun intended) in one way or another. For example, Van Noort explains that "Protestants usually mean by apostolicity, apostolicity of doctrine. That is all that is required, they say, and it suffices." He then adds: "But Greek schismatics and Anglicans – at least a large number of them – require in addition to apostolicity of doctrine, some sort of apostolicity of government. They do not, however, specify *legitimacy* of the mode of succession."[18] Van Noort then gives the true understanding of this mark, as taught by the Catholic Church: "According to Catholic teaching, Christ's Church essentially and necessarily enjoys a triple sort of apostolicity: apostolicity of doctrine, government, and membership."[19]

The principal difference between the teaching of the Catholic Church and that of the Anglican and Eastern Orthodox sects regarding the mark of apostolicity, is apostolicity in government. This is because they lack legitimate apostolic succession (formal apostolic succession), which is also lacking in the Sedevacantist sects. In fact, it is apostolicity in government (the clearest mark of the true Church) that gives the Sedevacantist apologists the most difficulties. Their position forces them to openly depart from the teaching of the Church, or else invent wild theories to keep from having to reject what they know the Church teaches. We will address this thoroughly in a moment, but before doing so, we will first address apostolicity in *doctrine*, and apostolicity in *membership*.

---

[17] *Catholic Encyclopedia* (1913), vol. I, p. 648. Note that *The Catholic Encyclopedia* (15 volume set; 1907-1912) was released in 1913 by Encyclopedia Press, Inc. as a new edition called the *Original Catholic Encyclopedia* (original 15 volumes plus a new Volume 16 which is an Index). For ease of reference, we will simply refer to this resource as the "*Catholic Encyclopedia* (1913)."
[18] *Christ's Church*, p. 151.
[19] Ibid.

Apostolicity in Doctrine

Apostolicity in doctrine means the Church will always retain the same doctrines that it received from the Apostles.[20] The *attribute* of infallibility guarantees that the Church will never impose a heresy upon the faithful to be believed with the assent of faith. This is the biggest sticking point today for the Sedevacantists, since they believe that unity of doctrine no longer exists, and infallibility has been violated. About this, however, they are mistaken.

As history shows, apostolicity in doctrine will survive, even in a severe *doctrinal crisis within the Church itself*, such as the Arian heresy of the fourth century. During the Arian crisis, the faith of many was shaken and a majority of bishops knowingly, or unknowingly, drifted into heresy (about the doctrine of the divinity of Christ, no less). Fr. Jurgens, who edited the book *The Faith of the Early Fathers*, estimated that between 97 and 99 percent of the bishops in charge of the Church's dioceses drifted into heresy,[21] yet the Church never *definitively* taught heresy (by imposing it upon the faithful), and the true Faith continued to be professed by a majority of the laity.

While it may have seemed "impossible" for the bishops to have wavered in the faith to such an extent, it happened (and it is also worth noting that the Church has never taught that these 97 to 99 percent of bishops lost their office *ipso facto*, at the time[22]). This historical precedent serves as a useful reminder for our own times, by showing us what *can* and indeed *has* happened in the true Church. During the Passion of the Church, we can expect that God will allow the Church to endure everything that can be *permitted* without any of His promises being violated. Therefore, in times such as ours, it is always helpful to consider what *has* occurred in the Church, in order to know what *can* occur without the gates of hell prevailing.

Cardinal Newman, who studied the Arian crisis in depth, estimated the percentage of bishops who fell into heresy to be closer to 80 percent. He explains what transpired during this extraordinary crisis:

---

[20] Ibid.

[21] "At one point in the Church's history, only a few years before Gregory [Nazianzen]'s present preaching (A.D. 380), perhaps the number of Catholic bishops in possession of sees, as opposed to Arian bishops in possession of sees, was no greater than something between 1% and 3% of the total. Had doctrine been determined by popularity, today we should all be deniers of Christ and opponents of the Spirit." Jurgens, *The Faith of the Early Fathers*, vol. 2 (Collegeville, Minnesota: Liturgical Press, 1979), p. 39.

[22] This is one of the erroneous claims of the Sedevacantists.

"There was the temporary suspense of the function of *Ecclesia Docens* [the teaching Church – the hierarchy] as about 80 percent of the bishops fell into heresy. The body of bishops failed in their confession of the faith... The episcopate, whose action was so prompt and concordant at Nicaea on the rise of Arianism, did not, as a class or order of men, play a good part in the troubles consequent upon the Council; and the laity did. The Catholic people, in the length and breadth of Christendom, were the obstinate champions of Catholic truth, <u>and the bishops were not</u>. Of course, there were great and illustrious exceptions; first, Athanasius, Hilary, the Latin Eusebius, and Phoebadius; and after them, Basil, the two Gregories, and Ambrose; there are others, too, who suffered, if they did nothing else.[23]

After noting that some of the laity unfortunately followed the bishops into heresy, Newman went on to note that most of the laity held fast to the faith:

"And again, in speaking of the laity ... on the whole, taking a wide view of the history, <u>we are obliged to say that the governing body of the Church came short, and the governed [the laity] were pre-eminent in faith, zeal, courage, and constancy</u>. This is a very remarkable fact; but there is a moral in it. Perhaps it was *permitted* in order to impress upon the Church at that very time passing out of her state of persecution to her long temporal ascendancy, the greatest evangelical lesson, that, not the wise and powerful, but the obscure, the unlearned, and the weak constitute her real strength. It was mainly by the faithful people that Paganism was overthrown; it was by the faithful people, under the lead of Athanasius and the Egyptian bishops, and in some places supported by their Bishops or priests, that the worst of heresies was withstood and stamped out of the sacred territory."[24]

The Arian crisis is a parallel of the situation in which we find ourselves today, when vast numbers of Catholic bishops have been infected with the heresy of Modernism, just as the majority of the bishops in the fourth century were infected with the heresy of Arianism. But, in spite of the doctrinal crisis currently afflicting the Church's hierarchy, the true Faith is still professed with clarity by countless traditional-minded Catholics throughout the world (priests and laity alike), just as it was during the time of the Arian crisis.

---

[23] Newman, *Arians of the Fourth Century*, 5th ed. (London: Pickerins & Co, 1883), p. 445 (emphasis added).
[24] Ibid., pp. 445-446 (emphasis added).

Material Division

There can be a *material* division in the membership of the Church due to *errors of fact*, without there being a *formal* division. As was noted above, this occurred during the Great Western Schism, when the Church was divided (materially) into three major camps (Rome, Pisa and Avignon), due to there being multiple claimants to the papacy, combined with sufficient uncertainty as to who was the true Pope. This material division was due to an *error of fact* (who is the true Pope?).

Just as there can be an error of fact *in government*, so too can there be an error of fact *in doctrine* – that is, an error in knowing what is to be assented to by faith. Those who adhere to the Magisterium as the rule of faith, yet profess a false doctrine, or refuse to accept a true doctrine, because they mistakenly believe that what they profess or reject is in accord with the teaching of the Church, are not truly in heresy. Cardinal Billot explains that heresy consists in rejecting the Magisterium as the rule of faith, not simply in adhering to an error because one mistakenly believes it is taught by the Church. In discussing formal and material heresy, the Cardinal said, "the nature of heresy consists in withdrawal from *the rule* of the ecclesiastical Magisterium, which does not take place" if there is "a simple *error of fact* concerning what the rule dictates [i.e., what the Church teaches]."[25]

One of the characteristics of Modernism is ambiguity, confusion and doublespeak, which obscures the Faith itself, resulting in confusion for the faithful in knowing what, precisely, the Church teaches. During the Modernist crisis of our day, the object of Faith (what must be believed) has been obscured by error and ambiguity - at the hands of the very leaders of the Church, no less (just as in the Arian crisis). But in spite of this crisis in the Faith that God has permitted, none of the recent Popes have *definitively imposed* any heretical doctrines upon the Church as matters of faith (which the charism of infallibility would not permit). As we will show in more detail in Chapter 13, none of the novelties, ambiguous formulations, or apparent errors of Vatican II (which have contributed greatly to the confusion and material divisions we see today) were proposed as doctrines that require the assent of faith.[26] Therefore, there has been no formal rupture in the

---

[25] Billot, *De Ecclesia Christi*, 3rd ed. (Prati: ex officina libraria Giachetti, 1909), p. 292 (translated by John Daly). The full quotation is provided in Chapter 4.
[26] As we will later see in Chapters 13 and 14, the teachings of Vatican II only require a "religious observance" which is not equivalent to an assent of faith. We we will also see that religious assent is not unconditional and may be suspended under certain circumstances.

Faith – neither in what has been *proposed* as a matter of Faith, nor what must be *assented to* by faith.

To further clarify, a *formal* division occurs when there is a break in a principle of unity, and not when this or that member (or group of members) is discontinuous in some way with the whole. A formal doctrinal division *in the faith* would occur, for example, if the Pope *imposed* an error or heresy to be believed by all the faithful *with the assent of faith*. Not every doctrinal teaching of a Pope, catechism, or even a council is proposed as an *object of faith*. Only those doctrines that have been proposed *infallibly* are to be assented to with the assent of faith.[27] Doctrines that are not proposed infallibly are only adhered to with a *religious assent*, which is an assent of obedience, and not of faith. This is why a *formal division* in the Faith would only occur if the Church *infallibly* taught an error (which is a contradiction), since only that which has been proposed *infallibly* is assented to with the assent of faith. As we will demonstrate in future chapters, this has not occurred, and cannot occur by virtue of the negative protection of infallibility. Therefore, the errors and novelties that have spread throughout the membership of the Church cannot be said to have caused a *formal* rupture in the Faith, even though there is a material doctrinal division within the membership of the Church.

Notwithstanding the fact that the Modernist prelates have blurred certain teachings by an ambiguity that lends itself to an erroneous, and at times even heretical understanding, all Catholics still profess the same Creed on Sunday, and no errors or heresies have been infallibly proposed and imposed upon the Church, which means the Church today continues to be united (objectively) in what must be assented to *by Faith*. It is important to note, however, that the Church's unity in doctrine is not conditioned upon how many people actually adhere to what the Church officially teaches, much less how correctly each person understands every aspect of the faith; rather apostolicity in doctrines means that the doctrines officially taught by the Church and imposed upon all *as a matter of faith*, have been believed by the Church, at least implicitly, since the beginning.

Let us turn again to the Arian crisis to see what parallels we can find between that doctrinal crisis and the one we face today. St. Basil, one of the relatively few stalwart bishops who lived during the Arian crisis, describes what he and the faithful endured during that period in which the Church appeared to be almost entirely overtaken by heresy:

---

[27] This point will be discussed at length in Chapter 13.

"The danger is not confined to one Church...This evil of heresy spreads itself. The doctrines of Godliness are overturned; the rules of the Church are in confusion; the ambition of the unprincipled seizes upon places of authority; and the chief seat is now openly proposed as a reward for impiety; so that he whose blasphemies are the more shocking, is more eligible for the oversight of the people. Priestly gravity has perished; there are none left to feed the Lord's flock with knowledge; ambitious men are ever spending, in purposes of self-indulgence and bribery, possessions which they hold in trust for the poor. The accurate observation of the canons are no more; there is no restraint upon sin. Unbelievers laugh at what they see, and the weak are unsettled; faith is doubtful, ignorance is poured over their souls, because the adulterators of the word in wickedness imitate the truth. Religious people keep silence, but every blaspheming tongue is let loose. Sacred things are profaned; those of the laity who are sound in faith avoid the places of worship, as schools of impiety, and raise their hands in solitude with groans and tears to the Lord in heaven. ... What is most melancholy of all, even the portion among us which seems to be sound [in faith], is divided in itself, so that calamities beset us like those which came upon Jerusalem when it was besieged."[28]

The Arian crisis is an historical example of how the Church suffered a very severe *material* division in *doctrine*; a majority of the bishops drifted into heresy, and the Pope himself signed a semi-Arian (ambiguous) profession of faith.[29] The Church was shaken to its core, just like today. Yet, the Pope did not *impose* the Arian heresy upon the Church. For this reason, the Arian crisis serves as a near identical parallel of today's crisis. Those who remained strong in the faith refused to attend Mass at churches infected with Arianism, just as many Catholics today, who have remained strong in the faith, refuse to attend Mass at churches infected with Modernism. St. Basil further explained what the faithful endured:

"Matters have come to this pass: the people have left their houses of prayer, and assembled in the deserts, - a pitiable sight,

---

[28] St. Basil, *Second Letter to the Bishops of Italy and Gaul*, taken from Newman, *The Church of the Fathers*, (London: Buns, Oates, and Company, 1868), pp. 76-77.

[29] After a lengthy historical study of case of Pope Liberius, Hefele wrote: "We therefore conclude without doubt that Liberius, yielding to force, and sinking under many years of confinement and exile, signed the so-called third Sirmian formula, that is, the collection of older formulas of faith accepted at the third Sirmian Synold of 358. He did not do this without scruples, for the Semi-Arian character and origin of these formulas were not unknown to him." *A History of the Councils of the Church: From the Original Documents*, vol. 2 (Edinburgh, Scotland: T & T Clark, 1876), p. 245.

women and children, old men, and men otherwise infirm, wretchedly faring in the open air, amid the most profuse rains and snowstorms ... To this they submit, because they will have no part in the wicked Arian leaven."[30]

Those poisoned with the Arian heresy referred to these faithful Catholics by the derogatory term of "country-Christian," which became a badge of honor to those who remained firm in the faith.[31] In an exact parallel of today, St. Basil described the one "offense" that was not tolerated by those infected with the Arian heresy, which just happens to be the same offense that is not tolerated today by the Modernists: *"Only one offense is now vigorously punished,"* wrote St. Basil, *"an accurate observance of our fathers' traditions."*[32]

St. Athanasius, one of the greatest defenders of the Faith during the crisis, was banned from his diocese five times, spent seventeen years in exile, and suffered an unjust excommunication from the Pope.[33] By all appearances, St. Athanasius was an excommunicated schismatic, but in reality he was one of the greatest defenders of the Faith the Church would ever know.

The Arian heresy shows us what God can permit His Church and the faithful to endure, without the gates of hell prevailing, and without the apostolicity of doctrine being lost. By serving as a precedent for today, we can see how God draws good out of the evils that afflict the Church. If our current crisis is a foreshadowing of the great apostasy (as many believe), it will also serve as a useful precedent for those who live during that time. And, no doubt, the crisis during the final

---

[30] Newman, *Arians of the 4th Century* (London: Pickering and Co., 1883), p. 459.

[31] "Clever and underhanded as they were, the Arians forgot about the laity, who gathered around loyal priests, kept the true faith and assembled for Mass outside the cities ... The derisive term, 'country Christians,' given them by the Arians became a badge of honor. The faithful laity and clergy kept the faith and, in 381, the Second Ecumenical Council was convened in Constantinople, the Creed completed and Arianism again condemned." Count Neri Capponi, "Time of Crisis; Times for Faith." https://www.ewtn.com/library/CANONLAW/CRIFAITH.HTM.

[32] Ibid. (emphasis added).

[33] "Some Catholic apologists have attempted to prove that Liberius neither confirmed the excommunication of Athanasius nor subscribed to one of the formulae of Sirmium [sic]. But Cardinal Newman has no doubt that the fall of Liberius is an historical fact. This is also the case with the two modern works of reference just cited and the celebrated *Catholic Dictionary*, edited by Addis and Arnold. The last named points out that there is 'a fourfold cord of evidence not easily broken,' i.e., the testimonies of St. Athanasius, St. Hilary, Sozomen, and St. Jerome. It also notes that "all the accounts are at once independent of and consistent with each other." Davies, Michael, *Apologia Pro Marcel Lefebvre*, (Kansas City, Missouri: Angelus Press, 1999), Appendix I.

apostasy, and reign of antichrist, will be *much* more difficult than the Arian crisis of yesterday and the Modernist crisis of today.

Apostolicity of Government and Membership

The Church is a monarchical society by divine institution. A monarchy is an unequal society in which some members govern and other members are governed. The bishops together with the Pope constitute the *Ecclesia docens* (the "Church teaching"); the faithful represent the *Ecclesia discerns* (the "Church taught"). The division between the teaching Church and the taught Church (the hierarchy and the laity) is not one of two separate societies, or even two halves of the same society with two distinct sets of members. Rather, the division is between those with the power, assisted by Christ, to define speculative and practical truth, on the one hand, and those who recognize this power, on the other. Although the hierarchy alone represents the teaching Church, because the bishops themselves must believe what the Church teaches, they, too, along with the laity, make up part of the believing Church.[34]

Apostolicity of *membership* is sometimes referred to as apostolic in *origin*.[35] It means that the Church as a whole remains *numerically one*[36] and the same *visible society* as that which existed during the days of the Apostles.[37] The hierarchy, which is the principal part of the Church (instituted directly by Christ), will remain numerically one with the apostolic college. In fact, the bishops collectively (the college of bishops[38]) form "one and the same *juridical person* with the apostolic

---

[34] "Inasmuch as they are the depositaries and the organs of the power of jurisdiction, the Pope and the bishops constitute the Church teaching [*Ecclesia docens*]; but inasmuch as they too have souls to save, minds and hearts to be dedicated to God, they are parts of the Church believing [*Ecclesia discerns*]... They are bound, like all other Christians, under pain of endangering their eternal salvation, to accept all utterances pertaining to the divine law, even when it falls to their lot to propose them solemnly to the world for the first time: thus, not to lose his faith. (...) As to decrees resting on ecclesiastical law that they themselves have promulgated, here again the hierarchy are [morally] bound to conform." Cardinal Journet, *Church of the Word Incarnate* (London and New York: Sheed and Ward, 1955), pp. 25-26.

[35] *The Church of Christ*, p. 80.

[36] "Numerically one" means one and the same moral body, even though the individuals that make up the body will continuously be replaced by others over the course of time.

[37] *Christ's Church*, p. 154.

[38] Due to a potential misunderstanding regarding the term *college of bishops*, we should note that individual bishops possess jurisdiction over their respective dioceses alone, while the Pope possesses supreme jurisdiction over the entire Church. The former is ordered to the good of a particular church; the latter to the good of the whole Church. Now, while the Pope alone possesses universal jurisdiction over the universal Church, he

college,"[39] just as the entire Church, as a whole, is one and the same *moral body* with the Church from the time of the Apostles. Individual members are "born" into the Church and then die, being replaced by others, so forth and so on, throughout the ages, but the *moral body* itself remains one. Regarding the numerical oneness of the Church, Van Noort wrote:

> "A moral body, despite the fact that it constantly undergoes change and renovation in its personnel, remains numerically the same moral body so long as it retains the same social structure and the same authority. ... Please note the word, *numerically* the same society. A mere specific likeness would never satisfy the requirements of apostolicity."[40]

Just as the *indefectibility* of the *visible society* refutes the Sedevacantist claim that the Church in 1958 morphed into a New Church after electing John XXIII (as we saw in the last chapter), so too does the numerical oneness of the Church refute this error. This is because the Church of October 27, 1958 (before electing John XXIII) is numerically one and the same Church as that which existed on October 28, 1958 (after electing John XXIII), and the Church of 1958 is numerically one with the Church that existed in January of 1966. Likewise, the Church of 1966 is numerically one with the Church of the Apostles, as well as with the Church of today. In other words, the Church that everyone, except the Sedevacantists, recognizes as the Catholic Church is numerically one with the Church of the Apostles. This demonstrates that the Catholic Church of today cannot be a New Church, as the Sedevacantists claim.

Furthermore, the Sedevacantist *sects* did not originate until the mid to late 1970s.[41] If the true Church defected in 1958, and there were no

---

can exercise this authority singularly, or jointly with the other bishops at an ecumenical council. In the later case, the bishops are invited to *participate* with the Pope in the exercise of his universal jurisdiction. The bishops collectively do not constitute a second supreme authority in the Church (which is the error of "collegiality"), but only *participate* in the authority that belongs properly to the Pope when gathered at an ecumenical council. Cardinal Journet explains that "the power to rule the universal Church resides first of all in the Sovereign Pontiff, then in the episcopal college united with the Pontiff; and it can be exercised either singly by the Sovereign Pontiff, or jointly by the Pontiff and the episcopal college: the power of the Sovereign Pontiff singly and that of the Sovereign Pontiff united with the episcopal college constituting not two powers adequately distinct, but one sole supreme power..." (Journet, *Church of the Word Incarnate*, p. 412).
[39] *Christ's Church*, p. 155 (emphasis added).
[40] Ibid.
[41] There were some individuals who questioned or rejected the Popes prior to the mid-1970s, but the Sedevacantist sects, as such, did not exist prior to that time.

Sedevacantist sects until 20 years later, where was the true Church during the two intervening decades? If this visible Church ceased to exist for a time (or morphed into a New Church during or after 1958), the gates of hell would have prevailed against the Church, which is contrary to the promise of Christ.

Apostolicity of Government

Apostolicity of government (mission or authority[42]) is not only the most distinguishing *mark* of the true Church, and the most important of the unities,[43] but it also represents the greatest difficulty for the Sedevacantists. Their position forces them to openly reject what the Church teaches, or else invent novel theories (based on no verifiable facts) in an attempt to justify their thesis.

Apostolicity in government means that "the Church is always ruled by pastors who form one same *juridical person* with the apostles. In other words, it is always ruled by pastors who are the apostles' *legitimate* successors."[44] As we have seen, just as the Church itself is numerically one with the apostolic Church, so likewise her hierarchy is numerically one with the apostolic hierarchy, which will always consist of *legitimate* successors of the Apostles. At this point, an important question arises: what makes a person a *legitimate* successor of the apostles? To answer this question, it is necessary to make a distinction between the power of *Orders* and the power of *jurisdiction*.

The Power of Order and Jurisdiction

The members of the teaching Church (the hierarchy) participate in the threefold office of Christ (who is Prophet, Priest, and King) by *teaching, sanctifying* and *governing the members of the Church*.[45] To

---

[42] Contrary to what some Sedevacantist apologists have claimed, *apostolicity in government* includes *mission* and *authority*. Van Noort: "Apostolicity of government – or mission, or authority – means the Church is always ruled by pastors who form one same juridical person with the apostles. In other words, it is always ruled by pastors who are the apostles' *legitimate* successors" (*Christ's Church*, p. 151).

[43] "Unity of government is by far the most important of the unities, because without it no other form of unity could be maintained for any length of time" (Berry, *The Church of Christ*, p. 47).

[44] *Christ's Church*, p. 151 (emphasis added).

[45] The power to teach "is the right and the duty to set forth Christian truth with an authority to which all are held to give internal and external obedience. The power to function as priest, or to minister is the power to offer sacrifice and to sanctify people through the instrumentality of outward rights. The power to rule or govern is the power to regulate the moral condition of one's subjects. Since this power is exercised chiefly

accomplish these duties, the members of the hierarchy possess the twofold power of *order* and *jurisdiction*.

The *power of order* corresponds to the office of *sanctifying*. The power is conferred by ordination to the diaconate, priesthood, or bishopric, and imprint an indelible character on the man's soul that can never be taken away. Even the reprobate clergy retain this *permanent* character as they are punished in hell. Holy Orders are concerned primarily with the worship of God and the sanctification of souls. The indelible character gives certain powers to the ordained, which are not possessed by laymen. For example, one who has been consecrated (ordained) a bishop is able to validly ordain another man to the priesthood or bishopric, even if the ordaining bishop has apostatized and left the Church. Similarly, a man ordained as a priest will always be capable of saying a valid Mass, even if he has been formally excommunicated. In such a case, the Mass he celebrated would be *illicit* (illegal), but it would nevertheless be *valid* due to the permanent indelible character received at ordination.

Jurisdiction pertains to the office of *teaching* and *governing* in the Church, and can only be given by a legitimate superior. Jurisdiction does not imprint an indelible character, neither is it a permanent quality that can never be revoked. Some sacraments (e.g., Penance and Matrimony) require jurisdiction to be valid. The sacrament of Penance requires *both* Orders (at least that of a priest) and jurisdiction.

In his Dogmatic Manual, *Christ's Church*, Van Noort writes the following about the power of order and jurisdiction:

> "The power of orders is the same as that of the priesthood. It has as its immediate object the worship (in the strict sense) of God, and also the internal sanctification of souls through the infusion of grace. It takes its name from the sacrament of orders or sacred ordination, by which it is conferred on a person.
>
> The power of jurisdiction is the moral power to place others under obligation, to bind and to loose, and comprises at once the two powers of teaching and ruling. It has as its immediate object the governing of the people in the realm of belief (through doctrinal decrees), and conduct (through disciplinary laws, juridical sentences, penalties). Finally, it directs the faithful in acquiring holiness through their own personal efforts. <u>This power is conferred on a person when a superior imposes it, or when the person is given a legitimate mission</u>. (…)

---

through legislation and then through judicial sentences and penalties, it comprises legislative, juridical and coercive powers." (Van Noort, *Christ's Church*, p. 33).

They differ in their *basic nature*. The power of orders is merely instrumental or ministerial. Since God alone can produce grace as its principal, efficient Cause, the official personnel of the Church... act merely as God's instruments, or, since they are rational beings, as His ministers. ...

The power of jurisdiction, on the other hand, involves not merely instrumental, but real principal causality."[46]

With this distinction in mind between the power of orders and the power of jurisdiction, we will now discuss apostolic sucession and then see what is required for a person to be a *legitimate* successor of the Apostles.

Apostolic Succession

Apostolic succession is the unbroken line of succession beginning with the Apostles, who were ordained by Christ (Mk. 3:14), down to the bishops of today. Because a bishop can only be ordained (consecrated) by the laying on of hands by one who is already a bishop, there is an unbroken *physical* connection between the Apostles (the first bishops) and those whom they consecrated down to our present day. The laying on of hands, during the ordination (or episcopal consecration), confers the power of orders on the ordained.

We see this succession beginning just after Pentecost, when the Apostles selected Matthias to succeed Judas Iscariot: "And praying they said: Thou, Lord, who knoweth the hearts of all men, show which of these two thou hast chosen, to take the place of this ministry and apostleship from which Judas hath by transgression fallen... And they gave them lots, and the lots fell upon Matthias, and he was numbered with the eleven apostles" (Acts 1:24-26). Later, we see Sts. Paul and Barnabas (both of whom are referred to as Apostles) being consecrated bishops by the laying on of hands, when the Holy Ghost said: "Separate me Saul and Barnabas, for the work whereunto I have taken them. Then they, fasting and praying, and imposing their hands upon them, sent them away" (Acts 13:2-3). Having been consecrated bishops, St. Paul and the other Apostles would go on to consecrate other men to the bishopric.[47] This succession has continued in the Church founded by Christ to our present day, without interruption.

---

[46] Ibid., pp. 48, 49 (emphasis added).
[47] For example, In Titus 1:5, St. Paul writes to Titus: "For this cause I left thee in Crete, that thou shouldest set in order the things that are wanting, and shouldest ordain priests in every city, as I also appointed thee." About this verse, St. John Chrysostom says, "here he [St. Paul] is speaking of bishops" since he says "as I also appointed thee" bishop.

Although valid orders makes a man a physical successor of the Apostles, they do not, in and of themselves, make a man a *legitimate* successor of the Apostles. This is clear from the fact that the character received at ordination remains even if a bishop were to apostatize and leave the Church, or be publicly excommunicated by the Church. In such a case, the character received at ordination, and the powers that go with it, remain. If a validly consecrated bishop left the Church and founded a new religion, he would still retain the power to consecrate bishops who would be *physical* successors of the Apostles (they would possess valid orders), but they would not be *legitimate* successors of the Apostles. To be a *legitimate* successor of the Apostles, one must possess the *authority* of the Apostles, and this authority comes with *jurisdiction*.

Legitimate Apostolic Succession

Episcopal *orders* (i.e., consecration to the bishopric) is the *material* aspect of apostolic succession; *jurisdiction*, which is the power to teach and govern in the Church, constitutes the *formal* aspect. Even members of a schismatic group, such as the Orthodox, possess *material* apostolic succession, but this does not make them *legitimate* successors of the Apostles. Fr. Berry explains:

"[S]ome knowledge of succession is necessary for a proper conception of apostolicity of *ministry*. Succession, as used in this connection, is the following of one person after another in an official position, and may be either *legitimate* or *illegitimate*. Theologians call the one *formal* succession; the other, *material.* A material successor is one who assumes the official position of another contrary to the laws or constitution of the society in question. He may be called a successor in as much as he actually holds the position, but he has no authority, and his acts have no official value, even though he be ignorant of the illegal tenure of his office. A formal, or legitimate, successor not only succeeds to the place of his predecessor, but also receives due authority to exercise the functions of his office with binding force in the society. It is evident that authority can be transmitted only by legitimate succession; therefore, the Church must have a legitimate, or formal, succession of pastors to transmit the apostolic authority from age to age."[48]

Chrysostom, Homilies on Titus, Homily II, Titus 1:5-6, Translated by the Rev. James Tweed, M.A., of Corpus Christi College, Cambridge; re-edited by the Rev. Philip Schaff, D.D., LL.D. See https://www.ewtn.com/library/PATRISTC/PNI13-11.TXT.
[48] Berry, *The Church of Christ*, p. 78.

R. P. Herrmann, in his book, *Theologiæ Dogmaticæ Institutiones*, elaborates on the same point:

> "Succession may be material or formal. Material succession consists in the fact that there have never been lacking persons who have continuously been substituted for the Apostles; formal succession consists in the fact that these substituted persons truly enjoy authority derived from the Apostles and received from him who is able to communicate it. For someone to be made a successor of the Apostles and pastor of the Church, the power of order — which is always validly conferred by virtue of ordination — is not enough; the power of jurisdiction is also required, and this is conferred not by virtue of ordination but by virtue of a mission received from him to whom Christ has entrusted the supreme power over the universal Church."[49]

Van Noort posed the question: "How can you be sure that this or that bishop should be counted as a legitimate successor of the apostles?" He responded as follows:

> "Obviously a man does not become a genuine successor to the Apostles merely by arrogating to himself the title of 'bishop,' or by carrying on in some fashion a function once performed by the Apostles. Neither is it enough for a man merely to possess some one, individual power, say for example, the power of *orders*. – The power of orders can be acquired even illicitly, and once acquired can never be lost. – What is required for genuine apostolic succession is that a man enjoy the *complete* powers (i.e., ordinary powers, not extraordinary) of an apostle. He must, then, in addition to the power of orders, possess also the power of *jurisdiction*. Jurisdiction means the power to teach and govern."[50]

In another place, he wrote:

> "Any man, then, who boasts of apostolic succession but is not united to the Roman pontiff, may indeed actually possess the power of orders; he may even by purely physical succession occupy a chair formerly occupied by an apostle - at least he could do so - but he would not be a genuine successor of the apostles in their pastoral office."[51]

---

[49] Herrmann, *Theologiæ Dogmaticæ Institutiones*, vol. I (Rome: Pacis Philippi Cuggiani, 1897), n. 282 (emphasis added).
[50] *Christ's Church*, p. 152 (emphasis in original).
[51] Ibid., p. 153.

It is a dogma of the Faith that the Church will always possess legitimate successors of the Apostles – that is, validly ordained bishops who *also* possess jurisdiction in the Church.[52] These men are not only the *physical* successors of the Apostles (material succession), but must have also received their apostolic *authority* (formal succession) to continue Christ's divine mission through His one true Church. Formal apostolic succession is the surest mark of the true Church because it distinguishes it from all others.[53] The *Catholic Encyclopedia* explains:

> "Apostolicity is the mark by which the Church of today is recognized as identical with the Church founded by Jesus Christ upon the Apostles. It is of great importance because it is the surest indication of the true Church of Christ. (…) This Apostolic succession must be both material and formal; the material consisting in the actual succession in the Church, through a series of persons from the Apostolic age to the present; the formal adding the element of authority [jurisdiction] in the transmission of power. It consists in the legitimate transmission of the ministerial power conferred by Christ upon His Apostles. … any concept of Apostolicity that excludes authoritative union with the Apostolic mission robs the ministry of its Divine character. Apostolicity, or Apostolic succession, then, means that the mission conferred by Jesus Christ upon the Apostles must pass from them to their legitimate successors, in an unbroken line, until the end of the world."[54]

Bishops Receive Their Authority from the Pope

From whom do the bishops receive the power of jurisdiction (authority), by which they become *legitimate* successors of the Apostles? They receive it directly from the Pope, *and only from the Pope.* Jurisdiction comes from a superior. Because the Church is by divine institution a monarchical society, only the head of this society – the Pope – receives his authority immediately and directly from Christ. The other bishops, as Pope Pius XII taught in *Mystici Corporis Christi*,

---

[52] "there will always be in the Church a body of men invested with that threefold power which the apostles enjoyed. This thesis is a dogma of faith…" (Van Noort, *Christ's Church*, p. 37).

[53] Dr. Ludwig Van Ott said: "In the unbroken succession of Bishops from the Apostles the *apostolic character* of the Church most clearly appears." (*Fundamentals of Catholic Dogma*, p. 308).

[54] *Catholic Encyclopedia* (1913), vol. I, p. 648 (emphasis added).

receive their jurisdiction *"directly* from the Supreme Pontiff" (and only *indirectly* from Christ).[55] Fr. Berry explains:

> "Jurisdiction is authority to govern and must be transmitted in the Church ... there can be no legitimate successor in the Church of Christ, who has not received jurisdiction either directly or indirectly from her *supreme authority*. But as will be proven elsewhere, the supreme authority in the Church of Christ was committed to St. Peter and his lawful successors, the bishops of Rome."[56]

When a Pope dies, the bishops retain the jurisdiction they previously received, but they can never obtain jurisdiction unless it is given by a Pope.

Formal apostolic succession, which is possessed by the body of *legitimate* bishops, is a perpetual and permanent reality in the Church, as we read in Van Noort's dogmatic manual, *Christ's Church*:

> "Proposition: *It was Christ's will that the sacred ruling power which had begun in the apostolic college should continue forever.*
>
> This proposition is concerned with the same threefold power which we have proved to have been given to the apostles [i.e., to teach, function as priests, and govern]. It asserts that this power was granted by Christ with the following stipulation: that it be handed on to an endless line of successors. We are not concerned at the moment with the subordinate co-workers of the apostles. The only point to be proven here is that it was Christ's will that the apostolic college should continue forever, <u>in such a way that there would always be in the Church a body of men invested with the threefold power which the apostles enjoyed [which includes jurisdiction]. This thesis is *a dogma of faith*, as we know, e.g., from the Council of Trent, Sess. 23, c. 4 (DB 960)."</u>[57]

---

[55] For centuries there were two general opinions regarding how a bishop receives his authority. The *minority opinion* held that authority was given to the bishop immediately by Christ at his ordination, and that the Pope merely designated him to a particular diocese, or perhaps fulfilled some *condition* required before Christ would immediately and directly grant the jurisdiction. The *majority opinion* held that jurisdiction comes to the bishop *directly* through the Pope, and only *indirectly* by Christ. In *Mystici Corporis Christi*, Pius XII gave his judgment by explicitly teaching the majority opinion: "Yet in exercising this office they [the bishops] are not altogether independent, but are subordinate to the lawful authority of the Roman Pontiff; and although their jurisdiction is inherent in the office, yet *they receive it directly from the Supreme Pontiff*" (No. 42; emphasis added).

[56] *The Church of Christ*, pp. 78-79.

[57] Ibid., p. 37 (italics in original; underline added). The Council of Trent, On the Sacrament of Order, Canon VI. — "If any one saith, that, in the Catholic Church there is not a hierarchy by divine ordination instituted, consisting of bishops, priests, and ministers; let him be anathema."

He went on to say:

> "The Church depends essentially on the teaching, priestly, <u>and ruling power of the apostles</u>. ... When our Lord gave the apostles their definitive mission to teach, sanctify, and rule, He went on to say, in the clearest terms: 'And behold I am with you all days, even to the consummation of the world'[58](Mt 28:20). But how could He possibly be forever present to the apostolic college, in the work of teaching, sanctifying, and ruling, unless that college itself were to last forever, unless <u>the apostles were to have a never-ending line of successors in their work as teachers, priests, *and rulers*</u>?"[59]

To be a successor of the Apostles in the office of *teacher* and *ruler* requires authority, which is received by *jurisdiction*.

While it is possible for there to be a time when there is no Pope (i.e., a temporary interregnum following the death of one Pope and before the election of another), there can *never* be a time in which the Teaching Body itself (the Magisterium) ceases to exist. As noted above, this is a dogma of the Faith, and therefore cannot be denied without embracing heresy.

In the magnificent book, *Manual of Dogmatic Theology* (1906), by Wilhelm and Scannell, we read:

> "The Indefectibility of the <u>Teaching Body</u>[60] is at the same time a condition and a consequence of the <u>Indefectibility of the Church</u>. A distinction must, however, be drawn between the Indefectibility of the Head [Pope], and the Indefectibility of the subordinate members [Bishops]. The individual who is the Head may die, but the authority of the Head does not die with him – it is transmitted to his successor. On the other hand, <u>the Teaching Body as a whole could not die or fail without irreparably destroying the continuity of authentic testimony</u>. Again, the Pope's authority would not be injured if, when not exercising it (*extra judicium*), he professed a false doctrine, whereas <u>the authenticity of the episcopal testimony would be destroyed if under any circumstances the whole body fell into heresy</u>."[61]

---

[58] The translation used in the original was replaced by the Douay Rheims translation.

[59] *Christ's Church,* pp. 37-38 (emphasis added).

[60] To be clear, the Teaching Body consists of the bishops who possess *jurisdiction* received from a Pope.

[61] Wilhelm, Joseph, and Scannell, Thomas, *A Manual of Catholic Theology,* vol. I, 3rd ed. (New York, Cincinnati, Chicago: Benzinger Bros., 1906), pp. 45-46.

This is yet another proverbial nail in the Sedevacantist coffin, since they claim that the Teaching Body *as a whole* fell into heresy, lost their jurisdiction, and ceased to be part of the Church (becoming a "New Church"). But if this would have occurred, the Church would have defected, since the indefectibility of the Teaching Body is linked to the indefectibility of the Church. As we have seen, the Sedevacantists don't merely profess a Church without a Pope, but also a Church without a legitimate Teaching Body (the Magisterium), which is not possible. As Fr. Tranquillo points out:

> "According to today's Sedevacantists, not only is the Chair of Peter vacant, but also all of the episcopal sees. Thus, one who wants to apply those theses to the current situation must recall that he is not putting forward a Church 'without Pope' (which happens on the occasion of every conclave), but a Church without any hierarchy on this earth, without a residential episcopate, and thus without the presence of ordinary jurisdiction."[62]

As we saw in Chapter 1, the Sedevacantist preacher, Gerry Matatics, publicly teaches that the Magisterium *no longer exists.* According to Mr. Matatics, all we have today are the writings of the Magisterium from the time when it did exist. He says: "there is no living voice of the Magisterium," but that "doesn't mean we're lost; it doesn't mean we're abandoned, because we've got *the Magisterium of the past.*"[63]

A "Magisterium of the past" does not suffice. Contrary to what Mr. Matatics publicly preaches in the name of Catholicism, it is a dogma of faith that the Church will always possess a college of bishops – that is, legitimate successors of the Apostles - who possess both the power of orders (material succession) and jurisdiction (formal succession). This is not something of the past; but a reality of the present. Of course, the only Church that even *claims* to have bishops who have received jurisdiction from the Pope is the Church that everyone, but Mr. Matatics and his Sedevacantist colleagues, recognizes as the Catholic Church.

Now, because only a Pope can grant jurisdiction, if Pius XII were the last true Pope (as most Sedevacantists claim), then there are no longer any bishops, *at all*, currently in charge of dioceses who possess jurisdiction. This would mean that *legitimate* apostolic succession

---

[62] Tranquillo, "Permanence of the Papacy, Permanence of the Church." Originally appeared in Italian in *Tradizione Cattolica*, n.1, 2014 (emphasis added).
[63] "Counterfeit Catholicism," disc 4 of 6, track 15.

would not even be found in the one and only Church that *claims* to possess bishops who received their jurisdiction from a Pope.

"Bishop in the Woods" Theory

Faced with the reality that the Sedevacantist position leads to a denial of the indefectibility of the Teaching Body (the Magisterium), the lay Sedevacantist apologist, John Lane, came up with a creative but unsuccessful attempt to solve the difficulty. He began by noting that a bishop cannot retire unless the resignation is accepted by the Pope. He then argued that if all the Popes from John XXIII forward were antipopes, it would mean that the resignation given by a bishop to one of these false Popes would not have been a valid resignation. Consequently, he reasoned, if any bishops were still alive who had received jurisdiction from Pius XII, they would continue to possess true jurisdiction today, even if they didn't know about it.

Mr. Lane presented this argument as a way to explain how it is possible for there to be a true Teaching Body (a bishop or two with jurisdiction) in existence today. He imagines that this theory (which is obviously built upon the false premise that we have not had a true Pope since 1958 to accept the bishops' resignations) allows Sedevacantists to reject all the conciliar Popes without having to admit that there are no bishops left with ordinary jurisdiction. Lane came up with this wild theory to avoid the obvious classification of his own position as heretical, which he knows it would be if no such bishops exist. Fr. Cekada, realizing how ridiculous Lane's theory is, referred to it as the "Bishop in the Woods" thesis. Mocking the theory invented by his fellow Sedevacantist, Fr. Cekada wrote:

> "Mr. Lane's Bishop in the Woods thesis, in fact, DEFEATS the two things about the Church it is supposed to save:
> a. Visibility - because no one can see this bishop.
> b. Apostolicity - for how can the Church be RECOGNIZED by the mark of apostolicity if no one can FIND the one bishop who is supposed to continue and embody it?[64]

In addition to the devastating objections Fr. Cekada raised, John Lane's theory creates a burden of proof that he cannot meet. Theorizing that there *could be* a bishop or two still living who were appointed by

---

[64] Fr. Cekada's complete comments can be read at http://www.tedeum.boards.net/thread/341/father-cekada-thread?page=2.

Pius XII, almost six decades ago,[65] is not the same thing as *proving* that they do, in fact, exist. And presenting the "Bishop in the Woods" as a mere "possibility" necessarily admits of the possibility that *they don't exist at all* – and, thus, that there are no legitimate bishops left. In fact, Mr. Lane actually *admits* that if there are no bishops left with ordinary jurisdiction, *then the Sedevacantist thesis is false.* But he attempts to escape the conclusion by shifting the burden of proof to his opponents. Here's what he says:

> "From this we conclude that the Church must always possess at least one bishop with ordinary jurisdiction or she would not be the Church. Now, if there is no such bishop, then either the proposition is not true – that is, we misunderstood the doctrinal point – or the *Sedevacantist* solution is wrong. Of course, until it is demonstrated that the Church does not possess even one bishop with ordinary jurisdiction, then there is no concrete problem. The problem is not just theoretical, but hypothetical."[66]

Notice that Mr. Lane puts the burden of proof *on others* to demonstrate that there is *not* a Pius XII bishop with jurisdiction. It's quite convenient for Mr. Lane to declare, on his own authority, that *all the bishops currently in charge of the episcopal sees lack ordinary jurisdiction,* and then tell his opponents that *they* must disprove his own theory by demonstrating that a Pius XII "Bishop in the Woods" *does not* exist.

Mr. Lane is guilty here of the logical fallacy known as Shifting the Burden of Proof.[67] Since it is Lane who is making the claim (that a Pius XII bishop with ordinary jurisdiction exists somewhere in the world),

---

[65] Because, according to the Sedevacantist thesis, the vacancies of the episcopal sees are lasting for generations and exceeding the average human lifespan, Sedevacantists are scrambling for new theories to buy more time. To give themselves more time beyond the death of Pius XII in 1958 to have valid bishops, we have seen that some Sedevacantists have begun to move the bar by suggesting that John XXIII may have been a valid Pope after all (since he didn't ratify Vatican II) and thus his episcopal appointments, through 1963, remained valid. Similarly, some Sedevacantists have suggested that Paul VI was a valid Pope until he ratified Vatican II at the end of 1965, and thus his episcopal appointments prior to that were valid. Of course, these arguments fail to account for the indefectibility of the visible social unit, which is the Church. And the longer the current crisis goes on, the more improbable, nay, ridiculous, the "Bishop in the Woods" theory becomes.

[66] Lane's comments are taken from his website at http://www.sedevacantist.com/viewtopic.php?f=2&t=429 (emphasis added).

[67] "Shifting the burden of proof is a kind of logical fallacy in argumentation whereby the person who would ordinarily have the burden of proof in an argument attempts to switch that burden to the other person, e.g.: If you don't think that the Invisible Pink Unicorn exists, then prove it!" See http://wiki.ironchariots.org/index.php?title=Shifting_the_burden_of_proof.

the burden of proof lies with him to demonstrate it, and is not up to anyone else to *disprove* it (how Lane would not be aware of such a rudimentary element of debate is quite surprising).

To illustrate the fallacy of Lane's reasoning, these authors claim that there are green men on Mars, and "until it is demonstrated" by Mr. Lane that Mars "does not possess even one" green man, "then there is no concrete problem," and we can assume green men on Mars exist. Unfortunately for Mr. Lane, the burden remains with him to prove a Pius XII bishop with ordinary jurisdiction exists, not on others to disprove it. But the problem with his "Bishop in the Woods" thesis doesn't end there.

Even if Lane were to prove the existence of a Pius XII bishop, he would still have the burden of proving that the bishop rejected "the Vatican II Church," and its Popes. In other words, he would have to find a *Sedevacantist* "Bishop in the Woods" who was never a member of the "New Church" (what the Sedevacantists call the Catholic Church after 1958). Why never a member of New Church? Because, according to the Sedevacantists' own position, the Vatican II Church is a false Church; and, according to their favorite canon from the 1917 Code, if a cleric publicly adheres to a non-Catholic sect (a false Church), he automatically vacates his office (Canon 188, §4), and hence loses his jurisdiction (which means the bishop's resignation would not have to be accepted by a true Pope). This would mean that if the Pius XII "Bishop in the Woods" adhered to the New Church that allegedly came into existence in 1958 (or 1965), even for a short time, he would have lost his jurisdiction *ipso facto*, according to their own logic and arguments.[68]

Now, dear reader, what seems more likely, that John Lane will prove that there is a Pius XII Bishop (consecrated six decades ago, which would put him well into his 90s if not over 100 years old), who is both a Sedevacantist and who was *never* a member of the "New Church," or that the Sedevacantist position is wrong?

Moreover, "the problem" of legitimate apostolic succession is not "hypothetical" as Mr. Lane claims, but *actual*, with *actual* (not hypothetical) consequences – no less than the defection of the Catholic Church founded by Christ. If John Lane cannot prove his case, then, in his own words, "the Sedevacantist solution is wrong," since the

---

[68] Even if there did exist a Pius XII bishop or two in the woods with ordinary jurisdiction, this Sedevacantist "solution" would still constitute a violation of the Church's indefectibility (since it maintains that the visible hierarchy fell away, causing the visible Church to morph into a New Church) and moral Catholicity (the Church can never be reduced to a small number of members), as we have seen.

proposition that there must always be *legitimate* successors of the Apostles is *de fide*. Indeed, Sedevacantism *is* wrong; and the *real* solution for Lane's difficulty is that the bishops of our day, currently in charge of the dioceses throughout the world, are the *legitimate* successors of the Apostles with ordinary jurisdiction - a reality that is staring Lane and his colleagues right in the face.

Fr. Cekada's "Solution"

Fr. Cekada evidently recognizes that the Sedevacantists bear this burden of proof that they cannot meet, which is why he coined and ridiculed Mr. Lane's "Bishop in the Woods" theory. But what is Fr. Cekada's solution to the problem? His "solution" is perhaps worse: Fr. Cekada's way around the problem is to explicitly *reject* the teaching of the Church (as expressed by Pius XII) by claiming that bishops today receive their jurisdiction *at ordination* (immediately from Christ) and *not* from the Pope (which is precisely what the Eastern schismatic bishops declared a millennium ago). In Fr. Cekada's own words:

> "If there is no true pope, as a sede like me would maintain, the provisions of ecclesiastical law pertaining to legitimacy of mission and apostolic succession can no longer be said to apply strictly. Nevertheless, this mission and command Our Lord gave to the apostles and those who would succeed them still applies as a matter of divine law,[69] because the divine law endures for all time, even when the provisions of human-ecclesiastical [law] can no longer be followed. Traditional bishops and priests received the obligation to continue this apostolic mission from Christ in virtue of their consecrations and ordinations."[70]

Notice, Fr. Cekada claims that "apostolic mission" (which requires jurisdiction) comes directly to Sedevacantist bishops *and priests*, by virtue of their ordination. He continues:

> "Despite the fact that their mission and succession did not come to them through the provisions of human-ecclesiastical law, their mission and succession is indeed apostolic as regards the divine law

---

[69] Fr. Cekada is fond of appealing to "divine law" to support his pet theories. As we will see in Chapter 5 and beyond, he also erroneously believes that a heretic loses his office for the sin of heresy under "divine law," without the authorities of the Church being involved in the process.

[70] Fr. Cekada's comments are taken from http://sedevacantist.com/viewtopic.php?f=2&t=1468.

because it is identical with the mission Christ gave to the Church."[71]

We see that the only way Fr. Cekada can defend his Sedevacantist position is to reject the teaching of Pius XII that bishops receive their jurisdiction (mission) "directly from the Supreme Pontiff." For Fr. Cekada, there is apparently no longer a distinction between the reception of orders and the reception of jurisdiction (a dogmatic distinction that is rooted in divine revelation and taught by the Church since the very beginning) because, well, *he doesn't think we have a valid Pope.*[72] What this shows is that just as Catholic truth builds upon truth, so the Sedevacantist error breeds more errors, as the rejection of one truth logically and necessarily leads to the rejection of the others.

John Lane, who, as we saw above, is guilty of his own fallacious reasoning on the question of jurisdiction, rightly criticized Fr. Cekada's un-Catholic position in no uncertain terms. After saying Fr. Cekada's position "just reeks of Protestantism," Lane went on to say:

> "Private judgement erecting ministers of Christ. No public authority involved. This is worse than Anglicanism, which at least replaced the authority of the Church with secular authority. It's one thing to defend another who is under attack when the police cannot be found; it's entirely another thing to don a uniform and pose as a cop. Who's the judge of the fitness of a potential bishop? The potential bishop (and his sidekick, perhaps)? What's the authority of a bishop without a mission from the Church? His own declarations to the effect that *his* Gospel is the true one? How does this differ from Protestantism? Does not every apologetics manual condemn this kind of theory on every second page? Fr. Cekada tells us, 'As regards hierarchy, mission and apostolicity, the short answer is this:...' He needs to give the long answer, ASAP. His short answer just opens the door to countless heresies, if it isn't heretical itself."[73]

Another one of Fr. Cekada's fellow Sedevacantists said, "it is not true that the power to teach and govern comes through consecration.

---

[71] Ibid.

[72] Fr. Cekada is being inconsistent in his own treatment of the power of orders and jurisdiction. As we will see in Chapter 18, Fr. Cekada claims that the form in the new rite of episcopal consecration is invalid because it does not univocally signify the grace of orders, only jurisdiction. But here he argues that the power of orders subsumes the power of jurisdiction as a matter of Divine law and the apostolic mission of Christ, at least during this time of crisis.

[73] http://www.sedevacantist.com/viewtopic.php?f=2&t=1468.

This is against the specific teaching of Pius XII, as everybody knows," and then added: "With defenders like Fr. Cekada, Sedevacantism doesn't need enemies..."[74]

As Lane rightly observed, Fr. Cekada's teaching "opens the door to countless heresies, if it isn't heretical itself," but the same is true with the Sedevacantist thesis as a whole. For it not only denies that the peaceful and universal acceptance of a Pope is an infallible sign of his legitimacy, as Cardinal Billot explained (as we saw in Chapter 1), but it also denies the indefectibility of the visible Church by claiming that the visible society, with its members, morphed into a New Church, with the *same* members. We also have the public profession of heresy by those who claim that the true Church today exists "in the hearts and minds" of true believers, who "profess the true Faith," and who are somehow spiritually united together without a Pope or hierarchy. Their loss of faith *in the Church* has caused them to deny the marks and attributes of the Church. They have been led right into the error of Protestantism, which substitutes visible *members* for the material and formal visibility *of the Church of Jesus Christ.*

When John Lane first discovered that Fr. Cekada explicitly denies that there are any bishops left with ordinary jurisdiction, he said: "I myself was shocked to discover that Fr. Cekada's 'sedevacantism' involves the explicit denial that the Apostles have any Successors at all today. This assertion is directly opposed to Tradition, as formulated at Vatican I."[75] He went on to say:

> "I have spent more than fifteen years combatting what I thought was an entirely unjust allegation against 'sedevacantism' - viz., that we hold that the hierarchy is extinct - only to discover that this is exactly what Fr. Cekada believes. Not only that, I found out also that he has held this view for many years. So the SSPX has not been unjustly defaming 'sedevacantism' - they have been justly and accurately opposing an <u>heretical theory</u> held by the most prominent 'sedevacantist' proponent in the English-speaking world."[76]

Unfortunately for Mr. Lane, while Fr. Cekada holds to a "heretical theory" about episcopal jurisdiction, Lane falls into a related heresy (which denies legitimate apostolic succession), unless he can prove that there is a Pius XII bishop somewhere out there with ordinary jurisdiction (contrary to the assessment of Fr. Cekada), and who was

---

[74] Ibid.
[75] http://www.sedevacantist.com/viewtopic.php?f=2&t=1443.
[76] Ibid.

never a member of the modern Church. Of course, even if there were such a bishop in existence, it would still mean the entire visible hierarchy defected, and this is itself contrary to the indefectibility of the Church, since the *visible* Church will always have a *visible* hierarchy. Therefore, Mr. Lane's "solution" is also heretical.

Supplied Jurisdiction?

Fr. Cekada should realize the implications that his theory (that there are no bishops left with ordinary jurisdiction) has on supplied jurisdiction,[77] which he and all his parishioners depend upon for the validity of the sacrament of Penance and Matrimony. In a recent article published in the *Courrier de Rome*, Fr. Tranquillo explains that supplied jurisdiction presupposes habitual (ordinary) jurisdiction in the Church. Because all jurisdiction comes to the Church through the Pope, if there is no Pope, *and if there are no more bishops who received jurisdiction from a valid Pope,* "then jurisdiction delegated in extraordinary fashion [i.e., supplied jurisdiction] would also no longer exist."[78]

---

[77] Church law teaches that in cases of necessity, clergy who do not possess faculties (i.e., ordinary jurisdiction delegated by a bishop), can still validly administer the sacraments that require jurisdiction (hearing confessions, witnessing Holy Matrimony). This is known as *supplied jurisdiction,* or *ecclesia supplet* ("the Church provides"). Supplied jurisdiction (foreseen in canon law), is based upon the highest law of the Church, which is the salvation of souls (Canon 1752, from the 1983 Code of Canon Law). If there are no priests available, or none who can be trusted (which, unfortunately, is often the case in today's crisis), the faithful are permitted to approach traditional Catholic priests to receive the sacraments, even if these priests lack faculties (ordinary jurisdiction). According to canon law, these priests may validly administer the sacraments, not only in matters of grave necessity (e.g., a person is in danger of death), but even when the faithful request the sacraments from them *for any just cause* (avoiding Modernist priests who are leading souls into error and endangering their eternal salvation, is certainly a most just, and even *necessary,* cause). For example, in the 1917 Code of Canon Law, canon 2261, §2 permits the faithful to even approach an excommunicated priest in time of necessity. It says that "… the faithful may *for any just cause* ask the sacraments or sacramentals of one who is excommunicated, especially if there is no one else to give them…" Many other canons in both the old and new Code recognize supplied jurisdiction in various circumstances, such as canons 207, 209, 882 and 2252 (1917 Code) and canons 144, 976 and 1357 (1983 Code).
[78] Fr. Tranquillo: "If ordinary jurisdiction were to disappear completely from the individuals living upon this earth … then jurisdiction delegated in extraordinary fashion would also no longer exist, because it is delegated by someone, in the terms of the law, and not by the 'Church,' as understood in the abstract. Certainly Canon Law makes use of the expression supplet Ecclesia, but theologically and metaphysically jurisdiction resides in men who have received it from the Pope (or from Christ, in the case of the Pope alone). It is not floating around in the air waiting for someone to grab it. … Now, if not only the Pope but also all of the local Bishops are missing, we must ask from whom a priest could receive jurisdiction, even if just to hear the confession of a dying person. The

If Fr. Tranquillo's conclusion is correct (supplied jurisdiction is delegated by those with ordinary jurisdiction), then this would mean that those Sedevacantist priests, such as Fr. Cekada, who deny there are any bishops left who received their jurisdiction from the Pope are, *according to their own position*, giving their flock invalid absolutions in the confessional (and Fr. Cekada's error that priests receive jurisdiction directly from Christ does not solve the problem, since his subjective error on this point of doctrine has no effect on objective reality).

If Fr. Tranquillo's conclusion is incorrect (and supplied jurisdiction is delegated by Church law, without the need for ordinary jurisdiction), Sedevacantists would still not benefit from the sacraments because they are in schism (they reject the Pope and the Church over which he rules).[79] This Catch-22 is a classic case of being "damned if you do and damned if you don't," because whether supplied jurisdiction is available or not, members of the Sedevacantist sect will not thereby profit, since outside the Church there is neither salvation, *nor remission of sin*.[80]

Unauthorized Shepherds

Some Sedevacantists, who are well aware that none of the Sedevacantist bishops or priests possess jurisdiction (and therefore have no true "mission" from the Church) claim it is forbidden to receive the sacraments administered by Sedevacantist clergy (which is at least being consistent in their position). Yet these individuals also claim it is forbidden to receive the sacraments from a priest in union with "the Vatican II Church," or even from traditionalist clergy (like those of the S.S.P.X.). Obviously this doesn't leave many options for receiving the sacraments. In fact, it leaves *no* options.

---

problem is thus not knowing if, in certain situations, the power can be delegated under extraordinary forms (this is completely beyond dispute), but by whom. If someone answers that one can receive it directly from Jesus Christ, he must know that, by doing so, he is creating an exception to the principle whereby all jurisdiction on this earth comes from the Pope, the only one who receives the power from Christ Himself." (Tranquillo, "Permanence of the Papacy, Permanence of the Church." Translated into French for the June 2014 issue of *Courrier de Rome*. Translated from French to English by Fr. Paul Robinson.)

[79] Even under the 1983 Code of Canon Law, schismatics incur *latae sententiae* excommunication (1364, §1), and excommunicated persons are forbidden from celebrating or receiving the sacraments (1331, §1, °2).

[80] Pope Boniface VIII: "With Faith urging us we are forced to believe and to hold the one, holy, Catholic Church and that, apostolic, and we firmly believe and simply confess this (Church) outside which there is no salvation *nor remission of sin*..." (Denz., 468).

For those in whom the disease of Sedevacantism has fully metastasized, *all* post-Vatican II clergy (including Eastern Rite and traditional clergy) *and even the Sedevacantist clergy*, are "unauthorized shepherds,"[81] who "true Catholics" must avoid. These Sedevacantists (who are known as "home-aloners") refuse to receive the sacraments *at all*, thereby depriving themselves and their families of the ordinary means of salvation - all because of the erroneous theory they have come up with to explain the crisis in the Church. These souls stay home on Sundays, reading their missal and attempting to elicit acts of perfect contrition, in the hope that God will directly absolve them of their grave sins (again, just like Protestants).

Mr. Matatics, who has embraced and publicly defends this position, recently explained how he fulfills his Sunday obligation. He wrote:

> "I unite myself and my family — as we do every Sunday and every holy day, and in fact every single day of the year as we gather for family worship — *with all true Catholics around the world* and down through the ages who by God's grace, accept all of the Church's teachings and strive to abide by all her laws."[82]

This is where the error of Sedevacantism logically leads: a complete *withdrawal* from the visible social unit of the Church and the God-given means of sanctification, by staying at home on Sundays, uniting in spirit "with all true Catholics around the word" (translation: those who

---

[81] This is the title of a talk and CD set sold by Mr. Matatics. In his talk, Matatics claims that if one holds that a person can be saved in the post-Vatican II Church, then there is no true state of necessity, and therefore they cannot argue that the S.S.P.X. bishops and priests have supplied jurisdiction. This is another example of how Sedevacantists overgeneralize their argumentation. Matatics fails to distinguish between absolute and relative necessity. While it is not *absolutely* necessary to approach traditional priests for salvation, one may certainly argue it is a *relative* necessity in the current crisis, due to the danger of attending Mass at the average *Novus Ordo* parish. During the Arian crisis, it was certainly *possible* to save one's soul by attending the Mass of a priest infected with the heresy, but it was dangerous to do so since the faithful usually end by believing what their priest teaches. For this reason, the faithful avoided the local churches and assembled in the desert, receiving the sacraments from Athanasius, an "excommunicated" priest who was apparently in schism (without ordinary jurisdiction). The statistics today show that a majority of *Novus Ordo* priests, and the vast majority of those who attend *Novus Ordo* parishes, reject the Church's moral teaching (e.g., birth control) and her doctrinal teaching (e.g., the true presence; the Catholic Church is the only true Church, etc.). The fact that only a small percentage of Catholics in the *Novus Ordo* still believe *all* that the Church teaches is proof that a state of necessity exists, even if it is only a relative necessity.
[82] Matatics, "Home (but not alone)" August 15, 2015 (Parenthetical comments removed and emphasis added). http://www.gerrymatatics.org/20150815.html.

also stay at home on Sundays), while imagining themselves to represent the true Church, which exists in "their heart and mind" (in other words, the invisible "Church" of true believers known to God alone).

But what is even more inexcusable is not that these individuals have erred in their private judgment about the crisis in the Church, and ended by going to such absurd extremes; but rather that some of them, who have not been "sent," nevertheless send their message across the world wide web, and even themselves personally across the country on speaking tours, in an attempt to persuade others that they, too, must follow their example *by completely avoiding Mass and the sacraments*. In true Protestant fashion, these lay preachers and self-appointed missionaries (who themselves have no mission), "preach" to already-scandalized and confused souls, which only causes greater confusion. And when the clergy warn their faithful to ignore these unbalanced individuals, they play the part of the victim who is being persecuted – like the prophets of old – for doing nothing more than preaching the truth.

What is most puzzling is that these lay preachers don't seem at all concerned that their private opinion (which they publicly proclaim to be "the truth") has continuously changed over the years (today *directly contradicting* what they taught yesterday).[83] This realization does not seem to hinder them in their efforts, nor does it cause them to think that if what they are preaching *today* is true, it means they were leading souls into error, schism, and heresy *yesterday*. But if, according to their own standard,[84] they were leading souls into error, heresy and schism yesterday, how can they be sure they are not doing the same today? Perhaps those who have spent *nearly their entire adult life* leading people astray were not cut out to be lay preachers of the Gospel, as they imagine themselves to be, but should instead keep their *continuously changing* position to themselves to avoid further harming souls. But, evidently, intellectual pride is not easily swayed by such thoughts,

---

[83] Mr. Matatics, whom we've referenced in this section, is a classic example. Matatics has gone from being an ordained Presbyterian minister, to a *Novus Ordo* Catholic, to a Traditional Catholic (attending both S.S.P.X. and Indult parishes), to an "independent chapel" Catholic, to a Sedevacantist "Catholic" (e.g., S.S.P.V., C.M.R.I.), and, finally, to a home-aloner.

[84] For example, Mr. Matatics used to teach that it was necessary to belong to the post-Vatican II Church; today he declares it to be a false Church. He used to promote the F.S.S.P.; now he claims their orders are invalid and they belong to a false Church. He used to preach that attendance at the S.S.P.X. was acceptable; now he says they are in schism. He used to teach that one should receive the sacraments from Sedevacantist clergy; now he claims they are unlawful shepherds. According to his own theories, he has been leading souls into error, schism and heresy almost his entire adult life. Only now is he preaching the "truth."

which only goes to show that the "diabolical disorientation" Lucia of Fatima referred to is not only found in the upper hierarchy, but in the lower ranks of the laity as well. What this also shows is that there are many victims in this crisis, and they are certainly not all on the Left.

But no matter what brand of Sedevacantism one follows, the question remains: Where is the visible Church? For Sedevacantists - especially those who follow the opinion of the Sedevacantist preacher, Gerry Matatics - the practical answer is that it no longer exists, no matter how they wish to spin it. Clearly, they have lost faith *in the Church* as she suffers her Passion (just as the disciples lost faith in Christ during His Passion). They've ended by *publicly professing* the Protestant heresy that the *visible* Church exists *"in the hearts and minds"* of true believers.[85]

Analogies and End Times Prophecies: More Grasping at Straws

Unable to point to a visible hierarchy with ordinary jurisdiction, Sedevacantists often resort to using analogies to defend their position. For example, they will say that just as Christ's dead Body was not visible to those outside His tomb (but was still visible in itself), so too could the alleged Pius XII "Bishop in the Woods" not be visible to the public, yet still exist. The analogy of the tomb, of course, could be twisted to mean many different things; and the physical Body of Christ in the tomb does not have a one-to-one correspondence with the promises Christ made to His Mystical Body, the Church. Furthermore, while Christ's Body may not have been visible to those outside the tomb, the faithful *knew exactly where His Body was*. Such is not the case with the alleged "Bishop in the Woods," since Sedevacantists don't even know *if* any such bishop exists, much less *where* he can be found.

---

[85] It should also be pointed out that if Pius XII were the last true Pope, then the Church has no way of electing a Pope according to its current legislation. Why? Because according to the laws for electing a Pope, which were established by Pius XII in 1945: "The right of electing the Roman Pontiff pertains solely and exclusively to the Cardinals of the Holy Roman Church" (*Vacantis Apostolicae Sedis*, No. 32). But all the Cardinals appointed by Pius XII are dead. If all the Popes after Pius XII were antipopes, it means the "Cardinals" they appointed are not true Cardinals, and therefore cannot legally elect a Pope. Ironically, Sedevacantists will appeal to Cajetan, who teaches that the Church can provide the means to elect a Pope if it is impossible to follow the laws of election (e.g., no Cardinal-electors). Yet, Cajetan also explicitly held that a heretical Pope does not lose his office until he is deposed by the Church. This is another example of how Sedevacantists "sift" the teachings of theologians, to find something that *appears* to support their thesis, just like they "sift" the Popes.

An analogy that can be drawn between the Body of Christ in the tomb, and that of the Church today, is that, although the Body of Christ was separated from the soul, and, in fact, dead; nevertheless, it remained hypostatically united to the Word of God. At that time, who, other than the Blessed Mother, would have possessed the faith to proclaim that the tortured, disfigured and dead Body of Christ was the Body of the Messiah and Son of God? To profess such a thing would have been considered blasphemous, yet that dead and disfigured Body was truly and inseparably united to the Word of God. Similarly, in the Passion of the Church today, although the Church is disfigured and apparently dying, it remains the true Mystical Body and Bride of Christ – united to the Word of God, who is Christ Himself, the Bridegroom. Just as the Body that laid in the tomb rose again, so too will the visible, post-conciliar Church along with its members rise again at the time appointed by God.

Sedevacantists will also refer to Our Lady's prophecy at La Salette, when She said "The Church will be in eclipse." Based on these mysterious words, they reason that just as the Church will be hidden by a foreign body (as the sun is hidden by the moon during an eclipse), so it will be with the true Church and the true bishops during the crisis. But this analogy also does not follow, since during an eclipse we *know* (and not just speculate) that the sun exists, and we also *know where it is* (behind the moon), just as the faithful knew the exact place of Christ's Body, in the tomb.

The Church of Christ today is eclipsed by the moral filth and doctrinal and liturgical aberrations caused by her bad members, which hides the beauty of her moral and doctrinal teachings. But just as it was during the Passion of Christ, the divine nature of the Church (her *binding* doctrinal and moral teachings) remains unchanged. Furthermore, during an eclipse, the light of the sun can be seen along the fringes, just as the light of the Church today is still seen today along the "fringes" (where tradition has been maintained).

Of course, such is not the case with the alleged "Pius XII bishops who never embraced the New Church" since no one knows if any exist, much less where they can be found. And in none of Our Lady's many prophecies about the ecclesiastical crisis of our times does She ever suggest the practical disappearance of the hierarchy or the reign of antipopes. On the contrary, according to Sister Lucia of Fatima, She says that there will be a "diabolical disorientation of the upper hierarchy," not a defection of the upper hierarchy. Her prophecy at La Salette is consistent with the reality that the true Church, rather than being reduced to an unidentifiable remnant of "true believers," will continue to exist *exactly as she always has* (like the sun during an eclipse), even though her brilliance will be obscured for a time.

Because their thesis reduces the visible Church to a mere remnant of "true believers" and a hierarchy that is no where to be found, most Sedevacantists also attempt to justify their position by arguing that we are currently living in the end times, when it is predicted that very few people will have the true faith. They point to biblical and extra-biblical prophecies about how the faith will be nearly extinct right before the Second Coming of Christ. As Our Lord said, "But yet the Son of man, when he cometh, shall he find, think you, faith on earth"? (Lk. 18:8).

For example, in his CD talk "Counterfeit Catholicism," Gerry Matatics compares the current crisis of the Church to the time of the Flood when eight people were saved, that is, those who were inside the ark, which he argues is a type of the Church in the end times.[86] Matatics plainly admits he believes we are living in the end times, as he applies the following words of Our Lord to our day: "And as in the days of Noe, so shall also the coming of the Son of man be" (Mt. 24:37). He also mentions St. Peter's reference to the nominal quota of the saved during the time of Noe - "wherein a few, that is, eight souls, were saved by water" (1Pet. 3:19-20).

In his talk, Matatics also refers to the Exodus where only two people (Josue and Caleb)[87] out of two million were allowed to enter the Promised Land (*cf.* 1Cor. 10:1-5). He likewise argues that these Israelites are another type of the Church in the end times, when most souls will be lost. St. Paul alludes to these Old Testament typologies and their importance in his first letter to the Corinthians: "Now all these things happened to them in figure: and they are written for our correction, upon whom the ends of the world are come" (1Cor. 10:11). Based upon these and other similar passages, as well as extra-biblical revelations about apostasy in the Church in the last days, Matatics and other Sedevacantists argue that the Church in the end times will be reduced to just a few, and that we are living in those days now. This is how they rationalize that the true Church has all but disappeared in our day, but not defected.

Now, assuming the number of the saved who are living during the end times will be small (which is likely, for Jesus said God will shorten

---

[86] "Counterfeit Catholicism vs. Consistent Catholicism," disc 4 of 6.
[87] See, for example, Num. 14:30,38; 26:65; 32:12. Matatics also refers to the Fall of Adam and Eve as a type of the Church in the end times, when there was, in his words, "100 percent apostasy."

the days of apostasy to save His remaining Elect; Mt. 24:22),[88] it does not follow that the members of the *visible society* will be reduced to only a few, since not all members of the visible society are necessarily saved. In fact, this is confirmed by 1 Corinthians, chapter 10, which Matatics cites in defense of his position. The passage speaks of a great number (an estimated 2 million) who belonged to the *visible society* – all of whom had been baptized "in the cloud, and in the sea" (v.2). They all "did eat the same spiritual food, And all drank the same spiritual drink" (v.4). This large visible society, which is partaking of the same spiritual food (i.e., the sacraments), is a type of the Catholic Church. St. Paul tells us, however, that with most of those in this visible society, "God was not well pleased" (v.5), and consequently they did not arrive at the Promise Land (Heaven).

This passage simply confirms that not all the members of the visible society are pleasing to God, nor will all be saved. That is the point St. Paul was making with the analogy, which is why he said: "Now these things were done in a figure of us, that we should not covet evil things … Neither become ye idolaters … Neither let us commit fornication … Neither let us tempt Christ: Neither do you murmur: as some of them murmured, and were destroyed by the destroyer. Now all these things happened to them in figure: and they are written for our correction, upon whom the ends of the world are come. Wherefore he that thinketh himself to stand, let him take heed lest he fall" (1Cor 10:6-12).

St. Paul was instructing the Corinthians (who were members of the Church) not to behave like the Israelites did during the days of Moses, lest the same thing happen to them. But this reference to the Israelites in no way helps Matatics' case, since he himself has withdrawn from the visible society and no longer "eats the same spiritual food," nor "drinks the same spiritual drink" as the members of the visible Church. This analogy applies to the visible society of the Church from which Matatics has publicly separated, and out of which he seeks to lead others. Neither does the analogy of the eight souls saved by water at

---

[88] When Matatics addresses the salvation of the Elect (on disc 6 of 6), he accuses Archbishop Lefevbre of being "grossly liberal" in his interpretation of the dogma "No Salvation Outside the Church" because the Archbishop said people of false religions can be saved *in* their false religions but not *by* their false religions. Matatics even says that Lefebvre "may have been a heretic" for holding that position. And yet Matatics himself, in the very same talk, admits that a Catholic can be saved in the *Novus Ordo* Church, which he repeatedly claims is a false Church and a false religion. Thus, by his own standards (and yet another example of inconsistency and duplicity), Matatics is also "grossly liberal" in his interpretation of "No Salvation Outside the Church" and "may even be a heretic" for holding his position.

the time of Noah help his case, since these souls were saved by remaining in the ark (representing the Church) which Matatics left.

For those who believe we are currently in the end times - that is, the time that immediately precedes the Second Coming of Christ - there are some important factors to consider.[89] For one, Our Lady's prophecies at Fatima reveal that a period of peace in the world *must* intervene between our current time, and the final apostasy and the reign of antichrist. These prophecies, confirmed by numerous miracles, reveal that the Pope *will* consecrate Russia to the Immaculate Heart, Russia *will* convert to the Catholic Faith, and a period of peace *will* be granted to the world (whether this happens after a great chastisement, presumably revealed in the Third Secret, remains to be seen).[90]

Setting aside the speculative question of how long the period of peace will last,[91] the bottom line is that these events (the consecration of Russia, Russia's conversion, a period of world peace) *have not yet taken place*. To argue that the final apostasy and reign of antichrist *precedes* the period of peace and conversion of Russia (as the Sedevacantists, who still believe in Fatima, must do) also contradicts the unanimous consent of the early Church Fathers and Doctors, including St. Thomas Aquinas, all of whom held that the final apostasy and appearance of antichrist comes *right before the end of the world*. We further note that there has been no significant, universal conversion of the Jews, to which Scripture alludes and many Fathers and Doctors of the Church teach must take place before the end of the world.

It is also worthwhile to consider that traditional Catholic commentaries make a distinction between the internal subversion of the Church (which we are currently experiencing through the Vatican II revolution) and the external persecution of the Church which will

---

[89] Note that some of the verses cited by Mr. Matatics are *not* referring to the state of the Church in our day, but rather *during the final apostasy that immediately precedes the Second Coming, at the end of time*. We see this in Jesus' own words, when, for example, in His reference to the Flood and the lack of faith on Earth, He explicitly refers to His Second Coming: "when he cometh" (Lk. 18:8), and "the coming of the Son of man" (Mt. 24:37).

[90] For a thorough yet easy-to-read treatment of Fatima, see John Salza's *A Catechism of Fatima – And the Related Crisis in the Church* (2015), available at http://www.john salza.com.

[91] Some prophets have even predicted that this will be a long period of peace, where a great Catholic king will reign and thwart the Church's enemies (St. Cataldus of the fifth century; Monk Adso of the tenth century; Abbot Joachim Merlin of the thirteenth century; Monk Hilarion of the fifteenth century; Telesphorus of Cozensa of the sixteenth century; Venerable Holzhauser of the seventeenth century; David Poreaus of the seventeenth century; Brother Louis Rocco of the nineteenth century; and Melanie Calvat at La Salette in the nineteenth century, among others). See Yves Dupont, *Catholic Prophecy: The Coming Chastisement* (Rockford, Illinois: TAN Books and Publishers, Inc., 1970, 1973).

lead to the final apostasy of the end times (which the Sedevacantists claim is happening now).[92] For example, in his classic commentary *The Apocalypse of St. John* published in 1921, Fr. E. Sylvester Berry says:

> "Satan will first attempt to destroy the power of the Papacy and bring about the downfall of the Church through heresies, schisms and persecutions that must surely follow [internal subversion]. <u>Failing in this he will then attack the Church from without</u> [external persecution]. <u>For this purpose he will raise up Antichrist and his prophet to lead the faithful into error and destroy those who remain steadfast</u>."[93]

Fr. Berry further explains that Satan will attempt to destroy the Church from without by raising up antichrist, *after* he realizes, during the reign of peace, that he cannot destroy the Church from within (by Modernism, homosexuality, etc). Fr. Berry says "Satan now realizes that victory will be difficult. His first attempt failed miserably. In this second conflict new tactics must be employed. He will now seek to lead the faithful astray by a false Messias whom he will raise up in the person of Antichrist."[94] Fr. Berry's opinion is that the end times apostasy comes *after* the internal subversion of the Church and the reign of peace promised by Our Lady of Fatima.[95]

---

[92] It is likely that, during this time, the persecution of the Church will lead her to go "underground." At this time, it would seem that Rome will become an enemy of the Church and be the seat of the antichrist as Our Lady revealed at La Salette. St. Paul says this final apostasy or "revolt" happens when "the man of sin [antichrist] is revealed, "who will "sitteth in the temple of God [the Church], shewing himself as if he were God" [an antipope] (2Thess 2:3-4). At this time, the true Pope is "taken out of the way," presumably by martyrdom (v.7). Just as the Church was persecuted by the Romans and went underground at her very beginning, so she will suffer the same at the end of time, but then at the hands of the antichrist. Fr. Berry says: "Those shall be days of great persecution in which the Church will suffer all the horrors of the early ages..." Fr. E. Sylvester Berry, *The Apocalypse of St. John* (Columbus, Ohio: John W. Winterich, 1921), p. 126.

[93] Ibid., p. 120.

[94] Ibid., p. 128.

[95] Our Lord Himself seems to reveal the sequence of events in the Gospel of St. Matthew. He first describes the period of time in which we are currently living (the "beginning of sorrows"), which is during the internal subversion of the Church and the looming chastisements that await us if Russia is not timely consecrated: "And you shall hear of wars and rumours of wars. See that ye be not troubled. For these things must come to pass, but the end is not yet. For nation shall rise against nation, and kingdom against kingdom; and there shall be pestilences, and famines, and earthquakes in places: Now all these are the beginnings of sorrows" (Mt. 24:6-8). Then Our Lord goes on to say: "But he that shall persevere to the end, he shall be saved. And this gospel of the kingdom, shall be preached in the whole world, for a testimony to all nations [the period of peace], and

In fact, Fr. Berry says that the vacancy of the papal office and reign of antipope(s) will occur, not during the period of internal subversion (the Vatican II revolution) which *precedes* the period of peace, but rather during the external persecution of the Church which *follows* the period of peace. The vacancy of the papal office will possibly be the result of the martyrdom of the true Pope and the difficulty the Church will have in electing a successor during this time of external persecution. Again, this reign of a false Pope (or Popes) is said to occur *in the last days of the Church*, during the time of antichrist and the final apostasy. Wrote Fr. Berry:

> "It is now the hour for the powers of darkness. The new-born Son of the Church [the Pope] is taken 'to God and to His throne.' Scarcely has the newly elected Pope been enthroned when he is snatched away by martyrdom. The 'mystery of iniquity' gradually developing through the centuries, cannot be fully consummated while the power of the Papacy endures, but now he [the Pope] that 'withholding is taken out of the way' [martyrdom of the Pope]. During the interregnum 'that wicked one [the antichrist] shall be revealed' in his fury against the Church."[96]

Fr. Berry's analysis is consistent with many other prophecies which predict the martyrdom of the true Pope and the reign of an antipope (presumably the antichrist or his false prophet) during the last days,[97] before St. Michael the Archangel destroys the antichrist and Christ comes in His glory to judge the living and the dead at the end of the world. While we don't wish to engage in endless speculation about these matters, the foregoing strongly suggests that we are *not* currently in the end times and the final apostasy. And even if we were in those days, it would in no way help the Sedevacantist thesis, since the visible Church will *never* be overcome by the gates of hell – not even during the reign of antichrist.

---

then shall the consummation come" [the final apostasy and reign of antichrist] (Mt. 24:13-14).

[96] *The Apocalypse of St. John*, p. 124.

[97] For example, John of Vatiguerro (thirteenth century); John of the Cleft Rock (fourteenth century); a Capuchin Friar (eighteenth century); the Ecstatic of Tours (nineteenth century); Bl. Anna-Maria Taigi (nineteenth century); and St. Pius X (twentieth century), among others.

Closing Comments

As we have seen in these first two chapters, the Church is an indefectible *visible society* possessing four marks and three attributes. The visible society is *numerically* one with the Church of the Apostles; it is a single moral body that will always remain the Church of Christ, in spite of any trials God wills to permit it to suffer. If this visible society had elected a false Pope and then morphed into a New Church in 1958 (or 1965, etc.) as the Sedevacantists claim, the Church would have defected. This, however, is contrary to the nature of the Church and the promises of Christ, her Divine Founder.

Furthermore, Sedevacantists not only fail to point to a Church in our time which possesses the marks and attributes of the Church, but their own communities have *none* of them. Thus, it is impossible for their sects to be "the true Catholic Church" as they claim (or even *part* of the Church, since they cannot even point to the visible and infallible Church of which they are part). And, as should be evident, it is impossible for them to claim that the true Church merely indwells in a remnant of true believers, without embracing the Protestant understanding of the Church, which is precisely what they have done. As we have shown, the only Church that even claims to possess these marks and attributes is the Church that everyone in the world but the Sedevacantists recognizes as the Catholic Church. This means that if *this* Church is not the true Church, the true Church founded by Jesus Christ no longer exists.

While much more material could be provided on these matters, these first two chapters, in and of themselves, sufficiently demonstrate that the Sedevacantist thesis is completely erroneous, and, in fact, cannot be held without at least logically falling into heresy. It is simply an overreaction to the current crisis, fueled by a faulty understanding of the Church's attribute of infallibility. This is combined with a lack of faith in the promises of Christ, a presumption of the limits of God's permissive will, and the pride of private judgment.

Chapter 3 Terms and Explanations

Before proceeding with this chapter, it is critical to understand the terminology to be used. To that end, we have provided the following terms and explanations before the beginning of the chapter. Please read (and refer back to, as needed) these important terms to help facilitate comprehension. This chapter is foundational for the material that follows.

Body of the Church: The visible, social, ecclesiastical society founded by Jesus Christ for our salvation, whose members possess certain rights and privileges according to their station in the Church.

External Bonds of Union (with the Body): Profession of the true Faith, communion in the Sacraments (beginning with water baptism), and union with the Pope and hierarchy. These three bonds may be summarized as the bonds of faith, worship, and governance. By way of analogy, or metaphorically, the external bonds of union are themselves sometimes referred to as the "Body" of the Church.

Perfect and Imperfect Union with the Body: One has *perfect* union with the Body of the Church if he possesses all three external bonds of union. Perfect union with the Body is known as "*in re*" (in reality) and makes a man a *member* of the Church. One has *imperfect* union with the Body if he does not possess all three external bonds but *desires* to be a member of the Church (e.g., a catechumen who wills to enter the Church; or one publicly excommunicated who wills to return to the Church). Imperfect union with the Body is known as "*in voto*" (in desire). Note that one who has imperfect union with the Body is not yet (or no longer) a *member* of the Church as such.

Soul of the Church: The Holy Ghost, who is the Lord and Giver of life to the Church, and to those joined to the Church, either in reality or desire.

Internal Bonds of Union (with the Soul): The theological virtues of faith, hope and charity, as well as sanctifying grace and the other gifts of the Holy Ghost which dwell in a man's soul. The internal bonds of union are sometimes referred to analogously, or metaphorically, as the "Soul" of the Church.

Perfect and Imperfect Union with the Soul: One has *perfect* union with the Soul of the Church if he possesses all the internal bonds of union (e.g., a Catholic in a state of grace). One has *imperfect* union with the Soul if he has faith (and hope) but not charity (e.g., a Catholic in mortal sin). One has *no* union with the Soul if he has lost faith, since the theological virtues of hope and charity cannot remain when faith is lost.

Being a *member* of the Church: One who has perfect (*in re*) union with the Body of the Church, and consequently possesses the rights and privileges of Church membership. One who is externally recognized as a Roman Catholic in good standing is a *member* of the Church.[1]

Being *joined* to the Church: One who has *imperfect* union (*in voto*) with the Body of the Church (and thus is *not* a member of the Church as such). Referred to by Pope Pius XII as being *ordained* to the Church.

Salvation: Salvation is distinct from the concept of formal "membership" in the Church. Salvation requires *perfect* union with the *Soul* of the Church (through faith, hope, charity and sanctifying grace), as well as either *perfect* (*in re*) or at least *imperfect* (*in voto*) union with the *Body* of the Church. Thus, one can be saved by being *joined* to the Body of the Church *in desire*, even if he is not an actual "member" (as defined above).

---

[1] The "Roman Catholic Church" refers to all the churches (East or West) that are united to Rome.

Chapter 3

~ Church Membership and Bonds of Unity ~

In Chapters 1 and 2, we saw that the Church is a visible society, complete in and of itself, composed of a governing hierarchy and laity. We saw that the Church has *marks* by which it can be known, and *attributes* that perfect its nature. In this chapter, we will see that just as the true Church can be known by its *marks*, so too can the members of the Church be known by exterior *bonds,* which unite them to the visible society and to one another. We will see that there are both internal and external bonds of unity with the Church, and show what the minimum requirement is for a person to properly be considered a *member* of the Church. We will discuss various theological opinions regarding what, precisely, constitutes *membership* in the visible society, and consider some recent ambiguities and errors concerning this question. The information contained in this chapter will serve as a foundation for some of the arguments presented in future chapters; and the distinctions that will be discussed will be used to more clearly explain the errors of the Sedevacantist thesis as we go forward.

External Bonds of Unity

A person enters the Church through baptism, which infuses faith, hope and charity into the soul, and incorporates him into the visible society. While baptism is necessary for one to be a member of the Church,[1] baptism alone does not suffice for membership. Even members of heretical sects can receive valid baptism, yet those joined to heretical sects are not members of the Church,[2] since they are not part of the *visible society* which is the Church. To belong to the Church, in addition to receiving baptism, one must also be 1) united to the hierarchy (especially the Pope), 2) partake of the same sacraments, and 3) profess the true faith (must acknowledge the Church as the rule of

---

[1] "Through the waters of Baptism those who are born into this world dead in sin are not only born again and made members of the Church, but being stamped with a spiritual seal they become able and fit to receive the other Sacraments" (Pius XII, *Mystici Corporis Christi*, No. 18, June 29, 1943).

[2] The exception are those below the age of reason, who are incorporated into the Church even if baptized by a heretic; yet they cease to be considered members of the Church once they reach the age of reason and embrace the errors of their sect. See Pope Benedict XIV, *Singulari Nobis*, Nos. 13 and 14.

faith). These three external, visible bonds unite the members of the Church, and show which individuals belong to the visible society.

In his classic treatise, *De Ecclesia Militante* ("The Church Militant"), St. Robert Bellarmine, who is known particularly for his teaching on the nature of the Church,[3] defines the Church as the assembly of men who are united by these three visible bonds:

> "This one and true Church is the assembly of men bound together by the profession of the same Christian faith and the communion of the same sacraments, under the rule of the legitimate pastors, and especially that of the Roman Pontiff, the one Vicar of Christ on earth. From this definition, it is easy to infer which men belong to the Church and which do not belong to it. There are three parts of this definition: the profession of the true faith, the communion of the sacraments, and the subjection to the Roman Pontiff, the legitimate pastor."[4]

In the *original* schemas prepared for the Second Vatican Council, we read that the members of the Church are those who have been baptized and possess these three external bonds of union:

> "According to the most ancient tradition, only they are called members of the Church, in the true and proper sense, in whom the Church, one and indivisible, indefectible and infallible, comes together in unity of faith, sacraments and government. They, therefore, are truly and properly said to be members of the Church who, washed in the bath of regeneration [i.e., baptism], professing the true Catholic faith, and acknowledging the authority of the Church, are joined in its visible structure to its Head, Christ, who rules it through his Vicar, and have not been cut off from the structure of the Mystical Body because of very serious offenses."[5]

In his Apologetic and Dogmatic Treatise, *The Church of Christ*, Fr. Sylvester Berry refers to these external bonds of unity as *conditions* for membership in the Church. He also elaborates further on them by explaining that subjection to the hierarchy is essentially submission to the Church's *ruling authority,* while the profession of faith is realized by the external and public submission to the Church's *teaching authority as*

---

[3] The Fathers of the First Vatican Council drew heavily from the writings of St. Bellarmine when formulating their decrees and definitions on the nature of the Church.
[4] *De Ecclesia Militante*, ch.2.
[5] Dogmatic Constitution On the Church, ch. 2, The members of the Church Militant and Her Necessity for Salvation, No. 9. http://www.unamsanctamcatholicam.com/images/church%20schema.pdf.

the rule of faith.[6] As we will see below, "profession of the true faith" does not require that each member profess every aspect of the faith with theological precision and no admixture of error. What suffices for the profession of faith is that they acknowledge the Church as the *infallible rule of faith*. For this reason, Fr. Berry explains that "the profession of the faith practically resolves itself into submission to her teaching authority."[7] Regarding these conditions for membership, he writes:

> "...three *conditions* are absolutely necessary and of themselves sufficient for membership; viz.:
> (a) Initiation by baptism;
> (b) External profession of the true Faith which is had by submission to the teaching authority of the Church.
> (c) Submission to the ruling authority of the Church."[8]

He goes on to explain that *perfect observance* of the conditions (the "unities") is not absolutely necessary for a person to retain membership in the Church. He wrote:

> "These *conditions* may be briefly summarized in one phrase: the reception of Baptism, and the preservation of the unities – unity of faith, unity of worship, and unity of government; or in other words, reception of Baptism and submission to the teaching and ruling authority of the Church. It should be noted, however, that perfect observance of the unities is not required for mere membership in the Church; a person need not make an explicit profession of faith at all times; nor conform all his actions to it. He need not make a diligent use of the Sacraments at all times, neither must he be free from all infractions of Church laws and precepts."[9]

That the *unities* need not to be observed *perfectly* at all times is confirmed by the fact that a Catholic who has drifted away from the sacraments is not, for that reason alone, immediately considered a non-member of the Church. Furthermore, because the "profession of the true faith" means, practically speaking, the public submission to the Church's teaching authority *as the rule of faith*, this external bond does not require that every member profess each and every aspect of the

---

[6] St. Thomas explains: "Now it is manifest that he who adheres to the teaching of the Church, as to an infallible rule, assents to whatever the Church teaches..." ST, II-II, q. 5, a. 3.
[7] *The Church of Christ*, p. 126.
[8] Ibid. (emphasis added).
[9] Ibid. (emphasis added).

faith with theological precision; nor does the profession of a materially heretical *statement* sever one from the Church for heresy. The *Catechism of the Council of Trent* explains that "a person is not to be called a heretic as soon as he shall have offended in matters of faith; but he is a heretic who, *having disregarded the authority of the Church*, maintains an impious opinion with pertinaticy."[10]

This is confirmed by the fact that the Church does not immediately excommunicate (or consider excommunicated) every person who makes a false or even heretical statement. As we will see in later chapters, more is required before a person is cut off from the visible society for heresy. If those who simply made a heretical statement were "public heretics" who were immediately cut off from the Church (as many Sedevacantists believe), there would be few Catholics in the world, since most Catholics have said something that is materially heretical at one time in their adult life. Fr. Berry explains that those who recognize the Church as the rule of faith, yet who hold heretical doctrines are not, by that fact alone, considered to be heretics.[11] He explains:

> "A heretic is usually defined as a Christian, i.e., a baptized person, who holds a doctrine contrary to a revealed truth; but this definition is inaccurate, since it would make heretics of a large portion of the faithful. A doctrine contrary to a revealed truth is usually stigmatized as heretical, but a person who professes an heretical doctrine is not necessarily a heretic. *Heresy*, from the Greek *hairesis*, signifies a choosing; therefore a heretic is one who chooses for himself in matters of faith, thereby rejecting the authority of the Church established by Christ to teach all men the truths of revelation. (...) A person who submits to the authority of the Church and wishes to accept all her teachings, is not a heretic, even though he profess heretical doctrines through ignorance of what the Church really teaches; he implicitly accepts the true doctrine in his general intention to accept all that the Church teaches."[12]

Again, we see that the "profession of true faith," required for membership, is the external acknowledgment of the Church's teaching authority, and the public submission to it as the rule of faith. The

---

[10] *The Catechism of the Council of Trent*, p. 96 (emphasis added)
[11] Such a person would not be considered a heretic in the external forum. It is possible, however, for such a person to have committed the sin of heresy in the internal forum (which, as we will see, also does not, by itself, sever one from the Church).
[12] *The Church of Christ*, p. 128.

reason this is important is because many Sedevacantists erroneously believe that if a person makes a heretical statement, it means they no longer "profess the true Faith," and therefore have ceased to be members of the Church (since they believe that they lack an essential bond of unity). But, as Fr. Berry explained, this external bond is not immediately broken by those who make an erroneous, or even heretical statement. Hence, a Catholic who professes a heresy does not automatically cease to be a member of the Church. During the Modernist crisis of our day, in which the object of faith has been greatly obscured by "the Synthesis of all heresies," there may be many well meaning Catholics, and even prelates, who profess heresy, while publicly submitting to the Church as the rule of faith.

Example of Imperfect Observance of the Unities

The Sedevacantist writer, John Daly, cited an interesting example of how far a Catholic can go while still being considered a member of the Church. On January 10, 1907, during the pontificate of Pope St. Pius X, a parish priest submitted a question to a moral theologian on the staff at *L'Ami Du Clergé*,[13] concerning a family at his parish. The members of the family were all baptized Catholics and openly professed to being Catholic, but they had stopped regularly attending Mass, sent their children to Protestant schools, and from time to time attended Protestant services themselves. They even professed Protestant heresies about the Blessed Sacrament. According to Mr. Daly, they went so far as having "blasphemed the Blessed Eucharist to the parish priest, relying on typically Protestant arguments."[14] Even so, the family professed that they were Catholics, not Protestants, and wanted to have their newborn children baptized by the parish priest.

The priest contacted *L'Ami Du Clergé* for guidance in answering several questions. He wanted to know "whether the parents had incurred excommunication, whether they could be buried as Catholics, and whether, if he should manage to convert any of them, they would have to make a formal abjuration."[15]

L'Ami Du Clergé, a highly respected publication that was approved and even encouraged by Pope St. Pius X at the time, replied

---

[13] *L'Ami Du Clergé* (The Friend of the Clergy) was a French-language weekly magazine published between 1878 and 1969. Its purpose was to compliment and update the training of clergy, on all matters dogmatic, moral, liturgical, theological and historical, as well as provide assistance with questions related to canon law.

[14] John Daly, *Heresy in History*, May, 2000. http://www.strobertbellarmine.net/heresyhistory.html.

[15] Ibid.

by saying that the family's attendance at Protestant services was not proof that they intended to leave the Church, which, in fact, was confirmed by the fact that they publicly declared themselves to be Catholics. Because they continued to profess being Catholics, the moral theologian concluded that "these poor misguided souls had no wish to *knowingly* and *willingly* reject the dogma of the Church concerning the Holy Eucharist."[16] Mr. Daly concluded his comments on this case by saying:

> "So in evaluating the questions posed by the parish priest, the Ami du Clergé replied that the culprits were still members of the Catholic Church, were not excommunicated, had no need to make formal abjuration of their errors, but only to repair the scandal given..."[17]

This historical example from the days of Pope St. Pius X shows us just how "imperfectly" a Catholic can observe the external bonds of unity while still being considered a *member* of the Church. This also shows how rash the Sedevacantists are when they declare that anyone who makes a heretical statement, or multiple heretical statements over a period of time, is therefore a "public heretic," and consequently has cut himself off from the Church, since he no longer "professes the Faith."

Now, you may be wondering if there is a difference in this respect between a layman and a member of the clergy who professes heresy. In Chapter 6, we will consider examples of *prelates* who publicly professed errors and heresies, yet were not considered by the Church or their contemporaries to have severed their external bond of union with the Church. One example we will consider concerns a priest, who was a doctor of theology and university professor (obviously a highly-educated Catholic) who not only professed errors and heresies, but whose errors and heresies were formally condemned by the Church at the time, even though he, himself, was not publicly excommunicated by the Church, or named in the condemnation. We will see that St. Bellarmine, who lived through these events and knew the man personally, always considered him to be a Catholic in good standing and member of the Church. This case alone proves that Bellarmine, himself, does not agree with the Sedevacantist position that all who publicly profess heresy immediately sever their bond of union with the

---

[16] Ibid.
[17] Ibid.

Church.[18] We will see throughout this book that misinterpreting and misapplying the teaching of St. Bellarmine is quite common amongst the Sedevacantist apologists.

Internal Bonds of Union

Just as man possesses visible and invisible elements (body and soul) so, too, the visible Church possesses visible and invisible bonds of unity. The invisible spiritual bonds unite men spiritually to Christ and to His Church. These internal bonds of union are the theological virtues (faith, hope and charity), sanctifying grace, and the gifts of the Holy Ghost. These are considered special *properties* of the *visible society* which is the Church. Msgr. Van Noort explains:

> "...there are in the Church just as there are by nature in man two elements, one visible and one invisible. ... the Holy Spirit and His works are by the institution of Christ the special property of that visible society which is the Church, inasmuch as they can never fail to be found therein and cannot, in the ordinary course of events, be obtained outside of it."[19]

In *Mystici Corporis Christi,* Pope Pius XII explained the external bonds and the internal bonds of ecclesiastical unity as follows:

> "Now, since its Founder willed this social body of Christ to be visible, the cooperation of all its members must also be externally manifest through their profession of the *same faith* and their sharing the *same sacred rites*, through participation in the *same Sacrifice*, and the practical observance of the *same laws*. ... These juridical bonds in themselves far surpass those of any other human society, however exalted; and yet another principle of union must be added to them in those three virtues, Christian faith, hope and charity, which link us so closely to each other and to God."[20]

There is a deep relation between these internal and external bonds: for interior *faith* leads to the profession of faith, as St Paul says: *"credidi*

---

[18] For example, the Sedevacantist blogger, Steve Speray, maintains that anyone who is judged by *private judgment* to have made a heretical *statement* is a "public heretic," and therefore no longer a member of the Church. He has arrived at this erroneous position based upon his private interpretation of certain canonists. (See Speray, "Robert Siscoe and Catholic Family News Present Another False Argument Against Sedevacantism," September 18, 2014).

[19] *Christ's Church*, p. 225.

[20] *Mystici Corporis*, Nos. 69-70, June 29, 1943 (emphasis added).

propter quod locutus sum – "I have believed, therefore I have spoken" (2Cor. 4:13; Ps. 115:1). *Hope* leads to desire and to prayer, and thus to worship and the sacraments. *Charity* leads to obedience - "He that hath my commandments, and keepeth them; he it is that loveth me" (Jn. 14:21) - and hence to true submission to Magisterial authority.

In *De Ecclesia Militante*, St. Bellarmine discusses both the *external* bonds (which alone suffice for one to be a member of the Church) and the *internal* bonds which unite men *interiorly* to Christ and to His Church. He explains that none of the internal bonds are required for one to be a true *member*[21] of the visible society that is the Church. This is evident from the fact that if any interior spiritual property was required for a person to be a member of the Church, the Church would no longer be a visible society whose members could be known. Hence, if the interior virtue of faith were necessary for Church membership (as some Sedevacantists believe[22]), the true Church would not be a *visible society*, but an invisible Church of *true believers* known to God alone. But an "invisible" Church, where members are known to God alone, is the heresy of Protestantism.[23] In fact, this is the argument used by Bellarmine himself to explain why the external bonds of union *alone* suffice for one to belong to the Church. He wrote:

> "Now there is this difference between our teaching and all the others [the heretics discussed previously], that all the others require internal virtues to constitute a man 'within' the Church, and hence make the true Church invisible. But, despite the fact that we believe that all the virtues, faith, hope, charity, and the rest, are to be found within the Church, we do not think that any internal virtue is required to bring it about that a man can be said absolutely to be a part of the true Church of which the Scriptures speak, but [what is

---

[21] Bellarmine uses the terms "belong to the Church," "member of the Church," "part of the Church," and "in the Church" synonymously. (Fenton, "Membership in the Church," *American Ecclesiastical Review*, vol. CXII, n. 4, April, 1945, p. 293).

[22] For example, the Sedevacantist Richard Ibranyi teaches that an "occult heretic" (which is someone who has secretly lost interior faith) is not a "member" of the Church. He writes: "Therefore if an occult (secret) formal heretic held an office, he would automatically lose it because he is not a member of the Catholic Church and non-members of the Catholic Church cannot hold offices in the Catholic Church." (Ibranyi, "Cajetan's and Bellarmine's Heresies on Formal Heretics and Loss of Papal Office," November, 2013).

[23] "In opposition to the Catholic view of the church as a corporate, visible, and hierarchized clerical body, the Protestant magisterial reformers of the sixteenth century developed the concept of the church as the communion of true believers. As true believers are only known to God, by necessity this church could not take on a visible, social form." Van der Veer, Peter *Conversion to Modernities: The Globalization of Christianity* (London: Routledge, 1996), p. 73.

required] is only the outward profession of the faith and the communion of the sacraments, which are perceptible by the senses. For the Church is a visible and palpable assembly of men, just as the assembly of the Roman people or the Kingdom of France or the Republic of the Venetians."[24]

The sufficiency of the external bonds *alone* for Church membership is confirmed by considering that the rights and duties of Catholics in good standing are not based upon any internal theological virtues. For example, a Catholic's external bonds *alone* permit him to receive the sacraments in the Church (e.g., Holy Matrimony, Confirmation), irrespective of his internal virtues.[25] This is evident when we consider that a member of the Church must follow the laws of the Church for his marriage to be valid, while a baptized non-Catholic can be *validly* and *sacramentally* married without having to do so. This is because baptized non-Catholics (non-members) are dispensed from the canonical form of Matrimony (which is part of the Church's positive law), whereas *members* of the Church are not.[26] Since the dispensation from the canonical form for marriage is not based upon whether the Catholic possesses any of the theological virtues, Church law reflects Bellarmine's opinion that the external bonds alone suffice for Church membership. Therefore, as Bellarmine's teaching confirms, the loss of interior faith does not cause a Catholic to cease being a member of the Church.

Body and Soul of the Church

Pope St. Pius X and St. Bellarmine (among others) use the terms Body and Soul of the Church to refer to the external and internal bonds of union. This terminology, which is used in a metaphorical sense,[27]

---

[24] *De ecclesia militante*, ch. 2. (emphasis added).
[25] The state of grace is only required to receive these sacraments *worthily*, but it is not required by Church law to receive them *validly*.
[26] Those who receive baptism are subject to the positive law of the Church by virtue of their baptism; baptized individuals who are not members of the Church (e.g., Protestants) are then dispensed from certain positive laws, such as those pertaining to marriage.
[27] The terms *Body* and *Soul* are only used analogically or metaphorically when describing the inner and outward bonds of union with the Church. The inward bonds of unity are not *literally* the Soul of the Church, and the outward bonds are not *literally* the Body. Rather, the *Soul* of the Church is more properly the Holy Ghost, as taught by Popes Leo XIII (*Divinum illud*) and Pius XII (*Mystici Corporis*). The inward bonds of unity are those *invisible* realities that unite a man to the *Soul* of the Church. The *Body* of the Church is the visible society, which Msgr. Fenton describes as "the one Visible Mystical Body of Jesus

can be helpful in understanding how one person can be more perfectly united to the Church than another. It is also useful in understanding the various ways in which one who is not a formal *member* of the Church can be united *imperfectly* to her. However, before proceeding, an important word of caution should be mentioned regarding the use of these terms.

During the first half of the twentieth century, certain theologians began using the *Body* and *Soul* terminology in an imprecise manner.[28] This imprecision led some theologians to imply, and others to explicitly teach, that the Roman Catholic Church (the "visible Church") was the Body, while the Mystical Body of Christ (an "invisible Church") was the Soul. This error eventually developed into the erroneous notion that there are two separate and distinct Churches: The Roman Catholic Church (the "Body"), and the Mystical Body of Christ (the "Soul"), which merely "subsists" in the Roman Catholic Church, yet at the same time was a larger entity.

To avoid this error, it is important to note that the *Soul* and *Body* are not two separate Churches, nor does the Soul merely "subsist" in the Body, while simultaneously serving as the Soul to heretical sects or non-Catholic religions. Rather, the *Soul* and *Body* are two distinct elements of the *one* true Church of Christ, which is the Roman Catholic Church, similar to how the soul and body of man are two distinct aspects of one and the same person.

In his manual of Dogmatic Theology, *Christ's Church*, Van Noort wrote: "The Soul and Body of the Church are not two Churches, the one invisible and the other visible, but together they form the one

---

Christ on earth." The outward bonds are those *visible* realities that unite a man to that visible society. For this reason, Fenton noted that when the terms "soul" and "body" are used to signify the internal and external bonds of unity, they are "metaphorical names applied to two distinct sets of forces or factors that function as bonds of unity within the Church Militant of the New Testament." Fenton, *The Catholic Church and Salvation*, 1958 (New York: Seminary Press, Round Top, 2006), pp. 176-177; also see Fenton, "The Use of Terms Body and Soul of the Church with Reference to the Catholic Church," *American Ecclesiastical Review*, vol. CX, January 1944.)

[28] The late Msgr. Joseph Clifford Fenton published several articles in the *American Ecclesiastical Review* in which he strongly resisted this erroneous use of the terms. See, for example, the above-mentioned article "The Use of the Terms Body and Soul of the Church with Reference to the Catholic Church," *American Ecclesiastical Review*, vol. CX, January 1944, pp. 48-57. Pope Pius XII also responded to this error in the encyclical *Mystici Corporis Christi* (1943) and then again in *Humani Generis* (1950), when he taught that "the Mystical Body of Christ and the Roman Catholic Church are one and the same thing." For those who used the terms erroneously, see Paul Vigue, *Ecclesia*, edited by Agrain, published by Bloud et Gay (Paris, 1933), p. 101; and Karr, *Religions of Mankind*, translated by E.I. Watkins (New York: Sheed and Ward, 1938), p. 242.

Church, which is at once visible and endowed with interior life."[29] Cardinal Ottaviani, Pro-Prefect for the Holy Office, also said: "There is only one true Church of Jesus Christ... The visible Church and the Mystical Body of Christ *are one and the same reality* considered from different aspects."[30]

When properly understood, the terms Body and Soul (which were used by Pope St. Pius X in his own catechism[31]), and the realities they signify, can serve as a useful analogy for understanding the nature and being of the one Church of Christ, as well as further explaining the ways in which the internal and external bonds unite men to the Church. The distinction is also quite effective for understanding some of the errors of Sedevacantism which will be discussed later.

In *De Ecclesia*, Bellarmine explained the Body and Soul of the Church as follows:

> "We must note what Augustine says in his *Breviculus Collationis*, where he is dealing with the conference of the third day, that the Church is a living body, in which there is a <u>Soul</u> and a <u>Body</u>. The internal gifts of the Holy Ghost, faith, hope, charity, and the rest are the <u>Soul</u>. The external profession of the faith and the communication of the sacraments are the <u>Body</u>.[32]
>
> Hence it is that some are of the <u>Soul</u> and of the <u>Body</u> of the Church, and hence joined both inwardly and outwardly to Christ the Head, and such people are most perfectly within the Church. They are, as it were, living members in the body, although some of them share in this life to a greater extent, and others to a lesser extent, while still others have only the beginning of life and, as it were, sensation without movement, like the people who have only faith without charity.

---

[29] *Christ's Church*, p. 225.

[30] *Acta*, Series II, vol. II, pt. III, pp. 994-995 (emphasis added).

[31] Catechism of Pius X: "**Question 22:** In what does the Soul of the Church consist? **Answer:** The Soul of the Church consists in her internal and spiritual endowments, that is, faith, hope, charity, the gifts of grace and of the Holy Ghost, together with all the heavenly treasures which are hers through the merits of our Redeemer, Jesus Christ, and of the Saints. **Question 23:** In what does the Body of the Church consist? **Answer:** The Body of the Church consists in her external and visible aspect, that is, in the association of her members, in her worship, in her teaching-power and in her external rule and government." Roberts, Marshall, *Catechism of Pope St. Pius X*, (Winchester, Virginia: St. Michael Press, 2010, Lulu.com), p. 41.

[32] As mentioned above, the terminology is here being used in a *metaphorical* sense, to describe the internal and external bonds that unite man with the Soul (Holy Ghost) and the Body (the visible society).

Again, some are of the soul and not of the body, as catechumens and excommunicated persons if they have faith and charity, as they can have them.

And, finally, some are of the body and not of the soul, as those who have no internal virtue, but who still by reason of some temporal hope or fear, profess the faith and communicate in the sacraments under the rule of the pastors. And such individuals are like hairs or fingernails or evil liquids in a human body.[33]

The internal spiritual bonds unite a man to the Soul of the Church, while the visible bonds unite him to the Body. Now, we have seen that the external bonds alone suffice to render a man a *member* of the Church, but it is possible for some members of the Church to be more perfectly united to the Church than others, as Fr. Fenton teaches:

"There is no doubt whatsoever about the fact that one man can be more perfectly united to the Church than another. All acknowledge that a Catholic in the state of grace is living consistently with his membership in the Church, while a Catholic in the state of mortal sin is not."[34]

Perfect and Imperfect Union

One is *perfectly* united to the Soul of the Church when he possesses all three theological virtues – faith, hope and charity - and is thereby living the supernatural life of grace. He is *imperfectly* united to the Soul of the Church when he possesses the supernatural virtue of faith (or both faith and hope), yet is cut off from the life of grace and charity (i.e., a Catholic in mortal sin).

One is *perfectly* united to the Body of the Church (the visible society) when he is a *member* of the Roman Catholic Church (meaning he possesses all three *external bonds* of unity). On the other hand, a person is *imperfectly* united (*ordained*[35]) to the Body (the visible society) when he is not an actual member of the Church but *desires* (implicitly or explicitly) to enter the Church, either for the first time (e.g., catechumen) or by returning after being expelled (i.e., excommunicate).[36] Pope Pius XII referred to those imperfectly united to

---

[33] *De Ecclesia Militante*, ch. 2.
[34] Fenton, "Membership in the Church," *American Ecclesiastical Review*, vol. CXII, n. 4, April, 1945, p. 295.
[35] This is the term (*ordinentur*) used by Pope Pius XII in *Mystici Corporis Christi* (No. 103).
[36] As Bellarmine says, because catechumens and excommunicated persons are outside the Church, and cannot receive the sacraments, "catechumens and excommunicated persons

the Body by an implicit desire, in *Mystici Corporis Christi*, when he spoke of "those who do not belong to the visible Body of the Catholic Church," but, nevertheless, "by an *unconscious desire* and longing they have a certain relationship (*ordinentur*) with the Mystical Body of the Redeemer."[37]

Because no one can obtain Heaven unless he dies with supernatural faith, hope and charity in his soul, it is clear that *perfect* union with the *Soul* of the Church is *absolutely necessary* for salvation. On the other hand, since one can be united to the Body of the Church *'in voto'* (by desire) or *'in re'* (actually), *imperfect* union with the Body can suffice for salvation.

To illustrate this point, let us imagine a man who was validly baptized in a Protestant sect as an infant, and raised as a Protestant. Let us also imagine that when he reached adulthood, through prayer and study, he arrived at the firm belief that the Roman Catholic Church is the true Church of Christ and immediately began taking instructions from a priest. In addition to believing all that the Church teaches, during the time of his instruction, but before being formally received into the Church, he receives a special grace from God enabling him to make an act of perfect contrition for his past sins, and thereby obtained the state of grace.

If the man died in this state, before being formally received into the Church, his perfect union with the *Soul* of the Church, combined with his desire to formally enter the *Body* of the Church, would suffice for salvation. Just as the will and intent to sin satisfies the conditions for mortal sin (*cf.* Mt. 5:28), so too the will and intent to formally join the Church can suffice in place of actual membership in certain circumstances. Hence, in order to obtain salvation, a person must die perfectly united to the *Soul* of the Church (he must possess faith, hope and charity), and be united to the *Body* at least *in voto* (imperfectly). Thus, Bellarmine says: "When we say 'Out of the Church there is no salvation,' it must be understood of those who belong to the [Body of the] Church neither *in fact* nor or *in desire...*"[38]

---

are excluded [not members of the *Body*], because the former are not yet admitted to the communion of the sacraments, while the latter have been sent away from it" (*De Ecclesia Militante*, ch. 2).

[37] "*etiamsi inscio quodam desiderio ac voto ad mysticum Redemptoris Corpus ordinentur.*" Pius XII, *Mystici Corporis Christi*, No. 103.

[38] *De Baptismo* IV 22, cited in Fr. Berry, *The Church of Christ*, p. 137.

Material Heretics Are Not Members of the Church

Material heretics are those baptized individuals who do not accept the Church's teaching authority due to ignorance of the Church. Since these people do not acknowledge the Church as the *rule of faith*, they lack what is necessary for the "profession of the true faith" which, as we have seen, is necessary for one to be a member of the Church. The term "material heretic" is an objective classification, independent of the subjective state of the soul. A person baptized and raised in a Protestant sect, for example, who is ignorant of the Church, is classified as a material heretic, even if he possesses interior faith (which is possible). As Cardinal Billot explains, even if such a person is in good faith, he is still not a *member* of the Church:

> "Heretics are divided into formal and material. Formal heretics are those to whom the authority of the Church is sufficiently known; while material heretics are those who, being in invincible ignorance of the Church herself, in good faith choose some other guiding rule. So the heresy of material heretics is not imputable as sin, and indeed it is not necessarily incompatible with that supernatural faith which is the beginning and root of all justification. For they may explicitly believe the principal articles [of Faith], and believe the others, not explicitly, but implicitly, through their disposition of mind and good will to adhere to whatever is sufficiently proposed to them as having been revealed by God. In fact they can still belong to the body of the Church by desire, and fulfill the other conditions necessary for salvation. Nonetheless, as to their actual incorporation in the visible Church of Christ, which is our present subject, our thesis makes no distinction between formal and material heretics, understanding everything in accordance with the notion of material heresy just given, which indeed is the only true and genuine one."[39]

The Cardinal goes on to explain that if one considers a person who professes subjection to the Church's Magisterium in matters of Faith (i.e., Catholics) to be a material heretic for inadvertently holding an opinion contrary to what the Church has defined, then "material heretics" would be members of the Church. But, as the Cardinal explains, this is not the proper definition of a material heretic (although it is not uncommon for this incorrect definition to be used). He explains

---

[39] Billot, *De Ecclesia Christi*, 3rd ed. (Prati: ex officina libraria Giachetti, 1909), p. 292 (translated by John Daly).

that the nature of heresy is a withdrawal from the Church as the *rule of faith:*

> "For, if you understand by the expression material heretic those alone, who, while professing subjection to the Church's Magisterium in matters of faith, nevertheless still deny something defined by the Church because he did not know it was defined, or, by the same token, hold an opinion opposed to Catholic doctrine because he falsely thinks that the Church teaches it, it would be quite absurd to place material heretics outside the body of the true Church; but on this understanding the legitimate use of the expression would be entirely perverted. For a material sin is said to exist only when that which belongs to the nature of the sin takes place materially, yet without advertence or a deliberate will. But the nature of heresy consists in withdrawal from the rule of the ecclesiastical Magisterium, which does not take place in this case, since this is a simple error of fact concerning what the rule dictates. And therefore there is no scope for heresy, even materially."[40]

According to the proper use of the term, material heretics (baptized non-Catholics) are not members of the Church, even if they are in good faith, whereas Catholics who inadvertently profess material heresy remain true members. The difference is that the former do not recognize the Church as the rule of faith (and therefore do not profess the true Faith), while the Catholic does, even if he professes a material heresy.[41]

Whether the Virtue of Faith is Necessary for Membership

A question that divided theologians for centuries is whether a person must have the interior virtue of faith *in addition* to the external bonds of union to be considered a "member" of the Church. Over time, however, the position of Bellarmine (that interior faith is *not* necessary) has become the common opinion of the Church's theologians, and for good reason, as it more easily resolves difficulties and is more consistent with the positive law of the Church. While the contrary opinion has never been condemned by the Church, Msgr. Fenton

---

[40] Ibid.

[41] Canon 731.2 of 1917 Code of Canon Law says that heretics who "err in good faith" (material heretics) are "outside the Church." Ludwig Ott also states that "public heretics, even those who err in good faith [material heretics], do not belong to the body of the Church." *Fundamentals of Catholic Dogma*, p. 311.

explains that the opinion of Bellarmine now holds a privileged status in Catholic theology. He writes:

> "The opinion that a man devoid of faith can be a real member of the Catholic Church is recognized, even by those who do not accept it, as being more commonly held than its opposite. As a *doctrina communior* it has a sort of privileged status in the field of Catholic theology."[42]

In *The Church of Christ*, Fr. Sylvester Berry lists a number of theologians who fell on either side of this question. He wrote: "Many, such as Bellarmine, Cornelius a Lapide, Perrone, Palmieri, Straub, and Billot, maintain that they [who lack interior faith] are true, even though very imperfect, members of the Church. Suarez, Franzelin, Billuart, Dorsch, and others hold that they are not members, and, therefore, belong to the Church in appearance only."[43]

The differing views appear to be a result of the perspective from which the theologians approached the question. For those who viewed the question from the point of view of interior union with Christ and *salvation*, the inward virtue of faith was considered absolutely necessary for one to be a *member* of the Church (since the loss of interior faith causes a *complete severing* of supernatural *union* with Christ). Others, such as the fifteenth century Dominican, Cardinal John de Torquemada (or Turrecremata) went even further by maintaining that *any* mortal sin resulted in loss of membership in the Church, since mortal sin deprives the person of charity and sanctifying grace, and therefore of perfect union with Christ.[44]

The opinion that interior faith is necessary for membership gradually decreased due to the problematic consequences of the position, and the opinion that any mortal sin (resulting in the loss of charity and sanctifying grace) severed one from membership in the Church[45] was explicitly contradicted by Pope Pius XII in *Mystici*

---

[42] Fenton, "The Status of St. Robert Bellarmine's Teaching about the Membership of Occult Heretics in the Catholic Church," *American Ecclesiastical Review*, vol. CXXII, no. 3, p. 221.

[43] *The Church of Christ*, p. 133.

[44] Fenton, "Membership in the Church," *American Ecclesiastical Review*, vol. CXII, n. 4, April, 1945, p. 293.

[45] A Catholic who commits a mortal sin (excluding sins against the Faith) becomes a "dead member" of the Church. Roberts, *Catechism of Pope St. Pius X*, Q. 26., p. 42. A Catholic who sins mortally against the Faith in the external forum completely severs himself from the Body of the Church.

Corporis Christi.[46] Some others, who viewed the question from the point of view of salvation, such as Wycliff, Huss and Calvin, went even further by claiming that only the *predestined* (those who would actually attain the Beatific Vision) were "members" of the Church. This view was formally condemned by the Council of Constance.[47]

For those, such as Bellarmine, who rightly viewed the question from the point of view of exterior union with the *visible society*, neither the loss of sanctifying grace, nor the loss of interior faith, severed one from the Body of the Church, that is, from actual "membership" in the visible society. This is because the loss of the interior virtues (faith, hope and charity) occurs in the internal (invisible) forum and therefore cannot be seen. Consequently, the loss does not deprive one of the rights and privileges of a Catholic in the *external* (visible) forum, nor does it have any effect on the person's standing in the visible society. This explains why the common opinion maintains that the loss of interior faith does not cause a person to cease being a member of the visible Church.

Scripture also confirms that the visible bonds alone suffice for Church membership, since it consistently refers to membership in the *Body*, without regard to any of the interior, supernatural virtues of her members. For example, St. Paul tells the Corinthians: "Now you are the body of Christ, and members of member" (1Cor. 12:27). He also tells the Romans: "So we, being many, are one body in Christ, and every one members one of another" (Rom. 12:5); and "by the body of Christ, that you may belong to another" (Rom. 7:4). St. Paul further says: "For as the body is one, and hath many members; and all the members of the body, whereas they are many, yet are one body, so also is Christ" (1Cor. 12:12). St. Paul also refers to Christ's "body, which is the Church" (Col. 1:24) and says "Christ is the head of the Church. He is the saviour of his body" (Eph. 5:23).

We also have the example of our Lord not excluding the faithless Judas Iscariot from the Last Supper. St. Augustine, along with the other Fathers, held that Judas was amongst those in the Gospel of John, Chapter 6, who "believed not" (v. 64),[48] and Our Lord Himself, at the time, went so far as to call him a "devil" (v. 72). Yet, in spite of the loss

---

[46] "For not every sin, *however grave it may be*, is such as of its own nature to sever a man from the Body of the Church..." (Pius XII, *Mystici Corporis Christi*, No. 23).
[47] Denz., 627. For a thorough treatment of the topic of predestination and the errors of Calvinism, see John Salza's *The Mystery of Predestination – According to Scripture, the Church and St. Thomas Aquinas* (Charlotte, North Carolina: TAN Books and Publishers, Inc., 2010), available at http://www.johnsalza.com.
[48] *Commentary on the Gospel of John,* tract 27, St. Augustine.

of interior faith, Judas was invited to the Last Supper along with the other Apostles. St. Thomas explained why:

> "Since Christ was to serve us as a pattern of justice, it was not in keeping with His teaching authority to sever Judas, a hidden sinner, from Communion with the others without an accuser and evident proof, lest the Church's prelates might have an example for doing the like…"[49]

In the reply to an objection in the same Article, St. Thomas further explained:

> "The wickedness of Judas was known to Christ as God; but it was unknown to Him after the manner in which it is known by men. Consequently, Christ did not repel Judas from communion; so as to furnish an example that such secret sinners are not to be repelled by other priests."[50]

In this example, we see that Our Blessed Lord Himself treated an unbeliever as a "member" of His Church. Since Judas was united externally to Christ, he was invited to the Last Supper, and treated *externally* as one of the faithful.

Following the example of Our Lord, the Magisterium also treats those who are united to the Body of the Church externally as "members" of the Church. For example, Pope Pius XII defines the "Church" as "all the <u>members</u> of His Mystical <u>Body</u>."[51] Pope Leo X says "those who "<u>belong</u> to the one universal <u>Church</u>, outside of which no one at all is saved," are those "<u>belonging</u> to the one same <u>body</u>."[52] Pope Pius XI teaches that "whosoever therefore is not united with the <u>body</u> is no <u>member</u> of it, neither is he in communion with Christ its head."[53] Pope Clement XIV says, "One is the <u>body</u> of the <u>Church</u>, whose head is Christ, and all cohere in it."[54] In reference to the Church, Pope Pius IX teaches that "they, as <u>members</u> associated in one head, coalesce into one <u>bodily</u> structure."[55] Pope Eugene IV similarly says "that the unit of this ecclesiastical <u>body</u> is so strong that only for those who abide in it are the same sacraments of the <u>Church</u> of benefit for

---

[49] ST, III, q. 81, a. 2.
[50] Ibid., III, q. 81, a. 2, ad 2.
[51] *Mystici Corporis*, No. 30.
[52] *Fifth Lateran Council*, Session 11, December 19, 1516.
[53] *Mortalium Animos*, No. 10, January 6, 1928.
[54] *Cum Summi*, No. 3, December 12, 1769.
[55] Vatican Council I, Session 4, ch. 2.

salvation."[56] In these and other passages, neither Scripture nor the Magisterium makes interior virtue a requirement for actual membership in the Church. As noted previously, if the external bonds *alone* did not suffice for membership, the true Church would not be a visible society, but an invisible Church.

Ultimately, however, the divergent opinions regarding whether the virtue of faith is necessary for one to be considered a "member" of the Church is only a speculative question with no practical difference. This is because, on the practical level, all agree that those who retain the visible, external bonds of union *alone* (even if they have lost the faith internally), continue to be *treated* as actual members of the Church in good standing, and consequently possess equal ecclesiastical rights and duties, whether they possess the virtue of faith or not.

As we will see later, this applies equally to members of the hierarchy, which means that even if prelates (the Pope, bishops, priests) happen to lack interior faith (which is known with certainty to God alone), they nevertheless retain the rights and duties of a member of the Church according to their position, including ecclesiastical office. Hence, if a member of the hierarchy happens to lose the faith, he does not, by that fact alone, lose his office (jurisdiction).[57] As we will see in Chapter 5, this point is affirmed even by the minority of theologians who hold that interior faith is necessary for one to be considered, technically, a "member" of the Church.

Non-Members and the Soul of the Church

In the next chapter, we will discuss the dogma "No Salvation Outside the Church," and explain how it is *possible* for one to be saved without being a formal "member" of the Church. In trying to answer this question, certain theologians fell into an error that essentially split the Church in two. This confused ecclesiology resulted, in part, from an incorrect understanding of the *Soul* of the Church, which was considered to be *separate and independent* of the visible society, constituting a Church in itself with its own "members."

Whereas Bellarmine's ecclesiology rightly holds that "there is only one *ecclesia*, and not two,"[58] this Modernist theory resulted in the concept of two Churches, or at least two distinct modes of *membership* in the one true Church: namely, membership with the Body, and

---

[56] Council of Florence, *Cantate Domino*, 1441.
[57] Theologically speaking, there is no metaphysical incompatibility between the lack of interior faith and habitual jurisdiction.
[58] *De Ecclesia Militante*, ch. 2

"membership" with the Soul. This resulted in the error that the Mystical Body of Christ (the "Soul") is one Church, and the Roman Catholic Church (the "Body") is a separate Church. Instead of simply saying it was possible for a person who was not yet an actual "member" of the Church to be saved, Modernists came up with the notion of a second Church, with "members" of its own; or, two different modes of "membership" in the one Church. Responding to this error, Fr. Fenton said:

> "They have arrived at the implication that, in some way or another, all of those men and women who are eligible for salvation, or in the state of habitual grace, must be members of the Church. They have not considered the classical doctrine, a commonplace in scholastic ecclesiology since the days of Thomas Stapleton and St. Robert Bellarmine, that a man <u>may be saved</u> either by being a member of the Church <u>or by intending to enter this society as a member</u>. In their anxiety to find a sort of membership which would apply to all men of good will, they have voided the term 'member' of its essential meaning, and they have thus occasioned confusion about the nature of the Catholic Church itself."[59]

Pope Pius XII also responded to this error (which essentially split the Church in two) in *Mystici Corporis,* and again in *Humani Generis,* when he taught that "the Mystical Body of Christ and the Roman Catholic Church are one and the same thing;"[60] and referred to those who were undermining this truth as being "deceived by imprudent zeal for souls."[61]

The answer for understanding how *non*-members of the Church can be saved is not to treat the *Body* and *Soul* as separate entities, as if there are two separate Churches or two separate modes of membership in the Church, which does violence to the nature of the Church itself. Rather, the solution is to simply realize that one can be saved by being a *member* of the Church <u>or</u> by *desiring* to enter the Church as a member. In either situation, however, it is absolutely necessary for salvation that the person dies in a state of grace, that is, with the theological virtues of faith, hope and charity in his soul.

In summary, the Church is a visible society with both internal and external bonds of union. The external bonds of union are the profession of the true faith (which is primarily shown by a submission to the

---

[59] Fenton, "Membership in the Church," *American Ecclesiastical Review,* vol. CXII, n. 4, April, 1945, p. 303 (emphasis added).
[60] *Humani Generis* (August 12, 1950).
[61] Ibid.

Magisterium *as the rule of faith*), participation in the same sacraments, and union with the Church's hierarchy, especially the Pope. The external bonds alone suffice for one to be considered a true *member* of the Church. The internal bonds of unity are faith, hope and charity, which unite a man more perfectly to Christ and His Church, and without which no one can be saved. In the next chapter, we will address the dogma, *Outside the Church there is no Salvation*.

Chapter 4

~ Church Membership and Salvation ~

As we have seen, the virtue of faith is not necessary for a person to be a *member* of the visible Church, but supernatural faith (and not mere natural knowledge of God based upon reason) is absolutely necessary for man to possess supernatural grace and to achieve his ultimate end (the Beatific Vision). In Chapter 5, we will consider the virtue of faith in relation to jurisdiction in the Church. Before doing so, however, it seems opportune to further discuss the necessity of faith, and the necessity of the Church, for *salvation*.

This chapter is intended primarily to counter an overreaction on the Right, to an opposite error of the Left. The error on the Left is religious indifferentism, which maintains that all religions are more or less good and praiseworthy, insofar as they help man to live a better life. This error also maintains that salvation is attainable by the profession of any religion (or even no religion at all), as long as one lives a naturally good life and follows his conscience.

Those who possess the *sensus fidelium* (the sense of the Faith) immediately recognize this error. But some, who do not have complete knowledge about what the Church teaches, end up overreacting by embracing an opposite error on the Right – namely, that salvation is possible *only* for those who are formal *members* of the Catholic Church. Although this overreaction is understandable, it is not what the Church teaches. This chapter will address the specific details of the dogma "Outside the Church There is No Salvation," by showing how those who are not visible members of the Church can *possibly* obtain the Beatific Vision. In discussing the finer details of the dogma (what some wrongly call "exceptions"), we do not intend to imply that salvation for non-members is common. On the contrary, we believe attaining salvation without being a formal member of the Roman Catholic Church is likely very rare, especially in this day. *The point is not to open a door, but merely to remain faithful to the Church's teaching without distorting it either to the Left or to the Right.*

The Necessity of Faith and the Church for Salvation

The *habit of faith* is a supernatural virtue that resides within the intellect,[1] the purpose of which is to enable man, with the assistance of actual grace, to believe what God has revealed to be true, not on account of the intrinsic truth perceived by the natural light of reason, but because of the authority of God Himself, the Revealer, who can neither deceive nor be deceived.[2] The *formal object* of faith is the First Truth – God the revealer. The *material object* of faith consists of the truths revealed by God (contained in Scripture or Tradition) and proposed by the Church for belief. The *act of faith* is the intellectual assent to the truths revealed by God and proposed for belief by the Church.

Those who have not obtained the use of reason can be saved through the *habit of faith* infused in baptism (along with the other theological virtues and sanctifying grace), whereas an adult who has attained the use of reason is also obliged to make an *act of supernatural faith* (by accepting the truths of revelation) and perform works in charity to attain salvation,[3] because "faith without works is dead" (Jam. 2:26).

What Must Be Believed Explicitly?

While it is necessary for all who have attained the use of reason to assent to each and every article of faith that has been sufficiently proposed to them for belief, it is not necessary that every truth of the faith be believed *explicitly* for salvation. Because some articles of faith contain others implicitly (e.g., explicit belief in the Incarnation contains implicit belief in the human and divine wills of Christ), it suffices that some articles be believed *implicitly*, provided the person is so disposed that he is *willing* to believe all explicitly when they have been sufficiently proposed to him. St. Thomas says: "A man who *obstinately disbelieves* a thing that is of faith, has not the habit of faith, and yet he who does not explicitly believe all, *while he is prepared to believe all*, has that habit."[4]

Now, by considering the minimum that must be believed *explicitly* for an adult to possess supernatural faith and attain salvation, it will enable us to avoid a modern error on the Right, which has resulted

---

[1] ST, II-II, q. 4, a. 2.
[2] See, for example, the First Vatican Council, Session 4, ch. 3.
[3] Supernatural faith is an absolute necessity; good works are a relative necessity.
[4] ST, II-II, q. 5, a. 4, ad. 1 (emphasis added).

from an overreaction to an opposite error on the Left. The error on the Left is either an outright rejection of the dogma "Outside the Church There is No Salvation," or at least reducing the dogma itself to a "meaningless formula" as Pope Pius XII explained in the encyclical *Humani Generis*. This error of the Left has caused an opposite error on the Right, which departs from Tradition by maintaining that it is *impossible* for a person to be saved if they are not an actual member of the Church. The error on the Right is refuted by considering the minimum that must be believed *explicitly* for an adult to possess divine faith (and charity) and obtain salvation.

Four Necessary Truths

The theologians and Doctors are unanimous in holding that the two prime credibles – namely, that "God is" and "He rewards those who seek Him" (Heb. 11:6) – must be believed explicitly for an adult to obtain eternal salvation. In addition to these two revealed truths, St. Thomas Aquinas, St. Alphonsus Liguori and many others maintain that, after the promulgation of the Gospel, *explicit* belief in the Incarnation and the Blessed Trinity is also absolutely necessary for salvation. For example, St. Thomas says: "After grace had been revealed, both learned and simple folk are bound to explicit faith in the mysteries of Christ, chiefly as regards those which are observed throughout the Church, and publicly proclaimed, such as the articles which refer to the Incarnation..."[5] St. Thomas also says: "And consequently, when once grace had been revealed, all were bound to explicit faith in the mystery of the Trinity."[6]

Without discussing the controversy over why some theologians hold that explicit belief in the two prime credibles *alone* is absolutely necessary,[7] suffice it to say that all agree there are, at most, only four revealed truths that must be believed *explicitly* for an adult to possess the virtue of supernatural faith. As long as a person explicitly believes in these four truths, and is so disposed to believe the other articles of faith when they are proposed to him, he can obtain salvation, provided he has also obtained the state of grace and not lost it through mortal sin.

---

[5] ST, II-II, q. 2, a. 7.

[6] ST, II-II, q. 2, a. 8.

[7] We will discuss the degrees of necessity later in the chapter. For more on this topic, see Fr. Reginald Garrigou-Lagrange, *The Theological Virtues: I On Faith*, (St. Louis & London: Herder Book Co, 1964, originally published by Robert Berruti & Co., Torino, Italy, 1949, p. 225; and, Van Noort, *The Sources of Revelation*, (Westminster, Maryland: Newman Press, 1961), pp. 378-380.

Explicit Knowledge of the Church Not Necessary

Because knowledge of the Church itself is not one of the four truths that must be explicitly known, it is *possible* for a person to possess true supernatural faith without ever having known about the Church. While faith is absolutely necessary for grace and salvation, the necessity of knowing about the Church and belonging to the Church as a *member* can be supplied by an implicit desire to join her ranks, provided the person is unaware, through no fault of his own, that the Catholic Church is the true Church of Christ, yet "is prepared to believe all," to use the words of St. Thomas. In his magnificent book, *The Catholic Church and Salvation* (1958), Msgr. Fenton elaborated on this point:

> "The divine public revelation is composed of a certain number of truths or statements. It is quite manifest that genuine and supernatural divine faith can exist and does exist in individuals who have no clear and distinct awareness of some of these truths, but who simply accept them as they are contained or implied in other doctrines. But, in order that faith may exist, there certainly must be some minimum of teachings which are grasped distinctly by the believer and within which the rest of the revealed message is implied or implicit. Catholic theology holds that it is possible to have genuine divine faith when two, or, according to some writers, four of these revealed truths are believed distinctly or explicitly. There can be real divine faith when a man believes explicitly, on the authority of God revealing, the existence of God as the Head of the supernatural order, the fact that God rewards good and punishes evil, and the doctrines of the Blessed Trinity and of the Incarnation.
>
> It is definitely *not* a teaching of the Catholic theologians that there can be no true act of divine or supernatural faith apart from an explicit awareness and acceptance of the Catholic religion as the true religion and of the Catholic Church as the true kingdom of God. (...) True supernatural faith can exist even where there is only an implicit belief in the Catholic Church and Catholic religion. (...) A person *invincibly ignorant* of the true religion can attain eternal salvation. (...) Hence since it is possible for a man to have genuine supernatural faith and charity and the life of sanctifying grace, without having a distinct and explicit knowledge of the true Church and of the true religion, it is possible for this man to be saved with only an implicit knowledge and desire of the Church."[8]

---

[8] Fenton, *The Catholic Church and Salvation*, p. 69.

The desire to join the Church is *implicit*, if the person is responding to actual grace and truly seeking the will of God as far as he knows it, yet is unaware of the Church through no fault of his own. The desire to join the Church is *explicit* if he knows that the Catholic Church is the true Church, and explicitly desires to become a member (i.e., the catechumen).[9] Either can suffice for salvation in place of actual membership, provided it is informed by supernatural faith and perfect charity.[10] This also means that union with the Church, at least in desire, is absolutely necessary for salvation.[11] And, to be clear, while implicit desire to enter the Church can suffice for salvation, implicit faith alone will not suffice. This is because *implicit* faith in certain supernatural truths is dependent upon *explicit* faith in other, more general supernatural truths (e.g., the Trinity and Incarnation).

In his 1948 article, "The Theological Proof of the Necessity of the Catholic Church," Fr. Fenton explains how the theologians have always understood the teaching on actual membership vis-à-vis *desire* for membership in the Church:

> "...no theologian demands as absolutely requisite for eternal salvation any explicit belief in the Catholic Church itself. Hence it is obvious that the very *Schola Theologorum* (Theological Schools) which has insisted upon the validity of the doctrine that the Church is requisite for salvation, never intended to teach, *and cannot be interpreted as teaching*, that a man had to be an actual member of the Church, *or, absolutely speaking, even had to possess explicit knowledge of the Church* as God's kingdom on earth in order to attain eternal salvation. The men who have expounded the Church's teaching about its own necessity have always explained that teaching against the background of a theology which states that a man can be saved by a desire of the Church *even when that desire was merely implicit.*"[12]

Before proceeding, we will take this brief moment to note that while one cannot presume formal heresy for those who have never been members of the Church, we can do so in the case of those who have *left* the Church of their own free will (ex-Catholics). The First Vatican Council teaches "for those who have accepted the faith under

---

[9] Ibid., pp. 101-102.
[10] Ibid., p. 102.
[11] See, for example, *Christ's Church*, p. 264. Here, Van Noort mentions that the martyrdom of non-baptized children is the only exception to the principle that at least implicit desire to enter the Church is absolutely necessary for salvation.
[12] Fenton, "The Theological Proof of the Necessity of the Catholic Church, Pt. II," *American Ecclesiastical Review*, April 1948, p. 298, (emphasis added).

the Church's magisterium *can never have a just cause for doubting it.*[13] As St. Peter says: "For if, flying from the pollutions of the world, through the knowledge of our Lord and Saviour Jesus Christ, they be again entangled in them and overcome: their latter state is become unto them worse than the former. For it had been better for them not to have known the way of justice, than after they have known it, to turn back from that holy commandment which was delivered to them" (2Pet. 2:20-21).

Indeed, those who were raised Catholic or are adult converts to the true Church are *presumed* to be formal heretics for defecting from the Church because they have learned (and, thus, should know) that the Church is the infallible rule of Faith.[14] The First Vatican Council also condemned the view that Catholics and non-Catholics are in the same condition as regards their moral responsibility to the Church, indicating that while the latter may be excused for doubting dogmas while they investigate the Church, the former would be presumed culpable for doing so:

> "If anyone shall say that the condition of the faithful and of those who have not yet come to the true faith is equal, so that Catholics can have a just cause of doubting the faith that they have accepted under the Church's magisterium, by withholding assent until they have completed the scientific demonstration of the truth and credibility of their faith, let him be anathema."[15]

Now, with regard to ignorance of the true Church and salvation, in his 1863 encyclical *Quanto Conficiamur Moerore*, Blessed Pope Pius IX affirms the dogma that there is no salvation outside the Church, yet in the same paragraph explains that "they who labor in invincible ignorance of our most holy religion and who, zealously keeping the natural law and its precepts engraved in the hearts of all by God, and being ready to obey God, live an honest and upright life, can, by the operating power of divine light and grace, attain eternal life."

Note that such men do not obtain salvation merely by following the natural law and living a good moral life (a tenet of naturalism/Freemasonry), but "by the operating power of divine light and grace" which moves them to make an act of supernatural faith. If this faith is combined with an act of perfect contrition, or perfect

---

[13] Denz., 1794 (emphasis added).
[14] If this knowledge were lacking, it would almost certainly be *culpable* ignorance and therefore not morally excusable.
[15] Denz., 1815.

charity (which is possible), the person would obtain the state of justification even without being explicitly aware of the Church, or incorporated into it as an actual member. In such a case, the person would be united perfectly to the *Soul* of the Church through supernatural faith, hope and charity, and united to the *Body* of the Church by desire.

While such exceptional situations are not to be presumed upon, and may occur only in rare situations, it is possible for a person to obtain salvation in this fashion, as Pope Pius IX clearly teaches.[16] Simply because those on the Left err by making a rule out of the possible "exception" and thereby undermine the rule itself, is no reason to overreact in the other direction by denying the possibility and interpreting the dogma in a way in which the Church herself has never understood it.[17]

The prolific Sedevacantist writer, Richard Ibranyi, is a perfect example of an individual who has overreacted and fallen into error in the opposite direction. Mr. Ibranyi refers to the possibility that a person can obtain salvation without, technically, being a "member" of the Church as "the salvation heresy." He goes so far as to hold that Blessed Pius IX lost his office and became an antipope for teaching this traditional doctrine of the Church. In an article written against his fellow Sedevacantist, Hutton Gibson, Mr. Ibranyi accuses Mr. Gibson of what he calls the sins of "non-judgmentalism, and "non-punishmentalism." Wrote Mr. Ibranyi:

> "Pius IX taught the salvation heresy in 1856 in his allocution *Singulari Quidem* and in 1863 in his encyclical *Quanto Conficiamur Moerore*. Hence Pius IX automatically lost his office in 1856 and thus became an apostate antipope. ... He [Hutton Gibson] is also guilty of non-judgmentalism and non-punishmentalism. ... I pray that he will now see that Pius IX did publicly defect from the faith by denying the Salvation Dogma and

---

[16] We say salvation by *implicit desire to enter the Church* would seem to occur in rare cases due to the narrow scope of invincible ignorance, which, as St. Thomas teaches, is ignorance that "cannot be overcome by study" (ST, I-II, q. 76, a. 2). While we don't presume to set the boundaries of invincible ignorance for individual persons, overcoming ignorance of the Church through study would seem to be possible for the majority.

[17] Because one who desires to enter the Church is truly joined to the Church by that desire by means of supernatural faith, this imperfect union by desire (as opposed to perfect union through water baptism) is not an "exception" to the dogma "No Salvation Outside the Church." One must be joined to the Catholic Church as a member or in desire to be saved.

thus automatically lost his office and hence Hutton will no longer follow Pius IX in his heresy and in his damnation."[18]

Here we see what happens when a person overreacts to one error, and ends by falling into error in the opposite direction.

In his book on the early Church Fathers, Adrian Fortescue explains that heresies often arose in reaction to an error, and ended by going too far in the opposite direction:

> "It is never the case that one man out of sheer wickedness suddenly invents a false doctrine. (...) A movement begins, often very rightly, by a vigorous and extreme opposition to some patently false teaching. Then this way of looking at things crystallizes and hardens; it is taken up enthusiastically by some school, it becomes a point of honour with a certain party to insist upon it... At last, someone gets hold of the theory, oversteps every limit in his defense of it, and is eagerly supported by the rest of the party. And then he finds himself condemned by the Church."[19]

The erroneous teaching of Fr. Leonard Feeney, who held that water baptism (and formal membership in the Church) was absolutely necessary for salvation, is a perfect example of an overreaction to the error of the Left. In fact, Feeney's error by *excess* prompted the Holy Office, under Pope Pius XII, to issue a letter on August 8, 1949 to Archbishop Cushing of the diocese in Boston to address the problem.[20] The Letter affirms the teaching of Pope Pius IX that one may be saved without water baptism, and thus without being an actual "member" of the Church, so long as he is joined to the Church by desire:

> "[I]n order that one may obtain eternal salvation, it is not always required that he be incorporated into the Church actually as a member, but it is required that at least he be united to it by intention and desire. However, this desire need not always be explicit, as it is in catechumens; but, when a person is involved in invincible ignorance, God accepts also an implicit intention (*votum*) which is so called because it is included in that good disposition of

---

[18] Ibranyi, "Against Hutton Gibson," December 2012.
[19] Adrian Fortescue, *The Greek Fathers, Their Lives and Writings*, (San Francisco, California: Ignatius Press, 2007), p. 4.
[20] This letter from the Holy Office is also known as *Suprema haec sacra* or Protocol 122/49. While some dispute whether Pope Pius XII actually approved the Letter (*in forma specifica* or *in forma comune*), its Magisterial status is irrelevant to the fact that the Letter is in complete conformity with the constant teaching tradition of the Church.

the soul whereby a person wishes his will to be conformed to the will of God."[21]

The Letter goes on to note that this desire alone (i.e., *imperfect* union with the Body) will not suffice for salvation, unless it is accompanied by "supernatural faith" and "perfect charity" (*perfect* union with the Soul):

> "Nor must we think that any kind of intention of entering the Church is sufficient in order that one may be saved. It is requisite that the intention by which one is ordered to the Church should be informed by perfect charity; and no explicit intention can produce its effect unless the man has supernatural faith."[22]

The Letter from the Holy Office reflects the teaching of Blessed Pius IX, and the constant tradition of the Catholic Church.

Baptism of Desire

In his March 5, 1941 address to husbands and wives, Pope Pius XII expressed the perennial teaching of the Church, when he said:

> "In the case of other, more necessary sacraments, when the minister is lacking, he can be supplied through the force of divine mercy, which will forego even external signs in order to bring grace to the heart. To the catechumen who has no one to pour water on his head, to the sinner who can find no one to absolve him, a loving God will accord, out of their desire and love, the grace which makes them His friends and children even without Baptism or actual confession."[23]

Some modern Catholics have struggled with the difficulty of reconciling the teachings that: 1) Outside the Church there is no salvation, and yet 2) catechumens, who have not been incorporated into the Church by baptism, can be saved. Bellarmine noted the difficulty:

---

[21] *Suprema Haec Sacra*, English translation published in *American Ecclesiastical Review*, CXXVII, 4 (October, 1952).
[22] Ibid.
[23] *Husbands and Wives Ministers of the Sacrament*, Pius XII, cited in *Dear Newlyweds*, (Kansas City, Missouri: Sarto House, 2001), p. 13 (emphasis added).

"Concerning catechumens there is a greater difficulty, because they are faithful [interior virtue of faith] and can be saved if they die in this state, and yet outside the Church no one is saved, as [no one was saved] outside the ark of Noah..."[24]

After providing the explanation of others (such as Melchior Cano) to this question, Bellarmine gave his own answer to the apparent difficulty:

"I answer therefore that, when it is said outside the Church no one is saved, it must be understood of those who belong to her neither in actual fact nor in desire [desiderio], as theologians commonly speak on baptism. Because the catechumens are in the Church, though not in actual fact, yet at least in resolution [voto], therefore they can be saved."[25]

This explanation of Bellarmine is founded upon the teaching of the Council of Trent, which explains that one can be justified (obtain the state of grace) either by baptism ("the laver of regeneration") or by the *desire* for baptism. The Sacred Council teaches:

"And this translation [to the state of justification], since the promulgation of the Gospel, cannot be effected, without the laver of regeneration, or its desire [*aut eius voto*], as it is written; 'unless a man be born again of water and the Holy Ghost, he cannot enter into the Kingdom of God.'"[26]

Based upon this teaching of Trent, which reflects the constant teaching of the Church, Bellarmine explained that true conversion can "without doubt" supply for water baptism, provided one dies without water baptism through no fault of his own:

"But *without doubt* it must be believed that true conversion supplies for Baptism of water when one dies without Baptism of water, not out of contempt, but out of necessity... Thus also the Council of Trent, Session 6, Chapter 4, says that Baptism is necessary in fact or in desire (*in re vel in voto*)."[27]

---

[24] *De Ecclesia Militante,* bk. III, ch.2, *opera omnia,* Naples, 1872, p. 75.
[25] *Ibid.* Ch. 3, "Of those who are not baptized," p. 76.
[26] Denz., 796.
[27] *De Controversiis, "De Baptismo,"* bk. 1, ch. 6. As noted, St. Bellarmine based his teaching upon the doctrine of the Council of Trent on Baptism of Desire in her canon on justification (see Denz., 796) and in its Catechism, and which has been taught by the greatest saints, Fathers, Doctors and Popes of the Catholic Church (e.g., Cyprian,

Bellarmine's interpretation and application of Trent is consistent with the explanation of Pope St. Pius V, as set forth in the Catechism of Trent (or *Roman Catechism*), which is considered by many to be the greatest catechism the Church has ever produced. Pope Clement XIII declared that the Catechism of Trent contains "the common doctrine of the Church, from which all danger of doctrinal error is absent," and Pope Leo XIII confirmed "the exactness of its doctrine." In regard to adult baptism, the Catechism says, "should any unforeseen accident make it impossible for adults to be washed in the salutary waters, their intention and determination to receive Baptism and their repentance for past sins, will avail them to grace and righteousness."[28]

St. Alphonsus Liguori, another great Doctor of the Church (and the patron saint of moral theologians), teaches that Baptism of Desire is a *de fide* doctrine (requiring the assent of faith) based upon the teachings of the Council of Trent. He says:

> "We shall speak below of Baptism of water, which was very probably instituted before the Passion of Christ the Lord, when Christ was baptised by John. But baptism of desire is perfect conversion to God by contrition or love of God above all things accompanied by an explicit or implicit desire for true Baptism of water, the place of which it takes as to the remission of guilt, but not as to the impression of the [baptismal] character or as to the removal of all debt of punishment. It is called "of wind" ["*flaminis*"] because it takes place by the impulse of the Holy Ghost who is called a wind ["*flamen*"]. Now it is de fide that men are also saved by Baptism of desire, by virtue of the Canon Apostolicam, "de presbytero non baptizato" and of the Council of Trent, session 6, Chapter 4 where it is said that no one can be saved 'without the laver of regeneration or the desire for it.'"[29]

The Catechism of Pope St. Pius X (who was certainly no Modernist!) explicitly teaches Baptism of Desire:

> "**Question:** Can the absence of Baptism be supplied in any other way?
> **Answer:** The absence of Baptism can be supplied by martyrdom, which is called Baptism of Blood, or by an act of perfect love of

---

Ambrose, Augustine, Gregory Nazianzen, Bernard, Albert the Great, Bonaventure, Thomas Aquinas, Alphonsus Liguori, Pope Innocent, Pius V, Pius X, Pius IX and Pius XII).

[28] *The Catechism of the Council of Trent* (South Bend, Indiana: Marian Publications, Third Printing), p. 179.

[29] St. Alphonsus Liguori's *Moral Theology*, bk. 6, nn. 95-7 (emphasis added).

God, or of contrition, along with the desire, at least implicit, of
Baptism, and this is called Baptism of Desire."[30]

Further, St. Pius X had Baptism of Desire incorporated into canon
law which was promulgated by his successor, Pope Benedict XV.
Canon 737, §1 of the 1917 Code of Canon Law says: "Baptism, the door
and foundation of the Sacraments, in fact *or at least in desire* necessary
unto salvation for all, is not validly conferred except through the
ablution of true and natural water with the prescribed form of words"
(emphasis added).

We also read the following in the Douay Catechism (1649 A.D.):

"**Question:** Can a man be saved without baptism?

Answer: He cannot, unless he have it either actual *or in desire*,
with contrition, or to be baptized in his blood as the holy Innocents
were, which suffered for Christ."[31]

The Baltimore Catechism teaches the same doctrine:

"**Question**: How can those be saved who through no fault of their
own have not received the sacrament of Baptism?

Answer: Those who through no fault of their own have not received
the sacrament of Baptism can be saved through what is called
baptism of blood or of desire. (…)

Question: How does an unbaptized person receive baptism of
desire?

Answer: An unbaptized person receives baptism of desire when he
loves God above all things and desires to do all that is necessary for
his salvation.

(a) Baptism of desire takes away all sin, original and actual, and the
eternal punishment due to sin. It does not, however, imprint a
character on the soul nor does it necessarily take away all temporal
punishment due to actual sin.
(b) In the baptism of desire, there need not always be an explicit desire
to receive baptism of water."[32]

---

[30] Catechism of St. Pius X, (Australia: Instauratio Press, 1993), p. 71.
[31] *An Abridgment of the Christian Doctrine*, Composed in 1649 by Rev. Turberville, D.D., of
the English College of Douay (New York: John Doyle, 1833), p. 80.

The theology of the Tridentine Fathers (and the Catechisms which followed) was greatly influenced by the teachings of the Universal Doctor of the Church, St. Thomas Aquinas, whose *Summa Theologica* was placed alongside the Sacred Scriptures on the Altar during the Council of Trent. In the *Summa Theologica*, St. Thomas teaches the following about Baptism of Desire:

> "Moreover, the sacraments of grace are ordained in order that man may receive the infusion of grace, and before he receives them, either actually <u>or in his desire</u>, he does not receive grace. This is evident in the case of Baptism, and applies to penance likewise."[33]

In answer to the question, "are there three baptisms" (namely, baptism of water, desire, and blood), St. Thomas replies:

> "I answer that, as stated above (Question 62, Article 5), Baptism of Water has its efficacy from Christ's Passion, to which a man is conformed by Baptism, and also from the Holy Ghost, as first cause. Now, although the effect depends on the first cause, the cause far surpasses the effect, nor does it depend on it. Consequently, a man may, without Baptism of Water, receive the sacramental effect from Christ's Passion, in so far as he is conformed to Christ by suffering for Him [i.e., Baptism of Blood]. … <u>In like manner a man receives the effect of Baptism by the power of the Holy Ghost, not only without Baptism of Water, but also without Baptism of Blood</u>: forasmuch as his heart is moved by the Holy Ghost to believe in and love God and to repent of his sins: <u>wherefore this is also called Baptism of Repentance</u> [i.e., Baptism of Desire]."[34]

We can also point to those who taught Baptism of Desire prior to the time of St. Thomas to demonstrate that the doctrine is part of the Church's *constant* tradition. For example, only a few years before the Fourth Lateran Council, Pope Innocent wrote that a certain one "who

---

[32] Baltimore Catechism No. 3, Benzinger Brothers Inc. 3rd ed. (Colorado Springs, Colorado: The Seraphim Company Inc., 1987 1991, 1995), q. 321, q. 323, pp. 188-189.
[33] ST, Supplement 6, 1 (emphasis added). Note also that St. Thomas promoted his teachings on Baptism of Desire after the Fourth Ecumenical Lateran Council infallibly declared the dogma "No Salvation Outside the Church." Therefore, if Baptism of Desire were incompatible with this dogma, then St. Thomas, the Universal Doctor of the Church, would have been a public heretic, and the many Popes who publicly promoted St. Thomas in their papal teachings would have also been suspected of heresy! Those would include Popes St. Pius V, Urban V, Innocent VI, Bl. Pius IX, Leo XIII, St. Pius X, Pius XI, Benedict XV and Pope Pius XII.
[34] ST, III, q. 66, a. 11 (emphasis added).

had died without the water of baptism, because he persevered in the faith of holy mother Church and in the confession of the name of Christ, was freed from original sin and attained the joy of heavenly fatherhood."[35]

Pope Innocent, on another occasion, also confirmed the Church's teaching regarding Baptism of Desire in the case of a Jew who, when at the point of death and surrounded only by Jews, immersed himself in water and attempted to baptize himself. Even though this baptism was invalid, Pope Innocent said: "If, however, such a one had died immediately, he would have rushed to his heavenly home without delay because of the faith of the sacrament, though not because of the sacrament of the Faith."[36]

In the book *City of God*, St. Augustine (fifth century) wrote:

> *"Of the Death Which the Unbaptized Suffer for the Confession of Christ:*
> 'For whatever unbaptized persons die confessing Christ, <u>this confession is of the same efficacy for the remission of sins as if they were washed in the sacred font of baptism</u>. For He who said, 'Unless a man be born of water and of the Spirit, he cannot enter into the kingdom of God,' John 3:5 <u>made also an exception in their favor</u>, in that other sentence where He no less absolutely said, 'Whosoever shall confess me before men, him will I confess also before my Father which is in heaven;' Matthew 10:32 and in another place, 'Whosoever will lose his life for my sake, shall find it.' Matthew 16:25."[37]

Commenting on the teaching of St. Cyprian[38] (third century), who held that martyrdom could supply for baptism, St. Augustine also wrote:

> "I find that not only martyrdom for the sake of Christ may supply for what is wanting in baptism, but also faith and conversion of heart, if recourse may not be had to the celebration of the mystery for want of time. ... But the want is supplied invisibly only

[35] *Apostolic sedem*, letter to the bishop of Cremona, Denz., 388.
[36] *Debitum pastoralis offici*, letter to the bishop of Metz, August 28, 1206, Denz., 413.
[37] Augustine, *City of God*, Vol I, bk. XIII, (Edinburgh: T&T Clark, 1888), p. 527 (emphasis added).
[38] "Those who were caught and killed confessing the Name [of Christ] before they were baptized in the Church... holding the integral Faith and truth of the Church... were ... baptized by the most glorious and excellent Baptism, by which the Lord Himself said he had to be baptized [Lk. 12:50]. That those who are baptized in their own blood and sanctified by their passion were glorified and received the Divine promise, is taught to us by the Lord Himself in the Gospel, when He promised to the thief who believed and confessed [the Faith] that he would be with Him in paradise." (Cyprian, Epistle No. 74,1).

when the administration of baptism is prevented, not by contempt for religion, but by the necessity of the moment."[39]

Because true "faith and conversion of heart" can *supply* for water baptism for the catechumen, it means a catechumen can receive the salvific *effects* of water baptism (sanctifying grace and justification), even though his baptism is only that of desire.[40] This is why St. Paul in Hebrews 6:2 refers to "the doctrine of baptisms," in the plural.[41] If the catechumen receives the salvific effects of water baptism, he is not only joined to the *Body* of the Church (imperfectly) by desire, but joined to the *Soul* of the Church perfectly by faith, hope and charity. If he were to die in this state, he would *without a doubt* obtain salvation.

Moreover, the Catholic Church publicly manifests her faith in the deceased catechumen's external (though imperfect) union with the Body by burying him as one of the baptized. While canon 1239.1 of the 1917 Code of Canon Law prohibits those who died without baptism from receiving ecclesiastical burial, canon 1239.2 states: "The catechumens who with no fault of their own die without baptism, *should be treated as the baptized*" (emphasis added).

Modern Errors against Baptism of Desire

As we have seen, the doctrine of Baptism of Desire is rooted in divine revelation, and taught by the Church's greatest saints, Doctors, Popes and catechisms. Accordingly, the teaching is infallible at least by virtue of the Ordinary and Universal Magisterium, if not by the extraordinary Magisterium exercised at the Council of Trent.[42] In our

---

[39] *On Baptism, Against the Donatists*, bk. IV, ch. 22. St. Ambrose (third century) also explicitly taught the doctrine, specifically, that Valentinian, the catechumen who died before receiving baptism, received the effects of the sacrament through his desire: "Did he, then, not have the grace which he desired? Did he not have what he eagerly sought? Certainly, because he sought it he received it" (RJ, No. 1328).

[40] These effects include forgiveness of original and actual sin, infusion of sanctifying grace and the theological virtues, and union (albeit imperfect) with the Body of Christ, the Catholic Church, but would not include the indelible mark on the soul because Baptism of Desire (and blood) *is not the sacrament* in reality but only in desire.

[41] While there is only one sacrament of Baptism (Eph 4:5), St. Thomas says St. Paul refers to "baptisms" in the plural in Hebrews 6:2 to denote "Baptism of Water, of Repentance [desire], and of Blood [martyrdom]." ST, III, q. 66, a. 2. The "doctrine of baptisms," then, refers to the various means (water, desire, and blood) by which the salvific effects of the single sacrament of baptism may be obtained.

[42] For more on Baptism of Desire, see Tanquerey, *Dogmatic Theology*, vol II, (New York; Tournai; Paris; Rome: Desclee Company, 1959), pp. 225-229; *Summa Theologica*, III, q. 66, a. 11; Ott, *Fundamentals of Catholic Dogma*, pp. 356-357; Berry, *The Church of Christ*, p. 138; Van Noort, *Christ's Church*, pp. 256-264.

day, however, in which virtually every traditional doctrine of the Church is called into question, if not outright denied, Baptism of Desire has not been spared.

The denial of this particular doctrine is due, in large part, to a philosophical error known as *false cause* (*non causa pro causa*), which mistakenly attributes an *effect* to a *cause* that did not produce it. In this case, when in comes to baptism and salvation, the Liberals err by making a rule out of the exception, and end by destroying the rule. The rule is that baptism of water is necessary for salvation; the "exception" is that, in certain rare circumstances, the salvific effects of baptism can be supplied by the person's *desire* for baptism (when accompanied by supernatural faith and perfect charity). This means it is *possible* for a person to be saved without receiving water baptism. The Liberals use the possibility of an extra-sacramental effect (grace and salvation being attained without water baptism) to justify the false doctrine of universal, or near universal, salvation (which undermines, and eventually results in a denial of the dogma "No Salvation Outside the Catholic Church").

Some on the Right, whose *sensus fidelium* has alerted them to this error, have not correctly attributed the root cause of the error to the *overemphasis* of the exception, but instead *to the doctrine of Baptism of Desire itself*. Consequently, they end by believing that the doctrine of Baptism of Desire is itself the *cause* that led to the Liberal error of universal or near universal salvation, when in reality the true *cause* is an overemphasis on the exception (the "possibility") which leads to a destruction of the rule. This error of *false cause* thus *forces* them to "reinterpret" the Church's teaching, most notably that of the great Council of Trent, in a manner *entirely opposite* of the way in which all the Popes and theologians have understood and explained it.

Specifically, they are forced to argue that the Council did not actually teach that the desire for baptism can suffice for salvation, *unless the desire is accompanied by the actual reception of the sacrament itself*, which is exactly contrary to how the phrase in question has always been understood (this is the error of the so-called "Feeneyites"). One of the more clever ways they defend their novelty is by arguing that when Trent says a person cannot be justified "without the laver of regeneration <u>or</u> its desire," the "or" (Latin, *aut*) really means "and" (Latin, *et*), meaning both the "laver" of water <u>and</u> the "desire" for it are required (thereby eliminating Baptism of Desire).

For example, the Sedevacantist brothers, Peter and Michael Dimond of Most Holy Family Monastery, wrote:

"The baptism of desire people believe that the use of the word "or" (Latin: *aut*) in the above passage means that justification can take place by the water of baptism or the desire for it. But a careful look at the passage proves this to be false. The passage says that justification cannot take place without the laver of regeneration (water baptism) or the desire for it; in other words, both are necessary. Suppose I said, 'This shower cannot take place without water or the desire to take one.' Does this mean that the shower takes place by the desire to take a shower? Absolutely not. It means that both are necessary."[43]

Notice, these brothers, who claim to be "Traditional Catholics," depart entirely from Tradition, not only by rejecting Baptism of Desire, but also by inventing a novel interpretation of Trent to justify their error. And, as we have seen, their private interpretation is exactly contrary to the official interpretation of the Church and her theologians. No reputable theologian has ever interpreted Trent as teaching that the desire for baptism can only suffice when accompanied by water baptism (they say only that it can suffice in place of water baptism in certain circumstances). Furthermore, if both desire and water baptism were required, as the Dimond brothers claim, how would an infant below the age of reason (who cannot desire baptism) be sanctified by water baptism?

The entire corpus of Catholic teaching on Baptism of Desire refutes this argument, but we can also negate the claim on grammatical and contextual grounds as well. It is true that, on a purely grammatical basis, the Latin "*aut*" *could* mean either "or" (disjunctive use) or "and" (conjunctive use; this can also be the case in English). However, we can understand the true meaning of Trent's use of "or" (as regards the "laver of regeneration or its desire") by looking at how the Council uses "or" in other similar contexts. In doing so, we see that in the other instances where Trent uses "or" in the context of the sacraments, the meaning of "or" is, in fact, "or" and not "and." For example, in Chapter 14, when referring to the sacrament of Confession, the council says sins are "remitted together with the guilt either by the sacrament or the desire of the sacrament..."[44] Since man is forgiven of sin outside of the sacrament of Confession when he makes a perfect act of contrition, the "or" in this case means "or," not "and."

Similarly, Trent teaches that man can receive the fruits of Holy Communion through the actual reception of the sacrament or its desire

---

[43] Dimond, Peter, "Theory of Baptism of Desire, Short Refutation," http://www.most holyfamilymonastery.com/catholicchurch/theory-of-baptism-of-desire/#.VeTziq2FPmQ
[44] Denz., 807.

through spiritual communion.[45] In the Council's Decree on the Sacraments, Canon 4, we read:

> "If anyone says that the sacraments of the New Law are not necessary for salvation but are superfluous, and that without them or without the desire of them men obtain from God through faith alone the grace of justification, though all are not necessary for each one, let him be anathema."[46]

Therefore, on a contextual basis, the "or" in Trent's teaching on baptism (as with its teaching on Confession and the sacraments in general) clearly indicates the meaning "or" and not "and," just as the Popes and theologians have all understood it.

More importantly, as we have demonstrated, the Church has always interpreted Trent's teaching to include Baptism of Desire (and, thus, Trent's use of "or" in the disjunctive sense in its teaching on justification). This is also seen in the Holy Office's 1949 Letter *Suprema Haec Sacra*, issued during the reign of Pope Pius XII, which we examined earlier. The Letter not only teaches that the salvific effects of baptism can be obtained by the intention and desire to receive the sacrament, but also explains that "this is clearly stated in the Sacred Council of Trent." This is just one more official interpretation of Trent as teaching Baptism of Desire. From the Holy Office Letter:

> "In His infinite mercy God has willed that the effects, necessary for one to be saved, of those helps to salvation which are directed towards man's final end, not by intrinsic necessity, but only by divine institution, can also be obtained in certain circumstances when these helps are used only in intention or desire. This we see clearly stated in the Sacred Council of Trent, both with reference to the sacrament of regeneration (baptism) and with the sacrament of penance."[47]

---

[45] "Now as to the use of this Holy Sacrament, our Fathers have rightly and wisely distinguished three ways of receiving it. For they have taught that some receive it sacramentally only, to wit sinners: others spiritually only, those to wit who eating *in desire* that heavenly bread which is set before them, are, by a lively faith which worketh by charity, made sensible of the fruit and usefulness thereof: whereas the third (class) receive it both sacramentally and spiritually, and these are they who so prove and prepare themselves beforehand, as to approach to this divine table clothed with the wedding garment." (Denz., 807).

[46] Trent, Decree on the Sacraments, Canon 4 (emphasis added).

[47] *Suprema Haec Sacra*, English translation published in *American Ecclesiastical Review*, vol. CXXVII, 4, October, 1952 (emphasis added).

Here we see the Holy Office interpreting the Council of Trent as teaching that the intention and desire for baptism (when combined with supernatural faith and perfect charity) can produce the salvific effects of the sacrament which are necessary for salvation, which simply repeats the longstanding teaching tradition of the Church. This teaching, of course, directly contradicts the *novel interpretation* of the Council of Trent employed by those (e.g., "Feeneyites," Dimond brothers) who labor under the error of *false cause* and end by denying Church doctrine.

Needless to say, the Dimond brothers imagine that their novel interpretation of the Trent is the correct one. Based upon their private judgment, they reject what the Popes, Doctors, saints, theologians and catechisms have taught, and publicly declare the 1949 Letter of the Holy Office to be heretical.[48] They claim the letter is not an official document of the Church, since it was not published in the *Acta Apostolicae Sedis* (the journal of the official acts of the Holy See), even though the complete text (not available in Denzinger) includes the statement that after the Cardinals approved the document in plenary session on Wednesday, July 27, 1949, "the August Pontiff in an audience on the following Thursday, July 28, 1949, deigned to give [it] his approval."[49]

As we have demonstrated, not only does the letter reflect the longstanding tradition of the pre-Vatican II Church, but those who prepared the original schemas of Vatican II also considered it authoritative, since they cited it many times as a footnote. And, needless to say, the original schemas of Vatican II taught the traditional doctrine that the Dimond brothers declare (based upon their own private judgment) to be heretical.

The following is the original schema drafted for Vatican II, titled, Dogmatic Constitution on the Church, along with the original footnotes:

---

[48] Dimond brothers: "As explained in the section on Protocol 122/49 in our book, this heretical letter was written in 1949 by a member of the Holy Office to the modernist Archbishop of Boston, Richard Cushing. It is not the teaching of the Catholic Church... it teaches that people who are not members of the Church can be saved, which is heresy ...This letter is a heretical denial of the dogma Outside the Church There is No Salvation." (Most Holy Family Monastery internet article on Bishop Louis Vezelis). http://www.mostholyfamilymonastery.com/catholicchurch/bishop-louis-vezelis/#.Ve XK2a2FPmQ.

[49] *The Companion to the Catechism of the Catholic Church* (San Francisco, California: Ignatius Press, 1995), p. 360.

"The Holy Synod teaches, as God's Holy Church has always taught, that the Church is necessary for salvation[50] and that no one can be saved who, knowing that the Catholic Church was founded by God through Jesus Christ, nevertheless refuses to enter her or to persevere in her.[51] Just as no one can be saved except by receiving baptism - by which anyone who does not pose some obstacle to incorporation[52] becomes a member of the Church - or at least by desire for baptism,[53] so also no one can attain salvation unless he is a member of the Church or at least is ordered towards the Church by desire. But for anyone to attain to salvation, it is not enough that he be really a member of the Church or be by desire ordered towards it; it is also required that he die in the state of grace, joined to God by faith, hope, and charity.[54]"[55]

This traditional doctrine of the Church is explicitly denied by many today, such as the Dimond brothers, who claim to be "traditional Catholics," yet depart from Tradition based upon their own private judgment. And the Dimond brothers don't just reject this teaching of

---

[50] For the teaching of the Fathers, Ignatius of Antioch, Origen, Cyprian, Jerome, Augustine, Fulgentius, see Tromp, *De Spiritu Christi Anima*, pp. 210-13. For the teaching of the Church, see the *Athanasian Creed* (Denz., 40); Pelagius II, Letter *Dilectionis vestris* (Denz., 247); Innocent III, *Profession of Faith for the Waldensians* (Denz., 423); Boniface VIII, Bull *Unam sanctam* (Denz., 468); Clement VI, Epist. *Super quibusdam* (Denz., 570b); the Council of Florence, *Decree for the Jacobites* (Denz., 714); *the Tridentine Profession of Faith* (Denz., 1000); Benedict XIV, *Profession of Faith for the Maronites* (Denz., 1473); GregoryXVI, Enc. *Mirari vos* (Denz., 1613); Pius IX, Enc. *Quanto conficiamur moerore* (Denz., 1677); *Syllabus*, n. 16-17 (Denz., 1716-17); Pius XII, *Mystici Corporis* (*AAS* 35 [1943], pp. 242-243); *Humani generis* (Denz., 2319); *Letter of the Holy Office to the Archbishop of Boston, Aug. 8, 1949* (found in the Appendix to Fr.Tromp's third edition of *Mystici Corporis*).
[51] *Letter of the Holy Office to the Archbishop of Boston.*
[52] The obstacle may be posed both with regard to grace and with regard to the juridical effect; see CIC, can. 87. The obstacle to grace, for example, is had if an adult to be baptized does not want to abstain from mortal sin; there is an obstacle to membership, if an adult to be baptized lacks faith. In Church documents the limitation, "unless some obstacle is posed," is often presupposed. See the Tridentine Profession of Faith (Denz., 996), where it is said that "sacraments confer grace," without any restriction, in opposition to the Canon on Sacraments in general (Denz., 849). And a Sacrament is generally defined as 'a sensible sign instituted by Christ which confers the grace it signifies,' and no one requires the addition, 'to those who place no obstacle.'"
[53] Council of Trent, Decree on Justification (Denz., 796), collated with ch. 14, "on the lapsed" (Denz., 807).
[54] *Letter of the Holy Office to the Archbishop of Boston:* "Nor should it be thought that just any desire to enter the Church suffices for a person to be saved. It is required that the desire by which someone is ordered towards the Church be informed by perfect charity, nor can the implicit desire have an effect if the person does not have supernatural faith (Hb 11:6; Council of Trent [Denz., 801])."
[55] Dogmatic Constitution on the Church, ch. 2, The members of the Church Militant and Her Necessity for Salvation, No. 8.

the Church; they go further by declaring that those who accept it are heretics. In fact, they have publicly declared that their fellow Sedevacantists, who accept this teaching of the Church on Baptism of Desire, to be not only heretics, but "the scum of the earth," and even "abominable." From the official website of the Most Holy Family Monastery, we read:

> "In short, Tom D. [Note: Tom Drolesky, a fellow Sedevacantist] belongs to the crowd of <u>baptism of desire heretics</u> who not only believe that souls can be saved in false religions, but who detest and wish to extirpate faith in Jesus' dogma that 'unless a man is born again of water and the Spirit, he cannot enter into the Kingdom of God' (John 3:5). In other words, he's among the very worst of the false traditionalist heretics. <u>That crowd is accurately described as the scum of the Earth. They are abominable.</u>"[56]

Here we see what happens when individuals employ the Protestant doctrine of private judgment to interpret dogmas of the faith without reference to the Church's own interpretation and understanding. It leads them not only to directly contradict the perennial teaching of the Church (including that of her greatest saints and theologians), but also drives imbalanced souls to accuse those who disagree with them (i.e., those who *do* accept the teaching of the Church) of being abominable heretics. We will have more to say about these bitter fruits of Sedevacantism in the last chapter.

Necessity of Means and Necessity of Precept

To clarify matters further, it is important to understand the various kinds of necessity. The word *necessity* denotes a strict connection between different beings, or the different elements of a being, or between a being and its existence. It is a primary and fundamental notion, and it is important to determine its various meanings and applications in theology.[57]

The Church teaches baptism is *necessary* for salvation, and anathematizes those who say otherwise: "If anyone shall say that baptism is optional, that is, not *necessary* for salvation: let him be anathema."[58] But in what way is Baptism said to be *necessary*? As always, it is critical to make the proper distinctions, lest error result.

---

[56] See http://www.mostholyfamilymonastery.com/catholicchurch/gerry-matatics/#.V d8sTa2FPmQ.
[57] *Catholic Encyclopedia* (1913) vol. X, p. 733.
[58] Council of Trent, Canon 2, Denz., 861.

The Church distinguishes between the *necessity of means* (absolute or relative) and the *necessity of precept*. The former are the *means* to salvation, and are constituted such either *by their very nature* (absolute necessity) or *by divine institution* (relative necessity); the latter (necessity of precept) is necessary because it is prescribed by law.

Matters that are necessary for salvation by precept *alone*, are necessary because omitting them constitutes a sin, which itself is a hindrance to salvation. For example, attendance at Mass on Sundays and Holy Days is necessary by a necessity of precept, but if circumstances arose that prevented a person from fulfilling the precept due to no fault of their own (such as illness), the violation of the precept would not be a sin, and therefore would not be an obstacle to salvation.

Other matters, however, are so necessary that without them one cannot obtain salvation – that is, *he cannot be translated from the state of sin to the state of justification*. These are necessary for salvation by a *necessity of means*. Some of these matters are, *of their very nature*, so necessary that nothing can supply in their absence. Sanctifying grace, for example, is an *absolutely* necessary means of salvation, since those who die without the life of grace in the soul cannot obtain the Beatific Vision. Other things are necessary as a means of salvation, not of their nature, but *by divine institution*. These are referred to as a *relative* necessity of means, since the *necessary effect* can be obtained by *an act of the will* when the person is hindered from fulfilling the act itself.

The necessity of water baptism and of becoming a "member" of the Church, are necessary for salvation by a *necessity of precept* and also a *necessity of means*. But the necessity of means in both instances is only a *relative* necessity, not an *absolute* necessity. Hence, in both of these cases, the act itself (of being baptized or becoming a "member" of the Church) can be supplied by a positive act of the will (the desire and intent to fulfill the act) when the act itself is hindered through no personal fault. In the *Summa Theologica*, St. Thomas affirms this in the following objection and answer:

"Objection: the sacrament of Baptism is necessary for salvation. Now that is necessary 'without which something cannot be' (Aristotle's Metaphysics V). Therefore, it seems that none can obtain salvation without Baptism.

Reply: The sacrament of baptism is said to be necessary for salvation in so far as there can be no salvation for man unless he <u>at least have it in desire which, with God, counts for the deed.</u>"[59]

Fr. Berry explains this *unanimous teaching* of the theologians as follows:

"In regard to attaining salvation, theologians distinguish between those things which are necessary by a necessity of means, and those which are necessary by a necessity of precept. (…) Matters of mere precept are necessary because by omitting them we commit grievous sin. (…) The case is quite different with those things necessary as the *means to* salvation; they cannot be omitted without the loss of salvation, even though the omission be without fault on our part. In some cases the thing is *absolutely* necessary, because it is of such nature that nothing can supply for its absence; e.g., sanctifying grace is an *absolute* necessity, whose absence cannot be supplied by anything else. Other things are necessary, not by their very nature, but by divine institution. In regard to these things God is pleased to accept substitutes when the things themselves cannot be had. Such means of salvation may be called *relatively* necessary, to distinguish them from those of *absolute* necessity. Baptism is an example of a *relative* necessity for salvation; it is a necessary means of salvation, because Christ has so ordained, but if for any reason it is impossible to receive Baptism, its absence can be supplied by perfect contrition and a sincere desire to receive it."[60]

Fr. Berry goes on to explain that "membership in the Church is [also] necessary by the twofold necessity of precept and means" and then adds, "but the necessity of means is only *relative*," just as it is with baptism.

Msgr. Van Noort taught the same in his well-known theological manual, *Christ's Church*, when he explained that baptism and membership in the Church are necessary by a necessity of precept, and a *relative* necessity of means:

"Two general types of necessity are distinguished: necessity of precept and necessity of means.
Necessity of precept signifies the type of necessity which arises exclusively from a moral obligation. It conduces to salvation not so much by a positive causal influx as the removal of obstacles to

---

[59] ST, III, q. 68, a. 2 (emphasis added).
[60] *The Church of Christ*, p. 134.

salvation. If the precept is not observed, serious sin is committed; and sin itself is an obstacle to salvation. (...)

Necessity of means signifies that something – abstracting from any question of moral obligation, or sin – is a means requisite for salvation: it is a causal force positively leading to salvation in such a way that without that cause salvation simply cannot be attained. (...)

A thing may be necessary by a necessity of means either by its nature or by the positive ordinance of God. In the first case there is such an intrinsic relationship between means and end that no substitute can take its place. Such a means is said to be *absolutely* necessary. Such a relationship obtains in the natural order between the human eye and the act of seeing; in the supernatural order between grace and the beatific vision.

Necessity [of means] by a positive ordinance results from an extrinsic bond established between two things by God's fiat: [such as] the sacrament of baptism as a remedy for original sin. Such a means *can have a substitute*, or [said differently] the means can be supplied for in some other way than its actual use. In the supernatural order baptism of water is a necessary means for the remission of original sin and the reception of sanctifying grace. But a catechumen who is martyred for Christ before he can be baptized has his sins remitted, and receives sanctifying grace by his 'baptism of blood.'

Such necessary means, set up by God's ordinance, are said to be not absolutely, but *disjunctively* [i.e. relatively] necessary. That is, the means must be employed either actually or in desire (*in re* or *in voto*). Notice, however, that the external means as actually employed and the substitute for it – the internal desire of making use of the external means – are not two distinct and different means. Rather, they are related to one another as the *perfect* and *imperfect*, the full and partial use of one and the same means."[61]

Msgr. Van Noort goes on to address a point that was discussed previously in this chapter. He begins by noting that the Church is necessary for salvation, yet at the same time *explicit* knowledge of the Church itself is not absolutely necessary for salvation (for those who are invincibly ignorant of the Church). He then adds:

---

[61] *Christ's Church*, pp. 256-257.

"But if these two facts are simultaneously true: that the Church is necessary by a necessity of means for salvation, and yet, some men purely by accident can obtain salvation without actually becoming members of the Church, the consequence is that the Church is a means necessary for salvation not absolutely, but disjunctively [i.e. relatively]: one must be joined to the Church if not in fact (*in re*), at least in desire (*in voto*)."[62]

As we have seen, the Council of Trent reveals this distinction between *absolute* necessity and *relative* necessity of means in its teaching on the sacrament of Confession and other sacraments. As we pointed out, Trent teaches that sin may be forgiven, either "by the sacrament [of Confession] or the desire of the sacrament." Here Trent is talking about one who has perfect contrition but is unable to confess his sins to a priest. The spiritual "rebirth" or translation into the state of grace (here, through love of God and sorrow/repentance for sins) is an *absolute necessity* for justification (since grace is an *absolutely necessary means* for salvation), while the external reception of the sacrament is only a *relative necessity* of means (since an act of perfect contrition can suffice in its place).

If a person concedes that one can be forgiven of grave sin outside of the usual means of the sacrament of Confession (auricular confession to a priest) by means of a perfect act of contrition, then he should also concede that one can be born again outside of the usual means of the sacrament of Baptism (water). In both cases, man is freed from mortal/Original sin by the *absolute necessity* of a spiritual rebirth (infusion of grace into the soul) along with the *desire* for the actual exterior reception of the sacrament, which itself is only a *relative necessity*. In short, perfect contrition (in the case of mortal sin) and supernatural faith, hope and charity, along with the implicit or explicit desire for baptism (in the case of Original sin) can join one to the Mystical Body of Christ (even if it does not make one an actual *member* of the Church) and bestow the effects of Christ's Passion which are necessary for salvation.

If we apply the concept of absolute and relative necessity of means to union with the Body and Soul of the Church, it is clear that perfect union with the Soul (faith, hope and charity) is *absolutely necessary* for salvation, while the perfect union with the Body (actual membership in the Church) is only a *relative means* of necessity, which can be substituted by desire. The great Thomist, Fr. Reginald Garrigou-Lagrange, uses the terms Body and Soul in this context:

---

[62] Ibid., p. 264.

"It is necessary, of a *necessity of means*, to belong really to the soul of the Church; [it is necessary] for adults to belong to the body of the Church actually *(in re)* or by desire *(in voto)*. [63]

We also see this distinction in regard to the sacrament of Holy Communion. Jesus teaches that "Except you eat the flesh of the Son of man, and drink his blood, you shall not have life in you" (Jn. 6:54). But, as all admit, receiving Holy Communion is only a *relative* necessity of means, which can be supplied by desire alone. If those who deny Baptism of Desire were consistent in their exegesis, they would have to consider receiving the Eucharist as an *absolute* necessity of means (rather than a relative necessity), just like they do with water baptism, for Jesus said "unless/except" we do both of them[64] we have no life in us.[65]

This is the Church's understanding of the distinction between *absolute* necessity of means and *relative* necessity of means regarding baptism and membership in the Church for salvation. With so many errors on either side of the truth today, the only safe course is to hold fast to tradition, which, as St. Vincent of Lerins said, "can never be led astray by any lying novelty." Those who depart from tradition today are sure to fall into error in one direction or the other.

To summarize these points, while supernatural faith and sanctifying grace are, of their nature, an *absolute necessity* of means for salvation, water baptism and actual membership in the Church are only a *relative necessity*, which, in some cases, can be supplied by an act of the will.[66] As we saw, St. Thomas explains this point by noting that because the catechumen's *desire* for membership and baptism is itself a

---

[63] Garrigou-Lagrange, *De Revelatione*, (Rome, 1925), p. 615.
[64] "Unless a man be born again of water and the Holy Ghost, he cannot enter into the kingdom of God" (Jn. 3:5); "Except you eat the flesh of the Son of man, and drink his blood, you shall not have life in you" (Jn. 6:54).
[65] The Sacrament of Baptism produces a two-fold effect: it imprints an indelible mark on the soul and infuses into the soul sanctifying grace (and the theological virtues). When one obtains the state of justification through Baptism of Desire alone, they receive the *salvific effects* only (grace and the theological virtues), and not the indelible mark. (See ST, III, q. 36, a. 8.) Those who deny Baptism of Desire err by holding that the indelible mark is also necessary for salvation, which is yet another novelty that neither the Church nor her theologians have ever taught.
[66] Again, to use "membership" in the classical sense, it's best to say the person may <u>desire to belong</u> to the Church, but he does not <u>belong by desire</u> to the Church, because he does not become an actual member of (belong to) the Church by desire. Simply said, he does not enjoy the rights and privileges of the Church by desire alone. Accordingly, we say such a person (who has the Catholic "faith" and thus is not a Protestant) is not a "member" of the Church *as such*, but is "joined to" the Church.

grace willed by God, when the external act itself is hindered, the desire "with God, counts for the deed."[67]

After all, salvation is primarily the work of God, and although God has bound Himself by the visible sacraments, He is not *limited* by them. Since salvation *requires* that man be joined to the Church in reality or in desire ('*in re*' or '*in voto*'), it also means there are no exceptions to the dogma that outside the Catholic Church there is no salvation (*extra ecclesia nulla salus est*). To be saved, a person must be perfectly united to the Soul of the Church *in re* (in reality), and united to the Body at least *in voto* (by desire).

The Death of Fr. Hermann Cohen's Mother

We will end this chapter with the story of Fr. Hermann Cohen's mother, which serves as an example of how a person can obtain salvation through extraordinary means. The following account is taken from the 1883 book *The Life of Rev. Father Hermann* (no further commentary is required):

> "The last moments for Mrs. Cohen arrived on 13 December 1855. Father Hermann was preaching Advent in Lyons at the time and he announced this sad news to his friend in these terms: 'God has struck a terrible blow to my heart. My poor mother is dead ... and I remain in incertitude! However, we have so much prayed that we must hope that something has passed between her soul and God during these last moments that we cannot know about. ...' We can easily imagine the pain of Father Hermann in learning of the death of his mother. He had prayed so much, and had so many prayers said for her conversion, yet she came to appear before the tribunal of God without having received holy Baptism! (...) 'I also have a mother,' would he write one day, 'I have left her to follow Jesus Christ, she no longer calls me her 'good son.' Already her hair is silvered, already her brow is furrowed, and I am afraid to see her die. Oh! No, I would not like to see her die before loving Jesus Christ, and already for many years I await for my mother that which Monica awaited for Augustine...'
>
> God seemed to have despised all his prayers and rejected his loving and legitimate desires. His faith and his love were put through a harsh trial. Nevertheless, if his sorrow was deep, his hope in the infinite goodness of God would not allow itself to be struck down. (...) a short time later, he confided to the Cure' of Ars [St.

---

[67] See ST, III, q. 68, a. 2.

John Vianney] his disquiet about the death of his poor mother who died without the grace of Baptism. 'Hope!' replied the man of God, 'hope; you will receive one day, on the feast of the Immaculate Conception a letter that will bring you great consolation.' (…)

These words were almost forgotten, when, on the 8th December 1861, six years after the death of his mother, a Father of the Company of Jesus handed to Father Hermann the following letter. (The person who wrote this letter died in the odour of sanctity; she was well known in the religious and ascetical world, by her written works on the Eucharist.) The letter read: 'On the 18th October, after Holy Communion, I found myself in one of those moments of intimate union with Our Lord, where he made me so feel his presence in the sacrament of His love that Faith seemed no longer necessary to believe him there. After a short time, He had me hear His voice and He wanted to give me some explanations relative to a conversation that I had had the night before. I remember that, in that conversation, one of my friends (Anna) had manifested her surprise that Our Lord, who has promised to accord everything to prayer, had, however, remained deaf to those of Reverend Father Hermann, who had so many times addressed Him to obtain the conversion of his mother; her surprise went almost as far as discontentment, and I had had difficulty in having her understand that we must adore the justice of God and not to seek to penetrate its secrets. I dared to ask of my Jesus how it was that He, who was goodness itself, had been able to resist the prayers of Father Hermann, and not grant the conversion of his mother. This was His (Our Lord's) response:

'Why does Anna always want to sound the secrets of my justice and why does she seek to penetrate mysteries that she cannot comprehend? Tell her that I do not owe my grace to anyone, that I give it to whom I please and that in acting in this way I do not cease to be just, and justice itself. But that she may know that, rather than not keep the promises that I have made to prayer, I will upset heaven and earth, and that every prayer that has my glory and the salvation of souls for [its] object is always heard when it is clothed in the necessary qualities.' He added: 'And to prove to you this truth, I willingly make known that which passed at the moment of the death of the mother of Father Hermann.'

My Jesus then enlightened me with a ray of His divine light and had me understand or rather to see in Him that which I want to try to relate. At the moment where the mother of Father Hermann was on the point of rendering her last breath; at the moment that she seemed deprived of awareness, almost without life; Mary, our good Mother, presented Herself before Her Divine Son, and prostrate at His feet, She said to Him: 'Pardon and mercy, O my Son, for this soul who is going to perish. Yet another instant and she will be lost,

lost for eternity. I beseech you, do for the mother of my servant Hermann, that which you would like to be done for your own, if She was in her place and if you were in his. The soul of his mother is his most precious good; he has consecrated her to me a thousand times; he has consecrated her to the tenderness and solicitude of my heart. Could I suffer her to perish? No, no, this soul is mine; I will it, I claim it as an inheritance, as the price of your blood and of my sufferings at the foot of your Cross.'

Hardly had the sacred suppliant ceased speaking, when a strong, powerful grace, came forth from the source of all graces, from the adorable Heart of our Jesus, and came to enlighten the soul of the poor dying Jewess; instantly triumphing over her stubbornness and resistances. This soul immediately turned herself with loving confidence towards Him whose mercy had pursued her as far as the arms of death and said to Him: 'O Jesus, God of the Christians, God whom my son adores, I believe, I hope in Thee, have pity on me.' In this cry, heard by God alone and which came from the intimate depths of the heart of the dying woman, were enclosed *the sincere sorrow for her obstination and for her sins, the desire of baptism, the express will to receive it and to live according to the rules and precepts of our holy religion*, if she had been able to return to life. This leap of faith and hope in Jesus was the last sentiment of that soul; it was made at the moment when she [was] brought towards the throne of the divine mercy. Breaking away the weak bonds which held her to her mortal casing, she fell at the feet of Him who had been her Saviour (a moment) before being her Judge.

After having showed me all these things, Our Lord added: 'Make this known to Father Hermann; it is a consolation that I wish to accord to his long sorrows, so that he will bless, and have blessed everywhere, the goodness of the heart of my Mother and Her power over mine.' (...) What appears to add great authority to this letter, is that it had been announced six years in advance by the venerable Cure of Ars."[68]

---

[68] Fr. Canon Charles Sylvain, *The Life of Rev. Father Hermann, in religion Augustin-Marie of the Most Holy Sacrament, Discalced Carmelite* (Paris: Oudin, 1883), pp. 126-129 (emphasis added).

Chapter 5 Terms and Explanations

In this chapter we address the topic of the sin of heresy and its impact on ecclesiastical office. As with Chapter 3, it is critical to understand the terminology to be used. To that end, we have provided another brief set of terms and explanations at the beginning of the chapter.

Heresy: The post-baptismal denial or doubt of a truth which must be believed with divine and Catholic faith.

Matter of Heresy: The matter, or material aspect of heresy, is a belief or proposition contrary to what must be believed with divine and Catholic faith. The matter of heresy is the objective element of heresy.

Pertinacity: A term used to describe the *conscious* and *obstinate* denial or doubt of a truth of the Faith.

Form of Heresy: The form of heresy is pertinacity, which exists in the will. Pertinacity is the subjective element of heresy.

External Forum: The objective, external realm.

Internal Forum: The subjective, internal realm (conscience).

Material Heretic: This term is used to describe a validly baptized non-Catholic who professes to be a Christian, yet who has never been a member of the Catholic Church and therefore does not submit to the Magisterium as the rule of faith. This is an objective classification in the external forum, independent of a subjective judgment of guilt. Only non-Catholics can be material heretics.

Catholic in Material Error (heresy): A member of the Roman Catholic Church in good standing, who acknowledges the Church as the rule of faith, yet who has *mistakenly* embraced an error contrary to what must be believed with divine and Catholic faith. Such a person may be called an ignorant Catholic or a Catholic in material heresy, but not a "material heretic."

Formal Heretic (external forum): This term refers to a baptized Catholic who consciously and publicly dissents from a truth which must be believed with divine and Catholic faith, or has been declared a heretic by the proper authorities. This is also an objective classification in the external forum.

Formal Heretic (internal forum): One who has embraced a heresy (the matter) with pertinacity (the form). Such a person is guilty of the internal sin of heresy.

Crime of heresy: The canonical offense of heresy under the Church's positive law which requires proof of the external infraction (objective element) as well as pertinacity (subjective element). It may or may not be accompanied by a declaration from the Church.

Invincible Ignorance: The (involuntary) inability to know what one is bound to know. One is bound to know the articles of faith. St. Thomas defines invincible ignorance as ignorance "that cannot be overcome by study."[1]

---

[1] ST, I-II, q. 76, a. 2.

Chapter 5

~ Sin of Heresy and Loss of Office ~

We begin this chapter by addressing the matter and form of heresy. The *matter* of heresy is a belief contrary to a teaching of the Church (revealed in Scripture or Tradition) which must be believed with divine and Catholic Faith. The matter of heresy exists in the intellect and can be present with innocent ignorance or with sinful pertinacity in the will.

The *form* of heresy is pertinacity in the will. Pertinacity is another word to describe the *depravity* of the will in *obstinately* adhering to a heretical proposition. When a person *knowingly rejects* or *willfully doubts* a doctrine of the Church that must be believed by faith, he is guilty of *formal heresy* (the sin of heresy) in the *internal forum* (the realm of conscience).

Unlike the natural moral virtues which corrupt gradually over time, the theological virtues corrupt entirely when a person commits a single mortal sin contrary to the virtue. Consequently, if a person commits the sin of heresy, by denying a single article of faith, he immediately loses the interior virtue of faith completely. Just as one mortal sin removes *all* supernatural charity (and sanctifying grace) from the soul,[1] so too one mortal sin against the faith removes *all* supernatural faith.[2] St. Thomas says:

> "Just as mortal sin is contrary to charity, so is disbelief in one article of faith contrary to faith. Now charity does not remain in a man after one mortal sin. Therefore, neither does faith, after a man disbelieves one article...Therefore, it is clear that such a heretic with regard to one article, has no faith in the other articles, but only a kind of opinion in accordance with his own will."[3]

Now, since faith is "the foundation of the supernatural life," when the faith is lost, so too are the theological virtues of hope and charity, which, along with faith, constitute the internal bonds that unite a man to the Church. Therefore, when one loses the faith, he is completely severed from the Soul of the Church.

---

[1] *Cf.* 1 Cor 13:1-13.
[2] See, for example, Pope Leo XIII, *Satis Cognitum*, No. 9, June 29, 1896.
[3] ST, II-II, q. 5, a. 2.

However, as we discussed in Chapter 2, the loss of this interior faith does not, in and of itself, sever a man from the *Body* of the Church (the visible, ecclesiastical society founded by Christ). This is evident when one considers that the loss of internal faith does not, of itself, cause a Catholic to lose the rights and privileges of his membership in the Church. And if the Catholic who loses the interior virtue of faith happens to be a bishop or even the Pope, the visible and external bonds *alone* suffice for him to retain his office. This crucial point strikes at the heart of one of the principal errors of Sedevacantism.

In Chapter 2, we discussed the dispute over "membership" in the Church. We saw that certain theologians, such as Suarez, maintained that the loss of interior faith was incompatible with actual "membership" in the Church. He and others held this view because they considered the concept of "membership" from the perspective of union with Christ, rather than union with the Body of the Church (the visible, ecclesiastical society). However, although these theologians did not consider those who lost the faith to be, technically speaking, "members" of the Church, they nevertheless realized that the external bonds of union alone sufficed for a person to possess jurisdiction and hold office in the Church. They maintained that a heretic Pope, for example, while not a "member" of the Church (as they defined it) was *still* the head of the Church.

In other words, their opinion on "membership" (who can be called a "member" of the Church) only pertained to the speculative level, and had no practical effect on those who held office in the Church. This is clear from the following quotation from Suarez. Although he held that faith was necessary for "membership" in the Church, he conceded that faith was not necessary for a man to hold office and perform acts of jurisdiction in the Church:

> "Finally, the faith is not absolutely necessary in order that a man be capable of spiritual and ecclesiastical jurisdiction and that he be capable of exercising true acts which demand this jurisdiction...The foregoing is obvious, granted that, as is taught in the treatises on penance and censures, in case of extreme necessity a priest heretic may absolve, which is not possible without jurisdiction."[4]

---

[4] *De Fide*, disp. 10, section 6, nn. 3-10, p. 317.

Suarez also says:

> "The loss of faith for heresy which is merely internal does not cause the loss of the power of jurisdiction (…) This is proved in the first place by the fact that the government (ecclesiastical) would become very uncertain if the power depended on interior thoughts and sins. Another proof: given that the Church is visible, it is necessary that her governing power be in its way visible, *dependent therefore on external actions*, and not on mere mental cogitations."[5]

The French canonist Marie Dominque Bouix (d. 1870) teaches the same:

> "Faith is not necessary for a man to be capable of ecclesiastical jurisdiction and that he might exercise true acts which require such jurisdiction. For in case of extreme necessity a heretical priest can absolve, as is taught in the treatises on penance and censures, however absolution requires and supposes jurisdiction. Moreover, the power of orders, which in its way is superior, can remain without faith, that is, with heresy; therefore ecclesiastical jurisdiction can do so too…"[6]

Because interior faith is not necessary to obtain or hold office in the Church, St. Robert Bellarmine explains that a Pope who loses the virtue of faith does not, for that reason alone, cease to be Pope. This is evident since Bellarmine held that a Pope who is an occult (secret) heretic retains his office; and, to be clear, an occult heretic is one who is guilty of *formal heresy* – the *mortal sin* of heresy - in the internal forum (the realm of conscience), but which has not become public and notorious in the external forum (which will be discussed later).

In support of his position, Cardinal Bellarmine cites the authority of Melchior Cano, a theologian from the Council of Trent, who explains that since an occult heretic remains united to the Church by an external union, a Pope who is an occult heretic retains his office. Bellarmine also notes that this is the unanimous opinion of all the authors he cites in his book *De Ecclesia*:

> "[O]ccult heretics are still of the Church, they are parts and members… therefore the Pope who is an occult heretic is still Pope.

---

[5] *De Legibus*, lib. IV, ch. VII, n. 7, p. 360 (emphasis added).
[6] Bouix, Tract on the Pope, Tom. II, p. 662.

This is also the opinion of the other authors whom we cite in book *De Ecclesia*."[7]

Again, by referring to a Pope as an occult heretic, Bellarmine is *not* speaking of him being in *material* error. He is referring to a Pope who has committed the *sin* of heresy in the *internal forum* and thereby lost the faith *entirely*.[8]

The great twentieth century Thomist, Fr. Reginald Garrigou-Lagrange, elaborated on this teaching from Bellarmine. In the following quotation, note that Garrigou-Lagrange (along with Billuart whom he cites) held the minority opinion that the interior virtue of faith is necessary to be a *"member"* of the Church (for the same reasons discussed earlier), yet, at the same time, maintained that a Pope who loses the faith interiorly *will retain his office*. Garrigou-Lagrange writes:

> **"St. Robert Bellarmine's objection.** The pope who becomes a secret heretic is still an actual member of the Church, for he is still the head of the Church, as Cajetan, Cano, Suarez, and others teach.
>
> **Reply.** This condition is quite abnormal, hence no wonder that something abnormal results from it, namely, that the pope becoming secretly a heretic would no longer be an actual member of the Church, according to the teaching as explained in the body of the article, but would still retain his jurisdiction by which he would influence the Church [*the Body*] in ruling it. Thus he would still be nominally the head of the Church, which he would still rule as head, though he would no longer be a member of Christ, because he would not receive that vital influx of faith from Christ [*from the Soul*], the invisible and primary head. Thus in quite an abnormal manner he would be in point of jurisdiction the head of the Church [*the Body*], though he would not be a member of it."[9]

In fact, Garrigou-Lagrange explicitly uses the "body" and "soul" distinctions when addressing the jurisdiction of a heretical Pope:

---

[7] *De Romano Pontifice*, bk. 2 (emphasis added).

[8] This is confirmed from the fact that Bellarmine goes on to say that "the occult heretics are united and are members although only by external union," which means they are severed from the internal union with the Soul of the Church due to their loss of faith.

[9] *Christ the Saviour, A Commentary on the Third Part of St. Thomas' Theological Summa*, at http://www.thesumma.info/saviour/saviour37.php (emphasis added). Although the authors of this book disagree with Garrigou-Lagrange's opinion that the "secret heretic" is not a *member* of the Body of the Church (favoring the opinion of Bellarmine that he is *still* a member), we all agree that the occult heretic Pope still retains his office as Pope.

"This condition could not apply to the natural head in its relation to the body, but such a condition is not repugnant in the case of the moral and secondary head. The reason is that, whereas the natural head must receive a vital influx from the soul before it can influence the members of its body, the moral head, such as the pope is, can exercise his jurisdiction over the Church [*the Body*], although he receives no influx of interior faith and charity from the soul of the Church. More briefly, as Billuart says, the pope is constituted a member of the Church [*the Soul*] by his personal faith, which he can lose, and his headship of the visible Church [*the Body*] by jurisdiction and power is compatible with private heresy. The Church will always consist in the visible union of its members with its visible head, namely, the pope of Rome, although some, who externally seem to be members of the Church, may be private heretics."[10]

Consistent with the distinction between the *Body* and *Soul* of the Church, formal heresy can remain hidden in the internal forum (the internal sin of heresy), or it can be manifested in the external forum. Fr. Sebastian B. Smith confirms the same. In his classic book, *Elements of Ecclesiastical Law*, he says:

"*Formal heresy*, of which alone we here speak, is either *internal* - i.e., not manifested externally by any word or action; or *external* - i.e., outwardly expressed, in a sufficient manner, by words or actions."[11]

Formal heresy in the *internal* forum alone (secret or "occult" heresy), only severs a man from the *Soul* of the Church.[12] It requires formal heresy in the *external* forum to sever him from the *Body* of the Church - from the visible, ecclesiastical society founded by Christ. Hence, the loss of interior faith alone does not cause a Pope or bishop to lose his office.

As Suarez reasoned, if the virtue of faith were absolutely necessary for a man to hold office in the Church, one could never be absolutely certain if a man elected Pope was a true Pope or an antipope (a believer or a pretender), since, absent an extraordinary grace, men cannot see into the hearts of other men. If the sin of heresy *alone* were to cause the loss of office for a prelate (or prevented one from legitimately and

---

[10] Ibid.

[11] Smith, *Elements of Ecclesiastical Law*, (New York: Benzinger Br., 1881), third ed., p. 304.

[12] In the same treatise, Fr. Smith explains occult heresy as that which is "known to no one, or only to a few e.g., five or six persons - and which, moreover, is not yet brought before the judicial or external forum." Ibid., p. 304.

validly acquiring the office), Catholics could never be absolutely certain if a Pope who defined a doctrine, or ratified the decrees of a Council, was the Vicar of Christ or a public imposter who was secretly an antipope.

If that were the case, those who professed to be Catholic, yet rejected defined doctrines, could simply cast doubts upon the Pope who defined them in order to cast doubts upon the doctrines themselves. If the interior virtue of faith were necessary for a Pope or bishop to legitimately retain his office, a measure of doubt would always exist, and hence everything would be left to the private judgment of each individual to determine (as is the case with Sedevacantism). With wounded human nature as it is, this would wreak havoc in the Church with no certain means of resolution. For this reason, the theologians who disagreed on whether interior faith is required for Church "membership" all agree that the visibility of the Church is not dependent upon that which is hidden in the heart of man.

All the great theologians also recognize the distinction between being joined to the *Body* of the Church (for purposes of jurisdiction) and the *Soul* of the Church (for purposes of spiritual goods), especially when speaking about the Pope. For example, Bellarmine says that "the occult heretics are united and are members although only by external union [*the Body*]; on the contrary, the good catechumens belong to the Church only by an internal union [*the Soul*], not by the external."[13] While Suarez held that a Pope who is an occult heretic is not a "member" of the Church (the *Soul*), he did concede that he would still be the "head" of the Church (the *Body*). He says:

> "*The Pope heretic is not a member of the Church* as far as the substance and form [*the Soul*] which constitute the members of the Church; *but he is the head* as far as the charge and action [*the Body*]; and this is not surprising, since he is not the primary and principal head who acts by his own power, but is as it were instrumental, he is the vicar of the principal head, who is able to exercise his spiritual action over the members even by means of a head of bronze; analogously, he baptizes at times by means of heretics, at times he absolves, etc., as we have already said."[14]

Bouix (who, like Suarez, also held the opinion that internal faith was necessary for "membership" in the Church) responds to those who

---

[13] *De Romano Pontifice*, bk. 2 (emphasis added).
[14] *De Fide*, *disp.* 10, section 6 nn. 3-10, p. 317 (emphasis added).

would argue that a non-member of the Church cannot be the "head" of
the Church, by making the same distinction between the governing
power (which takes place in the *Body*) and the supernatural union
(which takes place in the *Soul*). He wrote:

> "To the argument that, not being a member of the Church, the
> heretical Pope is not the head of the Church either, (…) one can
> give the following answer: I concede that the Pope heretic is not
> member and head of the Church in so far as the supernatural life
> which commences by faith and is completed by charity, by which
> all the members of the Church are united in one body supernaturally
> alive [the *Soul*], but I deny that he might not be member and head of
> the Church as far as the governing power proper to his charge [the
> *Body*]. Indeed, it is not absurd that Christ wishes that the Pope (the
> same might be said of a bishop in relation to the diocese), while he
> might not be part of this body supernaturally alive due to heresy,
> should nevertheless still conserve the power of governing the
> Church, *exactly as if he had not lost the supernatural life* mentioned
> above."[15]

The Major Error of Sedevacantism

The false idea that the sin of heresy alone causes the loss of
ecclesiastical office is a principal error of Sedevacantism. Because
Sedevacantists know they have no authority to judge a Pope for the
crime of heresy under canon law, they appoint themselves as the judge
and jury of the sin of heresy by appealing to *Divine* law. The error of
the Sedevacantist, in this respect, is thus twofold: First, the sin of
heresy is a matter of the internal forum of which God alone is the
judge. Second, the sin of heresy alone *does not cause the loss of office.*

We cannot overemphasize this crucial point. The Sedevacantist
thesis has been erected upon the false foundation that the internal *sin* of
heresy (against *Divine* law) causes the loss of office and jurisdiction in
the Church. While many quotations from leading Sedevacantists could
be provided, let us look at just a few from Fr. Anthony Cekada, one of
the leading Sedevacantist priests in America, who has been teaching
this erroneous position for many years. In fact, this is Fr. Cekada's
favorite defense of Sedevacantism, which he uses in almost every one
of his "rebuttals" of his opponents' arguments (including attempts to
respond to articles written by the authors of this book).[16]

---

[15] Bouix, *Tract on the Pope,* Tom. II, pp. 661-662 (emphasis added).
[16] See, for example, Fr. Cekada, "Traditionalists, Infallibility and the Pope" (1995, 2006);
"Resisting the Pope, Sedevacantism, and Frankenchurch" (2005); "A Pope as a 'Manifest'

In response to an article written by Mr. Thomas Sparks, Fr. Cekada wrote his own piece called "Sedevacantism Refuted?" After conceding Mr. Sparks' point that a Pope cannot incur the ecclesiastical censure of excommunication because a Pope is not subject to canon law (which we will clarify in Chapters 9 and 10), Fr. Cekada says the following:

> "Like many who have written against Sedevacantism, one fundamental flaw runs through Mr. Sparks' article: he seems utterly unaware of the distinction between human ecclesiastical (canon) law and divine law, and how this distinction applies to the case of a heretical pope."

> "Heresy is both a crime (*delictum*) against canon law and a sin (*peccatum*) against divine law. The material Mr. Sparks quotes deals with heresy as a *delictum* and with the ecclesiastical censure (excommunication) that the heretic incurs."

> "This is mostly irrelevant to the case of a heretical pope. Because he is the supreme legislator and therefore not subject to canon law, a pope cannot commit a true *delictum* of heresy or incur an excommunication. He is subject only to the divine law."

> "It is by violating the divine law *through the sin (peccatum) of heresy* that a heretical pope loses his authority – 'having become an unbeliever [*factus infidelis*],' as Cardinal Billot says, 'he would by his own will be cast outside the body of the Church.'"[17]

Using his own words, Fr. Cekada "seems utterly unaware" that the sin of heresy does not, by itself, cause a Pope to "lose his authority." Notice also that Fr. Cekada ended by quoting Cardinal Billot as an authority in defense of his theory. What Cekada failed to mention (or even indicate by an ellipsis) is that he only provided his readers with *half* of the sentence. If one takes the time to look up the *complete* sentence, it becomes clear that the Cardinal is not speaking merely of the internal *sin* of heresy, but of public and notorious heresy, which is the canonical *crime* of heresy in the *external* forum. Here is the full sentence from Cardinal Billot:

---

or 'Public' Heretic" (2007); and, "Sedevacantism: A Quick Primer" (2013) at http://www.fathercekada.com.
[17] "Sedevacantism Refuted?" at http://www.traditionalmass.org/articles/article.php?id =15&cat name=10.

"Given, therefore, the hypothesis of a pope who would become <u>notoriously heretical</u>, one must concede without hesitation that he would by that very fact lose the pontifical power, insofar as, having become an unbeliever, <u>he would by his own will be cast outside the body of the Church.</u>"[18]

What the half sentence giveth, the complete sentence taketh away. Because "notorious heresy" is a "crime" under canon law (see canons 2197, 2° and 2197, 3° of the 1917 Code) means that Cardinal Billot, like his predecessor theologians, held that the *crime* of heresy (not the *sin* of heresy) causes the loss of ecclesiastical office. And, as we will see later, the person must be a public and notorious heretic by the Church's judgment, not simply by the private judgment of individual priests or Catholics in the pew.

For now, it is crucial to realize that, contrary to what Fr. Cekada and those Sedevacantists who follow him believe, the sin of heresy alone neither prevents a man from being elected Pope, nor does it cause a Pope to fall from the pontificate, since the *internal sin* does not sever the *external bonds* of unity, which themselves suffice for a Pope to retain his office. If the sin of heresy alone caused a Pope to lose his office, a Pope who fell into occult (secret) heresy would also cease to be Pope which, as we saw earlier, is not only contrary to the teaching of Bellarmime (the Sedevacantists' favorite theologian), but, as Bellarmine himself said, also contrary to "all the theologians" he cited in his book *De Ecclesia*.[19]

Another authority Fr. Cekada often cites in his articles is the well-known commentary on canon law by Wernz-Vidal. Yet this commentary also explicitly teaches that a heretical Pope loses his office, not for the sin of heresy, but for *the crime* of heresy, which Fr. Cekada himself denies. Speaking of the case of a manifestly heretical Pope, Wernz and Vidal say "the General Council declares the fact of <u>the crime</u> by which the heretical pope has separated himself from the Church and deprived himself of his dignity."[20]

Fr. Cekada's position is also contradicted by Suarez, Cajetan, and John of St. Thomas who, in his treatise on the deposition of a heretical Pope (found in *Cursus Theologici*), states no less than twelve times that it is the *crime* of heresy that causes the Pope to lose his office. For example, he says:

---

[18] *De Ecclesia*, 1927, 5th ed., p. 632 (emphasis added).
[19] *De Romano Pontifice*, bk. 2, ch. 30.
[20] Wernz-Vidal, *Ius Canonicum* (Rome, 1943), II, p. 518.

"By what power should a deposition happen with regard to the pope? The entire question hinges on two points, namely one, a declarative sentence, by which it is declared - but by whom? - <u>that the pope has committed the crime</u>... and two, the deposition itself, which must be done after the declarative judgment of the crime."[21]

And a little later:

"The Church is able to <u>declare the crime of a Pontiff</u> and, according to divine law, propose him to the faithful as a heretic that must be avoided. (...) the deposition of the pope with respect to the <u>declaration of the crime</u> in no way pertains to the cardinals but to a general council."[22]

Fr. Cekada will search in vain for a *complete* sentence from his theology manuals which says the internal sin of heresy *alone* severs one from the Body of the Church. As noted above, if his theory were true, the Church would never have certainty that an elected Pope was a true Pope or an antipope – a believer or a pretender – since man is unable to see into the heart of another man. Consequently, there would be no certainty regarding the Pope's binding decrees, and this uncertainty would infect the entire Church. This practical consequence alone is sufficient to reveal the error of Fr. Cekada's primary defense of the Sedevacantist thesis.

Fr. Cekada used the same fallacious argument in response to John Salza's article against Sedevacantism in the April 2011 edition of *Catholic Family News*.[23] In the article, Mr. Salza explains that expulsion from the Body of the Church is not a matter of sin in the internal forum, but requires a determination of the crime in the external forum. In Cekada's "rebuttal" article called "Salza on Sedevacantism: Same Old Fare,"[24] he begins by glibly stating: "Mr. Salza does nothing more than recycle the same mythical objections to Sedevacantism that I and others

---

[21] *Cursus Theologici* II-II, John of St. Thomas, *De Auctoritate Summi Pontificis, Disp.* II, Art. III, *De Depositione* (emphasis added).

[22] Ibid (emphasis added).

[23] Salza, "Sedevacantism and the Sin of Presumption," *Catholic Family News*, April 2011.

[24] http://www.fathercekada.com/2011/04/11/salza-on-Sedevacantism-same-old-fare/. By titling his article "Salza on Sedevacantism: Same Old Fare," displaying a picture of the salsa condiment on the web page, and referring to the author's arguments as "a dash of Salza," Fr. Cekada was evidently attempting to make fun of Salza's last name (which, incidentally, is of Italian, not Mexican, origin). Personal insults and juvenile *ad hominem* arguments are, unfortunately, very common among Sedevacantist writers (and, in this case, particularly unbecoming since they come from a priest). The bitter fruits of Sedevacantism are discussed in Chapter 21.

have answered over and over for at least twenty years." Then, under his subtitle "Crime and Sin Confused," Cekada actually *confuses* "Crime and Sin" as he unwittingly points out that Salza's arguments "pertain to the **canonical crime** of heresy…and not to the **sin** of heresy" (emphasis in original). Amen Fr. Cekada! We concur.

Fr. Cekada then repeats his error by boldly stating: "In the matter at hand, when canonists and theologians say that 'heresy' automatically deprives a pope of his office, they are referring to the **sin** of heresy, not to the **canonical crime** of heresy" (emphasis in original). Fr. Cekada goes on to provide two quotes from the canonist Michel who explains the requirements for the sin of heresy, but who *never* says such sin "automatically deprives a pope of his office," as Cekada claims. That is because the internal sin of heresy alone does no such thing, and not a single quotation cited by Fr. Cekada in any of his articles proves otherwise, which is why he is reduced to citing *half sentences* (out of context) to support his position.

But Fr. Cekada is a master of the rhetorical skills of the sophists (particularly with his use of ridicule and sarcasm), which enables him to appeal to the emotions, and hence the *will*, of his readers. This tactic serves to divert his readers' attention away from the *intellectual* deficiency and general weakness of his arguments, which, if he keeps them entertained and laughing, they are less likely to spot.

Unfortunately, this tactic seems to have worked, since a number of unsuspecting laymen have fallen for the "sin of heresy" theory of Fr. Cekada, and then used it in their own defense of the Sedevacantist position. One such person is Mr. Jerry Ming, who wrote an "Open Letter to John Vennari," the Editor of *Catholic Family News*, in response to the aforementioned article by John Salza which Mr. Vennari published in 2011. Here is an excerpt from the "Open Letter." See if any of it sounds familiar:

> "So, it should be clear to all, that heresy is a crime against canon law and a sin against the divine law. 'It is by violating the divine law through the sin of heresy that a heretical pope loses his authority – 'having become an unbeliever…' as Cardinal Billot says, 'he would by his own will be cast outside the body of the Church.'"[25]

---

[25] "Open Letter to John Vennari." http://www.novusordowatch.org/open_letter_to_ John _Vennari.htm.

Notice that Mr. Ming not only parrots Fr. Cekada (a common trait among Sedevacantists), but he even quotes the same *half sentence* from Cardinal Billot (out of context) to make his point!

This only goes to show the danger of following Sedevacantist priests, such as Fr. Cekada, without double-checking their sources to verify the accuracy of their teachings. To those who wish to presume the accuracy of their materials, we say *caveat emptor.*[26] One thing is certain, no matter what authorities Sedevacantists cite, or what quotations they marshal: Any citation suggesting that *formal heresy* causes the loss of ecclesiastical office will necessarily refer to the *crime* of heresy (formal heresy in the external forum), not the internal *sin* of heresy (formal heresy in the internal forum).

Another individual who has embraced Fr. Cekada's "sin of heresy" theory is Richard Ibranyi, who has authored numerous books in defense of the Sedevacantis thesis. Having fallen for Fr. Cekada's theory, Mr. Ibranyi has now gone on record and publicly declared that Cardinal Cajetan, and Cardinal Bellarmine himself, a saint and Doctor of the Church, are "notorious heretics" for holding that an occult heretic (one who is guilty of the internal *sin* of heresy) remains a member of the Church, and a Pope who is an occult heretic retains his office. Mr. Ibranyi warned his readers:

> "Beware of *notorious heretics*, such as Cajetan and Robert Bellarmine, who...deny the basic dogma that an occult formal heretic is not a member of the Catholic Church and not Catholic. They hold the *formal heresy, introduced by the scholastics*, that an occult formal heretic is a member of the Catholic Church and Catholic. Hence they believe that an occult formal heretic [internal forum] can hold an office because they heretically believe he is a member of the Catholic Church and Catholic."[27]

Notice in the above citation that Mr. Ibranyi accuses the scholastics of teaching what he calls the "formal heresy" that occult heretics are members of the Church. Does that mean Mr. Ibranyi considers the great scholastic theologians of the Church to be heretics as well, for holding that position? Indeed he does! Two months after publishing the above article (revised November 2013), he came out publicly and

---

[26] Latin, "Let the buyer beware."
[27] Ibranyi, "Cajetan's and Bellarmine's Heresies on Formal Heretics and Loss of Papal Office," originally published December 2012, (revised November 2013) (emphasis added). See http://www.johnthebaptist.us/jbw_english/documents/articles/rjmi/tr28_cajetan_bellarmine_heresies.pdf (emphasis added).

declared that all the Church's theologians from the year 1250 onward have been *apostates.* He wrote:

> "All of the theologians and canon lawyers from 1250 onward were apostates. Many theologians and canon lawyers before 1250 were also apostates, but each case must be studied individually."[28]

So, according to Ibranyi, *all* the Church's theologians and canon lawyers from 1250 onward were apostates, and those before 1250 will have to be judged on a case by case basis. This, of course, would include the Universal Doctor of the Catholic Church, St. Thomas Aquinas (d. 1274) and the many holy Popes and councils who have endorsed his teaching (even referring to St. Thomas' teaching as the philosophy and theology of the Church). In the same article, the author went even further by declaring that "all of the so-called popes and so-called cardinals from Innocent II (1130-1143) until today were and are apostate antipopes and apostate anticardinals."

But since these Popes and Cardinals were not declared guilty of the crime of heresy or apostasy by the Church, Mr. Ibranyi (as a disciple of Fr. Cekada) must hold that they are apostates because they lost the interior virtue of faith. And, of course, this conclusion assumes Mr. Ibranyi can peer into and judge the souls of men – men whom he never knew and who lived hundreds of years ago, to boot. To make such an assertion is to refute it. This, dear readers, is the spirit and hubris of the Sedevacantist position, whether the individual Sedevacantist goes back to the year 1130, 1250, or 1958, or any other random year that he arrives at by his private judgment. St. Thomas observed that a small error in the beginning (in principle) results in a big error in the end (in the conclusion). The conclusions of Mr. Ibranyi serve as a case in point.

Sedevacantist "Proof-Texts"?

Sedevacantists have managed to dig up a number of "proof-texts" in an attempt to defend their assertion that the internal *sin* of heresy alone severs a person from the *Body* of the Church (thus, causing a loss of office). As we will see, arguments based upon these texts were answered long ago by real theologians of the Church.

---

[28] Ibranyi, "No Popes or Cardinals since 1130," January 2014. See http://www.johnthe baptist.us/jbw_english/documents/articles/rjmi/tr37_no_popes_cardinals_since_1130. pdf.

St. Jerome

The first "proof-text" is a fourth century quotation from St. Jerome, whom Bellarmine quotes as saying:

> "...other sinners are excluded from the Church by sentence of excommunication, but the heretics exile themselves and separate themselves by their own act from the body of Christ."[29]

Sedevacantists have interpreted this quotation to mean that a Pope whom they *privately judge* to be a heretic automatically loses his office, which is not what St. Jerome said. John of St. Thomas explains that Jerome is referring to the *nature of the crime*, which severs one from the body of the Church with no *additional censure* attached to it. In this sense, the crime of heresy differs *in its nature* from other crimes, such as physically striking the Pope or procuring an abortion, which are crimes that only sever a person from the Church by virtue of the additional censure attached to the act.[30] As John of St. Thomas explains, by saying a heretic severs himself from the Body of the Church by his own act, does not exclude the necessity of the Church to render a judgment, especially when the person in question is the Pope. He wrote:

> "Jerome, when he says that a heretic cuts himself off from the body of Christ, does not exclude the judgment of the Church in such a grave matter as that of the deposition of the Pope, but he instead refers to the <u>nature of the crime</u>, which, of itself, cuts one off from the Church without any other further added censure of the Church, <u>provided, that is, that he be declared guilty by the Church</u>."[31]

As we see, saying that heresy *of its nature* severs a man from the Body of Christ does not preclude a judgment by the Church (who determines that the crime of heresy has been committed), especially if the person in question still professes to be a Catholic, and more so if the person is a prelate who holds office in the Church.

---

[29] Quoted by Bellarmine in *De Romano Pontifice*, bk. 2, ch. 30.

[30] See canon 2350 of the 1917 Code and canon 1398 of the 1983 Code of Canon Law. Fr. Cekada actually uses the abortion example in several of his articles to demonstrate the distinction between sin and crime, but does not take the logical next step in realizing that the *sin* of abortion (like the *sin* of heresy) severs one only from the *Soul*, not the *Body*, of the Church. See, for example, Fr. Cekada, "Traditionalists, Infallibility, and the Pope," Appendix 2: Heresy: The Sin vs. the Crime, p. 11.

[31] *Cursus Theologici* II-II, John of St. Thomas, *De Auctoritate Summi Pontificis, Disp.* II, Art. III, *De Depositione Papae*, p. 139.

Now, Fr. Sylvester Berry provided a slightly different translation of the citation from St. Jerome (along with a source reference for the quote), which more clearly shows that St. Jerome was juxtaposing the crime of heresy (which, by its nature, severs one from the Church) with other crimes (which sever one from the Church by an additional censure). Here is the translation provided by Fr. Berry:

> "An adulterer, a homicide, and other sinners are driven from the Church by the priests (i.e., by excommunication); but heretics pass sentence upon themselves, <u>leaving the Church of their own free will</u>" (Serm. 181; P.L. 38980).[32]

Notice this translation indicates that the heretic in question is one *who leaves the Church of his own free will*; it is not simply a Catholic who makes a heretical statement (which is how the Sedevacantists have interpreted the quote). A person who leaves the Church of his own free will (either by the crime of heresy and/or public defection, discussed later), thereby, without *additional censure*, severs the *external bonds* of unity, by rejecting the Church *as the rule of faith*, and separating from the Church's *governing authority*.

Needless to say, none of the post-conciliar Popes left the Church of their own free will. On the contrary, they all professed to being Catholic and they were all recognized by the Church to be members in good standing. Hence, nothing in this quotation from St. Jerome supports the Sedevacantist position that a Pope, who is recognized as Pope by the Church, yet is judged by *private opinion* to be a heretic, automatically loses his office.

Mystici Corporis Christi

A second "proof-text" the Sedevacantists use is taken from the encyclical *Mystici Corporis Christi* in which Pope Pius XII wrote:

> "For not every <u>offense</u> (*admissum*), although it may be a grave evil, is such <u>as by its very own nature</u> to sever a man from the Body of the Church, as does schism or heresy or apostasy."[33]

---

[32] *The Church of Christ*, p. 129.

[33] *Mystici Corporis*, No. 23, June 29, 1943. In the previous paragraph (No. 22), Pope Pius XII also emphasizes that he is speaking of the external bonds and the external acts or crimes (not internal sins) which can break those bonds ("separating themselves" from the "body" by leaving the Church, or being "excluded by legitimate authority"): "Actually only those are to be numbered among the members of the Church who have received the

Notice Pius XII explicitly states that he is referring to the "nature" of these "offenses" which is precisely what John of St. Thomas said St. Jerome was referring to. As mentioned above, the *nature* of these particular crimes (heresy, schism and apostasy) differs from that of other offenses which only severs one from the Church due to an *additional censure* attached to them. But, as John of St. Thomas explained above, this does not eliminate the need for the Church herself to render a judgment and declare the crime – *especially when the culprit is a prelate who holds office in the Church.* Pius XII did not teach that the internal sin of heresy alone causes a prelate to automatically lose his office without the Church itself rendering a judgment, which is how the Sedevacantists interpret the passage.

In fact, Msgr. Fenton addressed this point in an article published in the *American Ecclesiastical Review* in March of 1950. The purpose of Fr. Fenton's article was to show that this citation from *Mystici Corporis Christi* was in no way contrary to the teaching of St. Bellarmine, who, as we have seen, taught that the sin of heresy alone does not sever a person from the Body of the Church.

Fr. Fenton began by explaining that the teaching of Pius XII was identical to what Bellarmine himself wrote in the fourth chapter of *De Ecclesia Militante,* when he taught that heresy, schism and apostasy, *of their nature,* sever a man from the Body of the Church. Fr. Fenton wrote:

> "In the encyclical, the Holy Father speaks of schism, heresy, and apostasy, as sins [*admissum*] which, of their own nature, separate a man from the Body of the Church. He thereby follows the traditional procedure adopted by St. Robert himself in his *De Ecclesia Militante.* The great Doctor of the Church devoted the fourth chapter of his book to a proof that [public] heretics and apostates are *not* members of the Church."[34]

Fr. Fenton then noted that Bellarmine dedicated the tenth chapter of the same book (*De Ecclesia Militante*) to demonstrating that *occult* infidels or heretics (those guilty of the *sin* of heresy by an internal act) are really *members* of the Body of the Church:

---

laver of regeneration and profess the true faith and have not *separated themselves* from the unity of the *body* or been *excluded by legitimate authority*" (emphasis added).
[34] When Fr. Fenton refers to "sins" [*admissum*] in this section, he is referring to sins being established *as crimes in the external forum*, which by their nature sever man from the Body of the Church, but which do not exclude judgment by the Church.

"The tenth chapter of the same work is nothing more or less than a demonstration of the *fact* that occult infidels or heretics are really members."[35]

Fenton then noted that what Bellarmine himself wrote in the tenth chapter of the book (that the sin of heresy alone does not separate one from the body of the Church) was obviously not in contradiction to what he wrote in the fourth chapter of the same book (that public heretics are not members of the Church). Just as Bellarmine did not contradict himself in these chapters, so likewise, there's no reason to believe that when Pius XII repeated Bellarmine's teaching from chapter four, he intended to contradict what the saint wrote in chapter ten of same book. Fr. Fenton said:

"In writing what St. Robert [Bellarmine] included in his fourth chapter, the Holy Father must not be considered as denying what the same great Doctor of the Church taught in the tenth chapter of the same book."[36]

The correct interpretation of Pope Pius XII's teaching is not that he was referring to the internal sin of heresy alone, but to the public offense (the crime) of heresy, which, *of its nature*, severs a person from the Body of the Church *with no further censure attached to the offense*. It is also worth noting that the word *admissum* used by Pope Pius XII, which is sometimes translated as "sin" or "offense," also means "crime."[37] A *crime* is a *public offense*, not merely an internal sin. And the public crime must be determined according to the Church's judgment, not the private judgment of individuals that is opposed to the public judgment of the Church.[38]

Van Noort further elaborated on this point by explaining that the internal sin of heresy alone only separates a person from the Body of the Church dispositively. He said "internal heresy, since it destroys that interior unity of faith from which unity of profession is born,

---

[35] Fenton, "Status of St. Robert Bellarmine's Teaching about the Membership of Occult Heretics in the Catholic Church," *American Ecclesiastical Review*, vol. CXXII, no. 3, p. 219 (emphasis added)

[36] Ibid.

[37] Definition of *admissum*: "a wrong done, a trespass, fault, crime." - *Lewis and Short, A Latin Dictionary*; Founded on Andrews' edition of Freund's Latin dictionary (Oxford: Trustees of Tufts University, 1879).

[38] If the Church recognizes a prelate as a member of the Church in good standing, the private judgment of individuals who personally consider him to be a heretic, does not make him a "public heretic," since their private judgment would be contrary to the public judgment of the Church.

separates one from the body of the Church <u>dispositively</u>, but not yet formally."[39] In other words, the sin of heresy *disposes* a person to be separated from the *Body* of the Church, but the *actual* separation does not take place until pertinacity in the *external forum* is established and the Church renders a judgment (unless, of course, the person openly left the Church of his own free will). Because the Church itself does not judge internals (*de internis ecclesia non judica*), in order for the sin to be judged *by the Church*, it must be *public*.

One final point is that this particular Sedevacantist theory - that the internal sin of heresy alone severs a person from the Body of the Church[40] - actually approaches heresy, since it *logically* denies the dogma of the visibility of the Church. If an internal sin of heresy *alone* severed a person from the Body of the Church, the Church would no longer be a visible society, but an "invisible Church of true believers known to God alone," which is a heresy of Protestantism. As Pope Leo XIII said, those who "conjure up and picture to themselves a hidden and invisible Church are in grievous and pernicious error..."[41] Hence, those who privately interpret this excerpt of *Mystici Corporis Christi* (or any other citation they manage to dig up) as teaching that a mere internal sin of heresy severs a person from the Church are *logically forced* to embrace this "grievous and pernicious error." Such is the case with the promoters of Sedevacantism.

---

[39] *Christ's Church*, p. 242 (emphasis added). Using Thomistic terminology, we can say the separation from the Body due to internal sin alone is in *potency*, but not in *act*.
[40] For example, the Sedevacantist author Richard Ibranyi wrote: "An occult formal heretic is as much a formal heretic as a public formal heretic. ... both are not Catholic, and <u>both are not members of the Catholic Church.</u>" (Ibranyi, "Cajetan's And Bellarmine's Heresies On Formal Heretics And Loss Of Papal Office" (November 2013).
[41] *Satis Cognitum*, No. 3, June 29, 1896.

Chapter 6

~ Suspicion of Heresy ~

In the previous chapters, we have demonstrated that the sin of heresy alone does not sever a man from the Body of the Church. One who is a formal heretic in the secrecy of the internal forum remains a member of the Church and thus continues to possess all the rights and privileges of a member, including ecclesiastical office. When the sin of heresy is proven to be manifest in the external forum in a public and notorious way, it also constitutes the crime of heresy, which severs a man from the Body of the Church (more on this later in the book).

Before we address how the crime of heresy is proven, we believe it is important to demonstrate what factors merely render a man *suspect* of heresy – which does *not* result in the loss of office (a man *suspect* of heresy remains a *member* of the Church). Some of these factors are set forth in the Church's canon law, and they include the mortal sins of knowingly propagating heresy and taking part in worshiping with non-Catholics (*communicatio in sacris cum acatholicis*).

In this chapter, we will see how very patient and prudent Holy Mother Church is with her members before making a judgment of heresy, and just "how far" one can go while only being considered suspect of heresy. We should likewise exercise the same prudence in our personal judgments of other Catholics, especially when it concerns the Pope who has no judge on this Earth.

In his commentary on the 1917 Code of Canon law, Fr. Charles Augustine explains the meaning of *suspicion*: "Suspicion, in the psychological sense, is doubt, coupled with a positive leaning to one side; in our case, towards a heretical doctrine. In law it may be expressed by presumption or circumstantial evidence. It is, therefore, a judgment formed about someone without sufficient evidence on the ground of certain *indicia*."[1] Fr. Augustine goes on to explain that suspicion is generally broken out into three categories: light, vehement, and violent. *Light suspicion* is suspicion is based upon insufficient indications, and therefore often amounts to no more than rash judgment. *Vehement suspicion* is suspicion based upon effective signs and conclusions. *Violent suspicion* amounts to morally certain proof.

---

[1] Augustine, *A Commentary on the New Code of Canon Law*, vol. VIII, bk. 5, (London: Herder Book Co., 1918), p. 284.

The 1917 Code of Canon Law provides that those who commit the following acts are suspect of heresy:

1. The propagators of heresy and those who participate with non-Catholics *in divinis* (can. 2316);
2. Those who contract marriage under the condition of having their offspring educated in a non-Catholic sect and those who have their children baptized by non-Catholic ministers or educated in a non-Catholic denomination (can. 2319);
3. Those who desecrate sacred hosts or species (can. 2320);
4. Those who appeal from the Pope to a general council (can. 2332);
5. Those who remain under sentence of excommunication for more than a year (can. 2340);
6. Those who administer or receive the Sacraments simoniacally (can. 2371).[2]

In addition to these anti-Catholic activities specified under canon law, the highly respected commentary on the 1917 Code of Canon law by Wernz-Vidal also sets forth extra-canonical activities that are considered grounds for suspicion of heresy. They include taking part in the exercise of magic, charms or divination, and those who become members of sects which, whether openly or secretly, hatch plots against the Church.[3]

In other words, a Catholic can propagate heretical doctrines, participate in false worship with non-Catholics, baptize, raise and educate their children in non-Catholic sects, commit sacrilege against the Blessed Sacrament, take part in satanic "black magic," and formally join anti-Catholic sects and secret societies, and only be *suspected* of heresy. Even though these activities are objective mortal sins against the Faith, under the Church's law they are only *grounds* for *suspicion* that one is a heretic.

Because the propagation of heresy is such a serious assault on the Faith of the Church, Fr. Augustine sets forth four categories to morally distinguish the types of "propagators of heresy" (can. 2316):

a) *"Credentes* are such as externally profess the errors of heretics, e.g., by asserting that Luther or Döllinger were correct in their views, even though they may not know the particular errors of these leaders.

---

[2] Ibid., p. 280.
[3] Cited by Arnaldo Vidigal Xavier da Silveira in "Essay on Heresy," translated by John Daly. http://sedevacantist.com/essayonheresy.htm.

b)   *Receptores* are those who receive and shelter heretics, especially with the intention of hiding them from the ecclesiastical authorities.

c)   *Fautores* are such as favor heretics because of their heresy, by omitting to denounce them when required or demanded by their office, or by giving support to non-Catholic propaganda. This latter way of propagating heresy is followed by public and private persons who write for heretics, praise their methods and objects, recommend their work and give it material support, always provided that the heresy itself is the object of their mental and material favors.

d)   *Defensores* means those who defend heretics for the sake of heresy, orally, in writing, or by acts of defense proper. All such persons are suspected of heresy if they act of their own accord and knowingly. *Sponte* is opposed to compulsion and fear, and therefore implies full deliberation and a free will not hindered by any extrinsic or intrinsic impediment, such as fear of losing an office, or one's reputation, or customers. *Scienter* is opposed to ignorance, the object of which here is heresy, and means that these promotors or propagators of heresy must be aware that they are helping heresy as such."[4]

Thus, one who "externally professes the error of heretics," or who favors heretics "because of their heresy," or who "defends heretics for the sake of heresy, orally, in writing, or by acts," are only considered suspect of heresy. While a Catholic may be inclined to conclude that John Paul II, for example, was a heretic for worshiping with pagans and praising the errors of Martin Luther, the Church says these are only grounds for suspicion of heresy. One who commits these acts is not considered a "public heretic" (even if the scandalous acts are multiplied) and, if the person in question is a cleric, such activities do not deprive him of his ecclesiastical office.

Fr. Augustine explains the canonical process and penalties for those who are suspect of heresy:

"We now proceed to the penalties the Code inflicts on those suspected of heresy.

a) <u>They must, first, be warned</u>, according to canon 2307, to remove the cause of suspicion. A reasonable time should be granted for this purpose in the canonical warning.

---

[4] Augustine, *A Commentary on the New Code of Canon Law*, vol. VIII, bk. 5, pp. 288-289.

b) <u>If the warning proves fruitless</u>, the suspected person must be forbidden to perform any ecclesiastical legal acts, according to can. 2256. If he is a cleric, he must be suspended *a divinis* <u>after a second warning has been left unheeded.</u>

c) If, after the lapse of six months, to be reckoned from the moment the penalty has been contracted, the person suspected of heresy has not amended, he must be regarded as a heretic, amenable to the penalties set forth in canon 2314. Whilst the penalties enumerated under (b) are *ferendae sententiae*, to be inflicted according to can. 2223, 3, the penalties stated under (c) are *a iure* and *latae sententiae*.

Note that, since the *ferendae sententiae* penalties require a canonical warning and a clear statement of the time granted, the moment from which the penalty is contracted can be almost mathematically determined."[5]

As we can see, under the Church's positive law, if one commits an act that renders him suspect of heresy (e.g., externally professing heretical errors, worshiping with pagans, profaning the Eucharist, etc.), he is not considered a heretic until the above procedures have been followed. In his commentary on the 1917 Code, Fr. Henry Ayrinhac notes that a person's actions may render him suspect of heresy *de facto*, yet "the suspicion has no *canonical effect* until the warning has been given." He then goes on to explain the procedures and penalties:

"If a person who is suspected of heresy does not, after being duly warned, remove the cause of the suspicion, supposing that it is morally possible to do so, he should be debarred from the legitimate acts. A cleric should receive a second warning, and if this too remained fruitless he should be suspended *a divinis*. After inflicting these punishments, six months more may be allowed, and if at the end of this time the party suspected of heresy has shown *no signs of amendment*, he is to be considered as a heretic and punished accordingly."[6]

We can see the prudence and patience of Holy Mother Church with regard to such people. Under the Church's law, a prelate is not considered a heretic for engaging in any of the aforementioned activities until he has been duly *warned* by legitimate authority, and

---

[5] Ibid., pp. 286-287.
[6] Ayrinhac, *Penal Legislation in the New Code of Canon Law*, (New York, Cincinnati, Chicago: Benzinger Brothers, 1920), p. 198.

may not even be suspended from his official duties until he fails to heed a *second* warning. Further, the prelate must be given *six months more* to remove the cause for suspicion, and after that he is only considered a heretic by the Church if he shows *no signs of amendment*. Finally, even after the six month period in which amendment is to take place, if the suspect is a cleric, he is not immediately suspended or forbidden from performing ecclesiastical legal acts. Such penalties are not automatic, but must be imposed, *ferendae sententiae,* by the proper ecclesiastical authorities, who may have reason to refrain from putting them into effect.

If these canonical rules apply to all Catholics, their *principles* also apply to the Pope who is not subject to any jurisdiction in the Church and could only be "warned" as a matter of charity.[7] Sedevacantists may wish to argue that the conciliar Popes have repeatedly engaged in activities that are suspect of heresy well beyond any "six month" grace period, but such a period – which does not strictly apply to the Pope – would nevertheless have relevance only after charitable warnings were issued by the proper authorities. Thus, alleging that the conciliar Popes have persisted in their suspicious activities could prove nothing beyond the allegations themselves, and certainly does not prove public, notorious heresy or imply loss of office.

As we have seen, the sin of heresy (and thus the loss of the Catholic faith) in the internal forum does not sever a man from the Body of the Church, and neither do external actions which render a man merely suspect of heresy, notwithstanding how egregious, scandalous and sinful they are, and no matter how often the acts are multiplied. While the conciliar Popes have engaged in actions rendering them suspect of heresy, and may have even lost interior faith, these actions by themselves do not cause a Pope to lose his office.

Historical Examples

To illustrate these principles, let us consider the following hypothetical case. Let's imagine a bishop, or perhaps even an archbishop, who publicly preached heresy to a body of important governmental figures. Let's also assume the heresy in question was a public denial of a basic truth of the faith, such as the dogma that the

---

[7] Since canon law is a further specification of the principles of divine law applied to individual cases, even if one maintains that a Pope is not subject to canon law, the principles of canon law would still need to be followed as a matter of justice, according to the philosophical principle of reason that the "greater includes the lesser," according to Aristotelian/Thomistic tradition.

Pope is the head of the universal Church. Let's further assume the liberal media gleefully published this heresy throughout the region for all to read, thereby resulting in untold scandal to the faithful. And to take the matter even further, let's say this archbishop was warned that his belief was heretical by the Pope himself (thereby removing any chance of invincible ignorance), and yet retracted nothing.

Should such a man be considered a public heretic? And if so, would he have immediately lost his office? We venture to say that most, if not all, Sedevacantist apologists would respond in the affirmative before citing (out of context) excerpts from a litany of Church Doctors, saints and canonists to seemingly support their position. In fact, many would argue that a Catholic who remained in union with such a man should be considered a heretic himself.[8] Is this not the kind of argumentation Sedevacantists often engage in? Yet, this hypothetical scenario of the archbishop is not hypothetical at all. It is instead the historical case of Msgr. Darboy, Archbishop of Paris, who lived at the time of Pope Pius IX – the Pope in the above story who warned Darboy that his public position was heretical.

Archbishop Darboy

An account of the Darboy affair is found in the article "Heresy in History" written by a Sedevacantist author named John Daly, who no one can accuse of distorting the facts in order to undermine the position he himself holds. Mr. Daly begins his discussion of Msgr. Darboy as follows: "In 1865 Mgr. Darboy, archbishop of Paris and member of the French senate, expressed in an important speech to the senate ideas clearly opposed to the divinely instituted primacy of the Roman Pontiff over the entire Church, which, unlike papal infallibility, already belonged to the corpus of Catholic doctrine. The speech was a public defiance of the pope and a refusal to recognize the pope's ordinary and universal jurisdiction in the dioceses of France."[9]

Daly goes on to explain that Pope Pius IX himself, who was already aware of the ideas of the wayward bishop, "reprimanded him sternly in a private letter," in which he informed the archbishop that his public teachings were comparable to those of Febronius, who had been

---

[8] For example, to those Catholics who die in union with the conciliar Popes, Sedevacantist preacher Gerry Matatics claims that God "will credit to your account the faith of these men." That is, God will impute the alleged heresies of the conciliar Popes to those who die in willful union with these Popes, which will cause them to lose their souls. "Counterfeit Catholicism vs. Consistent Catholicism," disc 4 of 6, track 4.

[9] John Daly, *Heresy in History*, May, 2000. http://www.strobertbellarmine.net/heresy history.html.

condemned for his views, and also opposed the teaching of the Fourth Lateran Council. Mr. Daly notes that the letter from Pius IX also complained of Msgr. Darboy's presence at the funeral of a known Freemason, as well as other scandals in which Darboy was involved.

Mr. Daly goes on to explain that after months of delay, Msgr. Darboy finally replied to the Pope. Did Darboy retract his errors and offer an apology? Quite the contrary. Rather than renounce his errors, Daly tells us that Darboy "adopted a haughty tone to justify himself and rebuked the pope! *He retracted nothing* whatever of the errors which had been reported throughout France with glee by the anti-Catholic press!"

Then, in 1868, the events again surfaced when the private letter of the Pope was "leaked" and widely published. At the time, preparations were underway for the First Vatican Council. Prior to the council, Msgr. Darboy opposed the dogma of papal infallibility. "For more than five years, despite the rebukes of the pope and of the nuncio, he never withdrew his extremely public errors against the faith," writes Mr. Daly. "And then when the council proclaimed the dogmas concerning the pope, in 1870, he did not adhere to them."

It wasn't until March 2, 1871, almost six years after his infamous speech, that Msgr. Darboy at last informed the Pope, *via a private letter*, that he accepted these dogmas. Yet, in another act of defiance, he continued to delay executing his duty of promulgating the Council's decrees in his diocese. At last, he finally did so, which, according to Mr. Daly, "constituted an *implicit* withdrawal of the false doctrines he was on *public record* as holding, despite the rebuke of the pope, since 1865."

Now, to the Sedevacantists, we must ask the obvious question: From 1865 to 1871, was Msgr. Darboy a public heretic or not? If not, why not? The facts are the facts: Darboy, an archbishop of the Catholic Church, clearly *denied* a most fundamental dogma of the Faith (defined by Vatican I), and he did so in a public manner. Darboy was even *warned* by the Vicar of Christ himself, and yet *refused* to retract his public heresy – even refusing to do so after the Pope's written warning was "leaked" and published. Hence, Darboy showed *pertinacity* of the will in the external forum in denying a dogma of the Faith, after being warned by legitimate authority (the highest authority in the Church!). For the Sedevacantist, the Darboy affair is an "open and shut" case of public heresy and loss of ecclesiastical office.

After all, don't Sedevacantist apologists argue that when an external violation of the law occurs in the external forum, the existence of malice is presumed until the contrary is proven, citing canon 2200, §2? And don't they claim that the very commission of any act which signifies heresy (e.g., the statement of some doctrine contrary to a revealed and defined dogma), gives sufficient ground for the juridical presumption of "heretical depravity," and furthermore, that the burden of rebutting the presumption is on the person whose action has given rise to the imputation of heresy? And, further, don't they claim that, in the absence of such a rebuttal, all such excuses are presumed not to exist? And don't they conclude from this that a cleric who publicly professes heresy is considered by the Church to be guilty until proven innocent? And from this don't they draw the conclusion that if a Pope makes a heretical statement, the faithful should presume he is a "public heretic" and therefore not the Pope?[10] And, still further, don't they maintain that we are morally bound to withdraw from communion with the Pope *they personally declare* to be a public heretic – as well as those priests who dare to include his name in the canon of the Mass - lest we share in the heretic's guilt?[11] Indeed, this is precisely the line of argumentation consistently employed by Sedevacantist apologists.

Yet, in the Darboy case, we have the example of an archbishop who taught heresy in pubic, whose heresy was published throughout his country, who was warned in writing by the Pope about his heresy, and who "retracted nothing," even after the Pope's letter of warning was leaked to the public. Yet Blessed Pius IX – the very Pope who gave us the *Syllabus of Errors*, *Quanta Cura*, and ratified the First Vatican Council – remained in union with the man!

If the Sedevacantists were consistent, should they not conclude that Pope Pius IX was an antipope for remaining in union with a "public heretic"? If so, what would this say about the First Vatican Council that he convened and ratified, as well as his other decrees to which Sedevacantists often appeal? And, if they consider Msgr. Darboy to be a public heretic (which they would have to do if they were consistent in their argumentation), would not the entire diocese of Paris, clergy and laity alike, have simultaneously fell from grace by remaining in union with such a man?

Or, could it be that Pope Pius IX's approach was the correct one, and that the Sedevacantists are rash in judging that a cleric (including the Pope!) who utters heresy is automatically deemed a "public heretic" who has lost his office *ipso facto*? Could it be that the Sedevacantists' private judgment and application of the Church's law

---

[10] This is the exact line of argumentation used by Fr. Cekada in his article "Sedevacantism and Mr. Ferrara's Cardboard Pope," August, 2005.
[11] Cekada, "Should I Assist at a Mass That Names Benedict XVI in the Canon?"; and Sanborn, "Can We Go to The *Una Cum* Mass in a Pinch?" (more on this topic in Chapter 21).

on these matters is completely erroneous? Indeed it is, as this historical case shows, and as we will continue to demonstrate throughout this book.

Erasmus of Rotterdam

The historical example of the priest Erasmus of Rotterdam is also worth considering. Fr. Erasmus was born on October 27, 1466. At an early age, he was received among the Regular Canons of St. Augustine and made his religious profession. After taking his vows, he eventually grew weary of the religious life, sought a Papal dispensation which he received, and returned to the world. He showed an interest in literature and, after leaving the cloister began to write on theological matters. Although he was a man of great learning, his writings contained many egregious errors against the faith.

St. Alphonsus said that Erasmus wrote in an obscure manner concerning dogma, and began to criticize the Fathers of the Church. His errors eventually became more pronounced, which led the French Dominican theologian Noel Alexandre to say "the more works he wrote, the more errors he published."[12] Many Catholics openly accused him of heresy, and for good reason.

According to St. Alphonsus, Erasmus "called the Invocation of the Blessed Virgin and the Saints idolatry; condemned Monasteries, ridiculed the Religious...and condemned their vows and rules." He "was opposed to the Celibacy of the Clergy, and turned into mockery Papal Indulgences, relics of Saints, feasts and fasts, auricular Confession." As a prelude to Luther, he claimed "that by Faith alone man is justified, and even threw doubt on the authority of the Scripture and Councils." In one of his published books he even declared it "rash to call the Holy Ghost God."[13] Certainly, Erasmus was a forerunner of the Protestant revolt, and, if he persisted in these errors at a canonical trial, would be considered a heretic even by Vatican II standards.

But in spite of all his egregious, public errors against the Faith, Erasmus was not considered a public heretic by his contemporaries, or even by the Popes reigning at the time. Rather, as St. Alphonsus reported, Erasmus was "esteemed by several Popes, who invited him to Rome, to write against Luther, and it was even reported that Pope Paul III intended him for the Cardinalship." After listing the above errors and heresies, St. Alphonsus concludes his history on Erasmus of

---

[12] Liguori, *The History of Heresies, and Their Refutation*, vol. I, (Dublin: Published by James Duffy, Wellington Qua, 1847), Chapter XL, p. 291.
[13] Ibid., p. 292.

Rotterdam by saying: "We may conclude with Bernini, that he died with the character of an unsound Catholic, but not a heretic, as he submitted his writings to the judgment of the Church."[14]

Yet, what would Sedevacantists say about a Pope (or a Cardinal or bishop) if he called the Invocation of the Blessed Virgin and the saints idolatry, mocked indulgences, relics, fasting and confession, and declared it rash to call the Holy Ghost God, as did Eramus? Would they not publicly declare the "fact" that the man was a "manifest heretic," who lost his office *ipso facto* due to heresy? Or do these historical precedents teach us to reserve our judgments in favor of "the judgment of the Church" in such matters? The answer is clear.

Doctor Michel de Bay

One final example is that of Doctor Michel de Bay. The de Bay case is of particular interest because it involves St. Robert Bellarmine, whom Sededevacantists often cite as an authority for their position. Let us see how St. Bellarmine himself reacted to this professor and celebrated theologian of his own day who was publicly teaching heresy. Let us then compare this example of a saint and Doctor of the Church to the rashness of the Sedevacantist apologists in our day.

Doctor Michel de Bay was born in 1513. He completed his university studies at Louvain and was ordained in 1541. After serving as the principal for Standonk College from 1541 to 1544, he was given the chair of philosophy. He held this position until 1550 when he earned the degree of Doctor of Theology and was appointed President of the College Adrien. He was also invited to take part in the great Council of Trent.

In spite of his learning, he possessed a love of novelty and a disdain for Scholasticism. One author noted that "a pronounced vice in his character was the ease with which he called heretics all those who failed to agree with his theological ideas, which, of course, he considered to be manifestly the only orthodox ones."[15] Shortly after being appointed President of the College Adrien, he began to teach and spread errors and heresies. Finally, in 1561, Pope Pius IV, through Cardinal Granvelle, imposed silence upon him, which he failed to obey. On October 1, 1567, Pope St. Pius V signed the Bull, *Ex omnibus afflictionibus,* which condemned more than 70 of de Bay's propositions, with several being qualified as heretical. The Bull was sent privately to de Bay before being published. Michel de Bay refused to retract his

---

[14] Ibid.
[15] John Daly, "*Heresy in History,*" May, 2000.

errors, but instead defended himself. St. Pius V responded by publishing the condemned propositions, without, however, personally naming de Bay.

It was not until the papal Bull was sent to the university that he submitted to the condemnations (at least externally) and subscribed with the other professors. However, when the Bull was later made public, he again defended himself and his errors, which he claimed to be nothing but the teaching of St. Augustine. He defended himself by saying that if some of his teachings were "at variance with the terminology of the Scholastics, they were yet the genuine sayings of the Fathers."[16]

It was during this time that St. Robert Bellarmine arrived at Louvain as a professor of theology. From 1570 to 1576, he publicly opposed the errors of de Bay in his lectures, but without ever naming him personally. In speaking of him, as one author noted, "he always considered him as a learned Catholic, most worthy of respect, and at this time called him 'prudent, pious, humble, erudite.'"[17] In spite of this, St. Bellarmine continued to hope for a new condemnation of his errors. The second condemnation would come in the year 1579, after the election of Pope Gregory XIII, in the Bull *Provisionis Nostræ*.

Around this time, Bellarmine was replaced at Louvain by Venerable Leonard Lessius. By way of preparatory information, Bellarmine told Lessius that, in his opinion, the doctrine of de Bay and his disciples on predestination was *heretical*. Lessius later wrote to St. Bellarmine, who had been transferred to Rome, and informed him that de Bay "continued to spread his errors in private, even after the new condemnation, and sometimes even in public," and that "his numerous disciples propagated them with great enthusiasm."[18] Bellarmine advised Lessius to continue to oppose these errors in his lectures, but without ever naming de Bay personally or condemning the man who was the source of so much evil, and the precursor of the heresy of Jansenism.

After relating the history of Michel de Bay and St. Bellarmine in one of his articles, the Sedevacantist author, John Daly, posed the following question:

> "Now in the light of this account, one is forced to ask whether some Sedevacantists in our day are not very much prompter than St. Robert Bellarmine was in identifying pertinacity, and more

---

[16] *Catholic Encyclopedia* (1913), vol. II (*Michel de Bay or 'Baius'*), p. 209.
[17] John Daly, "*Heresy in History*," May 2000.
[18] Ibid.

animated by the bad example of de Bay himself than by the good example of St. Robert and of the Ven. Leonard Lessius."[19]

Daly concludes by saying:

> "[I]f the Church presumes all who go astray in doctrine to be pertinacious, St. Robert Bellarmine was clearly not aware of it. And while it can be possible to recognize someone as a pertinacious heretic even before the intervention of the Holy See, the fact remains that St. Robert was slower to draw that conclusion, *even after several Roman condemnations*, than some are today when relying only on their own judgment of what seems evident."[20]

We certainly applaud Mr. Daly for his honest and true assessment of the Sedevacantist mindset, but it is a mindset that he also ultimately embraces along with his Sedevacantist colleagues, who put "their own judgment of what seems evident" ahead of "the judgment of the Church," when it is a question of who holds the papal office.

In contrast, notice how their favorite saint, Robert Bellarmine himself, reacted when faced with a man of influence who was spreading heresies that had just been been formally condemned by the Church. Bellarmine did not declare de Bay a "manifest heretic" as Sedevacantists no doubt would, nor did he demand that others withdraw from communion with him lest they share in his guilt. On the contrary, while hoping for another condemnation of his errors (which was, in reality, not necessary), Bellarmine treated de Bay with respect and even referred to him as "prudent, pious, humble, erudite." Neither did Bellarmine assume pertinacity, even though one could have easily drawn such a conclusion, since de Bay was *personally warned* by two Popes (Pius IV and St. Pius V), and his errors were *formally condemned* by two Popes (St. Pius V and Gregory XIII). Yet de Bay continued to propagate his heretical teachings even after these warnings and condemnations!

With Mr. Daly, we must also ask if the Sedevacantists in our day are not "very much prompter than St. Robert Bellarmine was in identifying pertinicity, and more animated by the bad example of de Bay himself [who rashly accused others of heresy], than by the good example of St Robert and of the Ven. Leonard Lessius." The answer to this rhetorical question is obvious.

---

[19] Ibid.
[20] Ibid. (emphasis added).

These examples demonstrate the utter rashness of Sedevacantists in our day, who not only judge the conciliar Popes to be "public heretics," but also declare them to have lost their office, and strive to convince others that they too must withdraw from communion with them. As the above examples demonstrate, just because a reasonable person has *evidence* to conclude someone is in heresy, does *not* suffice to render him a "public and notorious" heretic, at least according to the canonical meaning of the terms, which we will discuss in the following chapters. While Daly's purpose for writing his article was to highlight the rash tendency among Sedevacantists who mutually condemn each other as heretics over doctrinal and liturgical issues (a bitter fruit of Sedevacantism that we will discuss in chapter 21), we maintain that *it is even more rash to condemn the Pope and declare, by private judgment, that he has lost his office* – an office which is the very bridge between Heaven and Earth.[21]

---

[21] The term "Pontiff" comes from the Latin *pons* which means *bridge*.

Chapter 7

~ Theological Censures and "Hereticizing" ~

In the last chapter, we considered activities that render a *person* suspect of heresy. In this chapter, we direct our attention to material *error* and dangerous modes of expression, and to the degrees of theological censure attached to them by the Church. The Church applies theological or dogmatic censures to errors commensurate with their deviation from Catholic truth and to modes of expression that permit or give rise to confusion or error. Since theological censures are directed to doctrines and modes of expression, they are not to be confused with ecclesiastical censures, such as excommunication or interdict, which are directed to *persons*.

Heresy constitutes the greatest form of deviation from Catholic truth, insofar as it represents an immediate and direct opposition to what the Church teaches to be contained in the revealed Deposit, and so to be held with divine and Catholic faith. As we have seen, those who embrace heresy with pertinacity of the will are heretics. The *lesser* degrees of error we will discuss do *not* constitute such direct opposition to the faith, but nevertheless represent dangers to the integrity of the revealed Deposit. These errors too are rightly censured by the Church, but those who hold them are not in heresy, even materially.

The information in this chapter is extremely important when we remember that a Pope could only lose his office for heresy, *and nothing less than heresy*, on the sliding scale of theological censures. In fact, as we will see in Chapter 9, the deviation must not only be materially heretical, but also formally heretical *in the external forum*.[1] With this understanding of the distinction between heresy in the first degree, and those errors which are *less* than heresy, we will see that statements of the conciliar Popes which are declared to be "heresy" by Sedevacantists and others, almost never (if ever) constitute heresy properly so-called, but instead are qualified by a lesser category of theological censure.

There are a significant number of censures listed by the theologians, but they are generally broken out into three main categories: (1) the import (doctrine taught); (2) the mode of expression

---

[1] Both the matter of heresy (heretical doctrine) and the form of heresy (pertinacity) can be public or occult (secret). See Augustine, *A Commentary on the New Code of Canon Law*, vol. VIII, bk. 5, p. 17. Formal heresy in the external forum requires that *both* the matter and form are public, not occult.

(the terminology used to express the doctrine); and, (3) the consequences of a particular teaching. We will discuss each of these categories individually.

The Doctrine

Heresy in the First Degree: As we have learned, heresy is the pertinacious rejection of a dogma that must be believed with divine and Catholic faith. A dogma is a *revealed truth* – a truth contained within the sources of revelation (i.e., Scripture or Tradition) – which has been *definitively proposed* as such by the Church. A revealed truth that has not yet been definitively taught by the Church is considered a "material dogma."[2]

The Church can propose a truth definitively either by a solemn decree, or by the force of the Ordinary and Universal Magisterium. The former occurs by a single definitive act of the Extraordinary Magisterium (a Pope or council defining a doctrine); the latter takes place by virtue of a multitude of non-definitive acts which, when taken as a whole, clearly make it known that the doctrine is taught by the Church as a truth of the Faith.[3] According to the First Vatican Council, revealed truths that have been believed "always, everywhere and by all" are considered infallible by virtue of the Church's Ordinary and Universal Magisterium, even if they have not been solemnly defined by a Pope or council.[4]

If a revealed truth has been proposed by a single definitive act of the Extraordinary Magisterium, the doctrine is *de fide definita* (defined as of the Faith). If it has been proposed by the coalescing of a multitude of non-infallible acts by the Church's Ordinary and Universal Magisterium, it is *de fide* (of the Faith).[5] Revealed truths that have been definitively proposed by the Church, whether by a solemn decree or by her Ordinary and Universal Magisterium, must be believed with divine and Catholic faith (*de fide divina et catholica*). The clear, direct and conscious rejection of such a teaching constitutes heresy pure and simple, or heresy in the first degree.[6]

---

[2] A material dogma is a truth contained within the sources of revelation, which has not yet been defined by the Church. See Ott, *Fundamentals of Catholic Dogma*, p. 6; also Van Noort, *The Sources of Revelation*, p. 229.

[3] *The Sources of Revelation*, pp. 222-223.

[4] Vatican I, *Dei Filius* (April 24, 1870).

[5] *The Sources of Revelation*, pp. 226-227.

[6] *Catholic Encyclopedia* (1913), vol. III, p. 256.

If a doctrine has been clearly proposed by the Church as a truth to be held definitively, but not proposed as a *revealed truth*,[7] the doctrine is held only with ecclesiastical faith (*fides ecclesiastica*), not divine faith. Ecclesiastical faith is faith based upon the authority of the Church teaching, not the authority of God revealing. If the doctrine is not proposed as a revealed truth, the denial of the doctrine does not constitute heresy properly so-called.

The following is taken from Fr. Ayrinhac's *Penal Legislation in the New Code of Canon Law* (1920):

> "Formal heresy supposes the rejection of a truth proposed by the Church for our acceptance and known to be contained in the deposit of faith. If the truth was not known to be proposed by the Church for our belief, the heresy would be only material. If the truth was proposed by the Church *but not as contained in the deposit of faith*, to reject it would be an act of disobedience but not of heretical unbelief."[8]

For a doctrine to be qualified as heretical, the proposition must clearly and directly contradict a truth that must be believed with divine and Catholic Faith, in a plain and unmistakable way, such that no other interpretation is possible. As we will further see, the proposition cannot depend upon one or more steps of reasoning to prove this direct contradiction. This is why most doctrinal errors, particularly those couched in ambiguous, Modernist terminology, fall into one of the follow lesser categories of theological error.

Proximate Heresy: If the doctrine has not been strictly *defined* by the Extraordinary Magisterium in a solemn decree, or *clearly proposed* by the force of the Ordinary and Universal Magisterium (a doctrine believed always, everywhere and by all), but is only held by a majority of the Church's theologians as being a *revealed truth* (contained in the Word of God), the rejection of the doctrine is considered only "an opinion approaching heresy" (*sententia haeresi proxima*).[9]

Smacking of Heresy: The phrase "smacking of heresy" refers to "a proposition which offers serious grounds for fearing a heresy may be

---

[7] For example, a *theological conclusion* taught by the Church is not a *revealed truth*, and not proposed for belief by the Church as a revealed truth. A theological conclusion is a conclusion derived from two premises, one of which is a revealed truth and the other a truth known by reason. When the Church teaches a theological conclusion, it is only held with ecclesiastical faith, not divine and Catholic faith. More on this in Chapter 13.
[8] Ayrinhac, *Penal Legislation in the New Code of Canon Law*, p. 183 (emphasis added).
[9] Ibid.

hidden within it."[10] Many statements of the conciliar Popes fall into this category of error.

Suspect or Savoring of Heresy: If it is not strictly demonstrable that a proposition is directly opposed to an article of Faith, but can only be established with a certain degree of probability, the doctrine is termed "savoring or suspect of heresy" (*sententia de haeresi suspecta, haeresim sapiens*).[11] Fr. Garrigou-Lagrange explains: "Savoring of heresy...implies a fear of the poison of heresy being concealed, chocolate-coated, so to speak, in a proposition open to ambiguity."[12]

Erroneous in Theology: A doctrine that does not directly contradict a revealed truth, but involves *logical consequences* that are at variance with what has been revealed is "theologically erroneous" (*propositio theologice erronea*).[13] For example, the denial of a theological conclusion is qualified as erroneous.[14] One might place the rejection of Limbo of the children (*limbus infantium*) in this category, since the denial of this doctrine can logically lead to the rejection of defined doctrines.[15]

In an article on judging heresy, which included a list of "pitfalls to be avoided," the Sedevacantist John Daly correctly includes the following as a pitfall:

> "Giving the name 'heresy' to an error which is opposed to a doctrine to be believed with divine and Catholic faith, where the opposition is not direct and manifest but <u>depends on several steps of reasoning</u>: in such cases the qualification 'heresy' is not applicable before a definitive judgment on the part of the Church."[16]

---

[10] *The Sources of Revelation*, p. 285.

[11] Ibid.

[12] *The Theological Virtues: On Faith* (St. Louis & London: B. Herder Book Co., 1964), p. 436.

[13] *Catholic Encyclopedia* (1913), vol. II, p. 256.

[14] Ibid., vol. III, p. 532.

[15] For example, the Council of Florence, teaches the following: "We define also that...the souls of those who depart this life in actual mortal sin, *or in original sin alone*, go straightaway to hell, <u>but to undergo punishments of different kinds</u>" (Denz., 693). Limbo is the outer fringe of "hell." It is commonly believed to be a place of natural happiness, with the only "punishment" being the pain of loss (deprivation of the Beatific Vision). If one denies the existence of Limbo, he is either forced to hold that unbaptized infants who die in original sin go to the hell of the damned, or else he is forced to reject the above teaching which states that "those who die in original sin *only* go straightaway to hell" – that is "Limbo." The doctrine of Limbo is a theological conclusion that reconciles the justice and mercy of God.

[16] John Daly, *The Right to Judge Heresy* (2000). http://www.strobertbellarmine.net/judge heresy.html.

Mode of Expression

In addition to censuring doctrines that more or less approach or favor heresy, theologians also categorize dangerous modes of expression, which obscure doctrine or insinuate error. Fr. J. F. Sollier, Professor of Moral Theology at Marist College in Washington, D.C., listed the following modes of expression in the article he wrote on *Theological Censures* for the *Old Catholic Encyclopedia*:[17]

Ambiguous: A proposition is ambiguous when it is worded so as to present two or more senses, one of which is objectionable. For example: "The Church of Christ subsists in the Catholic Church." The phrase can be understood to mean that the Church of Christ is one and the same thing as the Catholic Church (true), or it can be understood to mean the Church of Christ only subsists within, but is not *identical* with, the Catholic Church (false).

Captious: A phrase is captious when acceptable words are used to express objectionable thoughts. For example, a recent Modernist theologian declared that the Catholic Church, as we know it today, is *at least* 1,500 years old. The statement is technically true since the Church is at least 1,500 years old, but it gives the impression that the Catholic Church, as we know it today, might not be 2,000 years old, which is false. Another example is the often-quoted statement that "Catholics reject nothing that is true in other (read: false) religions." Certainly, the statement itself is true, but it is incomplete and misleading. Catholics do not reject what is *true* in other religions, but they reject false religions, as such, *entirely* because of the errors they contain. By omitting this explanation, the statement gives the impression that the Catholic Church partially accepts these false religions as being more or less good and praiseworthy.[18] This favors the error of indifferentism which, when taken to its logical conclusion, ends in the many

---

[17] *Catholic Encyclopedia* (1913), vol. III, p. 532.

[18] "Certainly such attempts can nowise be approved by Catholics, founded as they are on that false opinion which considers all religions to be more or less good and praiseworthy, since they all in different ways manifest and signify that sense which is inborn in us all, and by which we are led to God and to the obedient acknowledgment of His rule. Not only are those who hold this opinion in error and deceived, but also in distorting the idea of true religion they reject it, and little by little, turn aside to naturalism and atheism, as it is called; from which it clearly follows that one who supports those who hold these theories and attempt to realize them, is altogether abandoning the divinely revealed religion" (Pius XI, *Mortalium Animos*, No. 2, January 6, 1928).

scandalous and sacrilegious "prayer meetings" that some of the conciliar Popes have held over the years.[19]

Evil-Sounding: A phrase is evil-sounding when improper words are used to express otherwise acceptable truths. For example, describing Jesus Christ as the "Grand Architect of the Universe," when such a term is used by Freemasons to describe the god of Freemasonry.

Offensive: Speech is offensive when the verbal expression is such, so as to rightly shock the Catholic sense and delicacy of faith. For example, if someone were to say "there is no Catholic God,"[20] or Catholics should not breed "like rabbits,"[21] this speech would offend the Catholic sense and pious ears.

Novelty of words: In light of the terminology used by Pope St. Pius X against the Modernists in his classic encyclical *Pascendi*, we have included "novelty of words" as a distinct category deserving of theological censure. This phrase aptly expresses a confusing mode of speech that has been employed regularly during the post-conciliar era, namely, utilizing words which, due to their novelty, do not have a fixed and definite theological meaning. The lack of a clear and fixed meaning gives rise to confusion, as each person is left to determine for himself what the word or phrase means.

For example, the term "ecumenism" is bantered about in various and diverse contexts, and used to justify an entire un-Catholic mentality. What does this term mean exactly, in the post-conciliar era, and how does the meaning differ from the ecumenical movement that originated in Protestantism, and which was explicitly condemned by Popes Pius XI and Pius XII?[22] Are we to understand the term as referring to the process by which Catholics seek to persuade Protestants to reject their grievous errors and convert to the one true Church? Or does it refer to some nonsensical and illogical "unity in diversity" that seeks to bring about a *convergence* between Catholics

---

[19] For example, both John Paul II (in 1986 and 2002) and Benedict XVI (in 2011) held interreligious prayer summits in Assisi, Italy during which time the Popes prayed with the leaders of false religions.
[20] "I believe in God, not in a Catholic God, there is no Catholic God." (Pope Francis, "The Pope's Chat With an Atheist," Catholic World Report, by James V. Shall, S.J., October 4, 2013.)
[21] After telling a story of a woman he met in Rome who had given birth to seven children by Caesarean section and was pregnant with an eighth, Pope Francis said: "Some think that — excuse the word — that in order to be good Catholics we have to be like rabbits. No." National Catholic Reporter, "Francis lambasts international aid, suggests Catholics should limit children," by Joshua J. McElwee, January 19, 2015.
[22] See Pius XI's encyclical *Mortalium Animos* (1928) and Pius XII's Instruction *De Motione Oecumenica* (1949).

and Protestants,[23] without the latter entering the Church[24] and embracing the Catholic Faith whole and inviolate?[25]

Words Have "Substance" and "Accidents"

The very purpose of words is to convey a meaning. According to the philosophical terminology of Thomistic metaphysics, words and phrases have a *substance* and *accidents*. The *substance* is the meaning; the *accidents* consist of the terminology used to express the meaning. Traditional theological terms have fixed theological meanings. Hence, when the terms are used, the meaning is immediately known, or can be known. Novel or new terminology does not communicate the same fixed and known meaning. Consequently, when "the novelty of words" (*accidents*) is employed, the listener is left wondering what precisely is meant (*substance*). This results in confusion that breeds division.

For example, with respect to ecclesiology, modern churchmen often speak of "full" versus "partial" communion with the Catholic Church. What, precisely, does this terminology mean? Does "partial communion" refer to a baptized non-Catholic who is invincibly ignorant of the Church, but willing to believe all, and united to the Soul of the Church by supernatural faith (something that is known to God alone)? Or does it refer to all who consider themselves Christians and simply profess some faith in Christ? While it might theoretically be possible to reconcile the terminology with the Church's traditional understanding after making certain qualifications, the lack of a fixed and definite meaning of the words has given rise to much confusion in the area of ecclesiology (the study of the Church). This has resulted in a

---

[23] Fr. Joseph Ratzinger wrote: "The Catholic Church has no right to absorb the other Churches... [A] basic unity — of Churches that remain Churches, yet become one Church — *must replace the idea of conversion*, even though conversion retains its meaningfulness for those in conscience motivated to seek it"(*Theological Highlights of Vatican II*, New York: Paulist Press, 1966, p. 73).

[24] In 2001, Cardinal Kasper, the head of Pontifical Council for the Promotion of Christian Unity, expressed the same hermeneutic of rupture as Fr. Ratzinger, when he said: "The decision of Vatican II, to which the Pope [John Paul II] adheres and spreads, is absolutely clear: Today we *no longer* understand ecumenism in the sense of ecumenism of a return, by which the others should 'be converted' and return to being 'catholics.' This was expressly abandoned by Vatican II. Today ecumenism is considered as the common road: all should be converted to the following of Christ...and not the fact that we should become 'Protestants' or that the others should become 'Catholics' in the sense of accepting the confessional form of Catholicism" (Rome, Adista, February 26, 2001, p. 9).

[25] "Whoever wishes to be saved, needs above all to hold the Catholic faith; unless each one preserves this whole and inviolate, he will without a doubt perish in eternity" (Athanasian Creed).

distorted understanding of the nature of the Church itself. Such confusion is avoided when traditional terminology is employed.

The Consequences

A third category of censure is directed against "such propositions as would imperil religion in general, the Church's sanctity, unity of government and hierarchy, civil society, morals in general, or the virtue of religion, Christian meekness, and humility in particular."[26] This category includes statements that are derisive of religion, subversive of the hierarchy, and destructive of governments. It includes statements that are scandalous, pernicious, or dangerous to morals, as well as those that are conducive to idolatry, superstition, or sorcery.[27]

The aforementioned categories are rightly censured by the Church due to the evil effects that they can cause. Such erroneous propositions and modes of speech can undermine the faith and good morals without being qualified, strictly speaking, as heretical. Consequently, a person who expresses a proposition that is qualified by a lesser degree of censure, or who uses a manner of speech that undermines the Faith, cannot be regarded as a having taught heresy, unless he *directly* denies a revealed truth that has been definitively proposed by the Church. If an erroneous statement is *directly* contrary to a theological conclusion, or if it requires several steps of reasoning to demonstrate that a proposition is contrary to a defined dogma, the proposition itself cannot be qualified as heresy.

Heresy vs. "Hereticizing"

The very learned Brazilian layman, Arnaldo da Silveira, coined the term "hereticizing." The word refers to the act of employing doctrinal errors and modes of expression that favor and lead to heresy, and which therefore rightly deserve a censure, *without, however, explicitly crossing the line into heresy.* He wrote:

> "Symmetrically, the accusation of heresy must also have a strictly explicit foundation and not a broad, analogous or generic one. In order for a proposition to be formally called heretical it must frontally and precisely counter a truth of Faith defined by the extraordinary papal or conciliar Magisterium or by the infallible

---

[26] *Catholic Encyclopedia* (1913), vol. III, p. 532.
[27] Ibid.

ordinary Magisterium. If this opposition is not strict, one has a text close to heresy, with the flavor of heresy, suspected of heresy, favoring heresy, or deserving some other theological censure, but one does not have an heretical text properly speaking."[28]

He then explains what he means by the term "hereticizing":

"Many words ending in 'ize' have been introduced in Western languages, especially over the last century. (…) 'socializing' or 'liberalizing' policies; an action can be 'Protestantizing' or modernizing (…) In all these expressions, the 'ize' termination and its derivatives carry the notion of a tendency toward a certain goal, a development of things and ideas toward a certain end, a movement in a defined, though not very explicit direction. One example should suffice: a 'leftizing' or left-leaning measure does not carry an explicit and obvious leftist charge; it is not really leftist but leads to the left directly or indirectly, albeit in a little noticed and perhaps even subliminal way."[29]

He then adds:

"The concept of hereticizing comprises all theological censures that fall short of heresy."[30]

Hereticizing has been a characteristic of post-conciliar "catechesis," and certainly a tactic of the Modernists to subvert the Faith. But this "hereticizing," while no doubt harmful and even destructive to the Faith, does not constitute heresy in the first degree (not even on the material level). This manner of communication, which "falls short of heresy," does not, of itself, sever the external profession of faith that unites a man to the Body of the Church.

Because these lesser errors do not constitute a clear and direct denial of an article of the faith, regardless of how much damage they have caused, they cannot be qualified, strictly speaking, as heresy. Hence, a Pope who expresses propositions that are erroneous or savoring heresy, or who uses a manner of speech that is ambiguous or offensive, and which justly deserves to be censured by the Church, cannot be regarded as having *taught heresy*, unless he directly denied a revealed truth that has been definitively proposed by the Church.

---

[28] Arnaldo Xavier da Silveira, "On the Extrinsic Theological Qualification of the Second Vatican Council" (June 29, 2013).
[29] Ibid.
[30] Ibid.

Further, as we will see in Chapter 9, even if a Pope were to profess a doctrine that was clearly and directly contrary to an article of faith, this would only constitute the material aspect of heresy, which, of itself, does not suffice for him to be considered a "manifest heretic."

It is important to realize that the very technique of Modernism intentionally *avoids* such clarity, which equivocates on doctrine and gives rise to multiple interpretations and explanations. This tactic enables the Modernists to insinuate error into the minds of their victims without clearly and directly denying an article of Faith. It is certainly a diabolical tactic, no doubt permitted by God as a trial of faith, but it falls short of explicit heresy.

For example, as we have seen, Vatican II's ambiguous teaching that "the Church of Christ subsists in the Catholic Church," does not directly contradict a truth of the Faith, even though it has been used by the Modernists to undermine and distort the nature of the Church by implying that the Church of Christ is not identical with the Catholic Church,[31] but extends beyond its visible boundaries[32] into other "ecclesiastical communities."[33]

Likewise, the statement that man has a right to religious liberty and freedom of conscience is in itself perfectly orthodox, provided one understands it to mean that man has the right to embrace and publicly profess the one true religion established by Christ, and the right to refuse evil based on the dictates of a well-formed conscience. However, the statement would be erroneous if it meant that man has a moral right to violate the First Commandment by practicing a false religion,

---

[31] "Some say they are not bound by the doctrine, explained in Our Encyclical Letter of a few years ago, and based on the sources of revelation, which teaches that *the Mystical Body of Christ and the Roman Catholic Church are one and the same thing.*" (Pope Pius XII, *Mystici Corporis Christi*, No. 27, emphasis added.)

[32] For example, Cardinal Ratzinger said: "Vatican II did not use Pius XII's expression according to which 'the Roman Catholic Church is the only Church of Christ.' Instead, it preferred the expression 'The Church of Christ subsists in the Catholic Church...because,' he said, 'it wished to 'affirm that the being of the Church as such is a larger identity than the Roman Catholic Church.'" (Frankfurter Allgemeine, English translation taken from the newsletter of Fr. Jean Violette, S.S.P.X., Toronto, October, 2000.)

[33] On June 29, 2007, the Congregation for the Doctrine of Faith rejected Ratzinger's hermeneutic of rupture (see above footnote), by explaining that the word "subsists" is to be understood as a diachronic rather than a synchronic subsistence – that is, an historical subsistence. In other words, that the Church of the Apostles "subsists" in the Catholic Church today. The document says: "In number 8 of the Dogmatic Constitution *Lumen gentium* 'subsistence' means this perduring, historical continuity ... the word 'subsists' can only be attributed to the Catholic Church alone precisely because it refers to the mark of unity that we profess..." (CDF, "Responses To Some Questions Regarding Certain Aspects Of The Doctrine On The Church," Cardinal Levada, Prefect, Angelo Amato, S.D.B. Secretary, June 29, 2007).

or that he should be permitted to publicly violate a just moral law by appealing to his "conscience" which does not reproach him for doing so.

The phrase "the Old Covenant, never revoked by God"[34] also smacks of heresy, since it favors the modern heresy that the *Mosaic* Covenant was never revoked by God,[35] and consequently "is salvific for Jews" who reject Christ. As problematic as the statement is, however, because it does not specify if the "Covenant" in question is the *Abrahamic* Covenant, which is certainly an "old covenant" that was never revoked by God, or perhaps the books of the Old Testament (as some have argued), the phrase leaves just enough room to prevent it from being qualified as heretical.

Similarly, the Modernists' nauseating praise for false religions that Catholics have been forced to endure for the past 50 years[36] certainly smacks of heresy and religious indifferentism, yet falls short of explicit heresy since 1) it does not constitute a denial that the Catholic Faith is the only true religion, and 2) even false religions can be said to promote some natural (though not supernatural) goods. Also, the offensive and scandalous statement that Muslims and Catholics "together worship the same God,"[37] also stinks of heresy and indifferentism; but it does

---

[34] "The first dimension of this dialogue, that is, the meeting between the people of the Old Covenant, *never revoked by God*, and that of the New Covenant, is at the same time a dialogue within our Church, that is to say, between the first and second part of her Bible, Jews and Christians, as children of Abraham…" (Quoted from Darcy O'Brien, *The Hidden Pope* (New York: Daybreak Books, 1998), p. 316. This same text also appears in *Pope John Paul II: On Jews and Judaism, 1979-1986,* published by the National Council of Catholic Bishops, Washington, D.C., 1987, p. 35.)

[35] The teaching that the Mosaic Covenant, or the "Old Law," has been revoked, can be found in Heb. 7:18; 8:7,13; 10:9; 2Cor. 3:14; Col. 2:14; Pius XII's *Mystici Corporis,* No. 19, Benedict XIV's *Ex Quo Primum,* No. 61, the papal Bull, *Cantate Domino* from the Council of Florence, and the Catechism of the Council of Trent, among other places.

[36] "I gladly take this occasion to assure those who follow the Buddhist religion of my deep respect and sincere esteem." (John Paul II, *General Audience,* January 11, 1995, *L'Osservatore Romano,* January 18, 1995, p. 11.) "Yours is a proud and sturdy people…bearing splendid fruits in art, religion, and human living. Your ancestors embraced such overwhelming spiritual worlds as Confucianism and Buddhism, yet made them truly their own, enhanced them, lived them and even transmitted them to others." (John Paul II, *Address at Airport in Korea,* May 3, 1984.) "Praise to you, followers of Islam…Praise to you, Jewish people…Praise especially to you, Orthodox Church…" (John Paul II, *Address,* May 22, 2002, *L' Osservatore Romano,* May 29, 2002, p. 4.)

[37] "…the followers of Islam who believe in the same good and just God." (John Paul II, Sermon, October 13, 1989, *L'Osservatore Romano,* October 23, 1989, p. 12.) "Today I would like to repeat what I said to young Muslims some years ago in Casablanca: 'We believe in the same God…'" (John Paul II General Audience, May 5, 1999, *L'Osservatore Romano,* May 12, 1999, p. 11.) "…Muslims; these profess to hold the faith of Abraham, and together with us they adore the one, merciful God, mankind's judge on the last day." (John Paul II, *The Catechism of the Catholic Church,* para. 841, p. 223.)

not involve a direct denial of any dogma, and the proposition itself has never been formally condemned by the Church. In fact, Pope Gregory VII used the same terminology in a letter to Emir Anazir, the Muslim King of Mauretania, when he said:

> "This affection we and you owe to each other in a more peculiar way than to people of other races because <u>we worship and confess the same God</u> though in diverse forms and daily praises and adore him as the creator and ruler of this world. For, in the words of the Apostle, 'He is our peace who hath made both one.'"[38]

Furthermore, the false implication that all men are saved,[39] which undermines the dogma of Original Sin, No Salvation Outside the Church (and many other revealed truths), nevertheless leaves just enough wiggle room for the proposition to escape the censure of heresy, provided it is understood to mean that all men are saved

---

[38] Emerton, Ephraim, *The Correspondence of Pope Gregory VII*, (New York; Oxford: Columbia University Press, 1932), p. 94. Because "Allah" means God or the Divinity in Arabic, some have argued that the object of Muslim worship is the true God Who is the Divine and Eternal Creator, vis-à-vis the pagans who worship finite creatures (*cf.* Rom. 1:20-23; Acts 17:22-25), which is a practice that Muslims condemn. This conclusion presupposes that such Muslims are not guilty of the voluntary sin of unbelief (hatred of God or truth) in which case they would not know God "in any way at all, because the object of his opinion is not God" (ST, II-II, q. 10, a. 3). This would explain why Pope Gregory VII (1073-1085), would have written what he did to the Muslim King. Even if one maintains that Muslims do not worship the same God, the proposition has never been declared heretical by the Church. It is important to note, however, that if one maintains that Mulsims do worship the one true God, it is certain that the public worship they offer Him is *false worship*, which is displeasing to God and constitutes an objective mortal sin against the First Commandment. For example, to the question "How may the first Commandment be broken?" (Q. 1146), the *Baltimore Catechism* responds "by false worship." In answer to the question: "How do we offer God false worship?" (Q. 1148), the same Catechism replies: "A. We offer God false worship by rejecting the religion He has instituted and following one pleasing to ourselves, with a form of worship He has never authorized, approved or sanctioned."

[39] "The Redemption event brings salvation to all, 'for each one is included in the mystery of the Redemption....'" (John Paul II, *Redemptoris Missio*, No. 4, Dec. 7, 1990.) "We are not dealing here with man in the 'abstract,' but with the real, 'concrete,' 'historical' man. We are dealing with each individual, since each one is included in the mystery of the Redemption and through this mystery Christ has united himself with each one forever." (John Paul II, *Centesimus Annus*, No. 53, May 1, 1991.) "...Jesus makes us, in himself, once more sons of his Eternal Father. He obtains, once and for all, the salvation of man: of each man and of all..." (John Paul II, Homily, April 27, 1980, *L'Osservatore Romano*, June 23, 1980, p. 3). While the other conciliar Popes also engaged in "hereticizing," given the breadth and sheer volume of his material, John Paul II could be said to be "the Great Hereticizer."

potentially, (and therefore redeemed objectively) based upon their response to sufficient grace which God gives to all men.[40]

Countless other examples could be provided, but the point is that the "hereticizing" that Catholics have been subject to since the close of the Second Vatican Council, as damaging as it has been, does not "frontally and precisely counter a truth of Faith" defined by the Church, in the words of Silveira. Therefore, the scandalous propositions would not constitute heresy "before a definitive judgment on the part of the Church," in the words of Daly. Moreover, one who advances such teachings, or even one who helps to "propagate heresy" is not considered a "manifest heretic," but is only "suspect of heresy," as we saw in Chapter 6, and therefore remains in the Body of the Church. Modernists, as dangerous as they are, are usually subtle and crafty enough to avoid explicit heresy. This explains why Pope St. Pius X could refer to them as being "in the very womb and heart of the Church," and as putting "into operation their designs for her undoing, *not from without but from within*" the Church.[41] Notice, he refers to them as being *within* the Church.

When the Church condemned the writings of the notorious Modernist Pierre Teilhard de Chardin, it did not condemn his pernicious errors as *heresy,* but instead said "it is quite evident that in philosophical and theological matters the mentioned works are filled with ambiguities and even serious errors that offend Catholic doctrine."[42] Hence, his writings were only condemned for ambiguity and "serious errors," which are qualified by lesser theological censures than heresy. Because of the "hereticizing" employed by Teilhard de Chardin, and the extreme danger such errors pose to the Faith, the Holy Office exhorted "all Ordinaries as well as the Superiors of Religious Institutes, Rectors of Seminaries and Directors of Universities, to protect minds, particularly of the youth, against the dangers of the works of Fr. Teilhard de Chardin and his associates."[43]

In spite of his pernicious writings, the notorious Modernist remained "with the Church" and consequently was always treated as a Catholic in good standing (even though he may have rightly been

---

[40] To clarify, it is correct to say all men have been redeemed and thus have sufficient grace to save their souls, and that Christ has united Himself to all men potentially based upon man's response to that grace. Failing to qualify the remarks savors heresy and is rightly deserving of censure, but it does not render the statement itself heretical or even necessarily erroneous.

[41] Pius X, *Pascendi,* September 8, 1907.

[42] Letter from the Holy Office, Given at Rome, June 30, 1962, *L'Osservatore Romano,* July 1, 1962, p. 1.

[43] Ibid.

considered suspect of heresy). He died during the reign of Pope Pius XII, and in 1955 was buried as a Roman Catholic in the cemetery at the Jesuit novitiate, St. Andrew's-on-the-Hudson.

It is also important to remember that even if a *proposition* (the matter) is qualified as heretical, in order for a *person* to be considered a heretic in the external forum, pertinacity would also have to be sufficiently established.[44] If we recall the cases of Erasmus of Rotterdam and Michel de Bay, which were discussed in Chapter 6, we have historical examples of individuals whose errors likely crossed the line into heresy (certainly in the case of de Bay), yet whose lack of public pertinacity prevented them from being considered heretics by their contemporaries.[45]

Recalling what was discussed in Chapter 6, Erasmus referred to the Invocation of the Blessed Virgin and the saints as idolatry; he condemned monasteries, ridiculed the religious life and condemned their vows and rules; he opposed clerical celibacy; he mocked auricular confession (confession to a priest privately), papal indulgences, the use of relics of saints, and fasting. He taught that man is justified by faith alone (*sola fide*) and didn't hesitate to cast doubt upon the authority of the Scripture and ecumenical councils. He even went so far as to declare it "rash to call the Holy Ghost God."[46]

Yet, in spite of all this, St. Alphonsus Ligouri, a Doctor of the Church, concluded his history on Erasmus (in which the above-mentioned errors are all listed) by saying: "We may conclude with Bernini, that he (Erasmus) died with the character of an unsound Catholic, *but not a heretic...*" Why didn't St. Alphonsus consider him a heretic, when some of his errors would likely be qualified as materially heretical? The reason he gives is because Erasmus "submitted his writings to the judgment of the Church."[47]

In other words, in spite of the material errors and even heresies he publicly held, and in spite of his university training, his brilliant intellect, his "wonderful memory and an extraordinarily quick power

---

[44] The way in which pertinacity is established will be discussed in Chapter 9, "Proving the Crime of Heresy."

[45] Although in de Bay's case, one could argue that he was pertinacious, given his persistence in his heresies after being formally warned and his errors condemned (and by the Popes themselves). This case shows how St. Bellarmine viewed such a judgment to be a matter for the Church and not individual Catholics, including himself.

[46] All of these are listed by St. Alphonsus in his book *The History of Heresies and Their Refutation*, vol. I (Dublin: Published by James Duffy, Wellington Qua, 1847), Chapter XL, p. 291.

[47] Ibid., p 292.

of comprehension,"[48] there was not sufficient evidence to demonstrate the existence of pertinacity, and consequently Erasmus was not considered by St. Alphonsus to be heretic, but only an "unsound Catholic." The same can be said for the conciliar Popes, whose doctrinal errors have rendered them "suspect of heresy," but who cannot be said to have *willfully* departed from defined dogmas of the Faith. We will further address this issue of pertinacity in Chapter 9, in the context of the *crime* of "public and notorious" heresy.

---

[48] *Catholic Encyclopedia* (1913), vol. V, p. 510.

Chapter 8

~ Can a Pope Fall Into Heresy? ~

We will now begin to discuss the questions related to papal heresy and the loss of office for a heretical Pope. In this chapter, we will begin by considering two related questions: (1) Can a Pope fall into personal heresy internally? (2) Can a Pope profess errors and heresy externally?

It is the common opinion among theologians that a Pope can fall into personal heresy (internally), and even public and notorious heresy (externally). The Church has never taught that a Pope is *impeccable* (unable to sin), and there are historical examples discussed below where Popes have indeed taught errors – even errors that have been condemned by the Church and are now qualified as *heretical*. While the charism (supernatural gift) of infallibility will prevent a Pope from erring when he meets the necessary conditions, according to Our Lord's promise to St. Peter (*cf.* Mt. 16:18-19), this charism will in no way prevent the Pope from teaching error or heresy when he operates outside of these limited parameters, nor will it prevent him from committing actual sin. Consequently, infallibility will not prevent a Pope from committing the personal sin of heresy, nor will it prevent the Pope from teaching heresy publicly, when the conditions for infallibility are not met.

The common opinion that a Pope can become a heretic is taught in the consecration sermon of Pope Innocent III, who in 1198 said:

> "Truly, he [the Pope] should not flatter himself about his power, nor should he rashly glory in his honor and high estate, because the less he is judged by man, the more he is judged by God. Still the less can the Roman Pontiff glory because he can be judged by men or rather, can be shown to be already judged, <u>if, for example, he should wither away into heresy;</u> because he who does not believe is already judged. In such a case it should be said of him: 'If salt should lose its savor, it is good for nothing but to be cast out and trampled underfoot by men.'"[1]

The Abbé de Nantes provides another quote from the same Pope:

---

[1] Pope Innocent III, Sermon IV, *Between God and Man: Sermons of Pope Innocent III* (Washington, D.C.: Catholic University of America Press, 2004), pp. 48-49.

"The great Innocent III comments on this, applying it humbly to himself: 'For me the faith is so necessary that, whereas for other sins my only judge is God, for the slightest sin committed in the matter of the faith I could be judged by the Church.'"[2]

Pope Adrian VI (1522-1523) also stated that "it is beyond question" that a Pope can err in matters of faith, and even "teach heresy":

"I say: If by the Roman Church you mean its head or pontiff, it is beyond question that he can err even in matters touching the faith. He does this when he teaches heresy by his own judgment or decretal. In truth, many Roman pontiffs were heretics. The last of them was Pope John XXII († 1334)..."[3]

Accordingly, theologians throughout the centuries have held that a Pope can become a heretic.[4] For example, the sixteenth century Dominican, Domingo de Soto (d. 1560), taught:

"(...) though some masters of our time sustain that the Pope cannot be a heretic in any way, the common opinion is however the opposite one. For though he might not be able to err as Pope – that is, he could not define an error as an article of faith, because the Holy Spirit will not permit it – nevertheless as a private person he can err in faith, in the same way that he can commit other sins, because he is not impeccable."[5]

---

[2] *Serm. Consecrat. Pontif. Rom.*, P. L. CCXVII, col. 656.

[3] The text is taken from *IV Sentent, Quaestio de confirm.* Quoted by De Bossuet (d. 1704) in "Oeuvres complètes," Tome XVI (Paris: Adrien Le Clère, imprimeur-libraire, rue; Lille: L. Lefort, imprimeur-libraire, 1841), p. 686.; Original Latin also cited in "Paus Adriaan VI," by Andreas Franciscus Chrisstoffels (Stoomdrukkerij Loman, Kirkerger and Van Kersteren, Amsterdam, 1871), p. 96. According to Church historian and theologian Döllinger (writing under the pen name "Janus"), this comment was made while Pope Adrian was a Professor of Theology in Louvain prior to his election to the pontificate. Döllinger notes that the statement was well-known at the time since it was included in his principal work (see "The Pope and the Council," by "Janus," i.e., Johannes Joseph Ignaz von Döllinger), second edition (Rivingtons; London; Oxford; and Bambridge, 1869), p. 376. We should note that Döllinger denied the dogma of papal infallibility before and after it was defined. So while his historical research and facts may be of use, one should remain cautious with respect to the soundness of his judgment.

[4] Venerable Pope Pius IX also recognized the danger that a Pope could be a heretic when he said: "If a future pope teaches anything contrary to the Catholic Faith, do not follow him" (quoted by Fr. Boulet in "Is that Chair Vacant? An SSPX Dossier on Sedevacantism").

[5] Soto, Comm. in IV Sent., dist. 22, q. 2, a. 2, p. 1021.

In his famous book *The Catholic Controversy*, the great Doctor of the Church, St. Francis de Sales (d. 1622), wrote:

> "Under the ancient Law, the High Priest did not wear the Rational except when he was vested with the pontifical robe and was entering before the Lord. Thus we do not say that the Pope cannot err in his private opinions, as did John XXII; <u>or be altogether a heretic</u>, as perhaps Honorius was."[6]

Referring to the teaching of Pope Innocent III, Mattheus Conte a Coronata also said:

> "It cannot be proven however that the Roman Pontiff, as a private teacher, cannot become <u>a heretic</u> — if, for example, he would contumaciously <u>deny a previously defined dogma</u>. Such impeccability was never promised by God. Indeed, Pope Innocent III expressly admits such a case is possible."[7]

In the *Manual of Dogmatic Theology* (1906) by Wilhelm and Scannell, we also read:

> [T]he Pope's authority would not be injured if, when not exercising it (*extra judicium*), he *professed a false doctrine*... The Infallibility and Indefectibility of the Church and of the Faith require on the part of the Head [i.e., the Pope], that ... the law of Faith should always be infallibly proposed; but this does not require the infallibility and indefectibility of his own interior Faith and of his extrajudicial utterances."[8]

The Jesuit theologian Fr. Paul Laymann (d. 1635), who was considered "one of the greatest moralists and canonists of his time,"[9] explained that it is more probable than not that a Pope could fall into notorious heresy:

> "It is <u>more probable</u> that the Supreme Pontiff, as concerns his own person, <u>could fall into heresy, even a notorious one, by reason of which he would deserve to be deposed by the Church, or rather declared to be separated from her.</u> ... The proof of this assertion is

---

[6] St. Francis de Sales, *The Catholic Controversy* (Charlotte, North Carolina: TAN Books and Publishers, Inc., 1986), pp. 305-306.
[7] Coronata, *Institutiones Iuris Canonici* (Rome: Marietti, 1950), vol. 1, p. 316.
[8] Wilhelm, Joseph, and Scannell, Thomas, *A Manual of Catholic Theology*, vol. I, 3rd ed. (New York; Cincinnati; Chicago: Benzinger Bros., 1906), pp. 45-46 (emphasis added).
[9] *Catholic Encyclopedia* (1913), vol. IX (*Fr. Paul Laymann*), p. 95.

that neither Sacred Scripture nor the tradition of the Fathers indicates that such a privilege [i.e., being preserved from heresy when not defining a doctrine] was granted by Christ to the Supreme Pontiff: therefore the privilege is not to be asserted. The first part of the proof is shown from the fact that the promises made by Christ to St. Peter cannot be transferred to the other Supreme Pontiffs insofar as they are private persons, but only as the successor of Peter in the pastoral power of teaching, etc. The latter part is proven from the fact that it is rather the contrary that one finds in the writings of the Fathers and in decrees: not indeed as if the Roman Pontiffs were at any time heretics *de facto* (for one could hardly show that); <u>but it was the persuasion that it could happen that they fall into heresy</u> and that, therefore, if such a thing should seem to have happened, it would pertain to the other bishops to examine and give a judgment on the matter; as one can see in the Sixth Synod, Act 13; the Seventh Synod, last Act; the eight Synod, Act 7 in the epistle of [Pope] Hadrian; and in the fifth Roman Council under Pope Symmachus."[10]

Before proceeding, permit us a brief detour. We have already noted the deference that Sedevacantists give to the ecclesiology of St. Robert Bellarmine. As we will further demonstrate in the next chapter, their deference is based upon a misunderstanding of Bellarmine's teaching that a heretical Pope automatically "ceases to be Pope" without a declaration from the Church (Bellarmine was indeed referring to the divine consequence for the crime of heresy, but *after* having been determined by the Church and not private judgment – more on this later). However, Bellarmine also believed that a Pope could not actually fall into personal heresy, even though Popes Innocent III and Adrian VI expressly taught the contrary. The Sedevacantists generally side with Bellarmine, and not Popes Innocent and Adrian. Why?

Perhaps the Sedevacantists side with Bellarmine because this position (that a Pope cannot fall into heresy) makes their case much easier to "prove," since a "hereticizing" Pope could certainly be considered by a reasonable person to have lost interior faith. This is a common opinion among many traditional Catholics, to whom it seems likely that the Vatican II Popes lost the faith internally, due to their many words and actions which render them suspect of heresy and propagators of heresy. Accordingly, if the Sedevacantist can convince these Catholics that a true Pope cannot lose the faith, then these Catholics would be left to conclude that the conciliar Popes are not true

---

[10] Laymann, Theol. Mor., bk. 2, tract 1, ch. 7, p. 153.

Popes. Many Catholics have been deceived by this type of argumentation.

Further, because Sedevacantists base their thesis primarily upon the teaching of Bellarmine (who said a manifestly heretical Pope automatically loses his office), many of them exalt Bellarmine to a "super-Magisterial" status, and thus follow his position (that a Pope cannot be a heretic) over that of Popes Innocent and Adrian (who said a Pope can be a heretic). And they defend Bellarmine's opinion almost as if it were a dogma, even though Bellarmine himself admitted that the common opinion was contrary to his own.

To show the extent to which Sedevacantists go in defending Bellarmine, we can look to the example of the lay Sedevacantist apologist John Lane. Lane has gone so far as to publicly declare that the quote from Pope Adrian VI, who taught that a Pope can "teach heresy," is a fabrication. Lane even impugned the good name of Fr. Dominique Boulet who used this citation from Pope Adrian in his article "Is That Chair Vacant? A SSPX Dossier on Sedevacantism." In response to the article, Lane rashly accused Fr. Boulet of being *"deceived* by fraudulent quotes which he has *carelessly* lifted from some place unknown."[11] On his website, Lane further denigrates the priest with his smug comment: "Poor Fr. Boulet - he literally grabbed quotes from the Net, it seems, and cobbled them together."[12]

When Lane himself later discovered that the "unknown" sixteenth century citation was not simply grabbed from the Net, but quoted in an early twentieth century book (published in 1904),[13] Lane, with no evidence whatsoever, claimed that the quotation included in the book had been "invented" by the author (another rash and baseless accusation). Because the 1904 book had been placed on the Index, Mr. Lane used this fact to support his assertion that the quotation was "invented" by the author (as if the book being on the Index in any way implies that the quote was invented). When the same quotation was later cited by Robert Siscoe in an article published in *The Remnant* newspaper,[14] Mr. Lane referred to it on his website as the "invented quote from Pope Adrian VI, taken from a book [the 1904 book] which St. Pius X put on the Index." Lane then accused the non-Sedevacantist

---

[11] Lane, "Concerning a SSPX Dossier on Sedevacantism, By Rev. Dominique Boulet, SSPX" (emphasis added), which may be found at http://www.novusordowatch.org /sspx_dossier_sede. pdf.
[12] See http://www.strobertbellarmine.net/viewtopic.php?f=2&t=1387&view = previous.
[13] Book: *L'Infaillibilité du pape et le Syllabus*, (Besançon: Jacquin; Paris: P. Lethielleux, 1904).
[14] Robert Siscoe, "Can the Church Depose an Heretical Pope?," *The Remnant* newspaper (published online November 18, 2014), http://remnantnewspaper.com/web/index.php /articles/item/1284-can-the-church-depose-an-heretical-pope.

authors who have cited the quotation of being "complete charlatans without the slightest affection for the moral law or truth itself."[15]

In order to recover the good name of Fr. Boulet, and any others tarnished by the false accusations of John Lane, we provide an even more complete version of the quotation, in the original Latin, taken from the writings of an author *who died two centuries before Mr. Lane claims the quotation was "invented"* (which proves that the quotation was not "invented" by the author of the 1904 book, as Mr. Lane claims). The quotation from Pope Adrian VI was quoted by Bishop Bossuet (1627-1704) in his *Complete Works* edited and published in Paris in 1841:

> *"Ad secundum principale de facto Gregorii, <u>dico primo quod si per Ecclesiam Romanam intelligatur caput ejus, puta Pontifex, Certum est quod possit errare, etiam in his, quae tangent fidem, haeresim per suam determinationem aut Decretalem asserendo; plures enim fuere Pontifices Romani haeretici. Item et novissime fertur de Joanne XXII</u>, quod publice docuit, declaravit, et ab omnibus teneri mandavit, quod animas purgatae ante finale judicium non habent stolam, quae est clara et facialis visio Dei."*[16]

Since Mr. Lane did not hesitate to accuse those who cited the quotation (which he falsely claimed to have been "invented" and first published in 1904) as being "complete charlatans" who lack "the slightest affection for the moral law or truth itself," we hope that he offers a public apology for his rash judgement and slandering of the good name of Fr. Boulet.[17] If not, one might be led to conclude that it is the public slanderer himself (Mr. Lane) who lacks "the slightest affection for the moral law or truth itself." Having cleared up this point, which we hope will help serve to restore the good name of Fr. Boulet, we now return to our consideration of whether a Pope can fall into heresy.

While it is true that St. Bellarmine personally held to what he called the "pious opinion" of Albert Pighius,[18] namely, that a Pope could not

---

[15] http://sedevacantist.com/viewtopic.php?f=2&t=1771.
[16] De Bossuet, 'Oeuvres complètes', Tome XVI (Paris: Adrien Le Clère, imprimeur-libraire, rue; Lille: L. Lefort, imprimeur-libraire, 1841), p. 686 (underlined portion previously cited above in English).
[17] Calling Mr. Lane's offense the sin of detraction is giving Lane the benefit of the doubt, because "the detractor narrates what he at least honestly thinks is true. Detraction in a general sense is a mortal sin, as being a violation of the virtue not only of charity but also of justice." *Catholic Encyclopedia* (1913), vol. IV, p. 757.
[18] See *Hierarch. Eccles.*, bk. IV, ch. 8.

fall into *personal* heresy, Bellarmine himself, as we noted, admitted that "the common opinion is the contrary."[19]

Pastor Aeternus

Several years ago, a lengthy article was published[20] which attempted to interpret Chapter IV of Vatican I's Constitution, *Pastor Aeternus* as teaching that a Pope cannot fall into personal heresy (cannot lose the virtue of faith). The author essentially argued that the First Vatican Council raised to the level of dogma the opinion of St. Bellarmine and Albert Pighius (who both held the minority opinion that a Pope cannot lose his personal faith) and that, consequently, the contrary opinion can no longer be defended. Without getting into a detailed analysis of this author's novel interpretation of Vatican I (which, as far as we know, is shared by no one), suffice it to say that his private interpretation of *Pastor Aeternus* directly contradicts the official interpretation of the document given during the Council.

In his famous four-hour speech, delivered during Vatican I, Bishop Vincent Gasser, the official Relator (spokesman) for the Deputation of the Faith, stated that the Pighius/Bellarmine opinion was precisely *not* what the document intended to teach. During the speech, which provided the Church's official interpretation of the document to the Council Fathers, Bishop Gasser responded to what he called "a most grave objection that has been made from this podium, namely, that we wish to make the extreme opinion of a certain school of theology a dogma of Catholic Faith. Indeed this is a very grave objection, and, when I heard it from the mouth of an outstanding and most esteemed speaker, I hung my head sadly and pondered well before speaking. Good God, have you so confused our minds and our tongues that we are misrepresented as promoting the elevation of the extreme opinion of a certain school to the dignity of dogma...?"[21]

What was this extreme opinion Bishop Grasser spoke of? He goes on to explain:

> "As far as the doctrine set forth in the Draft goes, the Deputation is unjustly accused of wanting to raise an extreme opinion, namely, that of Albert Pighius, to the dignity of a dogma.

---

[19] *De Romano Pontifice*, bk. II, ch.. 30.
[20] James Larson, "The Sifting: The Never-Failing Faith of Peter." http://www.waragainst being.com/node/44.
[21] Rev. James T. O'Connor, *The Gift of Infallibility* (San Francisco, California: Ignatius Press, 1986), p. 58.

For the opinion of Albert Pighius, which Bellarmine indeed calls 'pious and probable,' was that the Pope, as an individual person or a private teacher, was able to err from a type of ignorance <u>but was never able to fall into heresy or teach heresy</u>."[22]

After quoting the text in which St. Bellarmine agrees with the opinion of Albert Pighius, Bishop Gasser concluded by saying "it is evident that the doctrine in the proposed Chapter [of *Pastor Aeternus*] is *not* that of Albert Pighius or the extreme opinion of any school..."[23]

Cardinal Camilo Mazzella (1833-1900), who served as the Prefect of the Congregations of the Index, of Studies, and of Rites, directly addressed the same point. He wrote:

> "(...) it is one thing that the Roman Pontiff cannot teach a heresy when speaking *ex cathedra* (what the council of the Vatican defined); <u>and it is another thing that he cannot fall into heresy, that is become a heretic as a private person. On this last question the Council said nothing</u>, and the theologians and canonists are not in agreement among themselves in regard to this."[24]

Suffice it to say that the teaching of Popes Innocent III and Adrian VI (that a Pope can fall into personal or even public heresy) is not contrary to the teaching of the First Vatican Council. Even if one were to argue that Popes Innocent and Adrian were teaching as private theologians and not in their capacity as Popes, their teaching would still be considered the common theological opinion and express the mind of the Church. This explains why the dogmatic manual of Msgr. Van Noort, which was published many decades after the Council, noted that "some competent theologians do concede that the Pope when not speaking *ex cathedra* could fall into *formal heresy*."[25] Clearly, neither Msgr. Van Noort, nor the other "competent theologians" he is referring to, considered this teaching to be at variance with Chapter IV of *Pastor Aeternus*.

Papal Infallibility

There is a great deal of confusion over the issue of papal infallibility, by which God prevents the Pope from erring when he

---

[22] Ibid., pp. 58-59 (emphasis added).
[23] Ibid.
[24] Card. C. Mazzella, *De religione et Ecclesia*, Sixth Edition, (Prati: Giachetti, filii et soc., 1905), p. 817, n. 1045 (emphasis added).
[25] *Christ's Church*, p. 294 (emphasis added).

defines doctrines for the universal Church. Many erroneously believe that the charism would prevent a man raised to the pontificate from erring when speaking on matters of faith and morals. In reality, the charism of infallibility only prevents the Pope from erring in very limited and narrowly defined circumstances. It is *not* a habitually *active* charism of the papal office.

As we saw in Chapter 1, infallibility is not to be confused with inspiration, which is a positive divine influence that moves and controls a human agent in what he says or writes; nor is it to be confused with Revelation, which is the communication of some truth by God through means which are beyond the ordinary course of nature.[26] Infallibility pertains to safeguarding and explaining the truths *already* revealed by God, and contained within the Deposit of Faith,[27] which was closed with the death of the last Apostle.[28] Because infallibility is only a negative charism (*gratia gratis data*), it does not inspire a Pope to teach what is true or even defend revealed truths, nor does it "make the Pope's will the ultimate standard of truth and goodness,"[29] but simply prevents him from teaching error under certain limited conditions.

During Bishop Gasser's address at Vatican I, he said:

> "In no sense is pontifical infallibility absolute, because absolute infallibility belongs to God alone, Who is the first and essential truth, and Who is never able to deceive or be deceived. All other infallibility, as communicated for a specific purpose, has its limits and its conditions under which it is considered to be present. The same is valid in reference to the infallibility of the Roman Pontiff. For this infallibility is bound by certain limits and conditions..."[30]

The First Vatican Council fixed the conditions for papal infallibility when the Pope exercises his Solemn or Extraordinary (Pontifical) Magisterium:

> "We teach and define as a divinely revealed dogma that when the Roman pontiff speaks *ex cathedra*, that is, when, in the exercise of his office as shepherd and teacher of all Christians, in virtue of his supreme apostolic authority, he defines a doctrine concerning faith or morals to be held by the whole Church, he possesses, by the

---

[26] *Catholic Encyclopedia* (1913), vol. III (*On Revelation*), p. 1.
[27] *Christ's Church*, p. 120.
[28] St. Pius X, *Lamentabili Sane*, No. 21, 1907.
[29] *Christ's Church*, p. 290.
[30] *The Gift of Infallibility*, p. 49.

divine assistance promised to him in blessed Peter, that infallibility which the divine Redeemer willed his Church to enjoy in defining doctrine concerning faith or morals."[31]

Here we see that the divine assistance of Christ is present only when a Pope, (1) using his supreme apostolic authority in the exercise of his office as teacher of all Christians, (2) defines a doctrine concerning faith or morals, (3) to be held by the universal Church. Such definitive acts of the Extraordinary Papal Magisterium are relatively rare, and generally issued to combat an error or settle a doctrinal controversy. Fr. Nau explains:

> "But this method of presentation, sometimes called the extraordinary Magisterium, is only an exceptional occurrence. It is most often used to reply to an error, or put an end to a controversy or, where the intention is to obviate in advance all possible doubts by solemnly pronouncing that a truth which is already admitted is now made a dogma of the faith."[32]

At the First Vatican Council, Cardinal Franzelin emphasized the same point in the context of the Pope's Extraordinary Magisterium when exercised through ecumenical councils:

> "It was never the aim of the holy Councils, in proposing the definition of a doctrine, to set forth Catholic doctrine in itself, in so far as it was already possessed by the faithful in complete tranquility – the aim is always to make clear the errors which are threatening some doctrine and to exclude them by a declaration of the truth which is directly opposed to such errors."[33]

With this as a background, let us now examine *Pastor Aeternus'* three required elements for papal infallibility, when exercised through the Pope's Extraordinary Magisterium, under the following headings:

---

[31] Vatican I, *Pastor Aeternus*, Chapter IV. Note that the Pope's Solemn or Extraordinary Magisterium is distinguished from the Ordinary and Universal Magisterium which can also teach infallibly when the teaching is (1) proposed as a revealed truth and (2) in accord with the universality of Catholic Tradition (Vatican I, *Dei Filius*). The infallibility of the Ordinary and Universal Magisterium will be discussed in Chapter 14. For now, we are addressing only the Pope's Solemn or Extraordinary Magisterium.
[32] Dom Paul Nau, *Pope or Church? The Infallibility of the Church's Ordinary Magisterium*, (Kansas City, Missouri: Angelus Press, 1998), p. 10.
[33] *Collectio lacensis.* T. VII *Friburgi Brisgoviae*, 1890, c. 1611-1612, cited in the above *Pope or Church?*, p. 16.

1. Matters of Faith or Morals

The first condition for papal infallibility is that it is limited to doctrinal definitions or final definitive statements *concerning faith or morals*. This scope of papal infallibility is the same with respect to any other organ of infallibility in the Church (e.g., ecumenical councils).[34] Theologians distinguish between primary and secondary objects of infallibility.

The *primary object* of infallibility consists of the truths that have been formally revealed by God, being contained within the sources of revelation – namely, Scripture or Tradition – and extends to both positive and negative decisions of a definitive nature. Positive decisions include such things as dogmatic decrees of a council, *ex cathedra* statements from a Pope, and official creeds of the Church. Negative decisions consist of "the determination and rejection of such errors as are opposed to the teaching of Revelation."[35] When the Church definitively proposes for belief a truth on faith or morals that has been formally revealed by God, it must be believed with *divine and Catholic faith*. Divine and Catholic faith is faith in the authority of God revealing and the infallible Church teaching.[36]

The *secondary object* of infallibility includes those matters which, although not formally revealed, are connected with and intimately related to the revealed Deposit. The secondary object includes such things as *theological conclusions* (inferences deduced from two premises, one of which is revealed and the other verified by reason) and *dogmatic facts* (contingent historical facts). These are so closely related to revealed truths that they are said to be virtually contained within the revealed Deposit.

With varying degrees of certitude, theologians also list *universal disciplines* and the *canonizations of saints* within this category (which we will address in Chapter 14 and 16, respectively). Van Noort explains that the secondary objects of infallibility "come within the purview of infallibility, not by their very nature, but rather by reason of the revealed truth to which they are annexed. As a result, infallibility embraces them only secondarily. It follows that when the Church passes judgment on matters of this sort, it is infallible only insofar as they are connected with revelation."[37] Secondary objects of infallibility

---

[34] *Christ's Church*, p. 291.
[35] Ott, *Fundamentals of Catholic Dogma*, p. 299.
[36] See Tanquerey, *Dogmatic Theology*, vol. 1, (New York: Desclée Company; Paris, Rome, Tournai), p. 204.
[37] *Christ's Church*, p. 110.

which have been definitively proposed by the Church are held with ecclesiastical faith. Ecclesiastical faith is based on the authority of the Church teaching, not on the authority of God revealing.[38]

It is *de fide* that the Church speaks infallibly when issuing a definitive and binding declaration on revealed truths (the primary object); but before the First Vatican Council could rule with certainty on whether or not the Church can make an *infallible* pronouncement on secondary objects, the Council was halted by the Franco-Prussian War, and the subsequent invasion of Rome, and it was never reconvened. The Church has never ruled definitively on whether infallibility embraces the secondary objects. For this reason, the position that the Church can teach infallibly on secondary objects is not *de fide* (of the faith), but is only considered theologically certain (*sententia certa*). Van Noort qualifies the canonization of saints by the lesser degree of certitude known as the *common opinion*.[39]

To conclude this point, the object of infallibility consists of doctrines concerning faith and morals that have been revealed by God (primary object), and matters that are intimately related to the revealed Deposit (secondary object). It is *de fide* (of the faith) that the Church speaks infallibly with respect to the former, and it is qualified as *theologically certain* that the Church's infallibility embraces the latter, at least to some extent, with the exception of the canonization of saints, which was only qualified by some as the *common opinion* prior to Vatican II (and, as we will see in Chapter 16, may no longer be the common opinion of today).

2.   Doctrines Defined for the Universal Church

The second condition for papal infallibility is the *clear intent* to *define a doctrine* concerning faith or morals to be held by the universal Church. The Pope commits the authority Christ granted to him only to the degree in which he intends to do so. If a Pope merely teaches a doctrine, yet does so without *intending* to issue a doctrinal definition for the universal Church, this condition is not satisfied. Consequently, the possibility of error is not excluded.

---

[38] See Tanquerey, *Dogmatic Theology*, vol. 1, p. 204.
[39] According to Van Noort, canonization of saints is only considered "the common opinion today" (see *Christ's Church*, p. 117). See also John Salza's article "The Validity of the Canonizations – Against a Fact There is No Argument," *The Remnant* newspaper, May 31, 2014 (www.johnsalza.com), which provides ample evidence that the canonizations of John XXIII and John Paul II are also not infallible (and even invalid) under the Church's current legislation.

Furthermore, the Pope must provide a *definition* of doctrine to which the faithful can intellectually assent. A definition is a clear statement of belief, a *proposition* which can be read, understood, and definitively held. If the Pope fails to provide an actual "definition," then such an act would clearly not fit the narrowly defined parameters of infallibility as defined in *Pastor Aeternus*.[40] Today, for example, we hear that we must accept ecumenism, collegiality, religious liberty, freedom of conscience, the "spirit of Vatican II", etc. without ever receiving a clear definition of what these terms mean. This is one of the distinguishing characteristics of Modernism, which abhors clarity and thrives in the murky waters of ambiguity and undefined terminology. But undefined or ambiguous expressions are not doctrinal definitions.

When Pius IX defined the dogma of the Immaculate Conception, he didn't simply say "we declare, pronounce and define that all Catholics must believe in the Immaculate Conception," and then leave Catholics with the job of figuring out precisely what the term meant. After using the *term* twenty six times in the Apostolic Constitution, when it came to the section in which the doctrine was defined, he explained precisely what is meant. He wrote:

> "We declare, pronounce, and define that the doctrine which holds that the most Blessed Virgin Mary, in the first instance of her conception, by a singular grace and privilege granted by Almighty God, in view of the merits of Jesus Christ, the Savior of the human race, was preserved free from all stain of original sin, is a doctrine revealed by God and therefore to be believed firmly and constantly by all the faithful."[41]

---

[40] We are speaking here of infallibility of the Extraordinary Magisterium. As will be discussed in Chapter 14, the Ordinary and Universal Magisterium is also infallible. This means that if a Pope is teaching what the Church has always taught, and what has always been believed to be an article or aspect of faith (even if not strictly defined), it is infallible. We have an example of this in Paul VI's encyclical *Humanae Vitae*, which condemned contraception. Even though the teaching in the encyclical was not infallible by virtue of the Extraordinary Magisterium (since Paul VI did not issue a "definition"), nevertheless, the teaching was infallible by virtue of the Ordinary and Universal Magisterium, and therefore requires the assent of faith. Cardinal Felici explained this following the issuance of the encyclical. From *L'Osservatore Romano*: "On this problem we must remember that a truth may be sure and certain, and hence it may be obligatory, even without the sanction of an *ex cathedra* definition. So it is with the encyclical *Humanae Vitae*, in which the pope, the supreme pontiff of the Church, utters a truth *which has been constantly taught by the Church's Magisterium* and which accords with the precepts of Revelation" (*L'Osservatore Romano*, October 19, 1968, p.3, emphasis added).
[41] Pope Pius XI, Apostolic Constitution *Ineffabilis Deus*, December 8, 1854.

The same clarity is required for infallibility to be engaged during a council. For example, when the Council of Trent defined the doctrine of transubstantiation, it defined precisely what is meant so that Catholics would know precisely what must be believed. The Council declared:

> "By the consecration of the bread and wine there takes place a change of the whole substance of the bread into the substance of the body of Christ our Lord and of the whole substance of the wine into the substance of his blood. This change the holy Catholic Church has fittingly and properly called transubstantiation" (Session XIII, chapter IV).[42]

The Council then anathematized anyone who denied this doctrine.

> "If anyone denies that in the sacrament of the most Holy Eucharist are contained truly, really and substantially the body and blood together with the soul and divinity of our Lord Jesus Christ, and consequently the whole Christ, but says that He is in it only as in a sign, or figure or force, let him be anathema" (Session XIII, Canon I).[43]

This shows the way in which the Church defines a doctrine. If a Pope or council fails to *define* – to provide a *clear* and *definitive* explanation of what must be believed - infallibility is not engaged.

When the First Vatican Council defined the infallibility of the Roman Pontiff, it referred to Our Lord's words in the Gospel of St. Matthew, chapter 16, as a basis for the dogmatic definition – "That thou art Peter; and upon this rock I will build my church, and the gates of hell shall not prevail against it" (v.18).[44] Note that in the very next verse, Our Lord says to St. Peter, "And I will give to thee the keys of the kingdom of heaven. And whatsoever thou shalt bind upon earth, it shall be bound also in heaven" (v.19). We thus see a connection between "the gates of hell" and St. Peter's "binding" authority. From this we can see that one of the guarantees associated with this divine promise is that *St. Peter and his successors will never "bind" the Church to heresy.*

This is because the "gates of hell" refers to heresy and heretics. For example, Pope Vigilius says "…we bear in mind what was promised

---

[42] Council of Trent, Concerning The Most Holy Sacrament Of The Eucharist, Sess. XIII, Chapter IV, DS 1642.
[43] Council of Trent, Canons on the Most Holy Sacrament of the Eucharist, Sess. XIII, Canon I, Denz. 1651.
[44] See First Vatican Council, Session 4, chapter 4 (July 18, 1870).

about the holy Church and Him who said the gates of hell will not prevail against it (by these we understand the death-dealing tongues of heretics)...”[45] Pope St. Leo IX also says: “The holy Church built upon a rock, that is Christ, and upon Peter...because by the gates of hell, that is, by the disputations of heretics which lead the vain to destruction, it would never be overcome.”[46] St. Thomas Aquinas also says: “Wisdom may fill the hearts of the faithful, and put to silence the dread folly of heretics, fittingly referred to as the gates of hell.”[47]

Thus, whether the “tongues” and “disputations” of heretics attack the Church from without or within (even by the tongue of the Pope himself), Christ will never allow the heresy to prevail against the Church, which would happen if the Pope “bound” the faithful to the heresy by imposing it as a matter of faith to be believed by the Church. But, as we have noted, to be protected by infallibility, the Pope's binding authority must be invoked intentionally and consciously - otherwise the act of binding cannot properly be said to have taken place.

Regarding the mode of expression for an infallible *ex cathedra* pronouncement, there is no specific formula required, nor is any type of solemnity necessary. What *is* necessary, however, is the Pope's *clear intention* of giving a definitive and universally binding decision.[48] This condition of infallibility also applies to the Pope whether acting alone, or within the context of an ecumenical council. What this means is that it is possible for a papal encyclical, or even a document issued by a general council of the Church that has been ratified by a Pope, to contain error, as long as the Pope (or council) did not intend to bind the Church to a doctrinal definition. Moreover, even when infallibility is engaged, it does not necessarily cover an entire document, but only the specific definitions, or definitive decisions, contained therein.

The following is taken from the pre-Vatican II manual of dogmatic theology by Msgr. Van Noort:

> “The Church's rulers are infallible not in any and every exercise of their teaching power; but only when, using all the fullness of their authority, they clearly intend to bind everyone to absolute assent or, as common parlance puts it, when they ‘define’ something in matters pertaining to the Christian religion. That is

---

[45] Pope Vigilius, *Second Council of Constantinople*, 553 A.D.
[46] Pope Leo IX, *In pax terra hominibus*, September 2, 1053 A.D.
[47] *Intro. To Catena Aurea.*
[48] The will of the Pope may discerned, for example, by the solemn nature of the instrument the Pope chooses to convey a pronouncement, and the mode of expression he uses in the pronouncement.

why all theologians distinguish in the dogmatic decrees of the councils or of the popes between those things set forth therein by way of definition and those used simply by way of illustration or argumentation. For the intention of binding all affects only the definition…And if in some particular instances the intention of giving a definitive decision were not made sufficiently clear, then no one would be held by virtue of such definitions, to give the assent of faith: a doubtful law is no law at all."[49]

Notice that even within dogmatic decrees issued by a Pope or council, only the *definitions* contained *within* them are protected by infallibility (e.g., dogmatic canons with their accompanying anathemas). Furthermore, it is necessary that the Pope's intention of giving a definitive doctrinal definition be made sufficiently clear for infallibility to be engaged. If the Church is left guessing, questioning, and endlessly debating whether the Pope (or council) intended to bind the universal Church to a particular teaching, it is a very good indicator that the definitive character is lacking for an infallible proposition. And our tradition has well established ways by which this definitive intent is made clear, for example, the use of the "*anathema sit*" formula, stating that one must believe this under pain of excommunication, or under pain of losing the faith, or similar such statements.

The Case of Pope John XXII

One example of a Pope publicly teaching error (which would later be condemned as a *heresy*), but without invoking his binding authority, is John XXII (1322-1334). The Pope taught publicly that the souls of the faithful departed would only possess the Beatific Vision after the Last Judgment. In a sermon delivered to a distinguished audience consisting of Cardinals, prelates, and theologians, the Pope taught: "The souls of the faithful departed do not enjoy that perfect or face to face vision of God, in which, according to St. Augustine (in Psalm XC, Sermon, No. 13), consists their full reward of justice; nor will they have that happiness until after the general judgment. When, and only when, the soul will be re-united to the body, will this perfect bliss come to man - coming to the whole man composed of body and soul, and perfecting his entire being."[50]

---

[49] *Christ's Church*, p. 104.
[50] The words of John XXII are recorded in Fr. V. F. O'Daniel, "John XXII And The Beatific Vision," published by The Catholic University Bulletin. vol. VIII, (Washington, D.C.: The Catholic University of America, 1912), pp. 56-57.

Pope John XXII taught that after being purified in Purgatory, the souls would be placed "under the altar" (Apoc. 6:9) while awaiting the General Resurrection of the Body. He claimed that during this time, the souls would be consoled and protected by the humanity of Christ, but would not possess the Beatific Vision.[51]

Pope John XXII taught this error in a tract published prior to his election (while still Cardinal di Osa), and also taught it publicly in a series of sermons he gave in Avignon, France during his reign as Pope. As Pope, he even tried to force it on the Faculty of Theology in Paris, before eventually retracting the error on his deathbed. The following account is taken from the 1913 *Catholic Encyclopedia*:

> "In the last years of John's pontificate there arose a dogmatic conflict about the Beatific Vision, which was brought on by himself...Before his elevation to the Holy See, he had written a work on this question, in which he stated that the souls of the blessed departed do not see God until after the Last Judgment. After becoming pope, he advanced the same teaching in his sermons. In this he met with strong opposition, [with] many theologians, who adhered to the usual opinion that the blessed departed did see God before the Resurrection of the Body and the Last Judgment, even calling his view heretical. A great commotion was aroused in the University of Paris when the General of the Minorites and a Dominican tried to disseminate there the pope's view (...) In December, 1333, the theologians at Paris, after a consultation on the question, decided in favor of the doctrine that the souls of the blessed departed saw God immediately after death or after their complete purification; at the same time they pointed out that the pope had given no decision on this question but only advanced his personal opinion, and now petitioned the pope to confirm their decision. (...) Before his death he [John XXII] withdrew his former opinion, and declared his belief that souls separated from their bodies enjoyed in heaven the Beatific Vision."[52]

After the death of John XXII, his successor, Pope Benedict XII, infallibly defined that the souls of the faithful departed, after being purified in Purgatory if necessary, do indeed possess the Beatific Vision prior to the Last Judgment.[53]

---

[51] Ibid. p. 56; Marc Dykmans in *Les sermons de Jean XXII sur la vision béatifique*, Rome: Gregorian University, 1973; see also Christian Trottman, *La vision béatifique. Des disputes scolastiques à sa définition par Benoît XII*, Ecole Française de Rome, Rome 1995, pp. 417-739).

[52] *Catholic Encyclopedia* (1913), vol. VIII, pp. 432-433.

[53] Bull *Benedictus Deus*, January 29, 1336.

After noting the formal condemnation of the error following the death of John XXII, the Catholic historian Roberto de Mattei said:

> "Following these doctrinal decisions, the thesis sustained by John XXII must be considered formally heretical, even if at that time the Pope sustained that it was still not defined as a dogma of faith. St. Robert Bellarmine who dealt amply with this issue in De Romano Pontifice[54] writes that John XXII supported a heretical thesis, with the intention of imposing it as the truth on the faithful, but died before he could have defined the dogma, without therefore, undermining the principle of pontifical infallibility by his behavior. The heterodox teaching of John XXII was certainly an act of ordinary magisterium regarding the faith of the Church, but not infallible, as it was devoid of a defining nature."[55]

The case of Pope John XXII proves that a Pope can teach public errors against the Faith – even errors contrary to *material dogmas*,[56] which, therefore, could later be declared *heretical*. While the infallible definition (that the departed souls of the just enjoy the Beatific Vision) was not issued until after the death of John XXII, this truth is part of the Deposit of Faith, which explains why the Pope's teaching was immediately and vigorously opposed by theologians (even as *heretical*) well beyond the confines of Avignon. As we saw, Pope Adrian VI called John XXII a "heretic" and, as de Mattei correctly notes, Pope Benedict XII's definition officially renders John XXII's teaching "formally heretical."

At the end of his recorded CD talk "Counterfeit Catholicism vs. Consistent Catholicism," the Sedevacantist preacher Gerry Matatics fields a question from an attendee who asks why Pope John XXII didn't lose his office for teaching heresy. After Matatics properly explains the three conditions for papal infallibility defined in *Pastor Aeternus*, he says that John XXII did not violate infallibility because he did not "impose" his error upon the universal Church (even though St. Bellarmine said John XXII did intend to impose it upon the Church).

Of course, if the failure to "impose" (using Matatics' own words) erroneous doctrines upon the Church saves John XXII from falling

---

[54] *Opera omnia, Venetiis,* 1599, Book. IV, chap. 14, coll. 841-844.

[55] De Mattei, "A Pope who Fell into Heresy, and a Church that Resisted: John XXII and the Beatific Vision," January 28, 2015 (emphasis added) at http://www.rorate-caeli.blogspot.com/2015/01/a-pope-who-fell-into-heresy-church-that.html.

[56] Material dogmas are truths contained within the sources of revelation, and therefore definable, but which have not yet been defined by the Church. See Ott, *Fundamentals of Catholic Dogma,* p. 6; and Van Noort, *The Sources of Revelation,* p. 229.

from office, then the same would also apply to the post-conciliar Popes, since none of them definitively "imposed" their errors upon the Church either (and the failure to meet this one condition alone means they have not violated infallibility, even if their errors qualified as material heresies). While the conciliar Popes may have urged the faithful to join them in the ecumenical venture of Vatican II, Catholics have *no* obligation to do so, and remain Catholics in good standing, even if they refuse those novel doctrines and practices that are not in conformity to Tradition. Mr. Matatics' admission is fatal to his own thesis. What applies to John XXII applies to John XXIII and the other post-Vatican II Popes as well.

The case of John XXII also shows us that there will always be "papaloters" who follow the Pope into any novelty or heresy whatsoever. For example, even though there was strong opposition to John XXII's teaching by the "traditionalist" Catholics (the "Recognize and Resist" camp of the day), the head of the Franciscans, Gerard Ordon, eagerly supported the Pope's novel teaching. Ordon and others (including a Dominican preacher in Paris) promoted the Pope's errors, which caused an uproar at the University of Paris. This resulted in its theologians publicly opposing *the Pope* (not just those who agreed with him, as we see by some "conservatives" in our day) and asking that he (the Pope) correct his error.

The case of John XXII further demonstrates that a Pope who teaches error publicly - even an error contrary to a *material dogma* - does not automatically lose his office for doing so, even though, no doubt, if faced with such a situation, some would overreact by declaring him to be a "false Pope." Such accusations were, in fact, levied against John XXII.

The *Catholic Encyclopedia* article on John XXII, which was cited above, spoke of the "great commotion" that ensued when certain individuals began to disseminate the Pope's error. As one would expect, at the time there were some unstable souls who went too far in their reaction to the papal crisis. One of these individuals was the rebellious William of Ockham, who has been called "the first Protestant."[57]

William of Ockham is commonly held to be a prime mover in the error of Nominalism, and advocated a "secular absolutism," that denied the right of the Popes to exercise temporal power, or to interfere in any way in the affairs of the Empire.[58] Although he was never formally condemned as a heretic, a commission of six theologians

---

[57] *Catholic Encyclopedia* (1913), vol. XV (*William of Ockham*), p. 636.
[58] Ibid.

appointed by the Pope drew up two lists of his doctrines which more or less approached heresy. During the doctrinal crisis caused by Pope John XXII, the unruly William of Ockham went too far by declaring the Pope to be a "false Pope" who lost his office due to heresy. He wrote:

> "Because of the errors and the heresies mentioned above and countless others, I turn away from the obedience of the false Pope...because of his errors and heresies the same pseudo-Pope is heretical, deprived of his papacy, and excommunicated by Canon Law itself, without need of further sentence...
>
> If anyone should like to recall me [to his obedience] ... let him try to defend his constitutions and sermons, and show that they agree with Holy Scripture, or that a Pope cannot fall into the wickedness of heresy, or let him show by holy authorities or manifest reasons that one who knows the Pope to be a notorious heretic is obliged to obey him" (*Tractatus de Successivis*)."[59]

Needless to say, the Church never agreed with the claim of "the first Protestant," who held that John XXII was a false Pope who lost his office for teaching heresy. But what the historical example of John XXII and William of Ockham shows us is that if faced with the crisis of a Pope teaching errors publicly, we should not be surprised to find an overreaction by unbalanced souls who rashly declare the Pope to have lost his office. Such an overreaction is precisely what we see with today's Sedevacantists, whose lack of stability and general spiritual disorder are no secret[60] (not to mention a lack of integrity, as we have unfortunately seen, for example, with Fr. Cekada and John Lane). In fact, one former Sedevacantist said that when he was entangled in the movement, he found nothing but spiritual disorder *in all the Sedevacantists he ever met* – himself included. He wrote:

> "I myself had once been a Sedevacantist. Only in retrospect can I honestly see the great bitterness and lack of charity that this led to on my part. I have found nothing but spiritual disorder – to one extent or another – in all the Sedevacantists I have ever met (myself included and foremost among them). It would be best to

---

[59] Cited in Rama Coomaraswamy's *The Destruction of the Christian Tradition* (Bloomington, Indiana: World Wisdom, Inc., 2006), p. 117.
[60] For example, the Sedevacantist apologist John Lane admitted that "people who get interested in Sedevacantism become unstable in their spiritual lives, confused ..., and very often more broadly disturb the peace of the parish. I've observed all of this myself, and so often that I can't answer it. It's true." (http://sedevacantist.com/viewtopic.php?f=2&t=1771).

210

leave out the numerous downfalls - in scandalous fashion - of bitter Sedevacantists."[61]

We will deal with the bad fruits of Sedevacantism in Chapter 21. For now, suffice it to say that every papal crisis has had those who overreact in one direction or the other, whether it be the William of Ockhams of the fourteenth century who separated themselves from John XXII, or the John Lanes of our day who have declared all the Popes for the past 50-plus years to be "antipopes." But to William of Ockham's credit, he did not go nearly as far as John Lane and his many Sedevacantist colleagues, who now claim that all the *other* Bishops of the world – or at least all who are in charge of the dioceses – have also publicly defected from the faith and lost their office.

An Ecumenical Council Condemns Sedevacantism

To curb such overreactions from unstable individuals, the Fourth Council of Constantinople (869-870) condemned anyone who separated himself from his Patriarch by private judgment (i.e., Sedevacantism) before the matter had been settled by a synod, attaching the grave penalty of excommunication to any monk or layman who did otherwise:

> "As divine scripture clearly proclaims, 'Do not find fault before you investigate, and understand first and then find fault.' And does our law judge a person without first giving him a hearing and learning what he does? Consequently this holy and universal synod justly and fittingly declares and lays down that no lay person or monk or cleric should separate himself from communion with his own patriarch before a careful inquiry and judgment in synod. (…) If anyone shall be found defying this holy synod, he is to be debarred from all priestly functions and status if he is a bishop or cleric; if a monk or lay person, he must be excluded from all communion and meetings of the church [i.e. excommunicated] until he is converted by repentance and reconciled" (Canon 10).[62]

As we can see, an ecumenical council of the Catholic Church has flatly condemned the Sedevacantist thesis. It has done so by condemning the error by which one, in an act of private judgment,

---

[61] Laszlo Szijarto, "Pope Sifting - Difficulties with Sedevacantism," *Angelus Press Magazine*, October 1995, pp. 11-16 (emphasis added).
[62] Fourth Council of Constantinople, Canon 10, (869-870), http://www.papal encyclicals. net/Councils/ecum08.htm.

separates himself from communion with his Patriarch or Bishop (the Pope is the Bishop of Rome). Clearly the John Lanes, the Gerry Matatics, and Fr. Cekadas of today think they know better than the Council Fathers of Constantinople and Pope Adrian, who ratified its decrees, since they themselves have done, and seek to persuade others to do, precisely what the Council expressly forbade, and to which it attached the grave penalty of excommunication.[63]

This condemnation of deposing lawful religious authority by private judgment is rooted in the divinely revealed words of Our Lord Himself, Who taught His disciples not to usurp such authority, even including the very high priest (Caiaphas) who put Him to death:

> "Then Jesus spoke to the multitudes and to his disciples, Saying: The scribes and the Pharisees have sitten on the chair of Moses. All things therefore whatsoever they shall say to you, observe and do: but according to their works do ye not; for they say, and do not" (Mt. 23:1-3).[64]

If Our Lord Himself acknowledged the legitimacy of the office-holders of the Old Covenant "church" (the successors to Moses), how much more does He will us to do the same for the office-holders of the New Covenant Church, and most notably the successors to St. Peter? Especially when Christ tells us to "hear the church" (Mt. 18:17) in the same Gospel?[65] Indeed, just as Christ instructed His disciples to

---

[63] And if anyone wonder if it is possible for an evil man to be elected and reign as a legitimate Pope, the Council of Constance (1414-1418) condemned the following propositions of Hus and Wycliffe: "if the Pope is foreknown and evil, and consequently a member of the devil, he does not have the power over the faithful given to him by anyone, unless perchance by Caesar." – CONDEMNED (Session VIII: error No. 8 of John Wycliffe). "If the Pope is wicked, and especially if he is foreknown to damnation, then he is a devil like Judas the apostle, a thief and a son of perdition and is not the head of the holy church militant since he is not even a member of it." – CONDEMNED (Session XV: error No. 20 of John Hus).

[64] John Lane argues that the comparison of Our Lord's recognition of the Mosaic hierarchy fails because "The Old Testament Church was not the perfect unity of Faith and Charity which the Mystical Body of Christ is, and therefore a lack of Faith did not result in loss of membership in that Church as it does in ours." But the fact that Our Lord forbade the usurpation of the authorities of the *imperfect* Old Testament church only underscores the recognition He wills us to give to those who hold offices in the perfect society of the Catholic Church, especially that of the Vicar of Christ. Also, we demonstrated in Chapter 3 that "a lack of Faith" does *not* "result in the loss of membership" in the Church, as Lane erroneously suggests. See Lane's "Concerning an SSPX Dossier on Sedevacantism, by Rev. Dominique Boulet, SSPX," at http:// www.novusordowatch.org /sspx_dossier_sede.pdf.

[65] There is an interesting parallel between these passages in St. Matthew's Gospel, chapter 18 and chapter 23. In Matthew 23, Our Lord tells His disciples to recognize the Jewish

recognize those who have "sitten on the chair of Moses," He requires the same from us for those who sit on the Chair of St. Peter.

The Case of Pope Honorius

The case of Pope Honorius (625-638) is another historical example of a Pope who not only fell into heresy, but was officially condemned by the Church as a heretic.[66] Pope Honorius promoted the heresy of the Monothelites who held that Christ had only one will.[67] The Pope did this in official letters to Sergius I, the Patriarch of Constantinople. The letters were sent at the time when St. Sophronius was defending the Faith by publicly opposing the Monothelite heresy (and for which Honorius actually rebuked St. Sophronius). This was also after Pope St. Leo the Great had defined the union of the two natures of Christ in A.D. 449 (which can be said to affirm the two wills, which the Monothelites denied),[68] and which was reiterated by the Council of Chalcedon in 451.[69]

In one of his letters to Sergius, Pope Honorius said: "As regards defining a dogma of the Church, while confessing there are two natures united in Christ, <u>we should not definitively state whether there are one or two operations</u> in the Mediator between God and men."[70] Pope Honorius refused to "confirm the brethren" by defending the Faith in the face of the Monothelite heresy, and consequently placed truth and error on the same level.[71] While some have argued that Honorius did not personally embrace the Monothelite heresy, his letter to Sergius suggests otherwise (as the Council of Constantinople itself remarked); and he certainly failed in his duty to condemn the errors,

---

religious authorities (vv.2-3) and then points out their "binding" teaching authority in the next verse (v.4). Similarly, in Matthew 18, Our Lord tells His disciples to "hear the church" (v.17) and then points out the Apostles' "binding" teaching authority in the next verse (v.18). Our Lord is revealing that no matter how evil His Popes may be, they not only hold valid offices, but also possess infallible teaching authority (which will be discussed in more detail beginning in Chapter 13).

[66] We could also point to Pope Liberius (352-366) who accepted a semi-Arian Creed and excommunicated St. Athanasius, and Pope Paschal II (1099-1118) who was accused of propagating heresy by promoting lay investiture (where secular powers used to name the next bishops and abbots) against the testimony of tradition and the explicit teaching of his immediate predecessor.

[67] Jesus Christ, who is true God and true man, has both a human and divine will.

[68] Denz., 143-144.

[69] Ibid., 148.

[70] Jacques-Paul Migne, Pope Honorius I, "*Epistola ad Sergium,*" *Patrologia Latina,* vol. 80, col. 475.

[71] Pope Honorius' actions are quite similar to those of the conciliar Popes, who have placed the Catholic religion on the same level as other religions.

which of itself amounts to an approval of them, according to the well-known statement of Pope St. Felix (483-492): "Not to oppose error is to approve it; and not to defend truth is to suppress it."

For his actions (and lack thereof), in the face of the Monothelite heresy, Pope Honorius was formally condemned as a heretic by three ecumenical councils of the Catholic Church (Constantinople III in 680-681, Nicea II in 787, and Constantinople IV in 869-870), as well as a local Church council (Trullo in 692).

In the Third Council of Constantinople, Session XIII (March 28, 681), we read:

> "After we had read the doctrinal letters of Sergius of Constantinople to Cyrus or Phasis and to Pope Honorius, as well as the letter of the latter to Sergius, we find that these documents [including the letter from Honorius] are quite foreign to the apostolic dogmas, also to the declarations of the holy Councils, and to all the accepted Fathers of repute, and [that they] <u>follow the false teachings of the heretics</u>; therefore we entirely reject them, and execrate them as hurtful to the soul. But the names of these men must also be <u>expelled from the holy Church</u>, namely, that of Sergius (...) <u>We anathematized them all</u>. And along with them, <u>it is our unanimous decree that there shall be expelled from the Church and anathematised, Honorius, formerly Pope of Old Rome</u>, because of what we found in his letter to Sergius that in all respects he followed his view and confirmed his impious doctrines...<u>To Honorius, the heretic, anathema!</u>"[72]

In Session XVI (August 9, 681), the council also declared: "Anathema to the heretic Sergius, to the heretic Cyrus, <u>to the heretic Honorius</u>, to the heretic Pyrrhus." In Session XVIII (September 16, 681), we further read:

> "The creeds (of the earlier Ecumenical Synods) would have sufficed for knowledge and confirmation of the orthodox faith. Because, however, the originator of all evil still always finds a helping serpent, by which he may diffuse his poison, and therewith finds fit tools for his will, we mean Theodore of Pharan, Sergius... <u>also Honorius, Pope of Old Rome</u>... so he [that is, the devil] failed not, by them, to cause trouble in the Church by the scattering of the

---

[72] Taken from Fr. Charles Joseph von Hefele, *A History of the Councils of the Church, from the Original Documents,* vol. V (Edinburgh: T&T Clark, 1896), pp. 166-167.

heretical doctrine of one will and one energy of the two natures of the one Christ."[73]

Pope St. Agatho died before the conclusion of the Council, which was ratified by his successor, Pope St. Leo II, who reigned from 681 to 683. In his letter formally confirming the decrees of the Council, Pope Leo said: "We anathematize the inventors of the new error, that is, Theodore, Sergius, ... and also Honorius, who did not attempt to sanctify this Apostolic Church with the teaching of Apostolic tradition, but by profane treachery permitted its purity to be polluted."[74] Note further that from the eighth to the eleventh century, all newly elected Popes had to swear in the Papal Oath before assuming office that they acknowledged Constantinople III had anathematized Pope Honorius (as seen in the *Liber Pontificalis* and *Liber Diurnus*). Also, the lessons in the Roman Breviary (for the office of St. Leo II), up to the sixteenth century, listed Honorius as among those anathematized and excommunicated by the same council.

Notwithstanding the foregoing historical facts affirming the Church's repeated condemnations of Pope Honorius as a heretic for following "the false teachings of the heretics" and its order for Honorius' letters to be burned,[75] the Sedevacantist author, John Lane, had the audacity to claim that "it is commonly admitted" that Honorius' letter to Sergius was "completely orthodox."[76] Commonly admitted by whom? Lane doesn't say, nor does he provide even a single citation to justify his gratuitous assertion. But whoever Lane is referring to, it obviously doesn't include the Popes and bishops gathered in the Councils who issued these condemnations, and those who, by a "unanimous decree," anathematized Honorius and expelled him from the Church.

---

[73] *A History of the Councils of the Church, from the Original Documents,* p. 183.
[74] *The Catholic Encyclopedia* (1913), vol. VII, p. 452. We also read in *The Prosphoneticus to the Emperor:* "...we cast out of the Church and rightly subject to anathema all superfluous novelties as well as their inventors: to wit...Honorius, who was the ruler of Rome, as he followed them in these things"; and in *The Imperial Edict Publicly Posted:* "As he [Emperor Constantine] recognized the five earlier Ecumenical Synods, so he anathematized all heretics...also Pope Honorius, who was their adherent and patron in everything, and confirmed the heresy." Nicea II declared: "We have also anathematized...the doctrine of one will held by Sergius, Honorius...or rather, we have anathematized their own evil will." Constantinople IV declared: "So, we anathematize...Honorius of Rome...who followed the false teachings of the unholy heresiarchs."
[75] *Catholic Encyclopedia* (1913), vol. VII, p. 452.
[76] Lane, "Concerning a SSPX Dossier on Sedevacantism, By Rev. Dominique Boulet, SSPX." http://www.novusordowatch.org /sspx_dossier _sede.pdf.

Lane's assertion that Honorius' "letter" was "completely orthodox" also does violence to the wording of the condemnation itself, which explicitly states that Honorius was anathematized "because of what we found in his letter to Sergius that in all respects he followed his view and confirmed his impious doctrines." How does Lane defend his position in light of the explicit wording of the Council texts? He does so by resorting to his old tactic of casting doubt upon its authenticity – just like he did with the earlier quotation from Pope Adrian. When faced with the clear and undeniable teaching of the Third Council of Constantinople, Lane had the hubris to claim that "the acts of the Council are of doubtful authenticity,"[77] even though they were ratified in their totality by Pope St. Leo II and have been universally accepted by the Church ever since! Once again, Lane doesn't provide a single quotation from any authority to justify his assertions.[78]

Of course, as a Sedevacantist, Lane *must* argue that Honorius wasn't *really* a heretic because he knows the Church, after anathematizing Honorius for heresy, did not nullify his papal acts, nor did the Church declare him an "antipope" who lost his office for heresy (a fact which by itself negates the Sedevacantist thesis). Thus, Lane and his Sedevacantist colleagues are forced to defend their position with allegations of inauthenticity (which, in this case, would have to include the condemnations found in *three* ecumenical councils!), as well as publicly impugning the good names of those who disagree with them, as if such smear tactics will intimidate others from challenging their assertions.

For example, reverting back to his old bag of tricks, Lane accuses Fr. Boulet - the same priest whom he falsely accused of being "deceived" and "careless" for citing what he claimed was an "invented" quotation from Pope Adrian - of being "rash and unnecessarily injurious to the reputation of a sovereign pontiff."[79] What was Fr. Boulet's crime? He dared to quote directly from the Third Council of Constantinople in his article against Sedevacantism. That's the offense for which Lane sought to discredit him. For Lane to refer to Boulet's scholarship as "rash" and "injurious to the reputation" of a

---

[77] Ibid.

[78] Lane says the theory of inauthenticity was taught by the historian Baronius, but conveniently failed to mention that this theory has long been abandoned. And Mr. Lane cannot claim ignorance of this fact, since the same encyclopedia article he cited, two paragraphs later, says "the theory (Baronius, Damberger) of a falsification of the Acts being now quite abandoned" (Hefele, III, 299-313)." *Catholic Encyclopedia* (1913), vol. IV (article on the Third Council of Constantinople), p. 310.

[79] Lane, "Concerning a SSPX Dossier on Sedevacantism, By Rev. Dominique Boulet, SSPX."

Pope for simply quoting an ecumenical council, when he himself has publicly declared the last six Popes to be "antipopes," is an example of stupefying hypocrisy.

As a backstop argument, Lane actually claims that if the decrees of the Council are authentic, Pope St. Leo II was at odds with the reasoning of the Council which he himself ratified, by claiming that Pope Leo did not condemn Honorius for teaching heresy or for believing it, but *only* because he "fostered it by his negligence."[80] In other words, even though Pope Leo approved the Council's condemnation of Honorius for positively "scattering" the "heretical doctrine" by his "letter," Lane wants us to believe that Leo disagreed with the Council's rationale, believing instead that this was a case of mere passive negligence on the part of the Honorius.[81] So, for John Lane, either the condemnations of Honorius by Constantinople III are inauthentic, or they are authentic, but not actually believed by the Pope who approved them. For Sedevacantists, the more problematic the historical facts are, the more desperate and indeed ridiculous their arguments to refute them become.

Also note that in the very article in which John Lane impugned the good name of Fr. Boulet for quoting the Council of Constantinople, Lane himself quotes from the 1913 *Catholic Encyclopedia* article on Pope Honorius. The reason this is significant is that the article itself *directly refutes Lane's assertion that Pope Leo only condemned Honorius for negligence*. It also directly contradicts Lane's claim that the view of Pope Leo differed from that of the council which he himself affirmed. For example, after citing an excerpt from Pope Leo's letter, in which the Pope formally confirmed the decrees of the council and explicitly referred to the "profane treachery" of Honorius, the *Catholic Encyclopedia* adds:

> "The last words of the quotation are given above as in the Greek of the letter, because … [some have] taught that by these words Leo II explicitly abrogated the condemnation for heresy by

---

[80] Lane wrote: "To quote these (possibly falsified) acts to the effect that Honorius's letter to Sergius was 'in complete disagreement with the apostolic dogmas and the definitions of the holy councils,' is therefore rash and unnecessarily injurious to the reputation of a sovereign pontiff, and furthermore, it is incompatible with the words of Pope Leo II, who condemned Honorius not for teaching heresy or for believing it, but because he … fostered it by his negligence." (John Lane, "Concerning a SSPX Dossier on Sedevacantism, By Rev. Dominique Boulet, SSPX," p. 12.)

[81] As the Scholastics say, this is a distinction without a difference, since a heretic can manifest his heresy both positively (affirming a heretical doctrine) or negatively (failing to deny a heretical doctrine). In Honorius' case, it could be said that he failed to deny a heretical doctrine, but he did so by the *positive* act of writing a letter.

the council, <u>and substituted a condemnation for negligence.</u>
Nothing, however, could be less explicit. (…) <u>Such a distinction
between the pope's view and the council's view is not justified by
close examination of the facts.</u>"[82]

The very article Lane himself cited directly contradicts his own
assertion – and it does so in multiple places. It is also interesting to note
that Lane failed to provide his readers with a proper reference for the
aforementioned *Catholic Encyclopedia* article he cited. Why would he fail
to provide a proper reference? Could it be because he did not want his
readers to look up the article for themselves and discover that his own
position is refuted by the very source he himself cites as an authority
for it? Like other Sedevacantists (recall Fr. Cekada's half sentence
hatchet job on the quote from Cardinal Billot), Lane provides his
readers with a snippet here and a sentence fragment there – just
enough to "prove" his point - *even though the very document he cites
explicitly contradicts his position.* Unfortunately, these are typical tactics
one finds by a close examination of the writings of Sedevacantist
apologists, such as Fr. Cekada and John Lane.

To further demonstrate the complete baselessness of Lane's claim
that the view of Pope Leo differed from that of the council that he
himself ratified, we can cite the letter of Pope Leo himself to the
Emperor of Constantinople. In the letter, the Pope explicitly states that
he anathematized Honorius because he "endeavoured by profane
treason to <u>overthrow</u> the immaculate <u>faith</u> of the Roman Church,"[83]
and not for mere negligence *alone*, as Lane claims. And, as we have
already noted, Pope Honorius was included in the lists of heretics
anathematized by the Trullan Synod, and by the seventh and eighth
ecumenical councils. Moreover, in the oath taken by every Pope from
the eighth to the eleventh century, we find a phrase condemning
"Honorius, who added fuel to their wicked assertions" (*Liber Diurnus*,
ii, 9). Lane's contention is also refuted by the many Catholic historians
who have unequivocally proclaimed that Honorius' condemnation was
for heretical "doctrine," not mere "negligence" (e.g., historian and
bishop of Rottenburg, Karl Joseph von Hefele (1809-1893); Henry R.
Percival (1854-1903), author of *The Seven Ecumenical Councils of the
Undivided Church*). Commenting on this point in his 1907 article, *The*

---

[82] *Catholic Encyclopedia* (1913), vol. VII, p. 452.
[83] "*Anathematizamus - nec non et Honorium [anathematizamus], qui hanc apostolicam ecclesiam
non apostolicæ traditionis doctrina lustravit, sed profana proditione immaculatam fidem
subvertere conatus est.*" (Mansi, Tom. xi. p. 731), cited in *A Textbook of Church History*, vol. I
by Dr. John C.L. Geiseleh (New York: Harper & Brothers, Publishers, 1857), p. 541.

Condemnation of Pope Honorius, Dom John Chapman, O.S.B. (the same author who penned the *Catholic Encyclopedia* article cited by Mr. Lane), wrote:

> "It has been sometimes said that St. Leo in these words interprets the decision of the Council about Honorius in a mild sense, or that he modifies it. It is supposed that by 'permitted to be polluted' Leo II means no positive action, but a mere neglect of duty, grave enough in a Pope, but not amounting to the actual teaching of heresy. If Leo II had meant this, he would have been mistaken. Honorius did positively approve the letter of Sergius, as the Council pointed out. Further, the merely negative ruling of the *typus* had been condemned as heresy by the Lateran Council. As a fact the words of Leo II are harsher than those of the Council. He declares that Honorius did not publish the apostolic doctrine of his See, and he represents this as a disgrace to the Church of Rome itself, as a pollution of the unspotted. This no Eastern Bishop had ventured to say. The anathemas on Pope Honorius have been again and again continued. A few years later he is included in the list of heretics by the Trullan Synod ...the seventh and eighth oecumenical Councils did the same."[84]

So much for Lane's attempt to impugn the good name of Fr. Boulet by claiming it is "rash and unnecessarily injurious to the reputation of a sovereign pontiff" and "incompatible with the words of Pope Leo II" to cite the Council of Constantinople in support of the mere "possibility"[85] of a Pope falling into heresy. Quite the contrary, it is John Lane who has injured the reputation of the Sovereign Pontiff (St. Leo II), by actually alleging that the sainted Pope disagreed with the very council he approved, that is, assuming Lane will finally concede the council's decrees are authentic. Pope Honorius was anathematized by the Church and condemned by three ecumenical councils *for heresy*, and for centuries he was listed among other heretics in the Roman Breviary and in the Papal Oath. As Fr. Chapman went on to say in the above article from the Catholic Truth Society:

> "Unquestionably no Catholic has the right to deny that Honorius was a heretic (though in the sense that Origen and

---

[84] Chapman, John, *The Condemnation of Pope Honorius*, (London, Catholic Truth Society, 1907) pp. 114-115.
[85] The passage from Fr. Boulet's article, which John Lane commented on, only cited the council to demonstrate the *possibility* that a Pope could fall into heresy. It was a very measured statement, yet Lane reacted to it, in his usual unbalanced manner, by launching into rash and false accusations that impugned the name of the good priest.

Theodore of Mopsuestia were heretics), a heretic in words if not in intention."[86]

In fact, Fr. Chapman wrote the same in the *Catholic Encyclopedia* article that John Lane cited in his *defense* of Honorious (without providing a proper reference): "It is clear that no Catholic has the right to defend Pope Honorius. He was a heretic, not in intention, <u>but in fact</u>."[87]

What John Lane has demonstrated is not only apparent dishonesty, but the blatant inconsistency between the Sedevacantists' private judgment of the post-Vatican II Popes, who have *not* been declared heretics by the Church, and their defense of Pope Honorius, who *has* been declared a heretic by the Church (albeit after his death)!

The case of "Honorius the heretic," however, does not in any way contradict the dogma of papal infallibility, but rather highlights the narrow scope of the charism. Even though his letter to Sergius was not a private letter, but rather an official papal communication, Pope Honorius did not intend to define a doctrine to be held by the universal Church[88] which, as we saw, is one of the conditions for papal infallibility. Since this condition was lacking, infallibility was not engaged. Commenting on Pope Honorius in light of Vatican I's definition of papal infallibility, Fr. Chapman wrote:

> "We judge the letters of Pope Honorius by the Vatican definition, and deny them to be ex-cathedra, because they do not define any doctrine and impose it upon the whole Church... the Pope was not defining with authority and binding the Church."[89]

Fr. Chapman also explained why the letters of Pope Honorius did not imply that the Church of Rome erred in the faith:

> "Rome has an indefectible faith, which is authoritatively promulgated to the whole Church by the Bishops of the Apostolic See, the successors of Peter and the heirs at once of his faith and of his authority. How was it possible to assert this, and yet in the same breath to condemn Pope Honorius as a heretic? The answer is surely plain enough. Honorius was fallible, was wrong, was a heretic,

---

[86] Chapman, John, *The Condemnation of Pope Honorius*, (London: Catholic Truth Society, 1907), p. 115.

[87] *Catholic Encyclopedia* (1913), vol. VII, p. 455.

[88] "His answer to Sergius did not decide the question, did not authoritatively declare the faith of the Roman Church, did not claim to speak with the voice of Peter; it condemned nothing, it defined nothing." Ibid.

[89] Chapman, *The Condemnation of Pope Honorius*, p. 110

precisely because he did not, as he should have done, declare authoritatively the Petrine tradition of the Roman Church. ... Neither the Pope nor the Council consider that Honorius had compromised the purity of Roman tradition, for he had never claimed to represent it."[90]

What the case of Pope Honorius shows is that it is possible for a Pope "by profane treason to overthrow the immaculate faith of the Roman Church" and *yet still retain his office*. What applies to Honorius, of course, applies to the conciliar Popes. Because they have not been declared heretics by the Church, they must be accepted as true Popes, even though many would argue that, like Honorius, they too have compromised "the immaculate faith of the Roman Church."

Pope Stephen and The Cadaver Synod

In the latter part of the ninth century and into the tenth century, there were rival camps battling to gain control of the papacy. During this period, the papacy fell into the hands of one or another from each of these rival groups.

In January of the year 897, Pope Stephen VI had decided to put his predecessor from the rival camp, Pope Formosus (891-896), on a mock trial for alleged violations of Church law. To that end, Pope Stephen had the body of Pope Formosus exhumed, clothed in his papal vestments, propped up on a throne, and placed on trial. A deacon was appointed to answer the charges on behalf of the corpse. During this synod, which came to be known as "The Cadaver Synod," Pope Formosus was found "guilty" of perjury, of having coveted the papal office, and of violating the canons of the Church. Pope Stephen ordered that three fingers on Formosus' right hand (those used to give the papal blessing) be cut off and his body thrown into the Tiber river. The election of Pope Formosus and all the official acts of his pontificate were rendered null and void, and his ordinations were declared invalid.

Pope Stephen declared the ordinations of Pope Formosus invalid because Stephen held the erroneous belief (common during the day) that in order for an ordination to be sacramentally *valid*, it also had to be canonically *licit*. Today, there is no question that this position was entirely erroneous.

Pope Stephen VI was succeeded by Pope Romanus, who agreed with the decision of Pope Stephen and the Cadaver Synod. Pope

---

[90] Ibid., p. 109.

Romanus was then succeeded by Pope Theodore II, who was a member of the Formosus camp. Immediately after being elected to the papacy, Pope Theodore convened a synod of his own and overturned the decision of Pope Romanus, Pope Stephen, and the Cadaver Synod. He declared the election and ordinations performed by Formosus to have been valid and restored the clergy to their office. Pope Theodore II's immediate successor, Pope John IX, held two synods, one at Rome and another at Ravena, both of which confirmed that the election and ordinations of Formosus had indeed been valid.[91] Then came Pope Sergius III (from the opposing camp), who held another synod that overturned the ruling of Popes Theodore II and John IX, and once again declared null the election and ordinations performed by Pope Formosus.[92]

During this tumultuous time for the Church and the papacy, there were at least five synods, all convened and overseen by the reigning Pope, which issued contradictory declarations. Moreover, three of these synods issued an erroneous decision that was rooted in a *doctrinal* error.[93]

During these events, which were well known to the Fathers of the First Vatican Council, there was no violation of papal infallibility, since the erroneous judgments rendered by the Popes were not intended to be a *doctrinal definition* (even though these Popes willed their decisions to be held by the universal Church). This historical example underscores in a most striking way that it is only when a Pope is *defining a doctrine* (a divinely revealed truth in Scripture or Tradition) that he is preserved from all error, according to the definition of Vatican I. A violation of infallibility would have occurred in these cases only if the Pope had *defined* that ordinations are sacramentally valid only when they are canonically licit, and not by simply *acting* on the

---

[91] *Cf. Catholic Encyclopedia* (1913), vol. VI, p. 141.

[92] Sale, George; Psalmanazar, George; Bower, Archibald; Shelvocke, George; Campbell, John; Swinton, John, *An Universal History: From The Earliest Accounts To The Present Time*, vol. XXV, London: Miller, John Rivington, S. Crowder, 1761, p. 264; also see *Catholic Encyclopedia* (1913), vol. VI, p. 141.

[93] The Catholic magazine, *The Month*, provided the explanation of Abbé Saltet, of the Institute Catholique de Toulouse, for this doctrinal error. Explaining why it was believed that for an ordination to be valid, it must also be licit, they explained that it "was largely, thinks the Abbé Saltet, because in that uncultured age, when the dicta of early Popes and Fathers were not known in their context, but only in short abstracts, and some, such as those of St. Augustine, were unknown altogether, the ambiguous utterances of some early authorities, under the prevailing influence on minds of the second of the two dogmatic principles above stated, were interpreted as testifying to a tradition in favour of rejecting all Orders unlawfully obtained." *The Month*, vol. CIX, (London: Longmans, Green, and Co. January – June 1907), p. 652.

erroneous belief. These extraordinary events show us that a Pope can not only embrace an error, but also act upon that error and thereby cause untold confusion and harm to the Church (here, spreading universal doubt in the Church about the validity of the sacraments due to defective ordinations).

One can only imagine the turmoil that the faithful experienced when a Pope declared that their clergy had not been validly ordained, which meant, of course, that the Masses they celebrated, the Confirmations they administered, and the absolutions they gave, were all invalid. These contradictory declarations from Popes and synods were followed by additional papal scandals, one after another, that lasted for over a century. Commenting on this difficult time in Church history, the Catholic magazine, *The Month* wrote:

> "The period of history to which these extraordinary proceedings belonged was the end of the ninth century, and the beginning of that century and a half during which the Holy See, under the disturbing influence of the feudal princes of the neighbourhood, was dragged through the mire of innumerable scandals."[94]

This chaotic time shows us what God can and does permit His Church to suffer. It shows us that He can allow incredible damage to be inflicted upon the Church by its human element (including bad Popes) without the gates of hell prevailing, that is, without infallibility being violated. These events also show just how gravely mistaken are those who extend papal infallibility beyond the strict limits established by the Church, which is precisely what the Sedevacantists of our day have done.

In attempting to explain how this "impossible" event occurred, the Sedevacantist writer, Steve Speray, was forced to deny that Pope Stephen was a true Pope. He wrote:

> "There is no question that Stephen's mental capacity was unstable. Because of his insanity, Stephen should be considered an antipope. One theologian says this isn't a novel understanding among canonists: 'Not few canonists teach that, outside of death and abdication, the pontifical dignity can also be lost by falling into certain insanity... (Introductio in Codicem, 1946 .D. Udalricus Beste).' Who would not think Stephen was mad after the cadaver synod? ... Stephen VI's case shows that either the Church has failed

---

[94] Ibid.

to view him as insane, or that She recognized an insane pope given that he is viewed as a true pope by his successors and placed on the official papal list."[95]

Notice that Mr. Speray reveals his loss of faith in the Church. He says that "the Church has failed" to recognize Pope Stephen as "insane," who, in Speray's opinion, was actually an insane antipope (note that Speray has no credentials in either theology or psychology). Thus, Speray effectively accuses the Catholic Church of defecting, since the more than 150 Popes who have succeeded Stephen VI have recognized him as a valid Pope. Yet, Steve Speray believes that the Church has been in error about this matter, *and for over a millennium.* This, of course, means that the Church defected over a thousand years ago, since it has recognized Stephen VI as a true Pope.

Mr. Speray's error is easily identified by seeing that he has extended infallibility beyond the limits established by the Church. Since a small error in the beginning is a big error in the end, the only way he can reconcile his personal belief with this historical event, is to claim that Pope Stephen secretly lost his office – even though no historian or theologian has ever suggested such a thing. Although Mr. Speray concedes that the Catholic Church recognizes Pope Stephen as a valid Pope, he is nevertheless forced, by his errors regarding papal infallibility, to declare him an antipope. The solution for Mr. Speray's difficulty is not to declare Pope Stephen an antipope, but to realize that he and his Sedevacantist colleagues have an entirely erroneous and un-Catholic idea of papal infallibility. This historical event shows us why the Church, guided by the Holy Ghost, defined papal infallibility by the strict parameters that it did.

3. *Exercise of Supreme Apostolic Authority*

The third and final condition necessary for papal infallibility is that the Pope teaches using his supreme apostolic authority. Two things are to be considered regarding this condition: (a) The Pope must be acting in his official capacity as Pope; and, (b) he must be using his supreme authority at its maximum power. Regarding the first point, Msgr. Van Noort explains:

[95] Speray, Steven, *Papal Anomalies and Their Implications*, Second ed. (Versailles, Kentucky: Confiteor, 2011), pp. 71-72.

"A man holding office does not always act in his *official* capacity. Again, if the same person holds several offices simultaneously, he does not have to be constantly exercising the highest function. We must keep these points in mind when discussing the pope's infallibility. He is not only the pope of the whole Church, he is also the local bishop of the diocese of Rome, metropolitan of its surrounding sees, and temporal sovereign of the Vatican state. Consequently, if the pope speaks merely as a private individual, or as a private theologian, or as a temporal sovereign, or precisely as ordinary of the diocese of Rome, or precisely as metropolitan of the province of Rome, he should not be looked on as acting infallibly. (...) As private theologian he might write a book on some aspects of the spiritual life. As a temporal sovereign of the Vatican state, he might issue decrees of taxes, or economic reform (...) Speaking precisely as ordinary of the diocese of Rome he might give a series of instructions or a retreat to the people of some definite parish in the city.

What is required for an infallible declaration, therefore, is that the pope be acting precisely as pope; that is, as the supreme shepherd and teacher of all Christians so that his decision looks to the universal Church and is given for the sake of the universal Church."[96]

With respect to the second point, namely, using his authority to its maximum power, the same pre-Vatican II dogmatic manual teaches the following:

"A man who acts in an official capacity does not always make use of his full power, of the whole weight of the authority which he possesses by his very position. ... Thus the pope, even acting as pope, can teach the universal Church without making use of his supreme authority at its maximum power. Now the Vatican Council defined merely this point: the pope is infallible if he uses his doctrinal authority at its maximum power, by handing down a binding and definitive decision: such a decision, for example, by which he *quite clearly* intends to bind all Catholics to an absolutely firm and irrevocable assent.

Consequently, even if the pope, and acting as pope, praises some doctrine, or recommends it to Christians, or even orders that it alone should be taught in theological schools, this act should not necessarily be considered an infallible decree since he may not intend to hand down a definitive decision. (...) For the same reason, namely a lack of intention to hand down a final decision, not all

---

[96] Ibid., pp. 292-293.

doctrinal decisions which the pope proposes in encyclical letters should be considered definitions. <u>In a word, there must always be present and clearly presented the intention of the pope to hand down a decision which is final and definitive.</u>"[97]

Clearly, infallibility does not cover all the teachings of a Pope on matters of faith or morals, but only those teachings which he intends to be definitive and binding upon the universal Church.

Sometimes a Pope may explicitly *decline* to engage his charism of infallibility, even when he is teaching the entire Church on matters of faith or morals. For example, Pope Benedict XIV's *De canonisatione sanctorum* (July 20, 1753) expressly affirms that this document has no other authority than that of a private author.[98] Pope Paul VI, who ratified the documents of the Second Vatican Council, also stated: "In view of the pastoral nature of the Council, it avoided any extraordinary statements of dogmas endowed with the note of infallibility."[99] In such cases, infallibility is not engaged, since the charism is only engaged when the Pope *intends* to engage it by using the full force of his pontifical authority.

To conclude this section, infallibility is a negative charism that *prevents* the possibility of error, but is only active when the conditions set down by the First Vatican Council are met. If *any single one* of these conditions is lacking, infallibility is not engaged and error is possible.[100] Therefore, when considering whether a Pope can teach errors to the Church regarding faith and morals, we must make three distinctions:

1) A Pope teaching as a private person.

2) A Pope teaching as Pope on matters of faith or morals, but not intending to define a doctrine.

3) A Pope teaching as Pope, defining a doctrine on faith or morals, to be held by the universal Church.

---

[97] Ibid., pp. 293-294.
[98] See Fr. Nau, *Pope or Church?*, p. 21. Nau also cites *Apostolici Ministerii* (September 16, 1747) and St. Pius X's words pronounced during the course of private papal audiences, Instruction of the Secretariat of State to the Bishops of Italy, July 28, 1904.
[99] General Audience address, January 12, 1966.
[100] As Dom Paul Nau explained, "if these conditions are not fulfilled, the term 'definition' cannot be used, nor can the pontifical judgment be considered as in itself infallible and irrefutable." *Pope or Church?*, p. 10.

It is only in the last instance that the charism of infallibility will prevent the Pope from erring. From this fact, it is evident that a Pope can err when teaching as a private theologian, and also when acting in his *official capacity* as Pope (as we saw in the cases of John XXII and Honorius), as long as he does not intend to define a doctrine on faith or morals to be held by the universal Church.[101]

The reason this is important is because some Sedevacantists erroneously believe that it is "impossible" for a Pope to make a heretical statement (i.e., contradicting a defined doctrine), believing that the charism of infallibility would prevent him from doing so. Based upon this first error, they arrive at the second, namely, that if a Pope says something that they believe to be heretical, it "proves" that he must have already lost his office (since, they believe, a true Pope cannot make a heretical statement). This is an entirely erroneous notion of papal infallibility. As we have seen, the charism of infallibility only prevents a Pope from erring when he is *defining* a doctrine for the universal Church (binding the universal Church). It does not prevent a Pope from erring (or making a heretical statement) when he is not intending to define, even if acting in his official capacity as Pope.

In light of the foregoing, we conclude this chapter by noting that it is certainly within the realm of possibility for a Pope to lose the faith internally, and he can without a doubt profess error externally, provided he does not meet the conditions set down by Vatican I for infallibility. To insist on the contrary, as do Sedevacantists, is to extend infallibility beyond its narrowly defined limits and commit the error of excess. It is to reject the teaching of Popes Innocent III and Adrian VI as well as the "common opinion" of the Church's theologians.[102] It is to deny the historical cases of Popes Honorius and John XXII. And, as we witnessed with the sad case of John Lane, it may even force one to cast doubt upon the authenticity of a general council that was ratified by a Pope, and which has been accepted by the universal Church for thirteen centuries. In the present ecclesiastical crisis, this error of *excess* (extending infallibility beyond the limits established by the Church) leads rapidly to one of the two opposite errors: Sedevacantism or "papolatry."

---

[101] *Cf.* Silveira, "La Nouvelle Messe de Paul VI: Qu'en penser," pp. 188-194.
[102] Soto, *Comm. in IV Sent.*, dist. 22, q. 2, a. 2, p. 1021;

Chapter 9

~ Proving the Crime of Heresy ~

We will now turn to the discussion of how a Pope loses his office for heresy. In this chapter, we will address the issue of how the crime of papal heresy is established by the Church. In Chapter 10, we will further address why it is necessary for the Church itself to establish the crime (as opposed to individual Catholics in the street doing so), and in Chapter 11 we will directly address the question of how a heretical Pope is "deposed" by the Church. In these three chapters, we will also elaborate at length on the similarities and differences between the opinion of the two Jesuits, Bellarmine and Suarez, and that of the two Dominicans, Cajetan and John of St. Thomas, regarding the complex issue of how a heretical Pope loses his office. This chapter is lengthy and contains some technical and weighty material. As an overview, following are some of the key points that will be covered:

- We will begin by defining the crime of heresy according to the various canonical definitions.
- We will then consider the importance of canonical warnings by showing what they accomplish, and then answer the objection which maintains that a Pope cannot be warned.
- We will also discuss the penalties for heresy under canon law, and see what is required for a prelate to lose his office for heresy.
- We will then explore the difference between *crime* and *punishment*, and show how this distinction synthesizes the teaching of Bellarmine and Suarez.
- Finally, we will end by discussing Canon 188, §4 (1917 Code) and Canon 194, §2 (1983 Code).

Let us begin by briefly recapping what we addressed in previous chapters about the two elements of heresy, namely, the matter and form.

The *matter* of heresy is a clear and direct denial of a doctrine that must be believed with divine and Catholic faith. Not all errors qualify, properly speaking, as heresy. Those errors which are not directly contrary to an article of faith, but depend upon several steps of reasoning to demonstrate the contradiction, cannot be qualified as heretical before a definitive judgment by the Church.

The *form* of heresy is pertinacity, or incorrigibility, which is the willful (conscious and obstinate) denial or doubt of a doctrine that must be believed with divine and Catholic faith. Pertinacity requires full knowledge (*scienter*) of the Catholic dogma and full consent (*volente*) in adhering to a heretical proposition. Without pertinacity in the will, the subjective element of heresy is not present, and, consequently, the person in question would not be a heretic properly so-called, since a heretic, according to the canonical definition, is one who "*pertinaciously* denies or doubts a truth of divine and Catholic faith" (canon 1325, § 2). If a person denies a dogma of the faith without pertinacity, he is not in heresy, but only in error, as St. Thomas explains:

> "Hence it is evident that a heretic who pertinaciously disbelieves one article of faith, is not prepared to follow the teaching of the Church in all matters; but if he is not pertinacious he is not in heresy, but only in error."[1]

In another place, St. Thomas quotes St. Augustine who confirms the same:

> "As Augustine says (Ep. xliii) and we find it stated in the Decretals (xxiv, qu. 3, can. *Dixit Apostolus*): 'By no means should we accuse of heresy those who, however false and perverse their opinion may be, defend it without obstinate fervor [pertinacity], and seek the truth with careful anxiety, ready to mend their opinion, when they have found the truth,' because, to wit, they do not make a choice in contradiction to the doctrine of the Church."[2]

Public and Occult

The *matter* of heresy can be public or occult (i.e., secret). If a person adheres to a heretical proposition internally, but does not profess it externally, the material aspect of the heresy is occult (*materialiter occultum*). If a person professes a heretical doctrine externally, the *heretical matter* would be public.

The *form* of heresy can also be public or occult. If one *knowingly and willfully* denies a dogma, yet does so without providing sufficient external evidence of same, pertinacity would be formally occult (*formaliter occultum*). If a person provides sufficient evidence of

---

[1] ST, I-II q. 5, a. 3.
[2] ST, II-II q. 11, a. 2, ad. 3.

pertinacity in the external forum – e.g., by openly leaving the Church, by publicly admitting to knowingly and willfully rejecting what the Church teaches on faith or morals, or by remaining obstinate after being duly warned by the proper authorities, the formal aspect of heresy would be public.

Public and Notorious

Canonists distinguish three kinds of crimes: occult, public, and notorious. A crime is occult if the criminal act is known to no one, or only a few.[3] A crime is public if the act "is already commonly known[4] or the circumstances are such as to lead to the conclusion that it can and will easily become so" (canon 2197, 1°).

Both "Matter" and "Form" Must Be Public

Canon law is only concerned with external violations of the law, not with internal acts that remain concealed in the heart. Because an essential element of heresy is pertinacity, in order for a person to be considered guilty of the canonical crime of heresy, *both* the matter and form must be *public*.[5] For this reason, pertinacity is considered an essential part of the *corpus delicti* (the body of the crime) of heresy. While the external presence of the material aspect alone (e.g., a heretical statement) may provide sufficient grounds for the *suspicion* of heresy, or the presumption of culpability by the ecclesiastical authorities, it does not provide the degree of *proof* necessary to constitute the public crime of heresy. This point is acknowledged by the Sedevacantist author John Daly, who wrote:

"The canonists have defined pertinacity as *recognition* or *awareness* of the conflict between one's belief and that of the

---

[3] Fr. Augustine teaches that the act can be known to as many as six persons while still being considered occult (*A Commentary on the New Code of Canon Law*, vol. 8, p. 17).

[4] There is a distinction between *public* and *commonly known*. According to the canonist Bouscaren: "'Commonly known' (*divulgatum*) means known to the greater part of the inhabitants of a place or the members of a community; but this is not to be taken mathematically, but in prudent moral estimation" (*Canon Law: A Text and Commentary*, 1951). A crime can be public, if it is not yet commonly known, but was committed under such circumstances that it can easily become commonly known.

[5] Fr. Augustine explains: "Every crime which is not public, says our text, is occult or secret. The Code distinguishes a twofold secrecy, viz.: merely material (*materialiter occultum*), which exists when the fact is unknown, or known only to the perpetrator and a few reticent persons; and formal (*formaliter occultum*), when the moral and juridical guilt is unknown" (Augustine, *A Commentary on the New Code of Canon Law*, vol. 8, p. 17).

Church. As such, pertinacity is essential to the canonical delict of heresy; it is part of the *matter* or (technically) *corpus delicti* of heresy. Hence it must be <u>proved</u> before anyone can be considered a heretic, and Canon 2200/2 with its presumption of culpability does not help to prove it…"[6]

"Notorious" Distinguished from "Public"

Canonists explain that a notorious crime differs from a public crime by the degree of inexcusability of the act. Regarding this point, Fr. Augustine explains:

"A crime is notorious *notorietate facti* [notorius by fact] when it is publicly known and has been committed under such circumstances that it cannot be concealed by any artifice or be excused by any legal assumption or circumstantial evidence. … Hence, not only the fact itself must be notorious, but also its criminal character. … It is this element of inexcusability or of knowledge of the criminal character of the deed that appears to distinguish a public from a notorious crime. For the text manifestly lays stress on *divulgation* with regard to public crimes, and emphasizes the criminal character *as known and inexcusable* [for a notorious crime]."[7]

As Fr. Augustine notes, the principle distinction between a *public* vis-à-vis *notorious* crime is that the latter relates *chiefly* to the inexcusability of (and, hence, moral responsibility for) the crime, while the former relates *chiefly* to the extent to which the crime is known or can be known.

Fr. Dominique Boulet explained that for "heresy to be Notorious, not only would the *heretical act* have to be widely known … but it would also have to be an act whose <u>criminality</u> had been <u>legally recognized</u>." In other words, since the crime of heresy requires both matter and form, for a crime to be considered notorious, pertinacity (the form) would have to be so evident and so inexcusable that it had become *legally recognized*, that is, acknowledged as criminal (morally imputable). Applying this to the case of a Pope, Fr. Boulet wrote:

---

[6] John S. Daly, "Pertinacity: Material and Formal Heresy," 1999. See http://www.sede vacantist.com/pertinacity.html. Daly correctly notes that an external violation of the law under canon 2200, §2 requires conscious dissent from an article of faith before guilt can be presumed. The objectively heretical statement alone does *not* create a presumption of guilt because it does not, by itself, establish a violation of law.

[7] Augustine, *A Commentary on the New Code of Canon Law*, vol. 8, p. 17.

"In other words, for the criminality of a Pope's heresy to be legally recognized, such that his heresy would be canonically Notorious, not only would a knowledge of his heresy [the matter] have to have spread widely through the Church, as we have seen above, but it would also have to have been *widely recognized* as a morally imputable crime."[8]

From this it is clear that the material act itself of saying or writing something *heretical* (not a lesser degree of error), does not, in and of itself, suffice for the crime to be notorious. Moral imputability (guilt) would also have to be publicly and legally recognized. This can happen in one of two ways: 1) by notoriety of law; or 2) notoriety of fact.

Notorious by Law and Notorious by Fact

Notoriety of law: The 1917 Code explains that a crime is "Notorious by notoriety of law, after a sentence by a competent judge that renders the matter an adjudicated thing, or after a confession by the offender made in court in accord with Canon 1750."[9] As Fr. Augustine explains, "extrajudicial confessions do not render a crime notorious by notoriety of law."[10] Because a sentence has not been passed on any of the conciliar Popes by a competent judge, and none have confessed their crime in a court of law, their alleged heresies cannot be considered notorious by notoriety of law.

Notoriety of fact: The same 1917 Code teaches that a crime is Notorious by notoriety of fact, if it is "publicly known and was committed under such circumstances that no clever evasion is possible and no legal excuse could excuse."[11] For a crime to be notorious by notoriety of fact, the offense must be such that it leaves no doubt as to the *culpability* of the crime, even without a legal trial. This means that the moral imputability (guilt) must be *publicly* known.

The 1943 commentary on Canon Law by Stanislaus Woywod confirms the same:

"An offense is Notorious by notoriety of fact, if it is publicly known and committed under such circumstances that it cannot be concealed by any subterfuge, nor excused by any excuse admitted

---

[8] Boulet, "Is That Chair Vacant? A SSPX Dossier on Sedevacantism," *Communicantes*, October - December 2004, No. 21 (emphasis added).

[9] 1917 Code of Canon Law, canon 2197, °2.

[10] Augustine, *A Commentary on Canon Law*, vol. 8, p. 16.

[11] 1917 Code of Canon Law, canon 2197, °3 (emphasis added).

in law, i.e., <u>both the fact of the offense and the imputability or criminal liability must be publicly known.</u>"[12]

Commenting on the same point, Fr. Boulet observes that the heretical act "would have to be widely recognized as both heretical *and morally imputable* - as pertinacious (persistent and determined to the point of stubbornness). That is to say, it must be not only *materially notorious*, the heretical act being widely known, but also *formally notorious,* the act being widely recognized *as a morally imputable crime of formal heresy.*"[13] For example, if a person openly and publicly left the Church and joined another religion, his own actions would render him notorious by notoriety of fact. In the case of the conciliar Popes, however, their "moral imputability" is not "widely known." In fact, even the allegation of *material* heresy would be rejected by virtually the entire Catholic populace.[14]

Thus, even if one were to argue that the conciliar Popes professed errors or even heresies publicly, it is certainly *not* the case that both the matter (heresy) and form (pertinacity) have been sufficiently demonstrated to the extent that "no clever evasion is possible." This is evident in light of the fact that the "conservatives" have made a career out of using "clever evasions" to excuse and explain away erroneous or even seemingly-heretical statements made by the conciliar Popes, which they would not be able to do if no clever evasion *were possible.*[15]

To cite just one recent example to demonstrate this point, Fr. Brian Harrison wrote a letter to the editor of *The Remnant* newspaper, in response to an article by John Salza on the validity of the canonizations of John XXIII and John Paul II. In his article, Mr. Salza accused these two Popes of teaching *errors* contrary to the faith, which should have automatically barred them from canonization under the Church's current legislation.[16] (It should be noted Mr. Salza did not make an accusation of formal *heresy*, but only material *error*.) Fr. Harrison responded as follows:

---

[12] Woywod, Stanislaus, *A Practical Commentary on the Code of Canon Law* (New York: Joseph F. Wagner, 1943), emphasis added.

[13] Boulet, "Is That Chair Vacant? A SSPX Dossier on Sedevacantism," No. 21 (emphasis added).

[14] This is the case at least up to and including Pope Benedict XVI.

[15] As we will further see, because there could be many different private opinions about "clever evasion," the Doctors and theologians *unanimously* conclude that, for a sitting Pope, the notoriety of fact of an alleged crime *is a judgment of the Church*. It is not a matter of private judgment.

[16] See John Salza, "Questioning the Validity of the Canonizations: Against a Fact There is No Argument," *The Remnant* newspaper, May 15, 2014; also available at http://www.johnsalza.com.

"I think your readers should be advised that what Mr. Salza peremptorily declares to be a 'fact' - namely, that 'the writings of John XXIII and John Paul II…contain teachings contrary to Catholic faith or morals' - is not clearly established at all. It's a mere allegation based on Mr. Salza's own *personal interpretation* of English translations of the writings of these two popes, and of certain traditional magisterial statements which he thinks they contradict."

Fr. Harrison then added parenthetically:

"Mr. Salza's interpretations, it need hardly be said, are not shared by the competent Roman Congregations that were required by church law to evaluate the writings of these two popes as part of the process for their canonizations."[17]

Similar excuses based upon "interpretation" have been used for years to defend the Vatican II Popes against the accusation of professing errors or heresy (and Fr. Harrison provided no arguments to rebut Salza's assertion of material errors in the teachings of John XXIII and John Paul II). Even if one does not concede the merits of this particular defense, if a "clever evasion" is merely *possible* (and the Modernists are most clever in their evasions of formal heresy), then notorious heresy does not exist. What this shows is that the conciliar Popes cannot be classified as public and notorious heretics *according to the canonical definition of the terms.*

Lowering the Burden of Proof

For years, Sedevacantist apologists have presented quotations from theologians and canonists who taught that if a Pope were to become a notorious heretic he would lose his office. Without ever defining the term "notorious," much less demonstrating how the recent Popes met the definition, these apologists would simply present quotations from their theology manuals as "proof" that the conciliar Popes were not true Popes. Over time, however, as they began to realize the difficult task they had in demonstrating that the recent Popes met the canonical definition of "notorious," they began to lower the burden of proof by shifting the emphasis away from the *notorious* aspect (moral imputability) to the *public* aspect (the extent to which the act has been divulged). For example, the Sedevacantist John Lane wrote:

---

[17] *The Remnant* newspaper, vol. 47, No. 9, May 31, 2014.

"I am not here arguing that Paul VI, John Paul II, or Benedict XVI have all been notorious heretics in the legal sense, although that case could be made" [NB: Of course, Lane doesn't even attempt to make the case for "notorious" heresy because he cannot, or he would have done so].

Then, in the next sentence, Lane says:

"I think it may easily be demonstrated that all three of these men have been *public* heretics, and that suffices."[18]

Suffices for what? To make his case easier to prove? And if the "public" element *alone* now suffices, what about all the quotes the Sedevacantists have been citing all these years, which say that a Pope who becomes a "notorious heretic" loses his office? Are they now going to reject these authorities and search for others whom they believe support their new position? For example, will they remove the following quotations from their websites?

"Given, therefore, the hypothesis of a pope who would become notoriously heretical, one must concede without hesitation that he would by that very fact lose the pontifical power, insofar as, having become an unbeliever, he would by his own will be cast outside the body of the Church." (Billot - *De Ecclesia*, 1927)

"Through notorious and openly divulged heresy, the Roman Pontiff, should he fall into heresy, by that very fact (ipso facto) is deemed to be deprived of the power of jurisdiction." (Wernz-Vidal, 1943)

"Not a few canonists teach that, outside of death and abdication, the pontifical dignity can also be lost by falling into certain insanity, which is legally equivalent to death, as well as through manifest and notorious heresy." (H. *Introductio in Codicem* [1946] - Udalricus Beste)

"If, however, God were to permit a pope to become a notorious and contumacious heretic, he would by such fact cease to be pope, and the apostolic chair would be vacant." (St. Alphonsus Ligouri)

"Given that, as a private person, the Pontiff could indeed become a public, notorious, and obstinate heretic [i.e. pertinatious]

18 Lane, "Concerning an SSPX Dossier on Sedevacantism, by Rev. Dominique Boulet, SSPX."

236

... he would fall by the very fact of heresy from his papal power, in so far as he would have been removed from within the Church's body on his own accord..." (Hervé, *Manuale Theologiae Dogmaticae* (1943) I.501)[19]

These and similar quotations have been copied and pasted on virtually every Sedevacantist website on the internet as "proof" that the conciliar Popes have lost their office. Now that they realize the recent Popes do not meet the definition of *notorious* (since their "pertinacity" or "guilt" is not "widely recognized"), we again ask, are the Sedevacantists now going to disregard these quotations, along with other similar quotations they've dug up over the years, since they set the bar too high for them to prove their case? And will they remove the quotations from their websites and include a note to their readers informing them that if they embraced the Sedevacantist position based upon any of these quotes, they must reconsider their position? Take a guess.

What the fluid approach of lowering the evidentiary bar demonstrates is that the Sedevacantists not only imagine themselves to be the judge and jury, *but lawmaker as well.* For they not only determine (by private judgment) that the burden of proof has been met, but also define what the burden of proof is! And when they are unable to meet the burden of proof that they themselves have established, they simply lower the bar.

As one might expect, this lowering of the bar did not stop with their reducing the criminal elements of heresy from "public and notorious" to simply "public." In response to a recent article written by Robert Siscoe, which demonstrated that the conciliar Popes cannot be considered as having lost their office due to the public crime of heresy,[20] the Sedevacantist blogger, Steven Speray, reduced the burden of proof so low that, according to him, the Pope *doesn't have to be a heretic at all* to lose his office for *heresy!* You read that correctly. After arguing for years that a Pope who becomes a "manifest heretic" automatically ceases to be Pope, we are now told that "a pope doesn't

---

[19] We note that all of these quotations (except from Hervé) were taken from Sedevacantist websites (none of them provided bibliographical references for the quotations). The quotation from St. Alphonsus is taken from *Verità Della Fede*, Pt. III, c. VIII. p. 10. He continued by saying: "But were he only a secret heretic, *and did not propose to the Church any false dogma,* no harm in that case would happen to the Church"(Ibid).
[20] "Can the Church Depose an Heretical Pope?," *The Remnant* newspaper, November 24, 2014 (online).

need to be a heretic at all to lose office, much less an obstinate manifest declared one."[21]

Showing a complete disregard for the laws of the Church and objectivity (not to mention equity and fairness), Mr. Speray now argues that "a pope must simply <u>appear</u> to be a heretic"[22] to *automatically* lose his office. And who, you may be wondering, is the judge that determines if the Pope *appears* to be a heretic? You guessed it. It's the individual Sedevacantist layman in the pew. Who else?[23] While this is not yet a mainstream position among Sedevacantists, it reveals the sliding scale of "justice" among them, and shows just how far some of them will go to defend their position.

As should be quite obvious, and as we will discuss in more detail in the next chapter, such a difficult and weighty matter is not left to the private judgment of individuals in the pew, many of whom are simply out to "prove" their case by any means possible (as the lowering of the bar demonstrates). The competent Church authorities *alone* have the right and duty to establish the crime and perform the ministerial functions necessary to remove a heretical Pope from office. This fact, of course, explains why no theologian who has addressed this issue (not one!) has ever taught that private individuals have the right, based upon their own private opinions, to declare that a man elected to the papal office by the Conclave, and accepted as Pope by the Church, is not a true and valid Pontiff.

---

[21] Speray, "Robert Siscoe and The Remnant's Latest Canon Law Fiasco," February 3, 2015. It should be noted that following Robert Siscoe's lengthy response (published by *The Remnant* newspaper) to the above-mentioned article, the author, Steven Speray, completely re-wrote his piece and re-published it on his website with no explanation and without changing the original date.

[22] Ibid.

[23] Herein lies the real problem. Because the Church itself is unable to judge internals (*de internis ecclesia non judica*), it cannot ascertain whether a Pope who publicly and pertinaciously denies a dogma externally, in the face of an ecclesiastical warning, is truly heretical *internally* (in his heart). Therefore, as John of St. Thomas himself notes, should a Pope shows himself to be a pertinacious heretic *externally*, he can be deposed by the Church, even if he is not truly heretical *internally*. But, as we have shown, the judgment would have to be made by the proper authorities in the Church (not private judgment) before the externally heretical Pope would lose his office. John of St. Thomas explains that "the pontiff cannot be deposed and lose the pontificate except if two conditions are fulfilled together: that the heresy is not hidden, but *public* and *legally notorious* [declared]; then that he must be incorrigible and pertinacious in his heresy. If both conditions are fulfilled the pontiff may be deposed, but not without them; and even if he is not unfaithful interiorly, however if he behaves externally as a heretic, he can be deposed and the sentence of deposition will be valid" (John of St. Thomas, *Cursus Theologici*).

Establishing the Crime through Warnings

While the Church does not possess the authority to judge a Pope as a superior judges an inferior, it certainly possesses the competency and the right to judge whether or not a *proposition* professed by a Pope is materially heretical. The Church's ability to judge papal heresy was taught by Pope Innocent III, Pope Adrian, St. Robert Bellarmine,[24] the famous Decretal *Si Papa*,[25] and remains the common teaching of the Church's Doctors and theologians. This is an objective judgment made by competent authorities, and therefore it makes no difference if the proposition was professed by a Pope or any other bishop. If any person (Pope or not) was to proclaim, for example, that "the resurrection of the body, is not a resurrection of physical bodies...but the resurrection of persons,"[26] the Church, or any Catholic who knows his Faith for that matter, can judge the *statement* to be heretical.

Again, such a determination would *not* constitute a judgment of the *person* of the Pope, because it is only an objective judgment of the proposition itself. For this reason, a council would certainly be permitted to judge whether or not the material aspect of a teaching professed by a Pope was heretical; but this objective judgment would not *yet* determine if the Pope himself was guilty of the crime of heresy, since the second element of heresy, pertinacity, would also have to be proven by the Church.

Establishing pertinacity is more difficult than judging the matter of heresy, because it involves something that exists within the internal forum (the realm of conscience). If a person does not openly leave the

---

[24] Bellarmine wrote: "Firstly, that a heretical Pope can be judged is expressly held in Can. *Si Papa dist*. 40, and by Innocent III (*Serm. II de Consec. Pontif.*) Furthermore, in the 8th Council, (act. 7) the acts of the Roman Council under Pope Hadrian are recited, in which one finds that Pope Honorius appears to be justly anathematized, because he had been convicted of heresy..." (*De Romano Pontifice*, bk. 2, ch. 30).

[25] "Let no mortal man presume to accuse the Pope of fault, for, it being incumbent upon him to judge all, he should be judged by no one, unless he is suddenly caught deviating from the faith"(*Si Papa Dist* 40). Latin found in Brian Tierney, *The Crisis of Church and State* (Englewood Cliffs, New Jersey: Prentice-Hall, 1964), p. 124.

[26] "One thing at any rate may be fairly clear: both John (6:63) and Paul (1 Cor. 15:50) state with all possible emphasis that 'resurrection of the flesh,' and the 'resurrection of the body,' is not a 'resurrection of physical bodies.' Thus, from the point of view of modern thought, the Pauline sketch is far less naïve than later theological erudition with its subtle ways of construing how there can be eternal physical bodies. To recapitulate, Paul teaches, not the resurrection of physical bodies, but the resurrection of persons, and this not in the return of the 'fleshly body,' that is, the biological structure, an idea he expressly describes as impossible..." Joseph Ratzinger, *Introduction to Christianity* (San Francisco, California: Ignatius Press, 2004) with a new Foreword by Cardinal Ratzinger dated April 2000, pp. 357-358.

Church, or publicly admit that he knowingly rejects what the Church definitively teaches on faith or morals (which none of the conciliar Popes have done), pertinacity would need to be established another way. The other way, according to Divine law and canon law, is by issuing an ecclesiastical warning to the suspect.

An ecclesiastical warning serves as an effective means for establishing pertinacity, since the response will determine, with a sufficient degree of certitude, whether or not the person who has professed *heresy* (not a lesser error) is truly pertinacious, rather than merely mistaken, or perhaps only guilty of a regrettable statement made out of human weakness, which might be a sin, but not necessarily the sin of heresy. Because pertinacity is itself a necessary element of heresy, it does not suffice that its presence be presumed; *it must be proven.* The warning accomplishes this by removing any chance of innocent ignorance, or giving the suspect an opportunity to affirm what was denied in a moment of weakness, such as the moment of weakness experienced by St. Peter, as recorded in the Gospels: "And again he (Peter) denied with an oath, I know not the man... Then he began to curse and to swear that he knew not the man" (Mt. 26:26,28).

For this reason, in order to establish pertinacity, canon law requires that a warning be given to a prelate before he is deposed for the crime of heresy.[27] This aspect of canon law is founded upon Divine law, as revealed in Scripture (*cf.* Tit. 3:10), and is considered so necessary that even in the extreme case in which a cleric publicly joins a false religion, he must be duly warned before being degraded.[28] As we will discuss in more depth later, because the Church has no authority over the Pope, these warnings would not be an act of jurisdiction (as they would for other Catholics), *but only an act of charity*, as St. Thomas teaches in regard to fraternal correction.[29]

---

[27] Canon 2314.1-2 says: "All apostates from the Christian faith and each and every heretic or schismatic: Unless they respect warnings, they are deprived of benefice, dignity, pension, office, or other duty that they have in the Church, they are declared infamous, and [if] clerics, with the warning being repeated, [they are] deposed."

[28] "A cleric must, besides, be degraded if, after having been duly warned, he persists in being a member of such a society (non-Catholic sect). All the offices he may hold become vacant, *ipso facto*, without any further declaration. This is tacit resignation recognized by law (Canon 188.4) and therefore the vacancy is one *de facto et iure* (by fact and by law)." Augustine, *A Commentary on the New Code of Canon Law*, vol. 8, bk. 5, p. 280 (emphasis added).

[29] On whether a man is bound to correct his prelate, St. Thomas teaches: "A subject is not competent to administer to his prelate the correction which is an act of justice through the coercive nature of punishment: but the fraternal correction which is an act of charity is within the competency of everyone in respect of any person towards whom he is

If a Pope who professed heresy or denied the Faith in a moment of weakness ("I know not the man") failed to correct himself following an ecclesiastical warning issued by the proper authorities, he would thereby demonstrate publicly that he had willingly and pertinaciously turned away from the Faith. His heresy, in the true sense of the word, would be manifest to all, and he would thereby render a judgment upon himself. He would be notorious with a notoriety *of fact*, and would become notorious *by law* once the his heresy was declared by the Church.

The eminent eighteenth century Italian theologian, Fr. Pietro Ballerini, who subscribed to Bellarmine's famous Fifth Opinion[30] (which will be discussed later), discussed how the warnings would serve to demonstrate pertinacity for a sitting Pope who publicly professed heresy. In the following quotation, Fr. Ballerini begins by responding to the question of who would be responsible for warning a Pope who publicly professed heresy, and then explains the effects that such a warning would produce:

> "Is it not true that, confronted with such a danger to the faith [a Pope teaching *heresy*], any subject can, by fraternal correction, warn their superior, resist him to his face, refute him and, if necessary, summon him and press him to repent? The Cardinals, who are his counselors, can do this; or the Roman Clergy, or the Roman Synod, if, being met, they judge this opportune. For any person, even a private person, the words of Saint Paul to Titus hold: 'Avoid the heretic, <u>after a first and second correction</u>, knowing that such a man is perverted and sins, since he is condemned by his own judgment' (Tit. 3, 10-11). For the person, who, <u>admonished once or twice</u>, does not repent, but continues pertinacious in an opinion contrary to a manifest or defined dogma - not being able, on account of this *public pertinacity* to be excused, by any means, of heresy properly so called, which requires pertinacity - this person *declares himself openly* a heretic. He reveals that by his own will he has turned away from the Catholic Faith and the Church, in such a way that now no declaration or sentence of anyone whatsoever is necessary to cut him from the body of the Church. Therefore the Pontiff who <u>after such a solemn and public warning by the Cardinals, by the Roman Clergy or even by the Synod</u>, would remain himself hardened in heresy and openly turn himself away from the Church, would have to be avoided, according to the precept of Saint Paul. So that he might not cause damage to the rest,

---

bound by charity, provided there be something in that person which requires correction." ST, II-II, q. 33, a. 4.

[30] See Silveira, "La Nouvelle Messe de Paul VI: Qu'en penser," p. 168.

he would have to have his heresy and contumacy publicly proclaimed, so that all might be able to be equally on guard in relation to him. Thus, the sentence which he had pronounced against himself would be made known to all the Church, making clear that by his own will he had turned away and separated himself from the body of the Church, and that in a certain way he had abdicated the Pontificate...”[31]

Here we see an adherent of Bellarmine's teaching regarding the loss of office for a heretical Pope explain how pertinacity (the formal aspect of heresy) is made public, or “manifest,” thereby rendering a Pope who professed heresy a manifest heretic. We see that pertinacity becomes public when the accused remains hardened in heresy, *but only following the twofold warning from ecclesiastical authority (“Cardinals,” “Roman Clergy” or “Synod”)* based on Titus 3:10.

Bellarmine himself mentions this twofold warning by St. Paul in Titus 3:10. In his response to the “Fourth Opinion” (that of Cajetan), he quotes St. Paul's teaching to Titus as his authority for why a manifest heretic is automatically deposed, and, in so doing, shows that a “manifest heretic” is one who shows himself obstinate (pertinacious) by remaining hardened in heresy following a twofold warning. He wrote:

> “For, in the first place, it is proven with arguments from authority and from reason that the manifest heretic is *ipso facto* deposed. The argument from authority is based on Saint Paul (Titus, 3:10), who orders that the heretic be avoided after two warnings, that is, after showing himself to be manifestly obstinate...”[32]

Bellarmine explains that one who remains in heresy following the twofold warning thereby shows himself to be manifestly obstinate, and, consequently, can be considered a manifest heretic.[33] It is clear that the proof of obstinacy (pertinacity) is established by the “two warnings” from the competent authorities. Hence, there is perfect continuity between the teaching of Bellarmine and that of Fr. Pietro

---

[31] *De Potestate Ecclesiastica*, (Monasterii Westphalorum, Deiters, 1847) ch. 6, sec. 2, pp. 124-125 (emphasis added).

[32] *De Romano Pontifice*, bk. 2, ch. 30.

[33] Fr. Sylvester Berry explains that manifest heresy is heresy that can be proved in a court of law. He wrote: “Both *formal* and *material* heresy may be public or occult. Heresy is *manifest* when publicly known to such an extent that its existence could be proven in a court of law” (*The Church of Christ*, p. 128).

Ballerini, cited above, who is a known supporter of Bellarmine's own position. Fr. Ballerini simply explained the position in more depth.

John of St. Thomas also cites Titus 3:10 (Divine law) as the basis for requiring warnings to determine pertinacious heresy. He says a Pope may be a public heretic, but will not lose his office before he is first warned and *declared incorrigible* by the Church (which renders him notorious by law). Commenting on a statement of Cajetan, who said a heretical Pope is not deprived of the pontificate and deposed by the mere fact of heresy alone, John of St. Thomas wrote:

> "The first point of Cajetan is obvious and is not contradicted by Bellarmine. The truth is evident for the following reasons: First, because the Pope, no matter how real and public may be his heresy, if he is prepared to be corrected, he cannot be deposed (as we have said above), and the Church cannot depose him, according to divine law, for she cannot or should not avoid him since the Apostle [Paul] says, 'avoid the heretic after the first and second correction'; <u>therefore, before the first and second correction he should not be avoided</u>, and consequently he should not be deposed; therefore it is wrong to say that the pope is deposed (*ipso facto*) as soon as his heresy is made public: <u>he may be a public heretic, if he has not yet been corrected by the Church, and not declared incorrigible</u> [i.e., notorious by law]"[34]

Cardinal Cajetan discusses the same verse from Titus, chapter 3, in his extensive and detailed treatise on the loss of office for a heretical Pope. After one of the most thorough treatments of the subject that has ever been written, Cardinal Cajetan addresses one final point. He wrote: "Only one point remains to be cleared up – namely, whether heresy alone suffices (the matter), or whether incorrigibility or obstinate perseverance in heresy (the form) is also required for deposing a pope."[35]

Cajetan then proceeds to give what he calls two "extreme opinions." One opinion holds that a heretical Pope cannot be deposed for heresy even if his crime has been publicly confessed (which, as we've seen, would render him notorious by notoriety of law). The other opinion maintains that a Pope can be deposed for a single lapse into heresy, without perseverance. After proposing the various

---

[34] *Cursus Theologici II-II De Auctoritate Summi Pontificis, Disp.* II, Art. III, *De Depositione Papae* (emphasis added).
[35] Cajetan, *De Comparatione Auctoritatis Papae et Concilii,* English Translation in *Conciliarism & Papalism,* by Burns & Izbicki (New York: Cambridge University Press, 1997), p. 101.

arguments presented in defense of each of the two "extreme opinions," he solves the difficulty by navigating the middle course, and this middle course just so happens to correspond to the divinely inspired instruction given by St. Paul to Titus. Cajetan says:

> "Accordingly, the middle and reasonable opinion is that a heretic pope <u>after two admonitions</u> must be deposed, since the apostle Paul, determining this point, says 'A man that is a heretic, after the first and second admonition, avoid' [Titus 3:10]. Assigning the reason why he is to be tolerated no longer, he adds, 'Knowing that he that is such an one is subverted' [vs. 11], where the interlinear gloss, at the word 'subverted' explains it as, 'lost'; and, at the phrase 'such an one,' it explains it as, 'incorrigible.' The meaning of the text is that, because human judgment is given according to what is found in most cases and according to common course, whoever declines for the first time from the faith which he professed by his own will to be true, <u>after one correction, a second time, and a third one after a second correction, is judged to deserve expulsion as incorrigible.</u> Therefore, a heretic pope delinquent in faith, <u>after a first and second admonition,</u> must be shunned by deposition. The faithful cannot shun him while he remains pope, since the salvation of all depends on him after the Lord Jesus, as is said in *Si Papa* [d. 40 c. 6].
>
> Because, therefore, the apostle commanded that a heretical man who offends against the faith <u>after two admonitions</u> should not be tolerated but shunned, the consequence is, first, that, no matter how ready a heretic pope relapsed <u>after two admonitions</u> may be to be corrected, he not only can but ought to be deposed – and rightly, lest human judgment be protracted infinitely;[36] it should rather be brought to an end at some prescribed point. A reasonable limit is defined as a <u>threefold offence with a twofold admonition.</u>"[37]

As we can see, Cajetan solved the difficulty by choosing the middle course, and he did so by simply adhering to the Divine law revealed by God through St. Paul.

Before continuing, it will be helpful to cite a passage from Cajetan which is found in the preceding chapter of his work. In this passage, he explains that a Pope cannot incur the ecclesiastical *censure* of excommunication, since the *censure* - a canonical penalty which strips

---

[36] Here Cajetan is referring to a Pope who would fall into heresy, and repent over and over again indefinitely. He says that in such a case God may forgive him, but the Church should nevertheless depose him, after the third relapse (which means after the second warning).

[37] *De Comparatione Auctoritatis Papae et Concilii*, pp. 102-103 (emphasis added).

the offender of his rights and privileges as a Catholic – is based upon positive law, which does not have coercive power over a Pope (more on this later). Cajetan begins by saying the notion that "the pope, falling into a condemned heresy, falls into excommunication, is false," and then adds:

> "Since every excommunication, which is an ecclesiastical censure (and that is our subject), is based on positive law, which does not have coercive power over the pope in the ecclesiastical forum, whereas excommunication implies coercion in the ecclesiastical forum, we must conclude that *the pope cannot incur any censure*. The doctors carry this point so far that St. Thomas says that the pope cannot confer upon anyone the power to excommunicate him. Albert the Great and Saint Bonaventure are of the same opinion, as Lord Juan de Torquemada reports of them."[38]

With this teaching of Cajetan in mind, we continue with his treatment of why a heretical Pope *must* be warned before being deposed for heresy. He notes that because other heretics may automatically incur *latae sententiae* excommunication (the censure) by operation of canon law[39] (to which the Pope is not subject), it is not *absolutely* necessary for the Church to issue warnings to these before declaring them excommunicated;[40] whereas in the case of a Pope, who is *not* subject to the ecclesiastical censure, the teaching of St. Paul to Titus *should logically be followed to the letter*. In Cajetan's own words:

> "The second consequence is that a heretic pope should not be deposed before the admonitions: for he is not excommunicated on account of heresy, but should be excommunicated by being deposed. Therefore, the apostle's command concerning the double admonition, which need not be observed [to the letter] in the case of others, who are inferiors, on account of the addition of excommunication *latae sententiae*, which the Church imposes on heretics, should be observed to the letter with him."[41]

---

[38] Ibid., p. 99.

[39] Here we can think of certain Catholic politicians who openly acknowledge and defy Catholic teaching (e.g. abortion) to the world, thereby establishing their pertinacity as notorious by notoriety of fact. As non-clerics, their excommunication may be recognized by the Church without the need for ecclesiastical warning or censure.

[40] "Neither is it always demanded in the external forum that there be a warning and a reprimand as described above for somebody to be punished as heretical and pertinacious, and such a requirement is by no means always admitted in practice by the Holy Office" (De Lugo, disp. XX, sect. IV, n. 157-158, cited in "Essay on Heresy," by Arnaldo da Silveira).

[41] *De Comparatione Auctoritatis Papae et Concilii*, p. 103.

Bellarmine Requires Ecclesiastical Warnings

As we have demonstrated, it is the consensus among theologians that a sitting Pope, who directly contradicts an article of faith, must remain obstinate in the face of an ecclesiastical warning before losing his office for the crime of heresy. Although Bellarmine and Cajetan differ on precisely *how* he would lose his office,[42] they both agree that the loss of office *must be preceded by a warning*.

In opposing Cajetan's position (that the Church plays a ministerial role in the fall from the Pontificate), Bellarmine employed the use of a syllogism to defend his own position. Bellarmine's opinion is that the loss of office would occur *ipso facto*, without the Church having to actually "depose" the Pope by performing a juridical act[43] that severs the bond uniting the man (the Pope) to the office (the pontificate), thereby resulting in the fall from office. The syllogism employed by Bellarmine is as follows:

Major: According to St. Paul, a heretic must be avoided after two warnings.

Minor: A Pope who remains Pope cannot be avoided (for how could the Church avoid its head?).

Conclusion: A manifest heretic cannot be the Pope.

Here is the syllogism as expounded by Bellarmine in *De Romano Pontifice*:

"The fourth opinion is that of Cajetan, for whom the manifestly heretical Pope is not *ipso facto* deposed, but can and must be deposed by the Church. To my judgment, this opinion cannot be

---

[42] Bellarmine maintains that the heretical Pope would be deposed by Christ after his heresy and pertinacity had been made sufficiently manifest to the Church (the declaration of the crime being the *dispositive* cause of the deposition); Cajetan, on the other hand, held that the Church itself would play a part in the deposition by declaring him to be avoided (*"vitandus"*) after he was shown to be obstinate, and then separating from him. According to this opinion, the act of separation (not the declaration of the crime itself) would be the *dispositive* cause of the deposition, insofar as it renders the Pope impotent and thus unable to govern the Church. Being rendered impotent, Christ would then sever the bond uniting the man to the pontificate. According to the opinion of both Bellarmine and Cajetan, however, the action of Christ is the *efficient* cause of the fall from office.

[43] A juridical act separating the Church from the Pope, as will be discussed in more detail later in this chapter.

defended. For, in the first place, it is proven with arguments from authority [Major] and from reason [Minor] that the manifest heretic is *ipso facto* deposed, <u>The argument from authority is based on Saint Paul (Titus, 3:10), who orders that the heretic be avoided after two warnings</u>, [Major] that is, after showing himself to be manifestly obstinate which means before any excommunication or judicial sentence (…). Now, a Pope who remains Pope cannot be avoided, for how could we be required to avoid our own head? [Minor] … therefore the manifest heretic cannot be Pope." [Conclusion]

What Bellarmine seeks to demonstrate by this syllogism is that, because Divine law teaches that we must avoid a heretic *after two warnings*, it is evident that a Pope who remains obstinate following two warnings, and who therefore *must* be avoided by the Church, can no longer effectively govern the Church. Because he can no longer rule the Church, Bellarmine (and Suarez also) maintains that he would fall from the pontificate *ipso facto*, once the crime had been established (once his heresy was public and notorious) and therefore before any public excommunication or juridical sentence by the Church.

It is important to note that the Major in Bellarmine's syllogism is taken from St. Paul's instruction to Titus that a heretic must be avoided "after two warnings." It is by remaining hardened in heresy, following the ecclesiastical warnings, that a sitting Pope would be considered a "manifest heretic" (who must be avoided), and consequently incapable of effectively ruling the Church. But this would not take place before the Church issues the necessary warning, and the Pope "show[s] himself to be manifestly obstinate," as Bellarmine noted. It also logically follows that the Church's judgment would have to be communicated to the faithful, either by a "declaratory sentence" of the crime (Suarez says this is the "common opinion") or a command to avoid the heretical Pope (Cajetan/John of St. Thomas).[44]

In the face of the plain meaning of Bellarmine's words, the only response of Sedevacantists, who claim to hold the position of Bellarmine, is to argue that Titus 3:10 does not require that the warnings come from any ecclesiastical authority, but instead can come from anyone. Then, all they have to do is claim that the Pope "must" have been warned by someone (or claim to have heard of someone who has rebuked/warned the Pope) in order to hold their position. But who are they kidding? It is evident that St. Paul is instructing a

---

[44] The opinion of Cajetan/John of St. Thomas will be discussed in depth in Chapter 11.

fellow bishop - Bishop Titus[45] - to render a judgment following two ecclesiastical warnings.

Warnings Must Come From the Church Authorities

The Church has always understood St. Paul's instruction on warnings to relate to ecclesiastical authority, which Sedevacantists would realize if they would read the various commentaries on the verse. For example, in the original annotations of the Rheims New Testament, it says:

> "These admonitions [of Titus 3:10] or corrections must be given to such as err, by our spiritual governors and pastors, to whom if they yield not, Christian men must avoid them."[46]

In his *Commentary on St. Paul's Epistle to Titus*, St. Thomas confirms that the admonitions spoken of in Titus 3:10 come from ecclesiastical authority. Speaking of a person who has deviated from the Faith, St. Thomas wrote: "Such a person should be warned, and if he does not desist, he should be avoided. And he [the Apostle] says, after the first and second admonition, for that is the way the Church proceeds in excommunicating."

In the *Summa*, St. Thomas confirms the same point when he notes that "the Church" condemns, not at once, but after the first and second warning, according to the teaching of St. Paul: He wrote:

> "On the part of *the Church*, however, there is mercy which looks to the conversion of the wanderer, wherefore she condemns not at once, but 'after the first and second admonition,' as the Apostle directs: after that, if he is yet stubborn, the Church no longer hoping for his conversion, looks to the salvation of others, by excommunicating him and separating him from the Church, and furthermore delivers him to the secular tribunal to be exterminated thereby from the world by death."[47]

---

[45] In his Commentary on St. Paul's Epistle to Titus, St. Thomas says "it is easy to gather from the foregoing that the aim of this letter is to instruct Titus how to govern his Church." This is also clear, for example, from what is written at the beginning of the epistle, where St. Paul says: "For this cause I left thee [Titus] in Crete, that thou shouldest set in order the things that are wanting, and shouldest ordain priests in every city, as I also appointed thee" (Tit. 1:5). It is clear that St. Paul is addressing a bishop regarding the discharge of his duties as bishop.

[46] Rheims New Testament, p. 549.

[47] ST, II-II, q. 11, a. 3, *sed contra*. St. Thomas also affirms the justice of capital punishment to the extent it is in proportion to the severity of the crime (and the death penalty is

In other words, just as the Church hopes for the person's conversion through the "two warnings," so the Church severs him from the Body of Christ if he fails to heed those warnings.

In a 1909 article published in *The American Catholic Quarterly Review*, Fr. Maurice Hassett confirmed that the admonitions spoken of by St. Paul must come from the proper ecclesiastical authorities:

> "From the earliest Christian times heresy was universally regarded as the most heinous of sins. The heretic, St. Paul instructs Titus, shall be admonished a first and a second time of the grave character of his offense; if he will not heed, he must be avoided by Christians as a man in evident bad faith, who stands self-condemned - Titus 3:10. (...) Heretics were consequently cut off from all association with the faithful, who must hold no relations with them so long as they obstinately refuse to heed the <u>official remonstrances of the Church authorities</u>."[48]

The 1913 *Catholic Encyclopedia's* article on heresy explains that Titus 3:10 is an example of early ecclesiastical law, which itself is based upon the words of Christ, as recorded in St. Matthew's Gospel, 18:17:

> "St. Paul writes to Titus: 'A man that is a heretic, after the first and second admonition, avoid: knowing that he, that is such a one, is subverted, and sinneth, being condemned by his own judgment' (Titus 3:10-11). <u>This early piece of legislation</u> reproduces the still earlier teaching of Christ, 'And if he will not hear the church, let him be to thee as a heathen and the publican' (Matthew 18:17); it also inspires all subsequent <u>anti-heretical legislation</u>. The sentence on the obstinate heretic is invariably excommunication."[49]

We see that the necessity of a warning is an application of the very words of Christ – "if he refuses to hear the Church" (Mt. 18:17), as applied to the case of heresy. And because the legislation itself – the application of Christ's words - is contained in Scripture, it too is a part of the same Divine law.

John of St. Thomas also addresses the Sedevacantist argument (i.e., that *anyone* can issue a warning) directly and explicitly when he notes

---

proportionate to the crime of harming "the salvation of others"). See, for example, ST, II-II, q. 11, a. 3; q. 64, a. 3; Gen. 9:6; Lk 19:27; Rom 13:4.
[48] Hassett, "Church and State in the Fourth Century," published in *The American Catholic Quarterly Review*, vol. 34, January - October, 1909, pp. 301-302.
[49] *Catholic Encyclopedia* (1913), vol. VII (article on heresy), p. 260.

that the "manifest heresy" of a Pope must be declared *by the Church* before he is to be avoided. He says:

> "[A] heretic should be avoided after two admonitions <u>legally made and with the Church's authority, and not according to private judgment</u>; indeed, great confusion would follow in the Church if it would suffice that this correction be done by a private man. Therefore, let no one say that a Pope, whose manifestly heretical acts <u>have *not* been declared by the Church</u>, is to be avoided. For the manifest heresy of a Pope cannot be made known to all without the testimony of others; but such testimony, <u>if its not made juridically</u>, does not oblige, and consequently no one would be obligated to avoid him. For this reason, it is necessary that, just as the Church designates him by virtue of the election and proposes him to all as elected, so too it is necessary, to depose him, that she declare him a heretic and proposing him to all as one must be avoided."

He then added:

> "So long as it has not been <u>declared to us juridically</u>[50] that he is an infidel or heretic, <u>be he ever so manifestly heretical according to private judgment</u>, he remains, as far as we are concerned, a member of the Church and consequently its head. Judgment is required by the Church. It is only then that he ceases to be Pope as far as we are concerned"[51]

Other examples from theological commentaries could be provided, but the point has been made: The requirement to prove pertinacity in the external forum through "two warnings" must be officially carried out by ecclesiastical authority (the legitimate trier of fact), and not individual Catholics who have no such authority. This is the true and unequivocal meaning of Titus 3:10 upon which St. Bellarmine relies.

Nestorius' Loss of Office? Objection Answered

We will now answer one of the common objections, raised by Sedevacantists, in their attempt to rebut the necessity of warnings before a prelate loses his office for heresy. To support their position, they go back sixteen centuries to the time of Nestorius, the Patriarch of

---

[50] Note that the object of the juridical act is "us," that is, the Church, and not the Pope himself, over whom the Church possesses no jurisdiction.
[51] *Cursus Theologici II-II De Auctoritate Summi Pontificis*, Disp. II, Art. III, *De Depositione Papae*, p.139.

Constantinople. They claim that Nestorius was deposed *ipso facto* by Divine law, the moment he began publicly preaching heresy. Based upon their assertion, they insist that the case of Nestorius proves that warnings are not necessary for a prelate to be deposed. We will allow the Sedevacantist blogger, Steven Speray, to present the standard argument. The following is taken from his response to an article by Robert Siscoe, which was published by *The Remnant* newspaper:

> "The Remnant also contradicts Pope St. Celestine I and St. Robert Bellarmine who both taught that warnings are not necessary to prove defection of faith. Bellarmine put it this way:
>
> 'And in a letter to the clergy of Constantinople, Pope St. Celestine I says: 'The authority of Our Apostolic See has determined that the bishop, cleric, or simple Christian who had been deposed or excommunicated by Nestorius or his followers, after the latter began to preach heresy shall not be considered deposed or excommunicated. For he who had defected from the faith with such preachings, cannot depose or remove anyone whatsoever.'"[52]

The first thing to note is that the above citation no where says "warnings are not necessary," as Mr. Speray claimed. After quoting the above citation, Mr. Speray proceeds to give us his interpretation:

> "In other words, Nestorius lost his office immediately after he began preaching heresy, which is why he had no authority to depose or remove anyone. It happens by Divine law, not by sentence of Church law."[53]

First, note that while Mr. Speray pretends to be giving us the teaching of Bellarmine, the quote he uses does not include any commentary from Bellarmine (Bellarmine was only quoting Pope Celestine). As we will see in a moment, Bellarmine had much more to say about the case of Nestorius than Mr. Speray knows. The reason Mr. Speray is not aware of Bellarmine's actual commentary about the case of Nestorius, is because it was never translated from the Latin and posted on Sedevacantist websites for Mr. Speray to read. Second, neither Bellarmine nor Pope Celestine said that Nestorius "lost his office" by "divine law" the moment he began preaching heresy, as Mr. Speray claims, which is why Mr. Speray was forced to begin his explanation by saying "in other words." Celestine said only that the

---

[52] Speray, "The Remnant's Latest Canon Law Fiasco," February 3, 2015.
[53] Ibid.

excommunications and depositions pronounced by Nestorius, after he began preaching heresy (in A.D. 428), were to be considered null and void. There is absolutely nothing about him losing his office by divine law (based upon the private judgment of individual Catholics) anywhere in the citation. But Mr. Speray "interprets" the quotation as saying that Nestorius lost his office, simply because the excommunications he pronounced were later overturned by the Church (as if it's not possible for a prelate to have maintained his lawful office, simply because some of his official acts were nullified at a later date).

In his book, *De Romano Pontifice* (the same book from which the quotation used by Mr Speray was taken), Bellarmine addresses the deposition of Nestorius directly (with his own commentary), and tells us that the deposition occurred by an act of the proper authorities, not by "divine law" *as interpreted and applied by the private judgment of individual Catholics*, as Mr. Speray would have his readers believe. In fact, it was the faithful Catholics who were scandalized by Nestorius' preaching who appealed to Rome for a condemnation and lawful deposition of their Patriarch, which is what ultimately occurred at the Ecumenical Council of Ephesus. In book one of *De Romano Pontifice*, we find Bellarmine's actual commentary on the deposition of Nestorius, and how he was deposed. He wrote:

> "No bishop can be shown to have either been deposed or excommunicated by the people, although many are found who were deposed and excommunicated by the Supreme Pontiffs and general Councils. Certainly, Nestorius was deposed from the episcopacy of Constantinople by the Council of Ephesus [A.D. 431], from the mandate of Pope Celestine, as Evagrius witnessed."[54]

And in book two of *De Romano Pontifice*, he taught the same:

> "The Council of Ephesus, as it is found in Evagrius,[55] says that it deposed Nestorius by a command of a letter of the Roman Pope Celestine."[56]

Here we see St. Bellarmine explicitly stating that Nestorius was deposed by the Council of Ephesus (A.D. 431) with the approval of the Pope, which shows that, according to Bellarmine, he did not

---

[54] Bellarmine, *De Romano Pontifice*, bk. 1, ch 6.
[55] Evagrius, Hist., bk 1, ch. 4.
[56] *De Romano Pontifice*, bk. 2, ch. 13.

immediately lose his office *ipso facto* by virtue of "divine law" the moment he began to preach heresy three years earlier (December of 428), as Mr. Speray claims.

Suffice it to say that Mr. Speray's interpretation of the case of Nestorius is entirely erroneous. Bellarmine's actual teaching, as evidenced by what we saw above, not only contradicts Mr. Speray's interpretation, but entirely undermines the Sedevacantist thesis: it shows that one who preaches heresy in public must still be deposed by the proper authorities in the Church, and not "declared deposed" by the private judgment of Catholics in the pew. We will have more to say about the case of Nestorius in the next chapter.

Canonical Penalties and Loss of Office

Before proceeding, it seems appropriate at this point to discuss the penalties under canon law which do, and which do not, result in the loss of ecclesiastical office. Addressing the procedural complexities of canon law with respect to the loss of office for heretical clerics, will show us just how seriously the Church views the question. If what follows is true for other clerics, how much more so with regard to a Pope who is above the positive law of the Church, as Cajetan explained above.

In canon law, there are two distinct penalties for heresy: a *censure* and a *vindictive penalty*. A canonical censure can be incurred in one of two ways: either *ferendae sententiae* (imposed as a result of the intervention of Church authority), or *latae sententiae* (that is, *ipso facto*, or automatically, by force of the law itself), when a law is contravened.

The Censure of Excommunication

The censure of excommunication (*latae sententiae*) is incurred automatically by one who knowingly commits any offense that carries the penalty. Such excommunications can be public or occult (secret), and require no warning or declaration, *per se*. However, although the censure of excommunication does not, of itself, require a declaration, canon law does require a declaration when the public good demands it, in order for it to have any canonical effect in the external forum. In other words, in those cases in which a declaration is required for the good of the Church, no one is presumed to have incurred the censure in the external forum without a declaratory sentence. And as canon 2223, §4 of the 1917 Code provides (and the canonists confirm), when the suspect involved is a cleric, *the public good demands it*. This means that a cleric is not considered to have incurred a censure of excommunication unless it has been declared by the Church.

Canon 2223, §4 sets forth the rules for when declaratory sentences are required:

> "In general, to declare a penalty *latae sententiae* is left to the prudence of the superior; but whether at the instance/request of a party who is involved, <u>or because the common good requires it so, a declaratory sentence must be given</u>."[57]

In his popular commentary on the 1917 Code of Canon Law, Fr. Augustine wrote:

> "The *censure* inflicted is excommunication incurred *ipso facto,* which *per se* requires not even a declaratory sentence. Only if, in the prudent judgment of the superior, the public welfare should require such a sentence, it *must* be pronounced. The *bonum publicum* (public good) certainly demands it in the case of clergymen."[58]

Prior to such a declaratory sentence by the Church, even if a cleric incurs hidden (occult) excommunication in the internal forum (which is possible), he will retain the rights and privileges of a Catholic in good standing in the external forum. This means that a cleric will not lose the power of jurisdiction as a result of incurring a (hidden) censure of excommunication, unless and until a declaration is issued by the Church. Further, as we will see in a moment in our discussion of vindictive penalties, a cleric suspected of heresy, who holds office, must be duly warned before a declaratory sentence can be issued.

The *Original Catholic Encyclopedia* explains the difference, on the practical level, between a cleric who has incurred an occult, or secret, excommunication (i.e., one that has not been declared) and a cleric who has incurred a public excommunication (i.e., one that has been declared and therefore has a canonical effect in the external forum):

> "The practical difference is very important. He who has incurred occult excommunication should treat himself as excommunicated and be absolved as soon as possible, submitting to whatever conditions will be imposed upon him, but this only in the

---

[57] *"Poenam latae sententiae declarare generatim committitur prudentiae Superioris; sed sive ad instantiam partis cuius interest, <u>sive bono communi ita exigente, sententia declaratoria dari debet</u>"* (canon 2223, §4, 1917 Code, emphasis added).
[58] *A Commentary on the New Code of Canon Law*, vol. 8, bk. 5., pp. 278-279.

tribunal of conscience; <u>he is not obliged</u> to denounce himself to a judge nor <u>to abstain from external acts connected with the exercise of jurisdiction</u> (…) According to the teaching of Benedict XIV, 'a declaratory sentence of the offence is always necessary in the external forum, since in this tribunal no one is presumed to be excommunicated unless convicted of a crime that entails such a penalty.'"[59]

What this shows is that it is possible for a cleric to incur the hidden censure of excommunication in the internal forum (by secretly being a member of the Masonic sect, for example), yet still be capable of valid "external acts connected with the exercise of jurisdiction," in the ecclesiastical forum. This point is also explained in canon 2264, which provides the following:

"an act of jurisdiction carried out by an excommunicated person, whether in the internal or the external forum, is illicit; and <u>if a condemnatory or declaratory sentence has been pronounced</u>, it is also invalid, without prejudice to c. 2264, §3; otherwise it is valid."

Notice that if a cleric incurs the hidden censure of excommunication, without a declaratory sentence being issued by the Church, his acts would be illicit, but they would nevertheless *remain valid*. And this is true even for a hidden excommunication which results from the sin of heresy. Commenting on the last four words of canon 2264 – "otherwise it is valid" - Fr. Raymond Taouk wrote:

"These last four words are highly significant. Let us assume that this Pope - the validity of whose election nobody is disputing - refuses to admit that he has now fallen into heresy. Then, since no other earthly person or authority would be competent to pass a condemnatory sentence against this Pope, it follows from the Church's law that, if he refuses to resign, all his acts of jurisdiction remain valid, even though they are illicit."[60]

What this demonstrates is that even if one personally believes that a cleric has incurred the censure of excommunication in the *internal forum* – for example, by joining the Masonic sect - it would be quite erroneous to conclude from this that such a one would have lost his office and jurisdiction. This is especially true if the person in question is

---

[59] *Catholic Encyclopedia* (1913), vol. V, p. 680 (emphasis added).
[60] Taouk, "What are we to think of the Sedevacantist Position?" http://www.catholicapologetics.info/modernproblems/currenterrors/sede.htm.

the Pope, since a Pope is not subject to ecclesiastical censure. As we saw earlier in the citation from Cajetan, a Pope is not able to incur the *censure* of excommunication *at all* (at least not in the *external forum*), since this is a matter of positive law, which has no coercive power over a Pope.

This point is important because some Sedevacantist apologists claim, based upon their own private judgment (and their private interpretation of canon law), that recent Popes incurred the *censure* of excommunication and thereby lost their office. Others claim that they incurred the hidden censure *before* being elected Pope, and therefore were not valid candidates for the office. For example, Sedevacantist preacher, Gerry Matatics, claims Cardinal Roncalli (elected as John XXIII in 1958), incurred the automatic *censure* of excommunication before being elected Pope. He claims that by incurring this hidden censure, he ceased to be a member of the Church, and therefore could not be validly elected Pope. Before responding to this point, we will allow Mr. Matatics to explain the *multiple ways* in which he personally believes Cardinal Ronacli incurred excommunication before being elected Pope.

> "Angelo Roncalli incurred automatic excommunication ... in several different ways. First of all, by fraternizing with a man who had been excommunicated [Vitandus] .... A Catholic is forbidden to support such a person... or they share his excommunication, they incur the equal censure, according to canon law. And that is exactly what Angelo Roncalli did. ... He utterly dispossessed himself of his membership in the Catholic Church. But you can also excommunicate yourself by becoming a Freemason, according to the 1917 Code of canon law... strike number two against Angelo Roncalli is that he was inducted into Freemasonry. A third strike against Roncalli is that he was a Socialist and a promoter of Communism. ... he did this before his election, when he was Cardinal of Vienna ... Every Catholic must reject him [as being Pope] for the ... reasons I have just given."[61]

He also accuses Roncalli of being a heretic (strike four) for promoting Talmudic Judaism, during this time, even though Pope Pius XII and all the bishops and Cardinals of the day considered him a Catholic in good standing (which would mean, even if Mr. Matatics were correct, that Roncalli would have been a secret, not public heretic). And how, you may be wondering, does Mr. Matatics know

---

[61] Matatics, "Counterfeit Catholicism vs. Consistent Catholicism," disc 2, tracks 4-12.

that Roncalli committed these acts which carry an automatic excommunication? He claims to have read about it in "books." In other words, he relies upon nothing but hearsay evidence that wouldn't be admissible even in a secular court of law (and "evidence" that was certainly dismissed by Pius XII and the entire College of Cardinals). Then, based upon what he claims to have read (he also provides no actual quotations with references), Mr. Matatics publicly declares, as a *fact*, that Cardinal Roncalli incurred the censure of excommunication, ceased to be a member of the Church, and therefore was not validly elected Pope. Summarizing his thesis, he said:

> "We saw that, because of this fourfold strike against him -
> being a heretic, an aider and abettor of excommunicated heretics, a
> promoter of ... Communism, and a member of Freemasonry, which
> automatically excommunicates you from the Church - Angelo
> Roncalli was no longer a member of the Catholic Church by the
> time of his election in 1958; and not being a member of the Church,
> we saw ... if a man is not a member of the Catholic Church, he
> cannot be the head of something that he is not even member of. It's
> that simple. It's that straightforward. It's that logical."[62]

Based upon the above erroneous reasoning, Mr. Matatics then "logically" concludes that the 1962 Missal, which was promulgated by John XXIII, "is not a legal Mass of the Catholic Church, because John XXIII was not a legal Pope of the Catholic Church."[63]

Obviously, there are a number of problems with Mr. Matatics' logic: First, just because he read somewhere that Roncalli (John XXIII) was guilty of the aforementioned acts does not prove anything, nor does it in any way confirm that he incurred the censure of excommunication. That Mr. Matatics would introduce as "proof" an alleged statement of an unidentified author whose assertion cannot be cross-examined shows how far-reaching he is willing to go to "prove" his case (Matatics would be laughed out of a courtroom for such a tactic). More importantly, Roncalli was treated as a prelate in good standing during the entire pontificate of Pius XII, and was even elevated to Cardinal by Pius XII in 1953 – which was *after* Mr. Matatics alleges that he incurred excommunication. Thus, Matatics would have us accept his judgment of Roncalli, and that of an unknown author, over the judgment of Pope Pius XII (whom Matatics recognizes as Pope) and the entire Church.

---

[62] Ibid., disc 4, track 3.
[63] Ibid., disc 2, tracks 4-12.

Second, even if Cardinal Roncalli did incur the censure (which neither Pius XII nor anyone else at the time evidently knew about), the hidden censure would not have caused him to lose any office that he held or cease being a member of the Church,[64] since, as we have seen, a declaratory sentence is required for a prelate to be considered excommunicated in the external forum. We also note that the activities Matatics mentions ("fraternizing" with excommunicates; promoting Socialism and Communism) would have only rendered Roncalli suspect of heresy in the external forum, without further ecclesiastical inquiry into the allegations.

Third, as we will discuss in Chapter 12, even if Roncalli had incurred the hidden censure of excommunication, it would not have prevented him from being elected Pope, since, as the law promulgated by Pius XII states:

> "No Cardinal can in any way be excluded from the active and passive election[65] of the Supreme Pontiff on the pretext or by reason of any excommunication, suspension, interdict, or other ecclesiastical impediment whatsoever. We in fact suspend these censures only for the effect of an election of this sort."[66]

So even if Cardinal Roncalli did incur the hidden censure of excommunication before entering the Conclave, it would have been lifted by virtue of ecclesiastical law. Mr. Matatics' entire case is based upon nothing but his own private judgment and misunderstanding of Church law. Unfortunately, this same error is repeated by many of his Sedevacantist colleagues, who are equally confused over this issue. This only demonstrates how gravely Sedevacantists err in their private interpretation of canon law, and in applying its penalties to prelates and Popes.

Some Sedevacantists contradict themselves by requiring a declaratory sentence for a cleric when it suits their own personal needs.

---

[64] It is commonly held that only those excommunicated by name (*vitandi*) cease to be *members* of the Church. To quote Fr. Devine: "It is more probably that the excommunicated, who are what are called *tolerated* [*tolerati*], and *not to be avoided*, remain members of the Church. In the case of the *non-tolerated*, and those to be avoided [*vitandi*], the words, or terms, in which the sentence of excommunication is inflicted, have to be examined, and the case has to be judged according to the sentence, whether it be or be not a total separation of communion with the body of the Church" (*The Creed Explained, an Exposition of Catholic Doctrine*, 2nd ed., p. 262).

[65] Active election refers to the act of electing a Pope; passive election refers to the act of being elected Pope.

[66] Pius XII, *Vacantis Apostolicae Sedis*, No. 34, 1945, A.A.S., vol. XXXVIII (1946), n. 3, pp. 65-99.

For example, the Dimond brothers of Most Holy Family Monastery attend Mass at a non-Sedevacantist parish that is in union with Pope Francis. Even though they declare Pope Francis to be an apostate antipope, and the Church over which he rules to be a false Church, they nevertheless attend Mass at a chapel that is in union with the "antipope," and which is a part of the Church they publicly denounce as a "false Church."[67] How do they justify this? They do so by claiming that attending Mass at the Church is permitted, *because the priest has not been declared a heretic by the Church*. That's right. And they even use the example of Martin Luther to defend their position. They say that while it is true that Luther was "an obvious heretic" (by private judgment) before he was excommunicated, he wasn't considered a heretic according to Church law (by the Church's judgment) until his heresy was declared by the Church. Here's what Peter Dimond says:

> "One point on which I spent some time in the debate was the distinction between the way the Church uses the term "heretic" in its dogmatic decrees and in its ecclesiastical law. We know that, according to the Church's dogmatic teaching, all who dissent from an authoritative teaching of the Church are heretics without any declaration. However, the Church's ecclesiastical laws have used the term in a different sense. The case of Martin Luther is a prime example. Martin Luther was an obvious heretic before he was declared to be such. Certainly we are not saying that you cannot recognize someone as a heretic until the Church's declaration. ... In studying the papal bulls relating to Martin Luther, one will discover that he wasn't considered to be a heretic in the Church's ecclesiastical law until he was declared such. At that point, the absolute obligation to avoid him was imposed.[68]

So the Dimonds admit that not even Luther was considered a heretic *according to the Church's law*, until he was "declared such" *by the Church*. Without realizing it, the Dimonds have just invalidated the entire Sedevacantist thesis by conceding that the declaration is necessary for a prelate to be considered a heretic *by the Church* (and by all the members of the Church), which is precisely what canon law

---

[67] For this, the Dimonds are condemned by their fellow Sedevacantists. For example, Richard Ibranyi wrote: "The Dimonds deny the Catholic Church's infallible teaching that Catholics are forbidden to knowingly pray in communion with heretics, which makes the Dimonds heretics and also guilty of other mortal sins. The Dimonds knowingly attend Mass at a meetinghouse of heretics (a non-Catholic church) and teach others that they can do the same." (Ibranyi, *Against Gerry Matatics*, November 2006).
[68]http://www.mostholyfamilymonastery.com/Articles/sacraments_from_undeclared_h eretics_debate.php (emphasis added).

requires. All the Dimonds need to do next is realize that a cleric does not *lose his office* until he is judged a heretic *by that same Church* (not by private judgment), and then they will be able to see their error. Of course, this will require that they abandon the error they learned from Fr. Cekada, which maintains that a Pope loses his office, *ipso facto*, by violating "Divine law" through committing the "sin" of heresy (as judged by private judgment).

What else the Dimond brothers don't realize is that the Church does not understand heresy one way for "dogmatic decrees" and another way for "ecclesiastical law" (which is why they were unable to cite any authority to support their assertion). Heresy is the post-baptismal denial or doubt of a truth that must be believed with divine and Catholic faith. The distinction they have spotted in their reading (but not understood) is between heresy in the internal forum (i.e., loss of faith) versus the external forum (i.e., public and notorious heresy, as judged by the Church). The Dimond brothers fail to understand that the sin of heresy alone, *which has not been judged and declared by the Church*, does not result in the loss of ecclesiastical office for a cleric.[69] The loss of office for a cleric is a vindictive penalty, and there is a process in Church law which must precede vindictive penalties.

Vindictive Penalties

We have seen that the *censure* of excommunication can be public or occult. We have also seen that while a cleric may incur an automatic (*latae sententiae*) occult *censure* of excommunication (e.g., by secretly becoming a Freemason), he is not considered to have incurred the penalty in the external forum unless and until it is declared by the Church (for a cleric, the good of the Church demands a formal declaration of the crime). This also means that the loss of office for a cleric must be imposed (*ferendae sententiae*) by Church authority[70] which makes the loss of office a "vindictive penalty." Note, however, that the imposition of the penalty must *always* be preceded by an ecclesiastical warning (usually two). This means that for a cleric to *lose his office* for the crime of heresy, he must be duly warned, and the excommunication must be imposed by a declaratory sentence by the Church. If a prelate had previously incurred a hidden (occult) excommunication (in the internal forum), his juridical acts would have

---

[69] We will discuss tacit resignation from office (canon 188) later.
[70] In the old 1917 Code, there was an exception to this rule for the more severe vindictive penalty (canon 188, §4). This topic will be discussed at the end of this chapter.

been illicit, but nevertheless remained valid until the declaration was issued.

Fr. Augustine explains vindictive penalties as follows:

> "The penalties here enunciated are twofold: *censure* and *vindictive penalties*; (…)

> b) The *vindictive penalties* inflicted are: (…) For clerics: privation of every benefice, dignity, pension, office, or charge which they may hold; also infamy and, *after a fruitless warning, deposition*. <u>A warning must precede these vindictive penalties</u> (…). The infamy inflicted on both laymen and clergymen, and the deposition pronounced against clerics, are *ferendae sententiae*. <u>Deposition requires a second warning</u> after the first one has been served, with the threat of privation and infamy."[71]

Here we see that all vindictive penalties must be preceded by a warning, while the vindictive penalty of *deposition* must be preceded by a *second* warning. Hence, according to canon law, which interprets and applies Divine law, the two warnings required by St. Paul (Tit. 3:10) must be issued to a cleric before he can be deposed for heresy. Of course, if ecclesiastical warnings are required before just any cleric can lose his office for heresy, how much more necessary are such warnings (a necessity which is rooted in Divine revelation) when the cleric in question is the Pope? To ask the question is to answer it.

No One Can Warn the Pope? Objection Answered

At this point, an objection needs to be addressed. Almost all Sedevacantists claim that a Pope who professes heresy cannot be warned by the Church. They say that a warning requires a judgment, and since "the First See is judged by no one" (even though they themselves judge the Pope!), no one is permitted to warn a Pope. They further maintain that a warning must come from a superior, and since the Pope has no superior on Earth, it follows that he cannot be warned.[72] In other words, Sedevacantists maintain that *no one* can *warn* the Pope (not even the College of Cardinals), yet individual Catholics

---

[71] Augustine, *A Commentary on the New Code of Canon Law*, vol. 8, bk. 5, p. 279.
[72] For example, the Sedevacantist blogger Steve Speray, wrote: "As I explained in the article, only superiors give warnings etc. and the pope has no superiors. Therefore, there are [sic] no such thing as proper authorities to issue two warnings to the pope." (Speray, "Robert Siscoe and Catholic Family News Present Another False Argument Against Sedevacantism," September 18, 2014).

with no authority can *judge* the Pope guilty of heresy and declare him deprived of his office. Sound reasonable?

Setting aside the inherent contradiction in their position, what they fail to understand is that a warning can be either an act of judgment (which is proper to a superior), or a work of mercy and therefore an act of charity. As an act of charity, an inferior can certainly warn, or fraternally correct, a superior, "provided," as St. Thomas noted, "there be something in the person that requires correction."[73]

Fr. Ballerini, who was cited at length above with respect to warning a heretical Pope, made this very point. He said "whatever would be done against him [a heretical Pope] before the declaration of his contumacy and heresy, in order to call him to reason, would constitute an obligation of charity, not of jurisdiction."[74]

Scripture itself provides an example of an inferior warning a superior, and the superior in this case just happened to be the Pope. In Galatians, Chapter 2, we read that St. Paul withstood St. Peter to his face "because he was to be blamed" (Gal. 2:11). That is, St. Paul, who taught Titus about the necessity of warnings, practiced what he preached in his public warning to St. Peter. Thus, Scripture reveals that we are permitted to fraternally correct a superior, as a matter of Divine law.

Also, in the context of St. Paul's warning of St. Peter, St. Thomas observes that "to withstand anyone in public exceeds the mode of a fraternal correction."[75] What St. Paul did by *rebuking* St. Peter in public exceeds a mere fraternal correction. Yet God willed the event to be recorded in Scripture for our instruction. What are we to learn from this passage? We learn that a public warning and even rebuke, of a superior (i.e., the Pope), exceeds what is permitted, *unless there is an "imminent danger" to the Faith*. In other words, what would be excessive in normal circumstances is justified when the Faith is endangered, and hence when the salvation of souls is at stake. St. Thomas wrote:

> "It must be observed, however, that if the faith were endangered, a subject ought to rebuke his prelate even publicly. Hence Paul, who was Peter's subject, rebuked him in public, on account of the imminent danger and scandal concerning the faith."[76]

---

[73] ST, II-II, q. 33, a. 4
[74] Ballerini, *De Potestate Ecclesiastica*, (Monasterii Westphalorum, Deiters, 1847), ch. 6, sec. 2, p. 125.
[75] ST, II-II q. 33, a. 4, ad. 2
[76] Ibid.

St. Thomas goes on to quote St. Augustine who said, "Peter gave an example to superiors, that if at any time they should happen to stray from the straight path, they should not disdain to be reproved by their subjects." Clearly, if a subject is permitted to fraternally correct a superior (which is what the warning would constitute), and if St. Paul (an Apostle and bishop) was justified in going further by *publicly* withstanding St. Peter to his face because of an imminent danger to the faith, it logically follows that the Church is able to issue a public warning to one of St. Peter's successors, if he too is endangering the faith by his words or actions.

In his Commentary on the Book of Galatians, St. Thomas makes an important observation about this incident between St. Paul and St. Peter. He notes that St. Paul was resisting St. Peter in the *exercise* of his authority, but not in his authority of ruling as such (which would be schismatic). He wrote:

> "[T]he Apostle opposed Peter in the exercise of authority, not in his authority of ruling. Therefore, from the foregoing we have an example: for prelates, an example of humility, that they not disdain corrections from those who are lower and subject to them; while subjects have an example of zeal and freedom, so they will not fear to correct their prelates, particularly if their crime is public and verges upon danger to the multitude."[77]

As we have demonstrated, a warning is an integral part of establishing the crime of heresy for a reigning Pope, which is why the Church's theologians agree that a reigning Pope must remain obstinate following an ecclesiastical warning, before being deprived of his office for heresy. Such a warning would not constitute an act of jurisdiction, but an act of charity, which would sufficiently demonstrate if the Pope were incorrigible in his heresy, rather than merely mistaken.

If a Pope were to obstinately refuse to heed these charitable warnings by retracting his heresy, his response would prove pertinacity in the external forum and the Church would declare him to have judged himself. This is indeed permitted, as Pope Innocent III explained when, during one of his own Coronation sermons, he said:

> "the Roman Pontiff...should not mistakenly flatter himself about his power, nor rashly glory in his eminence or honor, for the less he is judged by man, the more he is judged by God. I say 'less' because <u>he can be judged by men</u>, or rather <u>shown to be judged</u>, if

---

[77] *Super Epistulas S. Pauli, Ad Galatas*, 2: 11-14 (Taurini/Romae: Marietti, 1953) nn. 77.

he clearly loses his <u>savor to heresy</u>, since he 'who does not believe is <u>already judged</u>.'"[78]

If a Pope has shown himself incorrigible by remaining obstinate in the face of a public warning, the crime of heresy would be sufficiently established. This would pave the way for the divine punishment (loss of office), which would then be followed by the human punishment (excommunication).

Distinction Between the *Crime* and *Punishment*

One of the root errors of the Sedevacantist thesis is the failure to realize that the loss of office is consequent to (but not the direct consequence of) the *crime* of heresy, and not simply the *sin* of heresy. Those who erroneously believe the loss of office is a direct consequence of the sin of heresy (and loss of the virtue of faith) believe that if they personally become "morally certain" that the Pope has committed the sin, they are equally "morally certain" that he has lost his office. Such reasoning excludes, in their mind, the necessity for the Church itself to establish the crime. For those Sedevacantists who maintain, along with Bellarmine and Suarez, that the loss of office is consequent to (follows) the *crime* of heresy (and there are some who do recognize this point), they err by considering themselves, rather than the Church, to be the judge and jury of the *crime,* just as the others make themselves the judge and jury of the *sin*.

But both groups have failed to consider an important point. What they fail to realize is that it is God Himself who severs the bond that unites the man to the pontificate. The reason this is important is because the actions of man do not directly *cause* God to act. What this means is that neither the *sin* of heresy, nor the *crime* of heresy, as such, is the direct *cause* of the loss of office. In other words, not even the *crime* of heresy relates to the fall from office as an efficient cause producing an effect. Rather, the crime of heresy is an antecedent[79] which only *disposes*[80] the heretical Pope to be deprived of the pontificate. The loss of office itself occurs by a direct and immediate act of God.

This is similar to what transpires with the election of a Pope. During the election, the Cardinals elect the man who is to become

---

[78] *Between God and Man: Sermons of Pope Innocent III,* Sermon IV, pp. 48-49 (emphasis added).

[79] Antecedent: a thing or event that existed before or logically precedes another.

[80] The *dispositive cause* "prepares matter for a certain form, but does not induce that form…"(St. Thomas Aquinas, *Commentary on Aristotle's Metaphysics,* , bk. 5, less. 2).

Pope. This act of being elected only *disposes* him to receive the pontificate, but it does not make him Pope. The act of joining the *matter* (the man elected) to the *form* (pontificate), occurs directly and immediately by an act of God. If a Pope falls from the pontificate due to heresy, the contrary occurs: the Pope first becomes *disposed* for the loss of office, while the loss of office itself (disjoining the man from the pontificate) occurs immediately by an act of Christ.

Msgr. Van Noort used the concept of *dispositive cause* in his response to the objection that "the sin of heresy immediately severs a person from the Body of the Church." In responding, he explains that "internal heresy, since it destroys that interior unity of faith from which unity of profession is born, separates one from the body of the Church *dispositively,* but not yet formally."[81] In other words, the sin of heresy *disposes* a person to be separated from the Church, but the actual separation from the visible society does not occur until the crime has first been sufficiently established or the person has himself openly left the Church.

The same principle is true with the Pope's fall from the pontificate. Because it is God who severs the bond that unites the man to the pontificate (just as it was God who joined the man to the pontificate following the election), even a notoriously heretical Pope is only *disposed* to lose the pontificate, but neither the crime of heresy, as such, nor even the declaratory sentence of the crime directly *causes* the fall from office.

Again, the reason this point is significant is because, since the loss of office occurs immediately by an act of God, and *not* as a direct *consequence* of the crime, Christ can continue to give jurisdiction even to a notoriously heretical Pope as long as he is being recognized by the Church as its head. It is *possible* for Christ to sustain a heretical Pope in office because the relationship between heresy and jurisdiction is not one of total metaphysical incompatibility, and Christ will do so because He will not secretly depose a Pope while he is being tolerated by the Church and publicly recognized as its head. This is confirmed by the teaching of Pope Alexander III (d. 1181) who said "a heretic retains his jurisdiction *as long as he is tolerated by the Church*; he loses it at the time he is reprobated by Her."[82] This is also taught in the *Summa, Tractaturus Magister Gratianus*, which states that a heretic retains his power (*potestas*) as long as he is tolerated by the Church (*quamdiu*

---

[81] Van Noort, *Christ's Church*, p. 242.
[82] *Summa*, in C. 24, q. 1. p. 100. Peter Huizing, *The Earliest Development of Excommunication latae sententiae*," Studia Gratiana 3 (1955), p. 286.

toleratur ab ecclesia potest).[83] This, of course, makes perfect sense. For if God were to secretly sever the bond uniting the man to the pontificate, while the Church continued to recognize the man as Pope, the actions of God would effectively deceive His Church into following an antipope – that is, one lawfully elected and publicly presented to the Church as Pope by the authorities, yet secretly deposed by God.

Needless to say, such a result is not only impossible, for God cannot lie or deceive us, but in such a case the charism of infallibility would not prevent the man (recognized publicly by the Church as Pope) from doing what a true Pope could never do - namely, binding the universal Church to false and heretical doctrines. Such a catastrophe would be *possible* only if God Himself – by His own divine act - *secretly* severed the bond that united the man to the pontificate without the Church being aware of it. If such were to occur, the man elected Pope, and recognized as such by the Church, would be capable of doing what the Church teaches and believes cannot be done. The indefectible Church would be capable of defection, and it would have been made possible because of a *hidden act* of God. This reasoning explains why the crime of heresy must be determined by the Church, rather than by an act of private judgment, before Christ deposes a Pope for heresy.

This was confirmed by the great canonist, Fr. Paul Laymann, S.J. (d. 1632). In his classic book, *Moral Theology*, he explained that if a Pope were to fall into heresy, and even "notorious heresy," he would remain a true Pope as long as he was being tolerated by the Church and publicly recognized as its head. Listen to Fr. Laymann:

> "It is more probable that the Supreme Pontiff, as a person, might be able to fall into heresy and even a notorious one, by reason of which he would merit to be deposed by the Church, or rather declared to be separated from her. (...) Observe, however, that, though we affirm that the Supreme Pontiff, as a private person, might be able to become a heretic and therefore cease to be a true member of the Church, (...) still, while he was tolerated by the Church, and publicly recognized[84] as the universal pastor, he would really enjoy the pontifical power, in such a way that all his decrees would have no less force and authority than they would if he were

---

[83] Quoted in Huizing, p. 287.
[84] As will be discussed in the section on the peaceful and universal acceptance of a Pope, a Pope does not have to be accepted by a *mathematical unanimity*, but only a *moral unanimity* of the Church. This means that if one percent of those who profess to be Catholics do not accept him as Pope (such as the Sedevacantists), it would not mean he was not recognized publicly as the Pope.

truly faithful. The reason is: because it is conducive to the governing of the Church, even as, in any other well-constituted commonwealth, that the acts of a public magistrate are in force as long as he remains in office and is publicly tolerated."[85]

Reason itself confirms this teaching. For if a Pope were able to fall from the pontificate without the Church being aware of it, we would never know for sure which Popes in the past were true Popes, and which had crossed the line into heresy and lost their office. Hence, we would have no way of knowing if the definitive decrees of the various councils had been ratified by a real Pope, or by one who had lapsed into heresy for a time and secretly fallen from the pontificate. Consequently, the object of the Faith itself (the dogmas that must be believed) would be uncertain, and the determination of which dogmas were defined by true Popes, and which were not, would be left to the private judgment of individual Catholics in the pew to decide. The scrupulous would be paralyzed by doubt, and the unstable would fall into the most outrageous conclusions. Those who denied various dogmas would only have to cast doubt upon the Popes who defined them in order to justify their incredulity. With fallen human nature as it is, such uncertainly would quickly lead to confusion and division – just like we see in Protestantism, where everything is based upon each person's private judgment. For this reason, Billuart teaches that:

> "Christ by a particular providence, for the common good and the tranquility of the Church, continues to give jurisdiction to an even manifestly heretical pontiff until such time as he should be declared a manifest heretic by the Church."[86]

This common opinion was also confirmed by John of St. Thomas, who said a Pope who is manifestly heretical, *according to private judgment*, remains Pope until he is declared such by the Church:

> "So long as it has not been declared to us juridically that he is an infidel or heretic, be he ever so manifestly heretical according to private judgment, he remains, as far as we are concerned, a member of the Church and consequently its head. Judgment is required by the Church. It is only then that he ceases to be Pope as far as we are concerned."[87]

---

[85] Laymann, Theol. Mor., bk. 2, tract 1, ch. 7, p. 153 (emphasis added).

[86] Billuart, *De Fide*, Diss. V, A. III No. 3, Obj. 2.

[87] *Cursus Theologici II-II De Auctoritate Summi Pontificis*, Disp. II, Art. III, *De Depositione Papae*.

Reconciling Bellarmine and Suarez

The distinction between the crime of heresy, established by the ecclesiastical authorities, and the fall from the pontificate, by the direct action of God, will enable us to reconcile what has been incorrectly considered by some modern writers to be a contradiction between the teaching of Bellarmine and Suarez regarding the loss of office for a heretical Pope.

By way of background, we note that Bellarmine, in his treatise *De Romano Pontifice,* said there were five different opinions concerning the implications of a heretical Pope (with the Fourth and Fifth Opinion as the most commonly accepted). The well-read Brazilian scholar Arnaldo Xavier da Silveira, in his book 'La Nouvelle Messe de Paul VI: *Qu'en penser,'* and Fr. Dominique Boulet, of the Society of St. Pius X,[88] categorized various authors according to the five opinions laid out by Bellarmine. The Five Opinions, and the categorization of those holding the various opinions by these two authors, are as follows:

- First Opinion: The Pope can never fall into heresy (e.g., Bellarmine, Billot).
- Second Opinion: The Pope loses his office *ipso facto* for occult heresy (e.g., Torquemada). This opinion "has been completely abandoned by the theologians."[89]
- Third Opinion: The Pope never loses his office for manifest heresy (Bouix).
- Fourth Opinion: "The manifestly heretical Pope is not *ipso facto* deposed, but can and must be deposed by the Church."[90] (e.g., Cajetan, <u>Suarez</u>[91])
- Fifth Opinion: "The Pope who is manifestly a heretic ceases by himself to be Pope and head... and for this reason he can be judged and punished by the Church."[92] (e.g., Bellarmine, Billot).

---

[88] Boulet, "Is that Chair Vacant? An SSPX Dossier on Sedevacantism," online at http://www.fsspx.com/Communicantes/Dec2004/Is_That_Chair_Vacant.htm.
[89] Silveira, 'La Nouvelle Messe de Paul VI: Qu'en penser' (translated by J. R. Spann), p. 157.
[90] Bellarmine, *De Romano Pontifice*, bk. 2, ch. 30.
[91] As further explained below, listing Suarez as a supporter of the Fourth Opinion is erroneous because Suarez believed that a manifestly heretical Pope lost his office *ipso facto*, after the Church established the crime (pertinacity established through warnings). Thus, Suarez, like Bellarmine, actually held the Fifth Opinion.

Silveira and Boulet (who are not Sedevacantists) both include Francisco Suarez - one of the greatest theologians of his age[93] - as holding the *Fourth Opinion* along with Cajetan. Again, the Fourth Opinion is that the manifestly heretical Pope <u>does not</u> lose his office *ipso facto*, but must be deposed by the Church. This differs from Bellarmine's Fifth Opinion, which holds that a manifestly heretical Pope <u>does</u> lose his office *ipso facto*. Silveira and Boulet presumably include Suarez as holding the Fourth Opinion because Suarez says: "I affirm: if he were a heretic and incorrigible, the Pope would cease to be Pope <u>just when a sentence was passed against him for his crime, by the legitimate jurisdiction of the Church</u>.[94] Compare that statement of Suarez to what Bellarmine wrote about the Fifth Opinion:

> "Therefore, the true opinion is the fifth, according to which the <u>Pope who is manifestly a heretic ceases by himself to be Pope and head,</u> in the same way as he ceases to be a Christian and a member of the body of the Church; and for this reason he can be judged and punished by the Church. This is the opinion of all the ancient Fathers, who teach that <u>manifest heretics immediately lose all jurisdiction</u>..."[95]

The problem, which we have not seen addressed before, is that the Silveira/Boulet classification of Suarez as sharing the opinion of Cajetan (listed as the Fourth Opinion) is not correct.[96] Suarez did not agree with Cajetan, but instead held that a heretical Pope loses his office *ipso facto* (being deposed immediately by Christ), which is the Fifth Opinion. For example, Suarez explicitly teaches that a manifestly heretical Pope "<u>is *ipso facto* and immediately deposed by Christ,</u>"[97] which is not what Cajetan himself taught.[98] And to be clear, the

---

[92] Ibid.

[93] *Catholic Encyclopedia* (1913), vol. XIV (Francisco Suarez), p. 319.

[94] *De Fide*, disp. X, sect. VI, nn. 3-10, pp. 316-317.

[95] *De Romano Pontifice*, bk. 2, ch. 30. These other saints include Alphonsus Liguori and Francis de Sales, and theologians such as Billot, Wilhelm, Badii, Prummer, Wernz, Vidal, Beste, Creusen, Coronata, Attwater, Naz, Regatillo, and Iragui.

[96] John Salza first addressed this issue in his landmark article "Bellarmine against Suarez? Another Critical Error in the Sedevacantist Thesis," published in *The Remnant* newspaper, November 2014.

[97] *De Fide, Disp.* 10, Sect 6, n. 10, p. 317.

[98] The confusion over this point seems to stem from da Silveira's personal commentary on Bellarmines's Five Opinions (which has served as the basis for many other commentaries). Silveira's commentary on the Fourth Opinion does not accurately reflect the wording of Bellarmine. For example, Silveira said: "According to this fourth opinion, the Pope never loses the Pontificate by the very act of his fall into heresy. Rather, for his destitution to be effective, it is necessary that there be an act declaratory of his defection

"Fourth Opinion" enunciated by Bellarmine is none other than that of Cajetan himself. As we will see later, pre-Vatican II theologians who studied this question *in depth* stated that Bellarmine and Suarez held the *same* opinion regarding the loss of office for a heretical Pope. They placed Bellarmine and Suarez in one camp and Cajetan in another, and there is indeed a good reason for this.

Part of the confusion stems from a failure to realize that there are two separate declarations, or at least two separate acts of the Church, in the deposition of a reigning Pope who has professed heresy (here we intentionally distinguish a Pope who merely professed heresy, as opposed to a Pope who openly left the Church, which will be addressed later).

After the material and formal elements of heresy have been sufficiently established by the proper authorities, the Church determines that the Pope is guilty of the crime of heresy (and will likely also issue a declaratory sentence of the crime). At this point, according to the opinion of Bellarmine and Suarez, God *immediately* severs the bond that unites the man to the office, and he falls *ipso facto* from the pontificate (divine punishment), without being technically "deposed" by the Church.[99] The *ipso facto* fall from the pontificate is followed by a separate act of the Church – the declaration of deprivation - which merely confirms that the former Pope has fallen from his office due to the crime of heresy. This second declaration would presumably include a public excommunication of the former Pope (human punishment). The following is the sequence of events we have just described, which follows the opinions of both Bellarmine and Suarez (the opinion of Cajetan and John of St. Thomas will be discussed in depth in Chapter 11):

1.   The crime is established by the Church (<u>human judgment</u>). Suarez taught that the "common opinion" is that a *declaratory sentence*

---

in the faith... <u>on account of which Jesus Christ himself will depose the Pope.</u>" But in his actual explanation of the Fourth Opinion, Bellarmine does not say the heretical Pope is deposed *ipso facto* <u>by Christ</u>, but that he is "deposed by <u>the Church</u>." It should also be noted that a close reading of Cajetan's position shows that he does indeed believe the Church itself plays an actual part (albeit a ministerial part) in the deposition itself – that is, *the Church has a part to play in actually severing the bond that unites the man to the office,* which occurs after the crime has been established. The part played by the Church in the deposition is to legally separate from the heretical Pope. According to Cajetan, this act of legal separation contributes, in a ministerial way, to the loss of office. This certainly differs from the opinion of Bellarmine *and* Suarez.

[99] What we mean by "not technically 'deposed' by the Church" is that the Church herself plays no part when it comes to severing the bond that unites the man to the office.

would also be issued at this time. The establishment of the crime by the Church *disposes* the Pope to lose his office.

2. God Himself severs the bond that unites the man to the pontificate, and he falls, *ipso facto,* from office (<u>divine punishment</u>).

3. The Church issues the declaration of deprivation which confirms that the Pope has fallen from the pontificate, paving the way for the Cardinals to elect a new Pope. The former Pope is publicly excommunicated by the Church (<u>human punishment</u>).

In light of the sequence of events, we can see that when Suarez says "the Pope would cease to be Pope just when a sentence was passed against him for his crime," he is confirming that <u>the Church</u> must *first* establish <u>the crime</u> (by proving guilt) and then issue the declaratory sentence[100] before a sitting Pope loses his office for heresy (point #1 above). This effectively *disposes* the Pope for the fall from office, paving the way for the divine punishment (loss of office) - that is, the divine act of severing the man from the pontificate by Christ Himself.

Thus, when Suarez says the heretical Pope "is *ipso facto* and immediately deposed by Christ," he is referring to the divine punishment (point #2), by which Christ Himself *causes* the fall by severing the bond that unites the man to the pontificate, without any *further* part being played by the Church (which differs from the opinion of Cajetan[101]).

When Bellarmine says a manifestly heretical Pope is *ipso facto* deposed "before any excommunication or judicial sentence," he is confirming that the <u>divine punishment</u> - *ipso facto* loss of office (point

---

[100] In order to prevent the notion that the Church was inappropriately "judging" the Pope, some have maintained that the fall would technically take place before any declaratory sentence was issued. See, for example, Vermeersch, I. Creusen, *Epitome Iuris Canonici* (Rome: Dessain, 1949), p. 340.

[101] Again, Cajetan held that after the crime of heresy has been established, the Church plays a ministerial part in the fall from the pontificate. He bases his opinion on Divine law. He notes that, according to Divine law (Tit. 3:10), the Church has a right to separate from a heretic. Therefore, once the crime of heresy has been established by the Church, the Church can licitly separate itself from the heretical Pope. It accomplishes the separation by a juridical act commanding the faithful that the man must be avoided. This juridical act itself plays a "ministerial" part in the severing of the bond uniting the man to the office. We will explain this point in more detail later. For now, we simply note, again, that this teaching of Cajetan is essentially different from that of Suarez and Bellarmine, who both held that the heretical Pope is "*ipso facto*" and immediately deposed by Christ once the Church renders its judgment.

#2) - takes place *before* the <u>human punishment</u> excommunication by a juridical sentence (point #3).

What recent authors have failed to recognize is that Suarez and Bellarmine, in the above quotations, are actually addressing *two different aspects of the question*[102] and not expressing *two different opinions*. Because of this misunderstanding, some have failed to distinguish when the theologian is addressing 1) the crime of heresy, 2) the divine punishment for the crime, or 3) the human punishment for the crime (declaration of deprivation and excommunication of the former Pope). The result is that they see contradictions where no actual contradiction exists.

And it is not only with the distinction between the crime and punishment that Sedevacantists find apparent contradictions. For example, the Sedevacantist apologist, Richard Ibranyi, admits that when he reads the writings of canonists, he sees "a fog of contradictions" that leaves him in total confusion. He wrote:

> "... all the canonists are not clear ... Many contradict one another, and *even contradict themselves* regarding the teachings on heresy, heretics, culpability, and the incurring of penalties, etc. There are brief moments of clearness in their writings, *engulfed in a fog of contractions that leaves them, as well as the readers, in total confusion.*"[103]

The confusion is not the fault of the Church's trained canonists, but of the untrained reader. It is Mr. Ibranyi's lack of understanding of the terminology and distinctions that leaves him "in total confusion." This is why such complicated matters are not to be resolved by the private interpretation of individual Catholics in the pew. It is the same confusion and lack of understanding that has prevented him, and his Sedevacantist colleagues, from grasping the distinction between the crime (established by the Church) and the punishment that follows.

We can further illustrate the distinction between the crime and the punishment by considering our own American legal process, where the offense (the crime) must be proven by competent authority before the sentence (the punishment) is imposed. In fact, in secular criminal courts, both phases usually require separate legal proceedings. While not a perfect analogy, the investigation and removal of a heretical Pope

---

[102] Suarez is addressing the *ipso facto* loss of office, while Bellarmine is referring to the excommunication and juridical sentence that follows the loss of office.
[103] Ibranyi, "Against John Lane," December 2009 (emphasis added). See http://www.johnthebaptist.us.

would nevertheless parallel the secular process: the crime of papal heresy is determined by the Church (the competent authority), and the punishment is inflicted by both God (loss of office) and man (excommunication). This distinction between crime and the twofold punishment reconciles the apparently contradictory statements of Bellarmine and Suarez.

As further evidence that Bellarmine (d. 1621) and Suarez (d. 1617) held the same opinion regarding crime versus punishment, we note that the two lived at the same time, yet *both* held that their position represented the *common opinion* of the Fathers and Doctors of the Church. (And both Bellarmine and Suarez are held as eminent theologians.[104]) For example, after teaching that a heretical Pope ceases to be Pope upon a *declaratory sentence* of the Church, Suarez says, "This is the <u>common opinion among the doctors.</u>" However, when Bellarmine says a heretical Pope ceases to be Pope <u>automatically,</u> he says, "This is the teaching of <u>all the ancient Fathers</u> who teach that manifest heretics immediately lose all jurisdiction."

How can they both say that their seemingly contradictory opinions represented the common teaching of the Fathers and Doctors of the Church? Again, the answer is that they are not giving two different opinions, but are instead addressing two different aspects of the question: The crime "manifest heresy" is determined by the Church (common opinion number one), and the punishment is effected immediately by God (common opinion number two).

In fact, Bellarmine explicitly teaches that a heretical Pope will not be deposed by God without the judgment of men. He begins by noting that although a Pope is made Pope by God (God joins the man to the pontificate), it does not happen without the cooperation of man (the election); likewise, a Pope will not be removed by God without the judgment of men. In his refutation of the *Second Opinion* (which has been completely abandoned by theologians), Bellarmine wrote:

> "Jurisdiction is certainly given to the Pontiff by God, <u>but with the agreement of men</u> [i.e. the election] as is obvious; because this man, who beforehand was not Pope, <u>has from men</u> that he would begin to be Pope, therefore, <u>he is not removed by God unless it is through men.</u> But a secret heretic cannot be <u>judged by men</u>...heresy, the only reason where it is lawful for inferiors to

---

[104] Pope Paul V declared Suarez *"Doctor Eximius et Pius"* during Suarez's lifetime, and Bellarmine was formally declared a Doctor of the Church. For the meaning "Pious and Excellent Doctor," see *Catholic Encyclopedia* (1913), vol. XIV (Francisco Suarez), p. 319.

judge superiors ... <u>in the case of heresy, a Roman Pontiff can be judged</u>."[105]

Here, Bellarmine is saying that a Pope will not be removed by God (Divine punishment), before the crime of heresy has been "judged by man"[106] (human judgment).

There is another point we should mention. As we have seen, Suarez explicitly taught that a *declaratory sentence* of the crime is necessary before Christ would act by deposing a heretical Pope, whereas Bellarmine simply states that the crime must be "manifest," without specifying if it must be "manifest" to the Church by a declaratory sentence. Because Bellarmine in *De Romano Pontifice* did not specifically address whether the Church must issue a declaratory sentence of the crime, Sedevacantists have assumed he did not require a declaration of the crime before a Pope would lose his office for heresy. But this is a rash speculation on their part, and injurious to the good name of St. Bellarmine. The reason is because, as Suarez noted, requiring a declaratory sentence was the *common opinion* during the day in which he and Bellarmine lived; and, as Sedevacantists themselves like to point out (when it helps their position), departing from the "common opinion" of the theologians is, at minimum, an act of imprudence *and possibly a mortal sin.*[107]

Therefore, in charity, the Sedevacantists should presume that Bellarmine indeed required a declaratory sentence before the Pope would lose his office. Simply because he didn't directly address the matter[108] (at least not within the snippets posted on Sedevacantist

---

[105] *De Romano Pontifice*, bk. 2 ch. 30.

[106] Bellarmine held that a heretical Pope can be judged, as an exception to the general rule that "the First See is judged by no one." This text will be cited in the next chapter.

[107] Regarding this point, in response to the teaching of Van Noort, who taught that the infallibility of canonizations is only the "common opinion," a very popular Sedevacantist website wrote: "Now, some defenders of the 'recognize-and-resist' position, unfamiliar with Sacred Theology, will be quick to say, 'But this is just a theological opinion and therefore not binding.' But it doesn't quite work this way. By stating that the view that canonizations are infallible is the common opinion of theologians, Van Noort is saying that this position cannot be contradicted under pain (usually) of mortal sin. In 1951, Fr. Sixtus Cartechini, S.J., a dogmatic theologian teaching at the Gregorian Pontifical University in Rome, published an imprimatur book called *De Valore Notarum Theologicarum*, which means *On the Value of Theological Notes*. Cartechini explains that opinions held in common by all theologians are theologically certain, the denial of which constitutes, usually, a mortal sin of temerity."("Pope Francis to 'Canonize' John Paul II and John XXIII," http://www.novusordowatch.org/wire/john-paul-canonization.htm.)

[108] Note that when Bellarmine said a manifestly heretical Pope is deposed "before any excommunication or juridical sentence," he was not referring to the declaration of the crime, but to the *vitandus* declaration that Cajetan said plays an essential part in severing

websites) is no reason to think he departed from the common opinion of his fellow theologians. Furthermore, John of St. Thomas, a contemporary of Bellarmine, who knew his position well, stated that Bellarmine *did in fact hold the common opinion* that a heretical Pope would have to be "declared incorrigible" before he would be "deposed immediately by Christ."[109]

In support, then, of the *Fifth Opinion* - that a manifestly heretical Pope is *ipso facto* deposed by Christ (which is certainly <u>not</u> the Fourth Opinion of Cajetan) - Suarez says:

> "Therefore on <u>deposing</u> a heretical Pope, the Church would not act as superior to him, but juridically and by the consent of Christ, she would <u>declare</u> him a heretic [crime] and therefore unworthy of Pontifical honors; he would <u>then</u> *ipso facto* and immediately be <u>deposed by Christ</u> [divine punishment], and once deposed he would become inferior and would be able to be punished" [human punishment]."[110]

Notice the chronology: The Pope is <u>first</u> declared a heretic (crime); he is "<u>then</u>" *ipso facto* deposed by Christ; finally the former Pope is punished by the Church (e.g., public excommunication).

As we have seen, Bellarmine essentially agrees with Suarez:

> "The fifth opinion therefore is the true one. A pope who is a manifest heretic [crime established by the judgment of the Church, and possibly declared] automatically ceases to be pope and head [divine punishment], just as he ceases automatically to be a Christian and a member of the Church. Wherefore, he can be judged and punished by the Church [human punishment]. This is the teaching of all the ancient Fathers who teach that manifest heretics immediately lose all jurisdiction."[111]

Here we see that both Suarez and Bellarmine are simply stating that a manifestly heretical Pope (whose crime is judged by the Church and not the faithful) ceases to be Pope without the need of any further declaration, due to the nature of heresy itself. But again, since the

---

the bond uniting the man to the office – that is, in the actual deposition itself. A merely declaratory sentence of the crime is not a juridical act. Referring to the case of a heretical Pope, Wernz-Vidal wrote: "A declaratory sentence of the crime, however, is not excluded *as long as it is merely declaratory. This does not bring about the judgment of a heretical pope,* but rather shows that he has been judged" (*Ius Canonicum,* Rome: Gregorian, 1943. 2:453).

[109] *Cursus Theologici,* II-II, Disp. II, Art. III, *De Depositione Papae,* p. 138.
[110] *De Fide,* Disp. 10, Sect. 6, n. 10, p. 317.
[111] *De Romano Pontifice,* bk. 2, ch. 30.

actions of man do not *cause* God to act, heresy, even *formally declared* by the Church, only *disposes* the Pope for the loss of office, which occurs immediately by an act of Christ, and not as a direct consequence (*effect*) of the crime (as explained above). Moreover, when Suarez and Bellarmine say the heretical Pope can now be "punished," they are confirming that, having fallen from the pontificate, the Church can punish the *former* Pope, just as it does other heretics. Because Bellarmine and Suarez essentially agreed on both the crime and punishment aspects of this question, they could both say they held the "common opinion."

As mentioned above, John of St. Thomas (d. 1644), who was a contemporary of both Suarez and Bellarmine, and one of the greatest Thomists the Church has known, confirmed that Suarez and Bellarmine are in agreement regarding this question. He wrote:

> "Bellarmine and Suarez, however, believe that the Pope, by the very fact that he is a manifest heretic <u>and has been declared incorrigible</u> [crime], is deposed immediately by Christ the Lord [divine punishment], and not by any authority of the Church."[112] [Again, notice the "declaration" is past tense and the "deposition" is present tense, underscoring and confirming the chronology.]

Notice that John of St. Thomas, who studied the question thoroughly, and wasn't limited to a few English translations of Bellarmine posted on Sedevacantist websites, states that Bellarmine and Suarez *both* held that a manifestly heretical Pope would have to be "declared incorrigible" (declaratory sentence), before being deposed immediately by Christ (divine punishment). This is also the teaching of Fr. Ballerini (quoted earlier), who explicitly stated that a Pope who remained hardened in heresy, following the solemn warning by the authorities, "would have to have his heresy and contumacy publicly proclaimed."[113] Here we have a known adherent to Bellarmine's opinion saying that a heretical Pope would have to have his heresy declared by the Church.

And what is even more clear is that the position of Suarez is not that of Cajetan (the Fourth Opinion), since Cajetan held that a heretical Pope, who is declared incorrigible, would then have to be deposed by the Church (by a *Vitandus* declaration). It should also be noted that in the treatise in which John of St. Thomas said that Bellarmine and

---

[112] *Cursus Theologici* (Theological Courses), II-II, *De Auctoritate Summi Pontificis, Disputatio,* Disp. II, Art. III, *De Depositione Papae*, p. 138.
[113] *De Potestate Ecclesiastica*, pp.104-105.

Suarez agreed that a Pope would be deposed by God *after his heresy was declared by the Church*, he was defending the opinion of Cajetan (his fellow Dominican) against the opinion of Bellarmine and Suarez (the two Jesuits). He taught that Bellarmine and Suarez held the same opinion, which differed from the opinion of himself and Cajetan. This further confirms that Suarez did not agree with Cajetan. (As an aside, at the end of Chapter 11, we will see that John of St. Thomas refuted each and every one of Bellarmine's and Suarez' objections to Cajetan's opinion.)

Furthermore, Cardinal Journet (1891-1975), who studied Bellarmine, Suarez, John of St. Thomas, and Cajetan at length regarding this matter, also placed Bellarmine and Suarez in the same camp, and Cajetan and John of St. Thomas in the opposite camp. Speaking of the case of a Pope who "withdrew himself from the Church" (that is, openly left the Church), the Cardinal wrote:

> "Some, such as <u>Bellarmine and Suarez</u>, considered that such a Pope, withdrawing himself from the Church, <u>was *ipso facto* deposed</u>, *papa haereticus est depositus*. (...) Others, such as <u>Cajetan, and John of St. Thomas</u>, *whose analysis seems to me more penetrating*, have considered that even after a manifest sin[114] of heresy the Pope is not yet deposed, but <u>should be deposed by the Church</u>, *papa haereticus non est depositus, sed deponendus*. Nevertheless, they added, the Church is not on that account above the Pope.[115]

As we can see, Cardinal Journet, who personally considered the arguments of Cajetan and John of St. Thomas to be "more penetrating" than that of Bellarmine and Suarez,[116] explicitly stated that the two Dominicans (Cajetan and John of St. Thomas) held the contrary view of the two Jesuits (Bellarmine and Suarez). This further confirms our assertion that Suarez is most certainly not in agreement with Cajetan in holding the Fourth Opinion, as some modern writers have mistakenly

---

[114] Since the sin of heresy requires pertinacity, a manifest sin would require *manifest* pertinacity. In the case of a sitting Pope, this would require the intervention of the Church, as discussed above.

[115] Journet, *The Church of the Word Incarnate*, p. 483.

[116] Notice that Cardinal Journet did not believe, as do Sedevacantists, that just because Bellarmine is a Doctor of the Church his opinion must be correct and therefore embraced. The Church does not automatically adopt the opinions of her Doctors. For example, in the centuries-long debate over the Immaculate Conception between the Dominicans (who followed St. Thomas) and the Franciscans (who followed Scotus), the Dominicans did not claim victory simply because St. Thomas is the Common Doctor of the Church.

concluded.[117] For further clarification, see the Appendix chart at the end of the book.

From what we have seen, it is clear that the reason Sedevacantists pit Bellarmine against Suarez is because they have failed to distinguish between the crime (established by the Church) and the divine punishment for the crime (*ipso facto* loss of office). This causes them to conclude that Bellarmine's teaching (*ipso facto* loss of office) and Suarez's teaching (loss of office *following* the declaration of the crime of heresy by the Church) represent two contrary opinions. Sedevacantists then insist that because Bellarmine is a Doctor of the Church, and Suarez is not, Bellarmine's opinion must be true! While they are certainly entitled to prefer the opinion of a Doctor of the Church over a non-Doctor, such a preference serves no purpose when it is based upon a completely fallacious distinction, as it is in this case. Further, these Sedevacantists go out of their way to denigrate Suarez (as they do anyone who serves as an obstacle to their Sedevacantist position) in order to discredit his teaching, which, quite embarrassingly for them, is none other than the same opinion as that of Bellarmine, as we have demonstrated.

The following quotations demonstrate not only how the Sedevacantists have misunderstood Suarez's teaching, but also how they have attempted to undermine his good name and credibility. For example, in attempting to counter an argument presented by Christopher Ferrara, who pointed out that "nowhere does Suarez teach that any member of the faithful can declare that a Roman Pontiff has lost his office based on their own private judgment,"[118] Fr. Cekada, responded by impugning the reputation of Suarez with three flagrant falsehoods in two sentences. He wrote:

> "Suarez, who tended to lose most controversies with other Catholic theologians [falsehood #1], was the **only** theologian who held that position [falsehood #2]. The rest all taught [falsehood #3] that a schismatic pope loses the pontificate automatically because heresy and schism both represented 'defection from the faith.'"[119]

---

[117] We note that the treatises of all four theologians are highly complex. It is therefore understandable that Suarez could have mistakenly been included as holding the Fourth Opinion. In fact, Wernz-Vidal also mistakenly placed Suarez in the same camp as Cajetan.

[118] Christopher Ferrara, "Defending the Papacy, Opposing the Sedevacantist Enterprise, Part I," The Fatima Crusader, http://www.fatimacrusader .com/cr80/cr80pg08.asp.

[119] "Sedevacantism and Mr. Ferrara's Cardboard Pope," http://www.traditionalmass .org/articles/article.php?id=66&catname=14 (emphasis in original).

Another Sedevacantist who has attempted to discredit Suarez is John Lane. Lane, who has demonstrated that he does not truly understand Suarez' position, wrote:

> "Francisco Suarez did in fact hold the *discredited minority position* that a public heretic would have to be deposed by the Church. But since his time the [First] Vatican Council has decreed that the First See is judged by no one."[120]

First, as we have seen, Suarez explicitly taught that a heretical Pope is deposed "immediately by Christ" and thus held the *common opinion* on the question, not the "discredited minority opinion" as Lane falsely claims. Second, Lane evidently believes that the axiom "*Prima sedes a nemine iudicatur*"(the First See is judged by no one) first originated at the First Vatican Council in 1870. Mr. Lane will be surprised to learn that this famous axiom is found in councils dating back to the first centuries of the Church,[121] and was cited by Popes and theologians throughout the Middle Ages. For example, it was used by Pope St. Nicholas in *Proposueramus quidem* (685 A.D.),[122] by Pope St. Leo IX in the Epistle *In Terra Pax Hominibus* (1053 A.D.)[123] and by Pope St. Gregory VII, in *Dictatus Papae*, (1075 A.D.).[124] It is also quoted by John of St. Thomas and Cajetan in their treatises dealing with the loss of office for a heretical Pope. In fact, Suarez himself cites it in his refutation of Cajetan's opinion.[125]

Yet John Lane claims that "the First See is judged by no one" only originated *after* the time of Suarez, and then claims that because of this "new" teaching from Vatican I, Suarez' position is discredited! Such a statement reveals more about John Lane's knowledge of the subject

---

[120] "Anti-Sedevacantism: Is it Catholic?," http://www.sedevacantist.com/isitcatholic.html.
[121] For example, regarding the case of Pope Marcellinus (d. 304 A.D.), Cajetan wrote: "When the pope incurred the charge of idolatry, the council which was convened, seeing him contrite of heart, said, 'Judge yourself. The first see is not judged by anyone." (*De Comparatione Auctoritatis Papae et Concilii*, p. 101). The phrase is also found in the Synod of Parma (501-502 A.D.), convened by Theodoret to consider the charges again Pope Symmachus.
[122] "Neither by Augustus, nor by all the clergy, nor by religious, nor by the people will the judge be judged ... The first Seat will not be judged by anyone" (*Proposueramus quidem*, 865 A.D., Denz., 330).
[123] Denz., 352
[124] Pope Gregory VII, *Dictatus Papae*, No. 19, (1075, A.D.).
[125] "... in the time of Pope Marcellus [sic.; Marcellinus], when it declared "The First see is judged by no one," it said that concerning the very person of Marcellus [sic.; Marcellinus], who was certainly a private person." (Saurez, *De Fide, Disputatio* X, sect. 6, n. 9).

matter, than it does about the common opinion held by Suarez. But Lane didn't stop there. He went on to say:

> "It is true that some authorities have taught that in the extraordinary case of a *pope* falling into heresy (something the best authorities believe to be impossible), the loss of office would not occur, or would not be known, until after a declaration by a General Council or a Conclave. Who are these few? <u>John of St. Thomas, Suarez, Cajetan, Bioux. Not a canonised saint or a Doctor among them, and they constitute a tiny minority</u>."[126]

In typical fashion, Lane attempts to smugly denigrate the *"Doctor Eximius et Pius"* and other brilliant theologians, whose teachings represent an obstacle to his personal opinion. Denigration of those who disagree with his opinion is unfortunately a common tactic of the layman John Lane and his fellow Sedevacantists. In revealing that he too does not understand what Suarez actually teaches, Peter Dimond also attempts to denigrate the esteemed Jesuit theologian by referring to his teaching as his "fallible speculations from 400 years ago" and "the inaccurate speculations of Suarez"[127] – which would necessarily include the "fallible" and "inaccurate speculations" of Bellarmine "from 400 years ago" as well! Like John Lane, Peter Dimond completely misunderstands Suarez and Bellarmine, and thus reveals in plain view the errors of his own "inaccurate" and "fallible speculations."

A Pope Who Openly Leaves the Church

We have shown that a reigning Pope will not lose his office before the Church has established the crime, and most probably not before the Church issues a declaratory sentence.[128] However, we do concede that if a Pope were to openly and publicly *leave the Church* of his own will, as opposed to simply professing heresy,[129] a case could be made that

---

[126] "Responses to Some Anti-Sedevacantist Objections," http://www.the-pope.com/ contra _objections .html (emphasis added).

[127] "The Remnant and Robert Siscoe Refuted on Sedevacantism," http://www.most holyfamily-monastery.com/catholicchurch/remnant-robert-siscoe-refuted-Sedevacantis m/#.VE3JAl_u3VI.

[128] Of course, the exact *moment* in which God would depose the Pope is unknown. Whether it were to happen just before, during, or sometime after the Church declared the crime is open to speculation.

[129] A formal act of defection from the Catholic Church (*actus formalis defectionis ab Ecclesia catholica*) is an externally provable juridical act of departure from the Catholic Church, recognized in the 1983 Code of Canon Law as having certain juridical effects enumerated

God would sever the bond that united the man to the pontificate at the moment his public defection was acknowledged by the Church, even without a declaratory sentence of the crime (for example, if the Pope publicly declared he was no longer Catholic and then joined and became a pastor of the Lutheran sect).

This is because, in such an extreme case, the Church would no longer have reason to recognize, as its head, a man who no longer presented himself as such. In such a case, the crime of heresy (matter and form), would be sufficiently manifest by the actions of the Pope himself (notorious by fact), without the Church having to prove it, and no "clever evasion" by the public defector would be possible. (Note that "public heresy" and "public defection from the faith" are two different things. Sedevacantists have failed to grasp this point when they attempt to apply canon 188, §4, to the conciliar Popes.) Consequently, it is possible that, once this crime was acknowledged by the Church, God would immediately act by severing the bond uniting the man to the pontificate, without the need of an additional declaratory sentence. In this case, if a council did issue a *declaratory sentence*, it would merely confirm the fact of the crime by which the Pope had *already* lost his office.[130]

As we will see below in our discussion on canon 188, §4, the old 1917 Code of Canon Law taught that in the extreme case in which a prelate publicly defects from the Faith by joining a non-Catholic sect, he is deposed *without the need of a declaratory sentence*. Nevertheless, the formal deposition would have to be preceded by a *canonical warning* (to confirm pertinacity), but it would not require a declaratory sentence of the crime. In fact, this extreme case may be what Bellarmine was actually referring to in *De Romano Pontifice*, when he wrote:

> "This is the opinion of all the ancient Fathers, who teach that manifest heretics immediately lose all jurisdiction, and outstandingly that of St. Cyprian (lib. 4, epist. 2) who speaks as follows of Novatian, who was Pope [antipope] in the schism which occurred during the pontificate of St. Cornelius: 'He would not be able to retain the episcopate, and, if he was made bishop before, <u>he</u>

in canons 1086, 1117 and 1124. In 2006, the Pontifical Council for Legislative Texts specified in what a formal act of defection from the Catholic Church consisted. – see Pontifical Council for Legislative Texts, Vatican City, March 13, 2006, Prot. N. 10279/2006.

[130] This would correspond to what Fr. Wernz wrote when he said "a General Council declares the fact that a crime had been committed, a crime whereby the heretical pope on his own *had separated himself from the Church* and deprived himself of his rank" (Wernz, *Ius Decretalium*, 1913, II, p. 615).

separated himself from the body of those who were, like him, bishops, and from the unity of the Church.' According to what St. Cyprian affirms in this passage, even had Novatian been the true and legitimate Pope, he would have automatically fallen from the pontificate, if he *separated himself* from the Church.

This is the opinion of great recent doctors, as John Driedo (lib. 4 de Script. et dogmat. Eccles., cap. 2, par. 2, sent. 2), who teaches that only those *separate themselves* from the Church who are expelled, like the excommunicated, and those who *depart by themselves* from her or oppose her, as heretics and schismatics. And in his seventh affirmation, he maintains that in those who *turn away* from the Church, there remains absolutely no spiritual power over those who are in the Church. Melchior Cano says the same (lib. 4 de loc., cap. 2), teaching that heretics [those who have turned away from the Church] are neither parts nor members of the Church, and that it cannot even be conceived that anyone could be head and Pope, without being member and part (cap. ult. ad argument. 12)."[131]

By referring to heretics as those who "separate themselves from the Church," who "turn away from the Church," and who "depart by themselves from her," Bellarmine is referring not to those who merely profess a heretical proposition, but to those who openly leave the Church (no longer accepting the Church as the rule of faith). This is confirmed by the example Bellarmine used, which was that of Novatian (as recorded by Cyprian). Now, Novatian didn't merely say something heretical; he openly left the Church by adamantly refusing to recognize Pope Cornelius as the true Roman Pontiff, and then went further by eventually proclaiming himself to be Pope. Ironically, this is exactly what over a dozen Sedevacantist priests and laymen have done in our day, including David Bawden, who not only left the Church, but now proclaims himself to be "Pope Michael." But the point is that Novatian effectively joined a non-Catholic sect of which he declared himself the leader. He didn't simply make a heretical statement.

Fr. Mattheus Conte a Coronata discusses the case of Novatian in his own treatment of how a heretical Pope can fall from the pontificate. Fr. Coronata cited the same source of the story of Novatian that Bellarmine referenced, which is that which was was written by St. Cyprian. This is what Fr. Coronata wrote (the context is how a Pope would fall from office):

---

[131] *De Romano Pontifice*, bk. 2, ch. 30 (emphasis added).

"Third, if he would <u>separate himself</u> on account of an unjust cause from the communion of the whole Church and of all the Bishops ... [which] <u>as is shown in the divine Cyprian (bk. 4, epistle 2), Novatian did</u>, who was pointed out by Cyprian a little after as a Schismatic, and outside the bosom of the Church."[132]

We see that Novatian didn't merely say something heretical. He openly left the Church by declaring himself Pope, and thus was a public schismatic who set himself "outside the bosom of the Church." By citing the example of Novatian, it seems that when Bellarmine speaks of a "manifest heretic" automatically falling from office, he is not simply referring to a person who publicly professed heresy (as Sedevacanitsts have imagined), but one who openly left the Church by joining another religion or, in the case of Novatian, declaring himself Pope.

It is certain that Bellarmine did not consider a person who merely professed heresy in public to be a "manifest heretic," by the fact that Bellarmine himself considered Michel de Bay to be a Catholic in good standing, even though, as we saw in Chapter 6, de Bay publicly professed heresy, ignored Pope Pius IV who imposed silence on him (in 1561), and continued to teach his heresies "in public," even after they were formally condemned by the Pope. Yet, in spite of this, as the Sedevacantist John Daly noted, Bellarmine "always considered him as a learned Catholic, most worthy of respect, and at this time [that he was professing heresy] called him prudent, pious, humble, erudite,"[133] which would be a strange thing to do if Bellarmine considered him to be a "manifest heretic."

Now, if Bellarmine's use of the term "manifest heretic" referred not merely to someone who professed heresy, but to one who openly left the Church (thereby openly rejecting the Church as the infallible rule of faith), and if he did not require a declaratory sentence of the crime in such an *extreme* case, his thinking would have been in perfect harmony with canon 188, §4 of the 1917 Code, since, as we will see below, according to the 1917 Code, in the extreme case in which a prelate publicly leaves the Church, he is deposed without a declaratory sentence - *but not before a canonical warning*. There is certainly no "public defection from the faith" in the case of the conciliar Popes, all of whom, like Michel de Bay, continued to present themselves as members of the

---

[132] *Tractatus Postumus* (Liege, 1677), Tract I, Chapter XXI, n. II, p. 81, translated by Br. Alexis Bugnolo (emphasis added).
[133] John Daly, "Heresy in History," http://www.strobertbellarmine.net/heresyhistory.html.

Catholic Church. And, equally important, they have all been accepted as Pope by the universal Church (even Pope Francis professes membership in the Church, which means he has not publicly defected).[134] Without a clear and evident defection from the Church, the crime of heresy itself would have to be sufficiently established (and likely declared) by the Church before a Pope would lose his office - just as it would for any other prelate who was suspected of heresy.

Canon 188, §4 (1917 Code)

Before concluding this chapter, we will address canon 188, §4, which has been used by Sedevacantists for years to support their position. Even though they claim canon law does not apply to a Pope (when it presents an obstacle to their position), when they can "interpret" a particular canon as supporting the Sedevacantist thesis, they argue that such canon *does* apply to the Pope. The particular canon is then presented as absolute and irrefutable proof for their position. Their favorite "proof canon" of all is 188, §4 of the 1917 Code which provides the following:

> "There are certain causes which effect the tacit resignation of an office, which resignation is accepted in advance by operation of the law, and hence is effective without any declaration. These causes are... §4 if he has publicly defected from the faith."[135]

What exactly does the canon mean by "publicly defected from the Faith"? The Sedevacantists interpret it to mean that if they privately judge a Pope to be a heretic, he has therefore "publicly defected from the faith," which means his See (*Sede*) is vacant (*vacat*: hence *sede vacante*). But is this really what the canon under tacit resignation means? No, not at all. To quote Fr. Brian Harrison:

> "Canon 188, §4 states that among the actions which automatically (*ipso facto*) cause any cleric to lose his office, even without any declaration on the part of a superior, is that of 'defect[ing] publicly from the Catholic faith' ('*A fide catholica publice defecerit*'). However, to 'defect publicly' from the faith, in this context, clearly means something a lot more drastic than making heretical (or allegedly heretical) statements in the course of public speeches or documents. This particular cause of losing an

---

[134] Whether Pope Francis has been "peacefully and universally accepted" by the Church is addressed in Chapter 12.
[135] Canon 188, §4, 1917 Code of Canon Law (emphasis added).

ecclesiastical office is found in that section of the Code dealing with
the *resignation* of such an office (cc. 184-191), and is part of a
canon which lists eight sorts of actions which the law treats as 'tacit
resignations.' In other words, they are the sorts of actions which can
safely be taken as evidence that the cleric in question *does not even
to want to continue in the office he held* up till that time, even
though he may never have bothered to put his resignation or
abdication in writing."[136]

A simple review of the explanation of this canon, as found in the
canonical manuals, explains precisely what the Church means by
"public defection from the faith." The statement does not apply, as Fr.
Harrison correctly notes, to a person who merely makes a heretical
statement. Public defection from the faith refers to a prelate *who publicly
joins a false religion*, either formally or informally.

Fr. Augustine also explains the point at length:

"The vindictive penalties are rendered more severe in two
cases, which may be distinct, but may also occur by one and the
same act: *sectae acatholicae nomen dare* [formally] or *publice
adhaerere* [informally].

A *sect* means a religious society established in opposition to the
Church, whether it consist of infidels, pagans, Jews, Moslems, non-
Catholics, or schismatics. To become a member of such a society
(*nomen dare*) means to inscribe one's name on its roster. Of course,
it is presumed that the new member knows it is a non-Catholic
society, otherwise he would not incur the censure. If he hears of the
censure after he has become a member, and promptly severs his
connection, the penalty is not incurred.

The text also provides for cases of informal membership.
Publice adhaerere means to belong publicly to a non-Catholic sect.
This may be done by frequenting its services without any special
cause or reason, or by boasting of being a member, though not
enrolled, by wearing a badge or emblem indicative of membership,
etc. Those guilty of such conduct, whether laymen or clerics, render
themselves infamous (*infamia iuris latae sententiae*) and
consequently can. 2294, must be applied to them. A cleric must,
besides, be degraded[137] if, <u>after having been duly warned</u>, he
persists in being a member of such a society. All the offices he may
hold become vacant, *ipso facto*, without any further declaration.

---

[136] Harrison, "A Heretical Pope Would Govern the Church Illicitly but Validly," *Living
Tradition*, No. 87 (May 2000).
[137] Degradation is the sentence of Ecclesiastical Law, whereby a minister is deposed from
the ministry entirely, and not from a higher to a lower Order.

> This is tacit resignation recognized by law (Canon 188.4) and therefore the vacancy is one *de facto et iure* [by fact and by law]."[138]

Tacit resignation for public defection from the faith occurs when a prelate joins a non-Cathlic sect, not when he simply makes a heretical statement (judged so by private judgment). Canon 2314, §3 confirms this when it provides:

> "Canon 2314: (3) if they have joined a non-Catholic sect (*Si sectae acatholicae nomen dederint*) or publicly adhered to it (*vel publice adhaeserint*), they are *ipso facto* infamous, and clerics, in addition to being considered to have tacitly renounced any office they may hold, according to canon 188.4, are, if previous warning proves fruitless, to be degraded" (emphasis added).

Furthermore, as noted above in Canon 2314 and in the quotation from Fr. Augustine, even in this extreme case in which a cleric publicly defects from the faith by joining a non-Catholic sect, the prelate must be duly warned before being degraded or "deposed." Thus, even when a cleric openly leaves the Church (by joining another religion), thereby abandoning his office (which is *de facto* vacant due to his "tacit resignation"), he must first be warned by ecclesiastical authority before he is formally deposed (or degraded) by the Church.

This is also confirmed by Fr. Ayrinhac's commentary on the 1917 Code, wherein he notes that a cleric who "formally affiliates with a non-Catholic sect, or publicly adheres to it" is only deposed after being warned. Wrote Fr. Ayrinhac:

> "If they have been formally affiliated with a non-Catholic sect, or publicly adhere to it, they incur *ipso facto* the note of infamy; clerics lose all ecclesiastical offices they might hold (Canon 188.4), *and after a fruitless warning* they should be deposed."[139]

But the Sedevacantists have their own interpretation of this canon, quite different from that of the Church and her theologians. According to to the Dimond brothers, for example, "public defection from the faith" is the same as a public crime.

---

[138] Augustine, *A Commentary on the New Code of Canon Law*, vol. 8, bk. 5, pp. 279-280.

[139] Ayrinhac, *Penal Legislation in the New Code of Canon Law*, p. 193. Note: "A deposition is an ecclesiastical *vindictive penalty* by which a cleric is forever deprived of his office or benefice and of the right of exercising the functions of his orders." *Catholic Encyclopedia* (1913), vol. IV, p. 737.

In their book, *The Truth About What Really Happened to the Catholic Church*, in the section titled, "Answers to Common Objections Against Sedevacantism," the Dimonds ask the question: "What is a public defection against the faith?" Here is their answer: "Canon 2197.1, 1917 Code of Canon Law: 'A Crime is *public*: (1) if it is already commonly known or the circumstances are such as to lead to the conclusion that it can and will easily become so...'"[140]

Notice, they answer by providing the canonical definition of a public crime, as if "public defection of the faith" and "public crime" are one and the same thing. Instead of piecing together unrelated canons, why not simply quote what the Church and her canonists teach, or at least cite the canons (such as canon 2314, §3) that specifically reference and explain the canon in question? The answer, of course, is that doing so would undermine their Sedevacantist position, since the canonists all teach that public defection from the faith refers to those who publicly join a non-Catholic sect.

Clearly, canon 188, §4 in no way supports the Sedevacantist position, since: 1) none of the conciliar Popes have publicly defected from the faith by joining a non-Catholic sect; and, 2) they have not been warned (which the canon requires before deposition, or "degradation" occurs). Without even addressing whether or when canon law applies to the Pope, the foregoing analysis demonstrates that the Sedevacantists' effort to commandeer this canon in support of their thesis is categorically misapplied and thus completely erroneous. It also demonstrates why such critical issues are left to the public judgment of the proper authorities in the Church, and not the private judgment of individual Catholics in the street.

Canon 194, §2 (1983 Code)

Finally, in the 1983 Code of Canon Law, which is in force today, Canon 194, §2 (which is the equivalent of canon 188, §4 in the 1917 Code) expressly states that the removal from office due to public defection from the faith can only be enforced if it has been established *and declared* by the competent authority. From the 1983 Code:

> "The following are removed from an ecclesiastical office by the law itself:
>
> 1° a person who has lost the clerical state;

---

[140] Dimond, Michael and Peter, *The Truth about What Really Happened to the Catholic Church after Vatican II*, p. 308.

2° a person who has publicly defected from the Catholic faith or from the communion of the Church;

3° a cleric who has attempted marriage even if only civilly.

§2 The removal mentioned in Canon. 2 and 3 can be insisted upon only if it is established <u>by a declaration of the competent authority</u>."

Thus, according to the Code currently in effect, the removal from office must be established by a declaration from the competent authorities. The declaration makes the loss *effective*. It is similar to the loss of office, *by law,* for a bishop who reaches the age of seventy-five. He retains the office until the resignation is accepted. For a cleric who *publicly defects from the faith,* he will remain in office and all of the acts of his office will remain valid, until the Church declares him removed. The following commentary on Canon 194, 2° and 3°, is taken from *A New Commentary on the Code of Canon Law*:

"In the case of defection [194, 2°] or clergy attempting marriage [194, 3°], the declaration by competent authority is similar to the declaration at the end of a term of office or completion of age. The fact on which the loss of office is based does not depend on the authority's declaration, <u>but its effectiveness does. The officeholder remains in office, and the actions which require the office are valid, until the declaration or removal is communicated to the officeholder in writing</u>."[141]

There has been no such declaration for the conciliar Popes, nor for the other 5,000-plus bishops of the Catholic Church. What this shows is that neither the 1917 Code (188, §4), nor the 1983 Code (194, §2) supports the Sedevacantist position that the conciliar Popes (along with the other bishops) have lost their office *ipso facto* due to "public defection from the faith."

Unable to wield the "public defection" canons to their favor, the Sedevacantists are forced back to the unanimous teaching of the Doctors and theologians who maintain that the Church (again, the "competent authority" that Sedevacantists reject), and not private individuals, must determine the crime of public and notorious heresy for a Pontiff to lose his office – which has not taken place with the conciliar Popes.

---

[141] Beal, John; Coriden, James; Green, Thomas, *A New Commentary on the Code of Canon Law* (New York: Paulist Press, 2000), p. 227.

Canon 151 (1917 Code); Canon 154 (1983 Code)

Fr. Cekada recently discovered a new canon from the 1917 Code of Canon Law, which he has confidently brought forward in an attempt to defend his novel theory of *ipso facto* loss of office due to the "sin" of heresy, as discerned by private judgment. His reason for citing this particular canon is to "explain away" the teaching of the theologians who've stated that a declaratory sentence of the crime is necessary for a Pope to lose his office for heresy.[142] Fr. Cekada introduced this canon in a recent video he made defending the Sedevacantist thesis. In the video, Fr. Cekada illustrates his misunderstanding of the term "declaration," ironically, in the section of the video that he appropriately titled "Misunderstanding the Term 'Declaration.'"[143]

Fr. Cekada begins this portion of the video by admitting that "later theologians," who accepted Bellarmine's position regarding *ipso facto* loss of office for a heretical Pope, "nevertheless allude to some sort of declaration by the college of Cardinals or bishops."[144] Fr. Cekada then claims the "declaration" that these theologians are referring to is not a declaratory sentence *of the crime* (which, as we've seen, follows and confirms the Church's judgment), but merely an *administrative declaration*.

In his usual fashion, Fr. Cekada smugly and sarcastically attempts to ridicule John Salza, Robert Siscoe, Chris Ferrara and Brian McCall (whose articles the video was intended to refute) by saying if his "moonlighting lawyer friends had taken even a basic course in canon law, they would realize that the term 'declaration,' in this context, merely reflects a general principle laid down in Canon 151 regarding appointment to a church office."[145] Here is the canon Fr. Cekada is referring to:

> "An office that is vacant *de jure* [by law], but that perchance is still held by another illegitimately, can be conferred provided that, duly according to the sacred canons, this possession is *declared not to be legitimate* and that mention of this declaration is made in the letter of conferral."[146]

---

[142] Some theologians specifically refer to the declaratory sentence as a *condition* for the loss of office.

[143] Cekada, video called "Stuck in a Rut."

[144] Ibid.

[145] Ibid.

[146] Canon 151, 1917 Code of Canon Law (emphasis added).

Notice that the 'declaration' spoken of in this canon merely declares that an office, which is vacant by law, is being illegitimately occupied (the act causing the legal vacancy having already been judged by the Church). After referencing the above canon, Fr. Cekada provided the following explanation:

> "If a cleric illegitimately functions in an office, he has no right to – a cleric, say, whose installation as bishop of the diocese was forcibly imposed by the civil power - the prelate or electors who have the canonical power to confer the office may validly appoint someone else only if the illegal occupant's possession of it is declared not to be legitimate."[147]

As we can see, canon 151 applies to the case where an office has *already* been vacated by law and yet remains illegitimately occupied. Thus, a "declaration" under canon 151 merely serves to facilitate the legal removal of the illegitimate occupier of an ecclesiastical office, in order to fill the office with a lawful occupant. But how could *the Church* declare that the office is being occupied illegitimately without first establishing how or why the person is not a legitimate officeholder? How could *the Church* declare that a Pope legally lost his office for heresy, for example, without first establishing that he had, in fact, fallen into heresy? Clearly, before a declaration of illegitimacy could be issued, it would require a *prior judgment* that the Pope was not a legitimate officeholder. And this first judgment would have to come from the proper authorities of the Church, who, in Cekada's own words, "have the canonical power to confer the office." Just as the Church alone has the authority to confer the office, it alone has the authority to judge (and declare) that a cleric has legally lost his office.

To further highlight the error of Fr. Cekada's theory, a "declaration" under canon 151 is similar to an eviction notice after a real estate foreclosure. In the cases of both ecclesiastical office and real estate, the underlying cause (heresy/debtor default) that gave rise to the loss (office/property) has *already* been adjudicated by the proper authorities (the Church/secular court). Canon 151 has absolutely nothing to do with the *initial* determination (i.e., the crime of heresy) that gave rise to the vacancy, and the necessity of declaratory sentences in the case of heretical clerics (i.e., canon 2223, §4).

Yet, based upon this single canon of limited application, Fr. Cekada wants his flock to draw the *general conclusion* that every time the theologians speak of a *declaratory sentence* in relation to the loss of office

---

[147] Cekada, video called "Stuck in a Rut."

for a heretical Pope, it refers to a declaration *of illegitimacy*, and not a declaration *of the crime*. That is, Cekada wants us all to believe that the "declaratory sentence" refers exclusively to the limited case where the Church declares that the office is *already* lost – and, evidently, lost according to the private judgment of .001 percent of the Church! Not only is this theory nonsensical, but Cekada hoists himself on his own petard, by the very quotation he includes in his video (and shows who really needs the basic course in canon law).

The quotation comes from the well-known commentary on canon law by Wernz and Vidal, whom Cekada uses as an example of "later theologians" who adhered to Bellarmine's opinion, but who nevertheless spoke of "some sort of declaration." In the video, Fr. Cekada displayed the following quotation (below) on the screen as he *verbally* "read" the quotation. But, interestingly, Fr. Cekada chose to exclude a few key words from the quotation in his oral "recitation." What words did Fr. Cekada choose to exclude? Those that show these "later theologians" (Wernz and Vidal) were referring to the *declaration of the crime*, and *not* the *declaration of illegitimacy*, as Cekada contends. We will underline the part he quoted. The remainder is what he conveniently failed to cite.

> "A declaratory sentence of the crime, however, is not [to be] excluded as long as it is merely declaratory. This does not bring about the judgment of a heretical pope, but rather shows that he has been judged."[148]

Notice that Wernz and Vidal explicitly mention a declaratory sentence "of the crime," not simply a declaration "of illegitimacy," as Fr. Cekada would have his sect believe. Once again, Fr. Cekada conveniently omits (at least verbally) the part that completely contradicts his position – just like he did with the citation from Cardinal Billot, as we saw in Chapter 5.

Now, when Wernz and Vidal say that the declaration *of the crime* is "merely declaratory," they are simply noting that because the Church has no authority over the Pope, it cannot exercise an act that requires authority over him. Therefore, the Church does not technically "judge" a heretical Pope, as a superior judges an inferior, but merely declares the crime, thereby showing that he has already been judged, just as Pope Innocent taught.[149] Furthermore, the declaratory sentence *of the*

---

[148] *Ius Canonicum*. Rome: Gregorian 1943. 2:453.
[149] As we have noted previously in this chapter, there may be a second declaration (declaration of deprivation) that follows the loss of office, but the loss of office itself

crime is what establishes the *fact* that results in the loss of office, which means it would have to *precede* any declaration of illegitimacy (and which would be issued *only* if a Pope sought to retain the office *after* being declared a heretic and deposed from office).

As we saw earlier in this chapter, Suarez explained that the common opinion of the theologians is that the *ipso facto* loss of office would *follow* the declaratory sentence *of the crime*. "On deposing a heretical Pope," wrote Suarez, the Church "would *declare him a heretic* [declaratory sentence *of the crime*] ... he would then *ipso facto* and immediately be deposed by Christ."[150] But before a Pope is declared a heretic by the proper authorities (or at least before the crime is established), he remains the legal (legitimate) officeholder. Therefore, the canon cited by Fr. Cekada, which applies to *illegitimate* office-holders (based upon *the Church's* judgment and not private judgment), in no way applies to the recent Popes, who have not been judged heretics by the Church, and thus were lawful occupants of the papal office.

In fact, Fr. Cekada's fellow Sedevacantist, Bishop Sanborn, concedes this very point. Bishop Sanborn confirms precisely what we have written in this chapter, when he admits that a heretical Pope would have to be warned by the proper authorities, and the warning would have to be followed by a declaratory sentence issued by the Church, before he would cease to be a *legal* occupant of the papal office. Referring to the post-Vatican II Popes and bishops, Bishop Sanborn wrote:

> "...we do not have the authority to declare the sees legally vacant which these ... possess *de facto*. Only the authority of the Church can do that. ... [until it] is legally declared null and void by competent authority, the heretical 'pope' or 'bishop' is in a state of *legal possession* of the see... He can only lose that state of *legal possession* by legal deposition."[151]

---

would not precede the Church's judgment of the crime. Further, as Hervè teaches, the second declaration could only be made by a general council of the Church (the same council that established the crime). Hervè wrote: "Given that, as a private person, the Pontiff could indeed become a public, notorious, and obstinate heretic...only a Council would have the right to declare his see vacant so that the usual electors could safely proceed to an election." (Hervé, *Manuale Theologiae Dogmaticae* (1943) I.501, emphasis added).

[150] *De Fide, Disp.* 10, Sect 6, n. 10, p. 317.

[151] Bishop Sanborn, "An Emperor We Have, But No Bishop" (emphasis added).

We will have more to say about Bishop Sanborn's version of Sedevacantism in the next chapter.[152] We cite him now to show that even Sanborn realizes a Pope or bishop will occupy his office *legally* unless and until he is *legally declared* illegitimate by the competent authority. Only after a legal declaration by the Church would he be considered an illegitimate officeholder, if he attempted to remain in office. As this chapter has demonstrated, such a declaration of illegitimacy would necessarily be preceded by the Church's determination (and declaration) of the crime of heresy, which is the *unanimous* opinion of the theologians. What this shows is that canon 151 in no way applies to the current Popes, as even Bishop Sanborn would concede. Fr. Cekada's effort to commandeer this canon to his cause further reveals not only the errors of his own theory, but the error of the Sedevacantist thesis as a whole.[153]

---

[152] In the next chapter we will explain how Bishop Sanborn can concede that the recent Popes have been *legal* occupants of the papacy, yet not *true* Popes.

[153] Not surprisingly, Fr. Cekada's video "Stuck in a Rut" was not very well received – even by those who are open to the Sedevacantist thesis. Here are a few comments that were posted below the video: "Fr. Cekada's new sedevacantist argument … actually places him at odds with +Sanborn."… A former Sedevacantist wrote: "SVism is the ultimate 'rut.' Why? Because it solves nothing." Another added: "I find this phenomenon interesting. When Fr. Cekada tries to smile, his face actually produces a frown." http://www.cathinfo.com/catholic.php?a=topic&t=36977&min=1&num=3.

294

Chapter 10

~ The Church Must Judge the Crime ~

In the previous chapter, we explained how the crime of heresy of a Pope would be established, according to the consensus of the Doctors and theologians of the Church. We also distinguished between the crime of heresy (established by the Church) and the twofold punishment: the divine punishment (loss of office either *ipso facto* or by deposition), followed by the human punishment (excommunication). In this chapter, we further examine why the Church alone possesses the authority to judge the crime of papal heresy. We then consider some of the errors that individual Sedevacantists make when they attempt to judge the matter for themselves.

In the *Summa Theologica*, St. Thomas explains that just as it belongs to public authority alone to write the law, so too it falls to public authority alone to interpret the law and apply it to particular cases by rendering judgment. He wrote:

> "Since judgment should be pronounced according to the written law, as stated above, he that pronounces judgment, interprets, in a way, the letter of the law, by applying it to some particular case. <u>Now since it belongs to the same authority to interpret and to make a law</u>, just as a law cannot be made except by public authority, so <u>neither can a judgment be pronounced except by public authority</u>, which extends over those who are subject to the community."[1]

The Angelic Doctor goes on to explain that it is unlawful for a person to render a judgment he has no authority to make. He explains that those who do such a thing are guilty of the unlawful act known as "judgment by usurpation."

> "Judgment is lawful in so far as it is an act of justice. Now it follows from what has been stated above (1, ad 1,3) that three conditions are requisite for a judgment to be an act of justice: *first,* that it proceed from the inclination of justice; *secondly, <u>that it come from one who is in authority</u>; *thirdly,* that it be pronounced according to the right ruling of prudence. <u>If any one of these be lacking, the judgment will be faulty and unlawful.</u> *First,* when it is contrary to the rectitude of justice, and then it is called 'perverted'

---

[1] ST, II-II, q. 60, a. 6 (emphasis added).

or 'unjust': *secondly,* <u>when a man judges about matters wherein he has no authority, and this is called judgment 'by usurpation'</u>; *thirdly,* when the reason lacks certainty, as when a man, without any solid motive, forms a judgment on some doubtful or hidden matter, and then it is called judgment by 'suspicion' or 'rash' judgment."[2]

From what we have already presented and will continue to develop, it should be evident that only the proper ecclesiastical authorities possess the competency to render the necessary judgments in the deposition of a heretical Pope, just as only the proper ecclesiastical authorities have the authority to render such judgments for other bishops who deviate from the Faith (and who retain their office before being deposed by the Church). Further, because the *crime* of heresy is antecedent to the loss of office, as explained in the previous chapter, in order for a sitting Pope to be deprived of the pontificate by an act of God, the crime itself must first be established and declared (common opinion) by the legitimate authorities of the Church. In fact, the declaration of the crime by the authorities is considered to be a *condition* required for a Pope to lose his office. Regarding this point, John of St. Thomas wrote:

> "The pontiff cannot be deposed and lose the pontificate unless <u>two conditions</u> are fulfilled together: that the heresy is not hidden, but public and <u>legally notorious</u> (i.e., declared[3]); and then he must be incorrigible and pertinacious in his heresy. If <u>both conditions</u> are fulfilled the pontiff may be deposed, <u>but not without them</u>."[4]

Suarez mentions both of these conditions as well, and expressly states that the declaration must come from "the legitimate jurisdiction of the Church." He said:

> "I affirm: if he were a <u>heretic and incorrigible</u> [condition], the Pope would cease to be Pope just when <u>a sentence was passed against him for his crime</u> [condition], <u>by the legitimate jurisdiction of the Church</u>. This is the common opinion among the doctors."[5]

---

[2] ST, II-II, q. 60, a. 2 (emphasis added).

[3] A crime is *legally notorious* "after a sentence by a competent judge that renders the matter an adjudicated thing..." 1917 Code of Canon Law, Canon 2197, §2.

[4] *Cursus Theologici II-II De Auctoritate Summi Pontificis,* Disp. II, Art. III, *De Depositione Papae* (emphasis added), p. 133.

[5] *De Fide, disp.* X, sect. VI, nn. 3-10, p. 316 (emphasis added).

Suarez goes on to explain who in the Church would constitute "the legitimate jurisdiction" to pronounce the necessary sentence:

> "In the first place, who ought to pronounce such a sentence? Some say that it would be the Cardinals; and the Church would be able undoubtedly to attribute to them this faculty, above all if it were thus established by the consent or determination of the Supreme Pontiffs, as was done in regard to the election. But up to today we do not read in any place that such a judgment has been confided to them. For this reason, one must affirm that, as such, it pertains to all the Bishops of the Church, for, being the ordinary pastors and the pillars of the Church, one must consider that such a case concerns them. And since by divine law there is no greater reason to affirm that the matter is of more interest to these bishops than to those, and since by human law nothing has been established in the matter, one must necessarily sustain that the case refers to all, and even to the general council. That is the common opinion among the doctors."[6]

Suarez states that the "crime" must be determined by "the legitimate jurisdiction of the Church," and concludes that this is a general council (and even says this is the "common opinion among the doctors").[7] Suarez thus confirms what should be obvious, namely, that a reigning Pope is not declared a heretic as an exercise of private judgment by appealing to "Divine law" as the Sedevacantists imagine. Rather, ecclesiastical authority alone (an ecumenical council) is required to judge and declare the crime of heresy, which is a *condition* that must occur before a sitting Pope "would cease to be Pope." Suarez further reasons by saying:

> "[I]f the external but occult heretic can still remain the true Pope, with equal right he can continue to be so in the event that the offense became known, as long as sentence were not passed on him."[8]

"External but occult heresy" is heresy that has been externalized (not completely hidden in the heart), but known to only a few. Suarez reasons by noting that if a reigning Pope can remain Pope if his heresy becomes known only to a few, with equal right can he remain Pope if

---

[6] Ibid., pp. 316-317 (emphasis added).
[7] We further address the matter of the general council (perfect and imperfect) in the next chapter.
[8] Ibid., (emphasis added).

his heresy becomes more widely known, "as long as a sentence were not passed on him" by the Church.

Suarez then explains what would likely occur if the declaratory sentence from the proper authorities were not a necessary *condition* for a heretical Pope to lose his office. "In effect," he wrote,

> "there would arise doubt about the degree of infamy necessary for him to lose his charge; there would rise schisms [Sedevacantism!] because of this, and everything would become uncertain, above all if, after being known as a heretic, the Pope should have maintained himself in possession of his charge by force or by other."[9]

Do these prophetic words not reflect the situation today with Sedevacantists, who are probably more divided amongst themselves than were the Protestants 40 years after Luther publicly defected from the Church? For example, how many "Popes" have been elected to date by the various Sedevacantist sects? Well over a dozen! As we saw in the Preface, one of whom ("Pope Michael") was elected in 1990 by his parents and four other individuals, and who professes to have a grand total of 50 followers throughout the world.[10] During his reign as antipope, "Pope Michael" has seen the election of other Sedevacantist "Popes," such as Linus II (in 1994), Peter II (in 1995), Pius XIII (in 1998), another Peter II (in 2005), Leo XIV (in 2006), Innocent XIV (in 2007), Alexander IX (in 2007), Gregory XVIII (in 2011), and John Paul III (in 2015). Here we see what happens when individuals declare the Papal See vacant by their own authority, as well as the schisms that naturally follow - just as Suarez predicted.

To justify their actions, Sedevacantists will often cite the well-known quotation from St. Jerome, who said "heretics exile themselves and separate themselves by their own act from the body of Christ." This quotation is cited to defend their position that a Pope whom they have *personally judged* to be a heretic is not a member of the Church, and therefore not the Pope. John of St. Thomas addressed this erroneous interpretation directly, and even applied it to the case of a heretical Pope. He wrote:

---

[9] Ibid.
[10] "I estimate that there are about 50 members of the Catholic Church worldwide. Only those who accept me as Pope are truly members of the Church." *Pope Michael Documentary*. See program at https://www.youtube.com/watch?v=5NMWs5Ngz9o. Many Sedevacantists would agree with "Pope" Michael on the number of true Catholic believers in the world, even if they don't follow him as Pope.

"When St. Jerome says that a heretic separates himself from the body of Christ, <u>he does not exclude a judgment by the Church,</u> especially in such a serious matter as <u>the deposition of the Pope.</u> He refers instead to the nature of the crime, which is such *per se* to cut someone off from the Church, without any further censure attached to it – <u>yet only so long as it should be declared by the Church;</u> (…) be he ever so manifestly heretical according to <u>private judgment,</u> he remains as far as we are concerned a member of the Church and consequently its head."[11]

As one would expect, St. Bellarmine's thinking is perfectly consistent with that of Suarez and John of St. Thomas regarding this point. In his book, *De Membris Ecclesiae,* Bellarmine begins by citing Divine law (Jn. 10, Mt. 7, Gal. 1) to show that *heretical bishops* should not be listened to by the people. He then explains that heretical bishops *can only be deposed by the proper authorities.* This shows that, according to Bellarmine himself, a bishop who publicly professes heresy, yet who had not openly left the Church, would retain his office. Thus, a bishop who publicly professed heresy would not, by that fact alone, be considered a "manifest heretic" (according to Bellarmine's understanding of the term), since, in *De Romano Pontifice,* Bellarmine taught that manifest heretics *automatically* lose their office (and he made no distinction between a Pope and other bishops).

In the following quotation, Bellarmine uses the term "false prophet" to refer those who teach false doctrines, not those who make predictions that do not come to pass as the term is commonly understood today. He begins by explaining that the faithful can certainly distinguish a true prophet from a false one by "watching carefully to see if the one preaching says the contrary of his predecessors," and then, one paragraph later, he adds:

"We must point out, besides, that the faithful can certainly distinguish a true prophet from a false one, by the rule that we have laid down, but for all that, <u>if the pastor is a bishop, they cannot depose him</u> and put another in his place. For Our Lord and the Apostles only lay down that false prophets are not to be listened to by the people, and not that they depose them. <u>And it is certain that the practice of the Church has always been that heretical bishops be deposed by bishop's councils, or by the Sovereign Pontiff."</u>[12]

---

[11] John of St. Thomas, Disp. II, art. III 26 (emphasis added).
[12] *De Membris Ecclesiae,* bk. I, *De Clerics,* ch. 7 (Opera Omnia; Paris: Vivès, 1870), pp. 428-429 (emphasis added).

Here we see the true thinking of Bellarmine regarding the loss of office for a heretical bishop. He explains that a heretical bishop can be spotted by the faithful (who should not listen to him), but they "cannot depose him," or, what amounts to the same thing, "declare" him deposed due to "manifest heresy." Of course, if the judgment of the Church is necessary for other bishops to lose their office, how much more necessary is it when the bishop is the Supreme Pontiff? Contrary to the Sedevacantist "interpretation" of Bellarmine, the Doctor explicitly rejects the Sedevacantist thesis by teaching that heretical bishops must be deposed by the Church, and not by the private judgment of the faithful through some fallacious appeal to "Divine law."

As we've seen, Sedevacantists (such as John Lane) will likely object to the plain meaning of Bellarmine's words by saying that because "the First See is judged by no one," Bellarmine could not have meant that a council would oversee the deposition of a heretical Pope, since this would require a "judgment" which the Church is not permitted to render. They will then likely argue that this is why Bellarmine said a heretical Pope loses his office *ipso facto*, since he cannot be judged by the Church. But this is clearly not the case, since Bellarmine did not limit his teaching on the *ipso facto* loss of office to a manifestly heretical Pope, but argued that all manifest heretics immediately lose jurisdiction.[13] Yet, in the above citation, he explicitly states that heretical bishops (whose heresy can be identified by the faithful and is therefore public) can only be deposed by the Church. What this shows is that a "manifest heretic," according to Bellarmine, is one who is such by the Church's judgment, not by private judgment. Secondly, Bellarmine himself defended the opinion that a heretical Pope can be judged by a council, which eviscerates the Sedevacantist argument altogether, and further proves they have not understood Bellarmine's position.

In his response to the "Third Opinion" (i.e., that a heretical Pope *cannot* be deposed even if his heresy is manifest), Bellarmine objects by saying:

> "Firstly, because, that a heretical Pope can be judged is expressly held in the Canon, *Si Papa*, dist. 40, and with Innocent.

---

[13] "Therefore, the true opinion is the fifth, according to which the Pope who is manifestly a heretic ceases by himself to be Pope and head, in the same way as he ceases to be a Christian and a member of the body of the Church; and for this reason he can be judged and punished by the Church. This is the opinion of all the ancient Fathers, who teach that manifest heretics immediately lose all jurisdiction…" (*De Romano Pontifice*, bk. 2, ch. 30).

(Serm. II de Consec. Pontif.) And what is more, in the Fourth Council of Constantinople, Act 7, the acts of the Roman Council under [Pope] Hadrian are recited,[14] and in those it was contained that Pope Honorius appeared to be legally anathematized, because he had been convicted of <u>heresy, the only reason where it is lawful for inferiors to judge superiors.</u>"[15]

The above quotation from Bellarmine himself directly undermines the Sedevacantist's "interpretation" of Bellarmine, by demonstrating, quite clearly, that they are not in agreement with the Doctor of the Church when it comes to judging a heretical Pope. Their disagreement with Bellarmine is clearly evident by what John Lane wrote about Suarez. As we saw earlier, Suarez taught that a general council must oversee the deposition of a heretical Pope and issue a declaratory sentence of the crime. John Lane uses this teaching of Suarez as an opportunity to further denigrate him. Lane wrote:

"Suarez's idea that the Church could ... 'declare him a heretic' is completely indefensible. After all, what else is a 'juridical determination' but a public judgment? Suarez's argument that in such a case there would be no violation of the principle, The First See is judged by no-one, is hardly convincing, *and Bellarmine explicitly rejected it.* This is, indeed, one of Francisco Suarez's famous distinctions - a distinction without a difference, as the scholastics say. Suarez, with this doctrine, places the bishops in council over the pope, a notion now condemned explicitly as heresy."[16]

Lane's embarrassing misunderstanding of Suarez continues when he likewise accuses John Salza of heresy for teaching that the crime of papal heresy must be determined by the Church, before a Pope loses his office. In response, John Lane declared:

---

[14] Here are the words of Pope Adrian: "We read that the Roman Pontiff has always judged the chiefs of all the churches (that is, the patriarchs and bishops); but we do not read that anyone has ever judged him. It is true that, after his death, Honorius was anathematized by the Orientals; but one must remember that he was accused of heresy, *the only crime which makes the resistance of inferiors to superiors, as well as the rejection of their pernicious doctrines, legitimate*" (quoted in *La Nouvelle Messe de Paul VI: Qu'en penser'* by Arnaldo da Silveira, pp. 19-20, emphasis added).

[15] *De Romano Pontifice*, bk. 2 ch. 30, translation by Ryan Grant (emphasis added).

[16] John Lane, "Anti-Sedevacantism: Is it Catholic?"(2001) (emphasis added). See http://www.sedevacantist.com/ isitcatholic.html.

"Salza is a Conciliarist – he cheerfully asserts what every non-Gallican theologian since Cajetan has been at pains to deny – that the Church can judge a pope. ... Since this position is heretical, I don't think we need to concern ourselves any further with it."[17]

Lane declares Suarez and Salza's position to be heretical, since "the First See is judged by no one," even though Bellarmine, (whom Lane praises as the authority for his own position), explicitly states that "a heretical pope *can be judged*," and then justifies the statement by saying that heresy is the one case in which "it is lawful for inferiors to judge superiors." In fact, Bellarmine is much more explicit than Suarez regarding this matter. Suarez merely said the Church can declare the crime of a heretical Pope, whereas Bellarmine explicitly states that he can be "judged." This further confirms what we have already demonstrated – namely, that the Sedevacantists, such as John Lane and Fr. Cekada, have completely misunderstood Bellarmine's position; it also confirms that Suarez and Bellarmine held the same opinion, just as the pre-Vatican II theologians (John of St. Thomas, Cardinal Journet, and others) have said.

We should again note that there is a nuance in the notion of "judging" a Pope in the case of heresy, as we discussed in the last chapter,[18] but Bellarmine clearly taught that *in the case of heresy* the Pope (*the* "superior") can be "judged" by a council (his "inferior"). And, to be clear, Bellarmine does not say a *former* Pope (one who has already lost his office for heresy) can be judged. No, he explicitly states that "a heretical *pope* can be judged," thereby confirming that he will remain the Pope at least until he is judged guilty of heresy by the Church. According to Bellarmine, this judgment of the Pope is permitted, because heresy is the one case "in which *inferiors* are permitted to judge *superiors.*" If the heretical Pope had already fallen from office, *ipso facto,* prior to the Church's judgment (which is how Sedevacantists incorrectly interpret Bellarmine), the former Pope would no longer be "superior" to the council. In the next chapter, we will explain how the Church can oversee the deposition of a heretical Pope, while avoiding the heresy of Conciliarism. For now, we simply wish to show that even Bellarmine said the Church can "judge" a Pope in the case of heresy.

---

[17] http://www.sedevacantist.com/viewtopic.php?f=2&t=1757&start=0.

[18] The nuance is that the Church does not strictly judge the Pope. It judges the *matter* and performs the necessary functions to establish that he is *pertinacious,* thereby "demonstrating that he has already been judged" (Wernz, *Ius Decretalium*, 1913, vol. 2, p. 615).

Bellarmine goes on to explain that even if Pope Adrian relied upon a corrupted text from the Oriental bishops (which some believed to be the case), "nevertheless," wrote Bellarmine, "we cannot deny, in fact, that Pope Hadrian [Adrian], and with him the Roman Council, nay more the whole eighth General council judged that, <u>in the case of heresy, a Roman Pontiff can be judged.</u>"[19]

Is Mr. Lane now going to declare Bellarmine's position to be "heretical," as he did with Suarez (and Salza), since Vatican I taught that "the First See is judged by no one"?[20] Or will Lane admit that he has not properly understood Bellarmine's position, and consequently has been publicly misrepresenting it for years? Again, this misunderstanding is pervasive among Sedevacantist apologists, the vast majority of whom have not studied Bellarmine's writings in depth, but instead formed their opinion by reading small snippets of his writings posted on Sedevacantist websites.

It is important to note that when Bellarmine said the Church must oversee the deposition of heretical bishops (which obviously includes a heretical Pope), he was simply following the teaching of the aforementioned Fourth Council of Constantinople (869-870). This is another most devastating blow to the Sedevacantist thesis (and, this time, a Magisterial blow). The same council, which stated that "in the case of heresy, a Roman Pontiff can be judged," also forbade anyone to separate himself[21] from his patriarch (the Pope is the Patriarch of the West), before a careful inquiry into the matter by a synod. The council then attached the grave penalty of excommunication to any layman or monk who refused to heed this teaching of the council, which obviously applies to today's Sedevacantists. Again, Canon 10 of the ecumenical council says:

> "As divine scripture clearly proclaims, 'Do not find fault before you investigate, and understand first and then find fault.' And does our law judge a person without first giving him a hearing and learning what he does? Consequently, this holy and universal synod justly and fittingly declares and lays down that <u>no lay person or monk or cleric should separate himself from communion with his own patriarch before a careful inquiry and judgment in synod</u>, even if he alleges that he knows of some crime perpetrated by his

---

[19] *De Romano Pontifice*, bk 2, ch. 30. (emphasis added)
[20] As we saw in the previous chapter, the axiom "the First See is judged by no one" did not originate with Vatican I, as John Lane imagines, but has been used by Popes and councils since the earliest years of the Church.
[21] In Chapter 20, we will discuss the difference between a *formal* and *material* separation from heretical prelates.

patriarch, and he must not refuse to include his patriarch's name during the divine mysteries or offices. (…) If anyone shall be found defying this holy synod, he is to be debarred from all priestly functions and status if he is a bishop or cleric; if a monk or lay person, he must be excluded from all communion and meetings of the church [i.e. excommunicated] until he is converted by repentance and reconciled."[22]

Here we have an official teaching of the Church (not just an opinion of a theologian) which explicitly *condemns* the Sedevacantist position. By virtue of this decree of the Fourth Council of Constantinople, no layman or cleric "should separate himself from communion with his own patriarch" (his bishop or the Pope) before a lawful inquiry by competent ecclesiastical authority, lest he "be excluded from all communion" and separated from the Church. But this is precisely what Sedevacantists have done, and with regard to the Supreme Pontiff no less. This decree shows that the Sedevacantist position is formally condemned by the Church. Those individuals, such as John Lane, who have spent much of their lives attempting to persuade people to do *precisely what the Council forbade,* will have much to answer for in this regard on the day of judgment.

Mr. Lane actually mocks the idea that the Church herself must render a judgment for a prelate or Pope to lose his office, by arguing that any Catholic in the pew can judge "facts as facts without requiring Daddy to confirm them."[23] "Daddy" in this case, is the Catholic Church. What Mr. Lane is saying is that he can judge whether a prelate has lost his office for heresy, without needing Holy Mother Church [or "Daddy"] to render a judgment. Let us see how contrary the thinking of the arrogant layman, John Lane, is in comparison to the actions of St. Cyril of Alexandria, a Doctor of the Church, when he himself was faced with a prelate teaching heresy.

In the encyclical *Lux Veritatis,* Blessed Pope Pius XI discusses the response of St. Cyril to the heresy being preached *publicly* by one of his fellow Patriarchs, Nestorius of Constantinople. What did St. Cyril do when he received word of Nestorius' public heresy? Did he declare him a "public heretic" who had automatically lost his office? No, he did not. The first thing St. Cyril did was to publicly defend the true doctrine to his flock. Next, he sent a letter to Nestorius in an attempt to bring him back to the correct doctrine (*cf.* Mt. 18:15). When Nestorius publicly persisted in his heresy (thereby demonstrating his pertinacity

[22] Pope Adrian, The Fourth Council of Constantinople, Canon 10 (869 A.D.).
[23] http://sedevacantist.com/viewtopic.php?f=2&t=1757.

304

in the external forum), St. Cyril did not declare him deposed by "Divine law," as no doubt Mr. Lane and his fellow Sedevacantists would have done. Instead, the Patriarch and future Doctor of the Church (not a mere layman) appealed to the Pope to render a judgment (*cf.* Mt. 18:17) and refrained from taking any further action on his own authority. Furthermore, St. Cyril refused to cut off communion with Nestorius until he received a judgment from the Pope. Pius XI explains:

> "These evil dogmas [of Nestorius], which were not taught now covertly and obscurely by a private individual, but <u>were openly and plainly proclaimed by the Bishop of the Constantinopolitan See himself</u>, caused a very great disturbance of the minds of men, more especially in the Eastern Church. And among the opponents of the Nestorian heresy, some of whom were found in the capital city of the Eastern Empire, the foremost place was undoubtedly taken by that most holy man, the champion of Catholic integrity, Cyril, Patriarch of Alexandria. For as he was most zealous in his care of his own sons and likewise in that of erring brethren, he had no sooner heard of the perverse opinion of the Bishop of Constantinople than he strenuously defended the orthodox faith in the presence of his own flock, and also addressed letters to Nestorius and endeavoured in the manner of a brother to lead him back to the rule of Catholic truth.
>
> <u>But when the hardened pertinacity of Nestorius had frustrated this charitable attempt, Cyril, who understood and strenuously maintained the authority of the Roman Church, would not himself take further steps, or pass sentence in such a very grave matter, until he had first appealed to the Apostolic See and had ascertained its decision.</u> Accordingly, he addressed most dutiful letters to 'the most blessed Father [Pope] Celestine, beloved of God,' wherein among other things he writes as follows: 'The ancient custom of the Churches admonishes us that matters of this kind should be communicated to Your Holiness. . . ' (Mansi, l.c. IV. 1011.) <u>'But we do not openly and publicly forsake his Communion (i.e. Nestorius') before indicating these things to your piety</u>. Vouchsafe, therefore, to prescribe what you feel in this matter so that it may be clearly known to us <u>whether we must communicate with him</u> or <u>whether we should freely declare to him that no one can communicate with one</u> who cherishes and preaches suchlike erroneous doctrine. Furthermore, the mind of Your Integrity and your judgment on this matter should be clearly set forth in letters to the Bishops of Macedonia, who are most pious and devoted to God,

and likewise to the Prelates of all the East.' (Mansi, l.c. IV. 1015.)"[24]

Here we see the response of a "champion of Catholic integrity," a Patriarch and future saint and Doctor of the Church, when faced with a prelate publicly teaching heresy. He didn't declare, on his own authority (which was significant), that Nestorius was deposed *ipso facto* by "Divine law" and that he didn't need "Daddy" to judge the matter. No, he appealed to Rome and requested that the Pope render a judgment. He refused to overstep his own authority by taking matters into his own hands. The saint even stated, quite humbly, that he would *not* openly and publicly forsake communion with Nestorius *before receiving the judgment of the Pope*. Here we see how different are the actions of a Doctor of the Church in comparison to the rashness of the Sedevacantists of our day, such as John Lane.

In the last chapter, we saw that the Sedevacantist blogger, Steve Speray, used the case of Nestorius in a vain attempt to argue that prelates who *profess* heresy lose their office automatically, without needing to be warned or deposed by the Church. We also saw that Mr. Speray attempted to use a creative interpretation of Bellarmine to support his theory, when, in fact, Bellarmine himself explicitly stated, in a different chapter of the very same book, that Nestorius was deposed *by the Church* (at the Council of Ephesus) in the year 431, not automatically in the year 428 (when he began preaching heresy), as Mr. Speray claimed.

The Sedevacantist preacher, Gerry Matatics, also uses the case of Nestorius in an attempt to defend the Sedevacantist theory of automatic loss of office under "Divine law," as *discerned* and *declared* by private judgment. According to Mr. Matatics, "though Nestorius continued to occupy the patriarchal see of Constantinople *de facto* (in fact), as a heretic he could not do so *de jure* (in the eyes of the Church's law). Legally, his see was vacant (or *sede vacante*, to use the Church's legal terminology)."[25] Needless to say, Mr. Matatics did not cite a single authority in support of his assertion that Nestorius' see was *legally vacant* in the eyes of the Church law (because none exist). Mr. Matatics simply applied his own erroneous Sedevacantist principles of private judgment to the case of Nestorius, and then declared, on his own authority, that Nestorius *legally* lost his office the moment he professed heresy. Mr. Matatics then provides us with the reasoning he used to arrive at his conclusion. He wrote:

---

[24] Pope Pius XI, *Lux Veritatis*, Nos. 11-12, December 25, 1931.
[25] https://www.gerrymatatics.org/2009Feb09essay.html.

"Once an officeholder in the Church manifests his heresy (as Nestorius did in his Christmas Day homily [in 428]), <u>such a heretic no longer holds legal title to his office in the Church</u>. This follows from two fundamental principles of the Catholic Faith:

1) Heretics are not members of the Catholic Church, since the Church is "one body professing one Faith" (Ephesians 4:4-5).
2) No one can lawfully hold office in a body of which he is not even a member."[26]

Evidently, Mr. Matatics' private judgment of "fundamental principles of the Catholic Faith" does not correspond to the judgment of St. Cyril of Alexandria, Doctor of the universal Church, nor to that of St. Bellarmine, another Doctor of the Church, who affirms St. Cyril's treatment of Nestorius. Regarding the case of St. Cyril and Nestorius, Bellarmine wrote:

"St. Cyril of Alexandria.... in Epistle 18 to Pope Celestine, whom he calls 'Most Holy Father' at the beginning, he asks from him whether he would have it that Nestorius <u>was still communicated with at that time</u> [after preaching heresy], or whether he <u>was to be shunned by all</u>. All of which sufficiently shows in what place St. Cyril held the Roman Pontiff, since in the condemnation and deposition of Nestorius, he showed that he was nothing other than the executer and administrator of the Roman Pontiff."[27]

As we see, Bellarmine accurately relates that Cyril did not believe Nestorius automatically lost "legal title to his office" for publicly preaching heresy (much less by private judgment), as Sedevacantists imagine, but rather appealed to the Pope to render a judgment of the matter (whether Nestorius "was still [to be] communicated with" or "was to be shunned"). In the meantime, St. Cyril continued to recognize Nestorius as a *member* of the Church and Patriarch of Constantinople (and remained in communion with him), *until the Church itself [the Pope] rendered a judgment*. While Nestorius' heresy was steadfastly resisted by St. Cyril, as well as many of the faithful in Nestorius' own diocese (who were later praised for doing so), neither St. Cyril nor these faithful declared that Nestorius was not a member of the Church, nor that he "no longer holds legal title to his office."

---

[26] Ibid.
[27] Bellarmine, *De Romano Pontifice*, bk. 2, ch. 15.

Mr. Matatics' fellow Sedevacantist, Bishop Donald Sanborn (who has evidently studied these issues in more depth than Mr. Matatics), realizes that Nestorius did not *legally* lose his office when he began to preach heresy, as Mr. Matatics claims. In fact, one might be surprised to learn that Bishop Sanborn actually acknowledges that only the Church has the authority to declare an office vacant, and that up to that point the officeholder retains *legal* possession of the office.[28]

In an article about the case of Nestorius, Bishop Sanborn wrote the following in which he draws a parallel to our current day:

> "...despite his public heresy, it was still necessary that Nestorius undergo warnings by the Pope, and having repudiated the warnings, be officially excommunicated and deposed by the same. The case is strikingly close to our own. ... we do not have the authority to declare the sees legally vacant .... Only the authority of the Church can do that. ... until their designation to possess the authority is legally declared null and void by competent authority, the heretical 'pope' or 'bishop' is in a state of legal possession of the see, but without authority. He can only lose that state of legal possession by legal deposition."[29]

So Mr. Matatics' claim that Nestorius legally lost his office *ipso facto* (automatically) the moment he began to preach heresy, is not only contradicted by St. Cyril and St. Bellarmine, but even by one of his fellow Sedevacantists, who happens to be a bishop himself. But the problem with Mr. Matatic's theory does not end here, as we will now see.

Matatics' explanation of the Nestorius case (which is cited regularly by other Sedevacantist apologists as an example of an *ipso facto* loss of office), directly contradicts his explanation of the case of Pope John XXII (d. 1333). Why? Because Mr. Matatics and other Sedevacantists

---

[28] Bishop Sanborn is a different stripe of Sedevacantist. Contrary to many of his comrades, he acknowledges that a Pope (and bishops also) could only be deposed by the authority of the Church, but he still refuses to recognize the conciliar Popes as true Popes. According to Sanborn's theory, which was first propounded by Fr. Guérard des Lauriers in the late 1970s, the conciliar Popes were validly elected (they are "material" Popes), but their heresies impede them from receiving the authority (jurisdiction) of the office (they are not "formal" Popes). In Chapter 12, we will see how this novel theory also causes Bishop Sanborn to conclude that the Church's peaceful and universal acceptance of a Pope means only that he was validly elected to the office, but did not receive the authority (jurisdiction) of the office. As we will see, this theory is exactly *contrary* to what the Church's theologians have taught about the peaceful and universal acceptance of a Pope.

[29] Sanborn, "An Emperor We Have, But No Bishop," http://www.mostholytrinitysemin ary.org/An%20Emperor%20We%20Have.pdf.

claim that John XXII retained his office in spite of publicly professing heresy, since the revealed truth he contradicted had not yet been formally defined by the Church. Therefore, they say, Pope John XXII was not truly professing *heresy*, but only an *error* against the Faith.[30] Only after the truth was formally defined by the Extraordinary Magisterium, they argue, was the error he professed truly qualified as *heresy*.

The problem is that the same is true in the case of Nestorius. The dogma of *Theotokos* (Mary is the Mother of God) that Nestorius publicly denied (in 428) was not formally defined until the Council of Ephesus (in 431) which was three years after Mr. Matatics (and Mr. Speray) claim he lost his office "by Divine law" for public heresy. How can Sedevacantists declare Nestorius a "public heretic" for denying an *undefined* doctrine, yet *excuse* John XXII by arguing that the doctrine he denied had not been defined?[31] And if Nestorius allegedly lost his office for publicly denying an undefined dogma, why did John XXII retain his office when he did the same? It is a complete contradiction. But such contradictions are legion in the Sedevacantist world of private judgment.

Sanborn's "Material Pope" Theory

Regarding the teaching of Bishop Sanborn, although he concedes that the recent Popes have been validly elected to the office of St. Peter and *legally* retained the office, he nevertheless claims that they have not enjoy the *powers* of the office (i.e., jurisdiction/authority). He claims that their alleged "public heresies" (as *personally judged* by Sanborn) operate as an impediment to them receiving the power. Using Thomistic terminology, he argues that the heretic "Pope" (the matter) is

---

[30] For example, the Sedevacantist blogger, Steve Speray, wrote: "Pope John XXII taught the blessed souls do not attain the Beatific Vision until after the General Judgment. This only constituted a theological opinion in his day *because the particular judgment had not yet been defined*. Therefore, Pope John XXII erred, but not against the Catholic Faith, which defined the teaching after Pope John's death." (Speray, Vatican I's Declaration is Foundation for Sedevacantism, May 24, 2015). See https://stevenspray.wordpress .com/category/sede vacantism/.

[31] Bishop Sanborn argues that the reason Nestorius was a heretic is because he denied a doctrine of the Ordinary and Universal Magisterium. He wrote: "Nestorius' heresies were not specifically condemned by any act of extraordinary magisterium. He was considered a heretic because his denials and teachings ran contrary to the ordinary universal magisterium of the Catholic Church." (Sanborn, "An Emperor We Have, But No Bishop"). The problem with this assertion is that the doctrine denied by John XXII had also been taught by the Ordinary and Universal Magisterium. So if Nestorius was a public heretic, Sedevacantist logic demands that John XXII was a heretic as well.

unable to receive the authority (the form) of his office, since his heresy (the impediment) prevents the conjunction of the *matter* and *form*.[32] Therefore, according to Bishop Sanborn, the Pope is only a "material Pope."

This is an entirely fallacious argument for the following reasons. First, a man becomes Pope by receiving the powers of the office (i.e., jurisdiction/authority). As Cajetan said "a Pope is constituted Pope by the power of jurisdiction *alone*."[33] If he lacks jurisdiction, he is not the Pope, *even materially*. He would at most be a designee, but certainly not a *legal* officeholder or a "material Pope" as Sanborn argues. Second, appealing to Thomistic terminology and paying lip service to the necessity for the Church's authority to declare a Pope deposed does not save Sanborn's entirely novel theory from its familiar Sedevacantist defect: *private judgment by usurpation*.[34] Whether one claims that the *office* was lost (or never obtained) due to the *sin* of heresy (Fr. Cekada), or that the office was *legally* obtained, while the *powers* of the office were never acquired (Bp. Sanborn), it is still being determined and publicly declared by an act of *private judgment* (and contrary to the Church's judgment), which they have no authority to make.

So, while we applaud Bishop Sanborn for acknowledging that he does not possess the authority to publicly declare the papal see vacant, what he doesn't realize is that he also lacks the authority to publicly declare that a *legal* officeholder has lost his *jurisdiction*. In fact, the very notion that a man can *lawfully* hold an office, yet lose (or never acquire) the authority of the office, is absurd. If a person *lawfully* holds an ecclesiastical office, he possesses the *authority* of the office (which his lawful possession entitles him to receive). He may abuse the authority of his office, but the Church has never taught that a prelate can lawfully hold an office, yet fail to receive or lose the jurisdiction inherent in the office. And notice carefully what Bishop Sanborn has done: First, he professes an entirely novel doctrine which has no support in Catholic Tradition (i.e., that a man can legally hold office without having the authority of the office). Then, he applies this novelty to the last six Popes and *every single bishop in the world* in legal possession of an episcopal see, by declaring that they have no authority (even though Sanborn couldn't even name them all, much less know

---

[32] See, for example, Sanborn, "The Material Papacy," at http://www.sodalitiumpianum.com/index.php?pid=27.

[33] Cajetan, *De Comparatione Auctoritatis Papae et Concilii*, English Translation in *Conciliarism & Papalism*, p. 76.

[34] Sanborn makes a judgment of usurpation both over a question of law (whether one can legally hold an office without jurisdiction) and a question of fact (who lawfully holds offices and jurisdiction).

what they believe). So, we have a *conclusion* ("they lack authority") that is based upon 1) a rash judgment ("they are heretics"), and 2) a wildly novel doctrine ("that a person can *legally* hold office yet lack the authority of the office"), which has absolutely no support in Church teaching. And Bishop Sanborn has the gall to refer to himself as a *traditional* Catholic bishop.

The fundamental problem with Bishop Sanborn's theory is that, while the Church makes a distinction between Orders and jurisdiction, she makes no distinction between the lawful possession of an ecclesiastical office (which Sanborn admits the conciliar Popes and bishops have) and the rights and privileges inherent in the office (i.e., jurisdiction). Just as a legal member of the Catholic Church enjoys all the rights and privileges of being a member, so the bishops and Pope, who *legally* hold their offices, likewise enjoy the rights, privileges and powers of the office they hold, including jurisdiction.

Furthermore, notwithstanding the claims of Bishop Sanborn, heresy does not absolutely impede the "conjunction" of *matter* (officeholder) and *form* (authority), especially if the man is publicly acknowledged *by the Church's judgment* as a member in good standing and as lawfully holding the office in question (whether Pope or bishop). As Fr. Laymann explained, even in the case of a notoriously heretical Pope, "while he was tolerated by the Church, and publicly recognized as the universal pastor, <u>he would really enjoy the pontifical power, in such a way that all his decrees would have no less force *and authority* than they would if he were truly faithful</u>. The reason is: because it is conducive to the governing of the Church, even as, in any other well-constituted commonwealth, that <u>the acts of a public magistrate are in force as long as he remains in office and is publicly tolerated</u>."[35] Indeed, so long as the conciliar Popes have "remained in office" (an office Sanborn acknowledges they *lawfully* hold), then they enjoy the "pontifical power" (jurisdiction), and even if the Pope is in heresy, his acts "have no less force *and authority* than they would if he were truly faithful." The bishop's position (that the conciliar Popes are lawful Popes), then, is actually a most useful argument *against* the Sedevacantist thesis.

Unfortunately, our Sedevacantist bishop takes his case yet one step further, by giving practical advice to his flock which has been formally condemned by the Church. Based upon his utterly novel theory that a prelate can *lawfully hold* an office without possessing the *authority* of the office, Bishop Sanborn further declares – once again, on his own

---

[35] Laymann, Theol. Mor., bk. 2, tract 1, ch. 7, p. 153 (emphasis added).

authority - that the faithful "have the right and obligation *personally* and even *collectively* to cut communion with heretical prelates"[36] – that is, with those prelates who *legally* hold offices in the Church but whom the faithful *personally judge* to be heretics. Bishop Sanborn justifies this assertion by noting that some people during Nestorius' day did, in fact, sever communion with Nestorius before he was deposed by the Church. Sanborn points to the example of these individuals, *rather than the example of St. Cyril*, Doctor of the Church, to justify his position. And it's no wonder why.

The problem with Bishop Sanborn's chosen example is that after the Nestorian crisis, the Fourth Council of Constantinople (assembled in the very territory in which the Nestorian heresy originated!), not only confirms that the position of St. Cyril was correct, but *condemned* the notion that the faithful can sever communion with their Patriarch before the matter has been settled by the Church - which is precisely what Sanborn tells his flock they have a *right*, and even an *obligation*, to do. And, as we have seen, the Council went so far as to debar clerics (including bishops) from priestly functions and status, and attach an excommunication to any layman, who separated from their bishop based upon their private judgment of the alleged crime.

While the individuals who severed communion with Nestorius before he was deposed by the Church could perhaps be excused in their day, those who follow their example today cannot be excused, since we now have the teaching of an ecumenical council that formally condemns what they did. The council also condemns those prelates who refuse to include their Patriarch's name in the canon of the Mass, before the Church had rendered a judgment. Bishop Sanborn completely ignores this teaching as well, since he himself refuses to name the current Pope (his Patriarch) in his Mass. And Sanborn goes further by claiming it is forbidden for anyone to attend a Mass in which the Pope's name is mentioned.[37] Sanborn's argumentation, while more "sophisticated" than those of the lay preacher Gerry Matatics, suffers the same defect of judgment by usurpation, and is thus equally anathematized by the Council of Constantinople IV.

Private Judgment of "Facts" under "Divine Law"

We will now examine the Sedevacantist reasoning for why they imagine themselves justified in ignoring the explicit teaching of the Fourth Council of Constantinople (assuming they know about it) by

[36] Bishop Donald L. Sanborn, "An Emperor We Have, But No Bishop."
[37] This point will be addressed in Chapter 21.

formally separating themselves from their Patriarch (the Pope), before the matter has been resolved by the Church. We will reveal their errors in reasoning and judgment which further demonstrate why such a critical matter is not to be decided by the private judgment of individual Catholics.

We will begin by returning to one of the fundamental errors of Sedevacantism, which was addressed in Chapter 5, namely, the error that the loss of office for a Pope is merely a question of the *sin* of heresy under *Divine law* (and not a determination of the *crime* of heresy by Church authority), and that anyone in the Church can judge the case for themselves, declare it to be a "fact," and then claim, based upon the alleged "fact," that the Pope has lost his office.[38]

Notwithstanding that not a single theologian in Church history has ever said private individuals can personally judge (and declare deposed) a heretical bishop or Pope under Divine law independently of the Church's judgment, Sedevacantists will attempt to support their novel theory by arguing that, since the Pope is above canon law, the canonical *crime* of heresy cannot apply to him. By taking the question out of the realm of ecclesiastical law, and making it solely a question of a "fact" based upon Divine law (determined, of course, by their private judgment), the Sedevacantist thereby eliminates the need for Church authority to render the necessary judgments, and appoints himself as both judge and jury in the case.

What they have obviously failed to realize is that if the proper ecclesiastical authorities alone are permitted to judge heresy under ecclesiastical law, the same authorities alone would be the competent judge under Divine law. This Sedevacantist theory, which claims for them the right to make definitive judgments of who lawfully holds ecclesiastical office under Divine law (which they are not permitted to judge under canon law) has no basis in Catholic teaching or practice and is further untenable for the following reasons:

First, the determination of the internal sin of heresy (which they think results in the loss of office for a heretical Pope) is a judgment of the internal forum. Since not even the Church judges internals (*de internis ecclesia non judica*), neither can the Sedevacantists.

---

[38] As we saw in Chapter 5, Fr. Cekada wrote: "The material Mr. Sparks quotes deals with heresy as a *delictum* and with the ecclesiastical censure (excommunication) that the heretic incurs. This is mostly irrelevant to the case of a heretical pope. Because he is the supreme legislator and therefore not subject to canon law, a pope cannot commit a true *delictum* of heresy or incur an excommunication. He is subject only to the divine law" ("Sedevacantism Refuted?," August 2004), emphasis added.

Second, even if the internal sin of heresy were committed, it alone would not sever the Pope from the Body of the Church or cause him to lose his jurisdiction, as the unanimous teaching of the theologians makes clear (he would only be severed from the Soul of the Church, as explained in Chapter 3).

Third, the Sedevacantists contradict themselves when they claim canon law does not apply to the Pope, and then defend their position by appealing to canon law (as they regularly do), which amounts to playing both sides of the fence (it also violates the principle of non-contradiction by saying that canon law both applies and does not apply to the Pope at the same time).

For example, in response to a recent article published in *The Remnant* newspaper,[39] the Sedevacantist blogger Steven Speray attempted to defend the Sedevacantist position by citing canon 2314, §1 of the 1917 Code. He began by saying:

> "Can. 2314.1 n. 1 states that heretics, 'incur ipso facto excommunication.' This automatic censure[40] refers to the external forum,[41] and happens without warnings. Excommunicated persons can't hold office since they are not members of the Church[42] in the external forum."[43]

Then, in the *very same article*, only two paragraphs later, Mr. Speray directly contradicts himself when he says that the penalties of canon law do *not* apply to a Pope - including the very canon 2314, §1 that he previously cited as applying to a Pope. He wrote:

---

[39] Siscoe, "Can the Church Depose an Heretical Pope?," *The Remnant* newspaper , online (November 18, 2014).

[40] As we saw in the previous chapter, a Pope cannot incur the *censure* of excommunication in the external forum, since he is not subject to the Church's positive law.

[41] As we also saw in the last chapter, the censure is not automatic in the external forum for a cleric, as Mr. Speray claims. Rather, a declaratory sentence must be issued for a cleric to incur the censure in the external forum, since this is necessary for the good of the Church. But, as noted, a Pope is not subject to the Church's positive law and therefore cannot incur this censure.

[42] Without a declaration, a cleric remains a member of the Church in the external forum. This is true even if he has incurred an occult excommunication in the internal forum (which would be known to God alone).

[43] Speray, "Robert Siscoe and The Remnant's Latest Canon Law Fiasco," February 3, 2015. (As noted previously, Mr. Speray completely re-wrote his article after reading Mr. Siscoe's reply. Mr. Speray re-posted the new article, without changing the original date and without mentioning that it had been completely revised.)

"Popes and cardinals don't fall under the penalties of canon law. Therefore, canons <u>2314.1</u> n.2, 2223.4, and 2232, which require superiors, trials and condemnations, can't be applied anyway."[44]

So, on the one hand, Mr. Speray quotes canon 2314, §1 to support his position that a heretical Pope is automatically excommunicated, and then, two paragraphs later, says the penalties of canon 2314, §1 do not apply to a Pope! We have seen that such embarrassing contradictions are pervasive in Sedevacantist argumentation.

Fourth, canon law interprets and applies Divine law to the accused in accordance with principles of justice. Even if a Pope is not *subject* to canon law, the principles of canon law, which interpret and apply Divine law (such as the necessity of warnings), would have to be followed if a Pope were accused or suspected of heresy, both as a matter of justice as well as under the philosophical principle *omne majus continet in se minus* - "the greater includes the lesser." While there might be some modifications to canonical procedure since "the First See is judged by no one," the general principles of Divine law, as reflected and codified in canon law, would still apply.

Fifth, those who publicly defend the Sedevacantist position by appealing to either canon law *or* Divine law usurp an authority that does not belong to them since, as St. Thomas explained above, it belongs to one and the same public authority to write the law, interpret the law, and apply the law to particular cases.[45] As follows from the teaching of St. Thomas, it would be the Church (the competent "public authority" who alone has the authority to definitively interpret her laws and the laws of God), and not individuals Catholics, who would have the authority to interpret and apply the applicable laws in the case of a heretical Pope.

This erroneous reasoning makes it clear why individual laymen, and even individual priests, have no right to declare a Pope deposed (even if he were to publicly profess heresy) by an exercise of their private judgment through an appeal to either Divine law or canon law. Such judgments and declarations belong to the proper authorities alone. And the Sedevacantists' claim that their position is simply based on "fact" - a "fact" that is disputed by 99.99 percent of the Church's faithful, which means it is not an established fact at all[46] - does not nullify this necessity, nor does it in any way help their case.

---

[44] Ibid.
[45] See ST, II-II, q. 60, a. 6; and ST, II-II, q. 60, a. 2
[46] The Oxford Dictionary defines *fact* as: "a thing that is indisputably the case."

Private Judgment Includes Judging Pertinacity

The Sedevacantists' erroneous judgment of "facts" under "Divine law" includes, of course, their judgment of pertinacity (whether the Pope is consciously dissenting from Catholic teaching), since the Pope must be both a "public" *and* "notorious" (pertinacious) heretic before he will lose his office. However, knowing they cannot prove pertinacity solely by the Popes' Modernist words and actions (which they don't have the authority to do anyway), they are forced to get their "proof" another way. To that end, Sedevacantists retreat to the speculative realm of the Popes' academic backgrounds by referring to their education in theology and seminary training. On that basis, which is a classic example of *petitio principii*,[47] the Sedevacantist will plead, "C'mon, the conciliar Popes *must* know they are teaching heresy!"

For example, John Lane argues as follows:

> "Did John Paul II *know* that the Church teaches that we are forbidden to do the many, many, things he did, and that we are forbidden to believe in the heretical notions that he was plainly in love with, such as universal salvation? Well, he was granted a Doctorate in Sacred Theology by the *Angelicum*, and the sponsor of his thesis was the famous anti-Modernist Fr. Garrigou-Lagrange. It is ridiculous to suppose that such a student did not know the basics of the Catholic Faith. To review the facts is to behold the answer."[48]

Someone should explain to Mr. Lane that what one *ought* to "know" and what one *actually* knows (that is, understands) may be two different things, and this distinction is essential to any finding of fact. That John Paul II studied under Fr. Garrigou-Lagrange (whom Sedevacantists themselves disagree with on the question of loss of office of a heretical Pope[49]) does not in any way prove that John Paul II willfully dissented from Catholic teaching. Furthermore, neither John Lane nor his fellow judges of "fact" have sufficiently demonstrated that John Paul II taught even material heresy (that is, that he directly contradicted a dogma of the faith, without requiring additional steps of reasoning to demonstrate the contradiction).

---

[47] The logical fallacy of assuming the conclusion in the premise (begging the question, circular reasoning).
[48] Ibid., p. 36 (emphasis in original).
[49] As we saw in Chapter 5, Garrigou-Lagrange held that Christ could sustain a heretical Pope as head of the Church even after he ceased to be a "member" of the Church, so long as the Church continued to recognize him as Pope.

Nevertheless, Sedevacantists take this approach (pointing out the Popes' academic backgrounds) because they know the Popes' alleged "heretical" propositions *alone* do not prove the crime (much less the sin) of heresy. Thus, they are forced to reach for additional "evidence" to meet their self-assumed burden of "proving" pertinacity; but academic backgrounds, like objective words and actions, are simply not sufficient to do so. If it were, canon law would not require warnings and trials to establish the crime of heresy, but merely confirm that the person who professed heresy completed the required seminary training.

Moreover, what is good for the Sedevacantist goose is good for the Catholic gander. If Sedevacantists wish to point to objective words and actions that they believe serve as evidence for pertinacity, we can also refer to the conciliar Popes' own testimony, such as their personal subjective belief that Vatican II was in *conformity* with the teaching of the Church, however objectively wrong their assessments may have been. For example, when confronted with the allegation that he has Communist leanings, Pope Francis replied:

> "I'm sure that I haven't said anything more than what's written in the social doctrine of the Church...I am the one following the Church...And in this it seems that I'm not wrong. I believe that I never said a thing that wasn't the social doctrine of the Church. Things can be explained, possibly an explanation gave an impression of being a little 'to the left,' but it would be an error of explanation...all of this, is the social doctrine of the Church."[50]

That Paul VI, John Paul II and Benedict XVI all publicly lamented the disastrous effects of the Second Vatican Council is further evidence of their subjective intention *not* to depart from Church doctrine with their novel "pastoral" approach, even if one believes they did so objectively. In fact, this point was conceded by the Sedevacantist, Richard Ibranyi, who said:

> "John Paul II does not believe he is teaching contrary to Church dogma, at least it cannot be proven that he believes he is. JP2 not only verbally professes to be Catholic, he also verbally submits to the Catholic Church and the papacy."[51]

---

[50] Pope Francis (September 22, 2015). See Catholic News Agency's report at http://www.catholicnewsagency.com/news/full-transcript-of-popes-in-flight-interview-from-cuba-to-us-78637/.
[51] Ibranyi, "Against John Lane," December 2009 (emphasis added).

But if John Paul II does not *believe* he is teaching contrary to Church dogma, as Mr. Ibranyi concedes, then he isn't even guilty of the *sin* of heresy, much less the public *crime* of heresy. Ibranyi's statement is about the best and most succinct refutation of Sedevacantism that we have found!

Garrigou-Lagrange made another interesting observation, which is quite relevant to this point. He noted that the Modernist crisis in the Church has "been *not* of a crisis of faith, *but of a very grave malady of the intellect,* which conducts itself on the tracks of liberal Protestantism..."[52] In other words, Modernism is chiefly a disease of the intellect, which is where the virtue of faith resides. Hence, the faith is undermined indirectly by a direct attack on the intellect. As a result of this "grave malady of the intellect," it may well be that a prelate who is infected with Modernism subjectively *intended* to hold and profess the Catholic faith, in which case he would not be pertinacious, but only mistaken. This is particularly the case with the conciliar Popes who, unlike Protestant heretics, *claim* to be teaching the Catholic Faith. Because Sedevacantists rightly accuse the Vatican II Popes of being rank Modernists, they cannot exclude positive, prudent doubt that the conciliar Popes are only mistakenly in error, in which case they would not even be guilty of the internal *sin* of heresy.

Lastly, even if one became *personally* convinced that the recent Popes have been guilty of the *sin* of heresy, private judgment on this matter would have absolutely no effect whatsoever on the status of their pontificates since, as we have sufficiently demonstrated, the Church itself must establish the *crime* of heresy before a Pope will lose his office for the same.

The Distinction Between Questions of Fact and Law

To further illustrate the problem with the Sedevacantists' private judgment of sin under "Divine law" based on the "facts," let us consider the arguments of a Sedevacantist blogger who masquerades behind the pen-name "Gregorius." This individual wrote an internet piece called "The Chair is Still Empty"[53] for a popular Sedevacantist website. The piece was an attempted response to John Salza's 2010 and

---

[52] Taken from a quote on the cover of "The Essence and Topicality of Thomism," by Reginald Garrigou-Lagrange, a 1945 essay published in book form in 2013 (private publisher, translation by Alan Aversa), emphasis added.
[53] The article by "Gregorius" may be found at www.novusordowatch.com. Salza replied with a detailed response in an article called "The Chair is Empty? Says Who? John Salza Responds to Novus Ordo Watch" at http://www.johnsalza.com.

2011 articles on Sedevacantism which were published in *The Remnant* newspaper.[54] In Gregorius' response, which is filled with errors, misrepresentations, and presumptions (not to mention the perfunctory personal attacks and childish invective), Gregorius advances these erroneous Sedevacantist arguments to a tee.

For starters, Gregorius, bases his position on the "loss of office by the *sin* of heresy" theory of Fr. Cekada, which he has fallen for hook, line and sinker. Parroting Fr. Cekada almost verbatim, Gregorius wrote: "the Sedevacantist case is based on the *sin* of heresy, not the canonical delict."[55] Based on this theory of Fr. Cekada, Gregorius then imagines that if he personally "discerns" that the Pope has committed the sin of heresy, his private judgment constitutes a "fact." Hence, the loss of office, he claims, is not determined by Church law judged by the competent authorities, but by individual discernment of "facts" of which Gregorius, a private layman, is the judge.

For example, in addressing the determination of whether the conciliar Popes have been heretics who lost their office, Gregorius confidently tells us: "And this, we are bound to inform Mr. Salza, is not a matter of *law* but of *fact*." Of course, this gratuitous assertion ignores the very legal question that is at the heart of this issue: <u>Who</u> judges the facts? Church authority or individuals like Gregorius with no authority?

As we will see, whether a person (e.g., the Pope) is a heretic is, indeed, a question of *fact*; but the related questions, namely, *who* tries the facts, *who* renders a judgment against a reigning Pope, and *how* punishment for the offense is carried out, are questions of *law*, the details of which have been debated for centuries.

Gregorius then adds:

> "Salza's failure to properly distinguish law from fact is the most fundamental error of his entire piece. He makes everything into a matter of Church law, when the Sedevacantist position is based on the order of fact, not the order of law."[56]

But what Gregorius does not explain is what happens when individual Catholics in the pew disagree about the "facts"? When this happens, who decides who is correct? This dilemma underscores the

---

[54] Salza, "The Errors of Sedevacantism and Ecclesiastical Law" (2010) and "Sedevacantism and the Sin of Presumption" (2011), published in *The Remnant* newspaper and online at http://www.johnsalza.com.

[55] "The Chair is Still Empty," found at http://www.novusordowatch.org/the_chair_is_still_empty.htm.

[56] Ibid.

Protestant nature of Sedevacantism, where private judgment, and not the Church, serves as the final court of appeal. Let's consider an example of Sedevacantists who disagree over the "fact" about whether a Pope was indeed a manifest heretic who lost his office. Regarding Pope Honorius, John Lane wrote:

> "Pope Honorius was not a manifest heretic, and nobody has ever claimed that he was. ... even if we were to admit the claim that Honorius really was a heretic, which we do not admit, he was certainly not a manifest heretic, and thus his case has no bearing on the question of the incompatibility of the status of 'manifest heretic' and the possession of an ecclesiastical office."[57]

Mr. Lane believes Pope Honorius remained a true Pope, even though he was later condemned by the Church as a heretic. But the Sedevantist blogger, Steve Speray, reaches a completely different conclusion in response to the "question of fact." He claims that Pope Honorious lost his office and became an antipope. In response to an article that pointed out the difficulties that the case of Honorius presents for the Sedevacantist thesis, Mr. Speray wrote:

> "As for Honorius, he was not considered a pope after his heresy! The fact that he was at best doubtful afterwards, means *he must be considered an antipope.* So Honorius proves sedevacantism not disproves it."[58]

Notice, Mr. Speray simply asserts that Pope Honorius "was not considered a pope after his heresy," which is something the Church has never taught. Speray further tells us that Honorius was "at best" a "doubtful" Pope, which is also something the Church has never taught. Then, based on his own conjecture, Speray claims that "Honorius proves Sedevacantism." For Steve Speray, as for his Sedevacantist colleagues, his private judgment of the "question of fact" becomes a "fact" in itself that settles the matter; yet, as we saw, his judgment is exactly contrary to that of his fellow Sedevacantist John Lane.

Who decides who is right? To what higher authority can the Sedevacantists appeal? And what about the Sedevacantist author, Richard Ibranyi, who considers it to be a "fact" that all of the Popes since Innocent II (1130-1143) - 102 in all! - have been antipopes?[59] For

---

[57] Lane, John, "Concerning A SSPX Dossier On Sedevacantism."
[58] Speray, Steven, "Against John Salza."
[59] Ibranyi, Richard, "No Popes since 1130" (January 2014).

Mr. Ibranyi, it is a "fact" that these men were heretics, and therefore not true Popes. Again, who decides which person's answer to the "question of fact" is correct? That Sedevacantists all claim the conciliar Popes are antipopes does not resolve the problem, since the conclusion is still based on the same fundamental error of private judgment - which happens to be the source of the rest of their disagreements and divisions.

Needless to say, Gregorius' assertion that the loss of office is solely "based on the order of fact, not the order of law" is entirely erroneous and a gross oversimplification of this most weighty topic. As. Mr. Salza explained in his response to Gregorius, this complex question is not based solely "on the order of fact," but on what true legal scholars recognize as a "mixed question of fact and law" (*de facto et iure*).[60] The reason it is a mixed question of fact and law is because the Church cannot look solely to the law, or solely to the facts, to resolve the question of whether the Pope has lost his office, as we will explain in a moment. This mixed question of fact and law is not only recognized by secular legal scholars and practitioners (like Mr. Salza), but by the Church's canon lawyers as well.

For example, in his commentary on the 1917 Code of Canon Law, Fr. Augustine mentions the mixed question of fact and law as it relates to the *ipso facto* loss of office due to a "public defection from the faith" under canon 188, §4. Fr. Augustine explains:

> "A cleric must, besides, be degraded if, <u>after having been duly warned</u>, he persists in being a member of such a society (non-Catholic sect) [Fact]. All the offices he may hold become vacant, *ipso facto*, without any *further* declaration [Law]. This is tacit resignation recognized by law (Canon 188.4) and therefore the vacancy is one <u>*de facto et iure*</u> [from fact and law]."[61]

Fr. Augustine's statement that the determination of the loss of office (vacancy) is "from fact and law" (*de facto et iure*) highlights the point that the determination (of the vacancy) cannot be made solely by looking to the "facts" (as Sedevacantists claim) or the "law." The

---

[60] For example, in the case of *Canada v. Southam, Inc.,* 1 S.C.R. 748 (1997), Judge Frank Iacobucci explained: "Briefly stated, questions of law are questions about what the correct legal test is. Questions of fact are questions about what actually took place…And questions of mixed law and fact are questions about whether the facts satisfy the legal tests." This explanation from a civil court judge accurately describes the distinction between questions of fact and law - a universal distinction in both secular and canonical jurisprudence.

[61] Augustine, *A Commentary on the New Code of Canon Law*, vol. 8, bk. 5, p. 280 (emphasis added).

question under canon 188, §4 of whether a cleric has publicly joined a non-Catholic sect and "persisted" after being warned is a question of *fact*, and whether such a cleric automatically loses his office ("tacit resignation" under the same canon 188, §4) is a question of *law* – both of which must be established/decided by the Church.

As an aside, we mentioned that Canon 188, §4 is probably the favorite canon of the Sedevacantists. It is the canon they use most often to "prove" the conciliar Popes have lost their office, even though this canon applies to clerics who publicly join a non-Catholic sect, not to those who simply profess heresy. In fact, in Gregorius' article, he ends his piece by providing his readers with a scanned copy of canon 188, §4 – in Latin, no less – which is quite a curious thing for him to do when he maintains, *in the same article*, that "the Pope, being the Supreme Legislator, is, strictly speaking, above canon law" (the same contradiction we saw Mr. Speray make in his article). In any event, Gregorius, quite predictably, argues that canon 188, §4 is actually based on Divine law, and that he is thus rendering his judgment, not according to canon law (*which he cites in support of his position!*), but according to the "facts" under Divine law (of which he makes himself the judge). We have exposed the complete falsity of this position.

But let us further demonstrate why one cannot look *solely* to the "law" or to the "facts" to resolve the complex question of whether the Pope is a manifest heretic who has lost his office. The following illustrates the "question of fact" versus "question of law" distinction:

Question of Fact – Is the Pope a manifest heretic?
Question of Law – Does a heretical Pope lose his office for heresy? (If so, when, how and who judges?)

As we have seen, St. Bellarmine said there were five different opinions about the question of law, *none of which have been definitively adopted by the Magisterium.* This point alone demonstrates that the issue of Sedevacantism is not "solely a question of fact," but involves a more fundamental question of law that must be resolved first. Even if one agrees with Bellarmine's opinion on the question of law, that is, that a manifestly heretical Pope loses his office *ipso facto* and not by Church deposition, the opinion has not been adopted by the Church, and there are reputable theologians who disagree with this opinion.[62] And even

---

[62] Bellarmine himself admitted his position on this question of law was his subjective opinion and not absolute fact when he said that the Third Opinion (that a Pope cannot be deposed) was only "exceedingly improbable." He makes the same qualification in his response to the Fourth Opinion when he says "in my judgment, this opinion cannot be

assuming Bellarmine's position on *ipso facto* loss of office is correct, precisely when and how the loss of office occurs, and who has the authority to judge whether it has occurred, are *additional* questions of law which have been extensively debated for centuries. This point further proves that the question of the loss of office for a heretical Pope is a mixed question of fact and law, and not solely "based on the order of fact."

Sedevacantists cannot even get to first base with their "question of fact" approach until they resolve these "questions of law," and yet resolving these complex questions are not within their power (not even the Magisterium has chosen to settle these questions). The entire Sedevacantist case, as it relates to "law," rests upon nothing more than their own *private interpretation* of the *opinions* of certain theologians (especially that of Bellarmine, whom Sedevacantists have failed to understand), and which in no way constitutes the official teaching of the Church.

The fact that individual Catholics (even priests and bishops) have no authority to settle speculative questions of theology and law which have not been resolved by the Church was even conceded by Fr. Cekada, Bishop Sanborn, and seven of their colleagues.[63] In 1983, these nine priests (former members of the Society of St. Pius X) wrote a letter to Archbishop Lefebvre complaining that they were not permitted to question the validity of the New Mass and the new rite of ordination. They claimed that forbidding them to do so was infringing on their liberty since, as they said, these speculative questions had not been resolved by the Church (as if approving a rite of Mass and ordination did not constitute the Church's judgment on the matter). Here is what these nine priests wrote in their 1983 letter:

> "The present situation in the Church has generated many unprecedented problems of a theological and practical nature — for example the question of the *in se* [in itself] validity or invalidity of the New Mass... <u>The Society must not presume to settle such speculative questions in an authoritative and definitive fashion, since it has absolutely no authority to do so</u>. Any attempt by the Society to teach and impose its conclusions on matters of <u>speculative theology</u> as the only positions suitable for a Catholic to

---

defended" (we also note that when Sedevacantists cite this quotation, they often remove "in my judgment" from the quotation to give the appearance that Bellarmine's subjective opinion is an apparent statement of fact).

[63] The nine priests are Rev. Clarence Kelly, Rev. Donald J. Sanborn, Rev. Daniel L. Dolan, Rev. Anthony Cekada, Rev. William W. Jenkins, Rev. Eugene Berry, Rev. Martin P. Skierka, Rev. Joseph Collins, and Rev. Thomas P. Zapp.

embrace <u>is dangerous and opens the door to great evils, for it assumes a magisterial authority which belongs not to it but to the Church alone</u>.

Now, while in theory the Society may deny any claim to such teaching authority, <u>in practice it has acted as though it did have such an authority</u>."[64]

At the end of the letter, these nine priests (who were soon to be expelled from the Society), added the following "resolution":

"Respect for the magisterial authority of the Church as the sole arbiter of theological questions shall be enforced. Therefore, the Society shall faithfully adhere to the teachings of the Church, <u>but shall never usurp that teaching authority by attempting to settle definitively questions of speculative theology</u>."[65]

So, according to the reasoning of the priests who signed this letter (most or all of whom are now Sedevacantists), the Society of St. Pius X is not permitted to insist on the *validity* of a Mass that was approved by the Church, yet the Sedevacantists themselves are permitted to settle speculative questions of theology and law regarding when and how a Pope loses his office for heresy. In fact, Fr. Cekada and Bishop Sanborn are so dogmatic about their personal opinion regarding this matter, that they not only publicly declare that the last six Popes have been antipopes, but they go further by publicly declaring that it is forbidden to attend a Mass in which the Pope's name is mentioned in the canon (and this is the same Bishop Sanborn who concedes that the post-Vatican II Popes are *legal* Popes).[66] Clearly, these priests are guilty of doing precisely what they complained about in 1983 – namely, usurping Magisterial authority "by attempting to settle definitively questions of speculative theology," which have not been resolved by the Church. Indeed, in the Sedevacantists' own words, their entire thesis "is dangerous and opens the door to great evils, for it assumes a magisterial authority which belongs not to it but to the Church alone."

As we have seen, even if the question of *fact* (i.e., is the Pope a public and notorious heretic?) was established by the proper

---

[64] Letter of 'the Nine' to Abp. Marcel Lefebvre, (March 25, 1983; emphasis added), http://www.traditional mass.org/articles/article.php?id=48&catname=12.
[65] Ibid.
[66] This will be discussed in Chapter 21. We also note Fr. Cekada penned an article during the reign of Benedict XVI in which he argued that those who attended at a Mass in which Benedict's name was mentioned in the canon, would not only fail to fulfill their Sunday obligation, *but would receive no sacramental grace* (*cf.* Cekada, "Should I Assist at a Mass That Names Benedict XVI in the Canon?").

authorities, the question of *law* (exactly when and how does the Pope lose his office) remains unresolved. It is clear that the unresolved question of law, in and of itself, completely negates the Sedevacantist position, without even addressing the question of fact, which is likewise something Sedevacantists have no authority to judge.

Continuing with his theme that he can personally judge the Pope a public heretic under "Divine law," Gregorius says:

> "John Salza's error lies in his claim that 'Catholics are required to look to the ecclesiastical law of the Church to resolve' the issue of whether someone is a heretic or not. Note that Salza does not quote any proof for this claim - he merely makes the assertion, hoping everyone will accept it. But the assertion is false."[67]

This is quite an incredible statement, not only because Gregorius "does not quote any proof for *his* claim" (because there is none), but also because *all* of the theologians who addressed the hypothetical question of a heretical Pope since the sixteenth century (e.g., Cajetan, Bellarmine, Suarez, Francis de Sales, John of St. Thomas, Billuart, etc.) said the loss of office (loss of jurisdiction) was a result of the public *crime* of heresy, not simply the *sin* of heresy, as Gregorius maintains! This is why John of St. Thomas says that in the absence of ecclesiastical inquiry and public warnings, which are necessary to establish the crime, "the Church, <u>by divine law, *cannot*</u> declare him [a heretical Pope] deposed,"[68] which is exactly the *opposite* of what Gregorius and other individual Sedevacantists have done. Hence, Gregorius' appeal to Divine law to prove his case shows just how unread he and his colleagues are on these issues.

Gregorius then attempts to illustrate the Sedevacantist "loss of office due to the sin of heresy" theory with the following analogy, which further demonstrates the error of his position. He says:

> "While canon law can help us understand divine law, it is crucial not to mix the two or to reduce divine law to canon law. This is easily apparent when we consider, for example, that there is no ecclesiastical law against entertaining impure thoughts [an

---

[67] "The Chair is Still Empty," found at http://www.novusordowatch.org/the_ chair _is_still_empty.htm.
[68] "The pope insofar as he is externally a heretic, *if he is prepared to be corrected*, cannot be deposed (as we have said above), and the Church, by divine law, cannot declare him deposed…Therefore, it is false to say that a Pontiff is deposed by the very fact that he is externally a heretic: truly, he is able to be so publicly as long as he has not yet been warned by the Church…" (*Cursus Theologici II-II De Auctoritate Summi Pontificis,* Disp II, Art. III), p. 138 (emphasis added).

internal sin]. Are we, then, to conclude that it is not an offense against divine law? Are we to conclude that unless there be an ecclesiastical trial, no one can know if someone has entertained such thoughts? What if the person in question makes this fact manifest by his actions?"[69]

Putting aside the fact that this example of a sin of impure thoughts is not on point because it is not a sin against the Faith and thus doesn't involve the question of the loss of office (and hence doesn't carry with it our critical questions of law), there are a number of other glaring problems with his example (keeping in mind it is supposed to demonstrate by analogy how one can know if a Pope has lost his office for heresy).

First, Gregorius' analogy begins with the erroneous assumption that the *sin of heresy against Divine law* in the internal forum causes the loss of office in the external forum.[70] This is error number one.

Second, Gregorius imagines that *he* is the competent authority to judge whether the internal *sin* has been committed by examining the external actions of the individual, when not even the Church judges the internal forum. This is error number two.

Third, Gregorius' judgment is based upon his personal, unilateral discernment of the facts, without any due process for the accused. Even though the Church does not "judge a person without first giving him a hearing" (per the Fourth Council of Constantinople), in Gregorius' courtroom, the accused gets no hearing. This is error number three.

Fourth, Gregorius' judgment of the facts based upon his personal discernment *becomes a fact in itself*. Gregorius takes Descartes' fallacious dictum "I think, therefore I am" to a new level, for Gregorius' "discerns it, and therefore, it is." For example, he wrote:

> "So, all of Salza's points about how canon law allows only a Pope to judge a cardinal, etc., are not relevant to the issue of Sedevacantism, because we are not pretending to be judging a Pope or a cardinal in a canonical trial. Instead, we are merely *discerning* that a certain cleric does not profess the Catholic Faith and hence cannot be a member of the Church"[71] (emphasis added).

---

[69] "The Chair is Still Empty," http://www.novusordowatch.org/the_chair_is_still_empty.htm.

[70] We have also noted that the crime (not sin) of heresy is antecedent to, but does not directly cause, the loss of office, but merely disposes the Pope for the same (and that the divine separation of the Pope from his office is a direct action of Christ).

[71] "The Chair is Still Empty," http://www.novusordowatch.org/the_chair_is_still_empty.htm.

As applied to the Pope, because Gregorius "discerns" the subjective sin of heresy in the Pope's objective words or actions (which is not possible), his personal judgment also becomes objective fact. This "discernment," of course, is simply, in the words of St. Thomas, a "judgment by usurpation." And this is error number four.

Having pointed out these most basic errors, we might also mention some other errors and omissions in Gregorius' hypothetical. For example, the Church, under her own law, must prove (not just presume) that the alleged "actions" of an individual are manifestly contrary to Catholic doctrine, which means they are plain and unmistakable in themselves, and do not depend upon additional steps of reasoning (a nuance that Gregorius, in his faulty approach to the question, does not mention). Further, under the laws of the Church, what is "made manifest by his actions," in Gregorius' example, does not by itself prove any sin was committed, because it does not prove the person *consciously* departed from the teachings of the Church. The burden of proof cannot be sustained by looking at the objectively sinful actions alone (another nuance that Gregorius fails to mention).

Finally, even if the competent authority proves there was a conscious departure from Catholic teaching, the presumption of guilt is always rebuttable (*praesumptio iuris tantum*)[72] in the external forum. If the average Catholic is afforded the opportunity to rebut the canonical presumption of guilt in the external forum, then the Pope, who is judged by no one on Earth (and who is above the canonical element of presumption), is afforded the same dignity, as St. Thomas says, by "giving him the benefit of the doubt, because the judge ought to be more inclined to acquit than to condemn."[73] Gregorius, like the rest of his Sedevacantist brethren, fails to mention these important details as he plays lawgiver, judge and jury.

One wonders how Gregorius would "discern" the case of Archbishop Darboy, which was discussed in Chapter 6. Recall that in the presence of a large governmental body, Archbishop Darboy *publicly denied* a dogma of the faith (which constitutes heretical matter) and persisted in this denial *for years*, even after being warned by the Pope himself (demonstrating pertinacity). Yet, in spite of this, Blessed Pope Pius IX considered Archbishop Darboy to have retained his office, and even invited him to take part in the First Vatican Council.

If Gregorius had been alive at the time, would he have "discerned" that Archbishop Darboy "did not profess the faith" sufficiently to "be a member of the Church"? If so, his judgment of the "fact" would have

---

[72] A presumption that is considered true unless someone proves otherwise.
[73] ST, II-II, q. 70, a. 2, ad 2.

been in manifest opposition to that of Pope Pius IX. And what about the case of Michel de Bay, which we have also discussed in previous chapters? Not only did he profess heresy, but his heresies were condemned by the Pope at the time – and they were condemned as being *his* heresies, even though he was not personally named in the condemnation. Yet the whole time Bellarmine (and his contemporaries) continued to recognize de Bay as a Catholic in good standing.

If the Pope loses his office based upon the judgment of heresy rendered by individual Catholics, as Sedevacantists imagine, what happens if one Catholic judges the Pope to be a heretic, while another does not? If John judges the Pope to be a heretic, while Robert judges him to be a Catholic, does that mean he is the true Pope for Robert, but not for John? And if John later changes his judgment, would the non-Pope suddenly become Pope? Or is the Pope the Pope regardless of John and Robert's personal subjective judgment? Objectively, who is and who is not the Pope is not determined by the subjective judgment of each individual Catholic. And it is also clear from what was discussed in the last chapter that God will not secretly sever the bond that unites the man to the pontificate, without the Church knowing about it. This further explains why a judgment must be rendered by the Church, before an apparently heretical Pope is deprived of the pontificate.

John Lane takes the same facile approach in his argument that the conciliar Popes were never validly elected to begin with. He defends his claim by saying "only a Catholic is valid matter for the papacy (or any ecclesiastical office) and therefore a non-Catholic cannot under any circumstances hold an office."[74] Notice Mr. Lane declares, as an act of private judgment, that the conciliar Popes were not Catholic, even though all the Cardinals in the Conclave considered them members of the Church in good standing. In the world of Messrs. Gregorius and Lane, their personal opinion is fact, even when their private judgment is exactly contrary to the public judgment of the Church.

But none of this will persuade Mr. Lane since, like Gregorius, he considers his judgment of the facts to be fact itself, thereby usurping the legitimate authority of the Church. If John Lane says they were not Catholics prior to their election, this "fact" alone confirms for him that their elections were null and void. And it is worth noting that Mr. Lane and his colleagues also apply the same "logic" to the rest of the Church's hierarchy, claiming that all the bishops of the world (the entire *ecclesia docens*) have publicly defected from the Faith and are

---

[74] Lane, "Concerning an SSPX Dossier on Sedevacantism, by Rev. Dominique Boulet, SSPX," p. 10.

therefore illegitimate.[75] And they "discern" this "fact" without ever having met the men (much less cross-examined them), 99.9 percent of whom they could not even name. That is quite a remarkable ability of discernment.

Unfortunately, without realizing it, Mr. Lane and his Sedevacantist colleagues have embraced the Protestant mindset that is so common in the modern age. Relying upon their own private judgment, they make themselves the judge, jury and executioner. Lacking all humility, they consider themselves to be the competent authority to decide some of the most complex theological questions of "fact" and "law" that exist: questions of "fact" which they have no authority to judge, and complicated questions of "law" that have been debated by theologians for centuries, and which the Church herself has never resolved.

---

[75] For example, referring to the Church from 1958 forward, Gregorius said "its heads are not true Popes, nor is its hierarchy legitimate" ('The Chair is Still Empty').

Chapter 11

~ The Deposition of a Heretical Pope ~

In this chapter, we will examine the issue of how a heretical Pope is deposed. We will consider this complex and difficult question on both the speculative and practical level by consulting the theologians and canonists who have written on the subject over the centuries. We will employ the distinctions necessary to navigate through the minefield of possible errors that touch upon the matter, while carefully avoiding the heresy of Conciliarism.[1]

At the outset of this chapter, it is critical to recall the distinction between the *crime* of heresy and the twofold punishment of the crime. In Chapter 9, we demonstrated from the writings of Bellarmine, Suarez, Francis de Sales, John of St. Thomas and others that the *Church* (not individual Catholics) must *prove* (not presume) the Pope is guilty of the crime of heresy through a formal finding of fact before a reigning Pope loses his office for heresy. This finding of fact includes ecclesiastical warnings (as a matter of charity, not jurisdiction), which is based upon St. Paul's instruction in his Epistle to Titus, 3:10. If the Pope remains obstinate following these public warnings, he publicly manifests his pertinacity and "judges himself," thereby demonstrating to all that he is, in fact, a heretic.

After the Church establishes that the Pope is guilty of the crime of heresy, she renders a judgment of the same (and, as we will see, this is to be done during an "imperfect" ecumenical council). Whether it would be absolutely necessary for the Church to publicly issue a declaratory sentence of the crime to the Church (which was the common opinion during the days of Bellarmine and Suarez) is open to speculation; whether the Pope would be deposed *ipso facto* and immediately by Christ (Bellarmine/Suarez), or if the Church herself would play a part in the deposition by a juridical act that separated the Church from the Pope (Cajetan/John of St. Thomas), has been debated by the Church's theologians, as we have seen.

What is *unanimous*, however, is that *the Church* must establish that the Pope is guilty of the crime of heresy before a Pope will lose his jurisdiction. Because the Church is a visible society, the faithful must know if the Pope is indeed a heretic who is no longer their head, since Christ Himself will not deprive the Pope of his office while he is still

---

[1] Conciliarism is a heresy that holds that a council is superior to the Pope.

331

recognized as Pope by the Church. The Church's formal judgment of the crime is a *condition* necessary for a sitting Pope to be deprived of the pontificate for heresy. This is why Suarez said "if he were a heretic and incorrigible, the Pope would cease to be Pope just when a sentence was passed against him for his crime, by the legitimate jurisdiction of the Church."[2]

Bellarmine and Suarez held that upon the Church's adjudication of the crime, a heretical Pope loses his office *ipso facto* as a matter of Divine law, without the Church having to, technically, depose him (this is the "Fifth Opinion" of Bellarmine). This conclusion is based upon the understanding that only Catholics can hold office in the Church, and the manifestly heretical Pope – that is, one who has openly left the Church or been judged guilty of the crime of heresy by the Church - is not Catholic (he has separated himself from the Church). According to this opinion, he who is not a member of the Church cannot be its head.

Other theologians maintain that the Church plays a ministerial part in the deposition itself, over and above simply establishing and declaring the crime. They say that the Church would also declare the heretic Pope "*vitandus*" (to be avoided), thereby separating itself from the heretic Pope. According to this opinion, then, the loss of office would occur *by the Church separating from the Pope* (not the Pope separating from the Church). Because the Church has not spoken definitively on these matters, both opinions are permitted. According to both opinions, however, only a general council would have the authority to declare the See vacant, thereby informing the faithful that the former Pope is, in fact, no longer Pope.

In this chapter, we focus on the deposition itself, the questions that surround it, and the various opinions of the Church's theologians. Having explained the position of Bellarmine/Suarez in Chapter 9, this chapter will be primarily dedicated to explaining the position of John of St. Thomas and Cardinal Cajetan, who taught that the Church has a part to play in the deposition itself. We will see how they explained their position without claiming that the Church has authority over a reigning Pope (thus avoiding the heresy of Conciliarism).

We will begin by addressing the more fundamental question of whether a heretical Pope can, in fact, be deprived of the pontificate for heresy.

---

[2] *De Fide*, Disp. X, sect. VI, nn. 3-10, pp. 316-317.

Can a Heretical Pope Be Deposed?

The common opinion of theologians and canonists is that a Pope *can* be deposed for the crime of heresy. By the term "deposed" we mean the formal process by which the Church oversees the heretical Pope's removal from office, either by establishing the crime and declaring the See vacant (one opinion), or by depriving the heretical Pope of the pontificate by actually deposing him (second opinion). As we mentioned in the previous chapter, Arnaldo da Silveira examined the writings of 136 theologians on this question, and found only one (Bouix) who taught that a heretical Pope cannot lose his office, even if he were to fall into heresy.[3] All the others affirmed that a heretical Pope can, and indeed *should*, be deposed.

We will begin by citing several authorities confirming that a heretical Pope can be judged by the Church. For example, Pope Innocent III said:

> "Without faith it is impossible to please God.'... To this end faith is so necessary for me that, though I have <u>for other sins</u> God alone as my judge, it is only <u>for a sin committed against faith that I may be judged by the Church</u>. For 'he who does not believe is already judged.'"[4]

This same teaching is found in the famous Canon *Si Papa,* attributed to Pope St. Boniface, and contained in the famous Decretum of Gratian,[5] which reads:

> "Let no mortal man presume to accuse the Pope of fault, for, it being incumbent upon him to judge all, he should be judged by no one, <u>unless he is suddenly caught deviating from the faith</u>."[6]

The renowned canonist, Fr. Paul Laymann, also wrote:

---

[3] *'La Nouvelle Messe de Paul VI: Qu'en penser'.*

[4] Sermon 2: *In Consecratione,* P. L. 218:656 (emphasis added).

[5] The Decretum of Gratian, or *Concordia Discordantium Canonum* by which it is also known, is a collection of canon laws compiled and written in the twelfth century by a jurist known as Gratian, and used as a legal textbook. It forms the first part of the collection of six legal texts, which together became known as the *Corpus Juris Canonici*. It was used by canonists of the Catholic Church until Pentecost May 19, 1918, when a revised Code of Canon Law (*Codex Iuris Canonici*) promulgated by Pope Benedict XV on May 27, 1917, obtained legal force. The Canon *Si Papa,* which is contained in the Decretum of Gratian, is attributed to Pope Boniface – see *De Comparatione Auctoritatis Papae et Concilii,* p. 110.

[6] *Decree of Gratian* I, dist. 40, ch. 6.

"It is more probable that the Supreme Pontiff, as concerns his own person, could fall into heresy, even a notorious one, by reason of which he would deserve to be deposed by the Church, or rather declared to be separated from her. ... if such a thing should seem to have happened, it would pertain to the other bishops to examine and give a judgment on the matter; as one can see in the Sixth Synod, Act 13; the Seventh Synod, last Act; the eight Synod, Act 7 in the epistle of [Pope] Hadrian; and in the fifth Roman Council under Pope Symmachus: 'By many of those who came before us it was declared and ratified in Synod, that the sheep should not reprehend their Pastor, unless they presume that he has departed from the Faith'. And in Si Papa d. 40, it is reported from Archbishop Boniface: 'He who is to judge all men is to be judged by none, unless he be found by chance to be deviating from the Faith'. And Bellarmine himself, book 2, ch. 30, writes: 'We cannot deny that [Pope] Hadrian with the Roman Council, and the entire 8th General Synod was of the belief that, in the case of heresy, the Roman Pontiff could be judged.'"[7]

Theologians commonly understand the phrase "judging the Pope" in the sense of establishing that he has willfully deviated from the Faith, which demonstrates that he is *already* judged. In the following quotation from his Coronation Sermon IV, Pope Innocent III uses this terminology when he teaches that a heretical Pope "can be judged by men," and then adds "or rather *shown to be judged*":

"[T]he Roman Pontiff...should not mistakenly flatter himself about his power, nor rashly glory in his eminence or honor, for the less he is judged by man, the more he is judged by God. I say 'less' because he can be judged by men, or rather shown to be judged, if he clearly loses his savor to heresy, since he 'who does not believe is already judged' (John 3:18)..."[8]

Using this terminology of Pope Innocent III, the famous canonist, Fr. Wernz, also observed that the *declaratory sentence* of the crime of heresy "does not have the effect of judging a heretical pope, but of demonstrating that he has *already* been judged."[9]

Because a Pope obstinate in his heresy shows himself to be *already judged*, according to the words of Our Lord (Jn. 3:18), the great Master of the Dominican Order and advisor to Pope Clement VII, Cardinal

---

[7] Laymann, Theol. Mor., bk. 2, tract 1, ch. 7, p. 153.
[8] Sermon 4: *In Consecratione*, P.L. 218:670 (emphasis added).
[9] *Ius Decretalium* (1913) II, p. 615.

Cajetan, held that the Church can depose the Pope for the crime of heresy. For example, Cajetan says that "the pope *can be deposed* legitimately because, granted that power to depose the pope resides in the council apart from the pope, it must be able to assemble its scattered members, *in order to depose him*; otherwise, while a pope *who must be deposed* refused to summon a council, he could not be deposed."[10] He also says "in a case of heresy, the connection between the papacy and that particular person is subject to the decision of the Church and the universal council, so that he [the heretical Pope] *can be deposed*."[11]

Cajetan also explains that deposition must follow the *crime* of heresy. For example, he wrote: "the pope can be *deposed* for the *crime* of heresy."[12] And a little later: "But the pope is liable to the penalty of *deposition* on account of the *crime* of heresy, as the doctors generally say, influenced by [the canon] *Si Papa* (dist 40, ch 6)."[13]

Suarez likewise held that a Pope who has been found guilty of the crime of heresy "should be deposed" so that the Church can "defend herself from such a grave danger." He says:

> "I affirm: If he is a <u>heretic and incorrigible</u>, the Pope ceases to be Pope as soon as a declarative sentence of his <u>crime</u> is pronounced against him by the legitimate jurisdiction of the Church. This is the common position held by the doctors, and can be concluded from the first Epistle of Pope St. Clement I,[14] in which one reads that St. Peter taught that <u>the heretic Pope should be deposed</u>. The reason is the following: It would be extremely harmful to the Church to have such a pastor and not be able to defend herself from such a grave danger; furthermore it would go against the dignity of the Church to oblige her to remain subject to a heretic Pontiff without being able to expel him from herself; for such as are the prince and the priest, so the people are accustomed to be (...) heresy 'spreads like cancer,' which is why heretics should be avoided as much as possible. This is, therefore, all the more so with regard to an heretical pastor; but how can such a danger be avoided, unless he ceases to be the pastor?"[15]

---

[10] *De Comparatione Auctoritatis Papae et Concilii*, p. 66 (emphasis added).
[11] Ibid., p. 94 (emphasis added).
[12] Ibid., p. 105 (emphasis added).
[13] Ibid., p. 102 (emphasis added).
[14] John of St. Thomas also mentions this teaching of St. Peter found in the First Epistle of Clement the Corinthians. However, we have been unable to locate the quotation in the modern translations of the Epistle.
[15] *De Fide*, vol. XII (Paris: Vivès, 1958), p. 317 (emphasis added).

John of St. Thomas explains that there are three cases in which a Pope can be deposed: "The first" he writes,

> "is the case of heresy or infidelity. The second case is perpetual madness. The third case is doubt about the validity of the election. Concerning the case of heresy, theologians and Canon lawyers have disputed very much [about precisely how the Pontificate is lost]. It is not necessary to delve into this question now. However, there is an agreement among the Doctors on the fact that the Pope may be deposed in case of heresy. (...)
>
> A specific text is found in the Decree of Gratian, Distinction 40, chapter 'Si Papa,' where it is said: 'On earth, no mortal should presume to reproach the Pontiff for any fault, because he who has to judge others, should not be judged (judicandus) by anyone, unless he is found deviating from the Faith' (Pars I, D 40, c. 6). This exception obviously means that in case of heresy, a judgment could be made about the Pope.
>
> The same thing is confirmed by the letter of Pope Hadrian, reported in the Eighth General Council [IV Constantinople, 869-870], in the 7th session,[16] where it is said that the Roman Pontiff is judged by no one, but the anathema was made by the Orientals against Honorius, because he was accused of heresy, the only cause for which it is lawful for inferiors to resist their superiors.
>
> Also, Pope St. Clement says in his first epistle that St. Peter taught that a heretical Pope must be deposed. The reason is that we must separate ourselves from heretics, according to Titus 3:10: 'A man that is a heretic, after the first and second admonition, avoid him.' Now, one should not avoid one that remains in the [Sovereign] Pontificate; on the contrary, the Church should instead be united to him as her supreme head and communicate with him. Therefore, if the pope is a heretic, either the Church should communicate with him, or he must be deposed from the Pontificate."
>
> The first solution leads to the obvious destruction of the Church, and has inherently a risk that the whole ecclesiastical government errs, if she has to follow a heretical head. In addition, as the heretic is an enemy of the Church, natural law provides protection against such a Pope according to the rules of self-defense, because she can defend herself against an enemy such as a heretical Pope; therefore, she can act (in justice) against him. So, in any case, it is necessary that such a Pope must be deposed."[17]

---

[16] Mansi, *Sacrorum Conciliorum nova collectio amplissima* (Venice, 1771), vol. 16, col. 126.

[17] *Cursus Theologici II-II De Auctoritate Summi Pontificis*, Disp. II, Art. III, *De Depositione Papae*, p. 133 (emphasis added).

Fr. Mattheus Conte a Coronata taught the same in his seventeenth century book, *Tractatus Postumus*:

> "A Pontiff, lapsed into heresy, can most justly be deposed. Thus, Duvallius, above in q. 10. The reason is, that it is not credible that Christ wants to *retain* him as Vicar of His Church, who pertinaciously segregates (*segregat*) himself whole from Her, since Christ has especially commanded Her to hear His Voice as a faithful people, and to comply with Him, just as sheep hear the voice of their shepherd. The sheep hear His Voice and they follow Him. The sheep follow Him (*cf.* John 10:3-4). But far be it that the Church should hear a Pontiff lapsed into heresy, She who is rather bound to stop up Her own ears against his violent speech, lest She be infected by the venom of his doctrine; [rather] <u>his casting-out and new election ought to be urged by the assembly of the Sacred Cardinals</u>."[18]

More quotations could be provided, but suffice it to say that what we have just seen (that a Pope can be deposed for the crime of heresy) represents the common opinion of the theologians and canonists. The sole exception we are aware of is the French canonist Marie Dominique Bouix (d. 1870), who maintained that even if a Pope publicly fell into heresy he could not be removed from office. He wrote:

> "There is not sufficient reason to think that Christ had determined that a heretical Pope could be deposed. The reason allegeable in favor of that deposition would be the enormous evil which would come upon the Church in case such a Pope was not deposed. Now this reason does not hold: for, on the one hand, a Pope heretic does not constitute an evil so great that it necessarily leads the Church to ruin and destruction; and, on the other hand, the deposition would be a remedy much worse than the evil itself."[19]

If Bouix had lived to see our day, in which modern means of communication have made it possible for the scandalous words and actions of the conciliar Popes to be broadcast, instantly and continuously throughout the world, he may have had a different opinion about the harm that a heretical Pope can do to the Church. Nevertheless, since the Church herself has never spoken definitively on the question, it is permissible for Catholics to hold the opinion. In fact,

---

[18] *Tractatus Postumus* (Liege, 1677), Tract I, Chapter XXI, n. II, pp. 80-81, translated by Br. Alexis Bugnolo.
[19] Bouix, Tract. *de Papa*, tom. II, p. 670.

Bellarmine himself only referred to this opinion (held by Bouix) as being "exceedingly improbable,"[20] rather than certainly false.[21]

Who Would Oversee the Deposition?

John of St. Thomas explains that because the Church has a right, according to Divine law, to separate itself from a heretical Pope, it also has a right to the means necessary to accomplish such a separation. Now, since the only competent tribunal to oversee such a grave matter affecting the universal Church is a general council, it follows that the Church herself must possess the authority to convene such a council. He explains:

> "And now it remains to be explained by what authority this Council is to be called (...). I respond that such a council can be convened by the authority of the Church, which is in the bishops themselves, or the greater majority thereof. For indeed the Church has the right, by divine law, to separate herself from an heretical pope. Consequently she has the right, by the same divine law, to use all means of themselves necessary for such separation, and the means that are 'of themselves (per se) necessary' are those that are legally able to prove such crime; but one cannot prove the crime legally unless there be a competent judgment; and in such a grave matter as this, the only competent judgment is that of a general council. Because we are treating here with the Universal head of the Church, this pertains to the judgment of the universal Church, which is a General Council.
>
> And therefore I do not agree with Father Suarez, who believes this can be treated in Provincial Councils.[22] For truly a Provincial Council does not represent the universal Church, and therefore does not possess the authority to decide a matter which pertains to the

---

[20] *De Romano Pontifice*, bk. 2, ch. 30. Located in the section of the "Third Opinion."
[21] Recalling what was said about mixed questions of fact and law in Chapter 10, this statement of Bellarmine demonstrates, as we said, that the matters relating to law (i.e., if, how and when a heretical Pope can lose his office) have not been resolved by the Church. This is also seen in Bellarmine's objection to the Fourth Opinion, in which he said "*in my judgment*, this opinion cannot be defended," and not that it was certainly wrong.
[22] Suarez said a general council would oversee the deposition of a heretical Pope, but also, in the same treatise, said "perhaps it would not be necessary for a general council as such to meet, but it might be enough if in each region there met provincial or national Councils, convoked by the Archbishops or Primates, and that all arrived at the same conclusion." John of St. Thomas disagreed with this conclusion of Suarez.

universal Church. Nor would several Provincial Councils possess the authority to represent the universal Church."[23]

Regarding the separate question[24] of *who* within the Church would have the authority to convene the council, John of St. Thomas explains that since it has not been entrusted to anyone in particular, such a council could be convened by the Cardinals or the neighboring bishops (or even at the request of secular authorities, "the princes"). He wrote:

> "But if we should not speak of the authority by which such a matter is to be judged, but of the convocation of the council itself, and who has the authority to convene such a council, then I judge that it has not been entrusted to anyone in particular, and therefore can be convened either by the cardinals, who are able notify the bishops, or else by other neighboring bishops, who then notify the others so that they can be gathered; or even at the request of the princes, not as a summons having coercive force, as when the Pope convenes a Council, but as an denunciative convocation, whereby a crime is announced to the bishops in order that they may hastily gather together to remedy the matter. The Pope cannot annul such a Council … for the Church has the authority, by the divine right, to convene a council for this purpose, since she has the right to separate herself from a heretic."[25]

Perfect and Imperfect Councils

How can the Church convene a general council to oversee the deposition of a heretical Pope, when a general council must be *convened* and *overseen* by a Pope, either personally or through his legates? In answering this question, Cajetan makes the classical distinction between a *perfect* council and an *imperfect* council; or, as he puts it, an *absolutely* perfect council, and a perfect council *in relation to the present state of the Church*.

Cajetan explains that a perfect council *absolutely* is one in which the body is united to its head, and therefore consists of the Pope and the bishops.[26] Such a council has the authority to define dogmas and issue

---

[23] *Cursus Theologici II-II De Auctoritate Summi Pontificis*, Disp. II, Art. III, *De Depositione Papae*, p. 137.

[24] The first question was "by what authority is such a council convened." This second question is "who in the Church has the authority to summon the council." Note that both questions are "questions of law."

[25] *Cursus Theologici II-II De Auctoritate Summi Pontificis*, Disp. II, Art. III, *De Depositione Papae*, p. 137.

[26] *De Comparatione Auctoritatis Papae et Concilii*, p. 67.

decrees that regulate the universal Church.[27] A council composed of those members who can be found when the Church is in a given condition (e.g., with several doubtful Popes, or with one apparently heretical Pope), which Cajetan refers to as "a perfect council according to the present state" (i.e., an imperfect council), can only "involve itself with the universal Church up to a certain point."[28]

An imperfect council cannot define doctrines or issue decrees that regulate the universal Church, but only possesses the authority to decide the matter that necessitated its convocation. Cajetan notes that there are only two cases that justify convoking such a council: "...when there is a single heretical pope to be deposed, and when there are several doubtful supreme pontiffs."[29] In such exceptional cases, a general council can be called without the approval of, or even against the will, of the Pope. Cajetan explains:

> "A perfect council according to the present state of the Church [i.e., an imperfect council] can be summoned without the pope and against his will, if, although asked, he himself does not wish to summon it; but it does not have the authority to regulate the universal Church, but only to provide for the issue then at stake. Although human cases vary in infinite ways ... there are only two cases that have occurred or can ever occur, in which, I declare, such a council should be summoned. The first is when the pope must be deposed on account of heresy; for then, if he refused, although asked, the cardinals, the emperor, or the prelates can cause a council to be assembled, which will not have for its scope the care of the universal Church, but only the power to *depose* the Pope. (...)
>
> The second is when one or more Popes suffer uncertainty with regard to their election, as seems to have arisen in the schism of Urban VI and others. Then, lest the Church be perplexed, those members of the Church who are available have the power to judge which is the true pope, if it can be known, and if it cannot be known, [they have] the power to provide that the electors agree on one or another of them."[30]

The council of Constance is often cited as an example of an "imperfect council." It was convened during the Great Western Schism, when there were three claimants to the papacy and sufficient uncertainty as to which of the three was the true Pope. The council (not

---

[27] Ibid., p. 67.
[28] Ibid., p. 68.
[29] Ibid.
[30] Ibid., p. 70.

individual sects of clergy and laity with no official authority) ended the schism by deposing or accepting the resignation of all the papal claimants, which then paved the way for the election of Cardinal Odo Colonna, who took the name Martin V.[31]

Another council that is often mentioned is the Council of Sinuesso, which was convened by the bishops to oversee the matter of Pope Marcellinus (d. 304), who had offered incense to idols.[32] In our day, when the Church is, in the words of Our Lady of Akita, "full of those who compromise"[33] and infested by "traitorous co-religionists,"[34] such papal actions would likely be explained away, or else praised as positive ecumenical gestures in the "spirit of Vatican II." In the time of the early Church, however, when the faith was strong and the faithful were militant, there was a different reaction: After Pope Marcellinus committed the grave public sin against the Faith by offering incense at the altar of Jupiter, a council was convened and the compromised Pope, through shame, *deposed himself* and anathematized anyone who would bury his body.[35]

But this story of Pope Marcellinus has a happy ending; for the bishops were so edified by his public repentance, that they re-elected him to the papacy (following his resignation). Pope Marcellinus went on to die as a martyr for the Faith and is now a canonized saint. Here we see the good fruit that resulted from an imperfect council that was convened to oversee the deposition of a Pope. How different his end may have been had his scandalous actions been explained away or, worse still, defended and praised as a positive good.

---

[31] *Catholic Encyclopedia* (1913), vol. IV, p. 290.

[32] In a letter to the Emperor Michael in 865, Pope Nicholas wrote: "In the reign of the sovereigns Diocletian and Maximian, Marcellinus, the Bishop of Rome, who afterwards became an illustrious martyr, was so persecuted by the pagans that he entered one of their temples and there offered incense." (Rev. Reuben Parsons, *Studies in Church History*, vol. II, (Philadelphia, Pennsylvania: John Joseph McVey, 1900), p. 510.

[33] "The work of the devil will infiltrate even into the Church in such a way that one will see Cardinals opposing Cardinals, bishops against bishops. The priests who venerate me will be scorned and opposed by their confreres...churches and altars sacked; *the Church will be full of those who compromise* and the demon will press many priests and consecrated souls to leave the service of the Lord"(Our Lady of Akita, to Sr. Agnes Sasagawa, October 13, 1973).

[34] "When everything has been ruined by war; when Catholics are hard pressed by traitorous co-religionists and heretics; when the Church and her servants are denied their rights, the monarchies have been abolished and their rulers murdered... Then the Hand of Almighty God will work a marvelous change, something apparently impossible according to human understanding" (Bartholomew Holzhauser).

[35] See Hidgen, *Polychronicon Ranulphi Higden maonachi Cestrensis*, vol. 5 (London: Longman, 1865), p. 107.

"Judging" and "Separating" From a Heretical Pope

While the necessity of *separating* from a manifest heretic is a matter of both Divine law (Tit. 3:10; 2Cor. 6:14) and common sense, the more difficult questions the theologians have had to sort out is how a Pope can be judged guilty of heresy, and then deposed for the crime, without the Church claiming authority over him? Theologians have had to navigate through these difficult questions while carefully avoiding many errors - especially the error of *Conciliarism*, which maintains that a general council is superior to a Pope, and can exercise jurisdiction over the Pope.

Cajetan explains the nature of the problem:

> "Three things have been established <u>with certainty</u>, namely, 1) that the pope, because he has become a heretic, is not deposed *ipso facto* by human or divine law;[36] 2) that the pope has no superior on earth; and 3) that if he deviates from the faith, he must be deposed, as in C. *Si Papa* [D. 40 c. 6]. Great uncertainty remains concerning how and by whom the pope who *ought* to be deposed will [in fact] be judged to be deposed, for a judge, as such, is superior to the one who is judged. (…)
>
> For, if he is to be judged and deposed by a universal council, then it follows that the pope, while remaining pope, has the universal council superior to him, especially in the case of heresy. If, however, neither the council nor the Church is superior to him, <u>then it follows directly that a pope who has deviated from the faith *should be* judged and deposed</u>, yet no one could judge and depose him, which is ridiculous. What shall we say, therefore, to avoid both extremes? The only course to take is toward the middle, which is hard to reach; virtue indeed consists of reaching that goal, which usually results in the solution to many problems."[37]

---

[36] In this first point, Cajetan is referring to the sin of heresy as such, and not the public crime of heresy established by the Church. John of St. Thomas addresses this first point of Cajetan and notes that Bellarmine himself does not disagree. He wrote: "The first point of Cajetan is obvious and is not contradicted by Bellarmine. The truth is evident for the following reasons: First, because the Pope, no matter how real and public may be his heresy, by the moment he is eager to be corrected, he cannot be deposed, and the Church cannot depose him by divine right, for she cannot nor should she avoid him since the Apostle [Paul] says, 'avoid the heretic after the first and second correction'; therefore, before the first and second correction he should not be avoided, and consequently he should not be deposed; therefore it is falsely said that by the very fact that the pontiff is a public heretic he is deposed: truly he is able to be public [in his heresy] but not yet rebuked by the Church, and not declared as incorrigible." (*Cursus Theologici*).

[37] *De Comparatione Auctoritatis Papae et Concilii*, pp. 82-83.

Four Opinions
(Two Extreme Opinions and Two Middle Opinions)

Having presented the difficulty regarding how a heretical Pope can be deposed, Cardinal Cajetan discusses the four theological opinions: Of these four opinions, he refers to two "extreme opinions," and two "middle opinions."

Two Extreme Opinions

The two extreme opinions are:

1) That a Pope who commits the sin of heresy falls from the pontificate *ipso facto* without human judgment. To be clear, this opinion maintains that a Pope ceases to be Pope by merely committing the *sin* (the internal act) of heresy.
2) That the Pope has a superior over him on Earth, and therefore can be judged and deposed for heresy.

If opinion #1 were true, the Church would never know for sure if a person elected Pope and considered Pope by the Church was, in fact, a true Pope or false Pope – a true believer or a pretender. If opinion #2 were true, it would mean the Pope has a superior on Earth (a general council), which is the heresy of Conciliarism. Both of these "extreme opinions" are therefore shown to be false and consequently rejected.[38] Cajetan explains:

> "We say, therefore, that there are two extreme ways, both of them false: one is that the pope who has become a heretic is deposed *ipso facto* by divine law without human judgment; the other is that a pope, while remaining pope, has a superior over him on earth by which he can be deposed."[39]

Two Middle Opinions

Within the two "extreme opinions," Cajetan discusses what he calls two middle opinions:

1) The first middle opinion maintains that a Pope does not have a superior on earth *unless he has fallen into heresy*, in which case the

---

[38] Ibid., p. 83.
[39] Ibid.

Church would be superior to the Pope. This opinion, which was held by Azorius,[40] is a variant of Conciliarism, and is therefore rightly rejected; for a council has no authority over a Pope, even in the case of heresy.

2) The second middle opinion holds that the Pope has no superior on Earth, *even in the case of heresy*, but that the Church does possess a ministerial power when it comes to deposing a heretical Pope. The ministerial power is exercised by the Church performing the acts necessary to 1) judge and declare the heresy and 2) separate itself from the heretical Pope, in accordance with Divine law.[41] This opinion avoids the error of Conciliarism, since it does not claim that the Church has authority *over* the Pope; nor does this opinion hold the Church herself *punishes* the Pope by deposing him. Rather, the Church works with Christ in the deposition by performing the ministerial functions necessary for the deposition, while Christ himself authoritatively deposes the Pope, by severing the bond that joins him to the pontificate.

Cajetan explains the two middle opinions as follows:

> "The middle way too has a double aspect: one holds that although the pope, absolutely speaking, has no superior on earth, nevertheless he does have a superior on earth in the case of heresy, the universal Church [held by Azorius]. The other [middle opinion] holds that the pope has no superior on earth, either absolutely or in the case of heresy, but that he is subject to the universal Church's ministerial power exclusively in regard to deposition."[42]

Second Middle Opinion

With respect to the second middle opinion, which is defended by Cajetan, the ministerial function consists of those acts which are necessary for the Church to establish that the Pope is indeed a heretic by judging that he is guilty of the crime of heresy, and then separating from the heretical Pope by virtue of a juridical act, which declares that he must be avoided, according to the teaching of St. Paul (Tit. 3:10). As Cajetan makes clear, the act of the general council, in this case, is not one of *subjection* - that is, it is not an act of authority over the Pope, since the Pope is subject to no earthly power - but rather an act of

---

[40] Azorius, (II, tom. II, cap. VII).
[41] The necessity to separate from unbelievers is revealed in Scripture, for example, Num. 16:26, Gal. 1:8, 2Thess. 3:6, 2Cor. 6:7, Tit. 3:10 and 2Jn. 1:10.
[42] *De Comparatione Auctoritatis Papae et Concilii*, p. 83.

separation, according to which the Church separates herself from the heretical Pope. The act of separation is, in fact, the ministerial act performed by the Church, which is part of the deposition itself; and it is an act that the Church has the authority to perform, as Cajetan explains:

> "In short, no where do I find superiority or inferiority from divine law in the case of heresy, but [only] separation. Now it is obvious that the Church can separate itself from the pope only by the ministerial power whereby it can elect him. Therefore, the fact that it is laid down by divine law that a heretic should be avoided and banished from the Church does not create a need for a power which is greater than a ministerial one. [This ministerial power] consequently is sufficient [for the separation]; and it is known to reside in the Church."[43]

John of St. Thomas also comments on the fact that while the Church has no superiority over a Pope, it does possess the authority, by Divine law, to *separate* from him and avoid him, if he should fall into heresy. He explained that,

> "it can never happen that the Church has power over the pope formally... One cannot cite any authority stating that Christ the Lord has given the Church authority over the pope. Those who were cited in the case of heresy, do not indicate any superiority over the Pope formally, but only speak of avoiding him, separating from him, refusing the communion with him, etc., all of which can be done without requiring a power formally above the Pope's power."[44]

As Cajetan and John of St. Thomas teach, because the Church, by Divine law, possesses the right to separate from a heretical Pope, the Church must also possess the right to the means necessary to accomplish the separation. Now, because the Church has no authority over a Pope, it follows that these *necessary means* can be exercised toward a Pope without requiring authority over him. They respond by pointing to a "ministerial power" by which the Church can licitly *separate* herself from the Pope, without having to exercise authority over the Pope. The same would be true in the case of a wife who was forced to separate from an abusive husband. The act of separation

---

[43] Ibid., p. 84 (emphasis added).
[44] *Cursus Theologici* II-II *De Auctoritate Summi Pontificis*, Disp. II, Art. III, *De Depositione Papae,* p. 138 (emphasis added).

would not require her to have authority over her spouse *and head*. In like manner, the Church can separate from a heretical Pope, due to the grave danger that he would present, without, however, having to claim for itself an authority superior to him.

When and How Does the Pope Fall from Office?

One of the questions debated by the theologians is exactly when, and precisely how, the Pope falls from the pontificate. Does it take place immediately after the Pope's pertinacity has been manifested to the authorities who issued the warnings? Does it occur if and when the general council issues a declaratory sentence of the crime? Or does it occur if and when the Church formally separates from the Pope?

As we've mentioned, the Church has never definitively settled these questions. Consequently, the points are open to debate and indeed have been debated for centuries. Regarding these speculative questions, John of St. Thomas said, "theologians and canon lawyers have disputed very much,"[45] even though many Sedevacantists, who have formed their judgment based upon snippets of material posted on Sedevacantist websites, mistakenly believe the matter has been settled.

But notwithstanding the different opinions regarding precisely when and how a Pope falls from office, the *unanimous* opinion is that the Pope loses the pontificate *after* the Church (a general council) establishes the crime of heresy (and probably after the Council issues the declarative sentence).

As we've seen, John of St. Thomas, who was a young contemporary of both Suarez and Bellarmine, confirmed that these two great theologians agreed that the heretical Pope is deprived of the pontificate immediately by Christ, but only after he has been "declared incorrigible" by the Church. He says:

> "[O]nly Christ our Lord is superior to the Pope. And for that reason Bellarmine and Suarez judge that the pope, by the very fact that he is a manifest heretic and has been declared incorrigible, is deposed immediately by the Lord Christ, not by some other authority of the Church."[46]

---

[45] "Concerning the case of [deposition due to] heresy, theologians and canon lawyers have disputed very much." (*Cursus Theologici* II-II, *De Auctoritate Summi Pontificis*, Disp. II, Art. III, *De Depositione Papae*, p. 133.)

[46] *Cursus Theologici* II-II, *De Auctoritate Summi Pontificis*, Disp. II, Art. III, *De Depositione Papae*, p. 139. Note that, according to John of St. Thomas, Bellarmine held that the Pope must be "declared incorrigible" by the Church to be considered "a manifest heretic"

The Church's establishment of incorrigibility (pertinacity) is a *condition* for a Pope to lose his office for heresy, since pertinacity itself is an essential element of the crime of heresy. Some, but not all, hold that over and above *establishing* the crime, the Church must issue a *declaratory sentence.* These maintain that the declaration is another condition for the loss of office. As we have seen, Suarez said it was the common opinion that the Pope will only lose his office upon the declaratory sentence of the crime. For practical purposes, requiring a declaratory sentence as a condition for the loss of office solves a number of potential problems.

For one, what if the Pope renounced his heresy sometime after the warnings, but before the declaratory sentence was issued? What if some bishops at the council judged him incorrigible before he renounced his errors, while others had not yet reached a definitive judgment? If he recanted just before the declaration was read, would he still be Pope? If the declaration is a *condition* required before God will act by deposing a heretical Pope, the Church knows precisely how long an apparently heretical Pope would have to renounce his heresy – as long as it takes for the Church to establish that the Pope is pertinacious (condition 1) and issue the declaratory sentence (condition 2). After that, he would be able to renounce his heresy, but it would be too late for him to retain the papal office.

Because under Divine law it is necessary for salvation for every human creature to be subject to the Roman Pontiff, the Church must be involved in the deposition of a heretical Pope in some way, either by actually deposing him, or at least by establishing the crime and declaring him (or at least judging him) to be incorrigible. Knowing the precise *moment* during the council in which he loses his office is, in fact, not critical. In reality, it is merely an academic question for theologians to discuss.

What is necessary, however, is for the Church to be involved in the process by overseeing the matter so that, just as the Church presented him to the faithful as Pope following the election, it can declare him "non-Pope" following the deposition. This is necessary so the faithful will know that he is no longer Pope and therefore should not be recognized as their head. No such certainty would exist if the fall from office were dictated by the private judgments of individual Catholics (i.e., the Sedevacantists), who pretend to "discern" that the Pope is a heretic, and therefore has lost his office. This is why the Church itself must establish the crime before a reigning Pope loses his office.

(which means Bellarmine, like Suarez, believed in the necessity of a declaratory sentence of the crime issued by the Church).

Who in the Church Renders the Judgment of the Crime?

Who in the Church would possess the authority to make the definitive judgment that the Pope is guilty of the crime of heresy (and issue a declaratory sentence)? Would it be the Cardinals, who are responsible for electing the Pope, or a general council? John of St. Thomas answers this question:

> "It must be said that the declaration of the crime does not come from the Cardinals, but from a general council. This is evident, firstly, by the practice of the Church. For in the case of Pope Marcellinus, who offered incense to idols, a synod was gathered together for the purpose of discussing the case, as is recorded in Distinction 21, Chapter 7, (*"Nunc autem"*). And in the case of the [Great Western] Schism, during which there were three reputed pontiffs, the Council of Constance was gathered for the purpose of settling that schism. Likewise, in the case of Pope Symmachus, a council was gathered in Rome to treat the case against him, as reported by Antione Augustine, in his Epitome *Juris Pontifice Veteris* (Title 13, Chapter 14); and the sections of Canon Law quoted above show that the Pontiffs who wanted to defend themselves against the crimes imputed to them, have done it before a Council.
>
> Second, it is commonly agreed that the power of treating the cases of popes, and that which pertains to his deposition, has not been entrusted to the cardinals. For the deposition belongs to the Church, whose authority is represented by a general council; indeed, only the election is entrusted to the cardinals and no more, as can be clearly shown by reading those things which we have drawn out from the law in *Art. 1]*. Concerning this matter, let one consult Torquemada *(Summa, 1. 2, c. 93)*, Cajetan *(De Comparatione auctoritatis papae)*, and the Canonists *(On the Decretal of Boniface VIII (in 6th), chap. 'In fide de haereticis'* and the Decree of Gratian, Dist. *40)*."[47]

As we can see, John of St. Thomas says no less than a *general council* of the Church (a gathering of the world's bishops) must make the definitive judgment that the Pope is guilty of the crime of heresy. He bases his conclusion upon the historical examples of general councils being convoked to resolve the cases of Pope Marcellinus, the Great Western Schism, and that of Pope Symmachus.

---

[47] *Cursus Theologici* II-II, *De Auctoritate Summi Pontificis*, Disp. II, Art. III, *De Depositione Papae*, p. 137.

Declaration of Deprivation (Deposition)
Two Opinions

The crime of heresy having been established by the Church (and, according to the common opinion, a declaratory sentence issued), we now reach the final phase in the process: the *deposition* of the Pope (one opinion), or the *declaration* that he has already fallen from office (another opinion). This is where we find the difference between the opinions of Bellarmine/Suarez and that of Cajetan/John of St. Thomas.

Opinion of Bellarmine and Suarez

As we have seen, according to the opinion of Suarez and Bellarmine, once the Church establishes the crime (and issues the declaratory sentence of same), "he would be then *ipso facto* and immediately deposed by Christ" (Suarez),[48] "before any excommunication or judicial sentence" (Bellarmine).[49] Their reasoning is that, since a heretic is not a member of the Church, such a one cannot remain as its head. But one who has been declared a heretic (or openly left the Church) is not a member of the Church; therefore, etc. Not being a member of the Church, he is deprived of the pontificate immediately by God, at which point the former Pope "can be judged and punished by the Church,"[50] as Bellarmine himself taught.

According to this opinion, the declaration of deprivation (which follows the Church's judgment and declaratory sentence of the crime), which is issued by the general council, is merely a procedural matter declaring what has already taken place. The declaration does not relate to the "deposition" itself (since God has already severed the bond that unites the man to the pontificate), but simply declares the See vacant so that the Cardinals can move to the election of a new Pope.

According to the opinion of Cajetan and John of St. Thomas, however, the conciliar declaration doesn't merely declare that the Pope has fallen from office, but instead plays an integral part in the deposition itself. We will now examine their position in depth.

Opinion of Cajetan and John of St. Thomas

Cajetan and John of St. Thomas maintain that the fall from the pontificate occurs, not when the Church establishes the crime, but

---

[48] *Tractatus De Fide*, Disp. 10, Sect 6, n. 10, p. 318.
[49] *De Romano Pontifice*, bk. 2, ch. 30.
[50] Ibid.

rather when the Church, using the authority of a council, issues the declaratory sentence and commands the faithful *by a juridical act* that the man must be avoided (*vitandus*).[51] It is only then, they believe, and not merely when the crime has been established and declared by the Church, that Christ authoritatively deprives the Pope of his office. Hence, they maintain that the separation of the Church from the Pope is the *dispositive cause* for the loss of office, whereas Bellarmine and Suarez believe the *dispositive cause* is the Church's establishment of the crime, which itself separates the Pope from the Church. Notice that in both cases it is *separation* that disposes the Pope to lose the office: in one case, the Pope is separated from the Church; in the other, the Church separates from the Pope.

Having considered the opinion of Bellarmine and Suarez in Chapter 10, we will now consider the position of Cajetan and John of St. Thomas. Because we will rely heavily on the writings of John of St. Thomas, we will begin by telling a little about him.

John of St. Thomas is recognized as one of the greatest Thomistic theologians after the Angelic Doctor himself. The *Catholic Theological Dictionary* notes that "his contemporaries unanimously called him a second Thomas, a bright star in front of the Sun (St. Thomas Aquinas)," and went on to say that "His doctrine is none other than that of the Angelic Doctor, profoundly understood and faithfully expressed."[52]

He was born in Lisbon, educated at Coimbra University and then at Louvain University, before joining the Dominicans in Madrid at the age of 23. He was a long time professor at Alcalá (Madrid University) and during the last years of his life served as the confessor of King Philip IV of Spain. The *Catholic Encyclopedia* says of him:

> "No man enjoyed a greater reputation in Spain, or was more frequently consulted on points of doctrine and ecclesiastical matters. His theological and philosophical writings, which have gone through many editions, are among the best expositions of Thomas Aquinas's doctrine, of which he is acknowledged to be one of the foremost interpreters. Though he took an active part in the scholastic discussions of his times, his courtesy was such that he is said never to have hurt an opponent's feelings. So faithful was he to the traditions of his order and the principles of the Angelic Doctor that in his last illness he could declare that, in all the thirty years he

---

[51] Although this might occur simultaneously with the issuance of the declaratory sentence, it is this juridical act, and not the declaration of the crime, that produces the *dispositive cause*, according to this opinion.

[52] J.M. Ramírez, *Dictionnaire de théologie catholique*, "Jean de Saint-Thomas," col. 806.

had devoted to teaching and writing, he had not taught or written anything contrary to St. Thomas."[53]

As one might expect, John of St. Thomas' scholarly explanation of precisely how a heretical Pope loses his office is deep, thorough, and quite profound. He utilizes the clear distinctions of Thomistic philosophy and theology to explain, in precise metaphysical detail, the way in which the bond uniting the man to the pontificate is severed, thereby causing the Pope to fall from office. He also answers the objections that Bellarmine and Suarez presented against Cajetan's position. We will cite the objections of Bellarmine and Suarez, and the answers of John of St. Thomas, at the end of this chapter. For now, we present his magnificent explanation of how a heretical Pope falls from the pontificate.

How the Church Deposes a Pope

John of St. Thomas explains that after a heretical Pope has shown himself obstinate, after being duly warned, and the Church's judgment of the crime having been rendered, the Church, using the authority of the council, issues a decree commanding the faithful, by a juridical act, that, according to Divine law (Titus 3:10), the heretic Pope must be avoided. This effectively separates the Church from the Pope. Now, because a Pope cannot govern the Church as its head while simultaneously being avoided by those whom he is to govern, the Pope is effectively rendered impotent by this legal act of the council. Being incapable of ruling the Church due to the legitimate act of the Church, God Himself severs the bond that unites the man to the office, and he falls from the pontificate.

So, according to John of St. Thomas (and Cajetan), the Pope is not deposed *ipso facto* by Christ upon the Church's judgment that the crime of heresy has been committed; rather, the juridical act commanding the faithful that he is a heretic who must be avoided plays an integral *and necessary* part in the deposition itself. This differs from the opinion of Bellarmine/Suarez, who maintain that the Church plays no part in the actual fall from the pontificate. The Church's function simply establishes that the crime has been committed (and issues a *declaratory sentence* announcing its judgment), at which time Christ acts immediately by deposing the Pope, without the need of any juridical

---

[53] *Catholic Encyclopedia* (1913), vol. VIII, p. 479.

sentence issued by the Church. The difference is subtle and merely academic, but no doubt real.

Cardinal Journet wrote the following about the opinion of John of St. Thomas:

> "John of St. Thomas, whose analysis seems to me more penetrating [than that of Bellarmine and Suarez] (...) remark[s] on the one hand that in divine law the Church is to be united to the Pope as the body is to the head; and on the other hand that, by divine law, he who shows himself a heretic is to be avoided after one or two admonitions (Tit. iii. 10). There is therefore an absolute contradiction between the fact of being Pope and the fact of persevering in heresy after one or two admonitions. The Church's action is simply declaratory...then the authoritative action of God disjoins the Papacy from a subject who, persisting in heresy after admonition, becomes in divine law, inapt to retain it any longer. In virtue therefore of Scripture, the Church designates and God deposes. God acts with the Church, says John of St. Thomas..."[54]

John of St. Thomas is careful to note that the Church only plays a *ministerial* part in the act of deposition, rather than an authoritative part, since the Church has no authority over a Pontiff - even in the case of heresy. He employs the Thomistic concepts of *form* and *matter* to explain how the union between the man and the pontificate is dissolved. A distinction is made between the man (the matter), the pontificate (the form), and the bond that unites the two. He explains that just as the Church plays a ministerial role in the election of a Pope, so likewise she plays a ministerial role in the deposition of a heretical Pope.

During the election, the Church designates the man (the matter), who is to receive the pontificate (the form) immediately from God. Something similar happens when a Pope loses his office due to heresy. Since "the Pope is constituted Pope by the power of jurisdiction alone,"[55] (which he is unable to effectively exercise if he *must* be avoided by the Church), when the Church judges that the crime has been committed and then presents him to the faithful as one that must be avoided, the Church thereby induces a *disposition* into the matter (the man) that renders him incapable of sustaining the form (the pontificate). God freely responds to this legitimate act of the Church (which the Church has a right and duty to do in accordance with

---

[54] *The Church of the Word Incarnate*, p. 483.
[55] *De Comparatione Auctoritatis Papae et Concilii*, p. 76.

Divine law) by withdrawing the form from the matter, thereby causing the man to fall from the pontificate. In John of St. Thomas' words:

> "The authority of the Church has for its object the application of the power of the Pope (form) to a given person (matter), by designating that person by election; and the separation of this power from the person, <u>by declaring him to be a heretic and as one to be avoided by the faithful.</u> And so, because the declaration of his crime works like an <u>anticipatory disposition,</u> preceding the deposition itself, it relates to the deposition only ministerially; nevertheless it also reaches the form itself <u>dispositively and ministerially,</u> insofar as it <u>causes the disposition,</u> and thereby indirectly (mediately) influences the form..."[56]

He delves deeper into his explanation by noting that in deposing the heretical Pope, the Church acts directly upon the matter (the man), but only indirectly upon the form (the pontificate). He describes this point by using the analogy of procreation and death. He explains that just as the generative act of man does not produce the form (the soul), neither does that which corrupts and destroys the matter (disease, etc.) directly touch the form (the soul) - nor does the corrupting element *directly cause* the separation of the form from the matter (but only renders the matter incapable of sustaining the form) – so, too, is it with the election and deposition of a Pope. John explains:

> "Just as in the generation and corruption of a man, the begetter neither produces nor educes [develops] the form (the soul), nor does the corruptor (disease, etc.) destroy the form, but accomplishes the coming together (of the form and matter), or the separation (of the form from the matter) by way of affecting directly the dispositions of matter, and by this reaches the form mediately (indirectly)."[57]

To make this deep concept more comprehensible, we will cite the following explanation given by Fr. Paul Robinson, Professor of Dogmatic Theology at Holy Cross Seminary:

> "in all activities performed by created agents, we only affect accidental forms of things by acting on their matter, without being able to affect their substantial form directly. We can only cause the death of an animal, for example, by hitting it over the head or

---

[56] *Cursus Theologici* II-II, *De Auctoritate Summi Pontificis*, Disp. II, Art. III, *De Depositione Papae*, p.138 (emphasis added).
[57] Ibid.

something similar, i.e., by exerting external violence on it, but without somehow reaching into its being and wrenching out its substantial form. And so, we only *dispose* the matter of the animal for losing its substantial form, without having the power to take it away directly."[58]

In both the election and deposition of a Pope, the Church acts directly upon the matter (the man) and only indirectly upon the form (the pontificate). During the election, the Church designates the man who is to receive the form. This act of the Church *disposes* the man to receive the pontificate. God freely responds to this legitimate ministerial act of the Church, which it has a right to do, by joining the man to the pontificate, thus making him Pope. In like manner, when it comes to deposing a heretical Pope, the Church first judges the man a heretic[59] and then commands the faithful, by a juridical act, that he must be avoided. While the Church has no jurisdiction or authority over the Pope, it does possess jurisdiction over the faithful, and therefore can issue commands that they are obliged to obey.

Now, since Divine law teaches that a heretic must be avoided after two warnings, the Church has the divine right to command that a Pope, who has remained obstinate following the warnings and been declared a heretic by the Church, must be avoided. And because one who must be avoided cannot effectively rule the Church, this act of the Church *disposes* the Pope for the loss of office. God freely responds to this legal act of the Church by severing the bond that unites the form to the matter, thereby causing the man to fall from the pontificate. In the words of John of St. Thomas:

> "The Church is able to declare the crime of the pontiff and, according to divine law, propose him to the faithful as one who must be avoided, according to the manner in which heretics should

---

[58] Taken from a private email exchange between Fr. Paul Robinson and the authors of this book. This explanation follows Our Lord's words: "And fear ye not them that kill the body, and are not able to kill the soul: but rather fear him that can destroy both soul and body in hell" (Mt. 10:28).

[59] As we saw in Chapter 9, this is the same argument made by Bellarmine, when he said: "Jurisdiction is certainly given to the Pontiff by God, but with the agreement of men [i.e. the election] as is obvious; because this man, who beforehand was not Pope, has from men that he would begin to be Pope, therefore, he is not removed by God unless it is through men. But a secret heretic cannot be judged by men." The difference between the opinion of Bellarmine and John of St. Thomas is that Bellarmine held that he would be deposed by God at once, after being judged by man, whereas John of St. Thomas and Cajetan held that the Church would have to "depose" him by a ministerial act, after he was found guilty of the crime.

be avoided [Titus 3:10]. The Pontiff, however, by the fact of having to be avoided, is necessarily rendered impotent by the force of such a declaration, since a Pope who must to be avoided is unable to influence the Church as its head. Therefore, by virtue of such a power, the Church dissolves ministerially and dispositively the link of the pontificate with such a person. (...)"[60]

And a little later,

"Thus by declaring a pontiff as *Vitandus* [to be avoided], the Church can induce a disposition in that person (the matter) by which the pontificate (the form) cannot remain, and thus it [the union of form and matter] is thus dissolved ministerially and dispositively by the Church, and authoritatively by Christ; likewise by designating him by election, she ultimately disposes him to receive the collation of power [directly] by Christ the Lord, and thus [the Church] ministerially creates a pope."[61]

We can see that, according to this explanation, the Church does indeed play a part – a real *ministerial* part - in the act of deposition, after the crime has been established. As we have seen, this differs (albeit slightly) from the teaching of Suarez and Bellarmine, who said that a Pope is deposed, *ipso facto*, by Christ (once the Church judges the crime), without the need of any further juridical act on the part of the Church. This is the essential difference between the two positions which, in reality, represents no practical difference at all when considered from the perspective of the Catholic faithful. It is only an academic question about how the fall from office exactly occurs.

John of St. Thomas goes on to explain how two sets of canonical laws, which might appear to some to be in contradiction, are harmonized by his explanation. He says:

"[According to this explanation] the provisions of the law, which sometimes affirm that the deposition of the Pontiff belongs to God alone, and sometimes say that he can be judged by inferiors in case of heresy, are in harmony. Both are true. For on the one side, the 'ejection' or deposition of the Pope is reserved only to God

---

[60] *Cursus Theologici* II-II, *De Auctoritate Summi Pontificis*, Disp. II, Art. III, *De Depositione Papae*, p. 139.

[61] Ibid. Just as the authorities of the Church (and not the faithful) elect the Pope (acting directly upon the matter - which is the man elected), so the same authorities (and not the faithful) depose the Pope (acting directly upon the matter - which is the man deposed). And just as Christ acts directly upon the form by joining the man to the pontificate, so He also acts directly upon the form by severing the man from the pontificate.

alone authoritatively and principally, as stated in the Decree of Gratian, Distinction 79 (Pars I, D 79, c. 11) and in many other places of the law, which say that God has reserved to Himself the judgment of the Apostolic See. On the other hand, the Church acts ministerially and dispositively by judging the crime and proposing him to the faithful as one to be avoided, and in this way she judges the Pontiff, as stated in the Decree of Gratian, in Dist. 40, chapter "*Si Papa*" (Pars I, D 40, c. 6) and in Part II, Chapter "oves" (q. 7 c. 13)."[62]

The ministerial function of the Church, then, is to establish the crime, issue the declaratory sentence, and then command the faithful, by a *juridical* (and therefore binding) act, that the man must be avoided. It is this juridical act, rather than the crime itself, that induces the *disposition* into the matter that renders him incapable of sustaining the form (the pontificate).

Now, because the juridical act relates essentially to the loss of office, it is evident why the command to avoid the heretic Pope must come from the proper authorities. For if such a command came from one with no authority, it would not bind, and consequently none would be obliged to avoid the man. John of St. Thomas explains:

> "...a heretic should be avoided after two admonitions legally made and with the Church's authority, and not according to private judgment. For great confusion would follow in the Church if it would suffice that this warning could be made by a private individual, rather than by a declaration coming from the Church stating that all must avoid him. For the pope's heresy cannot be public [made manifest] to all of the faithful except by an indictment brought by others. But the indictment of an individual does not bind, since it is not juridical, and consequently none would be obliged to accept it and avoid him. Therefore, it is necessary that, just as the Church designates the man and proposes him to the faithful as being elected Pope, thus also the Church declares him a heretic and proposes him as one to be avoided.
>
> Therefore, we see that this has been practiced by the Church, when in the case of the deposition of the Pope, the cause itself was first addressed by the General Council before the Pope was declared not to be Pope, as we said above. Therefore, it is not because the Pope is a heretic, even publicly, that he will *ipso facto* cease to be

---

[62] Ibid.

Pope, before the declaration of the Church, <u>and before she proclaims him as 'to be avoided' by the faithful</u>."[63]

The Difference Between the Two Opinions

To reiterate for clarity, the principle difference between the two opinions is that Cajetan and John of St. Thomas maintain the Church plays a part in the deposition itself, by using the authority of the council to juridically command the faithful to avoid the heretical Pope. This act legally (Tit. 3:10) separates the Church from the Pope, thereby inducing a disposition into the *matter* that renders the man incapable of sustaining the form, at which time Christ authoritatively severs the bond that unites him to the pontificate.

Bellarmine and Suarez, however, maintain that a Pope, whose heresy has been judged by the Church to be manifest, is no longer a member of the Church and therefore "ceases to be Pope by himself, *without any deposition*," to quote Bellarmine directly.[64] According to this opinion, the Church does not actually depose the Pope, or even play an active part in the deposition, but only establishes the crime, at which time Christ Himself immediately removes the Pope from office. It should be noted, however, that according to both opinions, it is Christ, not the Church, who *authoritatively* deposes the heretical Pope (which we have referred to as "divine punishment").

Sequence of Events

Following are the sequence of events according to the two opinions. (Also see the Appendix chart at the end of the book.)

Bellarmine and Suarez

1) *Establishment of the Crime:* The criminal phase, in which the Church establishes the crime through warnings (and may also issue a declaratory sentence of the crime). We here remind the reader that Bellarmine himself defended the notion that a council can judge a Pope for heresy. And his wording makes it clear that the heretical Pope remains Pope (*superior* to the *inferiors* who are judging him) during the process and until the crime is declared. The crime

---

[63] *Cursus Theologici* II-II, *De Auctoritate Summi Pontificis*, Disp. II, Art. III, *De Depositione Papae*, p. 139 (emphasis added).
[64] *De Romano Pontifice*, bk. 2, ch. 30.

(established by the Church), by which the Pope ceases to be a member of the Church, is the *dispositive cause* for the loss of office.

2) *Divine Punishment/Deposition:* Automatic, *ipso facto* loss of office by an act of Christ, Who severs the bond between the man and the pontificate (this is the *efficient cause* for the loss of office).

3) *Declaration of Deprivation/Human Punishment.* The Church declares that the Pope has lost his office due to heresy. This merely confirms that the loss of office has *already* taken place. The former Pope is excommunicated and, if heresy is a violation of civil law, turned over to the secular power for punishment.

All three phases are seen in the following quote from Suarez:

> "Therefore on deposing a heretical Pope, the Church would not act as superior to him, but juridically and by the consent of Christ she would declare him a heretic [(1) *establishment of the crime*] and therefore unworthy of Pontifical honors; he would then *ipso facto* and immediately be deposed by Christ [(2) *divine punishment*], and once deposed he would become inferior and would be able to be punished [(3) *human punishment*]."[65]

Cajetan and John of St. Thomas

According to the view of Cajetan and John of St. Thomas, the sequence of events are as follows:

1) *Establishment of the Crime:* The criminal phase, in which the Church establishes the crime through warnings and issues a declaratory sentence of the crime. This phase precedes the actual deposition. John of St. Thomas was clear on this when he said: the deposition *facienda est post declarativam criminis sententiam* - "is to be done <u>after</u> a declaratory sentence of the crime."[66]

---

[65] *Tractatus De Fide*, Disp. 10, Sect. 6, n. 10, p. 318.
[66] *Cursus Theologici* II-II, *De Auctoritate Summi Pontificis*, Disp. II, Art. III, *De Depositione Papae*, p. 137 (emphasis added).

2) *Deposition/Divine Punishment:* The Church juridically commands the faithful that the Pope, who has been found guilty of heresy, must be avoided (*vitandus*). This juridical act causes the *disposition* that renders him incapable of governing the Church (the *dispositive cause* for the loss of office). *Divine Punishment:* Christ authoritatively severs the bond that unites the man to the office, thereby causing the man to fall from the pontificate (the *efficient cause* for the loss of office).

3) *Human Punishment:* The former Pope could then be excommunicated by the Church and/or punished by the civil authority.

None of the theologians we have consulted speak of a determined lapse of time that would be required between the aforementioned events.

Therefore, it would seem that a single document issued by the council could: 1) publicly declare that the Pope is guilty of the crime of heresy; 2) command the Church that he must be avoided ("*vitandus*"); and, 3) declare the See to be vacant, and publicly excommunicate the former Pope. Of course, the exact procedure would be determined by the proper authorities, but what is clear (and what Sedevacantists have failed to realize) is that whether one holds to the opinion of Bellarmine/Suarez, or that of Cajetan/John of St. Thomas, in both cases the Church (a general council) must render a judgment of the crime of heresy before a sitting Pope loses his office for heresy.

This was confirmed by Fr. Sebastian B. Smith in *Elements of Ecclesiastical Law* (1881). He explains that there are two opinions regarding the loss of the pontificate for a heretical Pope. One opinion (Bellarmine/Suarez) maintains that he falls, *ipso facto*, from the pontificate (the *crime*, established by the Church, being the *dispositive cause* for the loss of office), while the other (Cajetan/John of St. Thomas) holds that a heretical Pope is only deposable (the *juridical command* to avoid the heretic Pope results in the *dispositive cause*). After mentioning these two opinions, Fr. Smith explains that, according to both opinions, the heretical Pope must at least be declared guilty (declaratory sentence) of the crime of heresy by the Church. Fr. Smith wrote:

"**Question:** Is a Pope who falls into heresy deprived, *ipso jure*, of the Pontificate?

Answer: There are two opinions: one holds that he is by virtue of divine appointment, divested *ipso facto*, of the Pontificate; the other, that he is, *jure divino*, only removable. <u>Both opinions agree that he must at least be declared guilty of heresy by the Church</u> - i.e., by an ecumenical council or the College of Cardinals."[67]

Fr. Smith expressly states that "both opinions agree" that he must at least be declared guilty of heresy by the Church. If he is not found guilty, he remains a true and valid Pope. The teaching of Fr. Smith confirms John of St. Thomas' understanding of Bellarmine and Suarez's position, since he stated that "Bellarmine and Suarez" both held that a heretical Pope loses his office only if he is "declared incorrigible."

It should also be noted that Fr. Smith's book was carefully examined by two canonists in Rome following its initial publication. The Preface of the Third Edition explains that Cardinal Simeoni, Prefect of the Propaganda Fide, "appointed two Consultors, doctors in canon law, to examine the 'Elements' and report to him. The Consultors, after examining the book for several months, made each a lengthy report to the Cardinal-Prefect."[68] Their detailed reports noted five inaccuracies or errors that required revision. The above quotation was not cited as an error, or even a slight inaccuracy. Therefore, it remained in the Third Revised Edition from which the above quotation was taken. If the statement of Fr. Smith were incorrect, it would have been noted during the detailed examination by the canonists and revised; yet it wasn't. That means the statement is correct and thus reflects the mind of the Church on this matter.

Because the "two opinions" agree that a heretical Pope "must at least be declared guilty of the crime of heresy by the Church," there are actually *three* opinions to be noted, which, for the sake of simplicity and easy recall, could be classified as follows: 1) the "Jesuit" opinion (of Bellarmine/Suarez), 2) the "Dominican" opinion (of Cajetan/John of St. Thomas), and 3) the unanimous opinion. The *Jesuit* opinion is that a heretical Pope falls from office after the crime of heresy has been established by the Church. The *Dominican* opinion is that a heretical Pope falls from office only after the Church commands the faithful to avoid him. But the *unanimous opinion* is that "he must *at least* be declared guilty by the Church." The Sedevacantists accept the *Jesuit* opinion, yet nonsensically reject the *unanimous* opinion. But one cannot hold the *Jesuit* opinion (the Pope loses his office *ipso facto*), without also

---

[67] *Elements of Ecclesiastical Law*, p. 210 (emphasis added).
[68] Ibid., Preface, p. xi.

holding the unanimous opinion (the Pope must at least be declared guilty of the crime of heresy by the Church).

The Sedevacantist rejection of the unanimous opinion is clearly not the fruit of sound, scholarly research of the question, but rather a rash and superficial judgment based, in many cases, on snippets read on the internet, or even despair over the crisis. If Sedevacantists studied the issue in more depth, they would see, as "the second St. Thomas" explained, that "the pope does not cease to be the pope by the fact of being a heretic, before an ecclesial trial (and) sentence..."[69] Without a judgment by the proper authorities, a sitting Pope, who is "discerned" to be a heretic by private judgment, remains Pope. The visibility of the Church (both formally and materially) is too necessary for the contrary to be the case. It is not a coincidence that the Sedevacantists, who have rejected the last six Popes, now also reject the visibility of the Church, as we saw in Chapter 1.

One final point is that all agree that only a general council would have the right to declare the See vacant, not individual Catholics in the pew based on their own private judgment of the situation. The point is explained in J. M. Hervé's, *Manuale Theologiae Dogmaticae*, which says:

> "Given that, as a private person, the Pontiff could indeed become a public, notorious, and obstinate heretic...only a Council would have the right to declare his see vacant so that the usual electors could safely proceed to an election."[70]

So whether a heretical Pope is "deposed" by the ministerial actions of the Church (Cajetan and John of St. Thomas), or whether he loses his office *ipso facto* and immediately (Bellarmine and Suarez) is merely an academic question pertaining to the speculative order, since, on the practical level, both opinions agree that the Pope must have at least been judged guilty of the crime of heresy by the Church. Furthermore, only a general (ecumenical) council has the right to declare the See vacant. Before the actions of the Church, a Pope who is considered to be a heretic according to private judgment remains a true and valid Pope.

Popes Alexander VI, John XXII, and Honorius I were all accused of heresy by their contemporaries, yet none of them were declared deprived of the pontificate by the Church while still living. Consequently, they have always been considered to have remained

---

[69] *Cursus Theologici* II-II, *De Auctoritate Summi Pontificis*, Disp. II, Art. III, *De Depositione Papae*, p. 139.
[70] Hervé, *Manuale Theologiae Dogmaticae* (1943) I.501 (emphasis added).

true and valid Popes by the Church, even though Pope Honorius, after his death, was "expelled from the holy Church of God and anathematized"[71] for heresy, by the Third Council of Constantinople, as we discussed in Chapter 8. In spite of the fact that the 1913 *Original Catholic Encyclopedia* entry on Honorius says, "It is clear that no Catholic has the right to defend Pope Honorius. He was a heretic...,"[72] not even Pope Honorius is considered by the Church to have lost the pontificate while living.

From what we have seen, it is clear that the deposition of a heretical Pope is never a matter to be determined by private judgment, but rather requires the authoritative and definitive judgment of the Church. Throughout the centuries, some of the greatest minds in the Church have plumbed the theological depths of this most delicate question, and *none of them has ever taught that individual Catholics are permitted to judge a Pope guilty of heresy, declare him a "manifest heretic," and claim publicly that he is not the Pope.* Rather, they *all* hold that, in the rare case of a Pontiff who falls into heresy, *the Church* must oversee the deposition, and that it alone has the right to declare the See vacant. Thus, in obedience to Jesus Christ, we "hear the Church" by patiently waiting for her judgment, and do not take this gravest of judgments into our own hands.

Pope Liberius: Objection Answered

Sedevacantists will often cite the case of Pope Liberius, who was replaced by Pope Felix while still living, without a trial or even a fruitless warning. They will note that Bellarmine defended the actions of the priests of Rome who elected Felix. They will then argue that this proves that a Pope can lose his office without being warned by the Church. Here is the objection as formulated by one Sedevacantist blogger:

> "**Objection:** Bellarmine clearly rejects warnings as necessary to establish obstinacy before one is considered a manifest heretic when he wrote in the previous chapter 29 that Liberius defected by merely appearing to be a heretic. St. Robert Bellarmine writes:
> 'Then indeed the Roman clergy, stripping Liberius of his pontifical dignity, went over to Felix, whom they knew to be a Catholic. From that time, Felix began to be the true Pontiff. For

---

[71] *The Seven Ecumenical Councils of the Church*, Volume XIV, Henry Percival ed. (Oxford: James Parker and Company, 1900), p. 343.
[72] *Catholic Encyclopedia* (1913), vol. VII, p. 455.

although Liberius was not a heretic, nevertheless he was considered one, on account of the peace he made with the Arians, and by that presumption the pontificate could rightly be taken from him: for men are not bound or able to read hearts; but when they see that someone is a heretic by his external works, they judge him to be a heretic pure and simple, and condemn him as a heretic. (On the Roman Pontiff, 29).'[73]

According to Bellarmine, a pope doesn't need to be a heretic at all to lose office, much less an obstinate manifest declared one. If warnings are always necessary to establish obstinacy before being declared a heretic, then the brilliant Bellarmine made a horrible contradiction."[74]

Answer: First, the removal of Liberius, and the subsequent "election" of Felix,[75] *was made by the authorities in Rome* ("the Roman clergy"), not by an individual Catholic in the pew. Hence, Bellarmine's account of Liberius being replaced by Felix confirms what he wrote in *De Membris Ecclesiae*, namely, that heretical bishops are only to be deposed by the proper authorities, and not by the faithful.[76]

Also note that, at this time in history, the "Roman clergy" elected the Pope (like the Cardinals do today), and thus they had the

---

[73] Steven Speray's poor scholarship is further displayed by his citation to Bellarmine's *De Romano Pontifice*, book 2, chapter 29, when Bellarmine's quote actually comes from an entirely different book (book 4, chapter 9).

[74] This objection was made by Steven Speray, in an article titled "Robert Siscoe and The Remnant's Latest Canon Law Fiasco," (February 3, 2015), which was posted on his website (we critiqued parts of this article in Chapter 10).

[75] For centuries there was confusion between a saint and martyr named Felix, and the "Felix" elected to replace Liberius, who is now recognized as having been an antipope. During Bellarmine's day, the confusion had not yet been cleared up. It is evident that Bellarmine was mistaken over this historical matter, since he said: "unless we are to admit that Liberius defected for a time from constancy in defending the Faith, we are compelled to exclude Felix II, who held the pontificate while Liberius was alive, from the number of the Popes: but the Catholic Church venerates this very Felix as Pope and martyr." Thus, it seems as if Bellarmine felt compelled to defend the actions of the Roman clergy, due, at least in part, to the "fact" (error) that Pope Felix II is recognized as a saint. In reality, however, St. Felix is an entirely different person from antipope Felix who was "elected" to replace Liberius. Antipope Felix was rejected by the majority of the faithful in Rome at the time. About antipope Felix, the *Catholic Encyclopedia* says, "the laity would have nothing to do with him and remained true to the banished but lawful pope [Liberius]." *Catholic Encyclopedia* (1913), vol. VI, p. 30.

[76] "…if the pastor is a bishop, they [the faithful] cannot depose him and put another in his place. Our Lord and the Apostles only lay down that false prophets [heretical bishops] are not to be listened to by the people, and not that they depose them. And it is certain that the practice of the Church has always been that heretical bishops be deposed by bishop's councils, or by the Sovereign Pontiff." *De Membris Ecclesiae*, bk. I *De Clericis*, ch. 7. (Opera Omnia; Paris: Vivés, 1870), pp. 428-429.

responsibility for electing a new Pope when the See was vacant (which, as will be explained below, was the case at the time Liberius was in exile). Needless to say, there is nothing in the citation from Bellarmine about a Pope being declared "deposed" for heresy by private judgment, as our Sedevacantist blogger imagines, and if there were, Bellarmine would have indeed been guilty of "a horrible contradiction," since he explicitly taught that if a bishop falls into public heresy "they [the faithful] cannot depose him and put another in his place."[77]

Second, Pope Liberius had been banished by the Emperor Constantius to Berea in Thrace,[78] and consequently the papacy was in a state of *Sede impedita*. This is defined as "the condition of the total impossibility of exercising the function when, by reason of captivity, *banishment, exile*, or incapacity a diocesan bishop is clearly prevented from fulfilling his pastoral function in the diocese, so that he is not able to communicate with those in his diocese even by letter."[79] In the early years of the Church, when the papacy itself was in a state of *Sede impedita*, the Pope was considered to have resigned, and, consequently, his See was vacant. Therefore, the electors could either wait for the return of the Pope (which might never happen), or legitimately move to elect a new Pope without having to convene a council or oversee the deposition of the exiled Pope. The latter course of action was chosen by the Roman clergy in the case of Liberius, and the controversial election of Felix.[80] The following is taken from *The Church of the Word Incarnate*, by Cardinal Journet:

> "How can the pontificate, once validly held, be lost? At most in two ways: a) the first is … death, or that species of death which consists in the irremediable loss of reason, or as a result of the free renunciation of the pontificate as that of St. Celestine V. [In the early years] <u>The Pope was considered as having resigned when he was so placed that he could not possibly exercise his powers</u>: 'It appears that in those times, when a bishop was removed from his see by a capital sentence (death, <u>exile</u>, relegation) or by an equivalent measure emanating from the secular authority, <u>the see was considered as vacant</u>. It was under these circumstances that the

77 Ibid.
78 G.A.F. Wilks, *The Popes: An Historical Study, from Linus to Pius IX*, (London: Francis and John Rivington, St. Paul's Churchyard and Waterloo Place, 1851), p. 18.
79 Manuel Jesus Arroba Conde "Sede Vacante in History and Canon Law," published in *L'Osservatore Romano*, Weekly Edition in English, March 6, 2013, p. 5.
80 The *Catholic Encyclopedia* explains: "The majority of the Roman clergy acknowledged the validity of his [Felix's] consecration but the laity would have nothing to do with him and remained true to the banished but lawful Pope [Liberius]." (1913), vol. VI, p. 30.

Roman Church replaced in the third century Pontianus by Anteros, in the sixth century Silverius by Vigilius, in the seventh Martin by Eugenius'[81] (L. Duchesne, The Early History of the Church, vol. III, p. 160, note 1)."[82]

So, the answer to this objection is that because Pope Liberius was in a state of exile (having been banished to Berea by the Emperor), *he was considered to have resigned*. Since the papacy was considered vacant, the proper authorities could, if they so wished, elect a new Pope without having to depose the former Pope. Thus, it is clear that Liberius was replaced for an extraordinary circumstance (exile) and not for the crime of heresy, even if the clergy's suspicion of him being a heretic contributed to their course of action. And Liberius was replaced by the competent authorities (the priests of Rome), not by laymen in the pew. For a Sedevacantist to use the case of Liberius' being replaced by Felix as support for their thesis is the proverbial "grasping for straws," and shows only how sterile the Sedevacantist position truly is.

Bellarmine and Suarez's Objections
Answered by John of St. Thomas

In the interest of covering further ground and showing more of the genius of John of St. Thomas, we would like to conclude this chapter by providing the answers he gave to the objections made by Bellarmine and Suarez against the teaching of Cajetan. The profound responses of John of St. Thomas require no further commentary.

Suarez's Objection: "From this arises a third doubt: by what right could the Pope be judged by the assembly, being superior to it? In this matter Cajetan makes extraordinary efforts to avoid seeing himself forced to admit that the Church or a Council are above the Pope in case of heresy; he concludes in the end that the Church and the Council are superior to the Pope, not as Pope, but as a private person. This distinction, however, does not satisfy, for with the same argument one would be able to say it belongs to the Church to judge or to punish the Pope, not as Pope, but as a private person (...). Finally the Church cannot exercise any act of jurisdiction over the Pope, and on electing him does not confer the power upon him, but designates the person

---

[81] We note that one of the reasons that Liberius/Felix are not included in this short list is because most of the faithful never accepted Felix II as Pope, and instead received Liberius as Pope when he returned from exile.
[82] *The Church of the Word Incarnate*, p. 483.

upon whom Christ directly confers the power. Therefore on deposing a heretical Pope, the Church would not act as superior to him, but juridically, and by the consent of Christ, she would declare him a heretic and therefore unworthy of Pontifical honors; he would be then *ipso facto* and immediately deposed by Christ..."[83]

John of St. Thomas Answers: "Suarez reproaches Cajetan for saying that the Church, in the case of heresy, is above the Pope as a private person, but not as a Pope. But this is not what Cajetan said. He [Cajetan] holds that the Church is not above the Pope absolutely, even in the case of heresy, but she is above the bond joining the Pontificate to the person when she dissolves it, in the same manner by which she joined it by the election, which is the ministerial power of the Church; for without qualification Christ the Lord is the only superior [power] to the Pope. That is why Bellarmine and Suarez judge that the Pope, by the very fact that he is a manifest heretic *and has been declared incorrigible*, is to be deposed immediately by the Lord Christ, not by some other authority of the Church."[84]

Bellarmine's Objection 1: "The second affirmation of Cajetan, that the Pope heretic can be truly and authoritatively deposed by the Church, is no less false than the first. For if the Church deposes the Pope against his will it is certainly above the Pope; however, Cajetan himself defends, in the same treatise, the contrary of this. Cajetan responds that the Church, in deposing the Pope, does not have authority over the Pope, but only over the link that unites the person to the pontificate. In the same way that the Church in uniting the pontificate to such a person, is not, because of this, above the Pontiff, so also the Church can separate the pontificate from such a person in case of heresy, without saying that it is above the Pope."[85]

John of St. Thomas Answers: "When Cajetan says that the Church acts with authority (*auctoritative*) on the *conjunction* or *separation* of the pontificate with the person, and ministerially on the papacy itself, we must understand it in the sense that the Church has the authority to declare the crime of the Pope, just as she has [the authority] of designating the same man to be Pope; and that what she does with authority [to the matter] by such declarations, acts, at the same time,

---

[83] *De Fide*, Disp. 10, Sect 6, n. 10, vol. 12, p. 317.
[84] *Cursus Theologici* II-II, *De Auctoritate Summi Pontificis*, Disp. II, Art. III, *De Depositione Papae*, p. 138.
[85] *De Romano Pontifice*, bk. 2, ch. 30.

ministerially on the form to either join or to separate; for of itself the Church is unable to do anything to the form, absolutely and in itself, (*absolute et in se*), since the papal power is not subject to the authority of the Church."[86]

Bellarmine's Objection 2: "But contrary to this it must be observed in the first place that, from the fact that the Pope deposes bishops, it is deduced that the Pope is above all the bishops, though the Pope on deposing a bishop does not destroy the episcopal jurisdiction, but only separates it from that person."[87]

John of St. Thomas Answers: "We answer that it is not in the same manner that the Pontiff has power over the bishop when he deposes him, and the Church over the Pontiff: indeed, the Pontiff *punishes the bishop as someone who is subjected to him*, [the latter] being invested with a subordinated and dependent power, which [the former] can limit and restrict; and, although it does not remove the episcopate from the person [punished], nor destroys it, nevertheless he does it by the superiority he has on the person, including in this power which is subordinated to him. That is why he really removes the power to that person, and does not just remove that person from power. On the contrary, the Church removes the pontificate not by superiority over him, but by a power which is only *ministerially* and *dispositively*, in so far as she can induce a *disposition* incompatible with the pontificate, as it was said."[88]

Bellarmine's Objection 3: "In the second place, to depose anyone from the pontificate against the will of the deposed, is without doubt punishing him; however, to punish is proper to a superior or to a judge."[89]

John of St. Thomas Answers: "In response to the confirmation of the reasoning, the Pope is deposed against his will, in a *ministerial* and *dispositive* manner by the Church, *authoritatively* by Christ the Lord, so that through Him, and not by Church, he is properly said *punished*."[90]

---

[86] *Cursus Theologici* II-II, *De Auctoritate Summi Pontificis*, Disp. II, Art. III, *De Depositione Papae*, p. 139.

[87] *De Romano Pontifice*, bk. 2, ch. 30

[88] *Cursus Theologici* II-II, *De Auctoritate Summi Pontificis*, Disp. II, Art. III, *De Depositione Papae*, p. 140

[89] *De Romano Pontifice*, bk. 2, ch. 30.

[90] *Cursus Theologici* II-II, *De Auctoritate Summi Pontificis*, Disp. II, Art. III, *De Depositione Papae*, p. 140.

Bellarmine's Objection 4: "In the third place, given that according to Cajetan and the other Thomists, in reality the whole and the parts taken as a whole are the same thing, he who has authority over the parts taken as a whole, being able to separate them one from another, has also authority over the whole itself which is constituted by those parts. The example of the electors, who have the power to designate a certain person for the pontificate, without however having power over the Pope, given by Cajetan, is also destitute of value. For when something is being made, the action is exercised over the *matter* of the future thing, and not over the *composite*, which does not yet exist, but when a thing is destroyed, the action is exercised over the composite, as becomes patent on consideration of the things of nature. Therefore, on creating the Pontiff, the Cardinals do not exercise their authority over the Pontiff for he does not yet exist, but over the matter, that is, over the person who by the election becomes *disposed* to receive the pontificate from God. But if they deposed the Pontiff, they would necessarily exercise authority over the *composite*, that is, over the person endowed with the pontifical power, that is, over the Pontiff. Therefore, the true opinion is the fifth, according to which the Pope who is manifestly a heretic ceases by himself to be Pope and head, etc."[91]

John of St. Thomas Answers: "Regarding the latter reason, he who has power over the conjunction of the parties has power over the whole *simpliciter*, unless his power over the conjunction is *ministerial* and *dispositive*; we must distinguish between physical realities when the *dispositions* have a natural connection to the very being of the whole, in such a way that when the agent realizes [brings about] the combination [of form and matter] by producing the *dispositions* binding the two parts, it produces the whole *simpliciter*; and moral realities, in which the *disposition* made by the agent has only a moral connection with the form, in relation to a free institution, so that he who *disposes* [who causes the disposition] is not judged to have affected the whole [the conjuction] simply and authoritatively, but only ministerially. For example, when the Pontiff grants to anyone the power to designate a place to be favored to gain indulgences, or to remove such indulgences by declaring that the place is no longer privileged in such a manner, that designation or declaration does not remove or grant indulgences authoritatively and principally, but only *ministerially*."[92]

---

[91] *De Romano Pontifice*, bk. 2, ch. 30.
[92] *Cursus Theologici* II-II *De Auctoritate Summi Pontificis*, Disp. II, Art. III, *De Depositione Papae*, p. 140.

Chapter 12

~ Peaceful and Universal Acceptance of a Pope ~

Following the publication of a series of articles over the past ten years (by these authors and others) on the grave errors of the Sedevacantist thesis, Fr. Cekada, having not been able to offer a cogent response to the critiques of his theories, posted an article on his website declaring that "the Sedevacantist argument must change"[1] (which, of course, must be the case when the argument – that a Pope loses his office for the sin of heresy under Divine law – is false).

Fr. Cekada proceeded to inform his followers that Sedevacantists should no longer argue that the conciliar Popes lost their office due to heresy, but should instead insist that they were never validly elected to begin with. He explained that his previous research had not only revealed that "a public heretic automatically lost his office and papal authority," but also that "a public heretic could not become pope in the first place." Thus, the new argument goes like this: Jorge Bergoglio (Pope Francis) was a public heretic before being elected Pope, and therefore he could not have been validly elected Pope (because, as they say, a heretic cannot be elected Pope). Cekada explains: "It is to this theological principle (rather than 'loss of office') that Sedevacantists must now appeal … As a public heretic, he [Bergoglio] could not be validly elected pope."[2]

Fr. Cekada then proceeded to cite the following quotations he had discovered which, in his mind, confirm the veracity of his "new argument":

> "Those capable of being **validly** elected are all who are not prohibited by **divine** law or by an invalidating ecclesiastical law… Those who are barred as **incapable of being validly elected** are all women, children who have not reached the age of reason; also, those afflicted with habitual insanity, the unbaptized, **heretics,** schismatics…" (Wernz-Vidal, *Jus Canonicum* 1:415).

---

[1] The title of the article is "Bergoglio's Got Nothing to Lose, So The Sedevacantist Argument Must Change," (May 7, 2014). http://www.fathercekada.com/2014/05/07/bergoglio-hes-got-nothing-to-lose/.
[2] Ibid.

III. Appointment of the office of the Primacy. 1. What is required by divine law for this appointment: ... Also required for validity is that the appointment be of a member of the Church. <u>Heretics and apostates (at least public ones) are therefore excluded.</u>" (Coronata, *Institutiones* 1:312).

c) The law now in force for the election of the Roman Pontiff is reduced to these points... Barred as **incapable of being validly elected** are all women, children who have not reached the age of reason; also, those afflicted with habitual insanity, the unbaptized, **heretics** and schismatics..." (Badius, *Institutiones*, 160).

"For the validity of the election as regards the person elected, it suffices only that he not be barred from the office by divine law — that is, any male Christian, even a layman. The following are therefore excluded: women, those who lack the use of reason, infidels, <u>and those who are at least public non-Catholics.</u>" (Cocchi, *Commentarium* in C.J.C, 2:151).

"Any male who has the use of reason and who is a member of the Church may be elected. The following, therefore, are **invalidly elected**: women, children, those suffering from insanity, the unbaptized, **heretics,** schismatics." (Sipos, *Enchiridion I.C.*, 153). (Emphases in original).[3]

Apparently Fr. Cekada doesn't realize that his "new argument" suffers from the same fundamental defect as his old argument. It is simply another application of his same error which maintains that individual Catholics can determine for themselves who is a "true" member of the hierarchy, based upon nothing but their own private judgment of whether the person has or has not been guilty of the "sin of heresy against Divine law." Whether Fr. Cekada argues that the sin of heresy ("discerned" by private judgment) has *caused* the loss of office, or *prevents* one from being validly elected, the same fundamental error remains.

Fr. Cekada unwittingly acknowledges that his *new* argument is essentially the *same old* argument when he explains that his "new argument" is based upon "the sin of heresy against Divine law" just like the old one. Wrote Fr. Cekada:

"But note: the canonists ... explicitly state that it is <u>divine law that prevents a public heretic from being validly elected. This</u>

---

[3] Ibid.

means that the sin of heresy suffices to prevent someone from becoming a true pope. There is no requirement that he first be convicted under ecclesiastical law of the canonical crime of heresy before the impediment applies. In the case of heresy, warnings and the rest of the canonical rigmarole come into play only for the crime. These are not required as a condition for committing the sin of heresy against divine law."[4]

We have already refuted Fr. Cekada's "sin of heresy" argument *ad nauseam* (and we also note that the canonists Cekada cites never say that the sin of heresy precludes the member from being elected to office because, as we've seen, the sin of heresy alone does not sever membership in the Church). Nevertheless, we find it curious why Fr. Cekada would attempt to change the argument (or, rather, tell his followers that it changed when it really didn't) if he thought his original argumentation was sound. And how does it "change the argument" to claim that the sin of heresy prevents a Pope from being elected, as opposed to the sin of heresy causing a Pope to lose his office after election, when both are determined by private judgment? If private judgment did not suffice for his old argument, how will it suffice for his new one? This new angle certainly does not help Fr. Cekada's case.[5]

Rather, it reveals that Fr. Cekada, by his own admission, no longer wants to address "for the nth time," as he says, arguments like "one must have official warnings, the accused must be given an opportunity to mount a defense, some sort of tribunal must be convened, the excusing causes [that] canon law provides [for] must all be carefully considered, etc."[6] In other words, Fr. Cekada no longer wants to argue against the "unanimous opinion" of the Doctors and theologians that a heretical Pope can lose his office only after the Church herself establishes that he is guilty of the crime of heresy – and that is because Cekada *has no argument.* He has been "beat down," as they say; and rather than admit his error, he pretends to have come up with a new argument - a "new argument" which, he claims, has caused all the objections to his old argument to disappear. He imagines that if he simply claims the recent Popes were never validly elected to begin with, he can avoid having to address the objections.

---

[4] Ibid.

[5] The "new argument" merely highlights Cekada's anti-Catholic theory that while the Church is the interpreter of ecclesiastical law, individual Catholics, and not the Church, are the definitive interpreters of "Divine law."

[6] Cekada, "Bergoglio's Got Nothing to Lose, So The Sedevacantist Argument Must Change," (May 7, 2014).

For example, after listing seven objections to his old argument –
e.g. issuing warnings, the necessity of the Church establishing the
crime, permitting the Pope to defend himself, etc. - which he was never
able to answer (beyond *ad hominem* attacks and inappropriate name-
calling), this is what Fr. Cekada wrote:

> "Poof! In the face of the principle laid down in the foregoing
> section [i.e., his "new argument"], all these spurious objections
> disappear."[7]

Unfortunately for Fr. Cekada, his "new" argument does not make
these "spurious objections" – which include those made by Bellarmine,
Suarez, Cajetan, John of St. Thomas and the Council Fathers of
Constantinople IV – disappear. As we have seen, if the recent Popes
had been accused of heresy prior to their election, Church law would
have required that the necessary warnings be issued, and the accused
given the opportunity to defend themselves, before they were
considered heretics by the Church. But this never happened, which is
why they were all considered Catholics in good standing prior to their
elections. So Fr. Cekada's "new argument" does not make the
objections to his old argument disappear. Not only must he respond to
these "objections," as he calls them, but is bound by them insofar as
they represent the mind of the Church and the definitive teaching of an
ecumenical council. One also wonders how Fr. Cekada can be sure the
previous 259 men elected Pope before John XXIII, and recognized as
such by the Church for their entire pontificates, had not also committed
the "sin of heresy" sometime prior to their election, thereby rendering
the election null and void? Or does the alleged loss of office for the sin
of heresy apply *only* to the last six consecutive Popes and no one else?
Fr. Cekada doesn't say.

What is even more curious is not that Fr. Cekada has come up with
another nonsensical theory to defend his position, but rather that there
are actually some individuals who are unable to see the absurdity of it,
and instead fall for it, lock, stock and barrel. For example, soon after Fr.
Cekada posted the aforementioned article on his website, the
Sedevacantist blogger, Steve Speray, used it in an attempt to respond to
an article, by Robert Siscoe, which demonstrated that the recent Popes
cannot be considered to have lost their office for heresy. Following
lock-step behind Fr. Cekada, Mr. Speray wrote that "Sedevacantists

---

[7] Ibid.

hold that no true pope has been validly elected since 1958. Therefore, there is no office to lose."[8] How very convenient indeed.

Now, let's think a little more about this argument. How could John XXIII (Angelo Roncalli), for example, have been a "public heretic" prior to his election, without any of the bishops or Cardinals knowing about it? And keep in mind that this was in 1958. Pope Pius XII had just died and the crisis in the Church had not yet erupted. If John XXIII was a Cardinal in good standing during the entire reign of Pius XII, when exactly did he become a "public heretic"? Roncalli may have been suspect of heresy before being elected Pope (as some claim), but he was appointed Cardinal by Pius XII in 1953 and was recognized as a Catholic in good standing by the entire Church up to the death of Pius XII. As a Cardinal in good standing, Roncalli was allowed to participate in the Conclave and was elected by a majority vote. In light of these facts, how can anyone seriously contend that he was a "public heretic" prior to his election? Are we to believe that the *private judgment* of individual Catholics 50+ years later, overrides the *public judgment* of Pope Pius XII and the entire Church at the time? To ask the question is to answer it.

As should be clear in light of the material covered to this point, the quotations, from the canonists that Fr. Cekada discovered, are referring to individuals who are not *members* of the Church - that is, people who are *not* publicly recognized *by the Church* as Catholic. They certainly are not referring to prelates, recognized as Catholics in good standing by the Church, whom individual Catholics personally believe fell into the "sin" of heresy prior to their election. For example, Coronata says "Also required for validity is that the appointment be of a <u>member of the Church</u>." Sipos similarly says only one "who is a <u>member of the Church may be elected</u>." Referring to those who are not eligible to be elected Pope, Cocchi refers to "those who are at least <u>public non-Catholics</u>." These canonists are making a distinction between members of the Church (who are eligible for election) and non-members or "public non-Catholics" (who are not eligible for election). In order for a member of the Church to be expelled from the Body (and thus ineligible to be elected to office), he must be guilty of the crime of public and notorious heresy or have publicly defected from the Church. Neither is the case with the conciliar Popes, *either before or after their elections to the papacy*, which is why they were all recognized by the Church as members in good standing. If they were non-members of the

---

[8] Siscoe, Robert, "Answering a Sedevacantist Critic," *The Remnant* newspaper, March 18, 2015 (online).

Church (according to the Church's judgment), they would not have been allowed to enter the Conclave.

By way of illustration, "Pastor Bob" of the First Baptist Church of Rome would not be eligible to be elected Pope, since he is not a member of the Church. Pastor Bob is not a member of the Church because he is a public heretic *by the Church's judgment*. Because Pastor Bob is not recognized as being a member of the Church, he could not be elected Pope, since one who is not a member of the Church cannot be its head. However, a Cardinal who enters the Conclave in good standing with the Church (at least externally), even if he has internally lost the faith due to the "sin" of heresy, is certainly eligible to be elected Pope. If not, one would never know for sure if the person elected Pope was a true Pope or a false Pope.

Legislation for Pre-Election Excommunications

Over the centuries, to ensure the validity of papal elections, Church law has operated to remove any doubt that a man elected by a Conclave becomes the true Pope. After all, the assurance that a Conclave gives us a true Pope is among the most important of all assurances the Church could possibly give. To that end, Pope St. Pius X, for example, issued the following decree which removed excommunications and other ecclesiastical impediments that would prevent a candidate from being validly elected:

> "None of the Cardinals may be in any way excluded from the active or passive election of the Sovereign Pontiff under pretext or by reason of any excommunication, suspension, interdict or other ecclesiastical impediment."[9]

Pope Pius XII issued an almost identical decree which likewise removed the canonical impediment of excommunication as a bar to a valid election. In the Constitution *Vacantis Apostolicae Sedis,* we read:

> "None of the Cardinals may, by pretext or reason of any excommunication, suspension, or interdict whatsoever, or of any other ecclesiastical impediment, be excluded from the *active* and *passive* election of the Supreme Pontiff."[10]

---

[9] Pope Pius X, Apostolic Constitution *Vacante Sede Apostolica,* December 25, 1904; (in *Pii X Pontificis Maximi Acta,* III, 1908, pp. 280-282).
[10] Pope Pius XII, *Vacantis Apostolicae Sedis,* No. 34, December 8, 1945. Paul VI's 1975 legislation for papal elections contains almost identical language (see Paul VI, The

"Active" election refers to the act of electing a Pope. "Passive" election refers to the act of being elected Pope. Since the Church does not judge internals, and since the internal virtue of faith is not absolutely necessary for the exercise of the papal office, this decree of Pope Pius XII, which is similar to previous decrees of Popes Clement V (1317), Pius IV (1562), and Gregory XV (1621), removes any doubt that a man who is elected by the Conclave becomes the true Pope. Clearly, the mind of the Church has been, for centuries, to remedy (or heal in the root) all potential defects in a papal election.

Even if a Cardinal incurred the censure of excommunication for heresy, he could still validly vote for and be elected the Sovereign Pontiff, under the foregoing legislation. If it were not for this legislation, the Cardinals and all the faithful would never have a guarantee that a given election produced a valid Pope. Such a lingering doubt would erode the Church from within, for no one would know with certainty whether the elected Pope were really the true Pope. This confusion would lead to schism after schism, and the Church would go into a paralysis. To avoid such a catastrophe, the Church's law ensures the Pope-elect's candidacy by removing any impediments to his election.

What is Fr. Cekada's response to these decrees? An appeal to Divine law, of course. He says:

> "Pius XII's Constitution suspends impediments of ecclesiastical law only - censures such as excommunication, etc. (See para. 34: '...*aut alius ecclesiastici impedimenti praetextu.*') It does not and could not suspend impediments of <u>divine law</u>."[11]

Again, Fr. Cekada answers by returning to his same argument (see 2Pet. 2:22)[12] that the recent Popes have violated Divine law by committing the "sin" of heresy, and because Fr. Cekada personally believes they are guilty of this sin, he believes he is completely justified in declaring that their elections are null and void. If nothing else, Fr. Cekada is consistent. The problem is that he is consistently wrong. If the sin of heresy alone ("discerned" by private judgment) prevented a person from being elected Pope, we would have absolutely no way of knowing which of the 265 men elected as successors to St. Peter, and

---

Election Of The Roman Pontiff, No. 35, October 1, 1975), as does that issued by John Paul II in 1996 (John Paul II, *Universi Dominici Gregis*, No. 35, February 22, 1996).

[11] Cekada, "Sedevacantism Refuted?," August 2004.

[12] "For, that of the true proverb has happened to them: The dog is returned to his vomit: and, The sow that was washed, to her wallowing in the mire" (2Pet. 2:22).

recognized as such by the Church, were real Popes, and which ones were not.

Because this legislation is so damaging to the Sedevacantist argument, Peter Dimond tried to wiggle around its import in an exchange with John Salza in 2010.[13] When Mr. Salza showed that the legislation refuted Dimond's argument, Dimond attempted to limit the application of the law to "minor" crimes subject to excommunication, but not to "major" crimes (which distinction, by the way, no longer exists under canon law). Dimond said: "The refutation is as follows: Historically, excommunications were distinguished by the terms *major* and *minor*. Major excommunications were incurred for heresy and schism (sins against the faith) and certain other major sins. Those who received major excommunication for heresy were not members of the Church. Minor excommunication, however, *did not remove one from the Church*, but forbade one to participate in the Church's sacramental life."[14]

The "historical" distinction between minor and major excommunication, which Dimond referred to, has not existed since the nineteenth century; and when it did exist, a major excommunication could only be imposed following a canonical warning.[15] Furthermore, the legislation of both Pius X and Pius XII states that a Cardinal who enters the Conclave in external good standing with the Church is not excluded from being elected Pope *"for any excommunication ... whatsoever."* Dimond simply discovered that there used to be a distinction between major and minor excommunications, and then erroneously attempted to apply it to the current legislation in order to justify his position.

Acknowledging that his argument may actually be wrong, Dimond then said:

> "...let's assume *for the sake of argument* that Pope Pius XII's legislation did mean that a heretical cardinal could be elected pope. It still wouldn't make a difference. Notice what Pius XII says: 'We hereby suspend such censures solely for the purposes of the said election; at other times they are to remain in vigor.' This is an

---

[13] See "John Salza Responds to the Lies, Errors and Hypocrisy of Sedevacantist Peter Dimond" (2010) online at http://www.johnsalza.com.

[14] Dimond, "John Salza's Arguments Against Sedevacantism Crushed," http://www.mostholyfamilymonastery.com.

[15] "So grave were the effects of major excommunication that previous warnings were required before it could be imposed." Logan, Donald, *Excommunication and the Secular Arm in Medieval England: A Study in Legal Procedure From the Thirteenth to the Sixteenth Century* (Pontifical Institute of Medieval Studies; 1968), p. 15.

extremely important point. Pius XII says that the excommunication is suspended *only for the time of the election*; at other times it remains in vigor. This would mean that the excommunication for heresy would fall back into force immediately after the election and then the heretic who had been elected pope would lose his office! Thus, no matter what way you look at it, a heretic could not be validly elected and remain pope."[16]

Now, the Sedevacantists have put forward many bad arguments in defense of their position, but this one surely ranks as one of the worst. Does Dimond really believe that a censure, which is lifted by ecclesiastical law for the express purpose of ensuring the validity of an election, kicks back in immediately after the election, thereby causing the recently elected Pope to fall from office at the very moment the Cardinal Protodeacon is announcing to the Church *"Habemus Papam"*? This would render null the obvious *purpose* of the legislation, which is to ensure that the Cardinal who is elected Pope validly ascends to the papal throne, notwithstanding the existence of any pre-election excommunications (which, in the case of the conciliar Popes, do not exist). Furthermore, as we saw in Chapter 9, a censure is a part of the Church's positive law, which has no coercive power over a Pope. Therefore, once elected, the Pope will not automatically incur the censure and lose his office as Peter Dimond imagines.[17]

According to Fr. Cekada's "new argument" (discussed above), each and every Catholic in the pew would have to decide for himself which Popes committed the sin of heresy prior to their elections and which ones did not. Or, alternatively, under Fr. Cekada's "old argument," every Catholic would have to determine for themselves which Popes committed the sin of heresy *after* their elections (and thereby lost their office) and which ones did not. Pick your Sedevacantist poison. Either way, the verdict would be based upon nothing but one's own fallible, private judgment, which has no effect whatsoever on the status of a determined Pope when he is recognized as Pope by the Church's public judgment.

And if Fr. Cekada and Pete Dimond get to determine, based upon their private judgment, that the last six Popes were not true Popes, on what basis could they object to their fellow Sedevacantist, Richard Ibranyi, who now rejects the last 102 Popes? As we saw previously, Mr.

---

[16] Dimond, "John Salza's Arguments Against Sedevacantism Crushed," http://www.mostholyfamilymonastery.com.

[17] As we have also seen, the *censure* of excommunication alone does not cause a prelate to lose his office. The loss of office is a *vindictive penalty* that must be preceded by two canonical warnings.

Ibranyi claims to have discovered "conclusive evidence" that all of the Popes since Innocent II (1130-1143) were formal heretics and apostates. Mr. Ibranyi explains:

> "As of January 2014, I have discovered conclusive [yes, conclusive!] evidence that all the so-called popes and cardinals from Innocent II (1130-1143) onward have been idolaters or formal heretics and thus were apostate antipopes and apostate anticardinals. Also all of the theologians and canon lawyers from 1250 onward have been apostates. (See RJMI article and audio 'No Popes or Cardinals since 1130.') Hence all their teachings, laws, judgments, and other acts are null and void. Therefore, all of the ecumenical councils, canon laws, and other acts from Apostate Antipope Innocent II onward are null and void."[18]

Richard Ibranyi, who accepts Fr. Cekada's teaching that a man who is guilty of the "sin" of heresy, against Divine law, cannot be Pope (or a Cardinal, theologian, or canon lawyer), has judged that *every single Pope for the last nine centuries* has been guilty of such a sin, and was therefore an antipope. This would mean, of course, that all of the councils and infallible pronouncements since then have been null and void. If that were true, it would mean the last 12 councils (out of the 21 ecumenical councils assembled by the Church) would have been null, with the last true council being the First Lateran Council in 1123. This would obviously mean that the great council of Trent (1545-1563) and the First Vatican Council (1870), which defined some of the most important dogmas of the Catholic Faith (dogmas Ibranyi claims to believe), were false councils.

Unfortunately for Mr. Ibranyi, though, the nine valid councils he holds as legitimate would include the Fourth Council of Constantinople (869-870), which explicitly condemned the Sedevacantist theory of private judgment "deposition" by vigilante laymen like Mr. Ibranyi! Here we see where the utterly absurd theory of Fr. Cekada inevitably leads. Contrary to what Fr. Cekada would have his followers believe, a public heretic is not someone who is judged as such by *private judgment,* but one who is recognized as such by the *Church's judgment.* And he who is prayed for in the Canon of every Mass ("*una cum fámulo tuo Papa nostro*") is not a public heretic *according to the Church's judgment.*

---

[18] Ibranyi, "No Popes or Cardinals since 1130," January 2014.

Peaceful and Universal Acceptance

Just as we can be sure that a Pope will not lose his office for heresy without the Church herself knowing about it (since God will not sever the bond uniting the man to the Pontificate as long as he is recognized as Pope by the Church), so too can we rest assured that a man who is elected by the College of Cardinals, and peacefully accepted as Pope by the Universal Church, is, indeed, a true and valid Pope. We don't have to wonder if his election was null and void due to a "sin" of heresy committed prior to the election. On the contrary, once the man is accepted as Pope by the universal Church, we have *infallible certitude* that he is in fact a true and valid Pope. He may not be a good Pope, as history shows, but he will nevertheless be a true Pope.

Dogmatic Fact and Infallible Certitude

As we have discussed in previous chapters, during the First Vatican Council the Church infallibly defined that when she *definitively* teaches a truth revealed by God, she speaks infallibly. The truths revealed by God are known as the *primary object* of the Church's infallibility. When the Church definitively proposes a revealed truth, the doctrine must be believed with Divine and Catholic Faith, which is faith in 1) God revealing, and 2) the infallible Church teaching.

But, according to the teaching of the Church's theologians, the Church also speaks infallibly on other matters, which fall into the category of *secondary objects* of infallibility. These include (a) *theological conclusions* (i.e., inferences deduced from two premises, one of which is immediately revealed, while the other is a truth known by natural reason), (b) *dogmatic facts*, (c) *universal disciplines*, and the (d) *canonization of saints*. These secondary objects of infallibility are not believed with Divine and Catholic Faith, but with Ecclesiastical Faith, which is faith in the infallible Church teaching (but not in God revealing).

The peaceful and universal acceptance of a Pope falls into the category of a dogmatic fact. Theologians explain that the unanimous acceptance of a Pope, by the bishops and faithful, is an infallible sign – an "infallible effect"[19] - of his legitimacy. They explain that the unanimous acceptance does not *cause* the Pope to be a true Pope, but is instead an *effect* that would not be present unless the *cause* (a true Pope) was itself present. If the Church universally accepts a man as Pope, we

---

[19] Wernz-Vidal, *Ius Can.*, II. p. 520, note 171, cited in *The Theological Hypothesis of a Heretic Pope*, Silveira, p. 185.

have infallible certitude that he is, indeed, a true Pope. The reason the Church's infallibility extends to dogmatic facts is because they are so inexorably connected to dogma that without certain knowledge of the *fact* there would be no certain knowledge of the doctrines connected with it. For example, if it were not certain that Pius XII was the Pope, we would not have certitude that the Assumption, which he defined as a dogma, was infallibly true. The two truths are linked together in such a way that uncertainty concerning the former would result in doubt regarding the latter.

The following, taken from Fr. Sylvester Berry's Apologetic and Dogmatic Treatise, *The Church of Christ*, further explains these principles:

> "The extent of infallibility refers to the truths that may be defined by the Church with infallible authority. Some truths are directly subject to the infallible authority of the Church by their very nature [i.e truths revealed by God and contained within the sources of Revelation – Scripture and Tradition]; others only indirectly because of their connection with the former. The one set of truths constitutes the primary, the other secondary extent of infallibility." (...)
>
> This secondary or indirect extent of infallibility includes especially (a) theological conclusions, (b) truths of the natural order, (c) dogmatic facts, and (d) general disciplinary matters (...)
>
> DOGMATIC FACTS. A dogmatic fact is one that has not been revealed, yet is so intimately connected with a doctrine of faith that without certain knowledge of the fact there can be no certain knowledge of the doctrine. For example, was the [First] Vatican Council truly ecumenical? Was Pius IX a legitimate pope? Was the election of Pius XI valid? Such questions must be decided with certainty before decrees issued by any council or pope can be accepted as infallibly true or binding on the Church. It is evident, then, that the Church must be infallible in judging of such facts, and since the Church is infallible in believing as well as in teaching, it follows that the practically unanimous consent of the bishops and faithful in accepting a council as ecumenical, or a Roman Pontiff as legitimately elected, gives absolute and infallible certainty of the fact."[20]

---

[20] *The Church of Christ*, pp. 288, 289, 290.

Msgr. Van Noort offers similar commentary on the same point. He also notes that the infallibility of dogmatic facts is qualified as "theologically certain":[21]

> "Assertion 2: <u>The Church's infallibility extends to dogmatic facts. This proposition is theologically certain</u>. A dogmatic fact is a fact not contained in the sources of revelation, [but] on the admission of which depends the knowledge or certainty of a dogma or of a revealed truth. The following questions are concerned with dogmatic facts: 'Was the [First] Vatican Council a legitimate ecumenical council? Is the Latin Vulgate a substantially faithful translation of the original books of the Bible? <u>Was Pius XII legitimately elected Bishop of Rome</u>? One can readily see that on these facts hang the questions of whether the decrees of the [First] Vatican Council are infallible, whether the Vulgate is truly Sacred Scripture, <u>whether Pius XII is to be recognized as supreme ruler of the universal Church.</u>"[22]

In another place, Van Noort addresses the same point from the perspective of the Ordinary and Universal Magisterium:

> "Meantime, notice that the Church possesses infallibility not only when she is defining some matters in solemn fashion, but also when she is exercising the full weight of her authority through her ordinary and universal teaching. Consequently, we must hold with an absolute assent, which we call 'ecclesiastical faith,' the following theological truths: (a) those which the Magisterium has infallibly defined in solemn fashion; (b) those which the ordinary magisterium dispersed throughout the world unmistakably proposes to its members as something to be held (*tenendas*). <u>So, for example, one must give an absolute assent to the proposition: 'Pius XII is the legitimate successor of St. Peter'</u>; similarly … one must give an absolute assent to the proposition: 'Pius XII possesses the primacy of jurisdiction over the entire Church.' For — skipping the question of how it begins to be proven infallibly for the first time that this individual was legitimately elected to take St. Peter's place — <u>when someone has been constantly acting as Pope and has theoretically and practically been recognized as such by the bishops and by the universal Church, it is clear that the ordinary and universal</u>

---

[21] Because the Church herself has never defined if infallibility extends to the secondary objects, the proposition that it does is only qualified as *theologically certain*. If the Church were to ever define that infallibility does extend to secondary objects, the teaching would be *de fide* (of the faith).
[22] *Christ's Church*, p. 112 (emphasis added).

magisterium is giving an utterly clear-cut witness to the legitimacy of his succession."[23]

Cardinal Billot makes a number of interesting observations about this matter as well. In addition to explaining that the acceptance of a Pope by the universal Church is an infallible sign of his legitimacy, he also explains, quite logically, that the universal acceptance is an infallible sign of the existence of all the *conditions* required for legitimacy, such as membership in the Church (a condition which all Sedevacantists claim the conciliar Popes did not have). Another interesting and quite relevant point he makes is that God might permit an extended vacancy of the Apostolic See, *but he cannot permit the whole Church to accept a false Pope as being the true Pope* (which, it should be noted, presents more problems for the "Siri Theory"[24]). Here is Cardinal Billot's teaching on this subject:

"Finally, whatever you still think about the possibility or impossibility of the aforementioned hypothesis [of a Pope falling into heresy], at least one point must be considered absolutely incontrovertible and placed firmly above any doubt whatever: the adhesion of the universal Church will be always, in itself, an infallible *sign* of the legitimacy of a determined Pontiff, and therefore also of the existence of all the conditions required for legitimacy itself. It is not necessary to look far for the proof of this, but we find it immediately in the promise and the infallible providence of Christ: 'The gates of hell shall not prevail against it,' and 'Behold I shall be with you all days.' For the adhesion of the Church to a false Pontiff would be the same as its adhesion to a false rule of faith,[25] seeing that the Pope is the living rule of faith which the Church must follow and which in fact she always follows. As will become even more clear by what we shall say later, God can permit that at times a vacancy in the Apostolic See be

---

[23] *Sources of Revelation*, p. 265 (emphasis added).
[24] As we saw in Chapter 1, the Siri Theory, held by some Sedevacantists, maintains that Cardinal Siri was validly elected in the 1958 Conclave, taking the name Gregory XVII, but through coercion was forced to resign before being presented to the Church as Pope. They hold that a forced resignation is invalid and consequently Cardinal Siri (who publicly recognized John XXIII, Paul VI, John Paul I and John Paul II as valid Popes as well as the legitimacy of the changes spawned by Vatican II) remained the true Pope until his death on May 2, 1989.
[25] The Pope is the rule of faith to the extent that he infallibly proposes doctrines that must be assented to by faith. As will be explained in the next chapter, only truths infallibly proposed are assented to with the assent of faith. Personal opinions or non-infallible teachings of a Pope do not constitute articles of faith. Hence, John XXII was not a "false rule" of faith when he taught his error regarding the Beatific Vision.

prolonged for a long time. He can also permit that doubt arise about the legitimacy of this or that election. <u>He cannot however permit that the whole Church accept as Pontiff him who is not so truly and legitimately</u>.

Therefore, from the moment in which the Pope is accepted by the Church and united to her as the head to the body, it is no longer permitted to raise doubts about a possible vice of election or a possible lack of any condition whatsoever necessary for legitimacy. For the aforementioned adhesion of the Church <u>heals in the root all fault in the election and proves infallibly the existence of all the required conditions</u>."[26]

Bishop Sanborn's Novelty

Due to the problems that universal and peaceful acceptance presents for the Sedevacantist thesis, the Sedevacantist bishop, Donald Sanborn, came up with a novel explanation in an effort to get around it. He claims that the peaceful and universal acceptance of a Pope means only that the he was validly elected; *and not that the man elected actually became the Pope.* You read that correctly. Sanborn claims it only ensures a valid election, but not a valid Pope. The following is taken from an article the Bishop wrote in 2002, which is still posted on his website:

"Q. Can a papal election be convalidated by the general acceptance of the Catholic people?

A. Yes. This is generally conceded by Catholic theologians. The ultimate guarantee of a valid election is the universal acceptance of Catholics <u>that a certain man has been elected</u>. Note that <u>this pertains only to election</u>, i.e., designation, and <u>not to jurisdiction</u>. For the Catholic people cannot confer jurisdiction, but only confirm designation to jurisdiction."[27]

Now, this is quite a novel theory that the Bishop came up with.[28] Unfortunately, as is the case with most novel theories, it is entirely

---

[26] Billot, *Tractatus de Ecclesia Christi*, vol. I, pp. 612-613 (emphasis added).
[27] Bishop Sanborn, "Explanation Of The Thesis Of Bishop Guérard Des Lauriers," June 29, 2002. See http://mostholytrinityseminary.org/Explanation%20of%20the%20Thesis.pdf.
[28] As mentioned in Chapter 10, Sanborn is basing his position upon the thesis of Fr. Guérard des Lauriers (often referred to as the "Cassiciacum" thesis), which holds that each conciliar Pope was a *material* Pope (they held the papal office lawfully), but not a *formal* Pope (they did not receive the authority of the office). Sanborn likewise holds that "*Novus Ordo*" Catholics "are still legally Catholics" (ibid.), even though he also holds that they are not members of the Church but of a false religion. Thus, Sanborn has created a

erroneous. The peaceful and universal acceptance of a Pope does not simply guarantee that the man was validly elected, as the bishop claims; it guarantees that he is a *legitimate Pope* (that is, it guarantees that God joined the *form* to the *matter* following the election).

As we saw above, the peaceful and universal acceptance of a Pope is an infallible *effect* that the Pope is, in fact, a true Pope. The *cause* (true Pope) produces the *effect* (universal acceptance). Notice that the *cause* is not only a *valid election*, but a *valid Pope*. In fact, St. Alphonsus Liguori, Doctor of the Church, even teaches that the peaceful and universal acceptance of a Pope means that a Pope who was *not* legitimately elected, or somehow took possession of the pontificate by fraud, has nevertheless *become* a true Pope. Again, this shows that the universal acceptance does not simply guarantee that an election was valid (by curing any defects that may have existed in the election), *but that the Pope is a true Pope.* Here is what St. Alphonsus taught:

> "It is of no importance that in past centuries some Pontiff was illegitimately elected or took possession of the Pontificate by fraud; it is enough that he was accepted afterwards by the whole Church as Pope, since by such acceptance he would have become the true Pontiff."[29]

Cardinal Billot applies the teaching of the peaceful and universal acceptance of a Pope to the scandalous papacy of Alexander VI. He does so in order to demonstrate that he was a true and valid Pope, even though there were some in Alexander VI's day who believed him to be a public apostate. Girolamo Savonarola, the controversial Dominican monk, was one who denied that Alexander VI was a true Pope. In a letter to the Emperor, Savonarola wrote:

> "The Lord, moved to anger by this intolerable corruption, has, for some time past, allowed the Church to be without a pastor. For I bear witness in the name of God that this Alexander VI is in no way Pope and cannot be. For quite apart from the execrable crime of simony, by which he got possession of the [papal] tiara through a sacrilegious bargaining, and by which every day he puts up to auction and knocks down to the highest bidder ecclesiastical

---

fictional distinction that does not exist in reality, that is, that one can be a legal Catholic and office-holder in the Church, but not actually enjoy the legal rights, privileges and powers which are *necessarily concomitant* with that legal membership (and, remember, all this is discerned by private judgment, to boot). Needless to say, neither the Church nor any reputable theologian has ever taught such a thing; the theory is as false as it is novel.
[29] Liguori, *Verita della Fede*, in "Opera...,"vol. VIII., p. 720, n. 9.

benefices, and quite apart from his other vices - well-known to all - which I will pass over in silence, this I declare in the first *place and affirm it with all certitude, that the man is not a Christian, he does not even believe any longer that there is a God*; he goes beyond the final limits of infidelity and impiety."[30]

In spite of the scandals of Alexander VI's papacy, including the grave accusations of heresy, apostasy, and illicit acquisition of the Papal See through simony, leveled by his contemporaries, Cardinal Billot explains that the universal acceptance proves *certain* that Alexander VI was indeed a legitimate Pope. The Cardinal explains:

> "Let this be said in passing against those who, trying to justify certain attempts at schism made in the time of Alexander VI, allege that its promoter [Savonarola] broadcast that he had most certain proofs, which he would reveal to a General Council, of the heresy of Alexander. Putting aside here other reasons with which one could easily be able to refute such an opinion, it is enough to remember this: it is certain that when Savonarola was writing his letters to the Princes, all of Christendom adhered to Alexander VI and obeyed him as the true Pontiff. For this very reason, Alexander VI was not a false Pope, but a legitimate one."[31]

The same holds true for the post-conciliar Popes, who, in spite of accusations of heresy, were accepted as true Popes by the Church.[32]

In his book, *The Church of the Word Incarnate*, Cardinal Journet wrote the following about the validity and certitude of a papal election:

> "Validity and certitude of election: The [Papal] election, remarks John of St. Thomas, may be invalid when carried out by persons not qualified, or when, although effected by persons qualified, it suffers from defect of form or falls on an incapable subject, as for example one of unsound mind or unbaptized.
>
> But the peaceful acceptance of the universal Church given to an elect, as to a head to whom it submits, is an act in which the Church engages herself and her fate. It is therefore an act in itself infallible and is immediately recognizable as such. (Consequently, and mediately, it will appear that all conditions prerequisite to the validity of the election have been fulfilled.)

---

[30] Schnitzer, Savonarola, Italian translation by E. Rutili (Milan, 1931), vol. II, p. 303. Quoted in Journet's *The Church of the Word Incarnate*, p. 484 (emphasis added).

[31] Billot, *Tractatus de Ecclesia Christi*, vol. I, pp. 612-613 (emphasis added).

[32] As explained below, some have questioned whether Pope Francis has, in fact, been peacefully and universally accepted by the Church.

Acceptance by the Church operates either negatively, when the election is not at once contested; or positively, when the election is first accepted by those present and then gradually by the rest.[33] <u>The Church has the right to elect the Pope, and therefore the right to certain knowledge as to who is elected</u>."[34]

In spite of the *dogmatic fact* that the conciliar Popes have been true Popes, as evidenced by their peaceful and universal acceptance, some Sedevacantists, such as the Dimond brothers, have desperately appealed to a quotation from Fr. Edmund O'Reilly, which deals with the issue of how long the Church could potentially be without a Pope; this, however, is a different question from whether a Pope who is peacefully and universally accepted by the Church is, in fact, a legitimate Pope. In the quotation, Fr. O'Reilly says he personally believes it would be possible for God to leave the Church without a Pope for as long as the Great Western Schism lasted, which was 39 years (from 1378-1417). In Fr. O'Reilly's words:

> "We may here stop to inquire what is to be said of the position, at that time, of the three claimants, and their rights with regard to the Papacy. In the first place, there was all through, from the death of Gregory XI in 1378, a pope – with the exception, of course, of the intervals between deaths and elections to fill up the vacancies thereby created. <u>There was, I say, at every given time a pope, really invested with the dignity of the Vicar of Christ and Head of the Church</u>, whatever opinions might exist among many as to his genuineness; <u>not that an interregnum covering the whole period would have been impossible or inconsistent with the promises of Christ, for this is by no means manifest, but that, as a matter of fact, there was not such an interregnum</u>."[35]

Of course, Fr. O'Reilly's opinion about how long he believes it would be possible for the Church to be without a Pope (an opinion anyone is free to disagree with) does not impinge upon the theological certainty that the post-conciliar Popes, who were universally and peacefully accepted by the Church, were, in fact, legitimate Popes. Whether there could theoretically be a long papal interregnum

---

[33] *Cf.* John of St. Thomas, II-II, qq. 1-7; disp. 2, a. 2, nos. 1, 15, 28, 34, 40; pp. 228 et seq.
[34] *The Church of the Word Incarnate*, pp. 481-482.
[35] O'Reilly, *The Relations of the Church to Society – Theological Essays*, London: John Hodges, 1892. The Dimond brothers actually use this quotation from Fr. O'Reilly as one of their "Answers to the Most Common Sedevacantist Objections"; see http://www.mostholy familymonastery.com/21_Objections .pdf.

according to Fr. O'Reilly, or anyone else, does not mean that such an interregnum could occur *during the reign of a determined Pope who was elected by the Cardinals and peacefully and universally accepted as Pope by the Church.*

Clearly, Fr. O'Reilly is referring to interregnums that exist between the death of one Pope and the election of his successor. He is *not* speaking of an alleged "interregnum" that could possibly exist based upon accusations of papal heresy (and loss of office) by individual Catholics (who represent .001 percent of the Church) *after* the Pope has been peacefully and universally accepted. Fr. O'Reilly makes this clear when he defines interregnum as "the intervals between deaths and elections" of a Pope. Thus, Fr. O'Reilly's speculation about the possible length of an interregnum does not apply to our time, since the Church has had a continuous line of men who have been universally recognized by the Church as Pope during the post-conciliar period.

Furthermore, as Cardinal Billot taught in the earlier citation, "God can permit that at times a vacancy in the Apostolic See be prolonged for a long time" but "he cannot, however, permit that the whole Church accept as Pontiff him who is not so truly and legitimately."[36]

Also note that Fr. O'Reilly says that during the midst of the confusion of the Great Western Schism, "There was, I say, *at every given time a pope*, really invested with the dignity of the Vicar of Christ and Head of the Church." And yet, most Sedevacantists claim that we have not had a true Pope for nearly 60 years (except for the Conclavists who have elected their own "Pope"). If there was a true Pope during the Western Schism (even though there was not universal and peaceful acceptance, as large factions of Catholics disagreed with each other about who was the true Pope), how much more certainty do we have today that the conciliar Popes are true Popes, when they have been universally accepted by the Church?

Moral Unanimity

It should be noted that the universal acceptance does not have to be mathematically unanimous, but only practically unanimous. This common opinion of the theologians was explained by Fr. Sylvester Berry, who wrote:

"The practically unanimous consent of the Bishops and faithful in accepting a council as ecumenical, or a Roman Pontiff as

---

[36] Billot, *Tractatus de Ecclesia Christi*, vol. I, p. 613.

legitimately elected, gives absolute and infallible certainty of the fact."[37]

To state the obvious, it is not necessary that an elected Pope be accepted by 100 percent of faithful (what the theologians call a "mathematical unanimity"). No, infallible certitude only requires a *moral unanimity*. A moral unanimity is less than a mathematical unanimity, but certainly more than a mere mathematical majority of the faithful, for the word *unanimous* comes from the Latin *unus* (meaning "one") and *animus* (meaning "mind") – in other words, the acceptance of the Pope reflects the one mind of the Church, which is clearly the case with the universal and peaceful acceptance of the conciliar Popes. Since the conciliar Popes were accepted as true and valid Popes by at least a practically unanimous consensus of Church, to claim they were not true Popes amounts to a denial of the infallibility of the Church.[38]

Providential Q&A from 1965

The *American Ecclesiastical Review* contained a providential Question and Answer in its December 1965 issue. Considering that virtually all Sedevacantists reject the papacy of Paul VI (since it was he who ratified the documents of the Second Vatican Council and published the New Mass), it is quite interesting to note that in the very same month that Paul VI ratified Vatican II, Fr. Francis J. Connell explained the teaching of the peaceful and universal acceptance of a Pope, and applied it to Paul VI himself. The following is the Q&A from the December 1965 issue:

"**Question:** What certainty have we that the reigning Pontiff is actually the primate of the universal Church – that is, that he became a member of the Church through valid baptism, and that he was validly elected Pope?
Answer: Of course, we have human moral certainty that the reigning Pontiff was validly elected in conclave and accepted the office of Bishop of Rome, thus becoming head of the universal

---

[37] *The Church of Christ*, p. 290.
[38] Sedevacantist John Lane practically admits the same when he says: "Peaceful acceptance involves moral unanimity...Peaceful acceptance is rooted in the fact that the pope is the proximate rule of faith for the faithful, and therefore they cannot be mistaken about whom he is when they are (infallibly) taught by him." Comments take from http://www.sedevacantist.com.

Church. The unanimous consensus of a large group of Cardinals composing the electoral body gave us this assurance. And we also have human moral certainty that the reigning Pontiff was validly baptized, since there is a record to that effect in the baptismal register of the church in which the sacrament was administered. We have the same type of certainty that any bishop is the true spiritual head of the particular See over which he presides. This type of certainty excludes every prudent fear of the opposite.

But in the case of the Pope we have a higher grade of certainty – a certainty that excludes not merely the prudent fear of the opposite, but even the possible fear of the opposite. In other words, we have infallible certainty that the present Sovereign Pontiff [Paul VI] has been incorporated into the Church by a valid baptism and has been validly elected head of the universal Church. For if we did not have infallible assurance that the ruling Pontiff is truly in the eyes of God the chief teacher of the Church of Christ, how could we accept as infallibly true his solemn pronouncements? This is an example of a fact that is not contained in the deposit of revelation but is so intimately connected with revelation that it must be within the scope of the Church's magisterial authority to declare it infallibly. The whole Church, teaching and believing, declares and believes this fact, and from this it follows that this fact is infallibly true. We accept it with ecclesiastical – not divine – faith, based on the authority of the infallible Church."[39]

Based upon the Church's infallibility as it relates to dogmatic facts, Fr. Connell rightly explains that in the case of the Church's universal acceptance of a Pope, we not only *cannot* have "prudent fear of the opposite" (that he is not a true Pope), but cannot even have "*possible* fear of the opposite." In other words, it is not even *possible* to have any prudent, positive doubt that the validly elected Pope, accepted as such by the universal Church, is not a true Pope. This level of certainty is based upon the very infallibility of the Church, which cannot err on expounding dogma, nor judging facts which are necessary to believe the dogma. Hence, those Sedevacantists who deny the legitimacy of the post-conciliar Popes, who have been peacefully and universally accepted by the Church, are once again forced to deny the Church's attribute of infallibility - just as they are forced to deny the Church's attributes of visibility and indefectibility (as we saw in Chapter 1).

---

[39] *American Ecclesiastical Review*, vol. 153, Dec. 1965, p. 422 (emphasis added).

Controversy Over Pope Francis

In light of what we have learned regarding the theological certainty that a Pope who has been peacefully and universally accepted by the Church is, in fact, a legitimate Pope, we briefly address the controversy surrounding the unprecedented resignation of Pope Benedict XVI in February of 2013 (the first Pope to resign in 600 years) and the subsequent election of Argentinian Cardinal Jorge Bergoglio as Pope Francis. Without a doubt, many Catholics have questioned the propriety of these unexpected, nay shocking, events, and even whether the resignation and subsequent election are valid (thus, raising the question of whether there has been a peaceful and universal acceptance of Pope Francis). These questions have not come from fringe elements within the Church, but have been raised by some of the most prominent and respected journalists in Rome, such as Vittorio Messori and Antonio Socci. And the voices publicly questioning both the resignation and election have only increased as Francis' controversial papacy has progressed.

For example, Antonio Socci published an entire book titled *Non e' Francesco: La Chiesa Nella Grande Tempesta* (*It's Not Francis: The Church in a Great Tempest*) which challenges the canonical validity of Pope Benedict's resignation. There were also numerous stories suggesting that Pope Benedict was coerced into resigning following the "Vatileaks" scandal,[40] which, if true, could have rendered the resignation null.[41] Further questions were raised when Stefano Violi, esteemed Professor of Canon Law at the Faculty of Theology in Bologna and Lugano, published a study of Benedict's resignation in which he argues that Benedict did not, in fact, renounce the papal office (the *munus petrinus*), but only a portion of the active exercise of the

---

[40] Prior to the resignation of Pope Benedict, secret Vatican documents were leaked to the media, which revealed corruption, blackmail and homosexual conspiracies inside the Vatican (including a possible cover-up of the sexual crimes of the notorious Fr. Marcial Maciel Degollado, founder of the Legionaires of Christ). Investigation into the leak, which became known as "Vatileaks," resulted in a 300-page dossier, compiled by three Cardinals at the request of Pope Benedict. It was reported that this dossier was used to force Pope Benedict to resign the papal office. For example, following the papal resignation, *The Spectator* wrote: "The Italian newspaper *La Repubblica* has been publishing extraordinary claims that the 300-page Vatileaks dossier proves that Benedict was forced out by an 'underground gay network.'" (Gray, Freddy, "Sex, Lies and the Next Pope," *The Spectator*, March 2, 2013). After the resignation, the Vatileaks scandal and the 300-page dossier faded from the headlines and were not spoken of again.
[41] "A resignation made out of grave fear that is inflicted unjustly or out of malice, substantial error, or simony is invalid by the law itself" (canon 188, 1983 Code).

office (the *agendo et loquendo*).[42] To add to the controversy, following the resignation, Pope Benedict chose to retain his papal name and papal coat of arms, and continue to dress in the white papal cassock. He also wishes to be referred to as Pope (Pope Emeritus).[43] His trusted secretary, Don Georg Gänswein, even said that Benedict kept the title of "Pope" because "he considers that this title corresponds to reality."[44] Needless to say, this is an entirely unprecedented situation in the Church.

Coupled with the questions concerning the canonical validity of Pope Benedict's resignation, there have been added allegations of a conspiracy to elect Cardinal Bergoglio (Pope Francis). The conspiracy was first brought to light by Dr. Austen Ivereigh in his book *The Great Reformer*. After the book was published, the Belgian Cardinal, Godfried Danneels, admitted *publicly* to being part of what he called a secret "clerical mafia" (*The St. Gallen Group*), which conspired to push Benedict out and elect Bergoglio.[45] According to the laws established by John Paul II for papal elections, any secret pact or agreement which would *oblige* Cardinals to vote a certain way in a Papal election, carries an automatic excommunication,[46] although it would not necessarily invalidate the election.[47]

---

[42] See Siscoe, "In a Papal Diarchy, Which Half is Infallible," *The Remnant* newspaper, July 3, 2014; see also Ferrara, "Latest from Socci: The Papal Games," *The Remnant* newspaper, February 17, 2014.

[43] For more information, see Siscoe, Robert, "A Bishop Dressed in White," *The Remnant* newspaper, March 2013; Salza, John, "Who is the 'Bishop Dressed in White?,'" *Catholic Family News*, January 2015.

[44] See http://rorate-caeli.blogspot.com/2014/05/two-popes-has-papacy-become-diarchy.html.

[45] See Pentin, Edward, "Cardinal Danneels Admits to Being Part of 'Mafia' Club Opposed to Benedict XVI," *National Catholic Register*, September 24, 2015; also see the article with the same title by *Jeanne Smits, Lifesite News*.

[46] "The Cardinal electors shall further abstain from any form of pact, agreement, promise or other commitment of any kind which could oblige them to give or deny their vote to a person or persons. If this were in fact done, even under oath I decree that such a commitment shall be null and void and that no one shall be bound to observe it, and I hereby impose the penalty of excommunication *latae sententiae* upon those who violate this prohibition." John Paul II, *Universi Dominici Gregis*, No. 81, February 22, 1996.

[47] "No Cardinal elector can be excluded from active or passive voice in the election of the Supreme Pontiff, for any reason or pretext, with due regard for the provisions of No. 40 of this Constitution." (Ibid., No. 35). The legislation of Paul VI provides the same, and clarifies that the "any reason or pretext" includes excommunication: "No cardinal elector may be excluded from active and passive participation in the election of the Supreme Pontiff because of or on pretext of any excommunication, suspension, interdict or other ecclesiastical impediment. Any such censures are to be regarded as suspended as far as the effect of the election is concerned." (Paul VI, The Election Of The Roman Pontiff, No. 35, October 1, 1975).

The questions surrounding the allegedly coerced resignation of Pope Benedict and the conspiracy to elect Bergoglio has left many wondering if Francis is, in fact, the Pope, or if Pope Benedict has retained the papal office. Thus, in light of what we have just studied, some have questioned whether Pope Francis has been "peacefully and universally accepted" by the Church as Pope, since the controversial resignation and election call into question the "peaceful" aspect of Francis' acceptance, while the number of people (some openly and some secretly) who believe Benedict is still Pope raises questions concerning the "universal" aspect of Francis' acceptance. Indeed, whether there is or can be a "peaceful and universal acceptance" after such a controversial resignation and election is a legitimate question, and certainly puts a spotlight on the doctrine and how it would apply in this case. We mention this, not to argue that Francis is not Pope, but rather to point out that if the Church (a future Pope) were to declare Francis' election null, it would not violate the infallibility of the dogmatic fact that a Pope who *is* "peacefully and universally accepted" is, in fact, a true Pope.

We should also note, however, that just because a Pope has *not* been peacefully and universally accepted *does not mean he is not a true Pope*. This was the case during the Great Western Schism, when there was a true Pope reigning, even though he had not been accepted by the universal Church.[48] But in a case in which there is no peaceful and universal acceptance of an elected Pope, if the Church were to later nullify the election (e.g., by an act of deposition by an imperfect council, if the man were still living), this act would not infringe upon the Church's infallibility concerning dogmatic facts. Of course, any such determination could only be made by the proper authorities in the Church, and not by the exercise of the private judgment of individual Catholics.

Cum Ex Apostolatus Officio

Our analysis of this topic would not be complete without examining the papal Bull of Pope Paul IV, *Cum Ex Apostolatus Officio*, issued February 15, 1559, which is one of the favorite documents cited by Sedevacantist apologists in defense of their position. It is generally agreed that the purpose of the Bull was to prevent Cardinal Morone from being elected to the papacy. Pope Paul IV suspected Morone, a member of the humanist party, of being a heretic. In fact, Cardinal

---

[48] During this time the Church was divided over which of the two or three men claiming to be Pope was, in fact, the true Pope.

Pacheco wrote King Phillip II the day the Bull was issued, notifying him that it was aimed at Cardinal Morone.

After a brief opening paragraph, the Bull teaches that if a Roman Pontiff is found to have deviated from the Faith, he who is "judged by no one" can nevertheless be contradicted:

> "In assessing Our duty and the situation now prevailing, We have been weighed upon by the thought that a matter of this kind is so grave and so dangerous that <u>the Roman Pontiff</u>, who is the representative upon earth of God and our God and Lord Jesus Christ, who holds the fullness of power over peoples and kingdoms, who may judge all and be judged by none in this world, <u>may nonetheless be contradicted if he be found to have deviated from the Faith</u> (*possit, si deprehendatur a fide devius, redargui*). Remembering also that, where danger is greater, it must be more fully and more diligently counteracted."[49]

After teaching that it is licit to contradict a Roman Pontiff who has deviated from the faith *after* being elected, the Bull goes on to say that if a Bishop, Archbishop, Cardinal or even the Roman Pontiff himself, is found to have deviated from the faith *prior* to be being elected to office, his election is null and void:

> "if ever at any time it shall appear that any Bishop, even if he be acting as an Archbishop, Patriarch or Primate; or any Cardinal of the aforesaid Roman Church, or, as has already been mentioned, any legate, or even the Roman Pontiff, *prior* to his promotion or his elevation as Cardinal or Roman Pontiff, has deviated from the Catholic Faith or fallen into some heresy:
>
> (i) <u>the promotion or elevation, even if it shall have been uncontested and [accepted] by the unanimous assent of all the Cardinals, shall be null, void and worthless</u>."[50]

In light of this teaching, because the Sedevacantists *personally believe* the last six Popes deviated from the faith prior to their elections, they believe they are entirely justified in proclaiming their elections null, and then publicly declaring them to be antipopes. Our old friend Richard Ibranyi (who believes the past 102 Popes – *including Paul IV who issued Cum Ex Apostolatus* – have been false Popes), provides us

---

[49] Pope Paul IV, *Cum ex Apostolatus Officio*, February 15, 1559.
[50] Ibid.

with the Sedevacantist *interpretation* and *application* of the document in question.

In the following quotation, notice that Ibranyi's application of this document is rooted in Fr. Cekada's "sin of heresy against Divine Law" theory. Mr. Ibranyi begins by saying: "Even though Paul IV's Bull *Cum ex Apostolatus Officio* of 1559 is invalid and fallible because he was an apostate antipope, it nevertheless teaches the ordinary Magisterium dogma that all formal heretics, and hence <u>even secret ones</u>, cannot hold offices."

Then, after quoting the pertinent section of the *Cum Ex Apostolatus*, he writes:

> "<u>Therefore, even the **secret sin** of formal heresy bans one from holding offices in the Catholic Church</u>. Hence even if the so-called pope is unanimously elected, enthroned, and given 'universal obedience' and thus believed to be the pope by every Catholic in the world, he is not the pope if he has fallen into formal heresy."[51]

First, as we have amply demonstrated, the internal sin of heresy alone does not cause a prelate to lose his office, nor does it prevent one from acquiring office. If it did, Catholics would have absolutely no way of knowing which Popes and bishops of the past or present possessed jurisdiction, and which had secretly lost their office (or never acquired it in the first place) due to heresy.

Second, the judgment and determination that the one elected to the papacy fell into heresy, *prior* to his election, is not based upon the *private judgment* of individual Catholics, who *personally believe* a sin of heresy was committed before the election. The judgment would have to be rendered by the proper authorities before the election would be rendered null. As St. Thomas taught, a *public* judgment must come from the *public* authority. *Cum Ex Apostolatus* was a disciplinary decree that attached a retroactive penalty to one who was *authoritatively judged* by the Church (not by private individuals) to have deviated from the faith prior to their promotion or election.

This was confirmed by two canonists who lived at the time the Bull was issued. The canonist, Maurcus Antobius Borghesius, said "the Bull [*Cum Ex Apostolatus*] includes only those who were <u>caught, convicted or confessed to have fallen into heresy</u>."[52] The canonist, Antonio Massa,

---

[51] Ibranyi, "Banned from Office for Simony or Secret Formal Heresy," (February, 2013), at http://www.johnthebaptist.us/jbw_english/documents/articles/rjmi/tr31_banned_from_office_for_simony_heresy.pdf (emphasis added).
[52] Firpo, 1:235.

teaches the same: "The Bull of Pope Paul does not prescribe it in the manner of one having been discharged, <u>unless he being taken up in a crime either confessed of his own will or was convicted by others</u>" (*nec bulla Pauli pontificis modo defuncti id disponit, nisi ille in crimine deprehensus vel sponte confessus vel ab aliis convictus.*)[53] Without an authoritative judgment, the retroactive penalty would not occur. Put another way, the authoritative judgment is a *necessary condition* for the election to be rendered null.

Cum Ex Apostolatus: Neither Ex-Cathedra Nor Irrevocable

Not only have Sedevacantists failed to understand that the retroactive penalties listed in the Bull would only take effect upon a judgment by the proper authorities, but they've also failed to properly understand the nature of the document, imagining it to be an infallible *ex cathedra* decree, rather than merely a disciplinary document containing penal legislation. For example, a popular Sedevacantist website presented the following in their introduction to the papal Bull:

> "During the time of the Council of Trent Pope Paul IV issued his Apostolic Constitution *Cum Ex Apostolic (sic) Officio* of February 15, 1559. (…) <u>Because it deals with faith and morals and was issued *ex cathedra* (from the Chair of Peter) [it is] therefore considered not only infallible, but to be held in perpetuity</u>."[54]

The Sedevacantist, "Pope Michael" (elected "Pope" by six lay people, including himself and his parents), also claims that *Cum Ex Apostolatus* is infallible. In his book, *54 Years that Changed the World,* he wrote:

> "This Bull of Pope Paul IV deserves special consideration, especially in light of the fact that it has been ignored by many. … this Bull appears in the Fontes of the Code of Canon Law in several places. It is considered infallible because it teaches on a matter of Faith."[55]

---

[53] Firpo, 3.333.
[54] DailyCatholic.com at http://www.dailycatholic.org/cumexapo.htm.
[55] "Pope" Michael, *54 Years That Changed the Catholic Church: 1958-2012,* (CreateSpace Independent Publishing Platform, 2011), p. 33.

Mr. Ibranyi also attributed an infallible character to the document. The following was written before he discovered "conclusive evidence" that Pope Paul IV was an antipope:

> "In 1559 Paul IV in his *Bull Cum ex Apostolatus Officio* infallibly teaches that a so-called officeholder who is a formal heretic does not actually hold the office and thus all his acts are null and void even if everyone thinks he is an officeholder."[56]

The Sedevacantist website, Today's Catholic World, also declares *Cum Ex Apostolatus* to be an infallible *ex cathedra* document. In the unfortunate but common Sedevacantist tone, under the heading, "*Very Useful Idiots,*" the author writes:

> "The absolutely intellectually dishonest Phony Opposition false traditionalist groups, such as: the priestless SSPX, Una Voce, John Vennari's "Catholic" Family News, Michael Matt's (truly lost) Remnant etc., by willfully refusing to accept the Church's Ex Cathedra (Infallible) teaching of Cum ex Apostolatus Officio which unmistakenly [sic] condemns imposters like Ratzinger a.k.a Anti-Pope Benedict XVI …"[57]

As with all sophists, once one gets past their demagoguery, here riddled with inflammatory invective ("idiots," "dishonest," "false," "priestless," "lost," "imposters" – and all in one sentence!), one generally discovers the sheer barrenness of their argumentation, which seeks to appeal to the will, rather than the intellect. Not only does the author entirely mischaracterize the nature of the document (which was never intended to be an infallible decree), but reveals much about himself by cloaking his error in such demagoguery and insulting rhetoric.

During the debates surrounding the definition of papal infallibility, *Cum Ex Apostolatus Officio* was brought to light by the dissenters in an attempt to prevent the Church from defining the doctrine. Their mode of operation was thus: First, they attempted to attribute an infallible dogmatic character to the Bull. Next, they pointed to the various penal sanctions as being utterly tyrannical and contrary to Catholic principles. Finally, they argued that such tyrannical and unjust sanctions prove the Pope is not infallible.

---

[56] Ibranyi, "Putative Officeholders and Laws," December 2012, http://www.john thebaptist.us/jbw_english/documents/articles/rjmi/tr29_putative_officeholder_and_la ws.pdf.
[57] http://www.todayscatholicworld.com/jan09tcw.htm.

One of the main voices opposing the doctrine was that of Johann Joseph Ignaz von Döllinger, a fierce opponent of papal infallibility. In his famous book, *The Pope and the Council,* written under the pen-name Janus, Döllinger attempted to demonstrate the tyrannical and unjust character of *Cum Ex Apostolatus.* After listing a number of penal sanctions in the document, he wrote:

> "Such, then, is this most solemn declaration, issued as late as 1558, subscribed by the cardinals, and afterwards expressly confirmed and renewed by Pius V, that the Pope, by virtue of his absolute authority, can depose every monarch, hand over every country to foreign invasion, deprive every one of his property, and that without any legal formality, and not only on account of dissent from the doctrines approved at Rome, or separation from the Church, but for merely offering an asylum to such dissidents, so that no rights of dynasty or nation are respected, but nations are to be given up to all the horrors of a war of conquest. And to all this is finally subjoined the doctrine, that all official and sacramental acts of a Pope or Bishop, who has ever — say twenty or thirty years before — been heretically minded on any single point of doctrine, are null and void! This last definition contains so emphatic and flat a contradiction of the principles on the validity of sacraments universally received in the Church, although mistakes have sometimes been made about it at Rome, that they must have seemed to theologians utterly incomprehensible. The serious inconveniences which at former periods such doctrines had led to in the Church would have been reproduced now, had not even the most decided adherents of the infallibility theory, the Jesuit divines, shrunk from adopting the principle laid down by this Pope and his cardinals, though Paul IV threatened all who resisted his decrees with the wrath of God. Bellarmine himself, forty years later, said in Rome itself that a bishop or Pope did not lose his power by becoming or by having been a concealed (occult) heretic, or [else] everything would be reduced to uncertainty, and the whole Church thrown into confusion."[58]

Döllinger never accepted the dogma of papal infallibility and on April 18, 1871, one year after the close of the First Vatican Council, he was excommunicated by name for heresy; and although he never officially joined the schismatic Old Catholic Church, Döllinger's writings contributed greatly to its establishment.

---

[58] Janus, *The Pope and the Council,* (London, Oxford, Cambridge: Rivingtons, 1869), pp. 383-384.

In response to the arguments of Döllinger and company, the proponents of the dogma did not attempt to defend the Bull of Paul IV against accusations that the penalties were extreme, unjust, or harmful to the common good. Rather, they defended papal infallibility by noting that the Bull *was not a dogmatic decree* and, therefore, any problems with the document in no way undermined the infallibility of the Pope.

In an 1870 article that was published in *The Dublin Review*, the author confirmed that *Cum Ex Apostolatus* does indeed require careful consideration, due to the issues raised by Döllinger and company, but not because of any violation of infallibility, since, as he said: "there is literally no pretext for thinking that this Bull was dogmatic in any sense." He wrote:

> "The most formidable-looking of all Janus's citations [against papal infallibility] is Paul IV's Bull '*Cum ex Apostolatus officio*,' (p. 382): nor, indeed, do we at all deny that that Bull requires very careful consideration, though on totally different grounds from those alleged by Janus. But (...) There is literally no pretext for thinking that this Bull was dogmatic in any sense whatever: the only dogmatic statement which Janus quotes - that which he numbers '(1)' - so far from being defined in the Bull, comes in quite accidentally and parenthetically."[59]

Another authority confirming that *Cum Ex Apostolatus* is not an infallible *ex cathedra* decree is the Church historian, canonist, and first Cardinal-Prefect of the Vatican Archives, Dr. Joseph Hergenrother. In his 1876 book, *Catholic Church and Christian State*, he responds to the accusation of "Janus." In so doing, he readily concedes that the Bull "may be perhaps considered too severe, injudicious, and immoderate in its punishments," but he defends papal infallibility by explaining, in no uncertain terms, that the document is not an infallible decree, but only concerns penal sanctions. We cite the Cardinal at length:

> "Appeal is also made to the Bull of Paul IV., 'Cum ex apostolatus officio,' of 15th Feb. 1559,[60] to which our opponents are most eager to attach the character of a dogmatic ex-cathedra decision,[61] saying that if this Bull is not an universally binding

---

[59] Dublin Review, vol. XIV, New Series (London, Burns and Oats, January - April 1870), p. 204 (emphasis added).
[60] Lib. Sept. c. ix. de Haeret. v. 3. Raynald. a. 1559, n. 14, M. Bull. i. 840. Sentis, Lib. Septimus, v. 5, 23, p. 164 (citation in original).
[61] Janus, p. 405 seq. Schulte, ii. 12 (citation in original).

doctrinal decree (on the point of the Papal authority), no single Papal decree can claim to be such.[62] But none of the exponents of dogmatic theology have as yet discovered this character in the Bull,[63] which has been universally regarded as an emanation of the spiritual penal authority, not a decision of the doctrinal authority.[64] We see the tactics of the Church's opponents have been reversed: formerly the Jansenists and lawyers of the French parliament denied that the Bull 'Unigenitus' was dogmatic, though all Catholic theologians regarded it as such; now the Janus [i.e., Döllinger] party and jurists who protest against the Vatican Council assert that the Bull of Paul IV is dogmatic, though all Catholic theologians deny it to be such. In truth, neither the wording of this last-named Bull, nor its contents as a whole, nor the rules universally received among theologians, allow it to be regarded as a dogmatic decision. If there is to be a doctrinal decree binding on all, it is requisite that a [particular] doctrine to be held, or proposition to be rejected, be placed before the faithful in terms implying obligation, and be prescribed by the full authority of the Church's teaching office. This is not the case with this Bull.

True enough in the introduction the Papal power is spoken of, and in accordance with the view of it held universally in the Middle Ages. But here, as in every other Bull, the rule already spoken of holds good, that not the introduction and the reasons alleged, but simply and only the enjoining (dispositive) portion, the decision itself, has binding force. Introductions quite similar are to be found in laws relating purely to matters of discipline, as any one may see who consults the Bullarium.[65] As to the enjoining portion of the Bull in question, it only contains penal sanctions against heresy, which unquestionably belong to disciplinary laws alone."[66]

---

[62] Huber, p. 47 (citation in original).

[63] Professor Denzinger has collected all dogmatic decisions in his *Enchiridion Definitionum*, which since 1853 has gone through four editions, been recommended by many bishops, and much praised by the Holy Father. No theological reviewer in all of Christendom has complained of the omission of the Bull in question; all would much rather have considered a demand for its insertion ridiculous (citation in original).

[64] Dr. Fessler, p. 44. *Cf.* Anti-Janus, p. 168 seq. Votum on the Vatican Council, Mainz, 1871, p. 45 seq. (citation in original).

[65] E.g., Urban VIII. Const. 12, d. 7, Mart. 1624 (Bull. ed. Lux. t. v. p. 40): "*Romanus pontifex, in quo dispositione incommutabili divina providentia universalis Ecclesiae constituit principatum, auctoritatem a Christo per B. Petrum Apostolorum culmen sibi traditam intelligens, ut noxia evellat, et destruat, utiliaque plantet et aedificet,*" &c. The entire Bull relates to the Constitutions of the Fratres Reformati strictioris observantiae Ordinis S. Francisci. Similarly, Const. 64 d. 6 Feb. 1626, relating to the abolition of a congregation of Franciscans (ib. p. 119, § 1) (citation in original).

[66] Cardinal Hergenrother, *Catholic Church and the Christian State*, vol. I (London: Burns and Oats, 1876), p. 42.

Cardinal Hergenrother goes on to explain that *Cum Ex Apostolatus* was simply renewing earlier penal sanctions against heresy and adding *new penalties* which, by their very nature, are disciplinary:

> "(...) Paul IV renews the earlier censures and penal laws, which his predecessors, acting in concert with the emperors, had issued against various heresies; he desires that they be observed everywhere, and put in force where they have been unenforced.[67] The point, then, is about the practical execution of previous penal laws, which by their nature are disciplinary, and proceed not from divine revelation, but from the ecclesiastical and civil penal authority. Besides the renewal of old there is an addition of new punishments,[68] which equally belongs to the sphere of discipline. (...)
>
> The Pope does not here speak as teacher (*ex cathedra*), but as the watchful shepherd eager to keep the wolves from the sheep, [69]and in a time when the actual or imminent falling away even of bishops and cardinals[70] demanded the greatest watchfulness and the strongest measures. The Bull of Paul IV may be perhaps considered too severe, injudicious, and immoderate in its punishments, but it certainly cannot be considered an *ex cathedra* doctrinal decision. No Catholic theologian has considered it as such, or placed it in a collection of dogmatic decisions; and to have done so would have only deserved ridicule; for if this Bull is to be considered as a doctrinal decision, so must every ecclesiastical penal law. Papal Infallibility, it is most true, excludes any error as to moral teaching, so that the Pope can never [definitively[declare anything morally bad to be good, and vice versa; but infallibility only relates to moral precepts, to the general principles which the

---

[67] "*Omnes et singulas excommunicationis, suspensionis, et interdicti ac privationis et quasvis alias sententias, censuras, et poenas .... contra haereticos aut schismaticos quomodolibet latas et promulgatas apostolica auctoritate approbamus et innovamus ac perpetuo observari et in viridi observantia, si forsan in ea non sint, reponi et esse debere, nec non quoscunque .... (haereticos cujuscunque status) censuras et poenas praedictas incurrere volumus atque decernimus*" (citation in original).

[68] E.g., loss ipso facto of all offices and dignities, incapacity to hold others, confiscation of goods, etc (citation in original).

[69] Paul IV nowhere in the Bull calls himself "doctor"; he acts "*more vigilis pastoris, pro munere pastorali vulpes vineam Domini demoliri satagentes capere et lupos ab ovibus arcere*" (§ 1) (citation in original).

[70] As Bishop Victor of Bergamo (Raynald. a. 1558, n. 20), Bishop Jacob of Nevers (ib. a. 1559, n. 13), Archbishop Bartholomew (ib. a. 1560, n. 22), the Bishop of Nantes (ib. n. 35), Cardinal Chatillon Bishop of Beauvais (ib. a. 1561, n. 86), &c. *Cf.* the Brief of Paul IV against the bishops suspected of heresy, ib. a. 1559, n. 19: "*Cum sicut nuper*" (citation in original).

Pope prescribes to all Christians as a rule of conduct, not to the application of these principles to individual cases,[71] and thus by no means excludes the possibility of the Pope making mistakes in his government by too great severity or otherwise. (...)[72]

One of the potential problems with the penal sanctions enunciated in the Bull (which Cardinal Hergenrother said could be considered "severe," "injudicious" and immoderate") is that it could be interpreted by some to imply that a Pope could be peacefully and universally accepted by the Church, and then later declared to have never been validly elected, *which is not possible*.[73] Although the document does not explicitly teach this,[74] some Sedevacantists have interpreted it in this fashion and ended by denying the teaching regarding the peaceful and universal acceptance of a Pope. The problematic wording (which has led these Sedevacantists into error) is another clue as to the fallible, disciplinary nature of the now-defunct document.

Continuing with his commentary on *Cum Ex Apostolatus*, Cardinal Hergenrother responded to those who opposed papal infallibility by asserting that, if the Pope was really infallible, the document should have been covered by infallibility since it was directed to the entire

---

[71] *cf.* Suarez, *de Fide*, disp. 5, § 8, n. 7. Also Schaetzler, Die Papstliche Unfehlbarkeit, Freiburg, 1870, p. 197; and Merkle in the Augsburg Pastoralblatt, 11 Feb. 1871, pp. 47-50. (Citation in original).

[72] Cardinal Hergenrother, *Catholic Church and the Christian State*, pp. 42-43.

[73] In light of the earlier teaching about the "peaceful and universal acceptance" of a Pope, it could never happen that the election of a Pope, who was accepted peacefully and universally by the entire Church (not simply elected by the unanimous consent of the Cardinals), would later be rendered null, since, as we saw, the peaceful and universal acceptance of a Pope provides *infallible certitude* of his legitimacy, as well as all of the *conditions* required for legitimacy. The election or promotion of a bishop or Cardinal would not have the same guarantee, but such a guarantee does exist with a Pope. This means that if a papal election were ever rendered null after the fact (which some claim happened at the 1903 Conclave, when the Bishop of Kraków allegedly vetoed the election of Cardinal Mariano Rampolla, paving the way for the election of St. Pius X), during the time intervening between the election and the declaration rendering the election null, the Pope would not have been accepted peacefully and universally by the Church. Either his election (following a questionable resignation of a former Pope, for example) would be doubted by the faithful, or he would be doubtful for other reasons. Once thing is certain: it has never occurred, and will never occur, that a Pope who was peacefully and universally accepted by the entire Church, was later declared to have never been Pope due to a defect in the election.

[74] The document speaks of the Pope being elected by a "unanimous assent of all *the Cardinals*," and then to "the obedience accorded to such [the elect] by all." Neither of these fallible statements directly contradicts the teaching that a Pope who is peacefully and universally accepted by the Church is, in fact, a legitimate Pope.

Church (*ex cathedra*), and was published in solemn form. The Cardinal responded as follows:

> "But it is said: 'This Bull is directed to the whole Church, is subscribed by the Cardinals, and thus has been published in the most solemn form, and is certainly *ex cathedra*.'[75] <u>These characteristics, however, do not suffice for a dogmatic doctrinal decision.</u> ... The sort of proofs our opponents bring forward in this matter show an entire ignorance of Papal Bulls.[76] Compare, for example, another Bull of the same Pope directed against the ambitious endeavours of those who coveted the Papal dignity;[77] this Bull has equally the agreement of the Cardinals, is published out of the plenitude of the Papal power, is declared to be forever in force, threatens equally all spiritual and temporal dignitaries without exception, etc. And yet it is undoubtedly not in the least a dogmatic Bull."[78]

As the Cardinal explained above, just because a Magisterial document issued by a Pope teaches that it is to remain in force in perpetuity (*constitutio in perpetuum valitura*) does not necessarily mean it cannot be abrogated by a future Pope. It depends upon the *nature* of the decree (doctrinal versus disciplinary). According to the ancient principle "equals do not have power over equals" (*par in parem potestatem non habet*), a Pope cannot bind a future Pope to merely disciplinary matters and ecclesiastical governance. A Pope cannot change Catholic doctrine, or abrogate a defined dogma, but he can alter disciplines, such as the punishment for certain crimes.

We provide one final reference to confirm that *Cum Ex Apostolatus* is not an *ex cathedra*, irreformable decree, but only punitive legislation. In his book *True and False Infallibility of the Pope*, Bishop Joseph Fessler, the secretary of the First Vatican Council, responded to the argument of Professor von Schulte, another opponent of papal infallibility who used *Cum Ex Apostolatus* as his weapon of choice. Bishop Fessler wrote:

---

[75] Schulte, i. p. 34, n. 1 (citation in original).

[76] See my review of Schulte in the Archiv fur Kirchenrecht, 1871. vol. xxv. p. cxxix. § 17; also Fessler, I.e. p. 82 seq. (citation in original).

[77] Cap. i. *Cum secundum Apostolum*. 1. v. 10, *de Ambitu* in lib. vii. *Decret* (citation in original).

[78] Cardinal Hergenrother, *Catholic Church and the Christian State*, Vol I (London: Burns and Oats, 1876), pp. 44-45.

"Dr. Schulte proceeds with another Bull of Pope Paul IV [*Cum ex Apostolatus*], issued in the year 1559,[79] which is rightly described in the collection of Papal Bulls under the title of 'Renewal of previous censures and punishments against heretics and schismatics, with the addition of further penalties.' Why, the very title, which gives a true account of its contents, is of itself alone enough to show everyone who reads it, that this Papal delivery is not a definition *de fide*, and cannot, therefore, be an utterance *ex cathedra*. (…) it is beyond all question certain, that this Bull is not a definition of faith or morals, not an utterance *ex cathedra*. It is simply an outcome of the supreme Papal authority as legislator, and an instance of his exercising his power of punishing; it is not done in the exercise of his power as supreme teacher."[80]

In light of what we have seen, it is "beyond all question" that *Cum Ex Apostolatus* is not an *ex cathedra* and therefore irreformable decree, as some Sedevacantists have claimed, but is instead a document of penal legislation which, by its very nature, is only disciplinary. In fact, after a thorough study of *Cum Ex Apostolatus*, which included some of the above-cited quotations, one Sedevacantist was forced to concede this point. He wrote:

"Pope Paul IV's 1559 Bull, *Cum ex Apostolatus officio*, is often cited by many Catholics today for its significance in regard to the current crisis of the Church. Some of us have believed this to be an infallible document, and have used that point to add force to our [Sedevacantist] arguments. At other times we have, in thinking the Bull was infallible, declared as heretics those who seem to contradict the Bull. Although this papal bull is certainly significant for our times, we would be entirely mistaken and in error to refer to the Bull as infallible or dogmatic. *Cum ex Apostolatus Officio* is not infallible, nor dogmatic, but merely a disciplinary statute."[81]

After citing a number of reputable authorities confirming that the Bull was not infallible, the Sedevacantist author concluded:

---

[79] Vide the Bull *Cum Ex Aposlolalus*, in the Bullar. Rom., ed. cit. t. iv. p i. p. 354. "*Innovatio quarumcumque censurarum et poenarum contra haereticos et schismaticos,*" etc. (citation in original).

[80] Fessler, *The True and False Infallibility of the Popes* (New York: The Catholic Publication Society, No. 9, Warren Street, 1875), pp. 88-89.

[81] Christopher Conlon, "The Non-Infallibility of Cum Ex Apostolatus Officio," (2013). https://www.archive.org/details/TheNon-InfallibilityOfCumExApos latusOfficio.

"Some of the greatest Catholic experts on the subject have made it clear that *Cum ex Apostolatus officio* is not infallible, while the only persons of any standing who have considered it to be infallible have been excommunicated and opposed by the Church. The Catholic experts state that it is beyond certain that the Bull is not infallible, and that it is a ridiculous and enormous blunder to consider it to be such. In light of this information, we [Sedevacantists] are obliged to discontinue referring to *Cum ex Apostolatus officio* as infallible. Not only would it be very deceptive and dishonest to erroneously refer to the Bull as infallible, but such an erroneous statement greatly damages the argument we are trying to make, along with our overall credibility on religious matters."[82]

Now, since *Cum Ex Apostolatus* was only concerned with "the practical execution of previous penal laws, which by their nature are disciplinary," as Cardinal Hergenrother explained, its penalties could be, and indeed were, abrogated when the 1917 Code of Canon law came into force. Canon 5.2 explains:

"That which pertains to penalties, of which there is no mention made in this Code, be they spiritual or temporal, remedial or, as they call it, punitive, automatic or declared through a judgment, they are to be held as abrogated."

None of the prescriptions contained in *Cum Ex Apostolatus Officio* were included in the 1917 Code, and consequently they were all officially and authoritatively abrogated.

The Sedevacantist bishop, Donald Sanborn, also acknowledges the papal Bull is no longer in force. He further acknowledges that, as we explained above, the heretical prelate would have to be recognized as a heretic *by the law of the Church* (by the Church's judgment), and not simply by private judgment. Bishop Sanborn wrote:

"Cum ex apostolatus is an apostolic constitution, a law, made by Pope Paul IV, which says that if a pope should be a heretic, his elevation to this dignity would be null. It was made in order to ensure that no Protestant could ever become the Pope. It does not apply to the present case for two reasons. The first is that it is no longer the law. It was derogated (made obsolete) by the 1917 Code of Canon Law. The second reason, and the more important, is that even if it should for some cause still have force, it could only apply to Ratzinger if he were legally recognized as a public heretic. But,

---

[82] Ibid (emphasis added).

as we have seen, there is no legal condemnation of Ratzinger. <u>Before the law of the Church he does not have the status of heretic</u> because (1) he himself does not hold himself guilty of heresy, and (2) no legitimate superior holds him guilty of heresy."[83]

Cum Ex Apostolatus and Canon 188, §4

Faced with the proof that *Cum Ex Apostolatus* was abrogated when the 1917 Code came into force, some Sedevacantists will argue that its penal legislation was based, not merely on Church law, but on *Divine law,* and therefore remains in force. They will then point to the fact that *Cum Ex Apostolatus* is referenced as a footnote to canon 188, §4 (1917 Code), and then claim that this proves its automatic penalties are still in effect. This argument is erroneous for the following reasons.

First, there is no Divine Law (nor has there even been an ecclesiastical law) teaching that a prelate who is judged, by private judgment, to be a heretic automatically loses his office.

Second, as we have seen, canon 188, §4 applies to clerics validly elected to office, who publicly defect from the Faith by joining a non-Catholic sect *after* being elected, whereas the penalties contained in *Cum Ex Apostolatus* render null an election if it is shown that the cleric deviated from the faith *before* being elected. *Cum Ex* does not decree that a validly elected cleric who later "deviates from the faith" automatically loses office. So the *penalties* contained in *Cum Ex Apostolatus* and canon 188, §4 are clearly not the same.

Third, footnotes are not part of the Church's law (they have no authority in themselves), and are often cited (by editors) to show legislative history related to certain canons. As applied here, the footnote to *Cum Ex Apostolatus* is nothing more than a reference to prior *legislation* which prevented certain clerics from holding office in the Church. It's purpose is to simply provide some legislative precedent for the current legislation, not to affirm a mythical "Divine law" that prevents heretics from holding office based upon individual private judgment.[84]

Fourth, to further prove the foregoing point, it is certainly *not* a matter of Divine law that a person, who had once deviated from the faith, would be prevented from later being elevated to the office of bishop or Cardinal. For example, the great Cardinal Manning not only

---

[83] Bishop Sanborn, "Explanation Of The Thesis Of Bishop Guérard Des Lauriers," June 29, 2002.
[84] See, for example, Fr. Albert, O.P., "La Constitution Apostolique Cum ex Apostolatus de Paul IV," Le Sel de la Terre, No. 33.

deviated from the faith he received at baptism, but he went so far as to become a pseudo-bishop of the Anglican sect. Yet, in spite of this public defection, he was later received into the Church *and allowed to be raised to the office of bishop and then Cardinal*. This elevation to one of the highest offices in the Church occurred in spite of irrefutable *proof* that he had deviated from the faith *prior* to his elevation. If one claims that Paul IV's prohibition from being elevated to the office of bishop or Cardinal does not apply to those who deviate from the faith and then later convert, they will have to point to the section of *Cum Ex* mentioning this exception. Yet the section containing this exception will not be found, because it does not exist (and, because it would be disciplinary, it would still have been abrogated by the 1917 Code). In fact, this was one of the objections Döllinger raised against the document. He wrote:

> "And to all this is finally subjoined the doctrine, that all official and sacramental acts of a Pope or Bishop, who has ever - say twenty or thirty years before - been heretically minded on any single point of doctrine, are null and void!"[85]

The penal sanctions of *Cum Ex* make no exception for a person who deviated from the faith and then later renounced his error. The Bull simply states that the election of one who had previously deviated from the faith, or previously embraced a heresy, is null and void. Now, if Sedevacantists are going to argue that the penal sanctions in this Bull are still in force today, and that they take effect without an authoritative judgment by the proper authorities, they will have to explain how Cardinal Manning was elevated to bishop and then Cardinal during the reign of Pius IX, in the face of *irrefutable proof* that he had "deviated from the faith" prior to his election. The truth of the matter is that the penal sanctions in *Cum Ex Apostolatus* were never enforced, and consequently the legislation had slipped into obsolescence, even before it was abrogated when the 1917 Code of Canon law was enacted. The case of Cardinal Manning proves that someone who publicly defects from the Faith, is not barred by "Divine law" from being elevated to the episcopacy (or the papacy) at a later date.

It is interesting to note that the opponents of papal infallibility unearthed the Bull *Cum Ex Apostolatus* over a century ago (which had all but disappeared from the mind of the Church), in order to argue against the infallibility of the Pope, and then used the contents of the

---

[85] Janus, *The Pope and the Council*, pp. 383-384.

Bull to justify their separation from the Church. In our day, the exact same document – now legally defunct and thus void of any authority - has again resurfaced. This time it serves as the weapon of choice for the Sedevacantists, who use its contents, not to deny a particular charism of the Pope, but to reject the Pope himself and justify their *formal* separation from him, which, needless to say, places their souls in grave jeopardy.[86]

---

[86] In the Bull of Pope Boniface VIII, *Unam Sanctam*, promulgated November 18, 1302, the following was defined as a dogma of faith: "We declare, we proclaim, we define that it is absolutely necessary for salvation that every human creature be subject to the Roman Pontiff."

Chapter 13

~ Vatican II and Conciliar Infallibility ~

The adherents of the Sedevacantist thesis defend their position in two different ways, one of which corresponds to the realm of being, and the other to the realm of acting. Regarding the former, the Sedevacantists claim that the recent Popes have been heretics (in the realm of being) and therefore could not be validly elected, or, if they were elected validly, could not become[1] or remain Pope (because, they maintain, it is metaphysically impossible for a heretic to possess habitual jurisdiction in the Church). This aspect of Sedevacantism was addressed in the previous chapters.

In this chapter, we now switch gears and address the Sedevacantist arguments which concern the realm of acting. With this approach, Sedevacantists point to certain things that have apparently issued forth from the Church over the past 50 years, which they insist are contrary to the Church's infallibility. Since these acts are said to be a violation of the infallibility promised by Christ to His Church, they maintain that the Church from which they issued could not have been the true Church, and, consequently, its head could not have been a true Pope.

As one can see, this argument extends beyond the *person* of the Pope to encompass the entire *Ecclesia Docens*, or teaching hierarchy of the Church. According to this theory, there is not simply "a diabolical disorientation" of the upper hierarchy, as Sister Lucia of Fatima described it, but a complete defection of the upper hierarchy; not an infiltration and subversion of the Church by Freemasons and Communists, resulting in a corruption of its human element (which is undergoing a Passion similar to that which Christ endured), but the complete destruction of the visible Church which, in their opinion, has been replaced by a New Church.

In the following chapters, we will address the arguments corresponding to the realm of acting, and demonstrate that Christ's promise of infallibility has not been violated. We will demonstrate that the current ecclesiastical crisis is not "impossible"[2] as Sedevacantists claim, but rather a trial permitted by God to sift the wheat from the chaff. The current crisis also provides the faithful with an opportunity

---

[1] As we saw, according to the thesis of Bishop Guérard des Lauriers, he would only become a "materal Pope," not a "formal Pope."

[2] See John Daly, "The Impossible Crisis," *Four Marks*, April 2009. http://www.the fourmarks.com/articles.htm#crisis.

to secure their Election by demonstrating their fidelity to Christ and
His Church, according to the words of St. Peter, who said: "Wherefore,
brethren, labour the more, that by good works you may make sure
your calling and election" (2Pet. 1:10). While the current crisis is indeed
a faith-shaking trial - a trial that may even be approaching the limits of
what Providence will permit at this moment in history – it has not
violated a single promise of Jesus Christ.[3]

The Council

Their argument begins with the assertion that the Second Vatican
Council could not have come from the true Church. They maintain that
Vatican II met the conditions for conciliar infallibility, and therefore, if
it was truly a council of Christ's Church, it should have been free from
all error. But the documents of Vatican II contain errors, they say,
therefore it could not have been a council of the Catholic Church
overseen by true Pope. In other words, they claim that the errors of
Vatican II prove that Paul VI was not a true Pope, since infallibility
would have prevented a true Pope from ratifying such documents. For
example, Peter Dimond wrote:

> "We have exposed in detail the heresies of Vatican II. We have
> also shown that the men who implemented this non-Catholic
> Council were not true popes of the Catholic Church, but antipopes.
> Despite all of the evidence, some people remain unconvinced. They
> hold that there are indeed doctrinal problems with Vatican II; but,
> according to them, this is no problem for Paul VI because he did not
> infallibly promulgate any of the Vatican II heresies. 'The heresies
> of Vatican II don't matter,' they say, 'because Vatican II was not
> infallible!' We will now show that <u>if Paul VI had been a true pope,</u>
> <u>the documents of Vatican II would have been promulgated</u>

---

[3] Unless the conditional chastisement revealed in the Third Secret of Fatima soon befalls
us (which is certainly possible), the authors speculate that the crisis is *not* yet
approaching the limits of what God may ultimately permit. Pope Francis has caused
more harm to the Faith than his predecessors through his use of the media, but Paul VI
and John Paul II wrought their damage more in an *official* teaching capacity. Further,
traditional Catholicism is in a better place today than it was during the reign of Paul VI
and John Paul II (e.g., there are more traditional Masses and vocations; the S.S.P.X.
bishops are no longer excommunicated, the S.S.P.X. priests have been granted ordinary
jurisdiction to hear confessions directly by the Pope during the Year of Mercy, etc.).
Moreover, based upon many prophecies, the Church in the end times will undergo a
much greater trial of faith than we see today.

infalli̲b̲l̲y̲.̲ ̲T̲h̲i̲s̲ ̲w̲i̲l̲l̲ ̲p̲r̲o̲v̲e̲,̲ ̲a̲g̲a̲i̲n̲,̲ ̲t̲h̲a̲t̲ ̲P̲a̲u̲l̲ ̲V̲I̲ ̲.̲.̲.̲ ̲w̲a̲s̲ ̲n̲o̲t̲ ̲a̲n̲d̲ ̲c̲o̲u̲l̲d̲ ̲n̲o̲t̲ ̲h̲a̲v̲e̲ ̲b̲e̲e̲n̲ ̲a̲ ̲t̲r̲u̲e̲ ̲p̲o̲p̲e̲.̲"[4]

His fellow Sedevacantist comrade, John Daly, agrees. He wrote:

> "The truth is that Vatican II so plainly fulfils the *conditions* required for infallibility that not even Paul VI ever dared to deny this. Hence if its teaching contains egregious errors against the faith, this fact necessarily calls into question the papal status of Paul VI himself."[5]

Before proceeding with a critique of this Sedevacantist argument, note that it is not our intention to defend the orthodoxy of the conciliar documents, which we also believe are replete with poorly formulated and ambiguous assertions which lend themselves to erroneous and possibly even heretical interpretations. We wish only to demonstrate that Vatican II did not meet the conditions for infallibility. When the Church does not exercise her infallible teaching authority (which was the case during Vatican II), error is *possible*. Therefore, any errors contained within the conciliar documents do not constitute a violation of the Church's infallibility.

Conditions for Conciliar Infallibility

As we will further explain in the next chapter, the Church teaches infallibly either by the Extraordinary Magisterium, or the Ordinary and Universal Magisterium. In layman's terms, the Extraordinary Magisterium is exercised either by a solemn papal decree (called an *ex cathedra* or "from the chair" statement), or a dogmatic *definition* of revealed truth concerning faith or morals emanating from an ecumenical council (a rare gathering of the world's bishops in union with the Pope). This latter mode of infallibility is called "conciliar infallibility." In his classic book, *The Church of Christ*, Fr. Berry lists the three conditions required for conciliar infallibility:

> "Certain conditions are necessary for the exercise of infallible teaching authority by the bishops assembled in council, namely: a) the council must be summoned by the Roman Pontiff, or at least with his consent and approval... b) The council must be truly

---

[4] Dimond, *The Truth About What Really Happened to the Catholic Church After Vatican II* (Most Holy Family Monastery, 2007), p. 469 (emphasis added).
[5] Daly, "Did Vatican II Teach Infallibly?," Second Revised Edition, 2014 (emphasis added). http://www.novusordowatch.org/vatican-ii-infallible.htm.

ecumenical by celebration, i.e., the whole body of bishops must be represented. ... c) <u>Bishops assembled in a council are infallible only when exercising supreme authority as teachers of faith or morals by a definite and irrevocable decree that a doctrine is *revealed*</u>, and, therefore, to be accepted by every member of the Church. But since the bishops need not intend such an irrevocable decision at all times [during the Council], <u>it is necessary that an infallible definition be so worded as to indicate clearly its definitive character.</u>"[6]

Now, Vatican II met the first two conditions for conciliar infallibility, since it was (a) summoned by the Pope, and (b) truly ecumenical by celebration. But it did not meet the third condition, since the council proposed no *revealed truths* for belief "by a definite and irrevocable degree... so worded as to indicate clearly its definitive character." On the contrary, Paul VI himself explicitly stated that Vatican II intentionally *avoided* defining any doctrines. During a General Audience on December 1, 1966, Paul VI said:

"There are those who ask what authority, what theological qualification, the Council intended to give to its teachings, knowing that it <u>avoided issuing solemn dogmatic definitions backed by the Church's infallible teaching authority.</u> The answer is known by those who remember the conciliar declaration of March 6, 1964, repeated on November 16, 1964. In view of the pastoral nature of the Council, <u>it avoided proclaiming in an extraordinary manner any dogmas carrying the mark of infallibility.</u>"[7]

Although Vatican II was an ecumenical council, by deliberately *avoiding* defining any dogmas, one of the conditions for conciliar infallibility was clearly lacking, which means infallibility was not engaged during the Council. This fact necessarily *permits* the possibility of error in the texts of Vatican II. To claim otherwise is to extend Conciliar infallibility beyond its proper limits (which is precisely what the Sedevacantists have done).

One year after the close of the council, Cardinal Heenan commented on the *purpose* of the Second Vatican Council. He explained the council "deliberately limited its own objectives. There were to be no

---

[6] *The Church of Christ,* pp. 260-261 (emphasis added).
[7] Paul VI, General Audience December 1, 1966 published in *L'Osservatore Romano,* January 21, 1966. Paul VI also said "the Council...is a pastoral one" (Discourse at the Opening of the Second Session, September 29, 1963) and refers to "the pastoral character of this Council" (Letter to Cardinal Tisserant, September 9, 1963). John XXIII also said the Council is "predominantly pastoral in character" (Opening Address, October 11, 1962).

specific definitions. Its *purpose* from the first was pastoral renewal within the Church..."[8]

Since the express *purpose* of Vatican II was to be merely pastoral (and not to define revealed doctrine), it falls into a different category than the previous general councils of the Church. Paul VI himself explained this during a General Audience in 1975, when he said: "*differing from other Councils*, this one was not directly dogmatic but doctrinal and pastoral."[9] In 1988, during an address to the Chilean Bishops, the future Pope Benedict XVI, as Cardinal Ratzinger, complained that Vatican II was being treated as a "super-dogma" and admitted that, in reality, it defined no dogmas at all, and instead remained on the modest level, as a "merely pastoral [non-dogmatic] council." He said:

> "The Second Vatican Council has not been treated as a part of the entire living Tradition of the Church, but as an end of Tradition, a new start from zero. <u>The truth is that this particular Council defined no dogma at all, and deliberately chose to remain on a modest level, as a merely pastoral council</u>; and yet many treat it as though it had made itself into a sort of super-dogma which takes away the importance of all the rest."[10]

In an article titled *The Limits of Infallibility*, published in *The Tablet* in 1967, Bishop Butler from England said: "Not all teachings emanating from a pope or an Ecumenical Council are infallible. There is no single proposition of Vatican II - except where it is citing previous infallible definitions - which is in itself infallible."[11] One year later, in an article titled *Responsibility and Freedom,* published in the same periodical, the bishop again affirmed that Vatican II defined no dogmas: He wrote:

> "[C]ouncils normally define doctrines and promulgate laws. The first of them all, the first Council of Nicea, did both these things. It defined that the Son of God is of one substance with His Father, and it issued practical instructions which are today regarded as the first elements of Canon Law. (...) <u>Vatican II gave us no new dogmatic definitions,</u> and on the whole it preferred to leave legislation to other organs of the Church."[12]

---

[8] Heenan, *Council and Clergy*, (London: G. Chapman, 1966), p. 7.
[9] Paul VI, "Weekly General Audience, "August 6, 1975.
[10] Cardinal Ratzinger, Address to Chilean Bishops, July 13, 1988.
[11] *The Tablet*, November 25, 1967, vol. 221, No. 6653, p. 4.
[12] Ibid., March 2, 1968, vol. 222, No. 6667, p. 7.

The quotations could be multiplied, but what is clear is that Vatican II, although it was an extraordinary gathering of the world's bishops with the Pope, did not define, *and did not intend to define,* any doctrines. This means that Vatican II did not meet the conditions for conciliar infallibility. [13] Because infallibility was not engaged during the Council, it follows that errors in its formulations was *possible,* and not "impossible," as Sedevacantists claim.

It is also crucial to note that even if an ecumenical council *does* define doctrines (which was always the case until Vatican II), infallibility does not cover the entire document in which the definition is contained, but only the *specific definition* contained therein. In the article on infallibility written for the 1913 *Catholic Encyclopedia,* P. J. Toner explains that before giving the *assent of Faith,* "the believer has a right to be certain that the teaching in question is *definitive* (since only definitive teaching is infallible)," and then adds:

> "It need only be added here that not everything in a conciliar or papal pronouncement, in which some doctrine is defined, is to be treated as definitive and infallible. For example, in the lengthy Bull of Pius IX defining the Immaculate Conception the strictly definitive and infallible portion is comprised in a sentence or two; and the same is true in many cases in regard to conciliar decisions. The merely argumentative and justificatory statements embodied in definitive judgments, however true and authoritative they may be, are not covered by the guarantee of infallibility which attaches to the strictly definitive sentences — unless, indeed, their infallibility has been previously or subsequently established by an independent decision." [14]

Msgr. Van Noort also teaches that in the dogmatic decrees in which doctrines are defined, it is only the definitions themselves that are protected by the Church's infallibility. For this reason, the definitions alone require the *assent of faith* (as opposed to a lesser degree of assent, as will be explained later):

> "Finally, please note the term *definitions.* In the very dogmatic decrees issued by councils and popes it often happens that matters

---

[13] When Vatican II reaffirmed previously defined teachings (e.g., Divinity of Christ, the Trinity, etc.), it did not engage the Church's infallibility, but merely restated what had already been infallibly taught either by a solemn act of the Extraordinary Magisterium, or by the constant teaching of the Ordinary and Universal Magisterium, or both. The charism of infallibility itself was never engaged during Vatican II.

[14] *Catholic Encyclopedia* (1913), vol. VII, p. 800 (emphasis added).

are mentioned which are by no means meant to be defined... No assent of faith is exacted for such matters."[15]

In the following citation, Fr. Berry quotes St. Bellarmine's teaching that not everything contained in a council is covered by infallibility:

> "A large majority of the acts of councils are not infallible definitions, because they are not intended as such. 'Neither the discussions which precede a dogmatic decree, nor the reasons alleged to prove and explain it, are to be accepted as infallibly true; nothing but the actual decrees are of faith, and these only if they are intended as such.'[16],[17]

There is no specific formula required for an infallible teaching. What is required, however, is that "the infallible definition be so worded as to indicate clearly its definitive character,"[18] which, of course, requires the express *intention* of the Church to do so – an intention that was not only lacking at Vatican II, but specifically "avoided," according to Paul VI himself.

After further explaining that only the *definitions* contained within a conciliar document are covered by the Church's infallibility, Van Noort then notes that it is necessary that the *intention* of giving a definitive decision is made sufficiently clear. If the intention to define is not sufficiently clear, he explains, no one is required to give the assent of faith.

> "[T]he Church's rulers are infallible not in any and every exercise of their teaching power; but only when, using all the fullness of their authority, they clearly intend to bind everyone to absolute assent or, as common parlance puts it, when they 'define' something in matters pertaining to the Christian religion. That is why all theologians distinguish in the dogmatic decrees of the councils or of the popes between those things set forth therein by way of definition and those used simply by way of illustration or argumentation. For the intention of binding all affects only the definition, and not the historical observations, reasons for the definition, and so forth. And if in some particular instances the intention of giving a definitive decision were not made sufficiently

[15] *The Sources of Revelation*, pp. 221-222.
[16] Bellarmine, *De Conciliis*, I, 17.
[17] *The Church of Christ*, p. 261 (emphasis added).
[18] Ibid.

clear, then no one would be held by virtue of such definitions, to give the assent of faith: a doubtful law is no law at all."[19]

As we have seen, within conciliar documents infallibility is only engaged when the bishops, using their supreme authority, clearly intend to define a doctrine contained in the revealed Deposit. We have also seen that Vatican II intentionally *avoided* defining any doctrines. What this clearly shows is that, contrary to what Messrs. Daly and Dimond confidently proclaim, Vatican II *did not* meet the conditions for conciliar infallibility.

"Monolithic Infallibility"

The erroneous assertion that Vatican II met the conditions for conciliar infallibility is a manifestation of a fundamental error quite common amongst Sedevacantist apologists who, like their *Novus Ordo* counterparts, extend infallibility beyond the boundaries established by the Church. This is called the error of *excess*, and it fails to properly comprehend the nature and scope of infallibility, as well as the necessary conditions that must be present for it to be engaged.

The charism of infallibility does not reside in the mind of the members of the Magisterium as a permanent habit, but is dependent in its exercise upon an external help. The charism of infallibility is habitual only in the sense that it will remain with the Church forever, but it is only actually engaged when the Church meets the necessary conditions.[20] If each and every one of the conditions are not in place, the charism remains in a state of *potency*.

Since the guarantee of infallibility is limited to those revealed truths *definitively proposed* for belief by the Church,[21] it is within the realm of possibility that a Pope or council could err when not teaching *definitively*. In such a case, the principle enunciated by St. Thomas applies: *quod possibile est non esse, quandoque non est* – which can be loosely translated as "that which is not impossible, will sometimes be."[22] Arnaldo da Silveira applied this metaphysical principle to the teaching of a council specifically. After noting that a Pope can err if he does not meet the conditions for infallibility set down by the First Vatican Council, he wrote:

---

[19] *Christ's Church*, p.104 (emphasis added).
[20] *Cf. Christ's Church*, p. 120.
[21] The *secondary objects* of infallibility will be discussed in later chapters.
[22] The literal translation is: "that which possibly is and possibly is not, sometimes is not."

"[T]he same thing must be said in relation to the conciliar documents which do not fulfill the same conditions. … when a council does not intend to define dogmas, strictly speaking it can fall into errors. Such a conclusion follows from the symmetry existing between the pontifical infallibility and that of the Church, stressed by the First Vatican Council."[23]

The Brazilian scholar later coined the term "Monolithic Infallibility" to describe the error of those on the Right and the Left who extend infallibility beyond its proper limits. In response to this error of *excess*, he wrote:

"the notion of a monolithic infallibility inspires most of the sede-vacantists as well as the neo-conciliar supporters who attach dogmatic authority to Vatican II. This notion is also at the root of the doubts, perplexities and troubles that torment many faithful minds."[24]

He went on to explain what he means by the notion of infallibility that possesses a monolithic character:

"To absolutely deny the possibility of error or even heresy in a papal or conciliar document not guaranteed by infallibility is to assign to it a monolithic character, which is not what Our Lord intended and did when He established it."[25]

Then, describing the Sedevacantist argument to a tee, he wrote:

"Some claim that, although not always guaranteed by infallibility, a papal or conciliar doctrinal pronouncement cannot contain errors. This position is better stated as follows: 'To say that a teaching is not infallible does not mean that it may have an error, but merely that it is not formally guaranteed by the charisma of infallibility. However, even if not assisted by infallibility, this teaching still has the assistance of the Holy Spirit, and, therefore, the principle stands that it cannot contain errors.' The correct teaching, however, is completely different. This assistance promised to the Church can be absolute, ensuring the truth of the

---

[23] Silveira, "The Theological Hypothesis of a Heretic Pope," at http: //www.traditionin action.org/Questions/WebSources/B_612_AX-English.pdf.
[24] Silveira, "Monolithic Infallibility & Differences among Anti-progressivists," June 2, 2013 at http://www.arnaldoxavierdasilveira.com/2014/02/monolithic-infallibility-and.html.
[25] Ibid.

teaching, and it is so when the conditions for infallibility are met. However, when these conditions are not met, it is possible for man to refuse grace. (…) In sound logic, it is impossible to accept this inflated and monolithic notion of infallibility, which would lead to the absurdity of an 'infallible fallible.' (…)[26]

The Dominican Fr. Labourdette referred to the same error, which is, unfortunately, all to common today:

"Many persons have retained very naïve ideas about what they have learned concerning the personal infallibility of the sovereign pontiff in the solemn and abnormal exercise of his power and teaching. For some, every word of the supreme pontiff will in some way partake of the value of an infallible teaching, requiring the absolute assent of theological faith…"[27]

Sedevacantist bishop, Don Sanborn, like most Sedevacantists, is guilty of ascribing "monolithic infallibility" to the Magisterium. Without making any of the necessary distinctions, Bishop Sanborn teaches his flock that the Magisterium "is infallible, and is therefore *necessarily* traditional."[28] He goes on to say:

"To deviate from Tradition is to be in error. The very notion of infallibility includes that the doctrine which they teach is in conformity with Tradition. How could it be infallible if it deviates from Tradition? If their doctrine deviates from Tradition, there is but one thing to say: *they are not the authority*, since they manifest that they are not assisted by Christ in the promulgation of doctrine."[29]

Here is Sanborn's error: He effectively says "the Magisterium (i.e., the hierarchy) *is* infallible, and therefore its teachings conform to tradition." What he *should* have said is that "the ordinary Magisterium is infallible *when* it conforms to tradition." *When* members of the hierarchy teach in accord with tradition, they are infallible.[30] *When* they

---

26 Ibid (emphasis added).
27 *Pope or Church?*, pp. 3-4.
28 Sanborn, "Response to Bishop Williamson on the Subject of the Vacancy of the Roman See," http://www.novusordowatch.org/sanborn-response-williamson.pdf (emphasis in original).
29 Ibid (emphasis in original).
30 Here we are referring primarily to the infallibility of the Ordinary and Universal Magisterium ("OUM"), as opposed to a definitive decree emanating from the

deviate from Tradition, they are *not* infallible. As we will further see, this is why the First Vatican Council specified certain *conditions* for infallibility, as opposed to saying infallibility was some kind of permanent habit residing in the mind of the members of the Magisterium, which is what Bishop Sanborn's teaching would suggest.

Further, because Sanborn erroneously believes the members of the Magisterium must, of necessity, *always* teach in accord with tradition (infallibly so), he incorrectly concludes that any deviation from traditional teaching could not come from members of the true Magisterium. The root error of Bishop Sanborn is equating *authority* with *infallibility*. The consequent error (the error that follows) is concluding that the visible Church ceased to be the true Church sometime after the death of Pius XII. Here we have another perfect example of the axiom, "a small error in principle results in a big error in conclusion." One wonders if Bishop Sanborn's theory (the Magisterium is "infallible" and therefore "traditional") applies to Pope Liberius, or Pope Honorius, or Pope John XXII, all of whom possessed the charism of infallibility, yet each of whom deviated from the Faith (deviated from Tradition). It is obvious that their gift of infallibility did not make them *"necessarily* traditional" at all times, as Sanborn imagines. As we have demonstrated, Popes are *only* infallible when they teach definitively. Consequently, it is only when they define doctrines that they are prevented from departing from Tradition.

Bishop Sanborn and other Sedevacantists accuse Catholics with a proper understanding of these principles as having a Protestant spirit, since we are said to "sift" the Magisterium for what is true and false. Sanborn says: "Catholics consequently need not and may not sift the magisterium for error and heresy. The very purpose of the Catholic Church is to teach the human race infallibly in the name of Christ, who gives perpetual assistance ["monolithic infallibility!"] to the Church to do this precise thing."[31] Someone needs to inform Bishop Sanborn of the necessary conditions for infallibility to be engaged.

In a reply to Bishop Williamson (who has a correct understanding of these principles), Sanborn mocks Williamson's Catholic appeal to Tradition by saying: "Bishop Williamson's system of sifting the magisterium in order to determine its conformity to Tradition completely overturns the Catholic rule of faith, which is the *magisterium of the Catholic Church*. His system is essentially that of the Protestants.

Extraordinary Magisterium. The infallibility of the OUM will be discussed in the next chapter.
[31] Ibid.

They hold that each individual must decide for himself what is the true interpretation of the Scriptures."[32]

Putting aside the hypocrisy of the Sedevacantist bishop, whose private judgment and "sifting" goes well beyond deciding what doctrines are traditional, to deciding for himself who validly holds offices (true "Magisterium-sifting"), and who is and who is not a true Pope ("Pope-sifting"), Bishop Sanborn tells us that we cannot do what St. Paul commanded that we *must* do, namely, hold fast to Tradition. St. Paul says: "Therefore, brethren, stand fast; and hold the traditions which you have learned, whether by word, or by our epistle" (2Thess. 2:14). These "traditions" to which Bishop Williamson and all faithful Catholics appeal are no less than the *revealed truths* contained in the Deposit of Faith (received through both the written and oral Word) and proposed definitively by the Magisterium in the past.

The Council of Trent explained that it sets forth dogmatic teaching "so that all, making use of the rule of faith, with the assistance of Christ, may be able to recognize more easily the Catholic truth in the midst of the darkness of so many errors."[33] This is not a private interpretation of Tradition, but an intellectual assent to what the Church herself has definitively (and therefore infallibly) taught over the past 2,000 years, which all Catholics have the ability to do "with the assistance of Christ." Hence, belief is based upon the authority of *the infallible Church teaching,* and not on a *private judgment interpreting,* as in Protestantism.

Canon René Berthod, who was a distinguished Professor of Theology and director at the Seminary at Ecône for several years, replied to the type of argumentation made by Bishop Sanborn and his like-minded followers:

> "Conformity to Tradition is thus the ultimate condition of the infallibility of the ordinary magisterium. This condition does not, as some have protested, subject the magisterium to a Protestant-like free personal inquiry. This is not at all the case, for the Protestant free inquiry signifies the exclusion of the Church's tradition (*i.e.,* what the Church has always believed and taught). It goes contrary to the Catholic doctrine according to which the Bible is to be understood in the same way it has been throughout the centuries. The examination of particular acts of the magisterium to test their conformity to Tradition is a far cry from subjective Protestant judgment. It uses a genuinely objective criterion."[34]

---

[32] Ibid. (emphasis in original).
[33] Pope Pius IV, *Council of Trent,* Sess. 13, Chap. 4 (emphasis added).
[34] *Pope or Church?*, p. 60.

While we will have more to say on this subject later, for now, we note that when a Pope or council teaches *without* the intent of defining doctrines, a necessary condition for infallibility is lacking, and therefore the Church's promise of infallibility is not engaged. In such a case, error is possible. To claim otherwise is to depart from what the Church and her theologians teach, by adhering to the absurd notion of an "an infallible fallible."

"Religious Assent" vs. Assent of Faith

Catholics are subject to all that the Church teaches, but there are different levels of assent corresponding to a) the degree of *objective certitude* concerning the truthfulness of the doctrine proposed (i.e., proposed infallibly, or not proposed infallibly), and b) the *nature* of the doctrine itself (i.e., revealed or not revealed).

The Assent of Faith

Truths that have been *definitively proposed* by the Church possess the highest degree of objective certitude – an infallible certitude which admits of no doubt. Accordingly, these truths must be assented to with the highest degree of assent, which is the assent of faith.

There are two different categories of definable truths that must be assented to by faith: 1) revealed truths, and 2) truths that are only connected to revelation. The former are *formally* revealed. The latter are referred to as being *virtually revealed*. These two categories of truths are, of their nature, distinct, and consequently they are assented with different kinds of faith.

Formally revealed truths (those that are contained in Scripture or Apostolic Tradition) which have been *definitively proposed* by the Church must be believed with *divine and Catholic Faith*.[35] The rejection of such a teaching is heresy in the first degree.

Truths that are only *virtually revealed* (i.e., theological conclusions) and which have been *definitively proposed* (*de fide ecclesiastica definita*) by the Church are to be assented to with *ecclesiastical faith*.[36] The rejection of such a teaching is a mortal sin, but not heresy in the first degree.[37]

---

[35] "Divine and Catholic Faith" is faith in God revealing and the infallible Church teaching.

[36] "Ecclesiastical faith" is faith in the infallible Church teaching, but not in God revealing.

[37] Referring to "truths to be believed not with the necessity of divine faith but by ecclesiastical faith," Sixtus Cartechini explains that "it would always be a grave sin, at least of the vice of rashness (*saltem vitii temeritatis*), not to offer assent to these

Religious Assent

A third, lower level of assent, is owed to those doctrines which have been *authentically proposed* by the Magisterium, but not definitively, and therefore, not *infallibly proposed*. These include: a) *revealed truths* that have not been defined by the Church (i.e., material dogmas); b) *virtually revealed* doctrines that have not been defined; and c) doctrines that are not contained in the revealed Deposit at all (either formally or virtually), but which are more or less connected to the faith.[38]

Because the teachings contained in this third category have not been proposed infallibly, error remains a possibility. Consequently a lower level of assent is owed to these teachings. The lesser degree of assent corresponds to the lesser degree of objective certitude concerning the truthfulness of the doctrine taught. This lower level of assent is known as "religious assent" or "religious observance." The importance of this lesser level of assent will become clear by the end of this chapter.

Msgr. Van Noort provides us with a definition of the terms *religious assent*, and *authentically proposed*. Regarding religious assent, he explains:

> "Religious assent means an intellectual assent given out of a religious motive, i.e., out of a motive of obedience to the religious authority established (whether directly or indirectly) by Jesus Christ."[39]

Notice that the motive of *religious assent* is one of obedience, *not* of faith. Faith is a theological virtue and the assent of faith is absolute. Obedience is a moral virtue, and like all moral virtues consists of the *rational mean* between the two extremes of *excess* and *defect*, that is, between false obedience and disobedience.[40] "Religious assent" is not

---

definitions." Sixtus Cartechini, *De valore notarum theologicarum et de criteriis ad eas dignoscendas* (Rome: Gregorian University, 1951), p. 50.

[38] Regarding the non-revealed truths taught by the Church, Cardinal Journet wrote: "That the doctrinal magisterium, over and above its primary mission, which is to define certain truths with absolute authority and irrevocably, has a secondary mission, which is to teach other truths with a prudential authority and not irrevocably, is a point of doctrine that is certain." *Church of the Word Incarnate*, p. 349.

[39] *The Sources of Revelation*, p. 270

[40] "Obedience is not a theological virtue, for its direct object is not God, but the precept of any superior, whether expressed or inferred (…) It is, however, a moral virtue, since it is a part of justice, and it observes the mean between excess and deficiency. Excess thereof is measured in respect, not of quantity, but of other circumstances, in so far as a man

based upon the *infallible Church definitively proposing*, but merely the submission of the intellect and will that is owed, in justice, to a legitimate ecclesiastical authority teaching. Therefore, *religious assent* is not absolute and unconditional, since the doctrine taught is not *certainly* (infallibly) true. Only the *assent of faith* is unconditional and absolute, because the doctrines that are believed by faith are those alone which have been *infallibly* proposed, and therefore do not admit the possibility of error. As Cardinal Billot explained, "the command to believe firmly and without examination of the matter in hand... can be truly binding only if the authority concerned is infallible."[41]

Van Noort noted that "theological truths which the Church's Magisterium teaches *merely authentically*, must be held with a *religious assent*," and then he went on to explain what the Church means by a "merely authentic proposal":

> "A merely authentic proposal. An authentic teacher, i.e., endowed with real authority in the Church, means a teacher possessing the right and duty to teach doctrines on faith or morals in such fashion that the subjects are, for that very reason, namely, that it proceeds from such a person or group, bound to accept it."[42]

Van Noort then explains that "those who possess the fullness of this magisterial power [i.e., Pope or council] may exercise their teaching office without using its full authority, that is, without intending to hand down a strictly definitive judgment (as, for example, can very easily occur in encyclical letters of the popes)."[43] Thus, these non-infallible proposals emanating from the *authentic* Magisterium are only owed a *religious assent* (again, due to a legitimate ecclesiastical authority teaching, but not the infallible Church proposing).

Fr. Nicolas Jung elaborates on this point in his classic book, *Le Magistère de L'Église* (1935):

> "This is why we owe the 'authentic' Magisterium not a blind and unconditional assent but a prudent and conditional one: Since not everything taught by the Ordinary Magisterium is infallible, we must ask what kind of assent we should give to its various decisions. The Christian is required to give the assent of faith to all the doctrinal and moral truths defined by the Church's Magisterium.

---

obeys either whom he ought not, or in matters wherein he ought not to obey, as we have stated above regarding religion (92, 2)" (...) ST, II-II, q. 104, a 2, ad 2.

[41] *De Ecclesia*, thesis XVII.
[42] *The Sources of Revelation*, p. 268.
[43] Ibid., p. 268.

He is not required to give the same assent to teaching imparted by the sovereign pontiff that is not imposed on the whole Christian body as a dogma of faith. In this case it suffices to give that inner and religious assent which we give to legitimate ecclesiastical authority. This is not an absolute assent, because such decrees are not infallible, but only a prudential and conditional assent, since in questions of faith and morals there is a presumption in favor of one's superior... Such prudential assent does not eliminate the possibility of submitting the doctrine to a further examination, if that seems required by the gravity of the question."[44]

Speaking of the non-infallible teachings contained in papal encyclicals, Pope Pius XII stated: "Most often (*plerumque*) what is found to be taught in the encyclicals already belongs also to Catholic doctrine."[45] In other words, some things (those "less often" presented) in encyclicals may *not* be part of Catholic doctrine and thus subject to error. Msgr. Joseph Clifford Fenton explains that the faithful are required to submit to non-infallible teachings only with "internal *religious assent*." He then quotes from an article that was written by Pègues and published in *Revue Thomiste* in 1904. Pègues explains that the non-infallible teachings are owed a certain degree of mental assent (since they come from a legitimate authority), but, due to the possibility of error, they are *not* owed the assent of faith:

"the authority of the encyclicals is not at all the same as that of the solemn definition, the one properly so-called. The *definition* demands an assent without reservation and makes a formal *act of faith* obligatory. The case of the encyclical's authority is not the same. This authority (of the papal encyclicals) is undoubtedly great.... [but only] an internal mental assent is demanded. Ultimately, however, this assent is not the same as the one demanded in the formal act of faith. Strictly speaking, it is possible that this teaching (proposed in the encyclical letter) is subject to error. ... because God does not guarantee it as He guarantees the teaching formulated by way of definition."[46]

After quoting Pègues, Msgr. Fenton went on to explain that a "religious assent" is owed to those teachings of the Holy Father, which are not guaranteed by his infallibility:

---

[44] Nicolas Jung, Le Magistère de L'Èglise, 1935, pp. 153, 154; cited in *Clear Ideas, On the Pope's Infallible Magisterium, SiSiNoNo*, January 2002, No. 44.
[45] *Humani Generis* (August 12, 1950).
[46] Pègues, Article in the Revue Thomiste, November-December 1904, p. 531 – apud Choupin, Valeur..., pp. 54-55.

"Despite the divergent views about the existence of the infallible pontifical teaching in the encyclical letters, there is one point on which all theologians are manifestly in agreement. They are all convinced that all Catholics are bound in conscience to give a definite internal <u>religious assent</u> to those doctrines which the Holy Father teaches when he speaks to the universal Church of God on earth <u>without employing his God-given charism of infallibility</u>."[47]

Fenton further makes a distinction between ecclesiastical faith (which is owed to theological conclusions definitively proposed by the Church), and other teachings of the Holy Father which lack the definitive character necessary for them to be protected by infallibility, and which, consequently, are only adhered to with religious assent. Wrote Fenton:

"It is quite probable that <u>some</u> of the teachings set forth on the authority of the various papal encyclicals are infallible statements of the Sovereign Pontiff, demanding the assent of the *fides ecclesiastica* (*ecclesiastical faith*). It is absolutely certain that <u>all</u> of the teachings contained in these documents, and dependent upon their authority, merit at least an internal <u>religious assent</u> from all Catholics."[48]

In the aforementioned article by Bishop Butlet, "The Limits of Infallibility," he touches on this point. After saying "not all official teaching, of course, is infallible. … nor are all teachings emanating from a Pope or an Ecumenical Council infallible," he adds:

"However, to say that a piece of official teaching, whether of an individual bishop, a national conference of bishops, an Ecumenical Council, or a Pope, is not provably infallible is not to say that it is destitute of all magisterial authority. As there is a virtue of obedience by which we accept with our will what authority prescribes, so there is a virtue of docility which disposes us to accept with our intellect what authority teaches."[49]

Now, the average Catholic in the pew is not going to know which teachings are owed the assent of *divine and Catholic Faith*, which are owed *ecclesiastical faith*, and which merely require a *religious assent*. So there is little practical difference when considered from the perspective

---

[47] Fenton, "The Doctrinal Authority of Papal Encyclicals," *American Ecclesiastical Review*, vol. CXXI, August, 1949, pp. 136-150 (emphasis added).
[48] Ibid., pp. 210-220.
[49] *The Tablet*, November 25, 1967, vol. 221, no. 6653, p. 4.

of the average Catholic. But these distinctions are necessary for the theologians to draw, precisely because of the difference between truths *infallibly proposed*, and those taught *without involving the Church's infallibility*. These distinctions are also important for us to know during the present crisis, lest we fall into the error of *excess* and end by believing, as the Sedevacantists do, that an error in a Magisterial document constitutes a violation of the Church's infallibility.

"Religious Assent" is not Unconditional

As we've seen, only a *religious assent* is owed to the non-infallible teachings of the Magisterium since such teachings do not exclude the possibility of error. Because our assent to these teachings is not based upon the theological virtue of faith, but on the moral virtue of obedience – which is the rational mean between *excess* and *defect* – the "religious assent" *is not unconditional*. Van Noort explains:

> "Granted the need for submission to the *authentic* Magisterium, it still remains true that just as a merely authentic proposal by its very nature incomplete and provisory, so, too, is the *religious assent* due to it. Quite frequently the decrees of these congregations do not look to the truthfulness of a given doctrine, but rather to its *security*. Now the security of a doctrine, i.e., whether it is *safe* to admit or to teach this or that point, or whether religion would thereby suffer some injury, depends somewhat on the circumstances and, above all, on the present state of the question – something which may change with the addition of new evidence or argumentation."[50]

The German Jesuit and militant anti-Modernist, Christian Pesch (d. 1925), goes further by explaining that assent should prudently be suspended when there are sufficient motives for doubt. He also notes that this applies to the non-infallible teaching of the Papal Magisterium as well:

> "(...) one must assent to the decrees of the Roman congregations, as long as it does not become positively sure that they have erred. Since the Congregations, *per se*, do not furnish an absolutely certain argument in favor of a given doctrine, one may or even must investigate the reasons for that doctrine. And thus, either it will come to pass that such a doctrine will be gradually accepted in the whole Church, attaining in this way the condition of infallibility, or it will happen that the error is little by little detected.

---

[50] *The Sources of Revelation*, p. 273.

For, <u>since the religious assent referred to is not based on a metaphysical certainty, but only a moral and general one, it does not exclude all suspicion of error. For this reason, as soon as there arises sufficient motives for doubt, the assent will be prudently suspended</u>: nevertheless, as long as such motives for doubt do not arise, the authority of the Congregations is sufficient to oblige one to assent. <u>The same principles apply without difficulty to the declarations which the Supreme Pontiff emits without involving his supreme authority,</u> as well as the decisions of the other ecclesiastical superiors who are not infallible."[51]

Clearly, Pesch does not agree with Bishop Sanborn who equates authority with infallibility. Just because an authority may be infallible when certain conditions are satisfied, does not mean that the authority ceases to be an authority if he should error when not meeting the required conditions.

Franciscus Diekamp also does not agree with Bishop Sanborn, since he teaches that the religious assent owed to the non-infallible acts of the Papal Magisterium permits of exceptions, which would not be the case if everything that came from a Pope was infallibly true:

"These non infallible acts of the Magisterium <u>of the Roman Pontiff</u> do not oblige one to believe, and do not postulate an absolute and definitive subjection. But it behooves one to adhere with a <u>religious and internal assent</u> to such decisions, since they constitute acts of the <u>supreme Magisterium</u>[52] of the Church, and are founded upon solid natural and supernatural reasons. The obligation to adhere to them can only begin to terminate in case, and this only occurs very rarely, [when] a man [who is] fit to judge such a question, <u>after a repeated and very diligent analysis of all the</u>

---

[51] Pesch, Praelectiones Dogmaticae., vol. I, (Freiburg: Herder & Herder, 1898), pp. 314-315.

[52] As we address in the next chapter, Sedevacantists, such as John Daly, have argued, without citing any authorities to back up the claim, that the term "Supreme Magisterium" (an undefined term that Paul VI used to describe Vatican II) is another name for the Ordinary and Universal Magisterium (OUM). They then claim that because Dei Filius defined that the OUM is infallible, when Paul VI referred to Vatican II as the "Supreme Magisterium," he must have mean it too is covered by the Church's infallibility (See Daly's "Did Vatican II Teach Infallibly"). The problem is that no one has ever taught that the Supreme Magisterium is another name for the OUM. In fact, as Diekamp makes clear, the "Supreme Magisterium" is not, in fact, infallible, which means it's not the same as the OUM. To be clear, just because a teaching is not "infallible" does not suggest that it is erroneous; only that error is possible.

arguments, arrives at the conviction that an error has been introduced into the decision."[53]

Merkelbach, one of the leading Dominican moralists in Rome in the first half of the twentieth century, teaches the same. In his *Summa Theologiae Moralis*, he wrote:

> "When the Church does not teach with her infallible authority, the doctrine proposed is not, as such, unreformable; for this reason, if *per accidens*, in a hypothesis which is however very rare, after a very careful examination of the matter, it appears to someone that there exist very grave reasons contrary to the doctrine thus proposed, it will be licit, without falling into temerity, to suspend internal assent (…)"[54]

We can see that the *religious assent* due to non-infallible teachings is not unconditional. If a "merely authentic" teaching of the Papal Magisterium (Pope Francis, for example) appears to directly contradict a previous teaching of the perennial Papal Magisterium that was proposed with an equal or higher degree of certitude (such as those teachings contained in any of the anti-Liberal encyclicals of Leo XIII, the Syllabus of Bl. Pius IX, *Pascendi* of St. Pius X, *Quas Primas* or *Mortalium Animos* of Pius XI, or even the moral teachings of the post-conciliar Popes which are in accord with Tradition), a *legitimate motive* for withholding religious assent to the "authentic" teaching would exist. Similarly, if an *ambiguous* proposal appeared to contradict multiple *clear proposals*, withholding religious assent from the ambiguous proposal (which appeared to contradict the clear proposals) would be entirely justified until such time as the Church reconciled the apparent contradiction.[55]

---

[53] Diekamp, *Theologiae Dogmaticae Manual*, vol. I (Desclee, Parisiis – Tornaci-Romae, 1933), p. 72.
[54] Merkelbach, *Summa Theologiae Moralis*, vol. I (Desclee, Parisiis, 1931), p. 601.
[55] Archbishop Lefebvre provides us a great example of the *justifiable* withholding of assent to the teachings of Vatican II through his scholarly and well-reasoned objections to the council's teaching in *Dignitatis Humane* on religious liberty. In fact, in October 1985, Lefebvre submitted his famous *Dubia about Religious Liberty* to the Sacred Congregation for the Doctrine of the Faith which demonstrates that the council's teaching is incompatible with the Church's perennial condemnations of religious liberty. The authors have a copy of the Congregation's 21-page unpublished reply (dated March 9, 1987) to Lefebvre's *dubia* against Vatican II's teaching on religious liberty. The Congregation's reply does little more than repeat the teachings of *Dignitatis Humanae*, rather than reconcile them with *Quanta Cura* and the Syllabus of Errors. Furthermore, the Congregation admits the possibility of further study of the problem ("...demeure la possibilité d'une étude ultérieure de ce problème...").

The same applies to a council, should it formulate its teachings in such a way that they appear to contradict what was previously taught. If a council attempted to reconcile the Catholic Faith with the Masonic Principles of 1789 (condemned in the Syllabus of Pius IX and many other places), for example, and if the attempted reconciliation included the council teaching doctrines that had been previously condemned by the Church, a justification would exist for withholding religious assent. With this in mind, let us recall what Cardinal Ratzinger said about Vatican II:

> "If it is desirable to offer a diagnosis of the text [Gaudium et Spes] as a whole, we might say that (in conjunction with the texts on religious liberty and world religions) it is a revision of the Syllabus of Pius IX, a kind of countersyllabus. [...] Let us be content to say that the text serves as a countersyllabus and, as such, represents, on the part of the Church, an attempt at an official reconciliation with the new era inaugurated in 1789. (....) the one-sidedness of the position adopted by the Church under Pius IX and Pius X in response to the situation created by the new phase of history inaugurated by the [Masonic] French Revolution was, to a large extent, corrected *via facti*, especially in Central Europe, but there was still no basic statement of the relationship that should exist between the Church and the world that had come into existence after 1789. (...) Let us be content to say here that the text serves as a countersyllabus and, as such, <u>represents, on the part of the Church, an attempt at an official reconciliation with the new era inaugurated in 1789</u>."[56]

Cardinal Felici, the Prefect of the Supreme Congregation of the Holy Office, admitted the possibility of withholding religious assent from the teachings of Vatican II which are novel in character (such as those that seek to reconcile the Church with the Masonic Principles of 1789). Archbishop Lefebvre related the following in his book *An Open Letter to Confused Catholics*:

> "A non-dogmatic, pastoral council is *not* a recipe for infallibility. When, at the end of the sessions, we asked Cardinal Felici, 'Can you not give us what the theologians call the 'theological note of the Council?'' he replied, 'We have to distinguish according to the schemas and the chapters those which have already been the subject of dogmatic definitions in the past; <u>as for the declarations which have a novel character, we have to make</u>

---

[56] Ratzinger, *Principles of Catholic Theology*, pp. 381-382.

reservations.' Vatican II therefore is not a council like others and that is why we have the right to judge it, with prudence and reserve."[57]

To summarize, we have seen that there are at least three levels of assent[58] owed to the teachings of the Magisterium: the assent of (1) divine faith; (2) ecclesiastical faith; and, (3) religious assent/observance. These three levels of assent correspond to a) the degree of certitude concerning the truthfulness of the doctrine proposed, and b) the nature of the doctrine taught (formally or virtually revealed, or not revealed). Truths that have been *definitively* and therefore *infallibly* proposed must be accepted *by faith* - either that of divine and Catholic Faith (formally revealed truths), or ecclesiastical faith (virtually revealed truths). Truths that have been taught by the Magisterium authentically, but not infallibly, are only owed a *religious assent*, which is based upon the motive of obedience, and therefore is not unconditional.

Vatican II Owed Only Religious Assent

In light of the above explanation between the *assent of faith* due to *infallible* teachings, and the *religious assent* that is owed to *non-infallible* teachings, let us consider another argument put forward by the Sedevacantists to defend their assertion that Vatican II violated the Church's infallibility. In spite of the clear fact (admitted to by Pope Paul VI) that Vatican II intentionally avoided defining any dogmas (a condition required for conciliar infallibility), Sedevacantists will argue that the documents of Vatican II should have nevertheless been covered by the Church's infallibility *in toto*. They advance their argument by pointing to the "solemn" wording used by Paul VI when he ratified the documents (as if his closing statements could nullify any of the necessary conditions of infallibility decreed by the First Vatican

---

[57] Archbishop Marcel Lefebvre, *An Open Letter to Confused Catholics*, (Herefordshire, England: Fowler Wright Books Ltd., 1986), Chapter 14, p. 112 (also published by *Angelus Press*, 1992).
[58] Some reputable theologians have taught that the degree of assent owed to non-infallible teachings is only that of *respectful silence* (*silentium obsequium*). Others only permit the *respectful silence* when there is a serious reason to suspect error. For example, in the above citation from Merkelbach, he continued by saying: "if *per accidens*, ... it appears to someone that there exist very grave reasons contrary to the doctrine thus proposed, it would be licit, without rashness, to suspend internal assent; externally, however, the *respectful silence* would be obligatory, on account of the reverence which is owed to the Church" (ibid).

Council). In the following citation, John Daly uses this very argument. See if you can spot the error in his thesis:

> "Moreover, anyone who cares to consult the 1965 volume of the *Acta Apostolicae Sedis* can see at a glance that Paul VI promulgated the gravely erroneous religious liberty text and many others on 8th December 1965 with all the formalities that could be required if he had been a true pope promulgating sound and obligatory truth. Here is an extract: '…we order and command that all that the Council has decided in synod be <u>sacredly and religiously held</u> by all of Christ's faithful, unto the glory of God… These things we edict and prescribe, decreeing that this present letter must ever be and remain firm, valid and efficacious and obtain and retain its full and integral effects…Given at Rome, under the fisherman's ring…' Indeed there could be no doubting the obligatory character of doctrine so put forth, if only it had been put forth by a Catholic and had not been manifestly false and heretical."[59]

What John Daly clearly doesn't realize is that by only requiring that the teaching be "sacredly and religiously held," Paul VI is further confirming that Vatican II defined no doctrines, since infallible propositions would require the assent *of faith,* and not mere "religious" observance. The solemnity with which Paul VI chose to "dress up" the documents with his closing statements does not change this fact, and certainly does not change the requirements for infallibility set forth by the First Vatican Council. Because John Daly's motive, however, is to prove that Paul VI wasn't a true Pope, he perverts Vatican I's definition of infallibility to include non-definitive pastoral propositions, to defend his Sedevacantist thesis. This only shows how weak his case actually is.

Peter Dimond makes the same error. He wrote:

> "In his brief declaring the council closed, Paul VI again invoked his 'apostolic authority' and acknowledged that all the constitutions, decrees and declarations of Vatican II have been approved and promulgated by him. He further stated that all of it must be '<u>religiously observed</u> by all the faithful'!"[60]

Dimond then goes on to quote Paul VI saying:

---

[59] Daly, "Did Vatican II Teach Infallibly?," Second Revised Edition, 2014. http://www.novusordowatch.org/vatican-ii-infallible.htm (emphasis added).
[60] Dimond, *The Truth About What Really Happened to the Catholic Church After Vatican II*, p. 471.

"At last all which regards the holy ecumenical council has, with the help of God, been accomplished and all the constitutions, decrees, declarations and votes have been approved by the deliberation of the synod and promulgated by us. Therefore we decided to close for all intents and purposes, with our apostolic authority, this same ecumenical council called by our predecessor, Pope John XXIII, which opened October 11, 1962, and which was continued by us after his death. We decided moreover that all that has been established synodally is to be <u>religiously observed</u> by all the faithful, for the glory of God and the dignity of the Church and for the tranquillity and peace of all men."[61]

Dimond concludes by saying:

"There you have it. The apostate Second Vatican Council is to be 'religiously observed,' if you accept Paul VI. <u>There can be no doubt that if Paul VI was a true pope the gates of Hell prevailed against the Catholic Church on Dec. 8, 1965</u>. If Paul VI was the pope, Jesus Christ's promises to His Church failed. If Paul VI was the pope, all of Vatican II's teaching on faith or morals was promulgated infallibly (*ex cathedra*). But this is impossible – and anyone who would say that it is possible doesn't believe in Catholic teaching on the indefectibility of the Catholic Church. Thus we know that Giovanni Montini (Paul VI) was not a true successor of Peter, but an invalid antipope ...."[62]

Here we have a perfect example of the error of excess, and why self-appointed Sedevacantist apologists like John Daly and Pete Dimond have no business publicly writing about these matters. If they engaged in real scholarship, they would quickly learn the distinction between "religious observance" and the "assent of faith," and the corresponding difference between non-infallible and infallible teachings. Even a simple layman can understand the words of Paul VI, who said that Vatican II "avoided issuing solemn dogmatic definitions backed by the Church's infallible teaching authority."[63] Nowhere does Paul VI declare that the conciliar documents must be accepted with the *assent of faith*, because none of the novel teachings of Vatican II were definitively proposed as revealed truths; they were merely "pastoral" teachings from the "authentic" Magisterium.

---

[61] Ibid.

[62] Ibid., p. 472.

[63] Paul VI, General Audience, December 1, 1966 published in *L'Osservatore Romano*, January 21, 1966.

We can imagine how such self-assured proclamations from the likes of Daly and Dimond could influence those who are looking for simple solutions to explain the profound mystery of the Passion of the Mystical Body of Christ; but in reality their "solution" does no such thing. It is simply an error in *conclusion* based upon an error in *principle*. In the age of Faith, the local bishops would have quickly dealt with individuals such as Dimond and Daly. In our age of apostasy, however, they are allowed to spread their errors throughout the world via the internet, thereby causing untold confusion in the faithful who are already far too confused.

If we consider this from another perspective, we can see God's hand present at Vatican II. He was not present in the sense of preventing ambiguities and errors in the conciliar documents, but by *preventing* the Modernists from engaging the charism of infallibility and thereby violating one of His promises. God may have permitted a high degree of "terrible and distressing" things at Vatican II, to use the words of Fr. O'Reilly, but he did not permit a violation of the Church's infallibility - something that would indeed have been "impossible."

433

Chapter 14

~ Vatican II and the Ordinary and Universal Magisterium ~

In the previous chapter, we saw that the Second Vatican Council did not meet the *conditions* for conciliar infallibility, since it expressly avoided defining any doctrines. As Cardinal Ratzinger said, the Council "chose to remain on the modest level of a merely pastoral council." We also considered the different levels of assent that are owed to infallible and non-infallible teaching respectively, and saw that non-infallible teachings do not require the *assent of faith*, but only a *religious assent*, which is not unconditional. We saw that Paul VI himself not only admitted that Vatican II defined no doctrines (and therefore did not engage infallibility), but expressly taught, at the close of the council, that the teachings were only to be adhered to with a "religious observance," which is the level of assent owed to *non-infallible* teachings of the "authentic Magisterium." In this chapter, we will address the infallibility of the Ordinary and Universal Magisterium, and in so doing refute another error used by Sedevacantists to defend their thesis.

The Novel Theory of John Daly

In light of the clear evidence that Vatican II did not meet the *conditions* for conciliar infallibility, the Sedevacantist apologist, John Daly, came up with a new theory in an attempt to demonstrate that Vatican II still violated the Church's infallibility, even though it did not define any doctrines. This novel theory is another attempt to "prove" that Paul VI, who ratified the documents, could not have been a true Pope. While Mr. Daly acknowledges that Paul VI himself admitted that Vatican II explicitly "avoided proclaiming in an extraordinary manner any dogma carrying the mark of infallibility," he nevertheless claims that Vatican II met the *conditions* for infallibility in another way. He claims that because Vatican II was a gathering of the bishops of the world along with the Pope, its teachings constitute an act of *the Ordinary Universal Magisterium*. Now, since the First Vatican Council (1870) taught that the Ordinary and Universal Magisterium is infallible, Mr. Daly asserts that the teachings contained in the documents of Vatican II should have been covered *entirely* by the Church's

435

infallibility. Accordingly, he concludes that if the documents of Vatican II contain errors, it proves that Paul VI could not have been a true Pope, since the bishops throughout the world, when united to the Pope, teach infallibly.

Now, from what we have already seen, it should be evident that there is a flaw somewhere in Mr. Daly's reasoning. After all, *every* general council of the Church consists of the bishops of the world in union with the Pope, yet even in the councils in which dogmas are infallibly defined, only the *definitions* themselves are protected by the Church's infallibility, which, interestingly, even some Sedevacantists acknowledge. How, then, can Mr. Daly claim that *everything* in Vatican II should have been covered by Church's infallibility, when, in fact, unlike the other general councils, Vatican II issued no *definitions* at all? The fact that Mr. Daly has been spreading this error for years, and has been unable to see the evident problem with his reasoning, is actually quite telling in and of itself.

Before exploring the errors in Mr. Daly's novel theory, we will allow him to explain his position in his own words. Notice how Daly's presentation is another case of *petitio principii* (begging the question), that is, Vatican II met the conditions for infallibility because he says so:

> "Most traditional Catholics know that Vatican II taught heresies and other errors. They rightly refuse to accept this false teaching. But when asked how it can be right to reject the teaching of a General Council of the Catholic Church, they reply that Vatican II was a special kind of council; it was non-dogmatic and non-infallible. As such it could err, and did err, and Catholics may reject its errors without doubting the legitimacy of the authority that promulgated those errors. (…)
>
> This popular explanation rides rough-shod over Catholic doctrine and plain reality. The truth is that Vatican II so plainly fulfils the conditions required for infallibility that not even Paul VI ever dared to deny this. Hence, if its teaching contains egregious errors against the faith, this fact necessarily calls into question the papal status of Paul VI himself.
>
> To show that this is so, let us look more closely at the ways in which the Church infallibly teaches divine truth to her children. Here is what the 1870 Vatican Council taught:
>
> 'All those things are to be believed with divine and Catholic faith which are contained in the Word of God, written or handed down, and are proposed by the Church either by a solemn judgment or by her ordinary and universal magisterium to be believed as

divinely revealed.' (Dogmatic constitution *Dei Filius*, chapter 3, "Concerning Faith").

It is quite extraordinary how many traditional Catholics, including some Sedevacantists, have entirely forgotten one of these two means which the Church uses to teach us. It is very often asserted that only the solemn definitions of popes and councils oblige under pain of heresy and are protected by infallibility. Yet here we see just such a solemn definition stating that Catholics have an identical obligation to believe the Church's teachings (under pain of heresy) irrespective of whether this teaching is communicated by 'solemn judgments' or by the 'ordinary and universal magisterium.' Both are equally infallible."[1]

There are two fundamental errors in Mr. Daly's theory: 1) an incomplete understanding of the Ordinary and Universal Magisterium ("OUM"); and 2) a failure to realize that, just as there are conditions for Papal Infallibility and Conciliar Infallibility, so too are there conditions for a doctrine to be proposed infallibly by virtue of the OUM. Regardless of which *organ* of infallibility is doing the teaching (Pope, council, OUM), *what* is taught, and *how* it is being taught, must meet certain *conditions* for the Church's promise of infallibility to be guaranteed.

Conditions for Infallibility of the OUM

According to Vatican I's Dogmatic Constitution *Dei Filius* (the document upon which Mr. Daly bases his theory), a teaching is infallible by virtue of the OUM *only* when it is: 1) a *divinely revealed* truth; and, 2) *definitively proposed* as such by the Church. *Dei Filius* states:

> "All those things are to be <u>believed with divine and Catholic faith</u> which are contained in the Word of God, written [Scripture] or handed down [Tradition], and are <u>proposed</u> by the Church either by a solemn judgment <u>or by her ordinary and universal magisterium to be believed as divinely revealed</u>."[2]

---

[1] Daly, "Did Vatican II Teach Infallibly?," Second Revised Edition, 2014. http://www.novusordowatch.org/vatican-ii-infallible.htm.

[2] Dogmatic Constitution *Dei Filius*, chapter 3, "Concerning Faith."

Divinely Revealed Truths

The first condition for infallibility of the OUM (according to *De Filius*) is that the truth to be believed must be "divinely revealed." *Revealed truths* are those contained in either Scripture or Tradition (the Deposit of Faith), irrespective of whether they are later defined by a "solemn judgment" (Extraordinary Magisterium) or proposed by the Church's "ordinary and universal magisterium." Only *revealed truths*, which have been definitively proposed as such by the Church are believed with the assent of Divine and Catholic Faith (which is the level of assent specified in *De Filius*).

Now, the revealed deposit was closed with the death of the last Apostle, as Cardinal Journet explains:

> "The extra-ordinary light bestowed on the Apostles as founders of the Church enabled them to embrace, in the simplicity of a unique glance and in an eminent manner, the whole revelation of the New Law. What they have handed down to us, the explicitly revealed deposit, contains, either explicitly or implicitly, all the truths of the Christian faith. Henceforth we are not to expect any further revelation of the Spirit inaugurating some new age of the world, or any sort of advance on Christianity. The New Testament, the revealed deposit as it has come to us from the Apostles orally (Tradition) or in writing (Scripture), is final; it will be valid till the end of the world. The Church herself has no authority to modify it. Her mission is simply to keep it intact: 'O Timothy, keep that which is committed to thy trust, avoiding the profane novelties of words...'."[3]

The novelties of Vatican II are not part of the revealed Deposit, as Mr. Daly would no doubt concede, nor were they proposed as such during the Council. Because none of the errors or novelties Mr. Daly objects to in Vatican II are *revealed truths*, they are not included as part of the *object* of infallibility of the Ordinary and Universal Magisterium. This is the first error in Mr. Daly's theory.

The First Vatican Council taught that the Holy Ghost was not promised to the Pope so that he could reveal new (novel) doctrines, but only so he could protect what had been handed down to him from Apostolic Tradition:

---

[3] *The Church of the Word Incarnate*, p. 339.

"The Holy Spirit has never promised the successors of Peter a *revelation* which would allow them to divulge a <u>new doctrine</u>: but that, with the assistance of the Holy Spirit, they should preserve and faithfully set forth the holy deposit of Faith, that is to say, <u>the *revelation* which was made to the Apostles</u>."

Definitively Proposed

The second condition for the infallibility of the OUM is that the divinely revealed truth be *definitively proposed* as such by the Church.[4] This same condition exists for an infallible teaching of a Pope or council. As we will see in a moment, the difference is the way in which this condition is satisfied by the OUM.

When a Pope or council defines a doctrine, it is clearly proposed by the Church as being an article of faith. This removes any doubt on the part of the faithful regarding whether the doctrine is an article of Faith. Such clarity, however, is lacking with the teachings of the OUM. The principal way in which doctrines are known to belong to the Faith, by virtue of the OUM, is *by their conformity to Tradition*, that is, by the unanimous consent of the Fathers, the agreement of the Scholastic theologians, and the constant belief of the faithful. The continuous belief of these *witnesses* confirms the *revealed nature* of the doctrine, while the unanimous belief over the centuries provides the *definitive character* necessary for them to be taught infallibly.

In his lengthy explanation of the OUM, Fr. Adolph Tanquery included these "witnesses" as an integral *part* of the OUM. He wrote:

"The ordinary and universal magisterium is that which is carried on daily through the continuous preaching of the Church among all peoples. It includes:

1. The preaching and proclamations of the Corporate Body of Bishops;

---

[4] We also note that the Church can only define, as an object of divine and Catholic Faith, a "material dogma." Material dogmas are truths contained within the sources of revelation (Scripture or Tradition), and therefore definable, but which have not *yet* been clearly and definitively proposed by the Church. It is not necessary for a material dogma to have been taught *explicitly* from the time of the Apostles to be defined at a later date by the Church, but it must have been believed at least *implicitly*, even if somewhat obscurely. If the explicit nature only became evident over time, the explicit teaching would have to be in perfect continuity with what the Church had always explicitly believed. When a material dogma is defined, it is raised to the status of a formal dogma, which is a dogma in the true sense of the word, as defined by *Dei Filius*: 1) a *revealed truth* 2) that has been *definitively proposed* as such by the Church.

2. Universal custom or practice associated with dogma;
3. The consensus or agreement of the Fathers and of the Theologians,
4. The common or general understanding of the faithful."[5]

Canon Berthod explains that conformity to Tradition is a *condition* for the infallibility of the Ordinary and Universal Magisterium:

> "Ordinary acts of the Magisterium also received the guarantee of divine assistance in what they propose to be believed as *revealed truth*. Unlike the acts of the solemn Magisterium, though, they do not have the same definitive character, nor do they carry the anathemas by which recusants are formally excluded from the Catholic Faith. But for them to be considered as belonging to the Church's teaching, to which the divine promise [of infallibility] is attached, they cannot be taken separately, but must be consonant with the body of the Church's teaching: they are infallible only insofar as they fit into the constant teaching, only insofar as they reflect or echo the permanent teaching and unchanging Faith of the Church. In short, they are only infallible insofar as they agree with Catholic Tradition. Two conditions, then, are required: 1) the teaching must be proposed as a revealed truth; 2) it must be in accord with the universality of Catholic Tradition."[6]

The definitive character of the doctrines of the OUM is not known by a *single act,* as with the Extraordinary Magisterium, but rather by a multitude of acts which, when taken together, clearly and unmistakably confirm that the doctrine has been *definitively proposed* by the Church as "divinely revealed."[7] This means that what is being proposed (revealed truth) becomes *unmistakably definitive* by virtue of a collection of teachings over time and space. Such teachings of the OUM are *de fide* (of the Faith) and, although they have not been solemnly defined by the Extraordinary Magisterium (and are thus not *de fide definita*), they are just as infallibly true as a dogmatic definition.[8]

---

[5] Tanquerey, *A Manual of Dogmatic Theology*, vol. I, p. 176.
[6] *Pope or Church?*, p. 58.
[7] The 1913 *Catholic Encyclopedia* explains that "the *magisterium ordinarium* (Ordinary Magisterium) is liable to be somewhat indefinite in its pronouncements," and as a result can be "practically ineffective as an organ" of infallibility (vol. VII, p. 800).
[8] "A dogma in the strict and customary meaning of the term is a truth revealed by God and proposed as such for our belief by the Church. *This means a clear-cut proposal,* as we have previously explained. If the proposal is made by a solemn decree it is labeled as a *defined dogma*; if proposed by the ordinary and universal Magisterium it is described as a non-defined dogma, i.e. not defined solemnly. A dogma in the sense just explained is exactly the same as: a truth of Catholic Faith." Van Noort, *The Sources of Revelation*, p. 227.

Msgr. Van Noort explains the way in which a truth is definitively proposed by the Extraordinary Magisterium, and the way it is proposed definitively by the OUM:

> "Ways in Which the Church Proposes Revealed Truths: A proposal of a revealed truth by the Church, such as we have described above, can, according to the Vatican Council, take place in either of two ways: either by a solemn decree, or by the Church's ordinary and universal teaching.

> 1. Under the formula *solemn decree* are included the following: (a) definitions made by the pope when speaking *ex cathedra*; (b) definitions made by particular councils which have either been ratified by the pope in solemn form, or accepted by the universal Church. ... Finally, please note the term *definitions*. In the very dogmatic decrees issued by councils and popes it often happens that matters are mentioned which are by no means meant to be defined. (...)

> 2. The exercise of the ordinary and universal Magisterium (OUM) includes the whole gamut of diverse actions by which the pope and bishops dispersed throughout the world, either by themselves or through various kinds of helpers, *continuously* expound doctrine on faith and morals. This teaching is exercised first of all by explicit teaching, either oral or written. Secondly, it is also exercised by implicit teaching through the practices and liturgy of the Churches, by the promulgation of laws, by the approval of customs, by the recommendation of devotions, by the approval of books, and so forth.

> Clearly, if a truth is capable of being declared an object of divine-catholic faith through the force of this ordinary and universal teaching, there is required such a proposal as is <u>unmistakably definitive</u>. The proposal must be of such a nature that <u>without any misgivings, it is proven that the doctrine in question is taught throughout the entire world *as revealed*</u> and, consequently, as something necessarily to be believed by every Catholic."[9]

With regard to the "heresies and other errors" of the council that Mr. Daly calls into question, none of them (e.g., religious liberty, ecumenism, dialogue, collegiality) were classified by the council as "divinely revealed"; nor are they clearly and definitively proposed as such in the conciliar documents. Ambiguity, in fact, is one of the distinguishing characteristics of the conciliar documents. In a recent

---

[9] *The Sources of Revelation,* p. 222 (emphasis added).

article published in the Vatican's official newspaper, *L'Osservatore Romano*, Cardinal Walter Kasper explained why there is such confusion and apparent contradiction in the conciliar texts. He said:

> "In many places, [the Council Fathers] had to find compromise formulas, in which, often, the positions of the majority are located immediately next to those of the minority, designed to delimit them. Thus, the conciliar texts themselves have a huge potential for conflict, [and] open the door to a selective reception in either direction."[10]

Fr. Edward Schillebeeckx said the ambiguity in the conciliar texts was an intentional tactic of the progressive wing. He said:

> "We [progressives] have used ambiguous phrases during the Council and we know how we will interpret them afterwards."[11]

This ambiguity further demonstrates that lack of a definitive nature in the novelties found in the conciliar documents.

Further, if any *revealed truths* had been proposed in an *"unmistakably definitive"* manner by the Second Vatican Council, the *definitive proposal* would have constituted a solemn decree (a single definitive act), and therefore the teaching would have been protected by the Church's infallibility, not by virtue of the OUM, but by the Extraordinary Magisterium, since a general council is itself an extraordinary event during which infallibility is exercised in an extraordinary way (when the necessary conditions are met). And because a definitive character is also necessary for a doctrine to be infallible by virtue of the OUM, it is evidently false to assert, as Mr. Daly does, that the *non-definitive* teaching of Vatican II met the conditions for the infallibility of the OUM.

Where Vatican II "differed from other councils," is that it was an extraordinary event[12] (a general council) which specifically avoided teaching in an extraordinary manner.[13] The *form* (gathering of the

---

[10] Cardinal Walter Kasper, *L'Osservatore Romano*, April 12, 2013.
[11] Archbishop Marcel Lefebvre, *An Open Letter to Confused Catholics*, p. 111.
[12] During the closing speech, Paul VI said: "This council is completely terminated, this immense and *extraordinary assembly* is disbanded." (Vatican II Closing Speech, December 8, 1965).
[13] One day earlier, Paul VI said: "Today we are concluding the Second Vatican Council. [...] But one thing must be noted here, namely, that the teaching authority of the Church, even though *not wishing to issue extraordinary dogmatic pronouncements*, has made thoroughly known its *authoritative teaching* on a number of questions..." (Address during the last general meeting of the Second Vatican Council, December 7, 1965; AAS 58).

world's bishops) was *extraordinary*, but the *matter* (the teachings contained in the documents) were only *ordinary*. Therefore, its teachings will be infallible only if they were previously defined, or if they meet the *true* conditions for infallibility of the OUM - ("believed always, everywhere and by all") – which certainly do not apply to any of the novelties in the conciliar documents. And because the documents themselves were only part of the Ordinary (but not Universal) Magisterium, there was no single teaching of Vatican II in which the charism of infallibility was engaged to prevent the possibility of error. We finally note that not even the Extraordinary Magisterium can infallibly propose a novelty (such as ecumenism), with no foundation in Scripture or Tradition, as a dogma that must be believed with Divine and Catholic Faith. God would not permit it, and He did not permit it.

Msgr. Van Noort further explains that the definitive character of the doctrines of the OUM is known not by a single definitive act (such as an act of a council), but by "countless activities" – a multitude of non-infallible acts – which, when taken as a whole, make it clear that the particular doctrine has been clearly proposed as a revealed truth. He admits, however, that this "is frequently enough not too obvious." He also notes that one of the major signs that a doctrine has been sufficiently proposed as a *revealed truth* by the OUM is the universal and constant agreement of the theologians that the doctrine is a matter of divine faith. In his own words:

"Now, since a definitive proposal of this sort must blossom forth from countless activities which individually are neither definitive nor infallible, the existence of such a proposal (with the exception of some fundamental truth) is frequently enough not too obvious. The major signs of such a proposal are these: that the truth be taught throughout the world in popular catechisms, or, even more importantly, be taught by the universal *and constant* agreement of theologians as a matter belonging to faith.

The reason we prefer the agreement of theologians to the agreement of catechisms is that the latter, by the very fact of being intended for popular instruction, usually make no distinction between matters which must be held by divine-catholic faith and those which must be held by ecclesiastical faith, or simply as theologically certain. Furthermore, a papal document designates, as we have, the agreement of theologians as a *sign* of a definitive proposal by the Church. Listen to Pius IX: 'By divine faith are to be believed those things which, through the ordinary teaching of the whole Church throughout the world, are proposed as divinely revealed and, as a result, by the *universal and constant consent* of Catholic theologians are held to be matters of faith.'"[14]

In his July 1956 article "An Essay on the Authority of the Teaching of the Sovereign Pontiff," Dom Paul Nau explains the infallibility of the Church's Ordinary Magisterium as follows:

> "The infallibility of the Ordinary Magisterium, whether of the Universal Church or that of the See of Rome, is not that of a judgment, not that of an act to be considered in isolation, as if it could itself provide all the light necessary for it to be clearly seen. It is that of the guarantee bestowed on a doctrine by the simultaneous or continuous convergence of a plurality of affirmations or explanations, none of which could bring positive certitude if it were taken by itself alone. Certitude can be expected only from the whole complex, but all the parts concur in making up the whole."[15]

Since a definitive proposal from the OUM is known by the coalescence of a multitude of non-infallible acts over time and geographies which are in conformity with Catholic Tradition, it goes without saying that a *single, non-definitive* teaching of a "pastoral council" does not constitute an infallible teaching of the Church, either by virtue of the Extraordinary Magisterium, or the Ordinary and Universal Magisterium, as Mr. Daly imagines.

Revealed Truths vs. Disciplines

Mr. Daly's erroneous theory has unfortunately been adopted by a number of Sedevacantists, who have themselves used it in an attempt to "prove" that Vatican II violated the Church's infallibility, thereby further "proving" (as we noted earlier), that the Church from 1958 forward is not the true Church and the conciliar Popes not true Popes.

Furthermore, Mr. Daly's novel theory has even been extended by some to embrace other aspects of the faith, such as disciplines and liturgical matters, which are said to constitute a violation of the infallibility of the Ordinary and Universal Magisterium. Because of this additional error, it is necessary to clarify the *object of infallibility* specified by the First Vatican Council. Before doing so, however, let us again read the quotation from *Dei Filius* that Mr. Daly uses as the

---

[14] *The Sources of Revelation*, pp. 222-223.
[15] Entire article published in *Pope or Church?*, citation found on p. 18 (emphasis added).

authority for his position (noting the plain words of the document, such as "divinely revealed"). Note well the underlined key phrases:

> "All those things are to be <u>believed with divine and Catholic faith</u> which are contained in the Word of God, written or handed down, and are <u>proposed</u> by the Church either by a solemn judgment <u>or by her ordinary and universal magisterium to be believed as divinely revealed</u>."[16]

As was discussed earlier in this chapter, only truths *revealed* by God and *definitively proposed* by the Church are to be "believed with divine and Catholic Faith." These truths, of course, refer exclusively to those contained within the sources of Revelation, i.e., Scripture or Tradition, since only these have been revealed by God. This is further confirmed by the last underlined passage from *Dei Filius* which explicitly states that such teachings must be proposed "to be believed *as divinely revealed.*" Thus, the *object* of infallibility specified by the Council is *revealed truths*, and revealed truths only. It does not include universal disciplines or liturgical matters, as some Sedevacantists have erroneously imagined (we will address disciplinary infallibility in depth in Chapters 15 and 16).

Commenting on the above teaching from the First Vatican Council, Msgr. Van Noort explained the meaning of the phrase "as divinely revealed." He begins by saying, "the subject matter of divine-Catholic faith are all those truths proposed by the Church's Magisterium as *divinely revealed,*" and then adds:

> "Note the phrase: '*as divinely revealed.*' To meet this requirement the truths must: a) be contained in public revelation, the depositories of which are Sacred Scripture and divine apostolic tradition. ... b) It is more probable – in accord with what was explained in the preceding article about 'virtual' revelation – that the truths must be contained in the sources of revelation *formally.*"[17]

In the following quotation, Canon Berthod comments on the same teaching from the First Vatican Council, and explains that it does not refer to everything taught by the Magisterium, but only those teachings proposed as "revealed truth." He wrote:

---

[16] Dogmatic Constitution *Dei Filius,* chapter 3, "Concerning Faith."
[17] *The Sources of Revelation,* p.220.

"In the Conciliar definition [*Dei Filius*, chapter 3], the obligation to believe has a specific object: one must believe all that is contained in the deposit of revelation and what the Church proposes to be believed as <u>revealed truth. It does not designate, as is sometimes said, everything that the Magisterium proposes, but only those propositions the Magisterium propounds as revealed truth.</u>"[18]

Universal disciplines, the liturgy, and even theological conclusions do *not* fall within the category of formally "revealed truth." This means the infallibility of the Ordinary and Universal Magisterium, as taught by Vatican I, does not extend to these aspects of the faith. Neither would infallibility extend to the "pastoral" novelties of Vatican II, such as ecumenism which, as Cardinal Ratzinger himself admitted, has no foundation in the New Testament[19] (which confirms that they are not "revealed truths"). Novelties, disciplinary and liturgical matters, and other non-revealed aspects of the Faith lack the *quiddity*[20] necessary to be the object of an infallible teaching of the Ordinary and Universal Magisterium that must be believed with divine and Catholic Faith. Hence, by their very nature, these matters clearly fall outside the scope of infallibility of the OUM as taught by the First Vatican Council.

Formally Revealed and Virtually Revealed

Let's briefly explore the object of infallibility specified by the First Vatican Council by considering in more detail the two categories of *revealed truths*, discussed earlier in this chapter, as well as the two kinds of faith owed to them.

Formally Revealed: A truth is said to be formally contained in Revelation if it is taught in Scripture or Tradition, either explicitly or implicitly. A doctrine is *explicitly revealed* if it taught using terminology that is absolutely clear and unmistakable (e.g., the Divinity of Christ). A doctrine is *implicitly revealed* if it is contained in Scripture or Tradition in a vague fashion, not in precise terms, but in equivalent terms (e.g., the Assumption of Mary).[21]

Another way a doctrine is contained *implicitly* in the sources of Revelation is when the truth is deduced from two *explicitly revealed*

---

[18] *Pope or Church?*, p. 57 (emphasis added).

[19] In his 1966 book, *Theological Highlights of Vatican II*, Ratzinger wrote: "The ecumenical movement grew out of a situation unknown to the New Testament and for which the New Testament can therefore offer no guidelines."

[20] As we saw in Chapter 1, *quiddity* is a philosophical term which means the inherent nature or essence of someone or something. The "whatness" of the thing.

[21] *The Sources of Revelation*, p. 206.

premises. Van Noort uses the following as an example: a) "Grace is required for each and every supernatural work" (explicitly revealed); b) "the beginning of faith is a supernatural work" (explicitly revealed). The conclusion: "Grace is required for the beginning of Faith," is said to be implicitly, but *formally*, contained in Revelation.[22]

Virtually Revealed: A truth is said to be *virtually* contained within the sources of Revelation when the doctrine is not itself revealed (e.g., Limbo for deceased, unbaptized babies), but is deduced from two premises, only one of which is explicitly revealed (e.g., baptism is necessary for salvation), while the other is known by reason (e.g., deceased, unbaptized babies merit neither Heaven nor the pain of sense in hell).[23] As we have noted, another name for a truth only virtually contained in Revelation is a *theological conclusion*.

Divine and Catholic Faith vs. Ecclesiastical Faith

As we've seen, Divine Faith is faith in the authority of God revealing; Ecclesiastical Faith is faith in the authority of the Church teaching.[24] Truths that have been *formally* revealed by God must be believed with divine and Catholic Faith,[25] but according to a majority of theologians,[26] including Van Noort and Tanquerey,[27] Catholics are only required to accept truths *virtually* contained within the sources of Revelation with Ecclesiastical Faith. Msgr. Fenton, who happened to adhere to the minority opinion on this point, admitted that "a great number of the manuals of sacred theology, current in our time, assert that... the assent due to these teachings [truths virtually contained in Revelation] is that of a strictly Ecclesiastical Faith."[28]

The distinction between the two kinds of faith owed to the two categories of doctrine is due to the differing *motives* for belief, which correspond to the *authority* of the teacher. The teacher can be God, the Church, or man. The motive for believing a truth formally revealed by God is "the authority of God Himself revealing, who can neither

---

[22] Ibid., p. 207.
[23] Ibid., p. 206.
[24] Ibid., pp. 187-188.
[25] Ibidl, p. 195.
[26] Van Noort discusses both opinions and provides a compelling refutation of those who maintain that Divine and Catholic Faith is due to truths only virtually contained in Revelation (Ibid., pp. 209-210). Also see Tanquerey, *A Manual of Dogmatic Theology*, vol. I, p. 204.
[27] *A Manual of Dogmatic Theology*, vol. 1, p. 145.
[28] Fenton, "The Question of Ecclesiastical Faith," *American Ecclesiastical Review*, April, 1953.

deceive nor be deceived,"[29] whereas the motive for believing a truth only virtually contained in Revelation is the authority of the infallible Church teaching. Hence, Divine Faith is owed to the former, while only Ecclesiastical Faith is owed to the latter.

The term Divine and Catholic Faith is used to designate the kind of faith owed to doctrines that have been *revealed by God* and also *definitively proposed* by the Church. For example, the dogma of papal infallibility must be believed with Divine and Catholic Faith because it is both formally revealed (in Scripture and Tradition) and definitively proposed by the Church (*Pastor Aeternus*). However, when the Church tells us that Pope Pius X, for example, is among the blessed in Heaven, we believe it with Ecclesiastical Faith.

As we saw earlier, when the Church proposes a truth merely "authentically" (and not "definitively" as "revealed truth"), the motive is one of religious obedience only, and consequently the teaching is accepted with a religious assent. When a teaching is accepted on the authority of man alone (such as a scientist explaining his conclusions based on a study of empirical evidence), it is called human faith.[30]

The distinction between Divine and Catholic Faith and Ecclesiastical Faith is important because the definition from the First Vatican Council specifies that the subject matter for an infallible teaching of the Ordinary and Universal Magisterium consists of truths that "are to be believed with Divine and Catholic faith" which, according to a majority of theologians,[31] limits the scope of the subject matter to truths contained within the sources of Revelation *formally*.[32] As noted above, this necessarily *excludes* disciplinary and liturgical aspects of the faith, as well as novelties such as "ecumenism" and "interreligious dialogue," which do not even have a clearly defined meaning, and are most certainly not part of Revelation.

---

[29] *The Sources of Revelation*, pp. 197, 205.

[30] Ibid., p. 188.

[31] It should also be noted that the minority of theologians who hold that Divine and Catholic Faith is owed to truths only *virtually* revealed, all agree that such an assent is only owed when these doctrines have been "defined by the Church" (Ibid, p. 210).

[32] It should be noted that we are not addressing the question of whether the Church's infallibility extends to truths that are only virtually contained in the sources of revelation. The question is whether virtually revealed truths are to be adhered to with "Divine and Catholic Faith," since this is what the teaching from the First Vatican Council specifies as the object of the infallibility of the Ordinary and Universal Magisterium.

Truly Universal

Mr. Daly's private interpretation of the First Vatican Council also fails to comprehend that for a teaching of the Ordinary and Universal Magisterium to be infallible, it must be truly *universal* – that is, in conformity to what the Church has *always* taught and *always* believed (at least implicitly). In other words, it must be in conformity to Tradition. Again, Vatican I's *Dei Filius* states:

> "One must believe by divine and Catholic faith all that is contained in the word of God, whether written <u>or transmitted by Tradition,</u> and which the Church, whether by a solemn judgment or by her ordinary and universal Magisterium, proposes to be believed as revealed truth."

In order to justify his assertion that Vatican II violated the Church's infallibility, Mr. Daly actually denies this most fundamental teaching of the First Vatican Council. That is, he claims that for a teaching of the Ordinary and Universal Magisterium to be protected by infallibility, it only has to be universal *in place* (synchronic universality), and not also universal *in time* (diachronic universality), and therefore does *not* have to be "contained in the word of God," and "transmitted by Tradition." Of course, was necessary for Mr. Daly to make this erroneous claim in order to argue that Vatican II violated the Church's infallibility, since he knows full well that any errors or novelties found in the conciliar documents were not taught by the Church universally *in time*.

In limiting Sacred Tradition to just a *moment* in time, Daly not only perverts the very meaning of Tradition, but also concedes that the novelties of Vatican II were *never taught by the pre-conciliar Magisterium*. That is, they were not taught *universally in time* and hence cannot be "infallible." But for John Daly, infallibility has nothing to do with Tradition, much less "revealed truths" that are "definitively proposed." Rather, for Daly, every utterance from an ecumenical council – just because the utterance is voiced by a majority of bishops in time – is, and indeed, must be infallible.

We will allow Mr. Daly to explain it for himself. In his customary haughty tone, he wrote:

> "Other escapists, unwilling to falsify easily verifiable facts about the Council itself, have cheerfully altered Catholic doctrine instead. They claim in particular that the Ordinary and Universal Magisterium is infallible only when the teaching it proposes is not only taught by all the bishops <u>at a given moment</u> but can also be

shown to have been taught by them <u>over a very lengthy period</u>. To justify this claim they appeal to the famous 'Vincentian Canon' or touchstone of traditional doctrine: 'What has always been believed, everywhere, and by all.' (...) <u>But the requirement is in fact heretical!</u> (...) <u>The term 'universal' implies universality in place, not in time. In technical terms, it is synchronic universality, not diachronic universality, which conditions the infallibility</u>. (...). If flagrantly false doctrine is taught under conditions that ought to guarantee infallibility, it is not just the novelty that must be rejected, but the authority imposing it also, for legitimate authority cannot err in such cases and blatant error is therefore a sure proof of illegitimacy."[33]

The true "escapist" is Mr. John Daly, who has "escaped" from the very definition of Sacred Tradition with his Sedevacantist agenda. In fact, Daly's agenda leads him to accuse *the Church's* definition of Tradition as being "heretical," since *Dei Filius* defines Tradition as what has been "handed down," while John Daly says it's what is taught "at a given moment." If Daly's definition is correct, then why weren't the Arian bishops teaching infallibly when they said Christ was not equal to the Father? After all, almost the entire episcopacy[34] "at this given moment" in history embraced this Christological error. The answer? John Daly's definition of Tradition is erroneous and even heretical, - as heretical, in fact, as the most anti-Catholic Protestant's usage of the term.

Even the most unsophisticated reader will note that Mr. Daly did not cite a single source to support his novel statement that the word "universal" refers to universality in place only, and not also time. Nor did he provide a single quotation supporting his statement that "it is synchronic universality (in place), not diachronic universality (in time), *which conditions the infallibility*." That's because no such *Catholic* sources or quotations exist. Such *ipse dixit* assertions may impress Daly's

---

[33] Daly, "Did Vatican II Teach Infallibly?," Second Revised Edition, 2014 (emphasis added) at http://www.novusordowatch.org/vatican-ii-infallible.htm

[34] In the book, *The Faith of the Early Fathers*, Fr. Jurgens noted that at one point during the Arian Crisis, the percentage of bishops in possession of Sees, who adhered to the true Faith, as opposed to those adhering to the Arian heresy, "was no greater than something between 1% and 3% of the total." (Jurgens, *The Faith of the Early Fathers*, vol. 2, p. 39). While almost all of the bishops embraced the Arian heresy, a good share of the laity did not do so. And yet no theologian has ever taught that the episcopacy defected, especially due to the judgment of the laity who had no authority to depose their bishops. The defection theory would also not explain how all of these defecting bishops were reincorporated back into the Church, especially since most Sedevacantists maintain that public heresy or defection bars a man from attaining (or reattaining) ecclesiastical office under Divine law.

Sedevacantist audience, but they will not fool the Catholic with even a rudimentary understanding of the true meaning of Tradition.

Universal in Space and Time

For additional Catholic teaching that reveals the errors of John Daly's position, we can look to the instruction of René Berthod and his article on the infallibility of the Ordinary and Universal Magisterium. Berthod explains that the word "universal" in the phrase Ordinary and Universal Magisterium comprises *two* dimensions, namely, extension in space (synchronic universality) and duration in time (diachronic universality). He wrote:

> "It would be an abuse to declare irreformable all the acts of the ordinary Magisterium. In order for them to be preserved from error according to the divine promise, they must be universal, which means that they must teach what the Church has always believed and always taught since the time of the Apostles, since the revealed deposit was closed. The Magisterium is universal when it proclaims the Faith of the Church unaltered throughout history. The notion of universality comprises two dimensions: extension in space and duration in time. ... This is how the theologians have always understood it. ... For the authenticity of the Ordinary Magisterium to be guaranteed, it is necessary that its teaching be universal in scope, that is, in conformity to the constant teaching of the Church throughout the centuries. In other words, it must agree with Tradition... For the Ordinary Magisterium of the Church to be infallible, it must be universal in the full sense of the word, including both space and time."[35]

Here we see a real Church-approved theologian (with a mandate to teach about such matters) directly contradict the claims of John Daly (a layman with no authority) by explaining how the Church's "theologians have always understood" the term universal – an understanding that Daly publicly proclaims is "heretical." Perhaps Daly should add the word "heresy" (along with "Tradition") to the list of terms he needs to learn before publicly pontificating about these matters.

---

[35] *Pope or Church?*, pp. 58-59.

Synchronic and Diachronic Universality

Mr. Daly's absurd claim that synchronic universality alone conditions infallibility was also rejected by the post-conciliar Magisterium. In 1998, the Congregation for the Doctrine of Faith issued a clarification of John Paul II's 1989 *Professio Fidei*. The Doctrinal Commentary on *Professio Fidei*, signed by Cardinal Ratzinger, says:

> "The Magisterium of the Church, however, teaches a doctrine to be believed as divinely revealed (first paragraph) or to be held definitively (second paragraph) with an act which is either defining or non-defining. In the case of a defining act, a truth is solemnly defined by an 'ex cathedra' pronouncement by the Roman Pontiff or by the action of an ecumenical council. In the case of a non-defining act, a doctrine is taught infallibly by the ordinary and universal Magisterium of the Bishops dispersed throughout the world who are in communion with the Successor of Peter. (...) Consequently, when there has not been a judgement on a doctrine in the *solemn form* of a definition, but this doctrine, belonging to the inheritance of the *depositum fidei*, <u>is taught by the ordinary and universal Magisterium, which necessarily includes the Pope, such a doctrine is to be understood as having been set forth infallibly</u> (17)."[36]

Notice that the end of the last sentence includes a reference to footnote "17." The purpose of this footnote was to clarify how the word "universal," included in the name "Ordinary and Universal Magisterium," is to be understood. Cardinal Ratzinger explains that "universality" is understood *primarily* as referring to *diachronic universality* (universality in *time*), and not necessarily a *synchronic universality* (universality in *space*). Thus, Cardinal Ratzinger's explanation is the exact opposite of John Daly's assertion. Wrote Cardinal Ratzinger:

> "It should be noted that the infallible teaching of the ordinary and universal Magisterium is not only set forth with an explicit declaration of a doctrine to be believed or held definitively, but is also expressed by a doctrine implicitly contained in a practice of the Church's faith, derived from revelation or, in any case, necessary for eternal salvation, and attested to by the uninterrupted Tradition:

---

[36] *Doctrinal Commentary on the Concluding Formula of the Professio Fidei,* Congregation for the Doctrine of the Faith, published in *L'Osservatore Romano,* Weekly Edition in English July 15, 1998, pp. 3-4 (emphasis added).

such an infallible teaching is thus objectively set forth by the whole episcopal body, understood in a diachronic and not necessarily merely synchronic sense."[37]

Here we have an official explanation from the Magisterium confirming that universality refers *primarily* to a universality in *time* (i.e., Tradition) and not necessarily a universality in space, notwithstanding the claims of Mr. John Daly. Common sense alone dictates that what is taught "at a given moment" (based, perhaps, on social, cultural or even demonic influences) may not necessarily be what the Church has *always* believed, as we saw, for example, during the Arian crisis of the fourth century.

Professor de Mattei reiterated the Church's emphasis on diachronic universality (extension in time) as the earmark of Apostolic Tradition. He wrote:

> "The constitution *Dei Filius* of the First Vatican Council, ascertained, in chapter 3, that there can be truths that must be believed, with Divine and Catholic faith in the Church, without the need of a solemn definition, since they are expressed in the Ordinary Universal Magisterium. The conditions necessary for the infallibility of the Ordinary Universal Magisterium are that it concerns a doctrine with regard to faith or morals, taught authoritatively in repeated declarations by the Popes and bishops, with an unquestionable and binding character.
>
> The word universal is meant not in the synchronic sense of an extension of space in a particular historical period, but in the diachronic sense of a continuity of time,[38] in order to express a consensus that embraces all epochs of the Church.
>
> For example, in the case of birth control, since the 3rd century the Church has condemned artificial methods. At the beginning of the 19th century, when this problem surfaced again, the declarations by bishops, in union with the Pope, stated, at all times, as definitive and binding doctrine of the Church, that contraception was a mortal sin. The explicit declarations of Pius XI, Pius XII and of all their successors, confirmed traditional teaching. (...)
>
> Quite different is the matter regarding doctrinal innovations included in the documents of the Second Vatican Council. In those cases not only is an *ex cathedra* act missing by the Pontiff in union with the bishops, but none of the documents were exposed in a dogmatic manner, with the intention of defining a truth of the faith

---

[37] Illustrative Doctrinal Note of the conclusive formula of *Professio fidei*, June 29, 1998, nota 17.

[38] Here de Mattei references the above Doctrinal Note by Cardinal Ratinger.

or morality and of binding the assent of the faithful. In those documents there can only be some passages infallible where the perennial doctrine of the Church is confirmed. 'Catholic,' in fact, is that which is *universal*, not what is in a given moment 'in every place' believed by everyone - which can occur at a Council or a Synod - but what is perennially everywhere believed by everyone, without equivocations and contradictions."[39]

The Holy Office Letter, *Suprema Haec Sacra*, which we addressed in Chapter 4, also confirms that universality refers to that which has *always* been believed, when it teaches:

> "We are bound by divine and Catholic faith to believe all those things which are contained in the word of God, whether it be Scripture or Tradition, and are proposed by the Church to be believed as divinely revealed, not only through solemn judgment but also through the ordinary and universal teaching office (magisterium). Now along those things which the Church has always preached [universality in time], and will never cease to preach, there is also contained that infallible statement by which we are taught that there is no salvation outside the Church."[40]

Pope Pius IX's *Tuas Libenter* also confirms the universality in both time and space when it teaches that the Ordinary Magisterium is infallible[41] when it proposes a teaching that represents the "common *and constant* teaching of the Catholic theologians." The venerable Pontiff says:

> "Even in the matter of that subjection which must be given in the act of divine faith, it should still not be restricted to those things that have been defined in the obvious degrees of the Oecumenical Councils or of the Roman Pontiffs or this See, but must also be extended to that which is taught as divinely revealed by the ordinary Magisterium of the entire Church spread throughout the world

---

[39] de Mattei, "The Synod and the Ordinary Magisterium of the Church," December 10, 2014. http://rorate-caeli.blogspot.com/2014/12/the-synod-and-ordinary-magisterium-of.html.

[40] *Suprema Haec Sacra*, English translation published in Fenton's *The Catholic Church and Salvation*, (New York: Seminary Press, 2006), pp. 100-101.

[41] Some have made a distinction between the Ordinary Magisterium and the Authentic Magisterium, and argued that the Ordinary Magisterium is always infallible, whereas the Authentic Magisterium is not. This distinction is fine on the speculative level, but it would be difficult to apply it practically, since on the practical level one will have a difficult time making a distinction between the two. However, this distinction does explain why some theologians will speak of the Ordinary Magisterium being infallible.

[universally in space], and which, <u>as a result, is presented as</u> <u>belonging to the faith according to the common and constant</u> <u>[universally in time] agreement of the Catholic theologians.</u>"[42]

It is quite interesting to note that Mr. Daly himself quoted *Tuas Libenter* in the article we have been discussing. But what is most revealing is that he quoted it twice and, in both instances, chose to remove the portion that spoke of the universality in time! Here is one of the sections of Mr. Daly's article in which he cites the teaching of Blessed Pius IX. The ellipsis (three dots indicating something is missing) is in the original:

> "It should also be noted that when the Fathers of the 1870 Vatican Council were discussing the draft of *Dei Filius* before voting, questions were raised about the meaning of the word 'universal' in the expression 'Ordinary and Universal Magisterium' and the Council's official 'relator,' Bishop Martin, referred them to Pope Pius IX's *Tuas Libenter*. This document clarifies exceedingly well the obligations of the faithful regarding acts by which representatives of the teaching Church communicate doctrine to them. Here is the most relevant part, which confirms precisely the words of Mgr. Martin:
>
> 'Even limiting oneself to the submission made by the act of divine faith, this could not be restricted to those things that have been defined by the express decrees of ecumenical councils and by the decrees of this See, but must be extended also to what is passed on as divinely revealed by the Ordinary Magisterium of the whole Church spread over the world...' [*Tuas Libenter*]."[43]

So Mr. Daly chose to include the section referring to a universality in space - "the whole Church spread over the world" – yet removed the remainder of the same sentence that spoke of a universality in time – "the *common and constant* agreement of the Catholic theologians." And he conveniently removed the same part of the sentence *each time* that he quoted the document (which, as we have seen, is an editorial tactic commonly employed by Daly's colleagues, Fr. Cekada and John Lane, as well). Is it possible that Mr. Daly ran out of word space in his piece, or is it more likely that he intentionally removed the ending of the

---

[42] *Tuas Libenter,* English translation published in *The Catholic Church and Salvation*, by J. Fenton, (Seminary Press, New York, 2006), p. 4.
[43] Daly, "Did Vatican II Teach Infallibly?," Second Revised Edition, 2014. http://www. novusordowatch.org/vatican-ii-infallible.htm.

sentence because it completely eviscerates the entire thesis of his article? We shall let the reader decide.

Unfortunately, John Daly is not the only Sedevacantist to have pulled this fast one on his readers. In an internet piece written in response to an article published in *Catholic Family News*,[44] a Sedevacantist pontificator quoted *Tuas Libenter* and *removed the very same part*. Here is what he wrote (ellipsis in the original):

> "A plethora of magisterial sources teach that the charism of infallibility extends not only to solemn judgments, but to the ordinary and universal magisterium. ... When the Vatican I Fathers questioned the meaning of the word 'universal,' the answer was given from reference to Pope Pius IX's *Tuas Libenter* (12/21/1863): 'Even limiting oneself to the submission made by the act of divine faith, this could not be restricted to those things that have been defined by the express decrees of ecumenical councils and by the decrees of this See, but must be extended also to what is passed on as divinely revealed by the Ordinary Magisterium of the whole Church spread over the world...'"[45]

As we have seen throughout this book, such deliberate deception and editorial subterfuge is chief among the tactics one finds regularly in Sedevacantist writings. Willful omissions, use of sentence fragments and quotes taken out of context, coupled with sophistical argumentation and accusations of heresy against their opposition is par for the course for Sedevacantist apologists. To be fair, the internet pontificator almost certainly cut and pasted the quotation from Mr. Daly's article, without bothering to verify the source. But such shoddy, copy-cat research among Sedevacantist writers, which is motivated more by winning an argument than presenting the truth, becomes a case of the blind leading the blind (*cf.* Mt. 15:14).

In closing, while Vatican II was an extraordinary gathering of the world's bishops with the Pope, it did not teach infallibly either by virtue of the Extraordinary or the Ordinary and Universal Magisterium. The council's novel teachings on religious liberty, ecumenism, collegiality, interfaith prayer, interreligious dialogue and all the rest are not revealed truths from Scripture or Tradition (neither formally nor virtually), nor were they definitively proposed by the council as such. They not only lacked synchronic universality, since not

---

[44] Siscoe, "Can We Recognize and Resist?," *Catholic Family News,* January 2015.
[45] Speray, "Catholic Family News, Reprobated, Proscribed, and Condemned," March 4, 2015.

all bishops at the time accepted these teachings, but, as the Sedevacantist themselves proclaim, these novelites (e.g., religious liberty, ecumenism) are not part of Tradition, and therefore lack diachronic universality. Thus, in no way did the Second Vatican Council engage the charism of infallibility, which Paul VI and Benedict XVI have made clear.

Those, like the Sedevacantists, who have ascribed infallibility to Vatican II, have committed the error of excess, based upon their false Major Premise that whatever the Pope approves must be true and good because "the Pope is infallible." This small error in principle has led them to a big error in conclusion – the error of Sedevacantism and separation from the Church.

Chapter 15

~ Universal Disciplines and Infallibility ~

In this chapter, we will address another alleged violation of the Church's infallibility, which is that of universal disciplines. Sedevacantists will begin by citing reputable theologians who teach that the Church's infallibility extends to universal disciplinary laws. Next, they will argue that certain post-conciliar disciplines, such as female altar servers and Communion in the Hand (and the New Mass, which will be discussed in the next chapter) are harmful to the Faith. They will conclude by saying it is "impossible" for these disciplines to have been permitted by the Church founded by Christ, and consequently the Church that approved them could not have been the Catholic Church. We will allow Fr. Cekada to explain their position:

> "We have published this little summary of the argument many times over the past decades, and it will be helpful to do so again here. The argument is essentially the same for all the post-Vatican II 'popes,' even though its force has become much more evident with the arrival of Bergoglio.

- Officially-sanctioned Vatican II and post-Vatican II teachings and laws embody errors and/or promote evil.

- Because the Church is indefectible, her teaching cannot change, and because she is infallible, her laws cannot give evil.

- It is therefore **impossible** that the errors and evils officially sanctioned in Vatican II and post-Vatican II teachings and laws could have proceeded from the authority of the Church. (...)

- The best explanation for the post-Vatican II errors and evils we repeatedly encounter is that they proceed from individuals who, despite their occupation of the Vatican and of various diocesan cathedrals, publicly defected from the faith, and therefore do not objectively possess canonical authority."[1]

Now, we have already demonstrated that it is not "impossible" for the Pope to teach error when he does not exercise the charism of

---

[1] "Sedevacantism: A Quick Primer," February 2015, http://www.fathercekada.com /2013/11/19/Sedevacantism-a-quick-primer/.

infallibility, according to the parameters set down by the First Vatican Council. It is an historical fact that Pope John XXII publicly taught, and even tried to impose upon the faithful,[2] an error that was formally condemned as a heresy by his immediate successor.[3] This fact proves that Popes *can* teach error, since "against a fact there is no argument" (*contra factum non fit argumentum*).

Fr. Cekada's statement that "errors and evils" could *only* have come from those who have "publicly defected from the faith and therefore do not objectively possess canonical authority" is also false. As we have seen, according to canon law, a prelate "publicly defects from the faith" by *publicly* joining a non-Catholic sect, which did not happen with any of the post-Vatican II Popes or other members of the hierarchy who have, to use the words of Fr. Cekada, continue to occupy "the Vatican and of various diocesan cathedrals."

Like Bishop Sanborn, Fr. Cekada has fallen into the error of confusing authority with infallibility. As we saw in the previous chapter, this fundamental error, which Arnaldo da Silveira refers to as "Monolithic Infallibility," extends infallibility beyond the precise limits established by the Church. As we've seen in spades, this error is pervasive within Sedevacantism, and has caused its adherents to conclude that the visible Church has defected (a view which itself contradicts the doctrine of the indefectibility of the Church). We see this erroneous conclusion above, where Fr. Cekada asserts that the "best explanation" for the alleged violations of the Church's infallibility is that the hierarchy has defected. This may be the "best explanation" for Reverend Anthony Cekada, but it is *no* explanation at all for those who have retained their faith in the promises of Christ for His Church.

In this chapter, we will demonstrate that Fr. Cekada and his colleagues are wrong in claiming that the novel disciplines issuing from Vatican II have violated the Church's infallibility. God may have permitted much evil in the Church over the past 50 years, just as he permitted much evil to be inflicted upon Christ during His Passion, but He has remained faithful to all of His divine promises, and consequently has not allowed a single violation of the Church's infallibility.

---

[2] "When the Pope [John XXII] tried to impose this erroneous doctrine on the Faculty of Theology in Paris, the King of France, Philip VI of Valois, prohibited its teaching…" (de Mattei, "Pope Who Fell Into Heresy, a Church that Resisted: John XXII and the Beatific Vision," January 28, 2015).
[3] Benedict XII, *Benedictus Deus* of January 29, 1336 (Denz., 530); also see the Bull, *Laetentur Coeli,* (Pope Eugene IV) issued by the Council of Florence (Denz., 693).

Primary vs. Second Objects of Infallibility

As has been explained in previous chapters, theologians distinguish between *primary* and *secondary* objects of infallibility. The primary (direct) object of infallibility concerns the truths revealed by God contained in Scripture and Tradition (the Deposit of Faith). When these truths are *definitively proposed* by the Church, infallibility is engaged by the Divine Redeemer's promise, and the possibility of error is prevented.

There are also secondary (indirect) objects of infallibility, which include such things as theological conclusions, universal disciplines, dogmatic facts, and the canonization of saints (canonizations are addressed in Chapter 17).[4] These matters are not contained in the Deposit of Faith, but help to foster and preserve the integrity of revealed truth. While it is a common theological opinion that the Church's infallibility embraces the secondary objects, the Church herself has never definitively taught this, much less clarified to what extent infallible protection would be guaranteed.[5]

As we saw, the First Vatican Council narrowly defined the precise scope and parameters of papal infallibility. Whenever the Pope, as the universal pastor and teacher of all Christians, defines a doctrine on faith or morals to be believed by the universal Church, he teaches infallibly. Thus, we know with certainty the scope and parameters of infallibility as it relates to the *primary object* (faith and morals revealed in Scripture and Tradition). However, because the Church has not spoken definitively with respect to any of those matters that constitute the secondary object,[6] we do not have the same clarity regarding whether, and, if so, to what extent, infallible protection is guaranteed.[7]

---

[4] For example, the doctrine of the "immorality of the soul" is a theological conclusion deduced from divine revelation. That the Council of Nicea (325 A.D.) was an ecumenical council of the Catholic Church is a dogmatic fact. While these and other such truths are not part of the Deposit of Faith, they are essential to its preservation and transmission.

[5] "It is important to recall that the Magisterium has never definitively settled the question of whether it can speak definitively about a matter that is not in the deposit of revelation, and still less has it settled definitively the question as to the limits of such an object of infallible teaching." (Sullivan, Francis, *The Theologian's Ecclesial Vocation*, 56).

[6] A schema was drafted for discussion at the First Vatican Council, which was intended to define the paramaters for the Church's infallible teaching authority with respect to the seconday objects of infallibility. Due to the break out of the Franco-Prussian War, the schema was never acted upon. (*Schema Primum de Ecclesia*, Canon IX, Mansi 51.552.)

[7] "After Vatican I, the explicit distinction between two objects of infallibility, the primary object corresponding to revealed truths and a secondary object corresponding to non-revealed truths, became common in the manuals. In some cases, the second category was defined quite narrowly as those facts necessary to defend revelation, and, in other instances, defined quite broadly as facts merely "connected" to revelation. ... Bishop

Does infallibility extend to universal disciplinary laws? If so, is it only universally binding laws, or does it even include what the Church merely *permits?* And what do the theologians mean by saying a universal law cannot be spiritually *harmful?* Sedevacantists would have us believe the answers to these questions are settled, and yet they themselves disagree with each other about the answers.

For example, some Sedevacantists argue that Communion in the Hand is a harmful and sacrilegious discipline, which necessarily violates the Church's infallibility, while other Sedevacantists disagree. During a private conversation with an author of this book, one Sedevacantist apologist stated that he has no problem with Communion in the Hand, since it was permitted in the early Church, while another declares that such permission is "proof" that the post-Vatican II Church has defected.

Some claim that the 1917 Code of Canon Law contains evil and harmful disciplinary laws. For example, the Sedevacantist apologist, Richard Ibranyi, declares that canon 1258, which permits Catholics to passively attend the religious service of a non-Catholic sect,[8] is not only an evil law, but one that *causes* men to commit mortal sin. He wrote:

> "This [Canon 1258] is an evil law because it denies a doctrine that belongs to the ordinary magisterium, blasphemes God, creates scandal, and causes men to commit mortal sins. Hence, any pope or anyone else who supports and defends this evil law commits all of these mortal sins. ... it is a doctrine of the ordinary magisterium that Catholics are forbidden to even passively attend services in non-Catholic churches, which means being present but not participating in the services in any way. Hence Canon Law 1258, which teaches Catholics are allowed to passively attend non-Catholic services, is a mortally sinful law for violating a doctrine that belongs to the

---

Gasser, in his relation offered to the council, made explicit mention of the possibility of the Church's infallibility extending to non-revealed truths, but presents these as truths taught infallibly only to the extent that they are necessary to safeguard divine revelation." (Gaillardetz, Richard, *The Ordinary Universal Magisterium:*
Unresolved Questions, Theological Studies 63, 2002).
[8] 1917 Code of Canon Law: "Canon 1258. It is unlawful for the faithful to assist in any *active manner,* or to take part in the sacred services of non-Catholics. At funerals of non-Catholics, at their marriages, and similar solemnities, provided there is no danger of perversion or scandal, *passive or merely material presence* on account of a civil office or for the purpose of showing respect to a person may be tolerated for a grave reason..." (emphasis added).

ordinary magisterium, as well as for the other mortal sins mentioned above."[9]

Mr. Ibranyi then goes on to argue that this law is condemned by the Bible, both the Old and New Testaments, and is contrary to the previous teaching of the Magisterium. According to his private judgment, canon 1258, which was promulgated by the Pope for the universal Church (at least the Western Rite) is an evil law. He also declares that canon 1374 of the old 1917 Code, which tolerates the practice of Catholic children being educated in non-Catholic schools, is an evil law that leads to mortal sin. He says:

> "Canon 1374 is a mortally sinful law that offends God and leads Catholic children into mortal sins because it allows Catholic children to attend certain non-Catholic schools under the false premise that there can be such a thing as a non-Catholic school that does not endanger the faith and morals of Catholic children."[10]

Mr. Ibranyi cites other canons from the 1917 Code as well, which he personally judges to be evil and harmful to souls. Does that mean the 1917 Code violated the Church's infallibility on universal disciplines? To use Fr. Cekada's reasoning, should we conclude that, since the Church is indefectible, the "best explanation" for these "evil laws" is that they proceeded "from individuals who, despite their occupation of the Vatican and of various diocesan cathedrals, publicly defected from the faith, and therefore do not objectively possess canonical authority" (which would include the anti-modernist Popes Pius XI and Pius XII)? Are we to rely upon the private judgment of individual Catholics, such as Mr. Ibranyi and Fr. Cekada (who disagrees with Ibranyi regarding the 1917 Code), to inform us which laws are so evil and so harmful that they constitute violations of the Church's disciplinary infallibility, and therefore prove that the Church from which they proceeded was not the Catholic Church? For all sane Catholics, the answers are obvious.

The Scope of Disciplinary Infallibility

When we consider how narrow is the scope of *doctrinal* infallibility (as defined by the Church), is it reasonable to presume, as

---

[9] Ibranyi, "Bad Laws in the 1917 Code," October 2008 http://www.john thebaptist.us/jbw_english/documents/books/rjmi/br15_bad%20Laws_in_1917_Code.p df.
[10] Ibid.

Sedevacantists do, that *disciplinary* infallibility (which has *not* been
defined by the Church), is even broader? If it is not contrary to the
Church's *doctrinal* infallibility for a Pope to publicly teach error, as did
John XXII (which was certainly *harmful* to souls), should we really
presume that *disciplinary* infallibility operates more extensively, to
prevent *all* harmful laws and practices? Put another way, is it
reasonable to hold that disciplinary infallibility, which has not been
defined by the Church, affords greater and broader protection than
doctrinal infallibility, which has been defined?

To add to the lack of clarity over this matter, the Church's
theologians speak of papal infallibility as both applying and also not
applying to disciplines promulgated by the Pope. For example, in his
1892 book, *Christianity and Infallibility*, Fr. Daniel Lyons explained that
papal infallibility only applies to the Pope as teacher, not as legislator
(i.e., lawgiver). He wrote:

> "Again, the pope, as Supreme Head of the Church, combines in
> his person four distinct offices, namely: first, the office of Teacher,
> and Guardian of the Christian Revelation; secondly, the office of
> Legislator in Ecclesiastical matters; thirdly, the office of Judge in
> Ecclesiastical causes; fourthly, the office of Governor and Ruler of
> God's spiritual Kingdom on earth. In this fourfold character the
> Pope is Supreme, and has the plenitude of authority over the entire
> Church, and over every branch of it throughout the world. But, and
> mark this well, he is infallible only in the discharge of the office of
> Teacher and Guardian of Revelation. He is not infallible as
> Supreme Legislator, or as Supreme Judge, or as Supreme Ruler; he
> is infallible only as Supreme Teacher; for to the teaching office
> alone has infallibility been promised and to that office it is
> expressly restricted by the Vatican Council. Consequently,
> objections based on the acts of the Pope either as Legislator, Judge,
> or Executor, have no force against the dogma of Infallibility."[11]

On the next page, he explicitly teaches that a Pope is not infallible
in disciplinary matters:

> "Now, in Catholic belief and teaching, the Pope is not infallible
> in matters of discipline, or of government; he is infallible only in
> matters of faith and morals; that is, exclusively in the doctrines that
> are to be believed and the duties that are to be fulfilled under the
> Christian Dispensation. All objections to Infallibility, therefore,

[11] Lyons, *Christianity and Infallibility* (New York: Longmans, Green & Co , 1892), pp. 12-13
(emphasis added).

founded on Bulls, Briefs, Constitutions, or Letters of Popes, or Decrees of Councils dealing with any of the many points of discipline and government just mentioned are at once disposed of. They do not touch the doctrine; they are simply irrelevant."[12]

After stating above that "the Pope is not infallible in disciplinary matters," Fr. Lyons included a footnote qualifying the statement by explaining that infallibility *does* extend to disciplines in rare cases. The footnote says:

> "It may happen, <u>in some rare cases</u>, that discipline is so closely bound up with matters of faith and morals, or is so necessary to the conservation of their integrity and purity, as to be inseparable from them. <u>In such cases the Pope is infallible in the matter of discipline;</u> but then, in such cases, discipline comes under the head of faith and morals, and strictly appertains to the <u>office of teaching and guarding them</u>."[13]

So, on the one hand, we are told that "the Pope is not infallible in matters of discipline," and on the other hand are told that, "*in some rare cases*... the Pope is infallible in the matter of discipline." How are we to reconcile this difficulty by knowing when, according to these theologians, infallibility does extend to universal disciplinary laws? We do so by making a basic distinction that is invariably overlooked (or purposefully avoided) by Sedevacantist apologists. And the reason it is overlooked or purposefully avoided is because of how limited the scope of disciplinary infallibility actually is.

Doctrinal vs. Prudential Judgments

When explaining what is and what is not covered by disciplinary infallibility, the Church's theologians make a distinction between a twofold judgment contained in disciplinary laws: a *doctrinal judgment* (whether the law squares with revealed truth) and a *prudential judgment* (whether the law is prudent under the circumstances). The theologians explain that infallibility only extends to the doctrinal judgment, and not the prudential judgment.

In his classic book, *The Church of Christ*, Fr. Sylvester Berry explains why he believes that the Church's infallibility extends to disciplinary laws:

---

[12] Ibid., p. 14 (emphasis added).
[13] Ibid., p. 27 (emphasis added).

"Disciplinary Matters: Under this head are included the laws and precepts established by ecclesiastical authority for the regulation of worship or for the guidance for the faithful throughout the world. Such laws and precepts are necessarily subject to the infallible authority of the Church, <u>because of their intimate connection with doctrines of faith and morals</u>."[14]

He then goes on to explain the twofold *doctrinal* and *prudential* judgment contained in such laws:

"Hence, in making laws, the Church implicitly passes a twofold judgment: one of the doctrine, the other of prudence: she judges that the law is not opposed to any revealed truth, and that, under the circumstances, it will assist and guide the faithful in the performance of their Christian duties. <u>The Church is necessarily infallible in this doctrinal judgment</u>, for it she were not, the faithful might be led into errors in doctrine at any time. <u>But there is no promise that the rulers of the Church shall always enjoy the greatest degree of prudence; consequently, there is no guarantee that their laws and precepts will always be the best possible under the circumstances. Neither is the Church infallible in applying her laws to particular cases.</u>"[15]

The reason infallibility is believed to extend to the doctrinal judgment (implicit in a disciplinary law) is because infallibility is directly a property of the Church's *teaching* function (when she teaches doctrine on faith and morals), and *not* (or only *indirectly*) part of her governing power. Infallible protection does not extend to the prudential judgments of the leaders of the Church (e.g., *when* a law is promulgated; *whether* it is prudent under the circumstances; *how* a law is worded, etc.). Disciplinary infallibility is believed to mean only that a universal discipline imposed upon the universal Church cannot directly contradict an article of faith.

In condemning the Liberals of his day who were expressing a desire to change the Church's disciplines, Pope Gregory XVI notes that some disciplinary laws are rooted in the divine law:

"When they pretend that all the forms of the Church without distinction can be changed, are they not subjecting to this change <u>those points of discipline which have their foundation in the divine law itself</u>, which are <u>joined to doctrines of faith</u> by so close a bond

---

[14] *The Church of Christ*, p. 291 (emphasis added).
[15] Ibid. (emphasis added).

that the rule of faith determines the rule of action? Are they not trying, moreover, to make of the Church something human; <u>are they not openly diminishing her infallible authority</u> and the divine power which guides her, in holding that her present discipline is subject to decay, to weakness, and to other failures of the same nature, and in imagining that it contains many elements which are not only useless but even prejudicial to the well-being of the Catholic religion?"[16]

Pope Gregory here expresses the relation between infallibility and the Church's disciplinary laws which are rooted in "divine law" and "joined to the *doctrines* of the faith."

In his classic book, *The Church of the Word Incarnate*, Cardinal Journet explained that "the precepts of the divine law, revealed by God and proposed by the declaratory power, have to be extended and made precise in the precepts of the ecclesiastical law, promulgated by the canonical or legislative power."[17] He went on to note that the ecclesiastical laws (i.e., disciplinary laws) that relate to the Deposit of Faith fall into one of two categories: they will either be a *consequence* of a revealed truth, or the *determination* of a revealed truth. He explains both categories and provides examples:

"The first will be drawn from the revealed law by way of *consequence*... For example, there is a divine precept enjoining all to 'eat the flesh of the Son of Man and drink his blood' (John vi. 54), and another enjoining the sinner to have recourse to one who in Jesus' name can 'forgive or retain sins' (John xx. 23). But seeing how easily men lose sight of things invisible, these precepts might be neglected by many; wherefore the Councils of Lateran and of Trent, with a wisdom confirmed by experience, have concluded to the obligation of annual confession and Easter communion.

The other class of precepts are drawn from the revealed law by way of *determination*. There is a scriptural precept imposing self-denial and fasting; hence the Church has determined certain forms of self-denial such as abstinence and certain modalities of fasting. It is a divine precept that Christ is to be honoured wherever He is; and He is in the Eucharist; so that the Church has provided for the public veneration of the Blessed Sacrament in processions. It is a divine precept that the Flesh of the Son of Man is to be eaten and His Blood drunk; but the Body and Blood of Christ are found under both the sacramental species, so that the precept will be observed whether we communicate under one species or under both; and the Church can regulate the matter according to the needs of the age.

[16] *Quo Graviora* (October 4, 1833).
[17] *The Church of the Word Incarnate*, p. 361.

Since the end of the Middle Ages she has chosen to give
communion to the laity only under one species, and to the clergy
too when they are not saying Mass. The precepts … are the work of
the canonical or legislative power, <u>which is not supported by any
absolute assistance, but by a prudential or relative assistance.</u> They
constitute a secondary practical message of the Church."[18]

Notice that the examples given are applications of revealed truth to
practical behavior, and the laws in question are universally applied to
the entire Church. But even in this case, he holds that these disciplinary
laws are not supported by an *absolute* assistance, but only by a practical
or relative assistance. This differs from the divine assistance as it relates
to *doctrines* defined by the Church. For example, referring to the
primary object of infallibility, the Cardinal wrote: "In transmitting it
and in declaring its meaning, the Church enjoys an infallible and
absolute assistance."[19]

Like papal and conciliar infallibility, disciplinary infallibility would
not be a *positive* quality of a particular law or discipline. It would not
inspire a Pope to promulgate a law or establish a discipline (much less
a good one). Rather, it would be only a *negative* protection. This means
the Holy Ghost would merely *prevent* the Church from *imposing* a
universal law that *directly contradicts* a doctrine on faith and morals. Fr.
Peter Scott explains:

"This is a profound observation on the negative quality of
disciplinary infallibility. It cannot be some positive quality of an
ecclesiastical law, as it is commonly understood to be. It is simply
the purely negative fact that the Church's disciplinary law does not
contradict divine or natural law. Consequently, there can be in the
Church, and frequently have been, bad laws, laws that are not
adapted to the common good, laws that contain all kinds of errors of
fact and practice. St. Thomas Aquinas would say that such laws are
not laws at all, since they are no longer an ordering of reason to the
common good (I-II, 96, 4), and that consequently it makes no sense
to speak of their infallibility. However, we can certainly admit that
inasmuch as such universal 'laws' are promulgated by the highest
authority in the Church, that of the Pope, they benefit from this
purely negative infallibility of which we are speaking. God would
not allow the Pope to make a universal law, related to the salvation

---

[18] Ibid (emphasis added).
[19] Ibid.

of souls, that would contain a direct contradiction to a doctrine of faith and morals."[20]

As we've mentioned, those who hold that infallibility extends to disciplinary laws should not understand it to mean that the Church is unable to permit imprudent disciplines, such as allowing the use of female altar servers or receiving Communion in the Hand (neither of which are directly contrary to a revealed truth). Whether a disciplinary law is prudent under the particular facts and circumstances is obviously a much different question than whether it directly contradicts a revealed truth, and therefore leads to sin and spiritual harm. There's no doubt the assistance of the Holy Ghost helps to guide the Church even in its prudential judgments, but, as history shows, the Church's authorities are certainly capable of resisting grace.

The theologians also note that disciplinary infallibility would only extend to laws intended for the universal Church, and then only when the Church engages its canonical or legislative authority *fully*, rather than merely partially. In this we see the symmetry between disciplinary infallibility and papal infallibility, which is only engaged when the Pope uses the *fullness of his authority* to define a doctrine of faith or morals *for the universal Church*. Cardinal Journet wrote:

> "When we speak of measures of general applicability [universal laws] the expression should not be taken in a material way [as applying to each and every individual], but in a living, qualitative and formal way. It indicates ecclesiastical measures which are general in a threefold respect: (1) by their final cause, (2) their formal cause, and (3) their efficient cause. (1) First, they reflect the common good of the supernatural society, to which they are immediately ordered, and they are, on the supernatural level, what measures of public safety are on the natural [final cause]. (2) Then, they are laws in the strict sense [formal cause], not commands in the strict sense: law, says St. Thomas, defines the rule of the common good, command applies this rule to particular matters. (3) Lastly, they engage the prudential authority of the Church fully, not merely partially: they must be approved by the whole Church [efficient cause], by an oecumenical council, by the Pope, not merely by a number of bishops or the Roman Congregations with the Pope giving his approval only 'in forma communi.' Most of the measures in question will in addition be general in their material cause, that is

---

[20] "Does the Church's Infallibility Extend to Disciplinary Laws?," Questions and Answers, November 2008. http://www.angelusonline.org/index.Php?section=articles &subsection=show_article&article_id=2804.

to say the subjects to whom they apply: the laws on Easter Communion, on fasting and abstinence, concern all the faithful; some however may concern only particular regions, or particular categories of the faithful such as clerics or religious. However, in spite of all this, it will not always be easy to recognize measures that are truly general. ... <u>the best sign of the universality with which the Church intends to invest a law lies in the insistence with which she proposes, approves and recommends it during the course of the ages.</u>"[21]

Note that, in Journet's explanation, a *universal* law is one that is promulgated with the *full force* of the Church's Magisterial authority, or at least one that the Church has proposed, approved and recommended throughout the centuries. It also must be approved by an ecumenical council or the Pope; not approved directly by bishops (or a bishops' conference), with the Pope later granting his approval *in forma communi*. This encompasses virtually *all* of the novel disciplines issuing since the council (including the New Mass itself, discussed in the next chapter), which have been largely introduced through "bishops" conferences and "Roman Congregations" (using Cardinal Journet's words), or merely permitted as an "indult," and therefore lack the full force of the Church's teaching authority. A merely imprudent practice which 1) does not directly contradict a revealed truth; and 2) was not promulgated with the full force of the Church's Magisterial authority, will not be covered by the Church's infallibility.

The following will illustrate why theologians maintain that infallibility extends to universal disciplinary laws only as far as they directly relate to revealed truths. If a council of the Church were to issue a universal law limiting the number of children in a family, and permitting Catholics use contraceptives after they reached the requisite number, such a law would *directly contradict* a moral doctrine of the Church, and thereby lead directly to sin and error. Such a law would be contrary to the very mission of the Church. Or, if the Church were to issue a "non-discriminatory" universal law allowing couples of the same gender to marry, we would again have a disciplinary law *directly contrary* to a revealed truth, since, according to Divine law, marriage can only be between a man and a woman. Once again, such a law would be contrary to the mission of the Church as it would lead souls to eternal ruin. For this reason, although the Church herself has never defined it, theologians commonly hold that the Church's infallibility

---

[21] *The Church of the Word Incarnate*, p. 367 (emphasis added; numbers added for clarity).

extends to the universal disciplinary laws insofar as they are directly related to revealed truths.

On the other hand, if the Church were to issue a particular law (as an exception to the general law), which permitted Catholics who had been divorced and civilly "remarried" to receive Holy Communion, *on the condition that they lived together as brother and sister,* the law would in no way violate a doctrine of the Church. Such a law may lend itself to much abuse, but the permission itself would not be a violation of the doctrinal judgment contained in the disciplinary law, since it would not contradict any doctrine of the Church (i.e., marriage is indissoluable; fornicators and adulterers - which those living together as brother and sister are not - cannot partake of the Eucharist). Further, if a Pope were to delegate authority to a bishops' conference to decide disciplinary matters, and if the bishops permitted a discipline that contradicted a doctrine of the Church, this would also not violate the Church's infallibility, since the decisions of bishops' conferences are not protected by the Church's infallibility. In the current crisis, it would not be surprising if God permitted such an evil for our time, to further sift the wheat from the chaff.

We can apply these same principles to controversial legislation recently issued by Pope Francis which radically streamlines the process for obtaining marriage annulments.[22] The new law substantially alters the time-proven juridical process by requiring only one judge and one sentence (thereby abolishing the requirement for a second judgment of nullity to settle the matter), shortening the process and even making it free of charge. In fact, following the announcement of the *Motu Proprio,* reports emerged that a dossier was circulated around the curia by senior Vatican officials which expressed grave objections to the new disciplines.[23] While the Pope's new legislation is clearly imprudent and will likely serve as a springboard for even more abuses in regard to declarations of nullity, it does not directly contradict the Church's infallible *doctrinal* teaching on the indissoluability of marriage.

In light of current events, which have pitted "Cardinal against Cardinal," there is reason to believe that further disciplines which undermine traditional Catholic teaching on marriage and family could indeed be introduced under the current Pope, and perhaps even receive the approval of those Cardinals who are valiantly standing up

[22] Published under the title *Mitis Judex Dominus Iesus* (for the Latin church) and *Mitis et Misericors Iesus* (for the Eastern rite churches), announced September 8, 2015.
[23] See Edward Pentin's article "Pope Attacked Over Motu Proprio; Cardinal Kasper Reasserts His Proposal" (September 11, 2015), http://www.ncregister.com/blog/edward-pentin/pope-attacked-over-motu-proprio-cardinal-kasper-reasserts-his-proposal.

for the Church's moral doctrine in the face of unrelenting attacks from the Left.[24] Nevertheless, as long as a universal disciplinary law does not directly contradict a doctrine of the Church, it would not violate any presumptive disciplinary infallibility as it relates to the *doctrinal judgment*. Further, there are historical cases (as we will see later in this chapter) in which universal disciplines could be seen as contradicting a *doctrinal* teaching of the Church. Until the Church herself defines infallibility as it relates to the secondary objects, there will remain a measure of uncertainty as to whether and to what extent the Church's charism of infallibility applies to laws and disciplines.

Prudential Decisions and Experiential Knowledge

Regarding the non-infallible prudential decisions of the Church (which are certainly not covered by the Church's infallibility), Cardinal Journet makes an interesting observation when considered in light of the current ecclesiastical crisis. He notes that in the Church's relations with the world, there is a certain degree of assistance by the Holy Ghost, but one that will not spare the Church trials, or even prevent her from falling into positive errors. God permits the Church to learn, by experience, just as Christ Our Lord learned by experiential knowledge.[25] The difference, of course, is that Christ could not make a prudential error, but only learned by experience that which He already knew by infused knowledge and by virtue of the Beatific Vision that He possessed from the moment of His conception. The Church, on the other hand, is able to learn experientially through mistakes, which are permitted by God for a greater good.

The Cardinal notes that there is a certain degree of relative infallibility (which is more akin to Providence than infallibility properly so-called) in the Church's prudential relations with the world, but only insofar as it sustains the Church in her existence, enabling her to retain the visible and permanent character promised by Christ. He wrote:

> "All the problems concerning the concrete relations of the Church with the kingdoms of this world, with great political movements and great cultural orientations, are therefore bound to present themselves to the canonical power. To enable it to solve

---

[24] Cardinal Burke, for example, has spoken publicly and approvingly about individuals he has met who were civilly remarried and living together as brother and sister for the sake of their children.
[25] See, for example, ST, III, q. 12, a. 2.

them, the Holy Spirit will support it. But this divine assistance, which I have called *biological*, will be of a particular kind. <u>It will spare the Church neither trials, nor hesitations, nor disappointments, nor even indubitable errors. It will often seem to exert only a very remote control over her conduct, to abandon her to merely human light and human power, to leave her to achieve her education at her own risk and peril and at the price of bitter experience.</u> Even more than the assistance promised to the particular ecclesiastical precepts, this biological assistance will be in the proper sense fallible. And yet, of this too it may be said that it is, in a sense, infallible, since it will be always sufficient to assure a certain general direction, to save at least the minimum of temporal conditions needed to ensure the permanence of the Church and her uninterrupted visible presence on the stage of history."[26]

In light of these comments, we recall that Cardinal Ratzinger said three of the more controversial documents of Vatican II were intended to reconcile the Church with the world, specifically, with the new Masonic era that came upon the world following the Masonic French Revolution in 1789. Commenting on "the merely pastoral council," we saw (in Chapter 13) the future Pope actually admit that the conciliar documents serve as a "countersyllabus" which "represents, on the part of the Church, an attempt at an official reconciliation with the new era inaugurated in 1789."[27] Needless to say, such an attempt to reconcile the Church with the world would be a grave mistake in the Church's practical judgment, but it is an "indubitable error" that God in His Providence could will to permit.

St. Augustine explained that God permits evil (including errors in practical judgment) so that He can draw out of it a greater good. The experiential knowledge the Church gains from prudential mistakes is itself a positive good which God draws out from the evil. The various trials that have shaken the Church over the course of her existence (often due to the actions of her own members) have only left her stronger in the end, and provided experiential knowledge and precedents to help guide her in the present and future. God may permit churchmen to make horrible and costly mistakes, but He will never permit such mistakes to destroy His Church. While He allows the Church to learn hard lessons by experience, He will always provide sufficient assistance to preserve her to the end, in spite of the trials He wills to permit. Wrote Cardinal Journet:

---

[26] *The Church of the Word Incarnate*, p. 371.
[27] Ratzinger, Joseph, *Principles of Catholic Theology* (San Francisco: Ignatius Press, 1989), p. 379. (emphasis added).

"In assisting the depositaries of the power of jurisdiction [i.e., the Magisterium), God does not seek to dispense them from effort, reflection or hesitation. He sends them like labourers into the harvest, <u>allowing them to make all kinds of experiments, fortunate or otherwise, to be stored up in the memory of the Church and continually to enrich it with the passing of the centuries</u>. It may seem at times that He leaves her to be the sport of the winds, like the little boat on the Lake of Tiberias, but in reality He never ceases to watch over her, and it is His omnipotence that finally determines her line of movement through history. To adopt another comparison, just as the grace of predestination, without destroying man's liberty or sparing him trials, brings him infallibly to the goal of salvation, so the grace of divine assistance, without destroying the liberty of the jurisdictional power or freeing it from the obligation of enquiry, consultation, reflection and prayer, nevertheless directs its steps infallibly to the great ends that God has assigned it."[28]

Selective Sedevacantist Quotes and Omissions

It is quite revealing to note that when one reads Sedevacantist writings in which the infallibility of universal disciplines is addressed, the twofold judgment (*doctrinal* versus *prudential*) is rarely, if ever, mentioned, and the *universal* aspect is either ignored or downplayed. The fact that the prudential judgment is not covered by the Church's infallibility (meaning that the Church can permit imprudent and even somewhat harmful practices) strikes a critical blow to the Sedevacantist argument that "no error or evil can come from the Church" (that is, from the prudential decisions of the leaders of the Church).

We have an example of selective quotations and omissions in an article by Fr. Cekada, titled "Traditionalists, Infallibility and the Pope." The article consists mainly of quotations from canonists and theologians, whom Fr. Cekada presents as supporting the Sedevacantist position. In the section on universal disciplines, he quotes a number of authorities, yet, in each and every case, he removed any mention of the *prudential judgment,* providing his readers with only the portion of the quotation that relates to the *doctrinal judgment.* He thus cites the authorities who hold that the Church is infallible in its universal disciplinary laws, but fails to mention that the infallibility would only apply to the discipline insofar as it directly relates to revealed truth. In so doing, he leaves his reader with the impression that anything perceived (by private judgment, of course) as harmful in

---

[28] Ibid., pp. 331-332 (emphasis added).

a discipline permitted by the Church constitutes a violation of the Church's disciplinary infallibility.

Since the citations he quoted were, in fact, quite good (although incomplete) we will cite several of them now and provide our own commentary.

> "R.M. Schultes (1931): The question of whether the Church is infallible in establishing a disciplinary law concerns the <u>substance</u> of universal disciplinary laws — that is, whether such laws can be <u>contrary to a teaching of faith or morals</u>, and so work to the <u>spiritual harm</u> of the faithful,...
>
> Thesis. The Church, in establishing universal laws, is infallible <u>as regards their substance</u>.
>
> The Church is infallible in matters of faith and morals. Through disciplinary laws, the Church teaches about matters of faith and morals, not doctrinally or theoretically, but practically and effectively. <u>A disciplinary law therefore involves a doctrinal judgement</u>...
>
> The reason, wherefore, and foundation for the Church's infallibility in her general discipline is <u>the intimate connection between truths of faith or morals</u> and disciplinary laws."[29]

Notice that Fr. Cekada conveniently cut the sentence short immediately after it spoke of the "doctrinal judgment...," thereby eliminating any mention of the prudential judgment. Also notice in the above quotation that infallibility applies to the *substance* of the law (that is, whether the law is in accord with faith and morals), not the *accidents* of the law (whether the law is prudent in the circumstances). This is another critical distinction that Fr. Cekada fails to make in his "analysis."

The next partial quote that Fr. Cekada provides is from Serapius Iraqui and also contains some useful (but partial) information:

> "D) Disciplinary Decrees. These decrees are universal ecclesiastical laws which govern man's Christian life and divine worship. Even though the faculty of establishing laws pertains to the *power of jurisdiction*, nevertheless the *power of the magisterium* is considered in these laws under another special aspect, insofar as there must be <u>nothing in these laws opposed to the natural or positive law. In this respect, we say that the judgement of the Church is infallible</u>...

---

[29] *De Ecclesia Catholica*, (Paris: Lethielleux, 1931), pp. 314-317.

1°) This is required by the nature and purpose of infallibility, for the infallible Church must lead her subjects to sanctification through a correct exposition of doctrine. Indeed, if the Church in her <u>universally binding decrees</u> would <u>impose</u> false doctrine, by that very fact men would be turned away from salvation, and the very nature of the true Church would be placed in peril.

All this, however, is repugnant to the prerogative of infallibility with which Christ endowed His Church. Therefore, when the Church establishes disciplinary laws, she must be infallible."[30]

Once again, we draw your attention to the well-placed ellipsis, which comes right after the explanation of the infallibility of the *doctrinal judgment* ("universally binding decrees" that are "imposed") and before any discussion of the non-infallible *prudential judgment*. We also note the distinction that is made between the power of jurisdiction (governing power) and the power of the Magisterium (teaching power) as it relates to universal disciplines. As we noted above, the theologians hold that it is the Magisterial power (or teaching function) that is infallible insofar as the disciplinary law corresponds to revealed truth.

Every theologian we have consulted makes the clear distinction between the twofold judgment, and then explains that the Church is not infallible with respect to the prudential or practical judgment; yet every single citation provided by Fr. Cekada was missing this latter point. Was this omission merely a coincidence, or did Fr. Cekada *intentionally* remove those portions of the quotation, since including them would undermine his case?

In his theological manual, *Christ's Church*, Msgr. Van Noort also makes the clear distinction between the twofold judgment, and notes that the Church's infallibility would only extend to the doctrinal judgment. He also explains, and emphasizes, that disciplinary infallibility would only apply to disciplines applicable to the universal Church. He wrote:

"Assertion 3: The Church's infallibility extends to the general disciplines of the Church. This proposition is theologically certain.

By the term 'general disciplines of the Church' are meant those *ecclesiastical laws passed for the universal Church* for the direction of Christian worship and Christian living. Note the italicized words: *ecclesiastical laws*, passed for the *universal Church*.

The imposing of commands belongs not directly to the teaching office but to the ruling office; disciplinary laws are only indirectly an object of infallibility, i.e., only by reason of the doctrinal

[30] *Manuale Theologiae Dogmaticae* (Madrid: Ediciones Studium, 1959), 1:436, 447.

decisions implicit in them. When the Church's rulers sanction a law, they implicitly make a twofold judgment: 1) 'This law squares with the Church's doctrines on faith and morals'; that is, it imposes nothing that is at odds with sound belief and good morals.' <u>This amounts to a doctrinal decree.</u>

2. 'This law, considering all the circumstances, is most opportune.' <u>This is a decree of practical judgment.</u>

Although it would be rash to cast aspersions on the timelessness of a law, especially at the very moment when the Church imposes or expressly reaffirms it, still <u>the Church does not claim to be infallible in issuing a decree of practical judgment.</u> For the Church's rulers were never promised the highest degree of prudence for the conduct of affairs. But <u>the Church is infallible in issuing a doctrinal degree as intimated above</u> – and to such an extent that it can never sanction a universal law which would be at odds with faith or morality or would be by its very nature conducive to the injury of souls."[31]

This quotation from Van Noort reflects the common teaching of the theologians who hold that infallibility extends to universal disciplines, but *only to the doctrinal judgment contained within the law, and only when passed for the universal Church.* And, unlike Fr. Cekada, we removed nothing from the above quote.

The Sedevacantist bishop, Mark A. Pivarunas, employed the same cherry-picking technique as Fr. Cekada in a 1996 article he penned called "The Infallibility of the Church." Like the technique used by Fr. Cekada, the bishop cited the above quotation from Van Noort, but in so doing, he deleted an entire section, and he did so without so much as an ellipsis indicating that something had been removed.

Now, can anyone guess what section the bishop chose to remove? That's right, it was the *entire section* (more than two full paragraphs) in which Van Noort discusses the *non-infallible prudential judgment.* Pivarunas also removed a single sentence that was intended to draw attention to the fact that disciplinary infallibility applies to laws that are meant for the *universal* Church, as opposed to laws covering only one particular area, such as a diocese in America or Italy. He also conveniently failed to provide a complete footnote, but only mentioned that the citation was taken from Van Noort's book, *Christ's Church.*

Now, why would the Sedevacantist bishop have deleted the entire section that addresses the non-infallible prudential judgment (as well as the additional sentence drawing attention to the universal aspect of the law), and why would he have done so without giving his readers

---

[31] *Christ's Church*, pp. 114-115 (emphasis added; italics in original).

any indication that something had been removed? Could it perhaps be because he is unable to make a persuasive case that the novel disciplines of the conciliar Church, while imprudent, do not directly contradict any revealed truths? And did the bishop fail to give a complete reference to the book he was citing, and "forget" to include an ellipsis (both times) in order to eliminate the possibility that a curious reader would check to see what had been removed?

After cutting and splicing together his carefully selected quotations, the bishop wrote:

> "The reason for this lengthy explanation of the Church's property of infallibility is that <u>this is the strongest argument against the Conciliar Church of Vatican Council II</u>. For how could the Catholic Church faithfully, consistently and infallibly teach the same faith for 1900 years, and then suddenly propose, during the Second Vatican Council, false doctrines previously condemned by the past Popes and Councils (viz., ecumenism and religious liberty)?"[32]

Once again, we see the error of Monolithic Infallibility rearing its ugly, Sedevacantist head. Infallibility has limits and conditions required for its exercise, and neither the novel doctrines of Vatican II nor the novel disciplines that followed the council meet the specified criteria. Yet, as the bishop just admitted, the Sedevacantists' erroneous notion of infallibility (Monolithic Infallibility), is the *strongest* argument they have in defense of their position! If their "strongest argument" (Pivarunas) and "best explanation" (Cekada) is rooted in such a fundamental error, it surely does not bode well for their remaining arguments.

Bishop Pivarunas then proceeded to explain what divides Traditional Catholics (who have not formally separated themselves from the Church), from the Sedevacantists, such as himself (who have done so). Here is the bishop's explanation for this division:

> "Yet, it is <u>primarily</u> this issue of <u>infallibility</u> that divides those who call themselves traditional Catholics. Some traditional Catholics reject the errors of false ecumenism and religious liberty of the Second Vatican Council ... and yet insists that the very authors of these errors are still Christ's representative here on earth. ... Such a conclusion is nothing more than to deny the infallibility of the Church."[33]

---

[32] Pivarunas, "The Infallibility of the Church" (1996).
[33] Ibid. (emphasis added).

Bishop Pivarunas correctly notes that infallibility is the primary issue that divides traditional Catholics from Sedevacantists. And this admission leads to the inescapable conclusion that if the Sedevacantists' understanding of infallibility is erroneous, *then the Sedevacantist position is erroneous.* Indeed, it is this error that causes them to believe that the Church, currently undergoing its Passion, is no longer the true Church. Based upon this error, they separate from the Church and begin to attack her from without, like an enemy of Christ, with a greater and more bitter zeal than that of the Liberal and Modernists who attack her from within.[34] In fact, many Sedevacantists express delight in seeing the Church suffering this crisis, since the worse the situation gets, the easier it is for them to rationalize their position and draw scandalized souls to their cause. Hence, they rejoice when they should weep, and they laugh when they should mourn.

Before Our Lord's Passion, Jesus said to His Apostles: "Amen, amen I say to you, that you shall lament and weep, but the world shall rejoice; and you shall be made sorrowful, but your sorrow shall be turned into joy." Likewise, during the Passion of the Church, the Catholics lament and weep, while the Sedevacantists rejoice. For example, following the purported "canonizations" of John XXIII and John Paul II (addressed in Chapter 17) which inflicted a terrible wound on the Church, a Sedevacantist apologist posted an article on his website declaring: "This is a Great Day to Be a Sedevacantist!" He then wrote: "For all those anti-Sedevacantist traditionalists out there, this is about as bad as it gets for you!" Indeed, the enemies of Christ rejoiced in His sufferings just as the Sedevacantists rejoice in the sufferings of the Church, while the faithful weep and mourn Her Passion.[35] If the Catholic's sorrow "will be turned into joy" when the Church rises again, as Our Lord revealed, what will become of the Sedevacantist's rejoicing?

---

[34] We again note that St. Pius X referred to the Modernists as being *within* the Church, when he said "they put their designs for her [the Church's] ruin into operation not from without but from within" (*Pascendi*, September 8, 1907).

[35] This calls to mind the words of a wise priest who said: "The problem with many Sedevacantists is that they only consider the *antecedents* (i.e., their reasons for holding such position), and not the *consequences* of such position. They should rather consider the consequences, and run away from such grave error."

An Example of a Non-Infallible Discipline:
Female Altar Boys

While Sedevacantists are quick to claim that the post-conciliar Church has violated disciplinary infallibility, when it comes to providing concrete examples, there is disagreement among them. Nevertheless, they all agree that the conciliar permission of female altar boys, used in the *Novus Ordo* Mass, is a clear example of a "violation" of the Church's disciplinary infallibility. Therefore, we will use this as our example, noting that the following analysis can be applied to *any* of the conciliar disciplines that are believed to violate infallibility.

This novel practice of female servers, of course, is a manifestation of the feminist ideology that has pervaded much of the modern Church. The practice was resisted by the conservatives for decades, before John Paul II finally caved in and permitted the practice. In typical fashion, the "conservatives" promptly reversed course by declaring the practice to be perfectly acceptable and even "traditional," simply because the Pope approved it; the Sedevacantists, on the other hand, cheerfully proclaimed that the practice "proves" the Church after Vatican II is not the true Church of Christ. Both the "conservatives" and the Sedevacantists are gravely mistaken.

To recall what we've learned thus far, there are two considerations to determine if a universal discipline (here, female altar boys) is a violation of the Church's infallibility: 1) whether the practice is directly contrary to a revealed truth (doctrinal judgment), and 2) whether the practice was imposed as a universal law upon the entire Church. (The *prudential judgment* is not a consideration since infallibility does not embrace this aspect of the law.)

Doctrinal Judgment

First, the doctrinal judgment. Does the discipline permitting female altar servers directly contradict a revealed truth? Some Sedevacantists have argued that altar boys represent Christ as an extension of the priesthood, and therefore allowing female altar boys equates to contradicting the Church's doctrine on the all-male priesthood. This position was advanced by the Sedevacantist blogger, Steve Speray, in an article titled "Altar Girls are Impossible for the True Catholic Church." He wrote:

> "Altar boys, like priests, represent Christ through their extension
> to priests who carry out the sacrifice. The reason why females can't

480

serve at the altar as altar boys falls in line with the reason why they can't be priests."[36]

Of course, Mr. Speray cites no authority supporting his assertion that altar boys "represent Christ," and that is because none exist. It's not the altar boy who acts in *persona Christi*, but the priest himself, who offers the Sacrifice to the Father. Speray claims that the prohibition of female altar servers "falls in line with the reason why they can't be priests," but this is a fallacious argument. Women cannot be priests because they are invalid matter for the sacrament of Holy Orders. No such metaphysical impediment exists for females to serve at the altar because, unlike a priest or deacon, altar servers are *not* a level of Holy Orders.

After effectively stating that female altar servers equate to a female priesthood, Speray concludes that the presence of altar girls proves "the Vatican 2 Church and its popes are not Catholic." In another example of Monolithic Infallibility, he wrote:

> "One solid argument (perhaps the simplest) to prove Sedevacantism:
>
> The Catholic Church has infallibly taught that its disciplines can't be harmful or contrary to Divine law…
>
> Altar girls are outward signs used in the celebration of mass in the church of Vatican 2, which has been approved by John Paul II's official interpretation of the 1983 Code of Canon Law.
>
> The Vatican 2 church and its popes are not Catholic, thus they aren't part of the Catholic Church."[37]

Did you get all that? Here it is in a nutshell: "The Church's disciplines are infallible → John Paul II permitted female altar boys → The Vatican II Church and its Popes are not Catholic." Speray's condemnation of "the Vatican 2 Church and its Popes" evidently also includes the Vatican II Popes *prior* to John Paul II who *did not* permit female altar boys.

Needless to say, Speray is completely out to sea on these matters, leading with a confused *major premise* (which fails to distinguish

---

[36] Speray, "Altar Girls are Impossible for the True Catholic Church," January 7, 2015. Gerry Matatics makes this same argument in his CD talk "Counterfeit Catholicism vs. Consistent Catholicism."
[37] Ibid.

between prudential and doctrinal judgments) a faulty *minor premise* (that altar girls are contrary to Divine law), and then long-jumping to an erroneous conclusion (the Vatican II Popes are antipopes and the entire post-Vatican II Church "is not Catholic"). As we have seen, assuming infallibility extends to the doctrinal judgment contained within universal disciplines, the charism would certainly not prevent the Church from passing imprudent disciplines which do not directly contradict an article of faith. Consequently, imprudent disciplines in no way prove that they came from illegitimate authority. Because Speray fails to distinguish between the doctrinal and prudential judgment aspect of disciplines, he doesn't explain, much less prove, how a *liturgical permission* to use female servers could directly contradict a doctrine of the Church (and that is because it doesn't). Yet, for Steve Speray, female altar servers "is perhaps the simplest" argument for Sedevacantism (echoing the "best explanation" and "strongest argument" affirmations of Cekada and Pivarunas, respectively).

To be clear, we are not defending the practice of female altar servers. It is a scandalous practice and was rightly banned by the Church in the fourth century.[38] Nevertheless, serving at the altar is a liturgical function, and permitting women to perform liturgical functions is not *directly contrary* to any doctrine of the Church. In fact, in 1955 Pope Pius XII permitted women to serve in a liturgical function, which was previously limited to men[39] (more on Pius XII's liturgical reforms in Chapter 16).

Not a Univerally Binding Law

We have seen that the use of female altar servers, as imprudent as it may be, is not a violation of the Church's infallibility, because it does not directly contradict any revealed truth. But there is another consideration that should be addressed: the use of female altar servers is not *required* by any universal law of the Church. On the contrary, as

---

[38] "[the] general discipline of the Church [against female altar service] has been set in stone by canon 44 of the Collection of Laodicea which dates generally from the end of the 4th century and which has figured in almost all canonical collections of East and West." Martimort, op. cit., trans. by Michael Baker, The St. Joseph Foundation, Sydney, Australia, 1994), quoted in "Altar Girls: Feminist Ideology and the Roman Liturgy," by Fr. Brian Harrison, *Living Tradition*, No. 88, July, 2000.

[39] On December 25, 1955, Pope Pius XII issued the encyclical *Musicae Sacrae*, which, for the first time in recent history, permitted women to sing the liturgical texts in the choir (Ibid., No. 74), which itself is a liturgical function – one that Pius XII himself said is "immediately joined with the Church's liturgical worship" (Ibid., No. 41).

with Communion in the Hand,[40] female servers are merely permitted as an "indult," which is a conditional *permission*, at the bishops' discretion, to do what the general law of the Church *prohibits*.

The use of female altar servers is permitted based upon a 1994 interpretation of canon 230, §2. But the interpretation is worded as an exception to the general law, which itself *still prohibits the practice*. The law merely permits the bishops to allow female altar servers at their discretion. It reads:

> "If in this or that diocese (*Si autem in aliqua dioecesi*) the Bishop for particular reasons (*peculiares ob rationes*) permits females as well [as males] to serve at the altar…"[41]

In the official communication, in which the *Sacred Congregation for Divine Worship and the Discipline of the Sacraments* notified the Episcopal Conferences of the new interpretation, Cardinal Antonio Maria Javierre Ortas included the following explanation:

> "In communicating the above information to your Episcopal Conference, I feel obliged to clarify certain aspects of Canon 230, §2 and of its authentic interpretation:
> 1) Canon 230, §2 has a permissive and not a preceptive character: 'Laici . . . possunt.' Hence the permission given in this regard by some Bishops can in no way be considered as binding on other Bishops. In fact, it is the competence of each Bishop, in his diocese, after hearing the opinion of the Episcopal Conference, to make a prudential judgment on what to do, with a view to the ordered development of liturgical life in his own diocese.
> 2) The Holy See respects the decision adopted by certain Bishops for specific local reasons on the basis of the provisions of

---

[40] "In reply to the request of your conference of bishops regarding permission to give communion by placing the host on the hand of the faithful, I wish to communicate the following. Pope Paul VI calls attention to the purpose of the Instruction *Memoriale Domini* of 29 May 1969, on retaining the traditional practice in use. At the same time he has taken into account the reasons given to support your request and the outcome of the vote taken on this matter. The Pope grants that throughout the territory of your conference, each bishop may, according to his prudent judgment and conscience, authorize in his diocese the introduction of the new rite for giving communion. (Sacred Congregation for Divine Worship, Letter "En réponse à la demande," to presidents of those Bishop's Conferences petitioning the indult for communion in the hand, May 29, 1969: AAS 61 (1969), pp. 546-547; No. 5 (1969), pp. 351-353.

[41] *Cf. AAS* 86 (1994), pp. 541-542. Canon 230, §2 provides: "Lay persons can fulfill the function of lector in liturgical actions by temporary designation. All lay persons can also perform the functions of commentator or cantor, or other functions, according to the norm of law."

Canon 230, §2. At the same time, however, the Holy See wishes to recall that it will always be very appropriate to follow the noble tradition of having boys serve at the altar. As is well known, this has led to a reassuring development of priestly vocations. Thus the obligation to support such groups of altar boys will always continue.

3) If in some diocese, on the basis of Canon 230, §2, the Bishop permits that, for particular reasons, women may also serve at the altar, this decision must be clearly explained to the faithful, in the light of the above-mentioned norm..."[42]

Clearly, the permission to use female altar servers was not intended to be a *universally binding law*. The discipline has "a permissive and not a perceptive character" and is "not considered as binding on other bishops." Furthermore, the Holy See explicitly stated that it wished to reinforce "the noble tradition of having boys serve at the altar," and "the obligation" to support altar boys, which is "the norm" (or law) of the Church. Thus, the non-binding, liturgical permission in no way invokes the Church's disciplinary infallibility.

Commenting on the wording of the new official interpretation of Canon 230, §2, the canonist, Msgr. McCarthy, founder and director of the Oblates of Wisdom, wrote:

> "The implication is that the general liturgical norm *prohibiting* female altar servers remains in existence, so that, in general, women may not serve at the altar unless a local ordinary intervenes by a positive act and grants permission for his territorial jurisdiction. Thus, the Congregation has clarified the authentic interpretation to mean that an *indult* is given to diocesan bishops to permit the use of female servers."[43]

Fr. Brian Harrison offered his own observation on the wording of the new indult, as well as its practical implications:

---

[42] Vatican Communication on Female Altar Servers, Congregation for Divine Worship, Rome, 15 March 1994, signed by Cardinal Antonio Maria Javierre Ortas, Prefect (emphasis added). See https://www.ewtn.com/library/curia/cdwcomm.htm.

[43] McCarthy, "The Canonical Meaning of the Recent Authentic Interpretation of Canon 230.2 Regarding Female Altar Servers," Fellowship of Catholic Scholars Newsletter, December 1994, p. 15 (emphasis added). (Citation and footnote taken from *Living Tradition*, No 88, July, 2000.) The author also observes (p. 17) that in any case the 1994 authentic interpretation applies only to the Latin-rite Church, and that the canon law of all the Oriental-rite Catholic churches continues to forbid female altar service.

"If in fact the authentic interpretation of c. 230, §2, and accompanying Instruction constitute an indult - in other words, an exception to the rule, a concession to depart from the norm of exclusively male altar service - it should follow logically that nobody has the right to impose this exception on those who want to worship according to the norm. In other words, it should be acknowledged that priests and faithful who strongly object to celebrating, or assisting at, Masses served by women or girls have a right to be able to assist at Mass celebrated according to the norm."[44]

As we can see, the liturgical permission of female altar servers (and other such conciliar novelties) cannot be considered a universally binding law when it is *not* the law of the Church, but an *exception* to the law (and only in the Latin-rite). Moreover, the exception does not compel the bishops to grant the permission, nor does it compel any of the faithful, even in those dioceses where the bishop has granted the permission! It goes without saying that every Catholic has a right to worship according to the norms of the Church. This proves that disciplines of a "permissive character," which are exceptions to their related norms, could not participate in the charism of infallibility.[45]

Women Deacons?

In his CD set, "Counterfeit Catholicism vs. Consistent Catholicism," the Sedevacantist preacher, Gerry Matatics, argues that female altar servers are "*not possible* in the true Church" because "women are not called to the sacred ministry or to the extension of the sacred ministry that altar servers constitute."[46] He then said:

---

[44] Harrison, "Altar Girls: Feminist Ideology and the Roman Liturgy," *Living Tradition*, No. 88, July, 2000.

[45] We also note that novel laws are *superseded* by the law of *immemorial custom* as a matter of Catholic jurisprudence and ecclesiastical law (another matter ignored in Sedevacantist writings and speeches). Hence, the novel laws of the conciliar Church (e.g., sacramental sharing; cremation) in no way violate disciplinary infallibility, nor do they overturn the immemorial prohibition of these practices. For example, canon 26 of the 1983 Code says a centenary (100 year) or immemorial custom can prevail against a contrary canonical law, and canon 27 says "Custom is the best interpreter of law." Further, canon 28 says "Unless it makes express mention of them, however, a law does not revoke centenary or immemorial customs." Since the Church's immemorial customs are the best interpreters of law, and also prevail against the novel, "harmful laws" of the post-conciliar Church (which are mere permissions and not obligatory practices) means such new laws are not protected by the charism of infallibility.

[46] Matatics, "Counterfeit Catholicism vs. Consistent Catholicism," disc 1, track 8.

"The Church Fathers taught that for women to be in the sanctuary would be a profanation of the order which God has established. It cannot be, it is contrary to divine law, it is nothing the Church can change, they said. It is not a matter of discipline that the Church could relax. It is rooted in divine law itself."[47]

After waxing eloquently about why permission to use female altar servers "proves" that the Catholic Church today cannot be the true Church, he said "next they will have deaconesses."[48]

Now, admittedly, female deacons would be in a completely different category than female altar servers. This is because the diaconate is an ordained office - the last step before the priesthood - and only men can be sacramentally ordained to Holy Orders. It is metaphysically impossible for a woman to be ordained as a deaconess, just as it is metaphysically impossible for a woman to be ordained a priest; but there is no such metaphysical impossibility for women to serve at the altar.

During his talk, Mr. Matatics went on to say that some people argue that the reason there were no female altar servers or women deacons in the early Church, is because of the cultural norms of that day. He responded by saying this argument is entirely wrong, since the general culture in those days would have had no problem with women serving in such a capacity. He said: "It was only Israel... and then the Church, the new Israel, which stood out like a sore thumb, that did not have women as sacred functionaries within the temple, within the Church."[49] He said the real reason there were not female altar servers or deaconesses in the early Church is because it is "against Divine law."

Now, we can only imagine the enthusiasm and zeal with which Mr. Matatics would declare the Catholic Church today to be a false Church if it began allowing women to serve in the capacity of deacons. After all, if altar girls "prove" the Church is a false Church, how much more so would women deacons?

What Mr. Matatics and his fellow Sedevacantists will no doubt be surprised to learn is that the early Church did, in fact, have women deacons. That's right. The early Church allowed women to serve as deacons, and *for centuries*. In fact, the women deacons even went through an ordination ceremony, thereby giving the faithful the impression that they received the sacrament of Holy Orders (which, as

---

[47] Ibid.
[48] Ibid.
[49] Ibid.

we've mentioned, is metaphysically impossible). But how can this be the case when, according to Mr. Matatics, women deacons are against Divine law? These female deaconesses (and other women) even had a place in the sanctuary during the Mass – another thing that Mr. Matatics declared to be "impossible" and "contrary to Divine law." And if permitting female altar servers, as an exception to the rule, "proves" that the Catholic Church today is a "false Church" (as Mr. Matatics claims), what does the universal use of female deacons "prove" about the early Church?

If Mr. Matatics is going to be consistent, he would have to conclude that the early Church was also a false Church for permitting female deacons, which, according to him, is a violation of Divine law. There is simply no other conclusion that he can reach, based upon his own argumentation. And Mr. Matatics will have to go way back to discover precisely when the Church became a "false Church," since the first female deacon (Phebe) is mentioned in the Bible. The Bible clearly tells us that Phebe served "in the ministry of the Church" (Rom. 16:1) even though, according to Mr. Matatics, "women are not called to the sacred ministry or to the extensions of the sacred ministry."[50] Here we have Mr. Matatics directly contradicting the inspired Word of God. And Phebe wasn't the only deaconess. The 1913 *Catholic Encyclopedia* entry on *Deaconesses* begins by mentioning the deaconess Phebe, and then states that "it is not improbable that the 'widows' who are spoken of at large in 1 Timothy 5:3-10, may really have been deaconesses." It then adds:

> "In any case there can be no question that before the middle of the fourth century women were permitted to exercise certain definite functions in the Church and were known by the special name of *diakonoi* or *diakonissai*.
>
> Most Catholic scholars incline to the view that it is not always possible to draw a clear distinction in the early Church between deaconesses and widows (*cherai*). The *Didascalia, Apostolic Constitutions* and kindred documents undoubtedly recognize them as separate classes and they prefer the deaconess to the widow in the duty of assisting the clergy. Indeed, the *Apostolic Constitutions* (III, 6) enjoin the widows to be obedient to the deaconesses. It is probable also, as Funk maintains, that in the earlier period it was only a widow who could become a deaconess, but undoubtedly the strict limits of age, sixty years, which were at first prescribed for widows, were relaxed, at least at certain periods and in certain

---

[50] Matatics, "Counterfeit Catholicism vs. Consistent Catholicism," disc 1, track 8.

localities, in the case of those to be appointed to be deaconesses; for example, the Council of Trullo in 692 fixed the age at forty."[51]

The Church permitted women deacons at councils and in Apostolic Constitutions. As mentioned above, deaconesses even went through an "ordination" ceremony, and women - either deaconesses or widows (*cherai*) - also occupied a place in the sanctuary during Mass, even though, according to Mr. Matatics, "the Church Fathers taught that for women to be in the sanctuary would be a profanation of the order which God has established" and "contrary to Divine law."[52] According to the 1913 *Catholic Encyclopedia* article, this "violation of Divine law" (and disciplinary infallibility?) was practiced in the early Church:

> "There can again be no question that the deaconesses in the fourth and fifth centuries had a distinct ecclesiastical standing, though there are traces of much variety of custom. According to the newly discovered 'Testament of Our Lord' (c. 400), widows had a place in the sanctuary during the celebration of the liturgy, they stood at the anaphora behind the presbyters, they communicated after the deacons, and before the readers and subdeacons, and strange to say they had a charge of, or superintendence over the deaconesses. Further, it is certain that a ritual was in use for the ordination of deaconesses by the laying on of hands, which was closely modeled on the ritual for the ordination of a deacon."[53]

Clearly, Mr. Matatics is going to have to go way back beyond 1958 to find the origin of the "false Church" that he denounces and condemns in his talks.

A record of the ordination ceremony for deaconesses is found in Apostolic Constitutions[54] which date back to at least the fourth century. The following Constitution even gives what appears to be the form and matter of the rite. It reads:

> "Concerning a deaconess, I, Bartholomew enjoin O Bishop, thou shalt lay thy hands upon her with all the Presbytery and the Deacons and the Deaconesses and thou shalt say: Eternal God, the Father of Our Lord Jesus Christ, the creator of man and woman,

---

[51] *Catholic Encyclopedia* (1913), vol. IV, p. 651.
[52] Matatics, "Counterfeit Catholicism vs. Consistent Catholicism," disc 1, track 8.
[53] Ibid., (emphasis added).
[54] The Apostolic Constition is a "collection, in eight books, of independent, though closely related, treatises on Christian discipline, worship, and doctrine, intended to serve as a manual of guidance for the clergy, and to some extent for the laity." *Catholic Encyclopedia* (1913), vol. I, p. 636.

that didst fill with the Spirit Mary and Deborah, and Anna and Huldah, that didst not disdain that thine only begotten Son should be born of a woman. Thou that in the tabernacle of witness and in the temple didst appoint women guardians of thy holy gates: Do thou now look on this thy handmaid, who is appointed unto the office of a Deaconess and grant unto her the Holy Spirit, and cleanse her from all pollution of the flesh and of the spirit, that she may worthily accomplish the work committed unto her, to thy glory and the praise of thy Christ."[55]

As one can imagine, this universal discipline of "ordaining" women was not without its problems, and certainly resulted in harm to the faithful, particularly due to the abuses of excess. In fact, some women deacons began to claim for themselves the power to consecrate, which resulted in their offering of sacrilegious and invalid Masses! The *Catholic Encyclopedia* article on *Deaconesses* speaks of the "spasmodic attempts of certain [women] deacons to exceed their powers and to claim, for example, authority to consecrate."[56] It goes on to explain how the Church reacted to these abuses.

For example, the Council of Nicea declared that deaconesses, who had undergone an "ordination" ceremony, where, in fact, lay persons who did not receive a true sacramental ordination, while the Chaldean rite of ordaining women deacons states that "the laying on of hands" does not confer an ordination, but only a blessing – but neither condemned the practice of using female deacons. From the Chaldean rite:

> "The archdeacon presents the deaconess-candidate to the bishop; her hands are joined, and her head is bowed... Then the deaconess raises herself fully erect and the bishop places his hands on her head, but not in the manner of an ordination; rather, he gives her his blessing, recites a silent prayer over her and commands her to avoid pride."[57]

The *Catholic Encyclopedia* explains how the abuses were suppressed:

> "[T]he Church made itself heard in conciliar decrees, and the abuse in the end was repressed without difficulty. Such restrictive

---

[55] *Catholic Encyclopedia* (1913), vol. IV, p. 651. Taken from *Apostolic Constitutions* (Book VIII), Bartholomew, Section 3. Ordination and Duties of the Clergy par. XIX-XX.

[56] *Catholic Encyclopedia* (1913), vol. IV, p. 652.

[57] I. M. Vosté, *Pontificale iuxta ritum Syrorum orientalium,* id est, Chaldaeorum, Versio latina, Vatican 1937, p. 161.

measures seem to be found in the rather obscure 11th canon of
Laodicea,[58] and in the more explicit 19th canon of the Council of
Nicaea,[59] which last distinctly lays down that deaconesses are to be
accounted as lay persons and that they receive no ordination
properly so called (Hefele-LeClercq, Conciles, I, 618). In the West
there seems always to have been considerable reluctance to accept
the deaconesses, at any rate under that name, as a recognized
institution of the Church. The Council of Nismes in 394 reproved in
general the assumption of the levitical ministry by women; and
other decrees, notably that of Orange in 411 (can. 26) forbid the
ordaining of deaconesses altogether."[60]

Over time, the universal discipline of permitting women to act as
deacons, and the abuses that it brought with it, were brought to an end.
The *Catholic Encyclopedia* explains their gradual disappearance:

"In the time of Justinian (d. 565) the deaconesses still held a
position of importance. At the church of St. Sophia in
Constantinople the staff consisted of sixty priests, one hundred
deacons, forty deaconesses, and ninety subdeacons; but Balsamon,
Patriarch of Antioch about A.D. 1070 states that deaconesses in any
proper sense had ceased to exist in the Church though the title was
borne by certain nuns (Robinson, Ministry of Deaconesses, p. 93),
while Matthew Blastares declared of the tenth century that the civil
legislation concerning deaconesses, which ranked them rather
among the clergy than the laity had then been abandoned or
forgotten (Migne, P.G., CXIX, 1272). In the West in spite of the
hostile decrees of several councils of Gaul in the fifth and sixth
centuries, we still find mention of deaconesses considerably after
that date, though it is difficult to say whether the title was more than
an honorific name attributed to consecrated virgins and widows.
Thus we read in Fortunatus that St. Radegund was 'ordained
deaconess' by St. Medard (about A.D. 540 — Migne, P.L.,

---

[58] Council of Laodicea Canon 11: "The appointment of so-called female elders
(presbytides) or presidents shall not take place in the Church." (C. Hefele, A History of
the Councils of the Church, vol. II (Edinburgh: T & T Clark, 1896,) p. 305.
[59] Council of Nicea, Canon 19: "Concerning the former Paulinists who seek refuge in the
Catholic Church, it is determined that they must be rebaptised unconditionally. Those
who in the past have been enrolled among the clergy, if they appear to be blameless and
irreproachable, are to be rebaptised and ordained by the bishop of the Catholic Church.
But if on inquiry they are shown to be unsuitable, it is right that they should be deposed.
Similarly with regard to deaconesses and all in general whose names have been included
in the roll, the same form shall be observed. We refer to deaconesses who have been
granted this status, for they do not receive any imposition of hands, so that they are in all
respects to be numbered among the laity."
[60] *Catholic Encyclopedia* (1913), vol. IV, p. 652.

LXXXVIII, 502) So also the ninth Ordo Romanus mentions, as forming part of the papal procession, the *'feminae diaconissae et presbyterissae quae eodem die benedicantur'* and *diaconissae* are mentioned in the procession of Leo III in the ninth century (Duchesne, Lib. Pont., II, 6). Further the Anglo-Saxon Leofric missal in the eleventh century still retained a prayer *ad diaconissam faciendam* which appears in the form Exaudi Domine, common to both deacons and deaconesses. The only surviving relic of the ordination of deaconesses in the West seems to be the delivery by the bishop of a stole and maniple to Carthusian nuns in the ceremony of their profession."[61]

Here we have a universal discipline of the Church (present both in the East and West) of "ordaining" women as deaconesses – a practice that implies not merely a prudential error, but, one could argue, even a *doctrinal* error, since a case could be made that women deacons are contrary to the Divine law of a male-only clergy. Certainly, this was much closer to a *doctrinal error* contained in a disciplinary law, than any universal law of the post Vatican II era. Further, this discipline caused harm to the faithful, and even led to one of the gravest of all offenses against God – *idolatry* – since the female deacons would induce the faithful to worship bread and wine through their invalid Masses (which some attempted to celebrate)! It doesn't get much more "harmful" than that.

Now, if Sedevacantists like Steve Speray and Gerry Matatics are going to claim that the mere permission of female altar servers violates the Church's infallibility, and proves the Vatican II Church has defected, then how much stronger could a case be made against the early Church, which permitted females to be "ordained" and serve as deacons? One can only imagine what the Sedevacantists would say if the Church today began "ordaining" women deacons. "It is impossible!" they would say. "The true Church could never allow such a thing. The Church is infallible in her disciplines."

And what would this "harmful discipline" say about Pope Peter, who may have permitted Phebe (Rom. 16:1) to act as a deaconess during his day? Is Mr. Matatics now going to cast doubt upon the papacy of St. Peter himself, for permitting this violation of Divine law? And what does Mr. Matatics' preaching tell us about the inspired Word of God? After all, according to Mr. Matatics, it is "not possible" for the true Church to permit women altar servers, since, according to him, it is contrary to "the order which God has established" and "Divine law"

---

[61] *Catholic Encyclopedia* (1913), vol. IV, p. 652 (emphasis added).

itself for women to serve in the sacred ministry – or even in an extension of that ministry. Yet, the Bible itself tells us that Phebe "was in the *ministry* of the Church." Either Mr. Matatics has erred in his theology, or the Bible, Apostolic Constitutions and Church councils have all erred in their recording of history. Which seems more likely?

Again, it should be obvious that we are not defending the practice of female altar boys or women deacons. We freely concede that certain harm resulted from both of these practices (and therefore should be shunned by all the faithful). Our point is simply to show what is "possible" for God to allow in His Church without His gift of infallibility being violated. If the universal practice of permitting women deacons – even allowing them to undergo an ordination ceremony – is not contrary to disciplinary infallibility, then neither is altar girls or anything else that has occurred in the post-Vatican II Church.

To conclude, note well that we can easily apply the foregoing analysis (disciplinary vs. prudential judgment, and whether it was promulgated as a universal law) to *all* of the novelties issuing from the post-conciliar Church. They include female altar boys, lay lectors, Eucharistic "ministers," Communion in the Hand, Communion while standing, Communion under both species, the one-hour Eucharistic fast, mandatory abstinence from meat only twice a year, and so forth and so on. Imprudent? Yes. Impossible? No. Violative of the Church's disciplinary infallibility? Absolutely not.

Chapter 16

~ The New Mass and Infallibility ~

The liturgy of the Church falls into the category of a universal discipline, and is therefore commonly believed to be covered by the Church's infallibility. As we have seen, disciplinary laws contain two judgments, the prudential judgment (whether it is a good discipline under the facts and circumstances) and the doctrinal judgment (whether the discipline squares with Church doctrine). Only the doctrinal judgment of a universal discipline is covered by the infallibility of the Church. In addition, the law must be promulgated with the Church's full canonical or legislative authority, and *"imposed"* upon the Church (by universally requiring or permitting Catholics to do something). Only when these two conditions are met are the Church's disciplines infallible, or "spotless." As Pope Pius XII explains:

> "Certainly the loving Mother is spotless in the Sacraments, by which she gives birth to and nourishes her children; in the faith which she has always preserved inviolate; *in her sacred laws imposed on all;* in the evangelical counsels which she recommends; in those heavenly gifts and extraordinary graces through which, with inexhaustible fecundity, she generates hosts of martyrs, virgins and confessors."[1]

In his 1916 book, *Illustrations for Sermons and Instructions,* Fr. Charles Callan, O.P., explains infallibility in the context of liturgical matters.

> "Infallibility, then, is not the same thing as inspiration. ... It does not apply to any and every act of Pope or Church; but to teaching concerning faith and morals (...) it does not confer upon him [the Pope], whose prerogative it is, either sinlessness or freedom from liability to err in everything he may speak about, nor on every occasion on which he may speak. ... The infallibility of the Pope does *not* mean that he cannot sin; it does *not* mean that he cannot err in matters of science; it does *not* mean that he cannot err in political matters; it does *not* mean that he cannot err in his personal theological views; it does *not* mean that he cannot err in his private theological utterances relating to faith or morals; it does *not* mean that he cannot err in his personal decisions; <u>it does *not*</u>

---

[1] Pope Pius XII, *Mystici Corporis*, No. 66, June 29, 1943 (emphasis added).

> mean that he cannot err in his measures concerning the discipline
> and practice of the Church, for example: sanctioning or dissolving
> an Order, precepts of worship, ecclesiastical rules etc."[2]

Notice that a Pope is able to err in the precepts of worship, that is, in liturgical matters.

In his book *The Church of Christ*, Fr. Sylvester Berry gives two concrete examples of when infallibility would apply to liturgical matters: Communion under one species and the veneration of relics. Communion under one species reflects the Church's *doctrine* that our Lord is completely and substantially present in either the consecrated Host or Precious Blood, while the veneration of relics provides infallible certitude that such veneration is licit, according to the mind of the Church and the law of God. Fr. Berrry also explains how disciplinary infallibility applies to the prayers approved by the Church for universal use in public worship. He does not say that the prayers will necessarily be the best possible, but only that they will not be contrary to any revealed truths – that is, they will not be directly heretical. In his own words:

> "Disciplinary Matters: Under this head are included the laws
> and precepts established by ecclesiastical authority for the
> regulation of worship or for the guidance of the faithful throughout
> the world. Such laws and precepts are necessarily subject to the
> infallible authority of the Church, because of their intimate
> connection of faith and morals. For example, the law prescribing
> Communion under one species presupposes the doctrine Our Lord
> is present whole and entire under either form, and the laws
> concerning the exposition of relics likewise presuppose veneration
> of them is licit. (…)
>   Corollaries. A) The prayers prescribed or approved for
> universal use in public worship cannot be opposed to any revealed
> truth."[3]

In light of these explanations, it is clear that disciplinary infallibility, as it relates to liturgical matters, is actually quite limited. It only prevents the Church from imposing a universal law that is directly contrary to a revealed truth, or from approving a prayer, for universal use, which directly contradicts an article of faith. In other

---

[2] Callan, *Illustrations for Sermons and Instructions*, (New York: Joseph Wagner, 1916), p. 146, 147. *Imprimatur* by Cardinal John Farley, New York.
[3] *The Church of Christ*, p. 291.

words, the Church's universal laws and disciplines will never be heretical in their application.[4]

This brings us to the issue of the *Novus Ordo Missae*, or "New Mass," which was published by Paul VI in 1969. The Sedevacantists maintain that the New Mass violated the Church's infallibility because it contains doctrinal errors or omissions, and then insist that this "proves" Paul VI could not have been a true Pope.[5]

The first thing to note is that doctrinal errors and omissions in a missal, do not, in and of themselves, violate the Church's disciplinary infallibility. Disciplinary infallibility only guarantees that the practice (or prayer) will not implicitly contain a doctrinal error that *directly contradicts* an article of the Catholic Faith (i.e., it will not be heretical).[6] And this aspect of infallibility only applies when the disciplinary matter has been legally promulgated and imposed upon the universal Church, which did not occur with the New Mass, as even some Sedevacantists apologists acknowledge.

Not only did Paul VI *not* violate infallibility when he published the new Missal, but his peaceful and universal acceptance as Pope guarantees that he could not have done so. As we saw in Chapter 12, Paul VI's peaceful and universal acceptance by the Church as Pope is an *infallible sign* (which provides *infallible certitude*) of his legitimacy, which ensures that he could not have bound the Church to heresy. Since we have *infallible certitude* that he was the true Pope, if he would have violated the Church's promise of infallibility, the one to blame would not have been Paul VI, but God Himself, who would have failed to keep His promises. But this, of course, is not possible.

In this chapter, we will demonstrate that even if one holds that the liturgical aspects of the *Novus Ordo Missae* are evil (due to omissions and implicit errors against the Faith), one cannot claim that Paul VI violate the infallibility of the Church when he published the new Missal. This is because the new Mass was never *imposed* on the

---

[4] Recalling what we learned in Chapter 6, an error that does not *directly and manifestly* contradict an article of faith, but requires additional steps of reasoning to demonstrate the contradiction, does not qualify as heresy, but a lesser theological error.

[5] The Sedevacantists first assert that "the Pope cannot give evil to the Church" (Major). They then claim that the new Mass is evil (Minor). They conclude by saying this proves that Paul VI, who gave us the new Mass, was not a true Pope. They error in the Major, by imagining that the Pope is infallible even when he does not invoke his infallibility. The true Major is much more restricted: the Pope cannot error *when he invokes his infallibility*, which Paul VI did not do when he published the New Missal.

[6] Fr. François Laisney rightly observed: "Even those who (erroneously) claim the invalidity *per se* of the New Mass, a position which the Society of St. Pius X rejects, have never presented any positively heretical text in the New Mass" ("Is the Novus Ordo Missae Evil?" *Angelus*, March 1997).

universal Church by law. No doubt there was some trickery at work, as we will show, but the Holy Ghost did not permit the Pope to *juridically promulgate* the New Mass, nor did he permit him to *juridically abrogate* the Traditional Mass, which had been promulgated, in perpetuity, by Pope St. Pius V in the Bull *Quo Primum Tempore.*

St. Pius V's *Quo Primum Tempore*

In 1545, the Council of Trent (1545-1563) was convened to condemn the errors of Protestantism which had originated several decades earlier. These errors and heresies began to show themselves in "reforms" to the Mass, in which the innovators sought to bring the Mass more in line with the errors of Luther (such as less emphasis on the sacrificial nature of the Mass, which Luther denied). Since the law of prayer determines the law of belief (*lex orandi, lex credendi*), the Holy Council of Trent responded to this danger being posed by the innovators, by anathematizing anyone who said the "received and approved rites" of the Church could be despised, omitted or changed into new rites. It also directed that the Roman Missal be restored and codified so that the faithful would know, once and for all, what is the "received and approved rite" of Mass for the Roman Rite.[7]

To that end, Pope St. Pius V issued his papal Bull *Quo Primum Tempore,* which rendered a definitive application of the conciliar decree, by mandating a single missal to be used for the Roman Rite for the Latin Church, with some minor exceptions for missals that had been in use for more than 200 years. *Quo Primum* served as a unifying force in the Roman Rite, and a barrier of protection for the dangers threatening the Mass at the time.

The Missal promulgated by *Quo Primum* is irreformable, at least in its substances, since it reflects the substantial identity of the Mass of the Roman rite, and not even a Pope possesses the authority to abrogate a received and approved rite of Mass, or change it substantially. The Missals that have been issued since *Quo Primum* simply reflect accidental changes to the rite, while leaving the substantial identity in tact.

In *Quo Primum*, Pope St. Pius V promulgated the new Missal using the *full force* of his papal authority. He wrote:

---

[7] "If anyone says that the received and approved rites of the Catholic Church, accustomed to be used in the administration of the sacraments, may be despised or omitted by the ministers without sin and at their pleasure, or may be changed by any pastor of the churches to other new ones, let him be anathema." Canons on the Sacraments in General, Session 7, Canon 13 (March 3, 1547).

"We specifically command each and every patriarch, administrator, and all other persons or whatever ecclesiastical dignity they may be, be they even cardinals of the Holy Roman Church... to read the Mass according to the rite and manner and norm herewith laid down by Us and, hereafter, to discontinue and completely discard all other rubrics and rites of other missals, however ancient, which they have customarily followed... Furthermore, by these presents [this law], in virtue of Our Apostolic authority, We grant and concede in perpetuity that, for the chanting or reading of the Mass in any church whatsoever, this Missal is hereafter to be followed absolutely, without any scruple of conscience or fear of incurring any penalty, judgment, or censure, and may freely and lawfully be used. ... We likewise declare and ordain that no one whosoever is forced or coerced to alter this Missal, and that this present document cannot be revoked or modified, but remain always valid and retain its full force...

It is Our will, therefore, and by the same authority, We decree that, after We publish this Constitution and the edition of the Missal, the priests of the Roman Curia are, after thirty days, obliged to chant or read the Mass according to it; ... no one whosoever is permitted to alter this notice of Our permission, statute, ordinance, command, precept, grant, indult, declaration, will, decree, and prohibition. Would anyone, however, presume to commit such an act, he should know that he will incur the wrath of Almighty God and of the Blessed Apostles Peter and Paul."[8]

Not a New Mass

The Missal promulgated by Pope St. Pius V did not, as some mistakenly believe, promulgate a new Mass. It merely unified the celebration of the Mass, in the Traditional form, by requiring all priests of the Roman Rite to celebrate Mass using the same missal – a missal that had remained essentially unchanged for the previous one thousand years, and which extends back to the midst of the apostolic age from which it developed organically. As many scholars such as Jungmann, Fortescue and Knowles have demonstrated, the Roman Missal promulgated by St. Pius V, in 1570, was already compiled in its essentials at the time of Pope St. Damasus (in the fourth century) and is virtually unchanged from the time of Pope St. Gregory the Great (in the sixth and seventh century). For this reason, the Roman Missal (the

---

[8] Pope St. Pius V, Apostolic Constitution *Quo Primum Tempore,* July 14, 1570.

Traditional Mass) has historically been referred to as the Damasian-Gregorian liturgy.[9]

The great liturgist, Fr. Adrian Fortescue, wrote the following about the Missal promulgated by St. Pius V:

> "Essentially, the Missal of Pius V is the Gregorian Sacramentary [Circa A.D. 600]; that again is formed from the Galasian book, which depends on the Leonine collection. We find prayers of our Canon in the treatise De Sacramentis and allusions to it in the IVth Century. So our Mass goes back, without essential change, to the age when it first developed out of the oldest liturgy of all. It is still redolent of that liturgy, of the days when Caesar ruled the world and thought he could stamp out the Faith of Christ, when our fathers met together before dawn and sang a hymn to Christ ... there is not in Christendom another rite so venerable as ours."[10]

Did Paul VI Abrogate *Quo Primum*?

In its Constitution on the Sacred Liturgy, *Sacrosanctum Concilium* (December 4, 1963), the Second Vatican Council decreed a "reform" of the Roman Missal. What followed the council's decree in the years to come was a staggering number of pronouncements, which gradually introduced changes into Catholic worship that brought it more in line with the reforms of the Protestant innovators.[11] The earliest changes

---

[9] In his magnificent book, The *Reform of the Roman Liturgy* (1993), Msgr. Klaus Gamber wrote: "The Damasian-Gregorian liturgy remained in use throughout the Roman Catholic Church until the liturgical reform in our time. Thus, it is inaccurate to claim that it was the Missal of Pope Pius V [in the 16th century] that has been discontinued. Unlike the appalling changes we are currently witnessing, the changes made in the Roman Missal over a period of almost 1,400 years did not involve the rite itself. Rather, they were changes concerned only with addition and enrichment, etc." The *Reform of the Roman Liturgy: Its Problems and Background* (Fort Collins, Colorado: Roman Catholic Books, 1993).
[10] Fortescue, *The Mass — A Study of the Roman Liturgy*, (London: Longmans, Green & Co., 1950), p. 213.
[11] In 1965, the man Paul VI appointed to head the *Consilium for the Implementation of the Constitution on the Sacred Liturgy*, Annibale Bugnini, said: "We must strip from our Catholic prayers and from the Catholic liturgy everything which can be the shadow of a stumbling block for our separated brethren, that is, for the Protestants" (*L'Osservatore Romano*, March 19, 1965). The close confidant of Pope Paul VI, Jean Guitton (the only layman to attend Vatican II), said: "The intention of Pope Paul VI with regard to what is commonly called the Mass, was to reform the Catholic Liturgy in such a way that it should almost coincide with the Protestant liturgy. There was with Pope Paul VI an ecumenical intention to remove, or, at least to correct, or, at least to relax, what was too Catholic in the traditional sense in the Mass and, I repeat, to get the Catholic Mass closer

targeted the Traditional Mass,[12] until Paul VI released his Apostolic Constitution, *Missale Romanum,* on April 3, 1969, in which he announced the publication of the New Mass.[13] Following the issuance of *Missale Romanum*, the Congregation for Divine Worship (not Paul VI) "promulgated" the New Mass by issuing *Celebrationis Eucharistiae* on March 26, 1970.[14] Other pronouncements from the Congregation followed, even one that attempted to ban the old Mass by mandating the exclusive use of the New Missal.[15]

From the time these pronouncements were unleashed on the Church over four decades ago, Catholics were divided over their meaning and level of authority. Specifically, the Liberal and Neo-conservative Catholics argued that Paul VI legally abrogated *Quo Primum* and that the old Mass was forbidden. Traditional Catholics, on the other hand, maintained that the old Mass was never *juridically abrogated,* nor was the new Missal ever *juridically promulgated* as a binding law. In the midst of this confusion, the priests who continued to say the old Mass and refused to say the New were (and still are) persecuted by their Liberal-minded counterparts, their bishops and fellow priests.

The position of the Traditionalists with respect to the Old Mass was officially (although not publicly) vindicated during the reign of John

---

to the Calvinist mass." (*Apropos*, December 19, 1993 and again in *Christian Order*, October 1994.)

[12] For example, the Consilium (the Committee responsible for the liturgical "reforms") issued *Inter Oecumenici* in 1964 (which made many changes to the order of the Traditional Mass), *Nuper Edita* in 1965 (which introduced Mass facing the people) and *Tres Abhinc Annos* in 1967 (which introduced many additional changes to the Mass). It should also be noted that the Modernists' efforts to pave the way for the New Mass had already begun during the reign of Pope Pius XII, with the experimental Easter Vigil (1951), changes to the liturgical calendar, Collects and suppression of Octaves (1955), the Renewed Order for Holy Week (1955) and vocal participation of the faithful (1958).

[13] The Congregation for Divine Worship issued the General Instruction of the Roman Missal, or "GIRM," a few days later (April 6, 1969).

[14] As we will further discuss later in the chapter, because the New Mass was "promulgated" by the Cardinal Prefect of the Congregation for Divine Worship (and not the Pope), it not only fails to trigger the infallibility of the Church, but some also argue it is necessarily rendered null by *Quo Primum*, which *was* promulgated by the Pope (St. Pius V). An inferior cannot annul a superior's law. They further argue that the New Mass is technically illicit (illegal but not invalid) by virtue of being contrary to the legislation of *Quo Primum*.

[15] See the Notice *Conferentia Episcopalium* (October 28, 1974). It must be noted that this Notice, as with other pronouncements regarding the New Mass during the 1970s, was not signed by the Pope and did not appear in the *Acta Apostolicae Sedis* where new laws must be published to take legal effect (because Paul VI never mandated the exclusive use of the New Mass in the 1969-1970 decrees, the 1974 Notice would have been considered a new law requiring publication in the *Acta*).

Paul II, who appointed a commission of nine Cardinals[16] to study the issue and provide the answers to two questions:

1) Did Paul VI or any lawful authority legally suppress the Traditional Mass?
2) Was any priest free to say the Old Mass without special permission?

In a 1995 interview, Cardinal Stickler, who was one of the nine Cardinals, explained the findings of the Commission as well as some other interesting, behind-the-scenes information about the subject. The following is taken from the interview first published in *The Latin Mass Magazine*. We quote the Cardinal at length:

> "**Question:** Did Pope Paul VI actually forbid the Old Mass?
>
> **Cardinal Stickler:** Pope John Paul asked a commission of nine cardinals in 1986 two questions. Firstly, did Pope Paul VI or any other competent authority <u>legally forbid</u> the widespread celebration of the Tridentine Mass in the present day? <u>No</u>. He asked Benelli explicitly, 'Did Paul VI forbid the Old Mass?' He [Benelli] never answered - never yes, never no. Why? He couldn't say, 'Yes, he forbade it.' <u>He [Paul VI] couldn't forbid a Mass which was from the beginning valid and was the Mass of thousands of saints and faithful</u>. The difficulty for him [Paul VI] was <u>he couldn't forbid it</u>, but at the same time he wanted the new Mass to be said, to be accepted. And so he could only say, 'I want that the new Mass should be said.' This was the answer all the princes [Cardinals] gave to the question asked. They said: the Holy Father <u>wished</u> that all follow the new Mass.
>   <u>The answer given by eight cardinals in '86 was that, no, the Mass of St. Pius V has never been suppressed.</u> I can say this: I was one of the cardinals. Only one was against. All the others were for the free permission: that everyone could choose the old Mass. That answer the Pope accepted, I think; but again, when some bishop's conferences became aware of the danger of this permission; they came to the Pope and said: 'This absolutely should not be allowed because it will be the occasion, even the cause, of controversy among the faithful.' And informed of this argument, I think, the Pope abstained from signing this permission. Yet, as for the

---

[16] Cardinals Ratzinger, Mayer, Oddi, Stickler, Casaroli, Gantin, Innocenti, Palazzini and Tomko.

commission - I can report from my own experience - the answer of the great majority was positive.

There was another question, very interesting: 'Can any bishop forbid any priest in good standing from celebrating a Tridentine Mass again?' <u>The nine cardinals unanimously agreed that no bishop may forbid a Catholic priest from saying the Tridentine Mass.</u> We have no official prohibition and I think the Pope would never establish an official prohibition."[17]

In spite of the finding of the nine Cardinals, most bishops during the reign of John Paul II continued to forbid the Old Mass (either out of malice or ignorance) and persecute the priests who continued to celebrate it. Traditional priests were even labeled schismatic for celebrating the Tridentine Mass, and forced to endure an unimaginable crisis of conscience.

But in 2007, to the shock and dismay of the Left (and, no doubt, many on the Sedevacantist Right), Pope Benedict XVI issued the Motu Proprio, *Summorum Pontificum*, which publicly declared what had been concluded by the commission of nine Cardinals twenty years earlier. Contrary to what virtually all Catholics throughout the years had been led to believe, Pope Benedict confirmed that the Old Mass had never been juridically abrogated and, in indeed, was always permitted – just as the Traditional Catholics had always maintained.

In a statement that sent shockwaves throughout the Church, Pope Benedict declared:

> "I would like to draw attention to the fact that this Missal [the Traditional Mass] <u>was never juridically abrogated and, consequently, in principle, was always permitted.</u>"[18]

In remedying this grave injustice, the Pope stated the obvious:

> "What earlier generations held as sacred, remains sacred and great for us too, and <u>it cannot be all of a sudden entirely forbidden</u> or even considered harmful."[19]

For almost forty years, the entire Catholic world had been led to believe that the Old Mass was abrogated by Pope Paul VI, but this

---

[17] *The Latin Mass* magazine, Summer 1995, p. 14.
[18] Letter of his Holiness, Pope Benedect XVI to the Bishops on the Occasion of the Publication of the Apostolic Letter "Motu Proprio Data" *Summorum Pontificum* on the Use of the Roman Liturgy Prior to the Reforms of 1970, (July 7, 2007), emphasis added.
[19] Ibid., emphasis added.

impression was entirely false. The old Mass was never juridically abrogated, just as the New Mass was never juridically promulgated as a universally binding law. This injustice certainly underscores what God wills to permit His Church to suffer, and with regard to the *source and summit of Catholic worship*, no less. Indeed, God can and does permit such evils to afflict His Mystical Body, but never at the cost of compromising the Church's charism of infallibility. While this confusion concerning the Old vs. New Mass was (and still continues to be) a source of consternation among the faithful, it can hardly compare with other crises God has willed to permit, such as what we learned in Chapter 8, when God permitted synods, called and overseen by Popes, to issue erroneous decrees (e.g., mistakenly declaring that the ordinations performed by previous Popes were null and void), and then be contradicted by other synods, also called and overseen by Popes, which decreed the exact contrary.

While Traditionalists had always maintained what Pope Benedict XVI finally affirmed, the Liberals had consistently argued that the Old Mass was juridically repealed and the New Mass was juridically imposed. Some Sedevacantists, such as Fr. Cekada, ironically joined ranks with their counterparts on the Left by arguing that the New Mass was indeed the obligatory law of the land (no doubt because it helps the Sedevacantist case). For example, in response to an article written by Fr. Laisney, which clearly demonstrated that Paul VI never abrogated the Traditional Mass (the same conclusion reached by the Cardinals), Fr. Cekada sided with the very Progressives that he claims to loathe.

Because *Missale Romanum* was an Apostolic Constitution issued by the Pope himself (while subsequent pronouncements concerning the New Mass came from Vatican congregations and not the Pope), Fr. Cekada targeted *Missale Romanum* as the document he claimed violated the Church's infallibility (since he knows that a document issued by someone other than a Pope could not have done so). In his 2000 article, titled "Did Paul VI 'Illegally Promulgate' the Novus Ordo? The Society of St. Pius X and a popular traditionalist myth,"[20] Fr. Cekada's argues that in *Missale Romanum,* Paul VI legally promulgated the New Mass, imposed it upon the faithful as a universally binding law, and abrogated *Quo Primum* in the process. Let's take a look at Fr. Cekada's arguments to determine if he is telling the truth.

---

[20] http://www.traditionalmass.org/articles/article.php?id=19&catname=8.

Paul VI's *Missale Romanum*

Fr. Cekada begins his article by providing the following definition of "promulgation." He wrote: "The essence of promulgation is the public proposal of a law to the community by the lawmaker himself, or on his authority, so that the will of the lawmaker to impose an obligation can become known to his subjects."[21] Notice that Fr. Cekada concedes that a validly promulgated law or discipline of the Church "imposes an obligation" on the faithful. Fr. Cekada affirmed the same when he asked: "In this case, did Paul VI manifest his will to impose on his subjects an obligation (i.e the New Mass)?"

Fr. Cekada then answers his own question by saying: "Paul VI makes it abundantly clear that his will is to impose the obligation of a law on his subjects." As evidence for his assertion, Fr. Cekada points to the Consitution's mere announcement of the new missal, along with its introduction of three new canons ("Eucharistic prayers") and the consecration formulae to be used in each of the new canons. Based upon these changes, Fr. Cekada concludes: "The New Mass is promulgated, and the law is binding."

Fr. Cekada's claim is patently false. As one can plainly see by carefully reading the document, *Missale Romanum* does not "impose an obligation" upon the Church to use the New Mass, which is necessary *even according to Fr. Cekada's own definition*. In fact, *Missale Romanum* decrees *nothing* beyond what Fr. Cekada actually points out in his article: Paul VI decreed the *option* of using three new Eucharistic prayers, and he decreed that the same consecration formulae is to be used in each of these prayers.[22] That's it. As Fr. Paul Kramer explains, "the Constitution contains only two decrees: 1. We have decided to add three new canons to the Eucharistic prayer and, 2. We have directed

---

[21] Fr. Cekada cites M. Lohmuller, *Promulgation of Law* (Washington: CUA Press 1947), p. 4 (emphasis in original).

[22] While Fr. Cekada argues that *Missale Romanum* uses similar Latin terminology as that of *Quo Primum* (*normae, praescripta, statuta, proponimus, volumus,* etc.), he fails to distinguish between St. Pius V's use of these terms as applied to the promulgation of the Tridentine Missal *in toto*, and Paul VI's use of these terms as applied to only certain *components* found in the new missal that he *published* (consecration formula, canons). It is only these specific components that Paul VI set forth in *Missale Romanum*. Fr. Cekada points out that the heading of the Apostolic Constitution says the Roman Missal is "promulgated," but the content of the document itself decrees *only* the new canons and consecration formula (and even if one were to argue that the Constitution promulgated the new missal, it did not *impose* the missal on the Church as a universally binding law). Unfortunately, Fr. Cekada is as deceptive as was Paul VI in pretending to elevate the New Mass to a status it does not, and cannot, have.

that the words of the Lord be identical in each form of the canon."[23] In other words, while *Missale Romanum* announces the publication of the new missal, it only provides three new canons as *options* and mandates that all three use the same formulae for the consecration. The constitution legislates *nothing else* regarding the Mass. Fr. Paul Kramer astutely observed:

> "The mere publication of a new Missal does not effect the obrogation of previous legislation – there is no such thing as implied legislation. It must not be forgotten that it pertains to the very essence of law that 1) it must be preceptive in its wording if it is going to make something obligatory, 2) it must specify who are the objects of the law, and it must specify where and when the law will be in force, 3) the law must be publicly promulgated in the manner specified by law, by the competent authority."[24]

Paul VI's *Missale Romanum* did not promulgate the New Missal (the *Novus Ordo Missae*), as Fr. Cekada would have his readers believe. In fact, even some of Fr. Cekada's fellow Sedevacantists acknowledge this. For example, commenting on the aforementioned article by Fr. Laisney (who demonstrated that the New Mass was not juridically promulgated) and the article of Fr. Cekada (who argued the contrary), the Sedevacantist apologist, John Lane, wrote:

> "These texts and commentary demonstrate perfectly clearly what I have been saying: <u>Paul VI did not make any law permitting or obliging anybody to use the new missal</u>. Fr. Cekada cannot point to the requisite text - he highlights the promulgation, and the preceptive terminology, yet he signally fails to point to the part that says 'Persons X are permitted or obliged to do Y.'"[25]

While Paul VI's *Missale Romanum* decrees the usage of three new canons and requires that the same consecration formulae be used in each, it does not promulgate the New Missal, much less impose the New Mass as a universally binding law. One could certainly argue that the words and actions of Paul VI gave the *impression* that he was abrogating *Quo Primum* and imposing the New Missal upon the Church, *but he did not legally do so.*

---

[23] *The Suicide of Altering the Church's Faith in the Liturgy*, (Terryville, Connecticut: The Missionary Association, 2006), p. 134.
[24] Ibid., p. 135.
[25] Mr. Lane posted these comments on his website at http://www. sedevacantist.com.

Rather, *Missale Romanum* expresses Paul VI's "hope" and "wish" that the *New Mass* would be happily received by the faithful (which, by the way, it was not!). Paul VI said "we <u>hope</u> (*confidimus*) nevertheless that the Missal <u>will be received by the faithful</u> as an instrument which bears witness to and which affirms the common unity of all."; and, "<u>We wish</u> (*volumus*) that these Our decrees and prescriptions may be firm and effective now and in the future..." Far from "imposing" the New Mass as an "obligation" on the Church as Fr. Cekada contends, *Missale Romanum* does little more than express Paul VI's personal sentiments toward the faithful's reception of the New Mass and his hope for greater unity in the Church.

As Fr. Laisney correctly noted in his article:

> "Pope Paul VI did not oblige the use of his Mass, but only permitted it. <u>The word 'permitted' is not even used in the constitution</u>. *Missale Romanum*. He merely says... 'that he is confident that [his missal] will be accepted...' There is no clear order, command, or precept imposing it on any priest!"[26]

Notwithstanding the absence of legal language in *Missale Romanum* promulgating the New Mass, Fr. Cekada claims that, as long as Paul VI expressed his *will* to impose the New Mass as an obligation (as privately discerned, of course, by Fr. Cekada), this suffices to make the publication of his missal a universally binding law, even though an actual decree of promulgation does not exist (Cekada's theory would certainly be news to any Pope). Based on this, all Fr. Cekada believes he has to do is convince his readers that Paul VI *desired* to impose the new Protestant-flavored Missal on the Catholic world (even if he didn't actually do so) and he can then assert that Paul VI violated the Church's infallibility, and therefore could not have been a true Pope. That is the typical kind of argumentation one finds in Fr. Cekada's articles.

We respond to Fr. Cekada's theory of promulgation by the Pope's *personal hopes and wishes* and not the Church's *official legislative process* (as if Paul VI didn't know how to promulgate a law) by quoting Fr. Kramer, who said:

> "Notwithstanding the Pope's personal wishes and opinions expressed in an unofficial non-legal manner, <u>the legally expressed</u>

---

[26] Laisney, "Is the Novus Ordo Missae Evil?" *Angelus* (March 1997).

<u>will</u> of the Roman Pontiff did not impose the new rite of Mass on the Latin Patriarchate of the Church."[27]

Indeed, according to the Church's jurisprudence (as well as common sense), the will of the legislator is manifested *only* by the laws he *validly promulgates*, and not by the private interpretation of the Pope's non-legal and non-promulgated "hopes" and "wishes." In fact, the Church has strict requirements for the valid promulgation of laws *precisely to prevent* the faithful from having to personally discern what, in fact, is or was the will of the legislator. The legislation itself is what informs the subjects of the legislators will. But for those, such as Fr. Cekada, who must "prove" by any means possible that Paul VI was not a true Pope, they are forced to resort to such non-sensical arguments to make their case.

Then, in his typical insulting tone, Fr. Cekada says the following about Fr. Laisney, whose article, as we have noted, simply pointed out that the written legislation did not impose the New Mass on the Church (which Fr. Cekada essentially concedes). In response, Fr. Cekada wrote:

> "Father Laisney's approach to a pope's laws, and that of this theory's other adherents is, in fact, 'Canon-Law Protestantism' — interpret selected passages as you see fit, and no pope is ever going to tell you what they mean. And if you don't find the magic formula that you have decided is 'required' to compel your obedience, well, too bad for the Vicar of Christ on earth."[28]

This is the kind of rhetoric one continually finds in Fr. Cekada's writings. The use of insulting and sarcastic verbiage to denigrate others (here, a fellow priest) enables him to mask his own intellectually deficient, contradictory, and even absurd arguments. He criticizes Fr. Laisney for noting that Paul VI's written legislation did not promulgate the New Mass (an argument Cekada cannot obviously rebut), and then claims, in response, that the mere *will* of Paul VI (as discerned, of course, by Fr. Cekada) suffices to promulgate a universally binding law.

As we have noted, even some of Fr. Cekada's fellow Sedevacantists have spoken out against this absurd theory. For example, John Lane rightly observed:

---

[27] *The Suicide of Altering the Faith in the Liturgy,* p. 134 (emphasis added).
[28] "Did Paul VI 'Illegally Promulgate' the Novus Ordo?, The Society of St. Pius X and a popular traditionalist myth," February 2000.

"Fr. Cekada focuses solely on the fact that Paul VI expresses his 'will.' This is indeed necessary. But he has also to say what his will actually is. He has to make it known. He hasn't done so anywhere in this text [*Missale Romanum*]."[29]

Here Mr. Lane is simply stating what should be obvious to all. The Pope expresses his will through legislation.

Before moving on, we must comment on one more quotation from Fr. Cekada's article. Near the beginning, he wrote:

"While many traditional Catholics adhere to the position that the New Mass was illegally promulgated, advocates are especially numerous among the members and supporters of Archbishop Marcel Lefebvre's Society of St. Pius X (SSPX). The theory fits neatly into what one can only term the Society's Jansenist/Gallican [*Nota Bene*: heretical] concept of the papacy: The pope is 'recognized,' but his laws and teachings must be 'sifted.' You get all the sentimental benefits of theoretically having a pope, but none of the practical inconveniences of actually obeying him."[30]

In his typical bitter spirit, Fr. Cekada engages in name-calling and ridicule (even calling his opponents heretics) for those who acknowledge that Paul VI was a true Pope, yet resist his "legislation" on the grounds of the enduring validity of *Quo Primum,* coupled with Paul VI's non-binding "wish" that his problematic New Missal would be "received" by the faithful. But, in labeling "heretics" those who acknowledge that Paul VI was a true Pope, while resisting his non-binding liturgical reforms, Fr. Cekada indicts *himself* of the crime by his own standards since he himself does, with the liturgical reforms of Pius XII, precisely what he claims to be forbidden.

The Reforms of Pope Pius XII

Fr. Cekada's inconsistency is revealed in his own rejection of the liturgical reforms of Pope Pius XII, whom he recognizes as a true Pope! That's right, Fr. Cekada does exactly what he ridicules others for doing – namely, "recognizing" Pius XII as a valid Pope, while he "sifts" and even rejects his liturgical legislation.[31] He even claims that the 1955

---

[29] Comments takes from his website at http://www.sedevacantist.com/viewtopic.php ?f=2&t=1394.
[30] Ibid.
[31] See Fr. Cekada's articles: "Is Rejecting the Pius XII Liturgical Reforms 'Illegal'?" (April 27, 2006); and "The Pius XII Reforms: More on the 'Legal Issue,'"(July 11, 2006).

liturgical reforms of Pius XII are "harmful," while simultaneously claiming that it is impossible for a true Pope to give a harmful liturgical law. How, you may be wondering, does Fr. Cekada justify such a blatant contradiction between his teaching and his *praxis*? He does so by claiming that the liturgical laws of Pius XII only *became* harmful after they were promulgated. In explaining his position, he wrote:

> "A human ecclesiastical law that was obligatory when promulgated can become harmful (*nociva*) through a change of circumstances after the passage of time…this principle…applies equally to the 1955 reforms."[32]

You see, Fr. Cekada cannot accuse Pius XII of *promulgating* a harmful universal discipline, since this is exactly what he accuses Paul VI of doing, which he cites as "proof" that he was not a true Pope. Thus, to get around the obvious contradiction, Fr. Cekada argues that Pius XII did not promulgate harmful laws. Rather, argues Fr. Cekada, Pius XII promulgated good laws that only *became harmful at a later date* (the next decade!), due to "a change of circumstance." That is the argument he's forced to use to justify his actions.

Specifically, Fr. Cekada conveniently argues that Pius XII's changes to the Holy Week rites in 1955, while not harmful in themselves, transformed into harmful reforms with the benefit of "hindsight" (at which time he argues they "*ceased*" to be law). He claims they *became* harmful in the Traditional rite when they were incorporated into the *Novus Ordo Missae*.

This is an entirely fallacious argument, since the 1955 reforms were made to the *Traditional rite itself* (*not* the *Novus Ordo*) and thus must be judged, in that context, on their own merits (or demerits). The question is: Are the 1955 reforms of Pius XII harmful to the Traditional rite or not? Whether some of these changes were *also* incorporated into the *Novus Ordo* later is irrelevant to that question. If the 1955 reforms are considered harmful in the Traditional Roman Rite, they would have to be considered harmful in and of themselves, and therefore harmful when promulgated by Pius XII.

To answer the question, let us first take a brief look at the reforms of Holy Week that were promulgated by Pius XII in 1955. If Sedevacantists give an honest assessment of these reforms, and if they remain consistent with their views, they will likely be forced to conclude that many of these reforms were harmful *in themselves*. After

---

[32] "Is Rejecting the Pius XII Liturgical Reforms 'Illegal'?" http://www.traditionalmass .org/articles/ article.php?id=78&catname=6.

all, the 1955 reforms radically changed the Holy Week liturgies, irrespective of their introduction into the New Mass 15 years later.[33] Moreover, some of these reforms have absolutely no basis in the liturgical tradition of the Roman Rite, but are complete novelties.

For example, the 1955 rite for Palm Sunday eliminated the "dry Mass" which had for centuries included the Introit, Collect, Epistle, Responsory, Gospel, Preface and *Sanctus*. In the liturgy reformed by Pius XII, the priest blesses the palms at a "table" and "facing the people," and also chants the final Collect facing the people, with his back to the tabernacle. The Prayers at the Foot of the Altar and the Last Gospel were eliminated. If there are other ministers present, they read the Scriptures while the priest sits and listens (contrary to St Pius V's injunction that the priest recites all Scripture readings which is the ancient practice of the Roman Rite). Other elements, such as the ceremonial knocking at the Church door, the alternating choirs, and elements of the Passion (anointing at Bethany, setting of the guard at the tomb) were also eliminated. If these reforms were not harmful when promulgated, when and how, exactly, did they *become* harmful later? If they are not harmful under Pius XII, when and why are they harmful under Paul VI?

For Maundy Thursday, the Creed and Last Gospel were eliminated, the Washing of the Feet was inserted into the actual rite of the Mass, and the Collect which follows is recited by the priest facing the people with his back to the tabernacle. For Good Friday, the traditional ceremonies for the Mass of the Presanctified were eliminated. There is no solemn procession with the Blessed Sacrament from the Altar of Repose to the church proper. The priest chants the Solemn Orations from a book placed in the center of the altar, and the people recite the *Pater Noster* aloud with the priest – two novel reforms that have no foundation in the liturgical tradition of the Roman Rite.

If these reforms (e.g., suppression of prayers, Creed, Gospel and other ceremonies, the priest facing the people, etc.) have proven harmful in the *Novus Ordo*, then it is difficult to avoid the conclusion that they are harmful *in themselves*. That conclusion, however, would prove too much for Fr. Cekada's argument because, using his own criteria, it would "prove" that Pius XII violated the Church's disciplinary infallibility when he promulgated these reforms. Therefore, he claims that these radical reforms only *became* harmful at a later date.

---

[33] Pope Pius XII promulgated the Renewed Order for Holy Week in a document called *Maxima Redemptionis* (November 16, 1955), published in *the Acta Apostolicae Sedis* 47 (1955), pp. 838-841.

The 1955 revisions to Holy Week were not the only "harmful" reforms promulgated by Pius XII during his reign. Already in 1948, Pius XII approved a Commission on the liturgy (known as the Pian Commission) that would begin drafting the reforms that he would ultimately approve during the 1950s. For example, Pius XII approved an experimental Easter Vigil in 1951 which not only permitted the celebration of the Vigil on Saturday night instead of early Sunday morning (contrary to longstanding tradition), but also drastically changed rubrics of the rite.[34]

In the revised rite, prayers for blessing the Easter fire were reduced, a new ceremony for inscribing the Paschal candle was created, the triple candle used to bring the Easter fire into the church was eliminated, the novelty of the clergy and people carrying candles was introduced, the Prophecies were reduced from twelve to four, the priest sits and listens to the readings, he blesses the baptismal water facing the people, the faithful vocally recite the Renewal of Baptismal Vows in the vernacular, and the Last Gospel was abolished, among other things.

Thus, for the *most solemn celebration* in the Church's liturgical year, Pius XII abolished ancient prayers, eliminated parts of the Mass, created new rites, introduced the priest facing the people and desired a greater *physical* participation of the laity, even including their recitation of vocal prayers *in the vernacular* during the Mass! Such reforms certainly did not develop organically from the traditional Roman Rite, and many of them can even be traced to Protestant (Luther/Cramner) influences. Can you guess, dear reader, what Sedevacantists would have said about these reforms had they originated with Paul VI or John Paul II? Would they not have declared them evil in themselves, violative of the Church's disciplinary infallibility, and further "proof" that they were not true Popes?

In addition to the changes to Holy Week, in 1955 Pius XII also promulgated many drastic changes to simplify the rubrics and calendar of the Traditional Mass.[35] These included demoting certain feasts, eliminating certain Collects and the Last Gospel, and suppressing ten Vigils and fourteen Octaves (the continuous commemoration of the Church's most important feasts for a week following the actual feast), some of which were part of the Church's liturgical calendar for well over a thousand years! Finally, Pius XII promulgated an instruction on

---

[34] The decree is called *Dominicae Resurrectionis Vigiliam*, February 9, 1951, which was published in the *Acta Apostolicae Sedis* 43 (1951), pp. 128-129.

[35] The decree is called *Nostra Hac Aetate* (March 23, 1955), which was published in the *Acta Apostolicae Sedis* 47 (1955), pp. 218-224.

sacred music which also introduced a radical expansion of vocal participation of the congregation.[36] These changes would not only allow vocal participation for short responses (*"Amen," "Et cum spiritu tuo"*), server's responses (*"Domine, non sum dignus"*) and parts of the Ordinary of Mass (*Gloria, Credo, Pater Noster*), but when fully implemented, would even include the laity reciting the Prayers at the Foot of the Altar, the *Confiteor*, Propers (Introit, Gradual, etc.), *Kyrie*, Sequences and Tracts, Offertory, the *Suscipiat* prayer, *Sanctus, Agnus Dei,* and the Communion verse!

As we can see, Pope Pius XII was responsible for some of the most *drastic* changes to the Roman liturgy in the Church's history; a liturgy that had remained essentially unchanged for the previous 400 years by virtue of *Quo Primum.* For a ten year period (1948-1958), Pius XII promulgated or allowed liturgical novelties under the same rationale of the conciliar revolutionaries – for better "conformity" to "ancient liturgical traditions." However, the truth is that many of these changes under Pius XII, *were completely without precedent in the history of the Roman Rite.* Thus, it is entirely fair to say that the liturgical revolution began during the reign of Pius XII. The Modernists who followed him simply finished what he started, and incorporated into the *Novus Ordo much of what Pius XII had already approved* for the Traditional Roman Rite.

For Fr. Cekada to argue that these changes were not harmful *under Pius XII,* but only became harmful *during the reign of Paul VI* (which is how he justifies not using the revised missal of Pius XII) only reveals how barren his "harmful in hindsight" theory is. It is the proverbial case of "having your cake and eating it too." In Cekada's own words, Pius XII's papacy is "recognized," but his liturgical laws must be "sifted." Cekada gets "all the sentimental benefits of theoretically having a Pope (Pius XII), but none of the practical inconveniences of actually obeying" his liturgical legislation. Thus, Fr. Cekada continues to recognize Pius XII as a true Pope, but rejects his laws and says Mass at his Sedevacantist chapels according to pre-1950 rubrics.[37]

Fr. Cekada also advances other non-sensical arguments in addition to his absurd "harmful in hindsight" theory. For example, Cekada

---

[36] The decree is called *De Musica Sacra* (September 3, 1958), which was published in the *Acta Apostolicae Sedis* 50 (1958), pp. 630-633.
[37] John Salza has confirmed with a parishioner who attends St. Hugh of Lincoln (a Sedevacantist parish in Salza's hometown of Milwaukee) that Fr. Cekada celebrates Mass exclusively using pre-1950 rubrics when he says Mass at the chapel. And, in another example of hypocrisy, Bishop Dolan celebrates on occasion *Missae cantatae,* a concession to bishops allowed by Paul VI in *Inter oecumenici* (1964). Thus, according to his own standards, Dolan acknowledges and follows a law of a "false Pope."

claims that Pius XII's liturgical reforms were "mere human ecclesiastical laws" and thus "they no long [sic] bind on two grounds." In addition to being "harmful in hindsight," Fr. Cekada also argues that Pius XII's legislation "lacked one of the essential qualities of a law — stability or perpetuity — and are therefore no longer binding." Cekada even cites Bugnini (whom Cekada himself declares to be a Freemason) as his authority for this argument, since Bugnini said the reforms are "a bridge between the old and the new." Cekada's self-made "lack of stability" theory is just another fallacious argument to justify his rejection of Pius XII's reforms, while retaining "all the sentimental benefits" of recognizing the legitimacy of his papacy.

First, if the legislation of Pius XII, which radically transformed the Roman Rite, can be disregarded as "mere human ecclesiastical laws," then certainly the liturgical legislation of the Sacred Congregation for Divine Worship under Paul VI, which was *not* promulgated by Paul VI, can also be disregarded as "mere human ecclesiastical laws" that do not violate the Church's infallibility. Second, Fr. Cekada does not cite any authority (there is none) for his theory that certain validly promulgated legislation can be disregarded by *private judgment*, because one personally thinks the legislation "lacks stability." Third, the aforementioned legislation of Pius XII did not "lack stability" because most of the legal changes *were made a permanent part of the Traditional rites*, irrespective of their incorporation into the *Novus Ordo* years later.[38]

Being neither able to prove his fallacious assertions nor counter his opponents' arguments, Fr. Cekada is ultimately forced to make excuses for Pope Pius XII. For example, in his book *Work of Human Hands*, he claims that Pius XII "seemed to lack the common sense necessary for making sound practical judgments."[39] After proclaiming on the same page that "Pius XII lacked the practical sense to be a sufficiently ruthless exterminator" (of the Modernists around him), Cekada concludes, again on the same page: "This lack of practical judgment, I think, blinded Pius XII to the disconnect between the teaching of *Mediator Dei* and the liturgical changes he permitted to be introduced during his reign."[40]

---

[38] By permanent we mean mandatory and not optional (unless and until a future Pope changes the legislation). Interestingly, in light of this point, one must conclude that either the changes legislated by Pius XII were accidental only (and hence they also remain accidental in the *Novus Ordo* rites), or are substantial changes to the rites (in which case they are either legitimate for both the Old and New rites, or illicit for both the Old and New rites).
[39] Cekada, *Work of Human Hands* (West Chester, Ohio: Philothea Press, 2010), p. 64.
[40] Ibid.

This is another highly convenient argument from Fr. Cekada. First, if, according to Fr. Cekada, the many substantive (and completely novel) changes that Pius XII legislated into the liturgy were merely "practical judgments" (which did not contain doctrinal errors), then how did these same reforms, when later incorporated into the *Novus Ordo* by Paul VI, become evil doctrinal judgments that violated the Church's infallibility? As we saw in the previous chapter, infallibility only extends to the doctrinal judgment (not the practical judgment) contained in a disciplinary law. Further, if Pius XII can be excused for lacking "practical sense" and "practical judgment" in liturgical matters, then why can't Paul VI be excused for the same reasons? After all, Paul VI publicly lamented the effects of the conciliar reforms (almost all of which were not actually issued by him), even declaring that the smoke of Satan had unexpectedly entered the Temple of God.[41] Could Fr. Cekada's selective indictment of Paul VI, and his acquittal of Pius XII, be driven by his Sedevacantist agenda?

Fr. Cekada also pleads that the "Angelic Pastor" was tricked into promulgating the 1955 liturgical changes by the Freemason[42] and

---

[41] In a 2008 interview with the publication *Petrus*, Cardinal Virgilio Noè, who served as the Master of Liturgical Ceremonies during the Pontificate of Paul VI, revealed, for the first time, what Paul VI meant by the famous phrase "the smoke of Satan has entered the Temple of God." In responding to a question about this phrase, the Cardinal said: "You from *Petrus*, have gotten a real scoop here, because I am in a position to reveal, for the first time, what Paul VI desired to denounce with that statement. Here it is. Papa Montini, for Satan, meant to include all those priests or bishops and cardinals who didn't render [proper] worship to the Lord by celebrating badly (*mal celebrando*) Holy Mass because of an errant interpretation of the implementation of the Second Vatican Council. He spoke of the smoke of Satan because he maintained that those priests who turned Holy Mass into dry straw in the name of creativity, in reality were possessed of the vainglory and the pride of the Evil One. So, the smoke of Satan was nothing other than the mentality which wanted to distort the traditional and liturgical canons of the Eucharistic ceremony." (English translation by Fr. Zuhlsdorf, available at the webaddress http://www.wdtprs.com/blog/2008/05/petrus-amazing-interview-with-card-noe-paul-vis-smoke-of-satan-remark-concerned-liturgy/.)
[42] Although Bugnini never admitted to being a Mason, in his autobiography he admitted the following (speaking in the third person): "Toward the end of the summer a cardinal who was usually no enthusiast for the liturgical reform told me of the existence of a 'dossier' which he had seen on (or brought to?) the Pope's desk and which proved that Archbishop Bugnini was a Freemason." (Annibale Bugnini, *The Reform of the Liturgy 1948-1975* (Collegeville, Minnesota: The Liturgical Press, 1990), p. 91. Fr. Brian Harrison wrote the following about the finding of Bugnini's briefcase that contained the evidence of his Masonic affiliation: "I know that there are high-ranking Vatican officials, including at least one former Cardinal Prefect of a Roman Congregation, who believe that there have been and are Freemasons in high Vatican positions. I confess my own amazement when I came to realise that such ideas (whether true or false) do not originate solely amongst 'crackpot' conspiracy-theorists. (...) An internationally known churchman of unimpeachable integrity has also told me that he heard the account of the discovery of

architect of the New Mass, Annibale Bugnini. In his article, Fr. Cekada says: "the Mason's liturgical creations were presented to the sick pope for his approval by the two scheming modernists who will be major players in destroying the Church at Vatican II."[43] In his book, Cekada repeats the same theme: "But if you are a gravely ill 79-year-old pope who is a bit credulous, and your trusted Jesuit confessor[44] brings you a document to approve, telling you it is just fine because it was all put together by that smart, young liturgist Father Bugnini, what are the chances that you will say no?"[45] On these grounds, Cekada concludes: "Traditionalists...should ignore liturgical laws that were the dirty work of the man who destroyed the Mass."[46]

Again, how convenient for Fr. Cekada to make excuses for Pius XII, yet not permit any excuses for Paul VI. If Bugnini could have fooled Pius XII, then why could he not have also fooled Paul VI? Since Pius XII had *already approved* many of the changes that Bugnini sought to introduce into the New Mass, why not excuse Paul VI on the grounds that he was simply continuing the work initiated by his venerable predecessor and relying on the same advisors that Pius XII himself had trusted with the work? Furthermore, it could be argued that Paul VI was even less involved in the liturgical reforms than was Pius XII, having delegated all the reforms to congregations and bishops' conferences, and even admitting that he had not read *Missale Romanum* before signing the document.[47]

Moreover, while Pius XII may have been ill when he promulgated the 1955 reforms, this does not prove they were not validly promulgated, unlike the New Mass, which was *not* juridically promulgated by Paul VI. Further, Pius XII was *not* ill when he appointed the Pian Commission in 1948 and promulgated the experimental Easter Vigil in 1951, which *radically* changed the most solemn of all the rites of the Church (abolishing ancient prayers, introducing the priest facing the people and the faithful's recitation of vocal prayers in the vernacular). Again, what is conceded for Pius XII

---

the evidence against Bugnini directly from the Roman priest who found it in a briefcase which Bugnini had inadvertently left in a Vatican conference room after a meeting." Harrison, "A response to Michael Davies Article on Annibali Bugnini" (1989), http://www.ad2000.com.au/articles/1989/aug1989p18_635.html.

[43] "Is Rejecting the Pius XII Liturgical Reforms 'Illegal'?"

[44] Here Fr. Cekada is referring to Fr. Bea, whom Cekada describes as a "half-Jew, modernist and premier ecumenist at Vatican II" (Ibid.)

[45] *Work of Human Hands*, p. 65.

[46] Ibid.

[47] See: Fr. Laisney, "Is the Novus Ordo Missae Evil?," *The Angelus*, March 1997.

(misinformation, deception, lacking practical judgment) must also be conceded for Paul VI, as a matter of equity and fairness.

All of this demonstrates that Fr. Cekada is being inconsistent and quite hypocritical for rejecting Pius XII's liturgical reforms as being "harmful" while recognizing him as Pope, yet at the same time claiming that the harmful liturgical reforms of Paul VI (many of which were approved by Pius XII) "prove" that Paul VI was not a true Pope (since, as Fr. Cekada claims, a Pope cannot give "harmful" disciplinary laws). Thus, it is Fr. Cekada, and not Traditional Catholics, who has the "Jansenist/Gallican concept of the papacy," since he not only "sifts" the liturgical laws of the Popes he chooses to recognize, but also "sifts" the Popes themselves, telling his followers just who is a valid Pope and who is not (no "sifting" required for antipopes!). It's quite amazing how Fr. Cekada can hold these positions publicly with a straight face, but perhaps even more incredible is how many don't see (or don't *want* to see) the blatant contradictions in Fr. Cekada's position.

Manipulating the Text of *Missale Romanum*

Returning to the introduction of the *Novus Ordo Missae*, many were fooled by the editorial deception that made its way into the vernacular translations of Paul VI's *Missale Romanum*. This included both a gross mistranslation of one sentence, and the complete fabrication of another which did not appear in the original Latin. For example, in the original document, Paul VI begins his closing comments as follows:

> "Concerning all that we have just set forth regarding the new Roman Missal, We are pleased here to end by drawing a conclusion. (Latin: *"Ad extremum, ex iis quae hactenus de novo Missali Romano exposuimus quiddam nunc cogere et efficere placet."*)[48]

However, the English version blatantly mistranslates this sentence, in the most dishonest way, as follows:

> "In conclusion, we wish to give the force of law to all that we have set forth concerning the new Roman Missal."[49]

---

[48] *Acta Apostolicae Sedis*, April 30, 1969, vol. 61, No. 4, pp. 221–222. http://www.vatican.va/archive/aas/documents/AAS-61-1969-ocr.pdf.
[49] The mistranslation is on the version currently posted on the Vatican's website at: http://w2.vatican.va/content/paul-vi/en/apost_constitutions/documents/hf_p-vi_apc_19690403_missale-romanum.html.

Yes, the artisans of the revolution translated Paul VI's statement, "we are pleased here to end by drawing a conclusion" (the conclusion being Paul VI's hope and expectation for unity in the new missal), as "we wish to give *the force of law*" to the missal. Hardly an honest mistake. Moreover, the English translation contains the following *additional* sentence that is also not found in the original Latin:

> "We order that the prescriptions of this Constitution go into effect November 30th of this year, the first Sunday of Advent."[50]

Needless to say, the mistranslation and addition of the foregoing texts, no doubt manufactured by conciliar revolutionaries within the Vatican, only underscores the reality that the official Latin version of *Missale Romanum* does *not* "give the force of law" to the New Mass, nor it order "order" it to be obligatory for the faithful.[51] Commenting on

---

[50] Fr. Kramer notes that this additional clause is included in the version published in the *Acta Apostolicae Sedis* and thus has been officially incorporated into *Missale Romanum*. However, Fr. Kramer also correctly notes that Paul VI's statement "we order" ("*praescripsimus*") refers only to the three new "canons" and consecration formula (as will be discussed below). Hence, its inclusion does not change the fact that *Missale Romanum* does not juridically promulgate the New Mass, much less impose it as a universal binding law for the Church.

[51] The following is a comparison between the original Latin and the English translation with the additions (taken from the Vatican's website). *Original Latin (word for word in English):* **"Concerning all that we have just set forth regarding the new Roman Missal, We are pleased here to end by drawing a conclusion [correct translation].** In promulgating the official edition of the Roman Missal, Our predecessor, St. Pius V, presented it as an instrument of liturgical unity and as a witness to the purity of the worship the Church. While leaving room in the new Missal, according to the order of the Second Vatican Council, 'for legitimate variations and adaptations,' we hope (*confidimus*) nevertheless that the Missal will be received by the faithful as an instrument which bears witness to and which affirms the common unity of all. Thus, in the great diversity of languages, one unique prayer will rise as an acceptable offering to our Father in heaven, through our High-Priest Jesus Christ, in the Holy Spirit."

"We wish (*volumus*) that these Our decrees and prescriptions may be firm and effective now and in the future, notwithstanding, to the extent necessary, the apostolic constitutions and ordinances issued by Our predecessors, and other prescriptions, even those deserving particular mention and derogation."

English translation with errors: **"In conclusion, we wish to give the force of law to all that we have set forth concerning the new Roman Missal [mistranslation].** In promulgating the official edition of the Roman Missal, Our predecessor, St. Pius V, presented it as an instrument of liturgical unity and as a witness to the purity of the worship the Church. While leaving room in the new Missal, according to the order of the Second Vatican Council, 'for legitimate variations and adaptations,' we hope nevertheless that the Missal will be received by the faithful as an instrument which bears witness to and which affirms the common unity of all. Thus, in the great diversity of languages, one unique prayer will rise as an acceptable offering to our Father in heaven, through our High-Priest Jesus Christ, in the Holy Spirit."

the mistranslations and additions to the original text, Michael Davies wrote:

> "It would be possible to devote an entire book to the controversy surrounding MR [*Missale Romanum*]. Additions were made to the text after publication. (...) I am fortunate in possessing a copy of the first official edition of the *Novus Ordo Missae* published by the Vatican Press in 1969 which contains the original text. It is interesting to note that the Flannery collection of documents contains a translation made from this original version without the additions."[52]

The late Abbé George Nantes published an article in the June 1970 issue of *The Catholic Counter Reformation,* which addressed the outright fraud surrounding the publication of *Missale Romanum.* He explains the mistranslation (which was already present in the French version in 1970) as well as the additional sentence that was discovered by the Bishop of Nancy, France.[53] The following quotation is difficult reading, but due to its historical value, and to illustrate the deceptive means used to foist the New Mass on the Catholic world, we quote the Abbé at length. He begins:

> "I have here under my eyes, the photocopies kindly supplied to a friend from the Bishop's House at Nancy (France), and guaranteed to conform to the originals by Chancellor Dautrey, on the date of 13th May, 1970, and under the seal of this bishopric.
>
> In this document, Pope Paul VI cites his reform of the Mass within the continuity of the liturgical restoration of Pius XII and presents the new Ordo as a 'revision' and an 'enrichment' of the Roman Missal; and also as a 'new arrangement of texts and rites, in

---

"**We order that the prescriptions of this Constitution go into effect November 30th of this year, the first Sunday of Advent**" [Addition not in original text].

"We wish that these Our decrees and prescriptions may be firm and effective now and in the future, notwithstanding, to the extent necessary, the apostolic constitutions and ordinances issued by Our predecessors, and other prescriptions, even those deserving particular mention and derogation. Given at Rome, etc."

[52] Davies, *Pope Paul's New Mass* (Kansas City, Missouri: The Angelus Press, 1980), p. 51.

[53] A large portion of the article from Abbé Nantes was published in Fr. Wathen's book, *The Great Sacrilege* (Rockford, Illinois: TAN Books and Publishers, Inc., 1971). Fr. Wathen notes that already in 1971, the mistranslation was present in the English text. See also "L'interdit jeté sur la sainte Messe romaine" – in *La Contre-Réforme Catholique au XXe Siècle*, Saint-Parres-les-Vaudes (France), n. 33, June, 1970.

such a way that they express more clearly the holy things which they signify.'"[54]

The Abbé then notes the evil influence at work:

'The major innovation,' according to his expression, is the introduction of new Canons (the Pope uses the word: *Statuimus*) which are presented as ancient, though they are in fact very modern; and the modification of the formula of Consecration itself, on the pretext of making them all identical: *Jussimus*... The term 'mysterium fidei' is left out and placed within the context of an 'acclamation,' where it loses its original and full meaning. This rejection represents the work of very sinister influences.

The innovations which are referred to as minor, are concerned with simplification, suppression, or restoration of prayers and rites, the changing round of the order of readings, and the very considerable modifications of the liturgical calendar."[55]

From here, the Abbé points out the intentional fabrications in the document, which attempts to elevate *Missale Romanum* to a binding decree:

"The Pope then makes his concluding remarks — but here we must make a distinction between the Latin text and its so-called French translation [which is identical with the English translation]. The Latin text, the photocopy of the original text printed on the Vatican printing press and dated June, has two paragraphs here. The French text, photocopied from Documentation Catholique, in which it is quoted as a translation emanating from the Vatican Press Bureau, contains three, the second of which is an invention pure and simple. It does not exist in the Latin text, which alone is the authoritative one...

In the first paragraph of this conclusion of his discourse, the Holy Father expresses his *hope* that the new Missal will be received by all as a sign and instrument of unity: *'Confidimus.'* It is through an unheard of act of violence — abuse No. 1 — that the 'Press Bureau' invented the false translation, which I am now going to read out to you: 'In conclusion, we wish to give the force of law to all that we have set forth concerning the new Roman Missal.' This conclusion, with its formally legislative tone, is a fabrication,

---

[54] The Catholic Counter-Reformation in the XXth Century. No. 5, June, 1970. R. P. Georges de Nantes, Editor. Maison Saint-Joseph-10 Saint-Parres-lès-Vaudes, France, pp. 9–10 (emphases added). Letter found in Wathen's *The Great Sacrilege*, pp. 135-137.
[55] Ibid.

inserted in the place where the Pope had merely written, according to the faithful translation made by Abbé Dulac: 'Concerning all that we have just set forth regarding the new Roman Missal, We are pleased here to end by drawing a conclusion.' And this conclusion refers to the *confidence* that all will find again in this Missal their mutual unity. Whoever has transformed this 'confidence' into a 'Law' has lied. Having made such a good start, and while they were about it, they invented a second paragraph which does not exist at all in the original Latin text, as photocopied by your Bishop's House, which I have here under my eyes. Here then is the fraud: 'We order that the prescriptions of this Constitution go into effect November 30th of this year, the first Sunday of Advent.' This is the essence of the text and it is a forgery.

The last paragraph, if you read it as the third in the French or Italian [or English] text, does indeed give the impression of wishing to impose an obligation even if the subject-matter, and the precise extent, of this obligation are left indeterminate. This is what it says: 'We wish that these our decrees and prescriptions may be firm and effective now and in the future, notwithstanding, to the extent necessary, the apostolic constitutions and ordinances issued by our predecessors, and other prescriptions, even those deserving particular mention and derogation.' Read in the context of the original Latin text, that is to say, freed from the encumbrance of the two forged texts preceding it, these simple words cannot be placed in comparison with detailed instructions and concessions, firm, and intended to last in perpetuity. Here we have a simple statement of the *wishes* of Paul VI, a directive bereft of any indication that would imply a strict obligation, and one which is not accompanied by any threat of sanctions. The definite obligation of having to follow the New Ordo, which is supposedly contained in the Apostolic Constitution, springs therefore from two sentences, of which the one is an invention pure and simple and the other one contains a manifest mistranslation of the authentic text. The forged text issued by the 'Press Bureau' imposes an obligation: that is as much as to say that the true text imposes nothing of the kind. That was the thing to be proved! The Constitution *Missale Romanum*, in its authentic Latin text, does not impose an obligation. Paul VI does not impose an obligation to follow his Ordo Missae!

However, a communication I received yesterday made me think that Msgr. Pirolley (the Bishop of Nancy), though himself deceived in the first place, has now been put on his guard. I have here a second photocopy, handed out from [the] Bishop's House to another member of the diocese, of the famous text of the Pope's which obliges the whole world to follow his new Mass. Well, they had more sense this time and, with the help of paste and scissors, they have produced a photocopy, in both Latin and French, of the last of these paragraphs alone — the two preceding ones have disappeared! We may well quote La Rochefoucauld when he said that 'hypocrisy is a compliment paid by vice to virtue.' Here is Bishop's House at Nancy tacitly acknowledging the crime committed in Rome! This is a memorable date indeed!

The bishop of Nancy, having caught the intentional deception, responded by removing the paragraph containing the mistranslated sentence, as well as the one sentence paragraph containing the fabricated text, leaving only the final paragraph, which had not been altered by the Vatican "Press Bureau."[56]

To conclude, the Abbé rightly affirms the perpetual validity of *Quo Primum*, which no Pope can abrogate lest he incur the wrath of Sts. Peter and Paul:

> "…There is nothing that can validly annul the Bull of St. Pius V. Paul VI, in his Constitution, does not formally abrogate it, and if he takes the risk, together with those who embrace his reform, of incurring the wrath of the Blessed Apostles Peter and Paul, we still have to admit that he is not obliging anyone to follow him into this peril. He does no more than to express a simple and indefinite *wish*, together with the *hope* that all may find spontaneously a common unity in the practice of the new reformed form of worship."[57]

As we have demonstrated with the plain language of the official Latin version of *Missale Romanum*, which was confirmed by Abbé Nantes' interpretation and explanation, Paul VI neither abrogated the Old Mass nor legislatively imposed the New Mass. This fact has been reiterated over the years by many scholars, and, as we have shown, is even conceded by some of the more honest Sedevacantists. Fr. James Wathen (who was not a Sedevacantist) affirmed the true meaning of the "unedited" version of *Missale Romanum*:

> "…when the text is purged of its forgery and given its correct translation, we find that the whole weight of the document, and the Act of abolishing the Mass and of introducing its deceptive Semblance, rests on two words '*confidimus*,' 'we hope', 'we trust,' 'we have confidence that,' "we wish, etc., and '*volumus*,' 'we wish,' 'we desire', 'we would be pleased,' etc. Two words of such thin-voiced wistfulness are supposed to effectively command, nay, force the whole Latin Church to forsake its most precious Treasure, the most essential means for our salvation, to completely forget

---

[56] Ibid.
[57] Ibid.

over fifteen hundred years of tradition (figured most conservatively), to ignore the solemn promulgations, edicts, injunctions, instructions, and anathemas of most of the successors of the Great Fisherman, to bury in silence the rapturous prayers and encomia inspired by it in the Saints of the West, and, without question or hesitation, to begin the performance of a bureaucratic Composition, whose real meaning and purpose have been the subject of the most resentful criticism and telling attacks since it first saw the light of day. This truly is what our enemies may well describe as 'popery' in the authentic sense of the word! As if our religion were nothing more than the dumb and servile fulfillment of the Pope's mere *wishes*, totally unrelated to morality, Revelation, history, law, or even plain common sense!"[58]

The late Canon Gregory Hesse, who possessed doctoral degrees in both canon law and Thomistic theology, publicly held the same position – namely, that Paul VI did nothing more than publish a liturgical book with the *hope* and *wish* that it would be received by the faithful. As we have seen, there was much intentional trickery and deception involved in spreading the New Mass throughout the Western Rite (just as there was in illicitly suppressing the Old Mass), but Paul VI did not *impose* the New Mass on the Catholic world as a universal binding law, any more than he obliged all Catholics to attend Sunday Mass on Saturday evening (a practice, by the way, that was introduced by Pius XII).[59] Needless to say, Paul VI's mere "hoping" and "wishing" that the New Missal would be received as a sign of unity in the Faith is not equivalent to Paul VI promulgating a universally binding law.

Further Deficiencies of *Missale Romanum et al.*

Let's close our analysis by addressing the last sentence in *Missale Romanum* in which Paul VI states:

"We decree that these laws and prescriptions [the new canons and consecration formulae] be firm and effective now and in the future, notwithstanding, to the extent necessary, the apostolic constitutions and ordinances issued by our predecessors and other

---

[58] Wathen, *The Great Sacrilege*, pp. 139-140.
[59] See Pius XII's Apostolic Constitution *Christus Dominus* (January 6, 1953).

prescriptions, even those deserving particular mention and *derogation.*"[60]

Based upon this general reference to "apostolic constitutions…by our predecessors," Fr. Cekada cheerfully and triumphantly declares that Paul VI repealed *Quo Primum*. In Cekada's words: "This clause **expressly** abrogates *Quo Primum*" (emphasis in original). Fr. Cekada's exaggeration of what *Missale Romanum* actually decrees leads him, again, to this erroneous conclusion.

First, it should be noted that the Old Mass is, *at least,* an immemorial custom of the Church, and immemorial customs can only be repealed by *explicit* mention in the new legislation. Canon 28 of the current Code of Canon Law provides: "Unless it makes express mention of them, however, a law does not revoke centenary or immemorial customs, nor does a universal law revoke particular customs."[61] As Fr. Kramer correctly notes: "No post-conciliar papal legislation has dared to presume to attempt the suppression of the venerable Roman Rite of Mass, *which is more than just an immemorial custom* but is the universal and perpetual custom of the Latin Patriarchate, the suppression of which…would be contrary to the doctrine of the Faith."[62] Far from abrogating the immemorial rite of Mass "by express mention," Paul VI's *Missale Romanum* even fails to legally promulgate the New Mass as an *alternative* to the Old Mass.

Second, Paul VI's use of the term "derogation" is a dead giveaway to the limited scope of *Missale Romanum* and the enduring application of *Quo Primum*. A derogation strikes down *only* those statutes of previous law that must be nullified to make room for the new law. (Having to acknowledge the meaning and significance of this term may be why Fr. Cekada, in his article, translated the Latin *derogatione* as "amendment" and not "derogation.") As applied here, because *Missale Romanum* decreed only the use of three new "Eucharistic prayers" and the consecration formulae to be used, it only *derogated* (made an exception to) the prior legislation by allowing these new prescriptions.

---

[60] The Latin, which Fr. Cekada cites in his article, is: "*non obstantibus, quatenus opus sit, Constitutionibus et Ordinationibus Apostolicis a Decessoribus Nostris editis, ceterisque praescriptionibus etiam peculiari mentione et derogatione dignis.*"

[61] Fr. Cekada actually argues that the Notification *Conferentia Episcopalium* of October 28, 1974 - which was *not* issued or signed by the Pope, which does *not* refer to *Quo Primum* by "express mention," and which was *not* published in the *Acta Apostolicae Sedis* - still repeals the immemorial custom of the Damasian/Gregorian/Tridentine Missal celebrated by the Church for at least 1500 years! Cekada, of course, would not make such a silly argument if he could prove his case by using *Missale Romanum* alone (the only document in question issued by the Pope and published in the *Acta*).

[62] *The Suicide of Altering the Faith in the Liturgy*, pp. 135-136.

In all other respects, the prior legislation, including (and especially) the decree *Quo Primum*, continues to have the force of law. As Fr. Paul Kramer explains:

> "The key word in the last clause is 'derogation'. The new Missal of Paul VI is only a derogation, an exception, to the previous laws, which are still in force. (…) *Missale Romanum* of Paul VI is only a derogation of some of the provisions of *Quo Primum* which remains in force."[63]

Third, not only did Paul VI's *Missale Romanum* not officially promulgate the New Mass, but there is no future papal legislation published in the *Acta Apostolice Sedis* that "imposes as an obligation" the new missal on the Church. According to Canon 9 of the 1917 Code (which was in force when the New Mass was introduced): "Laws enacted by the Holy See <u>are promulgated by their publication in the official commentary *Acta Apostolicae Sedis*</u>, unless in particular cases another mode of promulgation is prescribed."[64] Commenting on this point, Fr. Laisney wrote:

> "A decree of the Sacred Congregation of Rites imposing the New Mass is not in the *Acta Apostolicae Sedis*. A decree of the Sacred Congregation of Rites (dated April 6, 1969)[65] is only at the front of the first edition of the *Novus Ordo Missae* itself, not in the *Acta Apostolicae Sedis*, where it must appear. In later editions of the New Mass it is replaced by a second decree (March 26, 1970) only

---

[63] Ibid., p. 134. Fr. Kramer also says: "It is, therefore, a misconception that the legislation instituting the New Mass imposes a new rite on the Roman Church in an obligatory manner. Cardinal Silvio Oddi's interview in the August 1988 issue of Valeurs Actueles made this clear when he said, 'It needs to be said that the Mass of St. Pius V has in fact never been officially abrogated.' It is also a false opinion that maintains that *Missale Romanum* abrogates *Quo Primum* and therefore effectively suppresses the traditional rite of Mass." Ibid., pp. 134-135.

[64] In response to Canon 9, Fr. Cekada simply says: "This is all that the Code requires and it suffices to make known the will of the legislator, the pope." One wonders how Fr. Cekada believes such a statement helps his case, since *none* of what "the Code requires" was satisfied with the publication of the New Mass (i.e., the required juridical promulgation by the Pope of a universally binding law published in the *Acta*). Having conceded that "the essence of promulgation" is the legislator's will "to impose an obligation" on the Church, Fr. Cekada cannot escape the legal fact that Paul VI in *Missale Romanum* did *not* impose the Mass on the Church as a binding law, and neither did the Congregation for Divine Worship (it merely "permitted" the New Mass in its attempted "promulgation").

[65] This is a reference to the decree *Ordine Missae* issued by the Congregation of Sacred Rites on April 6, 1969 and signed by Cardinal Benno Gut, the Prefect. The decree was never recorded in the *Acta Apostolicae Sedis*.

permitting the use of the New Mass. This second decree which only permits – not orders – its use is in the *Acta Apostolicae Sedis*. There is not a single theologian alive who would say the first or second decree is covered by the infallibility of the Pope."[66]

As we mentioned at the beginning of the chapter, the March 26, 1970 decree, *Celebrationis Eucharistiae,* which "promulgated" the New Mass, was issued by the Congregation for Divine Worship, and not the Pope. Moreover, this act of "promulgation" merely *permits* the New Mass; it does not impose the New Mass as binding legislation upon the Church.

What all this demonstrates is that Paul VI did not juridically promulgate the New Mass, much less "impose it as an obligation" upon the Church as a universally binding law. Therefore, Paul VI in no way violated disciplinary infallibility in connection with his publication of the New Mass. While the New Mass and the many abuses it has spawned has caused harm to the Body of Christ, God has willed to permit this without compromising the Church's infallibility.

---

[66] "Is the Novus Ordo Missae Evil?" *The Angelus* (March 1997).

Chapter 17

~ Canonizations of Saints
and Infallibility ~

On January 25, 1983, Pope John Paul II issued the Apostolic Constitution *Divinus Perfectionis Magister*, which abrogated centuries-old norms for the beatification and canonization process and introduced new norms and procedures.[1] The new process eliminated the stringent *juridical* method used by the Church for centuries, and replaced it with an *academic* approach to determine the sanctity and worthiness of the candidate. The new process also delegates the determination of the cause to the local bishop and not the Pope, and reduces the number of requisite miracles for sainthood from four to two or less.[2] The Catholic Historian, William Thomas Walsh, described the rigorous nature of the former process:

> "No secular court trying a man for his life is more thorough and scrupulous than the Congregation of Rites in seeking to establish whether or not the servant of God practiced virtues both theological and cardinal, and to a heroic degree. If that is established, the advocate of the cause must next prove that his presence in Heaven has been indicated by at least two miracles, while a cardinal who is an expert theologian does all he can to discredit the evidence - hence his popular title of *advocatus diaboli*, or Devil's Advocate. If the evidence survives every attempt to destroy it after months, years and sometimes centuries of discussion, he is then beatified, that is, he is declared to be blessed."[3]

As noted, the old process was abandoned in favor of an academic method. The formal legal proceeding which included the defense

---

[1] Note that the Holy See's procedures for beatification and canonization are matters of Church discipline and not dogma; hence, the Pope is not bound by the procedures of his predecessors and can change them at will. Paul VI, for example, modified the procedures by his Apostolic Constitution *Regimini Ecclesiæ Universæ* of August 15, 1967, and the *Motu Proprio, Sanctitatis Clarior* of March 19, 1969.

[2] Under the traditional process, two miracles were required for beatification and another two miracles for canonization. Under the new norms, only one miracle is required for each, and the Pope can even dispense with these reduced norms (which Pope Francis did in the case of John XXIII, to whom no miracle has been attributed since his beatification in 2000).

[3] William Thomas Walsh, *The Saints in Action* (New York: Hanover, 1961), p. 14 (emphasis added). Though Walsh died in 1949, *The Saints in Action* was not published until 1961.

lawyer and the Promoter of the Faith was eliminated, and replaced by a college of relators, whose task is to prepare a biography of the candidate, structured similar to a doctrinal dissertation, based upon documentation provided to them by the local bishop. The historical-critical biography now serves as the basis for determining the worthiness of the candidate.

The Promoter of the Faith (also known as the *Advocatus Diaboli* or "Devil's Advocate") has been replaced by the Prelate Theologian who has an entirely different role. While the job of the Devils's Advocate was to present any evidence *against* the orthodoxy and the sanctity of the candidate (essentially acting as a prosecutor), the main task of the Prelate Theologian is simply to choose the theological consulters and preside at the meetings.

In his book *Making Saints: How the Catholic Church Determines Who Becomes a Saint, Who Doesn't, and Why,* noted Catholic Journalist, Kenneth L. Woodward, explained that the announced goals of the reform were "to make the canonization process simpler, faster, cheaper, more 'collegial' and ultimately more productive." He went on to say: "At the core of the reform is a striking paradigm shift: no longer would the Church look to the courtroom as its model for arriving at the truth of a saint's life; instead, it would employ the academic model of researching and writing a doctoral dissertation."[4] He said the new process,

> "put the entire responsibility for gathering all the evidence in support of a cause in the hands of the local bishop: instead of two canonical processes, the Ordinary and the Apostolic as was formerly the case, there would only be one, directly by the local bishop. Second – and far more drastic – it abolished the entire series of legal dialectics between the defense lawyers and the Promoter of the Faith. ... Indeed, not only were the advocates stripped of their powers, so were the Promoter of the Faith and his staff of lawyers. After nearly six centuries the function of the Devil's Advocate had been eliminated."[5]

He continued:

> "In effect, the *relator* had replaced both the Devil's Advocate and the defense lawyer. He alone was responsible for establishing

---

[4] Woodward, Kenneth, *Making Saints: How the Catholic Church Determines Who Becomes a Saint, Who Doesn't, and Why* (New York: Simon and Schuster, 1990), p. 91.
[5] Ibid.

martyrdom or heroic virtue, and it was up to the theological and historical consultants to give his work a passing or failing grade."[6]

The elimination of the Devil's Advocate, whose duty was to protest against any violations of the procedures and insist upon the consideration of any objections raised against the orthodoxy or the sanctity of the candidate,[7] was a drastic change. In the monumental work by Prospero Lambertini (later Pope Benedict XIV), *On the Beatification and Canonization of Saints*, we read that the role of the Devil's Advocate was considered so essential that "no important act in the process of beatification or canonization is valid unless performed in" his presence.[8]

Following the implantation of the new procedures, certain individuals, whose causes would have likely been stopped in their tracks by the former rigorous juridical method, have passed through, and in record time. After the removal of the Devil's Advocate, objections put forward by members of the laity and hierarchy alike are regularly ignored. As one writer put it, "the challenges are neither acknowledged nor answered."[9] Questionable miracles are accepted[10] and individuals of highly questionable or positively doubtful orthodoxy and sanctity have been beatified, and others canonized. This has caused concern amongst many faithful Catholics and, not

---

[6] Ibid.

[7] *Cf. Catholic Encyclopedia* (1913), vol. I, p. 168.

[8] Ibid. In the traditional process, the Devil's Advocate subjected the details of the candidate's life to extreme rigor and analysis. In the case of St. Pius X (the last sainted Pope under the old process), in spite of the thorough investigation, the Devil's Advocate could find only that the Pope smoked a cigarette a day and said Low Mass in less than 25 minutes - hardly practices that would undermine his incontrovertible sanctity!

[9] John Vennari, "Doubt and Confusion: The New 'Canonizations,'" *Catholic Family News*, August 2013.

[10] For example, one of the alledged miracles attributed to Mother Teresa's intercession was the cure of a tumor in a women named Monica Besra, in September 1998. Despite claims of a miracle, however, Besra's own doctors insisted that the cure had nothing miraculous about it, but was instead the result of strong anti-TB drugs administered over a period of nine months. For example, Dr. R.K. Musafi said: "This miraculous claim is absolute nonsense and should be condemned by everyone. She had a medium-sized tumor in her lower abdomen caused by tuberculosis. The drugs she was given eventually reduced the cystic mass and it disappeared after a year's treatment." Mrs Besra's husband agreed that the cure was no miracle. "This miracle is a hoax," he said. "It is much ado about nothing. My wife was cured by the doctors." ("Medicine cured 'miracle' woman - not Mother Teresa, say doctors," by David Or, *The Telegraph*, October 5, 2003). Likewise Dr. T. K. Biswas, the first doctor to treat Mrs. Besra said, "With all due respect to Mother Teresa, there should not be any talk of a miracle by her. We advised her a prolonged anti-tubercular treatment and she was cured." ("Doctor claims pressure to ratify Teresa's 'miracle,'" by M. Chhaya, Rediff, October 19, 2002).

surprisingly, has been used by Sedevacantists as "evidence" that the visible Church has "defected," due to an alleged violation of infallibility.

Controversial Canonization

The propriety of many canonizations have been questioned in the post conciliar era, particularly during the reign of John Paul II, who canonized more saints during his pontificate than all of his predecessors combined, since Pope Sixtus V created the Congregation of Rites in 1588. Even in the eyes of many non-traditional Catholics, John Paul II's "saint factory" (as some have called it) has depreciated the cult of the *beati* and *sancti* and the honor due them. One of the more controversial canonizations orchestrated by John Paul II was that of Msgr. Josemaria Escrivá de Balaguer (1902-1975), founder of Opus Dei. Msgr. Escrivá's canonization, which was declared by John Paul II on October 6, 2002, went through rapidly, in spite of the fact that former members of Opus Dei who personally knew Msgr. Escrivá raised many serious objections, which were completely ignored.

Frustrated that their objections were not being considered, in a last ditch effort these former Opus Dei members wrote an Open Letter to Pope John Paul II in which they said: "It is because we believe that the truth has been in large part hidden that we now give our testimony in order to avoid a danger for the Faith brought about by the unjustifiable reverence for the man that you have the intention of canonizing soon." They went on to say that the authors of their Open Letter included "people who have intimately known Msgr. Escrivá and who can testify to his arrogance, to his evil character, to his improper seeking of a title (Marquise of Peralta), to his dishonesty,[11] to his indifference towards the poor, to his love of luxury and ostentation, to his lack of compassion, and to his idolatrous devotion towards 'Opus Dei.'"[12]

After having pointed out that the process was uncanonical and dishonest, the writers said the canonization "will stain the Church forever. It will take away from the saints their special holiness. It will call into question the credibility of all the canonizations made during your Papacy. It will undermine the future authority of the Papacy." Unfortunately, the Open Letter was also ignored. Commenting on this,

---

[11] The late Canon Gregory Hesse also stated that Escrivá was a public liar, by falsifying professional credentials in canon law as well as deceiving people about his ethnicity (Fr. Hesse claimed Escrivá was Jewish and that Escrivá denied it).

[12] Cited in John Vennari, "Doubt and Confusion: The New 'Canonizations,'" *Catholic Family News*, August 2013.

Fr. Peter Scott noted that "their supplication was not heard, and the ceremony took place as arranged on October 6, 2002."[13]

Kenneth Woodward, author of the above-cited book on canonizations, was also disturbed by the canonization of Escrivá. He said:

> "the only fair-minded conclusion I can reach, given the evidence of the *positio* itself and interviews with people in Rome involved in the process, is that Opus Dei subverted the canonization process to get its man beatified. In a word, it was a scandal — from the conduct of the tribunals through the writing of the *positio* to the high-handed treatment of the experts picked to judge the cause. That *Newsweek* caught Opus Dei officials making claims that were not true is a matter of record. Escrivá may have been a saint — who am I to judge? — but you could never tell from the way his cause was handled."[14]

The Canonizations of John XXIII and John Paul II

Two more canonizations that have caused controversy are those of John XXIII and John Paul II, which occurred simultaneously on April 27, 2014. The canonization ceremony was unique for many reasons: This was the first time two Popes were canonized in a single ceremony; the first time two living Popes (one a "Pope Emeritus") were present at the ceremony (Francis and Benedict); the first time a Pope got "fast tracked" (*Santo Subito!*) to sainthood under his own carry-over legislation (John Paul II);[15] and the first time any Pope was canonized under the new procedures. It was also the first time any Pope was ever raised to the altars after such a controversial pontificate (which goes for both John XXIII and John Paul II). Prior to this double canonization ceremony, only one Pope, who reigned in the previous 400 years, had been canonized, and only four had been canonized in the prior millennium.

In May 2014, *The Remnant* newspaper published an article written by Catholic apologist John Salza titled "Questioning the Validity of the

---

[13] Holy Cross Seminary Newsletter, November 1, 2002.

[14] "Fair to Opus Dei?" Letter to the Editor of *First Things*, No. 61, March 1996, pp. 2-7.

[15] Pope Benedict XVI authorized the opening of the cause for the beatification of John Paul II only one month after his death. The diocesan process concluded in less than two years, and only two more years to raise John Paul II to "Venerable." The speed at which John Paul II was canonized after such a controversial pontificate only adds to the controversy, in light of the lengthy process of pre-Vatican II canonizations. Thomas More and John Fisher, for example, were canonized *400 years* after their martyrdoms. St. Joan of Arc was canonized more than *500 years* after her martyrdom.

Canonizations."[16] In the article, Salza questioned the *validity* of the canonizations of John XXIII and John Paul II (and implicitly their infallibility), arguing that if the canonizations did not meet the *legal* requirements according to the Church's current legislation, then they would not be *licit* (and possibly not *valid*), which may cast doubt upon the question of their *infallibility* (assuming, of course, that infallibility presupposes a process that meets the Church's legal norms currently in place).

Salza noted that while the new norms are not nearly as rigorous as pre-Vatican II law, and delegate the determination of the cause to the local bishop (not the Pope), the new legislation still requires a candidate's writings to be free from doctrinal or moral error in order for the cause to proceed.[17] Specifically, the law provides that all published writings are to be "examined by theological censors," and if "the writings have been found to contain nothing contrary to faith and good morals,"[18] then the bishop is to also examine the candidate's unpublished writings, as well as all documents, which in any way pertain to the cause. The law then provides that "If the Bishop has prudently judged that, on the basis of all that has been done so far, the cause can proceed,"[19] he is to so proceed with an examination of witnesses.

When inquiries are complete, a report is prepared and the cause turned over to the Sacred Congregation for the Causes of the Saints. While in deference to his authority there is a presumption that the bishop's assessment is correct, Salza noted that reason alone dictates the presumption is rebuttable if there are notorious facts which contradict his conclusion. These are facts which the bishop would have easily discovered had he exercised reasonable care and "prudent judgment" as the Church's law requires.

In light of the current legislation, Salza went on to note that John XXIII and John Paul II (as well as Escrivá) have been accused – by both traditionalists and "conservatives"– of having written and done things in public that both violated Church law[20] and objectively deviated from

---

[16] Salza, "Questioning the Validity of the Canonizations – Against a Fact There is No Argument," *The Remnant* newspaper, May 31, 2014.

[17] Pope Francis did not declare that he was abrogating or even deviating from John Paul II's legislation. Rather, Pope Francis chose to act in accordance with John Paul II's legislation which requires the writings of John XXIII and John Paul II to be free from doctrinal or moral error.

[18] *Divinis Perfectionis Magister*, January 25, 1983. Section 1, paragraph 2.3.

[19] Ibid., Section 1, paragraph 2.4

[20] For example, the Catholic apologist Jimmy Akin (no friend to Traditional Catholics) noted that "liturgical law was disregarded *regularly* at John Paul II's major celebrations of

the Faith[21] (and which would have barred them from canonization under the old process). We have seen some of these deviations in Chapter 7 on Theological Censures and "Hereticizing," which illustrated several of John Paul II's ambiguous and erroneous formulations of Catholic doctrine.[22] Salza argued that any bishop who "prudently judged" this evidence in the objective order would have had grounds for stopping the causes of these two Popes from advancing to the Holy See. The one Bishop who did publicly object is Bishop Bernard Fellay, who said "we vigorously protest these canonizations."[23]

Salza also noted the irony that the novel principle of collegiality, embraced by John XXIII and John Paul II (which was used as the basis for placing the investigation and judgment in the hands of the local ordinary alone), effectively operates to remove any assurance of liceity (and validity), not to mention infallibility, from their own canonizations. This is because the bishop and his assistants are not protected with the "divine assistance" Christ promises to the successors of St. Peter, and therefore their judgments are not immune from error. The same, of course, can be said for the decisions of the Cardinal Prefect and his assistants in the Sacred Congregation for the Causes of Saints. The Pope, who is no longer the investigator of a cause, but rather an approver, simply rubber stamps a completely fallible process (a process whose results are determined by the bishop and approved by the Holy See, all before the final report reaches the Pope).

If the Pope is simply approving the judgment reached by the local bishop, it calls into question whether the declaration of canonization is

---

the liturgy." (Akin, "Vatican's Top Liturgical Liberal Steps Down," October 2, 2007, http://www.jimmyakin.com/2007/10/vaticans-top-li.html.)

[21] Fr. Brian Harrison (not considered a "Traditionalist" priest) wrote an article called "John Paul II and Assisi: Reflections of a 'Devil's Advocate'" which was published by the *Latin Mass Magazine*. In the article, Fr. Harrison argues that John Paul II promoted the error, condemned by Pius XI in *Mortalium Animos*, that "all religions are more or less good and praiseworthy," by his interreligious activities (e.g., Assisi prayer meetings). Fr. Harrison concluded that John Paul II was not fit for canonization because he displayed less than a heroic level of the cardinal virtue of prudence and the theological virtue of faith.

[22] These deviations are chronicled in Fr. Patrick de La Rocque's book *Pope John Paul II – Doubts About a Beatification* (Angelus Press). The material for the book was taken from a theological study that was submitted to the ecclesiastical authorities in charge of the diocesan process for John Paul II, *which was ignored*. Other works have also been published, for example, "Pope John XXIII: A Critical Judgment" (*SiSiNoNo*, May 1997); and, "Was the 'Good Pope' a Good Pope?" (*The Angelus* magazine, September 2000).

[23] "Comments taken from the Society of St. Pius X's website at http://www.sspx.org/en/news -events /news/we-vigorously-protest-these-canonizations-3956.

an act of the Pope's supreme Extraordinary Magisterium. By permitting the local ordinary to oversee the process, there is also less assurance of liceity (and validity) of these canonizations (especially when formal objections raised against the canonizations are repeatedly ignored).

Canonizations and Infallibility

Some of these recent, questionable canonizations have naturally led people to ask if canonizations are, indeed, protected by the Church's infallibility, as many pre-Vatican II theologians held, since it is related to revealed truth (although indirectly) and an exercise of the Church's teaching, and not merely legislative, power. The question then arises, if the Church's infallibility does extend to canonizations, is it due, in part, to the juridical process, or simply to the decree issued by the Pope? Or is it a combination of the two? If the procedures are an integral part of the guarantee of infallibility, what if the procedures are dispensed with, as in the case of John XXIII and others?[24] Another question is what exactly does canonization guarantee? Does it provide infallible certitude that the person lived a life of heroic virtue, or does infallibility only guarantee that the person died in the state of grace and possesses the Beatific Vision, which could even be the case of one who lived a scandalous life, yet converted before death?

As we have seen, the Church has only definitively declared that infallibility embraces the *primary* objects of infallibility, which are the truths formally revealed by God in Scripture and Tradition, which require the assent of faith. We recall that the First Vatican Council declared a Pope receives the "divine assistance" from the Holy Ghost only when he "defines a doctrine concerning faith or morals."[25] Declaring someone a saint, however, is a judgment of sanctity, strictly speaking, and not a declaration on faith or morals about a doctrine which is contained in the Deposit of Faith. Since the Church has never declared that infallibility extends to the *secondary* objects such as the canonization of saints (which comes under the category of disciplinary facts), we cannot answer these questions with certainty. We are

---

[24] As noted, John XXIII was canonized without a miracle being confirmed after his beatification, which is even required by the new procedures. See, Magister, Sandro, "Vatican Diary/In a few months, six new saints canonized outside the rules,"www.chiesa.espressonline.it, March 19, 2014, http://www.chiesa.espresso.repub blica.it/articolo/1350746?eng=y&refresh_ce.
[25] First Vatican Council, *Pastor Aeternus*, 1870.

therefore left to the opinion of theologians and historical precedents to help guide us in arriving at an answer.

The article on infallibility by the eminent theologian, Rev. P. J. Toner, for the 1913 *Catholic Encyclopedia*, provides an answer to several of these questions. We quote him at length since he also makes the distinction, alluded to above, between the primary and secondary objects of infallibility, which we have also discussed in several places throughout this book. He begins by saying, "In the Vatican definition, infallibility (whether of the Church at large or of the pope) is affirmed only in regard to doctrines of faith or morals," and then goes on to add:

"This, however, is clearly understood to be what theologians call the direct and primary object of infallible authority: it was for the maintenance and interpretation and legitimate development of Christ's teaching that the Church was endowed with this charisma. But if this primary function is to be adequately and effectively discharged, it is clear that there must also be indirect and secondary objects to which infallibility extends, namely, doctrines and facts which, although they cannot strictly speaking be said to be revealed, are nevertheless so intimately connected with revealed truths that, were one free to deny the former, he would logically deny the latter and thus defeat the primary purpose for which infallibility was promised by Christ to His Church. (...)

Catholic theologians are agreed in recognizing the general principle that has just been stated, <u>but it cannot be said that they are equally unanimous in regard to the concrete applications of this principle</u>. Yet it is *generally held*, and may be said to be theologically certain, (a) that what are technically described as 'theological conclusions,' i.e. inferences deduced from two premises, one of which is revealed and the other verified by reason, fall under the scope of the Church's infallible authority. (b) It is also generally held, and rightly, that questions of dogmatic fact, in regard to which definite certainty is required for the safe custody and interpretation of revealed truth, may be determined infallibly by the Church. Such questions, for example, would be: whether a certain pope is legitimate, or a certain council ecumenical, or whether objective heresy or error is taught in a certain book or other published document. ... (c) <u>It is also commonly and rightly held that the Church is infallible in the canonization of saints</u>, that is to say, <u>when canonization takes place according to the solemn process that has been followed since the ninth century</u>. Mere beatification, however, as distinguished from canonization, is not held to be infallible, and <u>in canonization itself the only fact that is infallibly</u>

> determined is that the soul of the canonized saint departed in the
> state of grace and already enjoys the beatific vision. "[26]

A few points are to be noted: First, it is not *de fide* (of the faith) that canonizations are protected by infallibility. It is, *at most*, qualified as "theologically certain," and according to some of the best pre-Vatican II theologians, it is considered only the "common opinion," which is certainly subject to change. Second, Rev. Toner notes that canonizations were commonly considered infallible when they take place "*according to the solemn process that has been followed since the ninth century.*" But what if a canonization takes place according to a new process, and what if the more lax requirements of the new process are themselves dispensed with, as in the case of John XXIII? Would the canonization still be considered infallible? Lastly, note that with canonizations, the only *fact* that is infallibly determined "*is that the soul of the canonized saint departed in the state of grace and already enjoys the beatific vision.*"[27] It is commonly believed that this is the only "fact" that canonization guarantees. [28]

The Object of the Infallible Judgment

The 1913 *Catholic Encyclopedia* article on beatification and canonization, written by Fr. Beccari, agrees with the position of Rev. Toner in maintaining that the *object* of the infallible judgment is only whether the person is in Heaven, and not that the person lived a life of heroic virtue.[29] Fr. Beccari begins by addressing this distinction (whether canonizations confirm only that the person is in Heaven, or also that he lived a life of heroic virtue). This is his reply:

> "I have never seen this question discussed; my own opinion is that nothing else is defined than that the person canonized is in heaven. The formula used in the act of canonization has nothing more than this:

---

[26] *Catholic Encyclopedia* (1913), vol. VII, p. 799 (emphasis added).
[27] We do note that some theologians maintain that canonization also implies that the person lived a life of heroic virtue.
[28] Dr. Ludwig Van Ott also said: "The canonization of saints" is "the final judgment that a member of the Church has been assumed into eternal bliss, and may be the object of universal veneration." *Fundamentals of Catholic Dogma*, p. 299.
[29] There is no question that the object of the investigation into the person's life is to determine if they lived a life of heroic virtue, but the question is whether the *infallible judgment* pertains to this aspect of canoniazation, or exclusively to the judgment that they are in eternal beatitude.

'In honour of . . . we decree and define that Blessed N. is a Saint, and we inscribe his name in the catalogue of saints, and order that his memory by devoutly and piously celebrated yearly on the . . . day of . . . his feast.'[30]

There is no question of heroic virtue in this formula; on the other hand, sanctity does not necessarily imply the exercise of heroic virtue, since one who had not hitherto practiced heroic virtue would, by the one transient heroic act in which he yielded up his life for Christ, have justly deserved to be considered a saint. This view seems all the more certain if we reflect that all the arguments of theologians for papal infallibility in the canonization of saints are based on the fact that on such occasions the popes believe and assert that the decision which they publish is infallible (Pesch, Prael. Dogm., I, 552)."[31]

Now, if the object of the infallible judgment is *only* whether the person is in Heaven, no one can object that infallibility has been violated on the basis that this or that person has been canonized, since even a hardened sinner is capable of performing "one transient heroic act," of yielding up his life for Christ at the moment of death, and thereby obtain the Beatific Vision. And if anyone maintains that someone who lived a horrible life and only converted on their deathbed cannot be recognized by the Church as a saint, they are going to have a hard time explaining how St. Dismas, the Good Thief, was raised to the altars. St. Dismas has been recognized as a saint by the Church for centuries; he has churches named after him; approved prayers directed to him; and His feast day on the universal calendar is March 25.[32]

Degree of Certitude

Regarding the degree of certitude that canonizations are, in fact, covered by the Church's infallibility, Van Noort qualified it as only being the "common opinion" - and this was *before* Vatican II, when the more stringent juridical process for canonizations was still being followed. In his dogmatic manual, *Christ's Church*, we read:

---

[30] *Ad honorem...beatum N. Sanctum esse decernimus et definimus ac sanctorum catalogo adscribimus statuentes ab ecclesiâ universali illius memoriam quolibet anno, die ejus Natali...piâ devotione recoli debere.*

[31] *Catholic Encyclopedia* (1913), vol. II, p. 367.

[32] We also note that not all canonized saints go immediately to Heaven as some think; it is likely that many canonized saints pass through the fires of Pugatory.

"Assertion 5: The Church's infallibility extends to the canonization of saints. This is the *common opinion* today.

Canonization (formal) is the final and definitive decree by which the sovereign pontiff declares that someone has been admitted to heaven and is to be venerated by everyone, at least in the sense that all the faithful are held to consider the person a saint worthy of public veneration. It differs from *beatification,* which is a provisional rather than a definitive decree, by which veneration is only permitted, or at least is not universally prescribed. Infallibility is claimed for canonization only; a decree of beatification, which in the eyes of the Church is not definitive, but may still be rescinded, is to be considered morally certain indeed, but not infallible. Still, there are some theologians who take a different view of the matter."[33]

We again note that Van Noort only qualifies the infallibility of canonization as "the common opinion *today.*" Some Sedevacantists will try to present the proposition as being a *de fide* teaching of the Church (which would mean it would be "impossible" for the Church to err in the judgment), but that is clearly not the case.[34] Neither is it impossible for the common opinion to change. For example, throughout the history of the Church (and certainly up to the eighteenth century), it was the common opinion (and some may have even qualified it as *de fide*) that the Earth was the center of the universe;[35] yet if you consult the modern theological manuals in the first half of the twentieth century, the common opinion is the contrary. We also saw that, as Suarez taught, it was the common opinion in his day that a Pope would only lose his office after being declared a heretic by the proper authorities, yet the Sedevacantists today not only explicitly reject this "common opinion," but they base their entire case upon the premise that it was *certainly* wrong.

---

[33] *Christ's Church*, p. 117.

[34] That is why none of the Church's theologians qualify the teaching as being *de fide.* Sedevacantists will cite seventeenth and eighteenth century saints and theologians (e.g., Bellarmine, Liguori) in support of the infallibility of canonizations, but the opinions of these men were obviously formed in light of the very different process for canonizations at that time than exists today.

[35] The position that the Earth is the center of the universe was even supported by three papal bulls in the seventeenth century (by Popes Paul V, Urban VIII and Alexander VII). These decrees have never been overturned by subsequent Popes.

Common Opinion Today?

The next question that arises is whether it is still the common opinion today that canonizations are protected by infallibility, following the implementation of the new and less rigorous procedures (which, in some cases, are even dispensed with). Theologically speaking, it could be argued (and some reputable theologians have argued) that the "divine assistance" Christ promised to St. Peter (as defined by Vatican I) would not apply to the Pope under the current, post-Vatican II procedures for canonization. This is because the Pope is *not engaged* in the investigatory process for which he would receive divine assistance from the Holy Ghost (assistance which the pre-Vatican II Popes presumably did receive because they were the ones conducting the investigation).[36]

Rather, in accordance with Vatican II's new principle of collegiality, the local bishop and his assistants are responsible for the investigation of the cause, and they receive no infallible assistance from the Holy Ghost in carrying out such duties. As John Paul II's legislation provides, pursuant to "the desires of Our Brother Bishops, who have often called for a simpler process [of canonization]...In light of the doctrine of the Second Vatican Council on collegiality, We also think that the Bishops themselves should be more closely associated with the Holy See in dealing with the causes of saints."[37]

And "more closely associated" with the causes they certainly are, for the bishops effectively create the entire case for canonization, to be voted upon by the Congregation for the Causes of Saints, which acts in an advisory and consultative role to the bishops. As Pope John Paul II's legislation explains, "It's [the Congregation for the Causes of Saints] duty is to deal with those matters which pertain to the canonization of the Servants of God by providing advice and guidelines to Bishops in the instruction of the causes, by studying the causes thoroughly and, finally, by casting its vote."[38]

Bishop Giuseppe Sciacca, a distinguished Canonist and Adjunct Secretary of the Apostolic Signatura, was recently interviewed by Andrea Tornielli about the infallibility of canonizations. The Bishop began by noting that canonizations "should not be considered infallible

---

[36] The "divine assistance" promised to the Pope would presumably apply not to his simple utterance of the words of canonization (the form), but indispensably to his investigation and determination of the qualification of the candidate (the matter), which process is now removed from the Pope and delegated to the local bishop and Vatican bureaucrats.

[37] *Divinis Perfectionis Magister*, Introduction.

[38] *Ibid.*, Section 2, paragraph 3.

according to the infallibility criteria set out in the First Vatican Council's dogmatic constitution 'Pastor aeternus.'" When pressed for clarification, he said:

> "What I am saying, is that the proclamation of a person's sainthood is not a truth of faith because it is not a dogmatic definition and is not directly or explicitly linked to a truth of faith or a moral truth contained in the revelation, but is only indirectly linked to this. It is no coincidence that neither the Code of Canon Law of 1917 nor the one currently in force, nor the Catechism of the Catholic Church present the Church's doctrine regarding canonizations."[39]

The bishop was then asked to comment on the teaching of Prospero Lambertini (later Pope Benedict XIV), who said the idea that canonizations are not infallible "smells of heresy." The bishop replied by saying: "His theory is not binding as it forms part of the work he did as a great canonist [before being elected Pope], but as part of his private studies. It has nothing to do with his pontifical magisterium." The bishop was then asked: "But there was a doctrinal text issued by the Congregation for the Doctrine of the Faith in May 1998 which also mentions infallibility in canonizations," to which he replied:

> "It is patently clear that the purpose of the passage in question is purely illustrative and is not intended as a definition. The recurring argument according to which the Church cannot teach or accept mistakes is intrinsically weak in this case. But saying that an act is not infallible does not mean to say that the act is wrong or deceiving. Indeed, the mistake may have been made either rarely or never. Canonization, which everyone admits does not derive directly from faith, is never an actual definition relating to faith or tradition…"[40]

After making several other comments suggesting that canonizations are, in fact, not protected by the Church's infallibility, Tornielli ended by asking, "And yet today, at the moment of the proclamation, the Pope says 'decernimus e definimus,' in other words 'we decree and define.' It basically sounds like a 'definition.'" Because this terminology could potentially lead to the mistaken notion that

---

[39] Tornielli, Vatican Insider, July 10, 2014, http://www.vaticaninsider.lastampa.it/en/the-vatican/detail/articolo/canonizzazioni-canonizations-canonizaciones -351 58/ (emphasis added).
[40] Ibid., (emphasis added).

canonization is equivalent to defining a dogma, the bishop replied by saying:

> "This is why I agree with some important canonists who suggest setting aside the formula currently used to define the truths of faith, proposing instead a more suitable formula: *'declaramus,'* 'we declare.'"[41]

The bishop was then asked to comment on the opinion that St. Thomas Aquinas (supposedly) believed the Church's infallibility extended to canonizations. The bishop responded:

> "Of course, I am well aware of that. Thomas Aquinas is the most prestigious author supporting this theory. But it should be said that the use of the concept of infallibility and of language relating to it, in a context that is so far from that of the 19th century when the First Vatican Council was held, risks being anachronistic. St. Thomas placed canonization half way between things that pertain to the faith and judgments on certain factors that can be contaminated by false testimonies, concluding that the Church could not make mistakes: in fact, he claimed that: 'thinking that judgment is infallible, is holy.' As I said before and I repeat again, the 'Pastor aeternus' rigorously defines and restricts the concept of papal infallibility which could previously [before being defined, have] also [been considered to] encompass and contain or be likened to the concepts of 'inerrancy' and 'indefectibility' in relation to the Church. Canonization is like a doctrine which cannot be contested but which cannot be defined as a doctrine of faith as all faithful must necessarily believe in it."[42]

---

[41] Ibid.

[42] Ibid (emphasis added). The bishop correctly noted that St. Thomas placed canonizations between matters of faith and judgments based on human testimony. St Thomas says "it is certain that it is *impossible* for the judgment of the universal Church to err in the things that pertain to the *faith*...But in the case of other *decisions* regarding *particular facts*, as when it is a question of possessions or crimes or something similar, it is *possible for the judgments of the Church to err* because of false witnesses. The *canonization of saints is midway between these two*." St. Thomas then says: "Nonetheless, since the honor we exhibit to the saints is a kind of profession of faith whereby we believe in the glory of the saints, *it is piously to be believed* that even in these matters the judgment of the Church cannot err." (*Quodlibetal*, IX, a. 16 ed. Frette or Vivès, Paris, vol. 15, p. 566). Note that St. Thomas says the infallibility of canonizations "is piously to be believed," which is different from the assent of Divine and Catholic faith that is required for Church dogma.

It seems quite clear that the distinguished Canonist and Adjunct Secretary of the Apostolic Signatura is not convinced that the Church's infallibility extends to canonizations, and he is not alone.

In a recent interview published in *Catholic Family News*, Professor Roberto de Mattei explained that some of the best theologians of today question the infallibility of canonizations. He said:

> "Infallibility of canonizations is not a dogma of the faith, it is the opinion of a majority of theologians, above all after Benedict XIV, who expressed it moreover as a private doctor and not as Sovereign Pontiff. As far as the 'Roman School' is concerned, the most eminent representative of this theological school, living today, is Msgr. Brunero Gherardini. And Msgr. Gherardini expressed in the review *Divinitas* directed by him, all of his doubts on the infallibility of canonizations. I know in Rome, distinguished theologians and canonists, disciples of another illustrious representative of the Roman School, Msgr. Antonio Piolanti, these harbor the same doubts as Msgr. Gherardini. They hold that canonizations do not fulfill the conditions laid down by Vatican I to guarantee a papal act's infallibility. The judgment of canonization is not infallible in itself, because it lacks the conditions for infallibility, starting from the fact the canonization does not have as its direct or explicit aim, a truth of the Faith or morals contained in Revelation, but only a fact indirectly connected with dogma, without being properly-speaking a 'dogmatic fact.' The field of faith and morals is broad, because it contains all of Christian doctrine, speculative and practical, human belief and action, but a distinction is necessary. A dogmatic definition can, never involve the definition of a new doctrine in the field of faith and morals. The Pope can only make explicit that which is implicit in faith and morals, and is handed down by the Tradition of the Church. That which the Popes define must be contained in the Scriptures and in Tradition, and it is this which assures the infallibility of the act. That is certainly not the case for canonizations. ... the doctrine of canonizations is not contained in the Codes of Canon Law of 1917 and of 1983, nor the Catechisms of the Catholic Church, old and new. Referring to this subject, besides the aforementioned study of Msgr. Gherardini, is an excellent article by José Antonio Ureta appearing in the March 2014 edition of the magazine *Catolicismo*."[43]

---

[43] "The 'Canonizations': CFN interviews Professor Roberto de Mattei," *Catholic Family News*, April 14, 2015 (emphasis added).

The interviewer then asked what he thought about the teaching of St. Thomas on the infallibility of canonizations. The professor replied:

> "We must first dispel a semantic misconception: a non-infallible act, is not a wrong act that necessarily deceives, but only an act subject to the possibility of error. In fact, this error may be most rare, or never happened. St. Thomas, balanced, as always, in his judgment, is not infallible to the end. He is rightly concerned to defend the infallibility of the Church and he does so with a theologically-reasonable argument, on the contrary. His argument can be accepted in a broad sense, but admitting the possibility of exceptions. I agree with him that the Church as a whole cannot err. This does not mean that every act of the Church, as the act of canonization, is in itself necessarily infallible. The assent which lends itself to acts of canonizations is of ecclesiastical faith, not divine. This means that the member of the faithful believes because he accepts the principle that the Church does not normally err. The exception does not cancel out the rule."[44]

He was then asked: "Do you hold that canonizations lost their infallible character, following the changing of the canonization procedure, willed by John Paul II in 1983?" He responded by saying that, although he does not personally consider the weakness of the new process to be decisive, he noted that some have argued this very point. He said:

> "This position is supported in the *Courrier de Rome*, by an excellent theologian, Fr. Jean-Michel Gleize. Moreover, one of the arguments, on which Fr. Low in the article on Canonizations in the Enciclopedia Cattolica (Catholic Encyclopedia), bases his thesis on infallibility, is the existence of a massive complex of investigations and findings, followed by two miracles which precede the canonization. There is no doubt that after the reform of the procedure willed by John Paul II in 1983, this process of ascertaining the truth has become much weaker and there has been a change of the very concept of sanctity."[45]

As we noted previously, during the old rigorous procedures, Van Noort only qualified the infallibility of canonizations as the common

---

[44] Ibid (emphasis added). Mattei's statement that St. Thomas "is not infallible to the end" seems a bit anachronistic, since St. Thomas did not claim to be infallible, and moreover, did not hold the infallibility of canonizations to be a matter of divine faith, the very conclusion with which de Mattei agrees.
[45] Ibid.

opinion. In light of the above testimony, one is certainly permitted to question whether it still the common opinion today, and even maintain that it is *no longer* the common opinion today.

One of the more penetrating treatments in modern times of the infallibility of canonizations was given by theology professor Fr. Jean-Michel Gleize (mentioned by de Mattei), in an article entitled "Beatification and Canonization Since Vatican II."[46] Fr. Gleize's article, which was published in the traditional periodical *SiSiNoNo* in June 2011, examines the traditional principles concerning beatifications and canonizations, and the difficulties that are raised under the new legislation. After stating that the infallibility of canonizations is a common opinion according to the theology manuals issued after Vatican I (and *before* Vatican II),[47] Fr. Gleize raises three principal objections to their infallibility under the new legislation: (1) inadequacy of procedure; (2) collegiality and, (3) heroic virtue.

Regarding inadequacy of procedure, Fr. Gleize first noted that "the guarantee of infallibility does not dispense its holders of due diligence." He cited the First Vatican Council, which teaches that,

> "The infallibility of the Roman Pontiff is obtained, not by way of revelation, nor by way of inspiration, but by way of divine assistance. That is why the pope, in virtue of his function, is bound to employ the means required in order to elucidate the truth sufficiently and to expound it correctly; and these means are the following: meetings with bishops, cardinals, and theologians, and having recourse to their counsels. ... when Christ promised divine assistance to St. Peter and to his successors, this promise also included the requisite and necessary means so that the Pontiff could state his judgment infallibly."[48]

---

[46] http://sspx.org/en/beatification-and-canonization-vatican-ii-1.

[47] As further addressed below, Fr. Gleize notes that Cajetan (d. 1534) and Augustine of Ancona (d. 1328) before him (who both thought a heretical Pope must be judged by a council), denied the infallibility of canonizations (after St. Thomas had written on the matter) on the ground that, because it is impossible for the Church to judge the internal forum, the Church cannot infallibly discern a person's sanctity. Fr. Daniel Ols, a Dominican priest and no less than a relator for the Congregation of the Causes of Saints under John Paul II, also held Cajetan's opinion and publicly affirmed the same in 2002 (at the time of Escrivá's canonization). John of St. Thomas and Dominic Bannez (two more Dominicans) also denied that the infallibility of canonizations is a dogma of the faith, as did Suarez and the Carmalites of Salamanca. As noted above, while St. Thomas himself (also a Dominican) defended the infallibility of canonizations, he qualified his opinion as something that is to be "piously believed," which is a lesser level of assent from that which we *must* believe as a matter of Divine and Catholic faith (see *Quodlibetal*, IX, a. 16).

[48] See http://www.sspx.org/en/beatification-and-canonization-vatican-ii-1 (emphasis added).

Fr. Gleize argued that the *divine assistance* promised to the Pope is compromised under the new procedures. Under the former legislation, the procedures for the canonization "relied upon a double process carried out at the time of the beatification, one that took place before the tribunal of the Ordinary acting in his own name" along with "another that depended exclusively on the Holy See."[49] As noted previously, according to the new norms, the process overseen by the Holy See has been eliminated. Furthermore, in the pre-Vatican II legislation, before the Pope signed the decree of canonization the Holy See held three consecutive consistories. These have also been eliminated in the new procedures. According to the new norms, the essential part of the inquiry is not made by the Holy See, but delegated to the local bishop, who does not possess the *divine assistance* promised to the Pope.

Fr. Gleize noted that the new procedures revert to what was in place before the twelfth century, in which the local bishop makes a *direct judgment* on the cause, which the Pope simply certifies. He wrote:

> "The legislation of the 12th century merged beatifications and canonizations as two non-infallible acts.[50] This is what keeps us from simply assimilating the canonizations proceeding from the [conciliar] reform to the traditional acts of the extraordinary teaching authority of the Sovereign Pontiff; in these [latter] acts the pope is satisfied with certifying the act of a local Ordinary. This constitutes a first reason warranting a serious doubt that the conditions required for the infallibility of canonizations have been met."[51]

In accordance with Vatican II's principle of collegiality, then, the new norms leave it to the bishop to make a direct judgment on the cause, with the Pope only reserving the power to confirm the bishop's judgment. Accordingly, it can be said that these canonizations are no longer personally infallible and definitive acts of the Pope (if, indeed, they were before), but rather acts of the Ordinary Magisterium which is not infallible in itself.

After listing several other problematic aspects of the new process, which casts further doubt upon the infallibility of canonizations performed under the new legislation, Fr. Gleize also notes some of the recent theologians who publicly question *or even deny* the infallibility of

---

[49] Ibid.

[50] Such is the opinion of Benedict XIV in his treatise *On the Beatification and Canonization of Saints*, Bk. I, Ch. X, No. 6.

[51] http://www.sspx.org/en/beatification-and-canonization-vatican-ii-1.

canonizations, including Fr. Daniel Ols, who served as relator for the Congregation for the Causes of Saints under John Paul II. Wrote Fr. Gleize:

> "Since Vatican II, some conciliar theologians have adopted this anti-infallibilist position. Some of them have alleged difficulties of an historical nature[52] to call in question the infallibility of canonizations...The opinion defended by Augustine of Ancona and Cajetan [against the infallibility of canonizations] was recently reprised by Fr. Daniel Ols, O.P., professor at the Pontifical University of the Angelicum and a relator for the Congregation for the Causes of Saints in a study[53] on the theological basis for the cultus of saints."[54]

Notwithstanding the efforts of many Sedevacantists to convince us that it is "impossible" for the Church to err in the canonization of a saint, the Church has never declared that infallibility extends to canonizations, and there are many reputable theologians today who believe that canonizations are not (and never were) covered by infallibility. In fact, not all Sedevacantists believe infallibility extends to the canonizations of saints. For example, Sedevacantist Richard Ibranyi wrote a lengthy internet piece titled "Canonizations are Not Infallible," in which he argues that canonizations were not infallible even under the old procedures.[55]

Ibranyi says, "the charism of papal infallibility applies only to doctrines on faith and morals that were revealed to the apostles. Consequently, Popes cannot infallibly define anything at all that has been revealed since the death of the last apostle." After quoting the pertinent section of Vatican I, he concludes: "Thus every person that died after the death of the last apostle is not subject matter for papal infallibility and hence cannot constitute an object of the Catholic faith because the saintliness of that person could not have been revealed to

---

[52] For example, the Benedictine De Vooght cites the famous case of St. John Nepomucene [or "John of Pomuk"] about whom some historical controversy exists, to conclude: "I believe that we can draw from the story of John of Pomuk the conclusion that the pope is not infallible in the canonization of saints" ("The Real Dimensions of Papal Infallibility," Infallibility: Its Philosophical and Theological Aspects, Acts of the Colloquium of the International Center for Humanist Studies and of the Institute for Philosophical Studies, Rome, February 5-12, 1970, pp. 145-149).

[53] Ols, "*Fondamenti teologici del culto dei Santi,*" AA. Vv. *Dello Studium Congregationis de causis sanctorum, pars theologica* (Rome, 2002), pp. 1-54.

[54] http://www.sspx.org/en/beatification-and-canonization-vatican-ii-1.

[55] http://www.johnthebaptist.us/jbw_english/documents/books/rjmi/br47_canonizations_not_infallible.pdf.

the apostles. That is one reason every heavenly apparition and message since the death of the last apostle, no matter how true it may be, cannot be infallibly approved by the pope."

Unfortunately, the reasoning used by Mr. Ibranyi is also fraught with errors. One thing he doesn't seem to understand is that just because Vatican I taught that the Pope is infallible when he defines a dogma, does not mean infallibility does not also extend to secondary objects (as is commonly believed, and even held by most Sedevacantists, as they accuse the Popes of violating disciplinary, not just doctrinal infallibility).[56] Vatican I purposely left the issue open and, in fact, intended to addressed the matter during the Council, which was unfortunately cut short by the Franco-Prussian war. Based upon the initial draft prepared for the council, it is likely that infallibility does embrace some aspects of the faith commonly categorized as secondary objects of infallibility, although which ones and to what extent remains unclear.[57]

Conclusion

We conclude this chapter by noting that it is not our intention to deny that canonizations are protected by the Church's infallibility, nor is it our intention to defend the recent controversial canonizations. Our point is simply to demonstrate that these canonizations cannot be presented as *certain* violations of the Church's infallibility for the following reasons:

1) The Church herself has never definitively declared if infallibility extends to canonizations, which are a secondary object of

---

[56] Ibranyi's faulty reasoning includes his claim that a Pope, or anyone else, can infallibly judge someone to be a "notorious sinner" but not a saint. In fact, Ibranyi actually claims that a Pope can judge the *internal forum,* or "the condition of a person's soul...when the person's original sin or mortal sin is notorious." Setting aside the fact that there is no such thing as "notorious" Original Sin (which is merely a *disposition* to sin; see ST, I-II, q. 82 a. 1. ad. 2), Ibranyi's argument reveals the cornerstone of Sedevacantism, which is the alleged ability to judge the internal forum (and then further err by claiming that "mortal sin" in the internal forum causes a loss of ecclesiastical office in the external forum).

[57] The Dimond brothers go to the opposite extreme by actually claiming that "a Canonization is an *ex cathedra* (infallible) pronouncement because it fulfills the three conditions required for a Pope to speak infallibly, as defined by Vatican I." But, as we've seen, a canonization is clearly *not* a doctrinal definition on faith or morals, and thus does not meet Vatican I's condition for infallibility. Driven by their Sedevacantist agenda to discredit the conciliar Popes at any cost, the Dimond brothers also disregard the teaching of St. Thomas, who said that canonizations are midway between "particular facts" (secondary objects) and matters of "faith" (primary object). See http://www.mostholy family monastery.com/catholicchurch/arecanonizations -infallible/.

infallibility, and therefore are not included in the definition of infallibility given at the First Vatican Council. [58]

2)   Even if a canonization does provide infallible certitude that the person is in Heaven, one would have to be able to demonstrate that the candidate was, in fact, *not* in Heaven to demonstrate any violation of what the Church's process guaranteed to be true.

3)   Finally, if one holds to the position that only a person who lived a life of heroic virtue can be raised to the altars (which is certainly not the common opinion), he will have to explain how St. Dismas, who, according to Tradition, lived a horrible life until the hour of his death (which even included mocking Our Lord on the Cross before his miraculous conversion),[59] has been recognized as a saint by the universal Church (East and West) for centuries. In fact, not only did St. Dismas *not* live a life of *heroic* virtue, but, according to the book *The Good Thief*, by Rev. Schmitt, none of the Fathers of the Church "recognized in him one laudable quality." [60]

In light of the foregoing, it is not possible for Sedevacantists, or anyone else, to present the recent controversial canonizations as "proof" that the visible Church has defected, and violated the promise of infallibility. The problem with the syllogism is as follows: The *major* premise (that the Church is infallible in canonizations), has not been definitively taught by the Church (and may no longer even be the common opinion); the *minor* premise (that a person recently canonized is not in Heaven) cannot be proved. Therefore the *conclusion* (that the

---

[58] Following the close of Vatican I, the Swiss Bishops issued a Pastoral Instruction which said: "The Pope is infallible *solely and exclusively* when, as supreme doctor of the Church, he pronounces in a matter of faith or morals a definition which has to be accepted and held as obligatory by all the faithful. Again: *It is the revelation given by God, the deposit of faith,* which is the domain perfectly traced out and exactly circumscribed, *within which the infallible decisions of the Pope are able to extend themselves* and in regard to which the faith of Catholics can be bound to fresh obligations." (Cuthbert Butler, O.S.B., *The Vatican Council, 1869-1870*, London: Collin and Harvill Press, 1962, first ed. 1930, p. 464.) In response to the Bishops' Pastoral Instruction, Dom Cuthbert Butler relates that Pius IX "wrote to the Swiss bishops that nothing could be more opportune or more worthy of praise, or cause the truth to stand out more clearly, than their pastoral" (Ibid., 465).
[59] See Mt. 27:44; Mk 15:32.
[60] "The Fathers of the Church ask, what were the crimes of Dismas? One St. Eulogius accuses him of having killed his own brother. Others reproach him with the crimes common to all thieves, viz: the robbery of travelers, and homicide. None of them recognize in him one laudable quality." Rev. Schmitt, *Dismas, The Good Thief*, 2nd ed. (Cincinnati, Ohio: Rosenthal & Co., 1892), p. 6.

Church has violated infallibility by canonizing someone who was damned) does not follow.

Chapter 18

~ The New Rite of Episcopal Consecration ~

As we have seen, Sedevacantists have historically maintained that the post-conciliar Popes and bishops have been public heretics (before or after their election) and hence could not hold office in the Church, but they originally maintained that they were, at least, validly ordained bishops. Over the past few decades, however, several Sedevacantists have penned articles casting doubt upon the validity of the ordination rites, approved by Paul VI in 1968, for both priests and bishops.

This argument is a *different* angle of attack against the Pope, as well as the other bishops, since it maintains that the post-conciliar hierarchy, ordained in the new rites, *are not even valid priests and bishops*. Following the election of Pope Benedict XVI (who, along with Pope Francis, was consecrated a bishop in the new rite), Sedevacantists have used this argument as further "proof" that Benedict and Francis could not be true Popes. For example, the Sedevacantist preacher, Gerry Matatics, wrote: "A man who is not a validly ordained bishop cannot function as the bishop of Rome," and then added: "But Joseph Ratzinger is not a validly ordained bishop, having received (in May 1977) the demonstrably invalid episcopal ordination rite promulgated in June 1968."[1] Mr. Matatics then referenced what he calls a "devastating" article by Fr. Anthony Cekada, which he believes demonstrates the invalidity of the new rite of episcopal consecration. We will analyze Fr. Cekada's article in depth in this chapter, since many well-meaning people have evidently been persuaded by it.

While most Sedevacantists argue that the new rite of ordination for *priests* is only "doubtful" (this will be addressed in the next chapter), most of them firmly hold, along with Mr. Matatics and Fr. Cekada, that the new rite for consecrating *bishops* is "Absolutely Null and Utterly Void."[2] Based upon this claim, they argue that even if the new rite of ordination for a priest is itself valid, it doesn't matter, since a priest can only be ordained by a bishop; and if the bishop was himself invalidly consecrated, the men whom he attempted to ordain would not be valid priests.

---

[1] Matatics, "Is Gerry Matatics a 'Sedevacantist'?," Gerry Replies (slightly revised November 21, 2007), https://www.gerrymatatics.org/GRIsGerry Sede.html.
[2] This is the title of the article by Fr. Cekada that we will critique later in this chapter.

And if the Sedevacantists can't persuade people that the new rites are, in fact, invalid, they have another argument ready and waiting: they say "a doubtful sacrament is no sacrament at all." They then insist that the mere *doubt* regarding the validity of the new rite of episcopal consecration means the bishop's ordination must be *considered* invalid, and consequently the priests, ordained by these "bishops," must be avoided.

This is one of the more oppressive tactics used by Sedevacantist clergy. By infusing doubt into the minds of their flock about the validity of the new ordinations and consecrations (using, of course, specious arguments), they are able to convince their congregants that there is nowhere else to go for the sacraments, other than their Sedevacantist chapels. Some members of the laity, having been persuaded by this argument, and unable to find a local Sedevacantist chapel, no longer attend Mass at all. They choose to stay home on Sundays rather than attend a "doubtful" Mass" (and are known as "home-aloners').

In this chapter, we will examine the new rite of episcopal consecration and demonstrate that there is no objective doubt as to its validity, provided, of course, that the rite be followed as it was approved by the Church in 1968. By way of background, we will show what is necessary for the validity of a sacrament and explain the difference between those sacraments in which Christ instituted the form and matter *in specie,* as opposed to merely *in genere.* After exploring the Church's sacramental theology, we will compare the new rite of episcopal consecration to other approved rites in the Church, the validity of which have never been questioned. Finally, throughout this chapter, we will address, in detail, the specific arguments presented by Sedevacantists (such as Fr. Cekada) against the validity of the new rite. Because of the length of this chapter, combined with the complexity of the material covered, we will first provide an overview of some of the key points that will be discussed.

- The Church has the authority to change the *form* (words used) for priestly ordination and episcopal consecration (consecrating a bishop).

- There are many different *forms* used in the various approved rites of the Church. Some of these *forms* differ greatly one from another.

- In order for a *form* to be valid, it must signify the sacramental effect. In other words, the *form* must convey what it is that the sacrament is intending to accomplish (i.e., ordaining a man as a bishop or priest). This is the key point of dispute regarding the new rite.

- We will demonstrate that the new rite of episcopal consecration does sufficiently signify the sacramental effect. In fact, a case could be made that the *new form* more clearly signifies the sacramental effect than does the *old form* of Pius XII.

- The new form of Paul VI is actually not new at all. It is taken from the Apostolic Tradition of St. Hippolytus, which dates to about the year 217, and some scholars even maintain that it is of apostolic origin. The form is also used in two rites of the East (Coptic and Maronite) which have always been accepted by the Church.

- The new form of Paul VI was approved by Cardinal Ottaviani, who raised no concerns over its validity. This was one year before the Cardinal *did* raise concerns over the new Mass, which suggests that he would have objected to the new *form* as well if he believed there were reasons to do so.

- The objections raised by Fr. Cekada and other Sedevacantist apologists, against the validity of the new rite, are addressed directly and refuted (noting also that some Sedevacantists accept the validity of the new rites and reject the argumentation of Fr. Cekada).

Moral Certitude

Before delving into the subject, we will begin by addressing the degree of certitude that one can have regarding the validity of a sacrament. Some mistakenly believe that to participate in a sacrament, one must have *absolute* metaphysical certitude that a sacrament is valid. They further believe that if there is the slightest doubt over the validity of a sacrament, it means the sacrament is "doubtful," and based upon the axiom "a doubtful sacrament is no sacrament," it must be avoided. This is not correct.

A person can never have absolute metaphysical certitude about the validity of a sacrament. It is impossible to know, for example, if a priest saying Mass has the correct intention, or even if he uses the correct words of consecration (during the silent canon of the Traditional Mass). One cannot know for sure if the bread and wine used in the Mass were switched out for invalid matter without the priest knowing about it. There is no way to know with certainty that a priest who gives absolution in the confessional was, in fact, validly ordained to the priesthood. There is *always* a certain degree of doubt that cannot be removed. For this reason, the greatest degree of certitude we can have about the validity of a given sacrament is that of *moral certitude*, not absolute metaphysical certitude. Cardinal Billot, when addressing an objection about a possible doubt over the validity of a sacrament, ended his lengthy explanation by saying: "Distinguish, therefore, moral certitude from that metaphysical certitude which is never required in things pertaining to human relations."[3]

St. Robert Bellarmine, when responding to an objection by the Protestant heretic John Calvin, who maintained that the hidden intention of the minister (which affects validity) destroys certitude that the sacrament is valid, wrote the following:

"I reply, a man ought not in this world to seek an infallible certitude ... But a human and moral certitude, in which a man may properly rest, we have from the sacraments, even if they depend upon the intention of another."[4]

Fr. Peter Scott elaborated further on this point:

"St. Robert Bellarmine points out that we can never have a certitude of Faith concerning the reception of a true sacrament, since no-one can see the intention of another. However, in truth, we can never have such a certitude concerning human events. The greatest certitude that we can have is a moral certitude, which is also the certitude that we can have about any contingent, singular reality."[5]

The manualist Msgr. Jean Marie Hervè explained that moral certitude suffices to dispel any reservations over the reception of the

[3] Billot, *On The Sacraments of the Church: A Commentary on the Third Part of St. Thomas*, vol. 1, Thesis XVIII, q. 64, a. 8.
[4] Bellarmine, *De Sacramentis*, bk. I, cited in *History of Christian Doctrine*, vol. II, by Henry Clay Sheldon (New York: Harper & Brothers, 1886), p. 193.
[5] Scott, *The Angelus*, Questions and Answers, October 2003.

sacraments. He wrote: "Concerning the validity of the sacraments one can have moral certitude, which suffices for acting prudently, and for dispelling anxieties of spirit."[6]

Requiring an absolute certitude on a practical matter about which only moral certitude is possible, is the error of Skepticism. The *Catholic Encyclopedia* explains this error as follows:

> "The Skeptic fails to distinguish between practical moral certainty which excludes *all reasonable* grounds for doubt, and absolute certainty which excludes *all possible* grounds for doubt. The latter can be had only when evidence is complete, proof wholly adequate .... In mathematics this is sometimes possible, though not always; but in other matters 'practical certainty' as a rule is all we can get. And this is sufficient, since 'practical certainty' is certainty for reasonable beings."[7]

Requiring absolute metaphysical certitude over the validity of the sacraments is a recipe for disaster. It will quickly lead to scruples of conscience and, if allowed to go to its logical conclusion, will end with the person being paralyzed with fear and/or avoiding the sacraments altogether (e.g., "home-aloner" Sedevacantists), since one can never remove all doubt. Christ, of course, does not require from us the impossible. He asks only that we act reasonably and prudently, and it is certainly *unreasonable* to seek metaphysical certainty over a matter in which only moral certitude is possible.

The Four Causes

Turning to the causes of the sacrament, a sacrament is a compound of *matter (material case)* and *form (formal cause)*. It is administered by a *minister* (the efficient cause) who must have the *intention (final cause)* of doing what the Church does. The validity of a sacrament is dependent upon all four causes, in such a way that if a single one is lacking, the sacrament will be rendered invalid.

Matter and Form

The *form* of the sacrament consists of the words that are spoken; the *matter* is the element or "sensible thing" of the sacrament. For Baptism, the *form* consists of the words, "I baptize thee in the name of the Father,

---

[6] Hervé, *Manuale Theologiae Domaticae*, vol. III, 1929.
[7] *Catholic Encyclopedia* (1913), vol. XIII, p. 517.

and of the Son, and of the Holy Ghost." The *matter* of baptism is the water. The *form* for the double consecration at Mass are the words, "This is My Body," etc., and "This is My Blood," etc. The matter is the bread and wine, which are transformed into the Body and Blood of Christ at the moment the words (form) are spoken over the elements (matter). As St. Augustine said: "The word is joined to the element, and the Sacrament is made."[8]

With respect to the sacrament of Penance, the form consists of the words of absolution ("I absolve you from your sins," etc.). The matter for this sacrament, however, differs from that of the others, and is referred to as "quasi-matter."[9] Rather than being something alone that is tangible, the matter for Penance consists of three parts: *contrition* (sorrow for the sins committed), *confession* (to the priest), and *satisfaction*.[10] These three acts of the penitent together constitute the *matter* for this sacrament.

The Form Determines the Matter

The *form* (the words) determines the *matter*. In other words, they tell us what the matter is intended to signify. For example, the words (form) "Take ye and eat, for this is My Body...This is My Blood," etc. determine that the bread and wine (matter) signify food for the soul, that is, the transubstantiated Body and Blood of Christ. The words (form) "I baptize thee..." determine that the water (matter) signifies the washing away of Original Sin. The imposition of hands is the *matter* for several levels of Holy Orders. The words used (the form) determine what the imposition of hands signifies – namely, the ordination to the diaconate, to the priesthood, or to the bishopric. Without the form (words), the matter would lack its signification. The Catechism of Trent explains:

> "Every Sacrament consists of two things: 'matter' which is called the element, and 'form' which is commonly called the word...In order to make the meaning of the rite that is being performed easier and clearer, words had to be added to the matter. For all signs, words are evidently the most significant, and without them what the matter of the sacrament designates and declares would be utterly obscure. Water, for example, has the quality of cooling as well as of making clean, and may be symbolic of either.

---

[8] In Joan., Tract. LXXX, 3.
[9] "The acts of the penitent, namely contrition, confession, and satisfaction, are the *quasi materia* of this sacrament" (Council of Trent, Sess. XIV ch. 3).
[10] "*Decretum pro Armenis*," Council of Florence, Denz., 699; Council of Trent, Denz., 896.

In Baptism, therefore, unless the words were added, it would not be certain which meaning of the sign was intended. When the words are added, we immediately understand that the Sacrament possesses and signifies the power of cleansing."[11]

Significatio ex Adjunctis

We have seen how the matter is determined by the form. Now, the form consists of a group of words, or individual words, which sometimes derive their signification, in part, from the context in which they are used. The context of a sacramental form consists of the words and prayers that surround it, as well as the general ceremony itself. This determination by the ecclesial, historical and liturgical "context," which helps to give the form its intended meaning, is known as *determinatio ex adjunctis* or *significatio ex adjunctis*. Depending upon which sacrament we are discussing, and upon which historical rite in the Catholic Church is under consideration, these surrounding words and prayers are sometimes necessary to confirm or clarify the meaning of the words that constitute the form, just as the form itself signifies (or determines) the matter.[12]

Determination *ex adjunctis* is so important that it can even invalidate a form which might otherwise be valid in a different context within the Catholic Church. For example, Pope Leo XIII acknowledged that the Anglican form for the ordination of a bishop might be valid in a Catholic rite, but in the Anglican ordinal it is invalid because the texts and ceremonies of Catholic England had been deliberately deformed by the innovators in such a way as to eliminate all references to strictly sacerdotal power.

Substance and Accidents of Words

Doctrinal errors (in the mind of the minister) do not *usually* invalidate a sacrament, but the words themselves, which make up the form, must at least be generally intended to *mean* what the Church understands by the use of the words. Now, words have a *substance* and

---

[11] *Catechism of the Council of Trent* (Rockford, Illinois: TAN Books and Publishers, Inc., 1982), pp.150-151.

[12] When the form and matter of the sacrament are valid, the sacrament is presumed to take place. However, it is possible that accompanying words and prayers during the ceremony could raise a positive doubt about the minister's intention. For example, if a bishop gives a sermon that expressly denies the sacrificial priesthood, there would be a positive doubt that he intended to confer the priesthood on the ordinands (and a conditional ordination would be justified to remove the objective doubt).

accidents. The substance is the *meaning*; the accidents are *the words used* to convey the meaning. If the words used (accidents) are *intended* to convey a meaning (substance) *different* than what the Church understands by the same words, the sacrament will not be valid. We have an example of this in baptism administered by Mormons. The Mormons use the correct words (accidents), since they baptize in the name of the Father, Son and Holy Ghost, but when they use these words, they mean something (substance) completely different than what the Church understands by the same words.[13] Therefore, even though the correct words are used, the Church has declared that the baptism administered in the Mormon sect is invalid.[14]

Minister and Intention

Sacraments also require a proper *minister*. Some sacraments, such as Baptism and Holy Matrimony, can be validly administered by a lay person. The others require a validly ordained priest (or bishop) to confect the sacrament. Some sacraments (Penance and Matrimony) also require that the minister be invested with jurisdiction by the Church (ordinary, or supplied based on necessity) for the sacrament to be valid.

The minister (efficient cause) must also possess the *intention* (final cause) to do what the Church does. The intention does not have to be *actual*, but only *virtual*. An *actual* intention is present when the intention itself is consciously willed *at the moment the act is performed*. A *virtual* intention is present due to a prior act of the will, which continues to exist implicitly until the act previously explicitly willed is completed. For example, if a priest recites the words of consecration during the Mass but, due to distraction or routine, does not consciously will to consecrate the elements *at the moment he speaks the words*, his virtual intention (his prior act of the will to perform a valid consecration) suffices to bring about transubstantiation.

The *Catholic Encyclopedia* explains the difference between an actual intention and a virtual intention:

---

[13] "The words Father, Son and Holy Spirit have for the Mormons a meaning totally different from the Christian meaning. The differences are so great that one cannot even consider that this doctrine is a heresy which emerged out of a false understanding of the Christian doctrine. The teaching of the Mormons has a completely different matrix." (Fr. Luis Ladaria, "The Question of the Validity of Baptism conferred in the Church of Jesus Christ of Latter-Day Saints" (*L'Osservatore Romano*, Weekly Edition in English, August 1st, 2001, p. 4, emphasis added).
[14] Ibid.

"The virtual intention is not a present act of the will, but rather a power (virtus) brought about as an effect of a former act, and now at work for the attainment of the end. The thing therefore that is wanting in a virtual, as contrasted with an actual, intention is not of course the element of will, but rather the attention of the intellect, and that particularly of the reflex kind."[15]

J.M Hervè explains that the a virtual intention suffices for the validity of a sacrament.

"For the validity of a sacrament, it is necessary that the minister have the intention of doing what the Church does; indeed, he must have an internal intention, *which must also be at least virtual…*"[16]

St. Thomas refers to the virtual intention as a "habitual intention," and notes that this suffices for the validity of a sacrament. The following is taken from the *Summa*:

"**Objection 3.** Further, a man's intention cannot bear on that to which he does not attend. But sometimes ministers of the sacraments do not attend to what they say or do, through thinking of something else. Therefore, in this respect the sacrament would be invalid through want of intention.

Reply to Objection 3. Although he who thinks of something else, has no actual intention, yet he has habitual intention, which suffices for the validity of the sacrament; for instance, if, when a priest goes to baptize someone, he intends to do to him what the Church does. Wherefore if subsequently during the exercise of the act his mind be distracted by other matters, the sacrament is valid in virtue of his original intention. Nevertheless, the minister of a sacrament should take great care to have actual intention. But this is not entirely in man's power, because when a man wishes to be very intent on something, he begins unintentionally to think of other things, according to Psalm 39:18: 'My heart hath forsaken me.'"[17]

The minister must have the intention to do what the Church *does*, but it is not necessary that he has the intention to do what the Church *intends*. In other words, it is not necessary that the minister intends the sacramental *effect*, or even that he *explicitly knows* what the sacrament accomplishes. This is clear from the fact that even a pagan is able to

---

[15] *Catholic Encyclopedia* (1913), vol. VIII, p. 69.
[16] Hervé, *Theologia Dogmatica*, vol. III, part IV, ch. IV, 474.3 (emphasis added).
[17] ST, III q. 64, a. 8.

validly baptize in a case of necessity, even if he doesn't know that baptism infuses faith, hope, charity and sanctifying grace into the soul, *ex opere operato.*[18] Neither does an explicitly heretical doctrine concerning the sacramental effect *necessarily* prevent the minister from validly administering the sacrament.

Most Protestant sects, for example, deny the doctrine of Original Sin, yet the Church has never declared that this heresy *necessarily* invalidates the sacrament of Baptism, the purpose of which is to wash way Original Sin through the infusion of sanctifying grace. In fact, in 1872, the Holy Office responded to the following question concerning a baptism performed by a Methodist minister:

> "1. Whether baptism administered by those [Methodist] heretics is doubtful on account of defect of intention to do what Christ willed, if an *express declaration* was made by the minister before he baptised [saying that] that baptism had no effect on the soul?
> 2. Whether baptism so conferred is doubtful if the aforesaid declaration was not expressly made immediately before the conferring of baptism, but had often been asserted by the minister, and the same doctrine was openly preached in that sect?
> Reply to the first question: in the negative, because despite the error about the effects of baptism, the intention of doing what the Church does is not excluded.
> The second question: provided for in the answer to the first."[19]

Here we see that even the public profession of the minister that baptism has no effect of the soul, does not nullify the intention, even if the declaration was made just prior to performing the baptism.

When would a proper intention be lacking? An obvious example would be the case in which a priest, during a Bible study, read aloud Jesus' words "This is my blood" from Scripture while he was drinking a glass of wine. In such a case, he would have no intention at all (neither actual nor virtual) of consecrating the wine, and therefore transubstantiation would not occur. Similarly, a priest who was eating bread at a restaurant and happened to use the words "this is My Body" in a sentence, would obviously have no intention to, and therefore would not, consecrate the bread.

Another obvious defect of intention would be the explicit resolution *not* to do what the Church does. Pope Alexander VIII

---

[18] Latin meaning "by the work worked." The efficacy of the sacrament is derived from the action of the sacrament and not from the merits or holiness of the minister.
[19] *Acta Sanctae Sedis*, vol. XXV, p. 246.

condemned the proposition that "A Baptism is valid when conferred by a minister who observes every external rite and form of baptizing, but within in his heart, resolves to himself: *not to intend what the Church does."* [20]

If a priest properly performs his priestly function according to an approved rite of the Church (using valid form and matter), a virtual intention is to be *presumed* (again, absolute certitude is never required). [21] St. Bellarmine said "there is no cause to doubt that the minister has the intention, unless he reveals its absence by some exterior sign." [22] When a Catholic priest performs a Catholic ceremony, and externally administers the sacraments according to an approved rite of the Church, the sacraments are presumed valid (proper intention being present). Doubts are raised only if he externally manifests his intention *not* to do what the Church does.

The Minister for Holy Orders

Before discussing the controversy surrounding the change in the form for Holy Orders, which some Sedevacantists claim invalidates the new rite of episcopal consecration, we will consider an interesting and little known point about the minister for priestly ordination - namely, who possesses the power to ordain a man to the priesthood. Many believe it is certain that only a validly consecrated bishop is capable of ordaining a man to Holy Orders. But this is not absolutely certain. In fact, as we will see, there exist four papal Bulls, issued by three separate Popes, which empower abbots, who were only priests (not bishops), to ordain their subjects to sacred orders. Two of these Bulls explicitly give the priest-abbot power to ordain other men to the *priesthood*.

Ordinary and Extraordinary Minister of Ordination

The bishop alone is the *ordinary minister* for the sacraments of Confirmation and Ordination. A priest is *certainly* an *extraordinary* minister for Confirmation, and, according to some theologians, *possibly* an *extraordinary* minister for priestly ordination.

---

[20] Pope Alexander VIII, Decree of the Holy Office, December 7, 1690, Errors of the Jansenists (Denz., 1318).

[21] The presumption may be rebuttable by evidence which raises positive, probable doubt about the minister's intention. The Church evaluates such evidence, for example, when investigating the validity of Protestant baptisms (of Catholic converts) and which sometimes necessitates the sacraments to be conditionally conferred.

[22] Bellarmine, *De Sacramentis*, bk. I. ch. 28.

Regarding Confirmation, the 1917 Code of Canon Law says "only a bishop is the ordinary minister of Confirmation. The extraordinary minister is a priest to whom a faculty has been granted by a common law or by a special indult from the Holy See."[23] In 1946, Pope Pius XII determined that parish priests can confer Confirmation, without receiving special permission, when their subject is in danger of death.[24]

In Tanquerey's *A Manual of Dogmatic Theology*, we read the following:

> "The extraordinary minister of Confirmation can be a simple priest, especially delegated by the Apostolic See. This is certain.
>
> From the Practice of the Roman Church - Many Roman Pontiffs have granted this power to priests; thus, in the 6th Century St. Gregory the Great, and later Nicholas I, John XXII, Urban V, Eugene IV, etc. from the Code 782, the extraordinary minister is a priest to whom either by common right or a particular indult of the Holy See this faculty has been granted. Cardinals, abbot or prelate nullius, vicar and prefect apostolic possess it. In the decree 'Spiritus Sancti Munera' concerning the administration of confirmation to those who are in danger of death from serious illness 'according to the general indult of the apostolic see' then, this faculty is given as to extraordinary ministers to territorial pastors and to other priests who are equal to them."[25]

The 1917 Code of Canon Law also mentions the ordinary and extraordinary minister for Holy Orders:

> "The ordinary minister of sacred ordination is a consecrated bishop; the extraordinary minister is one who, though without the episcopal character, has received either by law or by a special indult from the Holy See power to confer some orders."[26]

Note that the extraordinary minister for Holy Orders is one who does not possess "the episcopal character" (i.e., who is *not* a bishop). While the typical commentaries usually indicate this as referring to minor orders, there are four papal Bulls empowering abbots, who are only priests, to ordain men to Holy Orders; and two specifically permit

---

[23] Canon 781.

[24] Pius XII, *Spiritus Sancti Munera*, September 14, 1946, AAS, 38, 1946, p. 349.

[25] Tanquerey, *A Manual of Dogmatic Theology*, II. (New York: Byrnes, Desclee Co., 1959), p. 236.

[26] Canon 951 (emphasis added). We do note, however, that the Code does say "some orders," without specifying it is referring to those which imprint an indelible character.

them to ordain men *to the priesthood.*[27] Two of the Bulls were signed by Pope Boniface IX,[28] one by Pope Martin V,[29] and one by Pope Innocent III.[30]

Some reputable theologians have debated the exact meaning of the papal Bulls permitting priests to ordain, since it has always been the more common opinion that priests cannot ordain men to Holy Orders. In fact, Fr. Tanquerey, who held to this more common opinion, said: "It is certain that priests cannot be delegated as extraordinary ministers of the episcopacy and of the priesthood; *all agree on this.*"[31]

If a priest can indeed ordain (according to the two papal Bulls), the question then becomes whether the priest is given the power at his ordination (which is restricted by ecclesiastical law), or whether ordination only makes him capable of receiving the power by virtue of special jurisdiction delegated by the Pope. St. Jerome held to the former opinion. He maintained that "at his ordination a priest receives power to ordain which is immediately restricted by ecclesiastical law."[32] Ott held the same opinion. He wrote: "the requisite power of consecration [of ordaining a priest] is contained in the priestly power of consecration as '*potestas ligata.*' For the valid exercise of it a special exercise of the Papal power is, by Divine or Church ordinance, necessary."[33]

Others argue that at ordination the priest receives only the capacity, or status, enabling the Pope to grant him the power to ordain. In the former case, the power is actually received at ordination and immediately suppressed by Church law. In the latter case, the priest is

---

[27] Namely, *Sacrae Religionis,* and *Apostolicae Sedis Providentia.*

[28] *Sacrae Religionis,* February 1, 1400; and *Apostolicae Sedis Providentia,* February 6, 1403.

[29] *Gerente ad Vos,* November 16, 1427.

[30] *Exposcit,* April 9, 1489. All four of the aforementioned Bulls are printed in H. Lennerz, *De Sacramento Ordinis,* second edition (Rome: Pontificia Universitas Gregoriana, 1953), pp. 145-153 (Appendix I). In his popular book *Fundamentals of Catholic Dogma,* Ludwig Van Ott concludes that "a simple priest is an extraordinary dispenser of the Orders of Diaconate and Presbyterate, just as he is an extraordinary dispenser of Confirmation," while also noting that these papal decisions did not "touch infallibility." p. 459. In his 1956 book, *Ordination to the Priesthood,* Fr. John Bligh also says that it is "almost certain" that a priest is able to ordain other priests when delegated to do so by the Pope, based upon the above-cited papal Bulls. Bligh, *Ordination to the Priesthood* (London and New York: Sheed and Ward, 1956), pp. 8-9. Bligh further maintained that there is a distinction between the priest's "status" to ordain (a power that is in potency) and the actual "power" to ordain (which comes only from jurisdiction granted by the Pope). Ibid., p. 14.

[31] Tanquerey, A Manual of Dogmatic Theology, vol. II (New York: Byrnes, Desclee Co, 1959), p. 363 (emphasis added).

[32] Bligh, *Ordination to the Priesthood,* p. 13.

[33] Ott, *Fundamentals of Catholic Dogma,* p. 459.

only capable of receiving the power; the power resides with the Pope, who is able to confer it upon the priest in certain circumstances.[34]

Those who hold to the more common opinion (that a priest *cannot* ordain) have pointed out some obvious problems with the above attempted explanations. They note that if the priest possesses this power at ordination, which is *restricted by ecclesiastical law*, then why could not the Pope restrict such power in the bishops – especially in those bishops who abandoned the Church, thus rendering any continuation of priestly orders outside the Church impossible? And if the priest does not possess this power, but only receives it *by special jurisdiction delegated by the Pope*, the same impossible conclusion follows: such power is concomitant with jurisdiction, and therefore could be withdrawn by the Pope from any schismatic or heretical bishop, thus preventing the continuance of a schismatic/heretical "line" of successor bishops. Now, evidently the Church never believed the Pope could prevent a schismatic or heretical bishop from ordaining a priest. Therefore, how can one maintain that the power to ordain is derived from jurisdiction or from ecclesiastical law?

We present this little known material anecdotally, as a matter of interest and for its historical value, noting that we are dealing here with a question that has not been definitively resolved by the Church. In spite of the existence of the papal Bulls, it is the more common opinion today that a simple priest *cannot* ordain a man to Holy Orders (Archbishop Lefebvre held to this more common opinion). If the common opinion is correct (and invalid ordinations were approved for a time by the Holy See), this historical precedent would further underscore the strict limits of papal infallibility, and what God can allow His Church to suffer.

We will now further consider the matter and form of the sacraments.

In Specie and *in Genere*

Jesus Christ instituted all seven sacraments, but He only explicitly determined the matter and form for the sacrament of Baptism and the double consecration during the Holy Mass. For the other five sacraments, Christ left it to the Church to determine the matter and

---

[34] Fr. Bligh, who held to this latter opinion, wrote: "By their ordination priests are given this eminent status, and by reason of their status, they can, thereafter, as the four papal Bulls show, be given power to ordain; but the status is not identical with the power, and normally those who possess the status do not possess the power" (Bligh, *Ordination to the Priesthood*, p. 14).

form. Using theological terminology, we say that Christ instituted the form of Baptism and the consecration of the Eucharist *in specie* (in a specific way) and the form of the other five sacraments *in genere* (in a general way). This explains why there is such a great difference between the sacraments of Holy Orders and Confirmation in the various approved rites of the Church. The *Catholic Encyclopedia* explains:

> "Granting that Christ immediately instituted all the sacraments, it does not necessarily follow that He personally determined all the details of the sacred ceremony, prescribing minutely every iota relating to the matter and the form to be used. It is sufficient (even for immediate institution) to say: Christ determined what special graces were to be conferred by means of external rites: for some sacraments (e.g. Baptism, the Eucharist) He determined minutely (in specie) the matter and form: for others He determined only in a general way (in genere) that there should be an external ceremony, by which special graces were to be conferred, leaving to the Apostles or to the Church the power to determine whatever He had not determined, e.g. to prescribe the matter and form of the Sacraments of Confirmation and Holy Orders. (...) This...can solve historical difficulties relating, principally, to Confirmation and Holy Orders."[35]

Not only did Christ grant the Church the authority to determine "the matter and form for the Sacraments of Confirmation and Holy Orders," but the Church also possesses the authority to alter the matter and form that she has established for the *validity* of a sacrament. This explains the *direct contradiction* between the teaching of the Council of Florence (in the *Decree for the Amenians*) and that of Pius XII (in *Sacramentum Ordinis*), who overturned what the Council of Florence taught constitutes the matter for the valid conferral of the sacrament of Holy Orders.

The Council of Florence taught that the passing of the *traditio instrumentorum* (the chalice and patten) is part of the *matter* for Holy Orders:

> "The sixth sacrament is that of Order; its *matter* is that by the giving of which the Order is conferred: thus the priesthood is conferred by the giving of a chalice with wine and of a paten with bread; The *form* of the priesthood is as follows: 'Receive power to offer sacrifice in the Church for the living and the dead, in the name

---

[35] *Catholic Encyclopedia* (1913), vol. XIII, p. 299.

of the Father and of the Son and of the Holy Ghost.'" (Council of Florence)[36]

In *Apostolicae Curae*, Pope Leo XIII noted that when the traditional instruments are omitted from the ordination rite, the established custom is for the person to be conditionally re-ordained.[37]

An article in the *Catholic Encyclopedia* - written before Pius XII was Pope - further explains that the *traditio instrumentorum* are required as part of the *matter* for Holy Orders.

> "To understand clearly the extent to which the imposition of hands is employed in the Church at present it will be necessary to view it in its sacramental or theological as well as in its ceremonial or liturgical aspect. ... In the sacrament of Holy orders it enters either wholly or in part, into the substance of the rite by which most of the higher grades are conferred. Thus in the ordination of deacons according to the Latin rite it is at least partial matter of the sacrament; in conferring the priesthood there is a threefold imposition, viz.: (a) when the ordaining prelate followed by the priests, lays hands on the head of the candidate nil dicens; (b) when he and the priests extend hands during the prayer, 'Oremus, fratres carissimi,' and (c) when he imposes hands at giving power to forgive sins, saying 'Accipe Spiritum Sanctum.' The first and second of these impositions, combined, constitute in the Latin Church *partial matter* of the sacrament, the *traditio instrumentorum* being required for the adequate or complete matter."[38]

In light of these teachings that the tradition of the instruments are part of the matter for ordination, consider the following from the Sedevacantist Patrick Henry Omlor, who claims that the Church has no power to change, or even touch, the matter and form of *any* sacrament. He wrote:

> "In his bull, *Apostolicae Curae*, Pope Leo XIII lays down an important distinction: 'In the rite for the performance and administration of any sacrament a distinction is justly made between its 'ceremonial' and its 'essential' part, the latter being usually called its 'matter and form.' Thus, although the Church is forbidden to change, or even touch, the matter or form of *any* sacrament, She may indeed change or abolish or introduce something in the nonessential rites, or 'ceremonial' parts, used in

---

[36] Denz., 701.

[37] Leo XIII, *Apostolicae Curae*, No. 21, September 18, 1896.

[38] *Catholic Encyclopedia* (1913), vol. VII, p. 698.

the administration of the sacraments, such as processions, prayers or hymns before or after the actual words of the form are recited, etc."[39]

Now, notwithstanding the claim made by Mr. Omlor that "the Church is forbidden to change, or even touch, the matter or form of any sacrament," Pope Pius XII teaches in *Sacramentum Ordinis* a very important principle: "*Ecclesiam quod statuit etiam mutare et abrogare valere* – that which the Church has established she can also change and abrogate." Then, using the full force of his authority, he decreed that the *traditio instrumentorum* which the Council of Florence taught to be the matter for the sacrament of Holy Orders, was no longer required as the matter for Holy Orders. Pope Pius XII decreed:

> "Wherefore, after invoking the divine light, We of Our Apostolic Authority and from certain knowledge declare, and as far as may be necessary decree and provide: that the matter, and the only matter, of the Sacred Orders of the Diaconate, the Priesthood, and the Episcopacy is the imposition of hands; … It follows as a consequence that We should declare, and in order to remove all controversy and to preclude doubts of conscience, We do by Our Apostolic Authority declare, and if there was ever a lawful disposition to the contrary We now decree that at least in the future the *traditio instrumentorum* is not necessary for the validity of the Sacred Orders of the Diaconate, the Priesthood, and the Episcopacy. (…) in the Episcopal Ordination or Consecration, the matter is the imposition of hands which is done by the Bishop consecrator."[40]

Here we have a Pope explicitly *abrogating* the teaching of an ecumenical Council of the Church about what constitutes the matter for a sacrament. Thus, either Mr. Omlor's claim that the Church is forbidden to alter the form or matter of *any* sacrament is false, or Pope Pius XII did what the Church is forbidden to do. Which do you think is correct?

Pope Pius XII explained his ability to change what the Council of Florence taught about the matter of Holy Orders by noting that the tradition of the instruments had not been instituted as the matter of the sacrament by Christ Himself, but by the Church. Unlike Baptism and

---

[39] Omlor, "Has the Church the Right?," first published in *The Voice*, Canandaigua, New York, October 1969, included in *The Robber Church*, The Collected Writings 1968-1997 http://www.huttongibson.com/PDFs/huttongibson_robberchurch_book.pdf (emphases added).
[40] Pius XII, *Sacramentum Ordinis*, No. 4, November 30, 1947.

the double consecration at Mass, the form and matter for Holy Orders were only instituted by Christ *in genere*, and not *in specie*.[41] Pius XII explained that even if the tradition of the instruments were necessary for *validity* (not *liceity*) by the will and command of the Church in the past, the Church has the authority to *change* or *abrogate* what she herself instituted. He wrote:

> "Even according to the mind of the Council of Florence itself, *the traditio instrumentorum* is not required for the substance and validity of this Sacrament by the will of Our Lord Jesus Christ Himself. If it was at one time necessary, even for <u>validity</u> by the will and command of the Church, <u>everyone knows that the Church has the power to change and abrogate what she herself has established</u>."[42]

One can only imagine how Sedevacantists would have reacted had Paul VI directly contradicted the Council of Florence by claiming that the matter for the sacrament was different than what the council taught. After all, according to Mr. Omlor, the Church has no power to even touch the matter of the sacraments. If the Sedevacantists of our day had been around in Pius XII's day, no doubt some would have declared Pius XII to have violated the infallibility of the Church, by definitively teaching the contrary of an ecumenical council. As they do today, the Sedevacantists would have no doubt caused confusion among the faithful, as well as condemning their opponents as public heretics for remaining in union with "antipope" Pius XII.

But, in reality, Pius XII did not violate the Church's infallibility, nor was there even a contradiction between his teaching and that of the Council of Florence since, contrary to the claim of Mr. Omlor, the Church does indeed possess the authority to alter some determination of the matter and form for the sacraments, when such was instituted by the will and command of the Church, and not by Christ Himself.

In light of what we have seen, one can easily spot the error in a common Sedevacantist argument. The following is the objection and answer:

Sedevacantist Objection: In *Sacramentum Ordinis*, Pope Pius XII gave the *form* for the ordination of Bishops. In the new Rite of Paul

---

[41] For those sacraments instituted by Christ *in genere*; the *effects signified* were instituted by Christ; the *meaning* (substance) of the *form* was instituted by Christ, the *words used* (accidents) to express that *meaning* are determined by the Church. This explains why the *words used* differ in the different rites.
[42] Ibid. (emphasis added).

VI, only one single word remains. Everything else has been changed. But, as Patrick Henry Omlor said, "the Church is forbidden to change, or even touch, the matter and form of any sacrament." Therefore, Paul VI's form is clearly invalid.

Answer: Though the *meaning* of the form was instituted by Christ, all the words used to express that meaning have been chosen by the Church, who possesses the authority to change what she herself has established. The fact that there is such a great difference between the approved wordings of the form for Ordination in the different rites (East and West) proves that all the words of the form have been determined by the Church to express the meaning required by Christ; He did not require any particular word in *specie*. Therefore the fact that Paul VI changed all the words of the form, which had been entirely determined by the Church, does not in and of itself invalidate the sacrament it is intended to confect. One must consider whether the meaning is respected, and that is a judgment for the Church.

Here we see once again how a false premise (the Church cannot change what she had determined in the matter and form of any sacrament), leads to a false and destructive conclusion (the conciliar Church does not have valid priests). A small error in the beginning is a big error in the end, and this particular error has led many vulnerable souls *completely away from the Church*, where they no longer receive the sacraments (especially confession and Holy Communion) because they erroneously believe there are no more (or very few) valid priests. They end by depriving themselves the ordinary means of salvation based upon their own private judgment on a matter about which Christ gave *the Church alone* the authority to judge and determine.

The Limited Power of the Church to Change the Matter and Form

While the Church does have the power to change the specific *matter* and *form* of some sacraments (at least that which was not given directly by Christ), the Council of Trent teaches that the Church has no power to change "the *substance* of the sacraments" - that is, to change what Christ has instituted as sacramental signs, at least *in genere*, and as known from the sources of Divine Revelation. As we have seen, the substance (matter and form) of some sacraments (i.e., Baptism and the double consecration at Mass) were instituted by Christ *in genere et in specie*. With respect to the others, Christ left it to the Church to determine the precise form and matter to be used. What the Church herself has instituted, the Church has the authority to alter. If the Church instituted the words that constitute the approved form, for example, she herself has the authority to change the words of the form. In such a case, a change in the *formula* previously established by the Church does not, of itself, constitute a change in the *substance* of the sacrament. Michael Davies elaborated on this point in his book *The Order of Melchisedech*:

> "The Council of Trent declares that the Church has always possessed the power - in the dispensation or administration of the Sacraments - to determine or to change those things which she judges to be more expedient for those receiving them or for the reverence due to the Sacraments themselves, according to the circumstances of time and place. An exception is made with regard to the substance of a Sacrament which the Church has no power to alter - *salva illorum substantia*: provided their substance is retained (D. 93 1).
>
> The question immediately arises as to what belongs to the substance of a particular Sacrament, and the answer will depend upon whether Our Lord instituted it generically (*in genere*) or specifically (*in specie*). In the former case, He left it to the supreme authority of His Church to decide the particular signs which should signify and effect the sacramental grace. Where Christ instituted a Sacrament *in specie*, as regards either matter or form, the Church has no power to change them. Our Lord chose water for the matter of Baptism and bread and wine for the matter of the Holy Eucharist; nothing else can ever be admitted. (...) With regard to the form of a Sacrament, some Catholics have mistakenly identified the form itself with a particular formula employed by the Church to express it, and have concluded that this formula cannot be changed without invalidating the Sacrament. Hence, they have fallen into the error of believing that the Church has no power to make changes in the matter and form of any Sacrament, having mistakenly identified the matter and form in current usage with the substance of the Sacraments themselves, which Trent taught could not be changed. The view that the Church can make no change in the matter and form of any Sacrament is historically indefensible."[43]

---

[43] Davies, *The Order of Melchisedech: A Defense of the Catholic Priesthood* (1979) Appendix I: The Substance of a Sacrament. See http://www.catholictradition.org/Eucharist/melch isedech-appx1.htm.

The terminology of "matter" and "form" was borrowed from the metaphysics of Aristotle and his teaching of hylomorphism.[44] Once the metaphysical treatises of Aristotle were discovered in depth by Latin Christendom early in the second millennium, his philosophy was purified in the light of divine revelation, and the metaphysical terminology was used to more clearly express the truths of the Faith (reflected most brilliantly in the writings of St. Thomas Aquinas).

The new terminology was also used to articulate and better understand the apostolic doctrine regarding the sacraments. While Aristotle's metaphysics was useful in providing additional clarity (for example, by explaining that the *substance* of the bread and wine undergoes change at the consecration, while the *accidents* remain the same), it also caused some problems. For example, it resulted in some people believing that the Church is unable to change *anything* in the form and matter of certain sacraments.

In his 1956 book, *Ordination to the Priesthood*, Fr. John Bligh S.J., explained that this problem stemmed from the analogous use of the terms form and matter for the sacraments, as compared to the same terminology when used to describe the matter and form of living or physical beings. We will allow Fr. Bligh to elaborate on this point:

> "The official adoption of the terminology of 'matter' and 'form' had the unfortunate effect of encouraging theologians to think that the *essential rites* of every sacrament must be unchangeable. In the physical world wherever there is a distinction of matter and of substantial form, there are distinct bodies: this *form* plus this *matter* makes this body, and that *form* plus that *matter* makes that body. Hence the terminology of matter and form, borrowed from Aristotle's analysis of things in the physical world, suggested that a change of the matter and form of the sacraments would mean the introduction of new sacraments — of sacraments other than those instituted by Christ our Lord! Hence it was concluded that the Church has no power to alter the matter and form of any of the sacraments. This erroneous conclusion led to great difficulties when the printing of early liturgical books made it more and more clear that <u>the only part of the rite of ordination common to all parts of the Church in all times and places is the imposition of hands</u>. Those who held that the matter and form of the sacraments are immutable inevitably came to the conclusion that the imposition of hands has always been the matter of Orders."[45]

---

[44] Hylomorphism is a philosophical theory developed by Aristotle which conceives being as a compound of matter and form.

[45] Bligh, *Ordination to the Priesthood*, p. 55.

What is immutable in the matter and form of the sacraments is what Christ has instituted. St Augustine gives this principle: what is observed everywhere and from time immemorial comes from Christ. Hence, the imposition of the hands does come from Christ and the conclusion imposes itself; it is the divinely instituted matter of the Sacrament of Holy Orders and may not be changed by the Church. Now, the form (the words accompanying the imposition of hands) is not everywhere the same: hence it is clearly a determination by the Church. Yet it has always and everywhere been required that the *meaning* of the words signify the "fullness of the priesthood" for the bishops, the "second rank" for the priests, and a rank of "service" for the deacons. That is the institution *in genere*.

What is Required for a Valid Form

Earlier we saw that the *form* is what gives the precise meaning to the *matter*. The words of the form determine what the matter is intended to signify. Some Sedevacantists make the blanket claim that because the form for the new episcopal consecration differs from the traditional form, it has changed "the substance of the sacrament." They claim that *any* change in the words that make up the form in and of itself invalidates the sacrament (believing, as apparently Mr. Omlor did, that the Church is unable to make any changes to the formula she has established). These Sedevacantists err by strictly equating a change in what the Church had previously established as necessary to confect a sacrament with a change in the "substance" of a sacrament (which the Church has no power to do). When the Council of Trent says the Church cannot change "the substance of the sacraments," it is referring to what *Christ* instituted – that is, the Sacraments themselves, as well as that which, *by divine ordinance*, is necessary to confect the sacrament. Pope Pius XII confirms the same when he says:

> "For these Sacraments instituted by Christ Our Lord, the Church in the course of the centuries never substituted other Sacraments, nor could she do so, since, as the Council of Trent teaches (Conc. Trid., Sess. VII, can. 1, De Sacram, in genere), the seven Sacraments of the New Law were all instituted by Jesus Christ Our Lord, and the Church has no power over 'the substance of the Sacraments,' that is, over those things which, as is proved from the sources of divine revelation, Christ the Lord Himself established to be kept as sacramental signs."[46]

---

[46] *Sacramentum Ordinis*, No. 1, November 30, 1947.

Other Sedevacantists acknowledge that the Church has the authority to change the formula, but claim that the current prayer in the new rite of episcopal consecration does not satisfy the essential requirements for a valid form. This is the position of Fr. Cekada. In an article confidently titled, *Absolutely Null and Utterly Void*,[47] Fr. Cekada claims that the form used in the new rite of episcopal consecration lacks what is necessary to signify the sacramental effects, and therefore has changed "the *substance* of the sacrament."[48]

Fr. Cekada begins by asking: "What specifically are we looking for in the new rite of episcopal consecration? What must the words of a form for conferring Holy Orders express?" He then provides the following answer:

> "Pius XII, in his Apostolic Constitution Sacramentum Ordinis, laid down the general principle when he declared that for Holy Orders these <u>must 'univocally signify the sacramental effects</u> – that is, the power of the Order and the grace of the Holy Ghost.' Note the two elements that it <u>must univocally</u> (i.e., unambiguously) express: the specific order being conferred (diaconate, priesthood or episcopacy) and the grace of the Holy Ghost. So we must therefore ascertain whether the new form is indeed '<u>univocal</u>'[49] in expressing these effects."[50]

Before we look specifically at the form (the words) of the new rite, let's address Fr. Cekada's understanding of the term "univocal." Fr. Cekada presupposes, in effect, that a univocal form excludes the possibility of different meanings in different contexts, and for him, univocity is defined without regard to how *the Church* understands the words.[51] We also note that Pius XII did not say the words of the form have never been used in any other possible way in the history of theology, the Church or the liturgy. Rather, the Pope said that the words of the form do "univocally signify the sacramental effect" and then added an important phrase (which Fr. Cekada failed to include), namely, "which are accepted and used by the Church *in that sense*."

---

[47] This is the phrase Pope Leo XIII used in *Apostolicae Curae* (September 18, 1896), discussed later in the chapter, in declaring the Anglican orders invalid.

[48] "The new form for episcopal consecration … changes the substance of a sacrament as established by Christ." (Cekada, "Absolutely Null and Utterly Void," March 25, 2006).

[49] *Univocal* means: "Having only one meaning. Non-ambiguous." *Equivocal* means: "Open to more than one interpretation; ambiguous."

[50] Cekada, "Absolutely Null and Utterly Void," March 25, 2006 (emphasis added).

[51] Fr. Cekada may have acquired his theory from the late Dr. Rama Coomaraswamy, who advanced this theory in his 1981 book *The Destruction of the Christian Tradition*, to be discussed later.

Before commenting further on the part that Fr. Cekada conveniently left off, let us read the actual words of Pius XII. He wrote:

> "Wherefore, after invoking the divine light, We of Our Apostolic Authority and from certain knowledge declare ... that the form ... is the words which determine the application of this matter, which <u>univocally signify</u> the sacramental effects - namely the power of Order and the grace of the Holy Spirit - <u>and which are accepted and used by the Church in that sense</u>."[52]

By saying the form univocally signifies the sacramental effects, and then adding that the words are "accepted and used by the Church in that sense" (that is, as signifying the sacramental effects in a given liturgical context), does not exclude the possibility that some authors or branches of the Church have understood the words in a different sense – that is, different than how the Church understands the phrase in a specific liturgical context. In other words, the form univocally signifies the sacramental effect *because of how the Church understands the words, and the univocity needed for a sacramental form does not depend upon certain words never having meant anything else in 2000 years.*

Earlier we saw that words possess a substance and accidents. The substance is the *meaning*, and the accidents are the *words* used to convey the meaning. We also saw, as in the case of Mormon baptism, that the correct words (accidents) can be used in the administration of a sacrament, but if the meaning intended (substance) is different than what the Church understands by the same words, the different meaning will render the sacrament invalid.

Now, just because the Mormons understand the words "Father, Son, and Holy Ghost" differently from how the Church understands the words, that does not render the same words, when used by the Church, to be equivocal (open to more than one meaning), as opposed to univocal (having only one meaning). The reason is because the univocal signification of the words is based, as we have said, on *how the Church understands them*. The phrase "Father, Son and Holy Ghost" is "accepted and used by the Church" to refer *only* (univocally) to the three Persons of the Blessed Trinity, even though the Mormons give the phrase a different meaning.

So, by saying a phrase is univocal "when accepted and used by the Church" in a particular sense, does not exclude the possibility that someone else, for example a Mormon, or even Coptic Christian monks, may have used a word or phrase to mean something similar but

---

[52] Ibid.

different in a different context. Unfortunately, neither does it exclude the possibility that a Sedevacantist priest with an ax to grind might claim that because the word *could* mean something different than what the Church means, it renders the form equivocal and therefore invalid or at least doubtful.

The words of the form mean what the Church intends for them to mean; and this meaning suffices to render the words univocal, regardless of how anyone else understands the words. This will become evident when we consider the actual words (form) that Pius XII declared to be "univocal" in the sacrament of Holy Orders. We will see that these words, when considered in and of themselves, are actually quite equivocal.

In the following citation, Fr. Cekada provides us with the form of the traditional episcopal consecration rite under Pius XII, along with his own unexplained and undocumented conclusions on why the form is "univocal." He wrote:

> "In the same document, having laid down a general principle, Pius XII then declared that the following words, contained in the consecratory Preface for the Rite of Episcopal Consecration, were the essential sacramental form for conferring the episcopacy: 'Complete in thy priest the fullness of Thy ministry, and adorned in the raiment of all glory, sanctify him with the dew of heavenly anointing.' This form univocally signifies the sacramental effects as follows:
> (1) 'The fullness of Thy ministry,' 'raiment of all glory' = power of the Order of episcopacy.
> (2) 'The dew of heavenly anointing' = grace of the Holy Ghost.
>
> The question is whether the new form does the same."[53]

If you actually read this section of Fr. Cekada's article, you will notice that it reads just as it does above. We have omitted nothing. Fr. Cekada begins *and ends* his "analysis" on the univocality of the old rite precisely with the last sentence above, and then jumps directly into his analysis of the new rite. In other words, he provides no commentary discussing why the form of the old rite univocally signifies the High-Priestly power and the sanctifying and sacramental grace of the sacrament (that is, "the grace of the Holy Spirit"). His "analysis" consists merely of putting equal signs after the elements of the form, and then telling us that the form is univocal.

---

[53] Cekada, "Absolutely Null and Utterly Void," March 25, 2006.

For Fr. Cekada, it's as simple as this: the words "the fullness of thy ministry" and "raiment of all glory" = the power of the order of the episcopate, and the words "the dew of heavenly anointing" = the grace of the Holy Ghost. Period. Finito. End of story.

Now, dear reader, raise your hand if you believe that the words "dew of heavenly anointing," in and of themselves, univocally signify the Holy Ghost. Can there be no other *possible* meaning for this expression? Everyone who hears the phrase will immediately know that it refers to the Holy Ghost, and nothing but the Holy Ghost? Try asking ten people what these words mean, and see how many say: "It refers to the Holy Ghost, what else?" You can even consult the massive, pre-Vatican II *Enchiridion Liturgicum* of Professor Polycarpus Rado, O.S.B.,[54] and it doesn't agree with Fr. Cekada on the exact signification of "heavenly anointing." For the distinguished professor, the "heavenly anointing" signified *charisma episcopale,* not grace, like it does for Fr. Cekada.

Similarly, do the words "raiment of all glory" immediately bring to mind the office of bishop, and the office of bishop alone? Try asking the same ten people and see if anyone gets it right. In fact, our Hungarian Benedictine professor fails Fr. Cekada's exam again; *he* thought "raiment of all glory" signified the grace of the Holy Ghost, not episcopal power of order, which is what it means to Fr. Cekada. Even the phrase "fullness of Thy Ministry" does not exclude the possibility of another interpretation. In fact, this was even admitted by Fr. Cekada's fellow Sedevacantist, Richard Ibranyi, who said: "The term 'fullness (perfection) of Thy ministry' could apply to any ministry. It does not specifically say what ministry is being spoken of."[55]

Brother Ansgar Santogrossi, O.S.B., a monk of Mount Angel Abbey, who has taught at Mount Angel Seminary for over a decade, wrote an article critiquing and refuting Fr. Cekada's claim that the new rite of episcopal consecration is invalid. One of the points he made is that the word "ministry" is a generic term which, in and of itself, could mean many things. In fact, as he notes, the word is used in the form of ordination to the diaconate. He wrote:

> "Even though a bishop receives the plenitude of the sanctifying power of the priesthood, the formula itself [of the traditional rite]

[54] See vol. 2 of *Enchiridion Liturgicum* (Herder, 1961, p. 1019): "*[E]lectus nunc iam plus valet presbytero, nam 'caeleste unguentum' accepit, quo metaphorice charisma episcopale significatur, imo etiam 'ornamentis totius glorificationis' ditatur, i.e. habitibus infusis donisque Spiritus Sancti vigore pollentibus speciali gratiae sacramentalis.*"
[55] Ibranyi, "Validity of Paul VI's Diminished Rites" (July 2004) http://www.johnthe baptist.us/jbw_english/documents/books/rjmi/br29_paul_vi_rites.pdf.

does not say 'priesthood,' but rather 'ministry,' a generic term also used for the non-sanctifying (non-priestly) power of order a deacon receives. According to his own principles, how does Fr. Cekada know that the formula 'plenitude of the ministry' univocally signifies a bishop and not an archdeacon, since diaconate is also, and even etymologically (*diakonos*—minister), ministry? Traditional writings sometimes use *ministerium* in a sense which excludes priesthood, as when the famous medieval commentator Amalarius justified a certain detail of ordination ceremonies by the observation that a deacon is consecrated "not for *sacerdotium*, but for *ministerium*.'" [56]

He concludes by saying:

> "We see that Fr. Cekada's particular understanding of univocity of sacramental signification logically implies that a formula specified by Pius XII does not signify univocally." [57]

The reason the ambiguous phrases above ("remnant of all glory," "dew of heavenly anointing," and "ministry") are said to univocally signify the sacramental effect is not because the words themselves can have no other possible meaning, but because, as Pius XII said, "they are accepted and used *by the Church in that sense.*"

With this teaching of Pius XII in mind, let us now turn to Fr. Cekada's main argument against the validity of the new rite of episcopal consecration.

Governing Spirit (*Spiritus principalis*)

As we saw above in *Sacramentum Ordinis*, a valid form for Holy Orders must signify two things: "the grace of the Holy Ghost" and the "power of order." Fr. Cekada's principal argument comes down to the use of a single phrase in the new rite ("governing Spirit"), which he claims is not "univocal." While he concedes that the new form does sufficiently mention "the grace of the Holy Ghost," he denies that the form sufficiently signifies the particular "power of Order" (office of bishop) to which the priest is being raised. Following is the form of the new rite as provided by Fr. Cekada:

---

[56] Santogrossi, "A Refutation of Fr. Cekada's 'Proof' of the Invalidity of the New Episcopal Ordination Rites," published at *Rorate Caeli*, February 2, 2007. http://www.rorate-caeli.blogspot.com/2007/02/feature-article.html.
[57] Ibid.

"Paul VI designated the following passage in the Preface as the new form for the consecration of a bishop:

'So now pour out upon this chosen one that power which is from you, <u>the governing Spirit</u>, whom you gave to your beloved Son, Jesus Christ, <u>the Spirit given by him to the holy apostles, who founded the Church</u> in every place to be your temple for the unceasing glory and praise of your name."[58]

Fr. Cekada then adds:

"The dispute over the validity of the new Rite of Episcopal Consecration centers on this passage. At first glance, it does seem to mention the Holy Ghost. However, <u>it does not appear to *specify* the power of Holy Order being conferred</u> — the fullness of the priesthood that constitutes the episcopacy — that the traditional form so clearly expressed. So, is this new form capable of conferring the episcopacy?"[59]

This is the essence of Fr. Cekada's argument. He claims that the phrase "governing Spirit" (*Spiritus principalis*) does not univocally signify the office of bishop, and therefore the rite approved by Paul VI is "Absolutely Null and Utterly Void." Wrote Fr. Cekada:

"The form does seem to signify the grace of the Holy Ghost. But 'governing Spirit'? Lutheran, Methodist and Mormon bishops also govern. Can such a term univocally signify the power of Order conferred – the fullness of the priesthood? The expression governing Spirit – *Spiritus principalis* in Latin – is at the heart of the dispute over the validity of the new rite, for if it does not signify the fullness of the priesthood that constitutes the episcopacy, the sacrament is invalid."[60]

A little later he is even more insistent:

"The expression *governing Spirit* is not univocal – that is, it is not a term that signifies only one thing ... the expression is ambiguous – capable of signifying many different things and persons."[61]

---

[58] Cekada, "Absolutely Null and Utterly Void," March 25, 2006.
[59] Ibid.
[60] Ibid.
[61] Ibid.

As we see, Fr. Cekada objects to the use of the phrase "governing Spirit" because, as he says, "Lutheran, Methodist, and Mormon bishops (who do not have valid orders) also govern." But this has no relevance whatsoever to what the Church means by the use of the term.

Using Fr. Cekada's same reasoning, shouldn't the term "ministry" which is used in the traditional, pre-1968 episcopal rite of consecration, also be considered equivocal, since the Lutherans, Methodists and Mormons also use the term "ministry" as a referring to a function performed by one who has not received Holy Orders as a sacrament with an indelible character? Obviously, the answer is no, and that is because Fr. Cekada's reasoning is erroneous.

Irrelevant Distinction

Furthermore, Fr. Cekada's himself admits that the term *principalem* (Greek: *hegemonia*) refers to the episcopate. He wrote:

> "Latin and Greek dictionaries render the adjective governing as, respectively, 'Originally existing, basic, primary... first in importance or esteem, chief... befitting leading men or princes,' and 'of a leader, leading, governing' or 'guiding.' There is a related noun, hegemonia, which in general means 'authority, command,' and in a secondary sense means 'rule, office of a superior: episcopal... of a superior of a convent...'"[62]

Now, you may be wondering, if Fr. Cekada concedes that *principalem* (or the Greek equivalent: *hegemonia*) refers specifically to the office of the episcopate, how can he argue that the word does not suffice to confer the episcopate on a candidate? He does so by making a distinction between the power of orders and the power of jurisdiction, and then says the word principalem "does not connote the power of Order (*potestas Ordinis*), just jurisdiction (*potestas jurisdictionis*)."[63] Notice, he concedes that the jurisdiction (governing) aspect of the office is signified, but claims the power of order, or office, itself is not.

Without even mentioning that the definition cited by Fr. Cekada himself specifically refers to the "office" of the episcopacy (not simply the function of the episcopacy), we note that Fr. Cekada doesn't cite a single authority confirming that the power of Order must be explicitly signified in the form. And there's a good reason for that, since, as Br. Ansar noted, if what Fr. Cekada said were true, it would mean the

---

[62] Ibid.
[63] Ibid.

traditional form of ordination for priests (approved by Pius XII) would itself be invalid. He explains:

> "If one were to apply the principle of univocity of signification to the traditional Latin formulas with all the rigor Fr. Cekada demands for an episcopal ordination formula, one would be forced to draw an absurd conclusion: that Pius XII specified a sacramental form for priestly ordination which cannot be valid. For if the episcopal formula must signify the plenitude of the power of order or sanctification *qua* distinct from the power of jurisdiction, as Fr. Cekada requires, then the priestly ordination formula would logically have to mention the power to offer sacrifice, or at least *sacerdotium*. But such is not the case in the traditional priestly ordination formula."[64]

Fr. Cekada's claim that "governing" does not suffice since it only refers to episcopal jurisdiction and not the power of the episcopacy is entirely non-sensical. If the standard meaning of the term "governing" includes *episcopal* jurisdiction (as Cekada concedes), then obviously it connotes the episcopacal office and power, since by divine institution, episcopal power of order is *for* the spiritual and hierarchical perfecting of a diocese, at least by its nature.[65]

We concede with Van Noort (citing Zapalena) that under the old code of Canon Law and an earlier tradition, a layman "appointed [as Bishop] to a diocese, but not yet consecrated, possesses jurisdiction..."[66] This shows that jurisdiction does not necessarily require episcopal consecration. However, the granting of episcopal jurisdiction during a ceremony, the very purpose of which is to consecrate a man to the bishopric, is not equivalent to appointing a laymen as bishop of a diocese, before he undertakes such a ceremony. Granting episcopal jurisdiction during such a ceremony suffices to

---

[64] Santogrossi, "A Refutation of Fr. Cekada's 'Proof' of the Invalidity of the New Episcopal Ordination Rites, published at *Rorate Caeli*, February 2, 2007. http://www.rorate-caeli.blogspot.com/2007/02/feature-article.html.

[65] The great theologian Fr. Louis Billot — no modernist he! — wrote: "[T]he fullness of the priesthood (plenum sacerdotium) is in need of special grace which the simple priesthood does not need, most especially on account of the task and office of ruling to which it has a relation by its very nature."De Ecclesiae Sacramentis, v. 2, 4th edition, Rome, 1908, p. 307 (emphasis added). Papal diplomats and curial officials obviously receive episcopal ordination with no jurisdiction over a diocese. But that is only supplementary to the fundamental reason Christ instituted the episcopate among his Apostles, namely the sacramental perfecting of a local church (diocese), which explains why even diplomat-bishops are assigned a "titular" See over which they could at least in theory have episcopal jurisdiction!

[66] Van Noort, *Christ's Church*, p 325.

specify the sacramental effect of raising the man to the office of bishop. *But no such bishop ever validly possessed title to his diocese and the jurisdiction of the episcopal office if he did not manifestly intend to receive sacramental consecration.*

We also note that the words which surround the phrase "governing Spirit" make it clear that it is referring to the same Spirit that Christ gave to His Apostles (the first bishops). Here again is the prayer:

> "So now pour out upon this chosen one that power which is from you, <u>the governing Spirit</u>, whom you gave to your beloved Son, Jesus Christ, <u>the Spirit given by him to the holy apostles, who founded the Church</u> in every place to be your temple for the unceasing glory and praise of your name."[67]

If there were any doubt about what was meant by the phrase "governing Spirit," the words that surround it – the *signifcatio ex adjunctis* - make it manifestly clear.[68] The "governing Spirit" is the same Spirit given by Christ *to the Apostles* (the first bishops) to rule and govern the Church. In fact, one could argue that the form of the traditional episcopal consecration rite of Pius XII was *less* clear on this point. Asserting that the new form (which asks God to give the priest the governing Spirit of the Apostles) is equivocal, but the old form (which asks God to fulfill in the priest the completion of the "ministry") is univocal, is another Sedevacantist case of *petitio principii* (begging the question).

As we've mentioned, the reason why there is such a difference in the forms used for priestly ordination and episcopal consecration throughout the Church is because the exact words were not given by Christ. Unlike the form used for Baptism and the double-consecration at Mass, Our Lord only instituted the other Sacraments in general, and left it to the Church to determine the words that make up the form.

---

[67] Cabié, Robert, *The Church at Prayers: The Sacraments*, vol. III (Collegevile, Minnesota: Liturgical Press, 1988), p. 175.

[68] Note also that the term "High Priest" appears elsewhere in the same long prayer, all of which was called "the form" by Paul VI, just like the whole Roman consecratory prayer was called "the form" by Pius XII, even though just a few lines respectively were declared essential and necessary for validity. The *adjuncta* for "governing Spirit"are not only words in the same sentence, but also the word "High Priest" contained within the same overall prayer of invocation.

Sedevacantists' Admissions

Even some Sedevacantists have been forced to admit that "governing Spirit" is a univocal term that suffices for validity. Responding to an argument that was put forward by two Sedevacantist priests of the *Congregatio Mariae Reginae Immaculatae* (C.M.R.I.), Francisco and Dominic Radecki, the Sedevacantist author Richard Ibranyi wrote:

> "[T]hey have the audacity to say that the 'governing Spirit' mentioned in the form of the New Rite is 'obviously… not sufficient,' as if it does not refer to the Holy Ghost that is being poured out on the candidate. In fact, the form of the New Rite clearly defines this 'governing Spirit' as the same Spirit of Jesus Christ that was also 'given… to the holy apostles,' which is the Holy Spirit.
> Form of the New Rite: 'So now pour out upon this chosen one that power which is from you, the governing Spirit whom you gave to your beloved Son, Jesus Christ, the Spirit given by him to the holy apostles…" (Ordination of a Bishop, Prayer of Consecration, vol. 2, #26, p. 73)
> Could there be any clearer reference that this 'governing Spirit' is the Holy Ghost and that the New Rite asks for this to be poured out on the candidate (sanctify him). Yet, the Radecki brothers say that the words 'governing Spirit' obviously does [sic] not indicate the Holy Ghost. One must conclude that the Radecki brothers obviously have eyes that do not see and ears that do not hear, that they are liars."[69]

Even Mr. Ibranyi is compelled to concede the obvious by noting that the form specifically states that the governing Spirit is the same Spirit given by Christ "to the holy apostles…" – that is, *those chosen to govern the Church*. Another Sedevacantist, who Fr. Cekada quoted in one of his own articles, was forced to admit the same. He did so by pointing to the *significatio ex adjunctis*, that is, the words and prayers surrounding the form. In fact, it is evident that this Sedevacantist was duped by his own colleagues until he actually read the form of the new rite which, in his own words, was "earth-shattering." In making this confession while responding to their errors, he wrote:

---

[69] Ibranyi, 'Validity of Paul VI"s Diminished Rites' (July 2004) http://www.johnthe baptist.us/jbw_english/documents/books/rjmi/br29_paul_vi_rites.pdf.

"Sorry guys. I can no longer consider this rite invalid, at least not materially.

The prayer of consecration itself, in its ENTIRETY [*significatio ex adjunctis*] clearly and univocally denotes the grace of the holy spirit, that this grace is the gift of the high priesthood, and that the rank of bishop is being conferred, with some of the particular powers of bishops mentioned: 'Through the Spirit who gives the grace of high priesthood grant him **the power to... assign ministries as you have decreed, and to loose every bond by the authority which you gave to your apostles.'**

This, for me is earth shattering. There is absolutely no doubt as to the intention here. I agree Paul VI shouldn't have changed it, but I mean, LOOK. It clearly spells out the role of a Catholic Bishop."[70] (emphasis in original)

As you have just seen, while some Sedevacantists claim the new rite is "absolutely null and utterly void," others claim "there is absolutely no doubt" about its validity. Such "doctrinal" disagreements within Sedevacantism are as stark as they are within Protestantism, since they are based upon the same fundamental error of private judgment, and often result in them holding diametrically opposed positions on major issues (like whether a rite is valid or not).

Testimony of Dom Botte

Dom Bernard Botte, a monk of Mont César in Belgium, specialist in Oriental languages and a member of the Consilium that prepared the new Rite, explained the meaning of "governing Spirit" in the episcopal ordination of Hippolytus' Apostolic Tradition, noting why it was and would now be used for the consecration of a bishop. Speaking of the three levels of Holy Orders – namely, bishop, priest, and deacon, he wrote:

"The three orders have a gift of the Holy Ghost, but it is not the same for each. For the bishop, it is the Spiritus principalis [governing Spirit]; for the priest, who forms the bishop's council, it is the Spiritus consilii [the Spirit of counsel]; and for the deacon, it is the Spiritus zeli et sollicitudinis [the Spirit of zeal and solicitude]. It is clear that these distinctions are made according to the functions of each minister. Thus, <u>it is clear that principalis must be correlated with the specific functions of the bishop</u>. (…)"[71]

There we have it, and from a member of the commission that drafted the new rite, no less. "It is clear," says Botte, that the term "*Spiritus principalis*," in and of itself, refers to "the specific functions of the bishop" (and which *excludes* the functions of the mere priest and deacon). It is not even necessary to look to the surrounding words to understand the meaning. Dom Botte continues:

> "The author begins with the typology of the Old Testament: God has never left His people without a leader, nor His sanctuary without a minister; this is also true for the new Israel, the Church. <u>The bishop is both leader who must govern the new people</u>, and the high priest of the new sanctuary which has been established in every place. <u>The bishop is the ruler of the Church. Hence the choice of the [Greek] term *hegemonicos* [Latin: *principalis*] is understandable: it is the gift of the Spirit apt for a leader</u>. The best translation in French would perhaps be 'the Spirit of authority.' <u>But whatever the translation adopted, the meaning [substance] seems certain</u>. An excellent demonstration of this was made in an article by Fr. J. Lecuyer: 'Episcopat et presbytérat dans les écrits d'Hippolyte de Rome,' Rech. Sciences Relig., 41 (1953) 30-50."[72]

So, without even considering the *significatio ex adjunctis* within the same prayer, it "seems certain," according to one of the authors of the new rite, that the governing Spirit refers to the office of bishop. This means that the phrase, in and of itself, univocally signifies the sacramental effect *when understood as the Church herself understands the phrase* (and obviously without regard to how the term *could* be interpreted by a heretical sect).

Fr. Cekada should have no problem with our reliance upon one of the papal advisers and drafters of the new rite (Botte) to prove the meaning of "governing Spirit." After all, Fr. Cekada also relies upon the interpretations of papal consultants to discern the meaning of terms used in ordination forms. For example, Fr. Cekada appealed to the explanation of Rev. Francis Hürth (one of the drafter's of Pius XII's

---

[71] Dom Bernard Botte, "Spiritus Principalis (formule de l'ordination episcopale)," Notitiae, 10 (1974), 410. Quoted in "Why the New Rite of Episcopal Consecration is Valid," by Fr. Pierre-Marie, *The Angelus Magazine*, No. 54. Autumn 2005 (emphasis added).
[72] Ibid.

Sacramentum Ordinis) who explained what the word "ministry" means in the form of diaconal ordination.[73]

Objection of Rama Coomaraswamy

The late Rama Coomaraswamy also objected to the use of the term "governing Spirit." In his book *The Destruction of the Christian Tradition,* Coomaraswamy was one of the first Sedevacantists to presuppose the error that univocality in a sacramental form must exclude the possibility of different meanings in different contexts (which is the secular definition), rather than how the term is "used and accepted" by the Church (in the words of Pius XII) in a given context. The following argument of Dr. Coomaraswamy is another example of the absurd lengths to which Sedevacantists are forced to go to rationalize their position that the post-Vatican II Church has defected. Let us briefly evaluate Coomaraswamy's efforts.

Coomaraswamy begins by citing four *possible* translations /definitions of the word *principalem* (as in "Spiritus *principalis,*" or "governing Spirit"), which he found by consulting several Latin dictionaries. He then chooses the translation that best suits his purpose. The translation he chose is the "overseer" (he evidently didn't have Fr. Cekada's dictionaries which at least provide the terms "bishop," "ruler," "episcopal"). Having boxed the reader into his translation of choice, Coomaraswamy notes that the Anglican sect considers their bishop to be an "overseer" who does not have a higher ontological status than a priest. Having already considered the errors of Fr. Cekada's arguments, one can guess where this is going.

Next, Coomaraswamy refers to the Vindication of the Bull *Apostolicae Curae* of Pope Leo XIII (the Bull that declared the Anglican ordinations invalid). The Vindication states that the Anglicans' erroneous *understanding* (substance) of the *word* "bishop" (accidents) invalidates their episcopal consecration. (As noted above, the Anglicans' erroneous understanding is that the bishop is not of a higher rank than a priest, but is only an "overseer.") Lastly, through the use of some very twisted logic, Coomaraswamy reasons his way backwards by arguing that if the Church uses the word *"principalem"* (which is translated in one of Coomaraswamy's dictionaries as "overseer"), it must mean that *the Catholic Church* is *also* saying the bishop is not higher than a priest (and is instead only an "overseer")!

---

[73] See Cekada, "The 1968 Rite of Episcopal Consecration: Still Null and Void," p. 4.

We will allow Dr. Coomaraswamy to give us his argument in his own words. Under the heading "Spiritum Principalem – What is It?," he writes:

> "What does the word principalem mean? Cassell's New Latin Dictionary translates it as: 1) first in time, original; first in rank, chief; 2) of a prince; 3) of the chief place in a Roman camp. Harper's Latin Dictionary also translates it by the term 'overseer.' Now this latter term is of great interest because it is the one used by the Reformers to distort the true nature of a bishop. As the Vindication of the Bull "Apostolicae curae" points out:
>
> 'The fact that the Anglicans added the term 'bishop' to their form did not make it valid because doctrinally they hold the bishop to have no higher state than that of the priest—indeed, he is seen as an 'overseer' rather than as one having the 'fullness of the priesthood.'"[74]

So, Coomaraswamy objects to the use of the term "governing Spirit" (*Spiritum principalem*) because one of his dictionaries says the term *principalem* means "overseer," and the Anglicans understanding of the term bishop is only one of an "overseer" who does not have the fullness of the priesthood! And this is supposed to call into question the validity of a sacramental form approved by the Catholic Church, who has the correct understanding of the office of bishop!

Needless to say, if Coomaraswamy's fallacious reasoning were true, then *all* of the Church's *traditional* sacramental forms would be insufficient for validity, because terminology used in *each* of the forms of the seven sacraments are surely misunderstood by one non-Catholic sect or another (e.g., the Mormon's understanding of the terms "Father, Son and Holy Ghost"). As previously explained, how a heretical sect understands a term has no bearing whatsoever on the Church's understanding of the same term, nor does it in any way affect the validity of the Catholic rite (although it certainly bears upon the validity of the *non-Catholic* rite).

For example, the traditional Catholic priestly ordination rite uses the term "priest," which is a term that the Anglicans understand in an erroneous way (e.g., *not* one who offers sacrifice). Now, even though the Anglicans' erroneous understanding of "priest" is one of the reasons that *their* ordination rite is invalid, it is irrelevant to the meaning of the same term as "accepted and used" by the Catholic Church. If that were not the case, then the Anglicans' false

---

[74] Coomaraswamy, *The Destruction of the Christian Tradition*, p. 333.

understanding of "priest" would invalidate the Church's *traditional* rite of priestly ordination. And since their erroneous understanding of the word priest does not invalidate the Catholic Church's traditional form used for ordaining a priest, then obviously their misunderstanding of office of bishop in no way affects the validity of the Church's *new* rite of episcopal consecration. The absolute inanity of Coomaraswamy and Cekada's approach – which looks to the *form* and intention of non-Catholic rites (according to their understanding of the words) to determine the validity of Catholic rites – should be evident to all.[75]

New Rite Approved by Cardinal Ottaviani

It should also be pointed out that the new form of episcopal consecration was not just written overnight in a back room at the Vatican by Bugnini and a few fellow "brethren." The ordination rite was prepared by a committee of 40 prelates, including many bishops and Cardinals. It was authored and approved by the Consilium, and then sent for a second tier approval to the Congregation for the Doctrine of Faith, which was headed at the time by Cardinal Alfredo Ottaviani, who was one of the prelates most hated and feared by the Modernists. Ottaviani, who had served as head of the Holy Office under Pope Pius XII, approved the form containing the words "governing Spirit" without any reservations whatsoever. And he approved the new rite of episcopal consecration only a short time before presenting Paul VI with the landmark *Critical Study of the New Mass,* which later came to be known as *The Ottaviani Intervention.*

The very same Cardinal who boldly declared the new Mass to be "a striking departure of the theology of the Mass as formulated by the Council of Trent" had no problem with the new form of consecration (which, as we will see later, was not "new," but dated back to at least the early third century); nor did he object to the phrase "governing

---

[75] In *Apostolicae Curae,* Pope Leo XIII declared the Anglican rite of Orders null and void for "defect of form and intention." For Anglican ordination, the mere phrase "Receive the Holy Ghost" does not signify the grace of the sacrificing priesthood, and when "for the office and work of a priest" was added *a century later,* their power of ordaining was extinct. Further, Leo XIII said, the phrases "for the office of priest" (for ordination) and "bishop" (for episcopal consecration) which they later added are necessarily "understood in a sense different to that which they bear in the Catholic rite." Note that the Anglicans have a different meaning (substance) for the same words (accidents), just like the Mormons do for the words "Father, Son and Holy Ghost." Leo XIII went on to say that due to this different understanding (substance) which Anglicans have for the words (accidents), they "cannot be considered apt or sufficient for the Sacrament which omits what it ought essentially to signify."

Spirit," which Fr. Cekada and Dr. Coomaraswamy find so objectionable. Apparently they imagine themselves to be more knowledgeable on the subject than some of the Church's leading experts in the field at the time, who prepared the new rite.

These men included Fr. B. Kleinheyer, then professor at the seminary of Aix-la-Chapelle, author of a thesis on the ordination of the priest in the Roman Rite; Fr. C. Vogel, professor at Strasbourg, who had taken the succession from Msgr. Andrieu for editing the *Ordines Romani* and the *Romano-Germanic Pontifical*; Fr. E. Lengeling, professor of Liturgy at Munster-in-Westphalia (later Dean of the Faculty of Theology); Fr. P. Jounel, professor at the Superior Institute of Liturgy at Paris, and Msgr. J. Nabuco, Brazilian prelate and author of a Commentary on the Roman Pontifical. Surely, the qualifications of these men overshadow those of Fr. Cekada and Rama Coomaraswamy, who even departed from tradition by getting himself ordained to the priesthood as a married man (and by a married bishop, Lopez Gaston).

In his book, *The Reform of the Liturgy*, Annibale Bugnini, who was a member of the Consilium, discusses the response they received from the Congregation for the Doctrine of Faith (headed by Cardinal Ottaviani) after they completed their review of the new rite. He wrote:

"The completely positive answer from the Congregation for the Doctrine of the Faith was particularly pleasing and an occasion of both joy and surprise. (...) Here is what the Congregation said (November 8, 1967):

'Their Eminences of the Congregation for the Doctrine of the Faith carefully examined the matter at their plenary session on Wednesday, October 11, 1967, and came to the following decisions:

The new schema is approved with the following qualifications:

1. Number 89: in the questions asked of the candidate for the episcopal office, greater emphasis should be put on faith and its conscientious transmission; moreover, the candidate should be expressly asked about his determination to give obedience to the Roman Pontiff.

2. Number 96: <u>The text of Hippolytus, duly adapted, is acceptable</u>.

Regarding the approach: the mind of the cardinals is that liturgical innovations should be dictated by real need and introduced with all the precautions that so sacred and serious a matter requires.

Once the changes listed have been made in the Ordo, it is then to be studied by a joint committee, in accordance with the august decision of the Holy Father...'"[76]

Putting aside the animus that many Sedevacantists have toward Paul VI, the approval of the new rite of episcopal consecration by Cardinal Ottaviani, and other princes of the Church and experts in the field of sacramental theology, should, in and of itself, remove for them any *reasonable* doubt that form of the new rite is valid.[77]

Apostolic Tradition of Hippolytus

The new form of episcopal consecration was easily approved by Cardinal Ottaviani and the other experts because it was taken from the *Apostolic Tradition of Hippolytus,* which dates to at least the beginning of the third century. It is unclear who this Hippolytus actually was, and the historical record says he could have been a martyred saint recognized by the Church,[78] or an antipope (who may have been the aforementioned martyred saint, having converted), or another cleric of unknown origin (Hippolytus being a common name at the time), or even the pen-name of an unknown author.

While the *Catholic Encyclopedia* takes the position that St. Hippolytus temporarily separated from Rome and had himself elected as antipope after opposing Pope Callistus,[79] consensus is growing that the *Apostolic Tradition of Hippolytus* is of Syrian (or possibly Egyptian) origin, and very dissimilar to later Latin texts which we know originated in Rome. This would suggest that the Hippolytus of the *Apostolic Tradition* was an Eastern rite Catholic and, hence, not the antipope who opposed Pope Callistus. However, if the Hippolytus of the ancient rite was the antipope, he was given the grace to redeem himself by dying in union with Rome, as a martyr for the Faith. But no matter who Hippolytus was, the consecration rite attributed to him

---

[76] Bugnini, *La Riforma liturgica, 1948-1975* (Rome: CLV Edizioni liturgiche, 1983), p. 692 [English version for citations: *The Reform of the Liturgy 1948-1975* (Collegeville, MN: The Liturgical Press, 1990), p. 712]. This approbation was conveyed to Fr. Bugnini on November 8, 1967. The notification bears a protocol number (Prot. 578/67), but no signature, at least on the copy we consulted in the archives of the German Liturgical Institute (Trier), under "*Pontificale Romanum.*"

[77] In fact, our research reveals that Fr. Cekada could find only one bishop in the world, in Spain, who allegedly had a doubt about the valid signification of Paul VI's new form.

[78] The *Catholic Encyclopedia* (1913) refers to St. Hippolytus as "the most important theologian and the most prolific religious writer of the Roman Church in the pre-Constantinian era" (vol. VII, p. 361).

[79] Ibid.

spread far and wide throughout the early Church and is therefore a reliable witness to authentic tradition.[80] This rite has also served as the basis for several other ancient forms, all of which have been recognized as valid by the Church.

In his book, *Ordination to the Priesthood*, Fr. Bligh explains that Hippolytus' rite of consecration is amongst the oldest known to exist, and was itself based upon what was traditional at the time, and what St. Hippolytus believed to have been used by the Apostles themselves. A decade before the new rite was approved by Paul VI, Fr. Bligh wrote:

> "In order to understand how the rite of ordination has developed in the course of the centuries from its primitive simplicity to its present complexity, it is necessary to have some idea of the source-books in which this process of development is disclosed to us. (...)
> The earliest of such collections that has come down to us is the Apostolic Tradition of Hippolytus, compiled at Rome by ... Hippolytus about the year A.D. 217. <u>As Hippolytus was an extreme conservative in things liturgical,</u> and set out, as the title of his work indicates, to describe rites which he believed to be of apostolic origin, <u>it is safe to assume that his text records liturgical practice that was already traditional at the end of the second century,</u> when he was a young man. The original Greek of Hippolytus (Greek was still the liturgical language of the Roman Church) has not survived except in fragmentary portions, but the work had a wide circulation and is known to us through Latin, Sahidic (Coptic), Bohairic, Arabic and Ethiopic versions, which have been edited with English translations in recent times."[81]

Dom Botte, cited earlier, who headed one of the two study groups that prepared the new rite of episcopal consecration for Paul VI, explained how he came up with the idea of using the Hippolytus texts as the form. He notes that he pondered the question: "Should we create a new prayer from start to finish?," and then answered:

---

[80] After studying the history of St. Hippolytus, Fr. Cekada did not defend the notion that he is the same person as the antipope. In his article against the validity of the new rite of episcopal consecration, Fr. Cekada wrote: "The Jesuit expert on Eastern liturgies, Jean-Michel Hanssens, devotes nearly one hundred pages to trying to identify Hippolytus: Was he the same Hippolytus associated with an Easter computation table? The one represented by a statue? The one reputed to be a native Roman? Or the Egyptian one? The pope's counselor? Or the anti-pope? The priest Hippolytus? Or a bishop? Or the martyr? Or one of the several saints in the martyrology? The best we can manage is scholarly conjecture." Cekada, "Absolutely Null and Utterly Void," March 25, 2006.
[81] *Ordination to the Priesthood*, p. 24 (emphasis added).

"I felt myself incapable of this. It's true that some amateurs could be found who would be willing to attempt it – some people feel they have a special charism for composing liturgical formulas – but I don't trust these amateurs. Wouldn't it be more reasonable to seek a formula in the Eastern rites that could be adapted? An examination of the Eastern rites led my attention to a text I knew well, the prayer in the Apostolic Tradition of St. Hippolytus.

The first time I proposed this to my colleagues, they looked at me in disbelief. They found Hippolytus' formula to be excellent, but they didn't believe it had the slightest chance of being accepted. (...) If I was paying attention to this text, it wasn't because I had just finished a critical edition of it, but because my study of the Eastern rites made me notice that the formula always survived under more evolved forms. Thus, in the Syrian Rite the prayer for the patriarch's ordination was none other than the one in the *Testamentum Domini*, a reworking of the Apostolic Tradition [of Hippolytus]. The same is true for the Coptic Rite where the prayer for the bishop's ordination is close to that of the Apostolic Constitutions, another reworking of Hippolytus' text. The essential ideas of the Apostolic Tradition [of Hippolytus] can be found everywhere."[82]

He then added:

"I had provided the fathers with a synoptic table of the different texts with a brief commentary. The discussion was lively, and I understand why. What finally obtained a favorable vote was, I think, Pere Lecuyer's intervention. He had published in the *Nouvelle Revue Theologique* a short article showing how the text of the Apostolic Tradition agreed with the teaching of the ancient Fathers. During the session, when it was time to vote on this issue, he made a plea which convinced those who were wavering. Afterward, we invited him to join our work group, and he was a great help to us by his theological competence and knowledge of the Fathers."[83]

Fr. Cekada's Smoke and Mirrors

Confronted with the ancient and perhaps apostolic pedigree of the Apostolic Tradition of Hippolytus which is used in its essentials in the

---

[82] Fr. Pierre-Marie, "Why the New Rite of Episcopal Consecrations is Valid," originally published in *Sel de la Terre* (No. 54., Autumn 2005, pp. 72-129), translated into English and published by the *Angelus Press*.
[83] Ibid. (emphasis added).

1968 rite, Fr. Cekada attempts to impugn its stature with a number of irrelevant inquiries. He first questions its legitimacy on the ground that the author cannot be identified with certainty. Of course, the ability to identify with certainty the author of the Church's most ancient rites and customs is absolutely irrelevant to the Church's determination of a form's sacramental validity. Can Fr. Cekada identify each and every author of the other approved forms of episcopal consecration (such as the one approved by Pius XII?), or the original author of each and every prayer contained in the traditional Roman Missal that he daily celebrates? (Was it Pope Damasus? Pope Gregory? St. Peter or St. Paul? A combination of them?). Needless to say, St. Pius V in *Quo Primum* did not base his codification of the Roman Missal upon the specific identification of the authors of the rite. Simply confirming the various ancient usages and customs as conforming to and being derived from Tradition was sufficient for the saintly Pope.

Next, Fr. Cekada attempts to cast doubt by raising questions of "Origin" by asking: "Where did *The Apostolic Tradition* come from? Some say Rome; others say Alexandria, Egypt. More conjecture." Conjecture? What difference does it make where the ancient manuscript came from? The fact that the manuscript had such *wide circulation* in the early Church (throughout the East *and* West), is evidence of its conformity to tradition, and the inability to pinpoint its original source (from which Hippolytus received it) serves as evidence for its apostolic origin.

Fr. Cekada then raises questions about the "Age":

> "How old is it? 'Usually' dated around 215 AD, but 'the section dealing with ordination *may have been retouched* by fourth-century hands in order to bring it into line with current doctrine and practice.' Note: 'retouched.' More scholarly conjecture is needed to tell us which parts of the document were retouched."[84]

Again, whether the Church can identify the precise date of origin for an ancient form is irrelevant for determining sacramental validity. Does it really matter to Fr. Cekada whether Hippolytus' rite dates to the second, or third, or the fourth century? Why is the possibility that the form *may* (or may not) have been edited during the A.D. 300s to bring it into conformity with *current* doctrine and practice (as if the "current" doctrine and practice in the 300s was somehow in contradiction with the "previous" doctrine and practice of the first

---

[84] Cekada, "Absolutely Null and Utterly Void," March 25, 2006 (emphasis in original).

three centuries) considered a negative for Fr. Cekada? Especially when the style and various phrases from it are found in the Syriac and Coptic churches who have retained a hierarchy going back to the Apostles? (When the "uniate" Syrian Catholic and Coptic Catholic Churches were formed, their clergy and bishops were not reordained to make them valid.) Shouldn't Fr. Cekada and any other Catholic find comfort in a rite that proves to reflect the doctrine and *praxis* of large portions of the fourth century Church? What constitutes true "conjecture" is Fr. Cekada's intimation that the unidentified authorship, origin and age of the Hippolytus rite is a basis for questioning the validity of the 1968 rite.

Next, Fr. Cekada poses the question of "Manuscript Authority?" and notes that we don't have the originals, but only reconstructions of the fragments. So what? We don't have any of the original autographs of Sacred Scripture either. Neither do we have the original manuscripts of the Damasian/Gregorian sacramentaries. In fact, the Catholic Church does not need the originals, because she has the authority and divine assistance to recognize a rite formed gradually over time[85] that, in her judgment, is in conformity to apostolic Tradition. Same answer for Fr. Cekada's final question of "Liturgical Use?" Whether the rite of Hippolytus conforms exactly to what everyone else in Syria, Egypt or Rome was doing in the time of the author is irrelevant, because in those centuries the rites were still in a stage of growth, with local differences, and even improvisation (perhaps by a saintly martyr) and confessor bishops, who are or at least presumed to be guided by the Holy Ghost received in ordination. So much for Fr. Cekada's attempt to denigrate this ancient rite. That Fr. Cekada raises these unanswerable questions (which could not be answered for the form of any approved rite) only reveals the weakness of his own case.

Comparison of Rites

Returning to the actual text of the Apostolic Tradition of Hippolytus – the oldest extant rite known to exist – note that it uses the phrase "governing Spirit." The phrase is also used in both the Maronite and Coptic rites of the East, which have always been accepted by the

---

[85] Pius XII wrote: "As circumstances and the needs of Christians warrant, public worship is organized, developed and enriched by new rites, ceremonies and regulations, always with the single end in view, 'that we may use these external signs to keep us alert, learn from them what distance we have come along the road, and by them be heartened to go on further with more eager step; for the effect will be more precious the warmer the affection which precedes it' (St. Augustine)." (*Mediator Dei*, No. 22, November 20, 1947.)

Church. The following is a comparison of the form of St. Hippolytus, the new rite of Paul VI, and also those of the Maronite and Coptic rites.

> *St. Hippolytus' rite:* Now, pour forth on this chosen one that power which is from Thee, the <u>governing Spirit</u> (*Spiritus principalis*), whom Thou gavest to Thy beloved Son Jesus Christ, whom He gave to the holy Apostles, who founded the Church in diverse places as Thy means of sanctification, unto the glory and unceasing praise of Thy name."[86]

> *Paul VI's new rite:* "And now, pour forth on this chosen one that power which is from Thee, the <u>governing Spirit</u> (*Spiritus principalis*), whom Thou gavest to Thy beloved Son Jesus Christ, whom He gave to the holy Apostles, who founded the Church in every place as Thy sanctuary, unto the glory and unceasing praise of Thy name."[87]

> *Maronite Rite:* "Enlighten him and pour forth upon him the grace and understanding of Thy <u>governing Spirit</u> (*Spiritus principalis*), whom Thou hast bequeathed to Thy Son, our Lord Jesus Christ, Who was given to Thy saints, O Father, Who knowest the hearts of us all, pour forth Thy virtue upon this Thy servant, whom Thou hast chosen to be a patriarch, that he might shepherd Thy holy, universal flock."[88]

> *Coptic Rite:* "Thou, again, now, pour forth the power of Thy <u>leading Spirit</u> (*Spiritus tui hegemonici*), which Thou gavest to Thy holy Apostles, in Thy name. Bestow, therefore, the same grace, upon Thy servant, N. whom Thou hast chosen for the Episcopacy that he might shepherd Thy holy flock, and that he might be for Thee a minister above reproach."[89]

Regarding the slight difference in wording between the Maronite and Coptic rites, we note that the use of the term *"spiritus tui hegemonici"* (which is translated as "leading Spirit") is equivalent to the term "governing Spirit." The difference is due to the translation from Greek, to Latin, to English.[90]

---

[86] Cited in Fr. Pierre-Marie, "Why the New Rite of Episcopal Consecrations is Valid," originally published in *Sel de la Terre* (No. 54., Autumn 2005, pp. 72-129), translated into English and published by the *Angelus Press*.
[87] Ibid.
[88] Ibid.
[89] Ibid
[90] "Governing Spirit" is a translation of the Latin *"Spiritus principalis,"* which itself is a translation of the Greek *"pneuma hegemonikon."* The Latin translation used by Fr. Pierre-

Clearly, the use of "governing Spirit" in the context of bishops, metropolitans and patriarchal bishops is not foreign to the Church. It has been used since at least the late second century (if it is not of apostolic origin), and, as Dom Botte noted, refers specifically to the office of bishop, who is appointed to rule or "govern" the Church. This obvious episcopal duty was affirmed by St. Paul in his discourse at Ephesus when he declared: "The Holy Ghost hath placed you bishops, to rule the Church of God, which he hath purchased with his own blood" (Acts 20:28).[91] Given the association in tradition between "governing Spirit" and the order of bishops defined by a spiritual character which of its nature disposes to the reception of *supreme* governing power in the Church[92] - it is quite a stretch to believe with Fr. Cekada that when a Coptic bishop prays over an ordinand "*pour forth* the power of thy governing Spirit which thou gavest to thy holy Apostles"... *Nothing episcopal happens; no episcopal power is given, despite the historical associations and connotations.*

Because most people naturally find this implied claim of Fr. Cekada to be a stretch, they will understand why Fr. Calderon called the "governing Spirit" passage the "form" in the Coptic rite, "form" meaning "formal-*effective* sentence," when the sacramental effect is actually accomplished (Fr. Calderon's analysis is below.) There is nothing unusual here - with St. Thomas, many theologians have said that *the form* of consecration of the chalice is the whole sentence "this is the chalice of my blood of the new and eternal covenant, the mystery of faith . . .", even though they have also said that "this is the chalice of my blood" is effective.

Marie (*Spiritus tui hegemonici*) is more than simply a translation from Greek to Latin. It is a borrowing of the Greek word in a Latinized spelling. The same Greek word has been translated by others as "*principalem*," which was then translated as "governing." The original Greek word is the same.

[91] It is interesting to note that in the next two verses, St. Paul says: "I know that, after my departure, ravening wolves will enter in among you, not sparing the flock. And of your own selves shall arise men speaking perverse things, to draw away disciples after them (vv. 29-30). Here St. Paul prophesies that evil bishops will infiltrate the Church and rule "among" good bishops and lead the faithful astray (a prophecy fulfilled in our times). But they are still valid bishops, since it is implied that they have jurisdiction over "the flock."

[92] The Supreme Pontiff is not a higher sacred *order* to bishops, and he is after all a *bishop* with no territorial limits on his *episcopal governing* power; Vatican I defined his power as "episcopal." Even when, in the past, priests or deacons were at times elected Pope, they had to at least intend to receive episcopal consecration as a condition for their acceptance of the election and the possession of jurisdiction until consecration. And those bishops-elect of Rome who died before receiving episcopal consecration are often referred to in the ancient sources in a quite different way from all those who were consecrated.

Fr. Cekada attempts to muddy the waters by also arguing that the Maronite rite is a non-sacramental prayer for installing a Patriarch who is already a bishop when appointed. But this is irrelevant to the point we have proven, namely, that the term "governing Spirit" univocally signifies the *office of bishop*, irrespective of whether the man is being elevated to the office of bishop or installed as a Patriarch, since, obviously, a Patriarch has to be a bishop (he is a sort of Archbishop of Archbishops).

More Smoke and Mirrors From Fr. Cekada

Faced with the Eastern rite forms, which refer to the episcopate in the same terms as the new form of Paul VI, Fr. Cekada resorted to more smoke and mirrors to defend his thesis. After mentioning the irrelevant fact that the Coptic Catholics (who are part of the Catholic Church) "descend from monophysite heretics," Fr. Cekada goes on to compare apples and oranges, and then declares that the apples and oranges "cannot be equated." The "apple," in this case, is the long Preface of the Coptic rite (340 words); the "orange" is the short form of the new rite (containing 42 words). Fr. Cekada says that the Coptic rite has "a Preface of about 340 words long in a Latin version. The Paul VI form is 42 words long. The two forms, therefore, cannot be equated."

Now, why would Fr. Cekada compare the entire "Preface" of the Coptic rite, with the shorter operative essential "form" of the new rite, *and then refer to both of them as the "form"*?[93] Why didn't he compare the Preface of the Coptic rite to the Preface of the rite of Paul VI? That would be an apples to apples comparison. And if we were to compare the Preface of both rites (apples and apples), what would we find? We find that a majority of the 340 words of the Coptic Preface *also* appear in the Preface of the new rite of Paul VI, the preface which Paul VI declared to be the form of the sacrament, even though only one section was declared necessary for validity.

If you are wondering how Fr. Cekada could justify comparing the Preface of one rite with the form of another, and then refer to them both as the "form," here is the answer: the sacramental theology of the East is not as precise as that of the West. Because of this, the theologians of the East have not sought to determine what, exactly, constitutes the *formal effective* words/sentence for certain sacraments,

---

[93] In his critique of Fr. Cekada's article, Fr. Calderon wrote: "Fr. Cekada counts the words: 340 to 42! But he does not point out that the majority of these 340 words occur in the rest of the new preface." (Calderon, "In Defense of the Validity of the Rite of Episcopal Consecration: Replies to the Objections," November 2006.)

and therefore they include the surrounding prayers as being part of what they refer to as the "form." Both Pius XII and Paul VI referred in their apostolic constitutions to the *whole* consecratory or invocation-prayer as "the form." In the rite of ordination in the East, because they lack the clarity in distinguishing what precise words constitute the formal effective sentence, they will usually (if not always) include the entire Preface as being the "form." And, again, Pius XII did the same in 1947!

Fr. Cekada uses this lack of precision in Eastern sacramental theology as more smoke and mirrors to imply that the "form" used in the new Rite is much shorter than the form of the Coptic rite. What he doesn't tell his readers is that the reason the "form" is shorter, is because in 1898 a Coptic Catholic synod[94] referred to the entire Preface as the "form," whereas Pius XII and Paul VI, no doubt influenced by the precision of Roman jurisprudence, have applied this same precision to her sacramental theology in identifying what constitutes the few formal *effective* words vis-à-vis the surrounding words. It is these words *alone* (rather than the entire Preface), the words which Pius XII and Paul VI declared essential and necessary for validity, that the West usually calls the form.

Commenting on Fr. Cekada's sleight of hand tactic, Fr. Calderon wrote:

> "Fr. Cekada takes as the 'form' the entire Coptic preface (in reality, a single sentence must be 'formal-effective'); and, at the same time, he denies that the context of the new preface can take away the ambiguity of the 'formal-effective' phrase of the new rite. But one must choose: if the context does not determine the signification of the form, it would be necessary to identify the 'formal-effective' sentence of the Coptic rite and to compare it with that of the new rite; if, on the contrary, the context determines the signification, then it is necessary to compare one complete preface with the other complete preface. It is fallacious to compare a complete preface, on the one hand, with the 'formal-effective' sentence on the other."[95]

Fr. Cekada justifies his claim that the entire Preface of the Coptic rite is the form by citing Denzinger's *Ritus Orientalium,* which classifies the lengthy prefatory prayers as part of the sacramental form. But, as we have explained, this is *not* because the Church has ever declared

[94] Quoted Cappello 4:732; See Cekada, "Absolutly Null and Utterly Void,"p. 5.
[95] Ibid (emphasis added).

that the *entire* Preface constitutes the "formal-*effective*" words, but because of the less precise sacramental theology of the East. Fr. Cekada teaches *his own doctrine* about the Coptic form, namely that the entire form, or at least the passages including the establishing of houses of prayer and ordaining clergy, are necessary for validity. But the Church herself has never taught any such thing.

Fr. Calderon elaborates on this point by explaining, as we have above, that such compilations of works on the Eastern rites (e.g., Denzinger, Cappello) reflect the sacramental theology of the East. Fr. Calderon says:

> "It is necessary to bear in mind that Roman theology, imbued with a more rational and juridical spirit, has always sought to specify what constitutes the 'formal-effective' sentence in its various consecratory prefaces, whereas Eastern theology does not seek these specifications. That is why, for instance, the Romans arranged the Eucharistic consecration around the words of our Lord, thereby signaling that it is these words that effect transubstantiation; whereas the Orientals did not proceed in that manner, with the consequence that later they did not know whether the consecration occurred at that moment or during the *epiclesis* (the invocation of the Holy Ghost)."[96]

Fr. Calderon goes on to say:

> "If Denzinger presents the complete Eastern prefaces as 'forms,' it is because Eastern theology never determined with precision what constitutes, in each preface, the essential proposition (the 'formal-effective') that produces the sacramental effect. According to St. Thomas Aquinas' teaching, it must be a single, simple sentence (with a single subject and a single predicate, which can have several determining complements) that *produces what it signifies*."[97]

In Fr. Cekada's follow up article "Still Null and Void" (in which he attempted to respond to the grave objections to his first article), he

---

[96] "In Defense of the Validity of the Rite of Episcopal Consecration: Replies to the Objections," November 2006, at http://www.angelusonline.org/index.php?Section =articles&subsection=show_article&article_id=2551.

[97] Ibid. (emphasis added). St. Thomas also says: "Although it happens in every language that various words signify the same thing, yet one of those words is that which those who speak that language use principally and more commonly to signify that particular thing: and this is the word which should be used for the sacramental signification." ST, III, q. 60, a. 7, ad. 2. As applied here, relative to the three Major Orders (diaconate, priesthood, episcopacy), the term "governing Spirit" applies "principally" to the office of bishop.

simply repeats the same argument, when he writes: "The Coptic and Maronite <u>forms</u> consist of long Prefaces (about 340 and 370 words respectively)" and then says "unlike the Roman Rite, no one sentence in either is designated as the essential sacramental form." Again, as we have noted, this is because the sacramental theology of the East is less precise, not because the formal-effective words in the East constitute the entire Preface. But because the books that Fr. Cekada consulted on Eastern rites did not separate the one-sentence form from the entire Preface, *Fr. Cekada concludes that the entire Preface of the Coptic Consecratory Prayer is the sacramental form!*[98] We wonder whether Fr. Cekada really believes what he writes.

It is important to understand Fr. Cekada's error, because he points to elements within the Coptic *Preface* **or** entire Consecratory Prayer (which he erroneously claims is the "form") to argue for the invalidity of the *form* of the new rite. For example, in the section he titled "Coptic <u>Form</u>," Cekada says:

"The Paul VI Consecratory Prayer contains many phrases found in the Coptic <u>form</u>. It omits, however, three phrases in the Coptic <u>form</u> that enumerate three specific sacramental powers considered *proper to the order of bishop alone*: 'to provide clergy according to His commandment for the priesthood...to make new houses of prayer, and to consecrate altars.' This omission is significant, because the dispute over the validity of the <u>essential sacramental form</u> of Paul VI revolves around whether it adequately expresses the power of the Order being conferred — i.e., episcopacy."[99]

The error contained in this argumentation can hardly be overemphasized. First, the Coptic *effective* form does *not* contain these additional phrases; they are ancillary to the form. Fr. Cekada refers to the Coptic "form" four times in reference to these ancillary prayers (once in his subtitle, and three times in three sentences) but they are not part of the Coptic effective form, unless you agree with Fr. Cekada that nothing happens at the moment when the ordaining bishop asks God to actually do something to the recipient of the sacrament (that is, pour upon him the governing Spirit given to the Apostles). Second, while

---

[98] It is unclear why Fr. Cekada felt the need to "consult works that identify the Eastern Rite sacramental forms" in Denzinger et al. when Fr. Pierre-Marie's landmark 2005 study to which Fr. Cekada was responding included a side-by-side analysis of the 1968, Hippolytus, Coptic and Maronite rites. Perhaps Fr. Cekada wanted to give his readers the impression that his research sources were superior, even though there is no material difference in the presentation of these rites among the sources he said he consulted and what Fr. Pierre-Marie presented.
[99] Cekada, "Absolutely Null and Utterly Void," March 25, 2006 (italics in original).

the 1968 rite does not include the phrase "to provide clergy, make new houses of prayer, and consecrate altars," it does refer to the candidate as "this Thy servant, whom Thou has chosen <u>for the office of Bishop</u>,"[100] which necessarily signifies the "three specific sacramental powers" of the office. Furthermore, it specifically refers to the office of High Priest, which is proper to the episcopal order, just like "ordaining clergy" and "consecrating Churches" is in the Coptic consecratory prayer.

In summary, the form of both the Coptic rite and the new 1968 rite is the single "formal-effective" sentence, namely, "pour forth...governing Spirit...whom He gave to the apostles...for the glory of Thy name." And since Fr. Cekada is persuaded by word counts, we note that the Coptic form (the true form, not the entire Preface) is actually *shorter* than the new form of Paul VI.

Thus, when a *true* apples to apples comparison is made between the *forms* of the Coptic and the new rite, any reasonable person will conclude that the *longer* form found in the new rite, is just as valid as the *shorter* one found in the Coptic rite, the validity of which has never been doubted by the Church.

Conclusion

From what we have seen, there is no reasonable doubt whatsoever that the new rite of episcopal consecration, if followed according to the form established by Paul VI, is valid. The ancient form dates back to the early centuries of the Church and may even be of apostolic origin. The form served as the basis for other approved forms in the Church, which even the Sedevacantists admit. And last, but certainly not least, Paul VI's new form was approved by some of the most learned sacramental theologians in the Church, including Cardinal Ottaviani, whose actions demonstrate that he would have not been reluctant to issue the Pope a negative judgment regarding the new rite of episcopal consecration if he found it objectionable, just as he did with the New Mass two years later. In light of all this, we can have moral certitude on the validity of the new rite of episcopal consecration. For one to question its validity reveals either a gross ignorance of historical and ecclesiastical facts, the error of skepticism, or a harmful Sedevacantist agenda.

---

[100] Latin, "*huic servo tuo, quem elegisti ad Episcopatum*" (emphasis added).

Chapter 19

~ The New Rite of Ordination for Priests ~

In this chapter, we will briefly address the new rite of ordination for priests, also implemented by Paul VI in 1968. In the Latin original, the only difference between the form approved by Pius XII and that found in the new rite of Paul VI is a single Latin word: "*ut*," which means "so that." The following is an English translation of the two forms.

> *Form approved by Pope Pius XII:* "Grant, we beseech Thee, Almighty Father, to these Thy servants, the dignity of the Priesthood; renew within them the spirit of holiness, <u>so that</u> ['*ut*'] they may hold from Thee, O God, the office of the second rank in Thy service and by the example of their behavior afford a pattern of holy living."[1]

> [Latin: *Da, quaesumus, omnipotens Pater, in hos famulos tuos Presbyterii dignitatem. Innova in visceribus eorum Spiritum sanctitatis,* <u>UT</u> *acceptum a te, Deus, secundi meriti munus obtineant; censuramque morum exemplo suae conversationis insinuent.*][2]

> *New Form approved by Paul VI:* "Grant, we beseech Thee, Almighty Father, to these Thy servants, the dignity of the Priesthood; renew within them the spirit of holiness. May they hold from Thee, the office of the second rank in Thy service and by the example of their behavior afford a pattern of holy living."[3]

> [Latin: *Da, quaesumus, omnipotens Pater, in hos famulos tuos Presbyterii dignitatem; innova in visceribus eorum Spiritum sanctitatis; acceptum a te, Deus, secundi meriti munus obtineant, censuramque morum exemplo suae conversationis insinuent.*][4]

---

[1] Pius XII, *Sacramentum Ordinis*, November 30, 1947.

[2] Latin at http://www.papalencyclicals.net/Pius12/P12SACRAO.HTM.

[3] Taken from Davies, Michael, *The Order of Melchisidech – A Defence of the Catholic Priesthood*, Harrison, New York: Roman Catholic Books, 1979; 2nd edition 1993, Appendix XI, The Form for the Ordination of a Priest.

[4] Ibid. Some sedevacantists attempted to create controversy over the form by also noting that the phrase "*in hos famulos tuos*" was used in the *Pontificalis Romani Recognitio*, while the slightly different "*his famulis tuis*" was published in the AAS (even though practically all of them would admit the difference has no effect on the validity of the sacrament).

Clearly, there is no difference between the forms of Pius XII and Paul VI, other than a conjunction represented by a single Latin word, and which occurs *after* the bishop asks God to grant the candidate the dignity of the priesthood. The difference is immaterial, and thus the subtle change in the new form in no way renders it invalid (or even of questionable validity), by any stretch of the imagination.

The Dimond brothers, of course, disagree. They claim that "the omission of 'so that' gives rise to a relaxation of the naming of the sacramental effect (conferring the office of the second rank). In other words, removing 'so that' *presupposes an ordination which has already taken place, but is not taking place as the words are being pronounced*. Since the new rite purports to be the Roman Rite, this removal of 'ut' (so that) renders the new rite of *questionable validity*."[5] This "relaxation of meaning" theory is another example of the proverbial "grasping at straws."

In the first part of both the old and new forms, the bishop imposes his hands upon the candidate's head and, while doing so, beseeches Almighty God to "grant" him "the office of priesthood." These words (the form) determine the matter (imposition of hands) by univocally signifying the sacramental effect (the grace of the office of priesthood), as accepted and used by the Church in that sense. There is no "relaxation of meaning" (whatever that means) because *there is simply no other way the Church understands the meaning* of the matter and form of this sacrament (imposing hands and beseeching God to confer the priesthood). Thus, the form is univocal and the sacrament valid.

Further, moving to the second part of the form, omitting the conjunction "so that" (between the first clause which asks God to renew in the candidate "the spirit of holiness" and the second clause which asks God to grant the candidate to hold "the office of the second rank") in no way "relaxes" the sacramental signification or undermines the essential sense of the words, for a couple of reasons. First, because the bishop has already besought God to grant the candidate "the dignity of the priesthood" while imposing hands. The matter and form of this action univocally signifies the sacramental effect of Holy Orders.[6]

---

[5] Dimond, Michael and Peter, *The Truth About What Really Happened to the Church After Vatican II*, pp. 112-113.

[6] St. Thomas teaches: "Now it is clear, if any <u>substantial</u> part of the sacramental form be suppressed, that the <u>essential</u> sense of the words is destroyed; and consequently the sacrament is invalid. Wherefore Didymus says (De Spir. Sanct. ii): 'If anyone attempt to baptize in such a way as to omit one of the aforesaid names,' i.e. of the Father, Son, and Holy Ghost, 'his baptism will be invalid.' But if that which is omitted be not a <u>substantial</u>

Second, because imploring God to confer "the office of the second rank" [second clause] also univocally signifies the sacramental effect, independently of the preceding request to renew the candidate's "spirit of holiness" [first clause].[7] In other words, the candidate receives Holy Orders through the words "dignity of the priesthood" and "office of second rank" (which are both univocal) and not by a "renewed spirit of holiness" (which is equivocal and happens in the other six sacraments as well). This means the second clause is not dependent upon the first clause, and hence the conjunction "so that" is unnecessary.

The validity of the new form was even conceded by the Sedevacantist writer Richard Ibranyi who wrote:

> "Some, using a semantic argument, say that the words 'so that' in the Catholic Rite ('so that they may obtain...') are left out of the New Rite; thus, the New Rite does not mention or imply that God is giving the candidate the power of the priesthood, and this makes it invalid. Yet, the New Rite, using different words, expresses that same thing... In both rites, God clearly gives the power to the candidate. After reading the form of the New Rite, only those of extreme bad-will would say that God is not invoked to give the candidate the power of the priesthood."[8]

We quote Mr. Ibranyi here because he acknowledges that he himself had been deceived by Sedevacantist authors regarding the validity of the new rites for episcopal consecration and ordination. He admits that he had fallen prey to their erroneous arguments, and even outright lies, without taking the time to investigate the facts for himself. It wasn't until he took the time to read the new rite that he discovered he had been duped. He publicly retracted his former position by saying:

> "This article is a correction of my former position. I had originally taught that Paul VI's New Rites of Baptism and Holy Orders for making priests and bishops are doubtfully valid. I trusted what others had written about it. When I investigated the New Rites myself, I discovered that many ... had lied about them, or, like myself, trusted what others said. I am learning the hard way not to trust what any so-called Catholic says .... They all lie! I say lie

---

part of the form, such an omission does not destroy the <u>essential</u> sense of the words, nor consequently the validity of the sacrament." ST, III, q. 60, a. 8 (emphasis added).

[7] This means that if ordination to the priesthood does not take place in the first part of the form, it certainly takes place in the second part of the form.

[8] "Validity of Paul VI's Diminished Rites" (July 2004) at http://www.johnthebaptist .us/jbw_english/documents/books/rjmi/br29_paul_vi_rites.pdf.

because when one investigates their teachings on this topic or that, one discovers that <u>they have deliberately left out necessary information and even lie about what they left out. They mistranslate quotes or take them out of context</u>. And worse, when they are presented with the evidence they omitted that proves them wrong, they ignore it as if it does not exist or mangle its true meaning, which only exposes their extreme bad will to those of good will, to those who have eyes to see and ears to hear."[9]

Attacking the "Intention" of the New Rite

Because the new form is virtually identical to the traditional form (and most Sedevacantists will thus acknowledge how silly it would be to attack the nearly-identical form), they are forced to attack the validity of the sacrament by attacking the *intention* of the new rite instead. They do this by redirecting our attention to the prayers and ceremonies which surround the form (the *significatio ex adjunctis*), and claim that these elements lack what is required, thereby preventing the minister from "doing what the Church does." They justify their position by drawing attention to the papal Bull *Apostolicae Curae*, issued by Leo XIII, in which he declared the Anglican episcopal consecration to be invalid. They maintain that what was lacking in the Anglican ceremony is also lacking in the ceremony approved by Paul VI. And, so they argue, because Leo XIII declared that this ceremonial deficiency in the Anglican Rite renders null the intention to "do what the Church does," the same changes in the rite of Paul VI render it equally null.

In other words, they attempt to argue that if the notion of the sacrificial nature of the priesthood was removed from Paul VI's new rite, and this omission invalidated the Anglican rite (even though Leo XIII focused mainly on the invalidity of the Anglican *form*), then Paul VI's rite should also be void (that is, the *absence* of certain surrounding language in Paul VI's rite invalidates an otherwise valid form of ordination). The argument may appeal to those who are looking for excuses to reject the post-Vatican II Church, but it will not appeal to those who are learned in these matters.

First, as we saw in Pius XII's *Sacramentum Ordinis*, Christ gave the Church the authority to determine the words of the form for the

---

[9] Ibid. (emphasis added). In his piece, Ibranyi proceeds to discuss all of the lies and errors spread by his fellow Sedevacantists, primarily those contained in the book *What Happened to the Catholic Church*, written by two sedevecantist priests of the C.M.R.I., Frs. Francisco and Dominico Radecki. Ibranyi demonstrates the utter falsehoods contained in the book, by comparing what these two Sedevacantist priests claim about the new rite, and what Mr. Ibranyi found when he read the new rite for himself.

sacrament of Holy Orders. Second, Pope Leo XIII, in *Apostolicae Curae,* concluded that the Anglican rite of ordination was invalid by first looking to the form, and not the surrounding ceremonies (*significatio ex adjunctis*). Pope Leo concluded that the form was defective with the defect of intention being *evidenced* by this defect in form. Thus, any argument "against" the new rite must start with the *form itself,* which we have already shown to be valid, and then, secondarily, the prayers surrounding the form.

To prove the point, Leo XIII in *Apostolicae Curae* commences his analysis by looking to the form of the Anglican rite. The Pope points out that the words "Receive the Holy Ghost" in the Anglican "*form* of priestly ordination...certainly do not in the least definitely express the sacred Order of Priesthood (*sacerdotium*) or its grace and power, which is chiefly the power 'of consecrating and of offering the true Body and Blood of the Lord'...in that sacrifice which is no 'bare commemoration of the sacrifice offered on the Cross.'"[10] Further addressing the *form* of the Anglican rite (and not the surrounding prayers), Pope Leo says the fact that the Anglicans later added to the form the phrases "for the work and office of priest" (for ordination) and "bishop" (for episcopal consecration) "shows that the Anglicans themselves perceived that the first *form* was defective and inadequate."[11]

Continuing to focus on the *form,* Leo noted that these additions ("for the work and office of priest/bishop") "must be understood in a sense different to that which they bear in the Catholic rite,"[12] because the Anglicans do not believe in the *sacerdotium* in the Catholic sense, nor that bishops have a higher status than priests. In fact, Leo XIII said it is "vain" to plead for the validity of Anglican orders on the basis of its "other prayers," just as we maintain it is vain to plead for the invalidity of Paul VI's ordination rite on the basis of its other prayers in that rite, as we will further demonstrate.[13] Thus, Pope Leo's *primary* focus is on the *form* of the rite itself, and secondarily its accompanying prayers and ceremonies (which should also be the case when evaluating the validity of Paul VI's new rite). Indeed, the *form* (the words or accidents) of the Anglican rite does not properly determine the matter (the meaning or substance), since the matter (which is the

---

[10] *Apostolicae Curae,* No. 25, *cf.* No. 31.
[11] Ibid., No. 26 (emphasis added).
[12] Ibid., No. 28.
[13] Pope Leo XIII said: "In vain has help been recently sought for the plea of the validity of Anglican Orders from the other prayers of the same Ordinal" (Ibid., No. 27).

imposition of hands) "by itself signifies nothing definite, and is equally used for several Orders and for Confirmation."[14]

After Leo XIII establishes the defect in form, he turns to the defect in intention. The Pope says:

> "With this inherent defect of 'form' is joined the defect of 'intention' which is equally essential to the Sacrament."[15]

Pope Leo then explains that where the *form* (and/or matter) of a Catholic rite is changed, with the intention of introducing a new rite which is not approved by the Church, there will also be a defect of intention. As applied to the Anglican rite of ordination, not only was the form not approved by the Church, but it is defective. Furthermore, the entire rite has been divested of the Catholic understanding of the priesthood, which also evinces a defective intention. Pope Leo notes that "in the whole Ordinal not only is there no clear mention of the sacrifice, of consecration, of the priesthood *(sacerdotium)*, and of the power of consecrating and offering sacrifice but, as we have just stated, every trace of these things which had been in such prayers of the Catholic rite as they had not entirely rejected, was deliberately removed and struck out."[16] As we will see, no such omissions occur in the surrounding prayers of the new rite.

Pope Leo concludes by reiterating the Church's sacramental theology on form and intention:

> "The Church does not judge about the mind and intention, in so far as it is something by its internal nature; but in so far as it is manifested externally she is bound to judge concerning it. A person who has correctly and seriously used the requisite matter and form to effect and confer a sacrament is presumed for that very reason to have intended to do what the Church does. On this principle rests the doctrine that a Sacrament is truly conferred by the ministry of one who is a heretic or unbaptized, provided the Catholic rite be employed. On the other hand, if the rite be changed, with the manifest intention of introducing another rite not approved by the Church and of rejecting what the Church does, and what, by the institution of Christ, belongs to the nature of the Sacrament, then it is clear that not only is the necessary intention wanting to the

---

[14] Ibid., No. 24.
[15] Ibid., No. 33.
[16] Ibid., No. 30.

Sacrament, but that the intention is adverse to and destructive of the Sacrament."[17]

Attacking the prayers surrounding the form (rather than the form itself) is the approach of our usual suspects, Michael and Peter Dimond. In their book *The Truth about What Really Happened to the Catholic Church after Vatican II*, the Dimond brothers set their table by providing the following lengthy quotes from Leo XIII's *Apostolicae Curae*:

> "Pope Leo XIII, *Apostolicae Curae*, Sept. 13, 1896: 'For, to put aside other reasons which show this to be insufficient for the purpose in the Anglican rite, **let this argument suffice for all: from them has been deliberately removed whatever sets forth the dignity and office of the priesthood in the Catholic rite.** That form consequently cannot be considered apt or sufficient for the sacrament which omits what it ought essentially to signify.'

> Pope Leo XIII, *Apostolicae Curae*, Sept. 13, 1896: 'So it comes to pass that, **as the Sacrament of Orders and the true *sacerdotium* [sacrificing priesthood] of Christ were utterly eliminated from the Anglican rite, and hence the *sacerdotium* [priesthood] is in no wise conferred truly and validly** in the Episcopal consecration of the same rite, for the like reason, therefore, the Episcopate can in no wise be truly and validly conferred by it; and this the more so because among the first duties of the Episcopate is that of ordaining ministers for the Holy Eucharist and sacrifice.'

> Pope Leo XIII, *Apostolicae Curae*, Sept. 13, 1896: 'Being fully cognizant of the necessary connection between faith and worship, between '*the law of believing and the law of praying*,' under a pretext of returning to the primitive form, they corrupted the liturgical order in many ways to suit the errors of the reformers. **For this reason in the whole Ordinal not only is there no clear mention of the sacrifice, of consecration, of the sacerdotium [sacrificing priesthood], but, as we have just stated, every trace of these things, which had been in such prayers of the Catholic rite as they had not entirely rejected, was deliberately removed and struck out. In this way the native character – or spirit as it is called – of the Ordinal clearly manifests itself.** Hence, if vitiated in its origin it was wholly insufficient to confer Orders, it

---

[17] Ibid., No. 33.

was impossible that in the course of time it could become sufficient since no change had taken place.'"[18] (emphasis in original)

After providing these quotations, the Dimond brothers go on to claim that the new rite of Paul VI has removed these same surrounding elements, which they claim renders the intention of the minister deficient, just as it does for the Anglican rite (even though, again, the Anglican rite is invalid primarily due to defect in *form*. Unable to attack the actual form of the rite of Paul VI, they divert the reader's attention to the *significatio ex adjunctis* by saying "The biggest problem with the new rite of ordination is not the form, but the surrounding ceremonies which have been removed," and then write:

> "In the Traditional Rite, the bishop addresses the ordinands and says: For it is a priest's duty to offer sacrifice, to bless, to lead, to preach and to baptize.' This admonition has been abolished. (...)
>
> 'Receive the power to offer sacrifice to God, and to celebrate Mass, both for the living and the dead, in the name of the Lord.' This exceptionally important prayer has been abolished in the New Rite. (...)
>
> In the Traditional Rite, the new priests then concelebrate Mass with the bishop. At the end, each new priest kneels before the bishop who lays both hands upon the head of each and says: 'Receive the Holy Ghost. Whose sins you shall forgive, they are forgiven them; and whose sins you shall retain, they are retained.' This ceremony and prayer has been abolished."[19]

Based upon their assertion that certain language was removed from Paul VI's new rite, the Dimonds confidently conclude: "The New Rite of Ordination specifically eliminated the sacrificing priesthood."[20] As we will see, the Dimonds' entire case proves to be nothing less than a blatant misrepresentation of the content of the new rite (haven't we seen this show before?).

Does the rite of Paul VI really "eliminate the sacrificing priesthood," as the Dimonds claim? Does the new rite really remove mention of the priest forgiving sins? Did the new rite truly "abolish" those prayers, or did it simply replace them with others that have the same essential meaning? Let's find out. The following is taken directly from the new rite of priestly ordination:

---

[18] Michael and Peter Dimond, *The Truth about What Really Happened to the Catholic Church after Vatican II*, p. 114
[19] Ibid.
[20] Ibid.

"This man, your relative and friend, is now to be raised to the order of priests. Consider carefully the position to which he is to be promoted in the Church. ... He is called to share in the priesthood of the bishops and to be molded into the likeness of Christ, the supreme and eternal Priest. By consecration he will be made a true priest of the New Testament, to preach the Gospel, sustain God's people, and celebrate the liturgy, above all, the Lord's sacrifice."[21]

Then the bishop says:

"My son, you are now to be advanced to the order of the presbyterate. You must apply your energies to the duty of teaching in the name of Christ, the chief Teacher. ... Your ministry will perfect the spiritual sacrifice of the faithful by uniting it with Christ's sacrifice, the sacrifice which is offered sacramentally through your hands. Know what you are doing and imitate the mystery you celebrate. In the memorial of the Lord's death and resurrection, make every effort to die to sin and to walk in the new life of Christ. When you baptize, you will bring men and women into the people of God. In the sacrament of penance, you will forgive sins in the name of Christ and the Church. With holy oil you will relieve and console the sick. You will celebrate the liturgy and offer thanks and praise to God throughout the day, praying not only for the people of God but for the whole world."[22]

To affirm the candidate's intent to carry on the tradition of the Church, the bishop during the Examination asks:

"Are you resolved to celebrate the mysteries of Christ faithfully and religiously as the Church has handed them down to us for the glory of God and the sanctification of Christ's people?"[23]

To repeat a phrase we've used before, "there you have it." Here we see that in the new rite, the priest is told to "celebrate the liturgy, above all, the Lord's sacrifice"; he is told to unite himself to the "sacrifice which is offered sacramentally through your hands"; to "celebrate the mysteries of Christ"; to "baptize," and to "forgive sins in the name of Christ." Yet Pete and Mike Dimond have deceived themselves and others into believing that this traditional language has been removed

---

[21] All quotations are taken from the translation by the University of St.Thomas, located in Saint Paul, Minnesota, at http://www.stthomas.edu/ratio/.
[22] Ibid.
[23] Ibid.

from the new rite! Then, after shamelessly advancing this falsehood, they wrote:

> "Thus, the following words declared by Pope Leo XIII apply exactly to the New Rite of Paul VI. Pope Leo XIII, *Apostolicae Curae*, Sept. 13, 1896: 'For this reason **in the whole Ordinal not only is there no clear mention of the sacrifice, of consecration, of the sacerdotium** [sacrificing priesthood], **but, as we have just stated, every trace of these things, which had been in such prayers of the Catholic rite as they had not entirely rejected, was deliberately removed and struck out**. In this way the native character – or spirit as it is called – of the Ordinal clearly manifests itself.'
>
> The New Rite fits this description precisely. Could anyone deny this fact? No, to do so one would have to bear false witness. The New Rite of Ordination specifically eliminated the sacrificing priesthood. The intention it manifests is therefore contrary to the intention of the Church and cannot suffice for validity."[24]

By evaluating Dimonds' accusations in light of the actual language of the new rite cited above, the reader can surely discern who is guilty of bearing "false witness." It's Mike and Pete Dimond. Had the Dimond brothers actually taken the time to *read* the new rite, rather than rely upon the words of someone else (an approach that is all too common among Sedevacantists), they would not have embarrassed themselves by publishing what they did in their book.

Sedevacantist Rama Coomaraswamy made the same false allegation in his book *The Destruction of the Christian Tradition*. He said "the primary function of the priest is to offer the immolative sacrifice," and then added: "Nowhere in the new rite for ordaining priests is it made clear that he is given the power to offer sacrifice..."[25]

This same falsehood is repeated over again by one Sedevacantist author after another. Here we see how the errors of the Sedevacantist sect can so quickly spread. One person makes a false statement, and others believe it and spread it, without taking the time to check even the most basic facts (which is the *modus operandi* of those driven by an agenda and not by the honest the search for truth). As we saw earlier, to his credit, Mr. Ibranyi did take the time to investigate the claims of his Sedevacantist colleagues. And when he did so *he realized that he had been deceived*. As noted, Mr. Ibranyi initially made the mistake of relying upon information taken from a book published by the two

---

[24] *The Truth about What Really Happened to the Catholic Church after Vatican II*, pp. 116-117.
[25] Coomaraswamy, *The Destruction of the Christian Tradition*, p. 335.

Radecki brothers, priests of the C.M.R.I. sect. After reading the new rite for himself, Ibranyi wrote:

> "Not only does the New Rite mention a true sacrificial priesthood, priests that offer sacrifice, but it also mentions a priesthood that blesses, guides, preaches, and baptizes ... <u>One wonders what New Rite the Radecki brothers are referring to</u>. They also present the *form* of the New Rite dishonestly and deceptively: 'The words of the form have been essentially changed and do not in the least definitely express the Sacred Order of the priesthood, or its grace and power, which is chiefly the power of 'consecrating and of offering the true Body and Blood of the Lord.'' The intention of conveying the power of offering the Sacrifice of the Mass and of the forgiveness of sins, which are essential to the priesthood, is not present.' As shown above, <u>the form of the New Rite has not been essentially changed, and it does mention the priesthood</u>: 'grant to this servant of yours the dignity of the priesthood.' The Radecki brothers <u>dishonestly</u> said that the form of the New Rite does 'not in the least' mention the 'priesthood.'"
>
> They also <u>deceive</u> the reader when they say that the form of the New Rite does not mention 'the power of consecrating and of offering the true Body and Blood of the Lord,' or 'The intention of conveying the power of offering the Sacrifice of the Mass and of the forgiveness of sins.' Yet, the form of the Catholic Rite [meaning that of Pius XII] does not mention these either. To be consistent, the Radecki brothers would also have to invalidate the Catholic Rite [of Pius XII] for the same reasons. Just because these dogmas are not mentioned in the *form* of either rite, does not mean they are not mentioned elsewhere in the rites, the ceremonial parts. They are."[26]

Again, we commend Mr. Ibranyi for his honesty in publicly correcting his previous error, which he embraced by relying upon Sedevacantist priests with an agenda for his information (always a grave mistake), rather than looking into the matter himself. When Ibranyi took the time to check the facts, he learned that these priests had, to use his words, "dishonestly" presented the material and "deceived" him.

Regarding the arguments against the new rite presented by the Dimond brothers, while there is much more that could be said, we will only address one more alleged "omission," which they claim invalidates the new rite. They wrote:

---

[26] Ibranyi, "Validity of Paul VI"s Diminished Rites" (July 2004) http://www.johnthe baptist.us/jbw_english/documents/books/rjmi/br29_paul_vi_rites.pdf

"In the Traditional Rite, the bishop then intones the Veni Creator
Spiritus. While anointing each priest, he says: 'Be pleased, Lord, to
consecrate and sanctify these hands by this anointing, and our
blessing, that whatsoever they bless may be blessed, and
whatsoever they consecrate may be consecrated and sanctified in
the name of Our Lord Jesus Christ.' This prayer has been abolished.
And this prayer was so significant that it was even mentioned by
Pius XII in Mediator Dei #43:"[27]

Abolished? Just as Mr. Ibranyi asked about the Radecki brothers,
"one wonders what new rite the Dimond brothers are referring to." In
the equivalent prayer in the new rite (which takes place during the
anointing of hands), the *Veni Creator Spiritus* is in fact sung, and "the
bishop receives a linen gremial and anoints with chrism the palms of
the new priest as he kneels before him." The bishop then says: "The
Father anointed our Lord Jesus Christ through the power of the Holy
Spirit. May Jesus preserve you to sanctify the Christian people and to
offer sacrifice to God."

So, contrary to the statements given by the laymen from Filmore,
New York, the new rite indeed contains an equivalent prayer to the
Holy Ghost. Even if one were to prefer or even hold that the former
prayer is superior to the one used in the new rite, this opinion would
have no effect whatsoever on the validity of the rite itself. In fact, while
the Dimonds claim the prayer for the anointing of the priest's hands
"was so significant that it was even mentioned by Pius XII," *the prayer
was not part of the ceremony for the first seven centuries of the Church!* As
Fr. Bligh notes, "the earlier liturgical book containing an anointing of
the priest's hands is the so-called 'Missal of the Franks,' a Mass book
compiled for the Cathedral of Poitiers early in the eight century."[28]
Later in the eighth century, "the anointing [of the hands] at ordinations
was banned by an Edict of Charlemagne!" Why did Charlemagne ban
the anointing of the hands? Fr. Bligh explains that he did so because
"He imposed the use of the Gregorian Sacramentary obtained from
Pope Hadrian. This Sacramentary did not contain the anointing."[29]

Thus, Peter and Michael Dimond's public assertion that the change
in the prayer of the new rite for the anointing of hands invalidates or
even causes doubt about the priest's ordination only demonstrates that
they clearly have not studied this subject in any depth. (Or,
alternatively, they *have* studied the subject in depth and have chosen to

---

[27] *The Truth about What Really Happened to the Catholic Church after Vatican II*, p. 115.
[28] *Ordination to the Priesthood*, p. 129.
[29] Ibid., p. 130.

lie to the public.) If they had studied the ancient rites, they would know that the bulk of the ceremony surrounding the ordination of a priest only gradually developed over the centuries, from the early simplicity of the apostolic times, to the complexity of the modern rite.

After all, during the early years of the Church, the ceremony for ordination was quite short, and yet it was obviously still valid. If you read the account of Paul and Barnabas' ordination, as recorded in Acts chapter 13, it appears to have consisted of not much more than the laying on of hands and a short prayer. We read:

> "Now there were in the church which was at Antioch, prophets and doctors, among whom was Barnabas, and Simon ... Saul. And as they were ministering to the Lord, and fasting, the Holy Ghost said to them: Separate me Saul and Barnabas, for the work whereunto I have taken them. Then they, fasting and praying, and imposing their hands upon them, sent them away. So they being sent by the Holy Ghost, went to Seleucia: and from thence they sailed to Cyprus. And when they were come to Salamina, they preached the word of God in the synagogues of the Jews" (Acts 13:1-5).

According to what was recorded in Scripture, this ordination ceremony was certainly not elaborate, and yet it was the approved primitive rite of the Church, and therefore sufficed to confer a valid ordination/consecration upon Paul and Barnabas. In fact, when we refer back to the oldest known ordination ceremony, which goes back to the midst of the apostolic age, we learn that they were actually quite simple and short. For example, following are the entire rubrics and prayers for the ordination of a priest as found in *The Statutes of the Apostles*, compiled by St. Hippolytus, which Schermann dates to the first century:[30]

> "In the name of the Father and of the Son and of the Holy Spirit, one God. This is the Sinódos of the fathers, the Apostles, which they ordered for the direction of the Church (...)
> Statute 23: Concerning the ordination of presbyters. If the bishop desires to ordain a presbyter, he shall lay his hands upon his head; and all the presbyters shall touch him and shall pray, saying: My God, the Father of our Lord and our Saviour Jesus Christ, look down upon this thy servant, and impart to him the spirit of grace and the gift of holiness, that he may be able to direct thy people

---

[30] *Cf.* Schermann, Theodor, Ein Weiheritual der römischen Kirche am Schlusse der ersten Jahrhunderts, (München, Walhalla-Verlag, 1913).

with pure heart: as thou lookesdst upon thy chosen people and commendedst Moses to choose presbyters whom thou fillest with the Holy Spirit which thou grantedst to thy servant and minister Moses, so now, Lord, give to this thy servant the grace vouchsafed to us, whilst thou fillest us with thy worship in our heart, to glorify thee, through thy Son Jesus Christ, through who to thee be glory and power, to the Father and the Son and the Holy Spirit in the holy Church now and always and for ever and ever.

And all the people shall say: Amen and Amen. He is worthy of it."[31]

Commenting on the above ancient ordination rite for priests, Fr. Bligh said: "The whole ceremony would take only two or three minutes."[32] And notice what is missing from the above prayers: there is no mention of offering sacrifice and no mention of absolving sins.

Now, since Michael and Peter Dimond pretend to be experts on sacramental theology, perhaps they should use their imagined expertise to research and pass judgment on the ordination ceremony performed by the Apostles to see if it lacks the necessary prayers that they erroneously claim are missing from the new rite of Paul VI. Then they can inform us if the ordinations performed by the Apostles were also null and void.

Doubtful Dolan and More Hypocrisy

Before concluding this chapter, we would like to show how a Sedevacantist bishop responded when a number of Sedevacantist priests expressed doubt about his ordination to the priesthood. The main accuser, Fr. Clarence Kelly (now also a Sedevacantist bishop), claimed that Bishop Daniel Dolan's ordination to the priesthood was "doubtful" due to a defect in the matter (the ordaining bishop allegedly only imposed one hand, instead of two). Fr. Kelly demanded that Fr. Dolan cease and desist saying Mass and administering the other sacraments, until he could clear up the doubt. This is a helpful analogy because, like the Sedevacantist thesis, it involves both a question of fact (Was Dolan ordained with one-hand or two?) and a question of law (Is one-handed ordination valid?). Let us see how this Sedevacantist priest-turned-bishop responded to Fr. Kelly's accusations. We will begin by reading the letter Fr. Kelly sent to Fr. Dolan:

---

[31] This is a translation of the Ethiopic text, taken from: Horner, George, *The Statues of the Apostles or Canones Ecclesiastici*, (London, Williams & Norgate, 1904) pp. 127, 143-144; For the Latin text see E. Hauler, Didascalia Apostolorum, Leipzig, 1900, I, pp. 108-109.
[32] *Ordination to the Priesthood*, p. 32.

"Dear Fr. Dolan,

In the course of the research which was being done in reference to ordinations and episcopal consecration, it was discovered that sacerdotal ordinations done with one hand are dubious, and in the opinion of two authors, the case would have to be referred to the Vatican for judgment. (…)

Since your ordination was done with one hand, we must hold your ordination to be dubious, unless evidence can be brought forth that the one-handed ordination is certainly valid.

We therefore urge you ad cautelam to stop saying Mass, hearing confessions and administering the sacrament of Extreme Unction until this problem is resolved.

Please understand that our position in this matter is based purely on the dictates of Moral Theology, and has absolutely nothing to do with the disputes which exist between us.

We further urge you diligently to research the problem, and to let us know any findings which shed light on this issue.

Yours in Christ,

Fr. Thomas P. Zapp (administrator)
Rev. Donald J. Sanborn
Rev. Clarence Kelly (Superior)
Rev. Thomas Mroczka
Fr. Jenkins
Fr. Martin Skierka.
Fr. Ahern
Fr. Paul Bamberger
Fr. Joseph B. Greenwell"[33]

Needless to say, Fr. Dolan wasn't too happy with these priests questioning his ordination. Dolan responded to Fr. Kelly in a letter that charges Kelly and the other accusers of being driven by personal malice, and declares them guilty of a mortal sin for blackening his name by daring to question his ordination publicly. But what's most relevant to our discussion is that Fr. Dolan rightly declares in his letter that Fr. Kelly has *no authority* to determine whether he is a priest, since such a judgment usurps the Church's prerogative to judge facts that determine whether one validly holds office in the Church. That's right, the Sedevacantist clergyman Dan Dolan correctly maintains that the Church alone is the judge of whether he is a true priest, even though

---

[33] Letter from Fr. Kelly to Fr. Dolan, September 21, 1990, http://www.scribd.com/doc/246398985/1990-Letter-to-Dolan-on-One Handed-Ordination.

Dolan also believes he can judge whether the Pope is a true Pope. A greater example of hypocrisy is difficult to imagine. In Dolan's own words, to Fr. Kelly:

> "**The Church, not Father Kelly, investigates and decides the facts**. Those impugning the validity of an ordination present their case to the Holy Office, which conducts an investigation, hears the evidence of all parties, examines the witnesses and establishes what the *facts* are. Let's repeat that: the *Holy Office* investigates, weighs the evidence and establishes the facts. Nothing there or in Canon Law about *Father Kelly* investigating, weighing evidence and establishing facts. Nothing there or in Canon Law about a priest having to answer 'evidence' *Father Kelly* finds convincing. Ditto for the rest of the clergy who signed the letter to me."[34] (emphasis in original)

Here we have a Sedevacantist cleric declare that the determination of whether he is a true priest is a question of fact that must be "decided" by "the Church" and not private judgment, which is *completely contrary* to his Sedevacantist judgment of the "facts" that the conciliar Popes are not true Popes. While the validity of Dolan's ordination under the traditional rite is a question of fact for the Church, whether the conciliar Popes are heretics is also a question of fact for the Church. Both questions concern whether one validly holds office in the Church (the office of priesthood and the papacy), of which the Church alone is the judge (as Dolan argues). In either case, "the Church, not Frs. Dolan, Kelly or Cekada, investigates and decides the facts" and then renders her legal judgment based upon those facts.

Thus, for those who wish to challenge the conciliar Popes' claim to the papal office (the Sedevacantists), they have to "present their case to the Holy Office, which conducts an investigation, hears the evidence of all parties, examines the witnesses and establishes what the *facts* are." Continuing with the words of Fr. Dolan: "Let's repeat that: the *Holy Office* investigates, weighs the evidence and establishes the facts. Nothing there or in Canon Law about *Father Kelly* [*or Bp. Sanborn, Bp. Pivarunas, Fr. Cekada, Frs. Radecki, "Brs." Dimond, Messrs. Lane, Daly, Ibranyi, Matatics, Speray, et al.*] investigating, weighing evidence and establishing facts. Nothing there or in Canon Law about a priest having to answer 'evidence' *Father Kelly* [or any other Sedevacantist] finds convincing." If such principles of equity and fairness apply to a mere

---

[34] Fr. Dolan's reply to Fr. Kelly, October 5, 1990. http://www.scribd.com/doc/246049783/DOLAN-S-REPLY.

priest, how much more do they apply to the Vicar of Christ? The question, of course, is asked and answered.

We would also like to ask Fr. Dolan "what Holy Office" he is asking Fr. Kelly to petition, since both of them believe the post-conciliar Vatican hierarchy has completely defected from the Church, and thus there is no "Holy Office." After all, when Fr. Dolan wrote his response to Fr. Kelly in 1990, Cardinal Ratzinger was the Prefect for the Congregation for the Doctrine of the Faith (the conciliar "Holy Office"), whom both Dolan and Kelly held to be a "public heretic" (and also later rejected as "antipope Benedict XVI" due to his "public heresy"). Dolan does not say he is writing hypothetically in his letter, nor does he suggest an alternative venue for Fr. Kelly to resolve the question in the event the Church has defected (query whether Dolan would have publicized a favorable judgment on his ordination from Ratzinger had he received one). Funny how Dolan would appeal to an authority that both he and Kelly reject. It is evidently quite convenient for Dolan to appeal to Church authority when it will help his case, but it is the same authority that he actually rejects (or claims to reject) in his daily life. Thus, the Dolan case provides us with an example of theological schizophrenia, which is part and parcel of the disease of Sedevacantism.

Although Dolan attacked Kelly primarily on the ground that he was usurping the Church's role to judge facts that determine who has received valid Holy Orders, Dolan's ordination also involves a question of law – that is, whether a one-handed ordination is valid. In another example of Sedevacantist duplicity, Dolan accused Kelly of basing his conclusion (that a one-handed ordination to the priesthood is invalid) upon his own private interpretation of theologians. In fact, Dolan accuses Kelly of shady and even deceptive research tactics, which we have proven to be the actual case with many Sedevacantist writers.

This is because Fr. Dolan took the time to research the sources that, according to Fr. Kelly, teach that a one-handed ordination is doubtful. Guess what Fr. Dolan discovered? He discovered that the sources do not actually teach what Fr. Kelly claimed. While we do not take up the question of whether the imposition of one hand suffices for ordination to the priesthood (leaving that question to be resolved by the Church), we find it interesting to note that Fr. Dolan himself discovered precisely what we ourselves have found in writing this book (and what Mr. Ibranyi also discovered), namely, that Sedevacantist writers (both clergy and laity) consistently misquote their sources and misrepresent their positions. Read carefully Fr. Dolan's criticisms of Fr. Kelly:

"You misrepresent what your sources say. You state that sacerdotal ordinations in which the bishop imposes only one hand are 'dubious,' and give page references to two works. I looked up your references. Neither writer – one of whom left the priesthood – states that ordinations so performed are 'dubious.' This is another example of how… (ellipses in original)

You play games with Canon Law to bully your victims. The ever-lengthening list of targets – Sr. Cabini, Thuc bishops, Mr. St. Michael's, yours truly – all receive this treatment, and your method is writ large in your latest letter to me. When you want to paint someone as a public sinner, excommunicated, doubtfully ordained or a schismatic, you find a sentence or two in a book by a theologian or canonist. You twist its meaning, and strain to apply it to your victim's actions. Then, even though it be the opinion of just one author, you present it in terms of 'Canon Law requires,' or "Moral theology says." You then proceed to condemn the victim outright, or claim that there is a 'doubt' present which renders his actions suspect, or even better, sinful. 'This doubt must be resolved,' you then say, 'and till then, Father So-and-so (or whoever) must be avoided.' From then on, discussion becomes a futile exercise in resolving *Father Kelly's* 'doubts' and answering *Father Kelly's* questions, all of them based on your twisted interpretation of one or two author's opinions, which interpretation, of course, you will never give up. Your methods may mesmerize your priests and both bedazzle and bully the laity (used as they are to following), but I'm not fooled and you won't bully me."[35]

Can a better explanation be given of the *modus operandi* of Sedevacantists, who sit in private judgment over the validity of the Church's new rites? And by a Sedevacantist, to boot! While Dolan rebuked Kelly for concluding that a one-handed ordination is invalid based upon his personal reading of theologians, Dolan and his colleagues do exactly the same thing in their judgment of the new rites of episcopal consecration and ordination. They personally interpret their theology manuals, and make judgments of law that are reserved for the Church. They "then proceed to condemn the victim outright," that is, all those who were consecrated and ordained according to the new rites (noting that the primary "victim" of the Sedevacantists is the Vicar of Jesus Christ). As Dolan unwittingly makes quite clear, the Church alone is the judge of the proper matter and form of a sacrament, and not individual Catholics.

---

[35] Ibid.

Fr. Dolan accurately describes the tactics used by Sedevacantists, as the readers of this book have learned. How many times have we demonstrated that Sedevacantist apologists "find a sentence or two in a book by a theologian or canonist," only to "twist its meaning, and strain it to apply to their victim's actions"? We have seen this in spades with their mistreatment of St. Bellarmine, who said "the manifest heretic is *ipso facto* deposed," but at the same time condemned the deposition of heretical prelates by private judgment (the Sedevacantists failing to understand the distinction between the Church's determination of the crime and the speculative question of when a heretical Pope would lose his office after the Church's determination).

Indeed, Sedevacantists will use "the opinion of just one author" (e.g., Bellarmine) and wrongly say it is the teaching of the Church, and, moreover, *while completely misrepresenting the opinion!* Their "methods" may "bedazzle and bully the laity" (who fall for their nonsense), but they are not going to fool and bully Fr. Dolan, at least when he is the target of such methods. In this case, of course, the Sedevacantist tactics were used *against* a Sedevacantist, Fr. Dolan, who spotted them at once and pointed them out. In other cases, however, Dolan uses the same shameful and dishonest tactics on his own "victims."

Finally, Fr. Dolan proceeds to explain how prudently and circumspectly the Church herself proceeds when the validity of an ordination is deemed objectively doubtful. Compare what Fr. Dolan says below with the scandalous and irresponsible statements of Fr. Cekada, who publicly declares the new rite to be invalid, causing untold scruples for many in the pews:

> "Your scandal-mongering contravenes Catholic practice. When confronted with possible defects in the administration of Holy Orders, the Church protected the individual priest from scandal and the loss of his good name before clergy and laity alike. Doubtful ordinations were rectified under the Secrecy of the Holy Office (which bound under pain of excommunication), or even under the seal of confession. In a case of the latter, Vatican officials concealed a doubtfully ordained priest's identity not only from his diocesian bishop, but also even from *themselves*; they provided for the priests to be ordained conditionally in confession, so that his status would be revealed to no one and that his good name would be protected.
>
> Thus the Church. But imagine how such an unfortunate man would have fared under your system. It gives running the gauntlet a whole new meaning. You issue an indictment based on phony references, demand 'answers' from the designated culprit, and – as

in my case – hint, eo ipso, that yet another public denunciation will soon be forthcoming should your demands go unmet.

Your methods are utterly contemptible and unspeakably evil, and you are blind to the wisdom of the Church."[36]

Fr. Dolan ends by saying: "In blackening my name by attacking my ordination, you have committed a mortal sin. You, Father, and your confreres each owe me a retraction – not an apology - but a retraction."[37] He then said: "You must also repair the damage you have done so far..."[38] and added: "I have enclosed a simple retraction and pledge for each of you to sign and return to me."[39] As far as we know, no retraction was forthcoming from either Fr. Kelly or any of his confreres.

Isn't it interesting to see how Fr. Dolan responded when his fellow Sedevacantists dared to question his ordination? Yet what Bishop Dolan declares to be "utterly contemptible and unspeakably evil," when directed toward himself, are the very same methods used to cast doubt upon the new rites of ordination and consecration themselves, even though they were fully approved by the Church. By doing so, are these Sedevacantists not casting suspicion upon *all* of the priests who have been ordained since the new rite was introduced? If "blackening" Dolan's name by "attacking [his] ordination" is a mortal sin, how much more serious of a crime is it to blacken the name of virtually every priest who has been ordained over nearly the past 50 years?

Isn't this, in the words of Bishop Dolan, "scandal mongering" of the highest degree, which blatantly "contravenes Catholic practice"? If "the Church protects the individual priest from scandal and the loss of his good name before clergy and laity alike" when the validity of his ordination is challenged, how much more would Holy Mother Church wish to protect from such scandal and loss the countless priests who have been ordained in the new rite? And what of all the laity who are now tormented by the doubt caused by the reckless assertions of Fr. Cekada and those like him, who many misguided souls have unfortunately chosen to trust?

But, of course, by declaring that most of the Church's priests are not true priests, Fr. Cekada does help to preserve the survival of his own little sect, since the scandalized sheep who blindly follow him will

---

[36] Ibid.
[37] Ibid.
[38] Ibid.
[39] Ibid.

feel themselves to be trapped, imagining that they have nowhere else to go for valid sacraments.

And it's unlikely that Fr. Cekada will change his current position as he did after first declaring invalid the episcopal consecrations of Archbishop Pierre-Martin Ngô Đình Thuc (d. 1984). Fr. Cekada reversed his position years later,[40] when he decided to recognize, as valid, the "Thuc line" consecration of his long-time partner Dan Dolan. By recognizing, as valid, Dolan's episcopal consecration, it helped to solidify their Sedevacantist community at St. Gertrude the Great parish. If the souls deceived by Fr. Cekada and the rest of the Sedevacantist clergy would spend more time prayerfully seeking the truth instead of drinking the Sedevacantist Kool-Aid, they would quickly recognize that the arguments presented against the validity of Pope Paul VI's 1968 ordination (and episcopal consecration) rite, are, in the words of Pope Leo XIII, "Absolutely Null and Utterly Void."

---

[40] Dan Dolan was consecrated to the episcopacy on November 30, 1993 by Bishop Mark A. Pivarunas, who was consecrated by Bishop Moises Carmona, who received his own episcopal orders from Archbishop Ngô Đình Thuc, the former archbishop of Hué, Vietnam. In January 1983, Fr. Cekada, under the pen-name "Peregrinus," wrote an article for *The Roman Catholic* magazine called "Two Bishops in Every Garage" in which Cekada makes a strong case that Archbishop Thuc's episcopal consecrations were invalid. Ten years later, Fr. Cekada would reverse his position. See, for example, his article "The Validity of the Thuc Consecrations" at http://www.traditionalmass.org/articles/article.php?id=60&catname=13.

Chapter 20

~ We Recognize and Resist ~

We now reach the final argument put forward by Sedevacantists. This argument does not directly support their own position, but is instead used in an attempt to force Traditional Catholics to embrace the Sedevacantist thesis. They do this by claiming that it is absolutely forbidden to recognize a man as being Pope, yet resist his commands or his teachings – even if the teaching happens to depart from what the Church had consistently taught up to that time. They insist that it is forbidden to judge the teaching of one Pope in light of the perennial teaching of his predecessors, or the dogmatic decrees of ecumenical councils. They declare this to be "sifting the Magisterium." With this approach, we see, once again, that an error in the beginning is an error in the end.

The Sedevacantist Bishop Donald Sanborn articulated the position as he attacked Bishop Williamson for defending the stance taken by Archbishop Lefebvre, which was one of,

> "accepting Novus Ordo popes, but at the same time of sifting their teachings and disciplines for what is Catholic, and rejecting what is non-Catholic. He says that to do so by one's own personal choice is equivalent to heresy, but it is not equivalent to heresy if one makes the choice based on a two thousand year tradition."[1]

Bishop Sanborn argues that this course of action is not permitted. Yet, judging the teaching of the conciliar Popes in light of the teaching of the previous Popes and councils *is exactly what the Sedevacantists themselves do.* They use the same objective measure of Tradition to "sift" (and reject) the novel teachings of the Vatican II Popes. The only difference between the position of the Sedevacantists vis-à-vis Traditional Catholics, in this respect, is that rather than simply rejecting any novel teaching that is contrary to Tradition, the Sedevacantists go *further* by declaring that the Pope who gave or approved the novel teaching is not a true Pope (and the Church of which he is the head is not the true Church). Thus, the position of the Sedevacantists as opposed to faithful Catholics is *identical*, right up to the final *additional*

---

[1] Sanborn, "Response to Bishop Williamson, On the Subject of the Vacancy of The Roman See," at http://www.mostholytrinityseminary.org/Bishop%20Williamson%20Response .pdf

step taken by the Sedevacantists, which, as we have shown in the previous chapters, is a step that exceeds their authority and separates them from the Church.

As we will see in this chapter, resisting novel teachings of Popes, which depart from the consistent teaching of the Church, is itself in accord with Tradition. It finds support in the writings of the Church's theologians and the teachings of the Popes, and there are many historical examples of the faithful – including saints and future Popes – doing just that.

St. Augustine, for example, appealed to the decision of a former Pope (Innocent I) against the currently reigning Pope (Zosimus), when the latter refused to recognize the previous condemnation of the heretic Pelagius.[2] Pope Zosimus essentially reopened the door to the Pelagian heresy, which had just been definitively settled by his predecessor. The famous saying *"Roma locuta est, causa finita est"* (Rome has spoken, the case is closed)[3] comes from a sermon St. Augustine gave against the wavering of Pope Zosimus in the face of heresy. In other words, St. Augustine publicly "resisted" the current Pope by appealing to the teaching of a previous Pope.

Before discussing the writings of the Popes and theologians on resisting commands and teachings of superiors (including Popes), it will be opportune to consider the virtue of obedience (which, like infallibility, has been greatly misunderstood in the current crisis).

Obedience

In considering the issue of obedience, we should begin by noting that obedience should be directed *primarily* to God, and only secondarily to the laws and commands of men. In other words, when we obey a particular law enacted by man, we ought to obey it with a view to obeying God. Pope Pius XI teaches that it is unbecoming for men, who have been redeemed by the blood of Christ, to obey man *for the sake of man*. He wrote:

> "It is for this reason that St. Paul, while bidding wives revere
> Christ in their husbands, and slaves respect Christ in their masters,
> warns them to give obedience to them not as men, but as the

---

[2] *Cf. Catholic Encyclopedia* (1913), vol. XV, p. 764.

[3] St. Augustine did not use the exact expression. The phrase is derived from the following sentence that has essentially the same meaning. "For already two councils [Carthage and Mileve] on this question have been sent to the apostolic see [Rome]; and replies [of approval] have also come from there. The cause is finished" (Sermon 131, September 23, 417 A.D).

vicegerents of Christ; for it is not meet that men redeemed by Christ should serve their fellow-men. 'You are bought with a price; be not made the bond-slaves of men.'"[4]

Now, although our obedience should be directed *primarily* to God, we are obliged by God to obey the just commands of lawful authority. If we sought to obey God without submitting to the medium of just laws, how would we be sure we were truly obeying God, rather than our own self-will? We show our obedience to God by submitting to just commands proceeding from lawful authority; and God tells us that those who fail to do so will be condemned: "Let every soul be subject to higher powers: for there is no power but from God: and those that are, are ordained of God. Therefore, he that resisteth the power, resisteth the ordinance of God. And they that resist, purchase to themselves damnation" (Rom. 13:1-2).

The Rational Mean Between Two Extremes

While we are bound to obey just laws of lawful authority, we are not to obey thoughtlessly and without discretion. We must recall that there is a hierarchical order to the virtues. The lower virtues are subordinate to, and meant to, serve the higher. The highest virtues are the theological virtues (faith, hope and charity), which have God for their object. As St. Thomas says, the theological virtue of "Charity is a greater virtue than obedience."[5] The cardinal virtues (prudence, justice, fortitude and temperance) fall beneath the theological virtues. Obedience, which is a moral virtue, is subordinate to (and part of) the cardinal virtue of Justice. As St. Francis de Sales said: "Obedience is a moral virtue *which depends upon justice.*"[6]

Like all moral virtues, obedience is a balance point – the *rational mean*[7] - between *excess* and *defect*, and as such can be violated in either direction - that is, by disobeying a just command (defect), or by obeying an unjust and sinful command (excess).

---

[4] Pope Pius XI, *Quas Primas*, No. 19, December 11, 1925.
[5] ST, II-II, q. 104, a. 3.
[6] St. Francis de Sales, *The True Spiritual Conferences of St. Francis de Sales* (London: Richardson and Son, 1862), p. 145 (emphasis added).
[7] "In this sense every mean of moral virtue is a rational mean, since, as above stated, moral virtue is said to observe the mean, through conformity with right reason" (ST, I-II, q. 64 a. 2).

Just and Unjust Laws

St. Thomas explains that "Laws framed by man are either just or unjust. If they be just, they have the power of binding in conscience, from the eternal law whence they are derived..." Regarding unjust laws, he wrote:

> "...laws may be unjust in two ways: first, by being contrary to human good...as when an authority imposes on his subjects burdensome laws, conducive, not to the common good, but rather to his own cupidity or vainglory - or in respect of the author, as when a man makes a law that goes beyond the power committed to him - or in respect of the *form*, as when burdens are imposed unequally on the community, although with a view to the common good. The like are acts of violence rather than laws. (...)
>
> Secondly, laws may be unjust through being opposed to the Divine good: such are the laws of tyrants inducing to idolatry, or to anything else contrary to the Divine law: and laws of this kind must nowise be observed, because, as stated in Acts 5:29, 'we ought to obey God rather than man.'"[8]

The unjust laws that St. Thomas refers to as "acts of violence, rather than laws" do not bind in conscience, "except perhaps in order to avoid scandal or disturbance."[9] The second category of unjust laws mentioned by the Angelic Doctor – namely, those "contrary to the Divine law" - can *never* be obeyed, but must be steadfastly *resisted*.

When the command of one superior is contrary to the command of a higher authority, we must resist the former and obey the latter. In such a case, resistance to a lower authority is not disobedience, but rather *obedience* to the higher authority. Pope Leo XIII said:

> "where the power to command is wanting, or where a law is enacted contrary to reason, or to the eternal law, or to some ordinance of God, obedience is unlawful, lest, while obeying man, we become disobedient to God."[10]

In another place, Leo XIII explained that those who refuse to obey unjust laws cannot be rightly accused of disobedience:

---

[8] ST, I-II q. 96, a. 4.

[9] Ibid.

[10] Pope Leo XIII, *Libertas*, June 20, 1888 (emphasis added).

"The one only reason which men have for not obeying is when anything is demanded of them which is openly repugnant to the natural or the divine law, for it is equally unlawful [for authorities] to command [their subjects] to do anything in which the law of nature or the will of God is violated. If, therefore, it should happen that any one is compelled to prefer one or the other, viz., to disregard either the commands of God or those of rulers, he must obey Jesus Christ ... <u>there is no reason why those who so behave themselves should be accused of refusing obedience</u>; for, if the will of rulers is opposed to the will and the laws of God, they themselves [the authorities] <u>exceed the bounds of their own power and pervert justice</u>; nor can their authority then be valid, which, when there is no justice, is null."[11]

In his classic book, *Handbook of Moral Theology*, (1916), Rev. Anton Koch further explains:

"Unjust laws do not bind in conscience because they 'are acts of violence rather than laws,' as St. Thomas says. In regard to the above, the following principles should be borne in mind: a) No one is obliged to obey a precept which it is morally impossible for him to fulfill. ... A law which runs counter to the moral law of nature, not only does not oblige in conscience, but must be resisted passively. <u>Authority</u>, be it civil <u>or ecclesiastical</u>, can never oblige a man to commit even a venial sin, for we must obey God rather than man. Such has always been the will and the teaching of the Church."[12]

Now, just as it would be wrong to obey a sinful command, or a command that is morally "contrary to reason," so too is it wrong to obey a command that is repugnant to the Faith. This is evident when we consider that the purpose of the lower virtues is to serve, not undermine, the higher. Faith, being a theological virtue, should never be put at risk under the specious pretext of "obedience."

Resisting Unjust Laws and Commands

As we have seen, superiors are not to be blindly obeyed in all things. St. Thomas said: "It is written: '*We ought to obey God rather than men.*' Now sometimes the things commanded by a superior are against

---

[11] Pope Leo XIII, *Diuturnam Illud*, 1881 (emphasis added).
[12] Koch, *Handbook of Moral Theology* (London: B. Herder Book Co, 1918), p. 166 (emphasis added).

God. Therefore, superiors are not to be obeyed in all things."[13] He went
on to explain why this is so:

> "As stated above, he who obeys is moved at the bidding of the
> person who commands him, by a certain necessity of justice, even
> as a natural thing is moved through the power of its mover by a
> natural necessity. That a natural thing be not moved by its mover,
> may happen … on account of a hindrance arising from the stronger
> power of some other mover; thus wood is not burnt by fire if a
> stronger force of water intervenes. In like manner … a subject may
> not be bound to obey his superior in all things. First on account of
> the command of a higher power. For as a gloss says on Romans
> 13:2…: 'If a commissioner issue an order, are you to comply, if it is
> contrary to the bidding of the proconsul? Again, if the proconsul
> command one thing, and the emperor another, will you hesitate, to
> disregard the former and serve the latter? Therefore, if the emperor
> commands one thing and God another, you must disregard the
> former and obey God.'"[14]

Now, this principle applies equally to a Pope, who is also a man.
Should a Pope command anything contrary to the natural or Divine
law, or to the common good (which must ultimately be ordered to the
salvation of souls), he must not be obeyed, but resisted. Suarez
confirmed this, when he wrote:

> "If [the Pope] gives an order contrary to good customs, he
> should not be obeyed; if he attempts to do something manifestly
> opposed to justice and the common good, it will be licit to resist
> him; if he attacks by force, by force he can be repelled, with a
> moderation appropriate to a just defense."[15]

Juan Cardinal De Torquemada, O.P. (d. 1468), who was selected to
represent the King of Castile and his religious order at the Council of
Florence, explained how broadly a Pope could exceed his authority, in
which case he must be resisted. He wrote:

> "Although it clearly follows from the circumstances that the
> Pope can err at times, and command things which must not be done,
> that we are not to be simply obedient to him in all things, that does
> not show that he must not be obeyed by all when his commands are
> good. To know in what cases he is to be obeyed and in what not, it

---

[13] ST, II-II, q. 104, a. 5.
[14] Ibid.
[15] Suarez, *De Fide*, (Paris: Vivès, 1958), vol. XII, p. 321.

is said in the Acts of the Apostles: 'One ought to obey God rather than man;' therefore, <u>were the Pope to command anything against Holy Scripture, or the articles of faith, or the truth of the Sacraments, or the commands of the natural or divine law, *he ought not to be obeyed*</u>, but in such commands, to be passed over (despiciendus)."[16]

Torquemada is clear that a Pope can exceed his authority in commanding things that are not only contrary to the natural law and common good, but also the perennial disciplines and worship of the Church ("the truth of the Sacraments") and even the dogmas of the Faith itself ("Scripture" and "the articles of faith"). In such a case, Torquemada's solution is not that of the Sedevacantists, which is to declare the Pope a heretic who is no longer Pope. Rather, it is to recognize and resist the Pope, who "ought not to be obeyed."

Torquemada then went on to quote Pope Innocent III, who said a Pope should not be obeyed if he goes against the universal customs of the Church:

> "Thus it is that Pope Innocent states (in De Consuetudine) that it is necessary to obey a Pope in all things as long as he does not himself go against the universal customs of the Church, but should he go against the universal customs of the church, he ought not to be obeyed..."[17]

Here, Pope Innocent III, who, as we saw in Chapter 8, taught that a Pope can "wither away into heresy," similarly teaches that the Pope can in fact "go against the universal customs of the Church" and when he does so, "he ought not to be obeyed" (*not* that "he must be declared deposed by private judgment").

Fr. Nicholas Gruner (d. 2015) had a great command of these principles. In his article "The Fatima Message and Problem of False Obedience," he synthesizes these principles as follows:

> "Now, since all authority comes from God, we obey men because - and *only* because - their authority ultimately is based upon God's authority. And this obedience, where it does not contravene God's law, is actually an act of justice - of giving to another, and ultimately to God, what is due. But God does not give any man the

---

[16] *Summa De Ecclesia.*, pp. 47-48, cited in Newman, John Henry, *A Letter addressed to His Grace, The Duke of Norfolk* (London: BM Pickering, 1875), p. 52.
[17] *Summa De Ecclesia.*, cited in Coomaraswamy, *The Destruction of the Christian Tradition*, p. 110.

authority to command, nor anyone the right to *obey* a command, that contravenes the commands He has given us, including the Decalogue and the law of the Gospel, which is the 'positive law' of Christ the King. Moreover, all authority on earth is limited by God's decree. Not even the Pope has unlimited authority. And we know the limitation of the Pope's authority by Revelation, Scripture, Tradition, and the teachings of the authentic Magisterium, both Ordinary and Universal, as well as the Extraordinary Magisterium in its dogmatic definitions."[18]

Negative Commands

Now, just as it is sometimes necessary to disobey a *positive* command (a command to *do* something), so too is it sometimes necessary to disobey a *negative* command (a command *not* to do something).[19] This is the case when obedience to a negative command would prevent a person from *doing* what justice and charity *demand*. For example, if a superior forbade an inferior from paying a bill that he owed in justice (and if the superior did not make other arrangements to ensure the bill was paid), obedience to that command would be unjust, and therefore excessive. In this case, obedience would not be in accord with justice or charity. For this reason, Pope St. Gregory the Great said:

> "Know that evil ought never to be done by way of obedience, though *sometimes* something good, which is being done, ought to be discontinued out of obedience."[20]

Notice St. Gregory does not say that which is good ought *always* to be discontinued out of obedience, but only *sometimes*; that is, when it is not contrary to justice to obey. This also brings up the notion of "blind obedience" which must be properly understood. Blind obedience does not imply that one must obey without discretion, nor that one must obey a command he knows to be sinful. As Pope Benedict XIV

---

[18] See http://www.fatima.org/news/newsviews/newsviews090910.pdf (emphasis in original). Note that Fr. Gruner also refers to Cardinal Ratzinger's comment on the limits of papal authority, who said: "The pope is not an absolute monarch whose will is law, but is the guardian of the authentic Tradition, and thereby the premier guarantor of obedience."

[19] We say sometimes, because it is never permissible to act contrary to the natural or Divine law, although it is sometimes permissible to act contrary to human positive law and particular commands.

[20] *Moralium*, bk. V, ch. 10, quoted in Coomaraswamy, *The Destruction of the Christian Tradition*, p. 121 (emphasis added).

observed, the notion of blind obedience is meant to check prudence of the flesh (craftiness and self-will), not the prudence of the spirit:

> "A superior is not to be obeyed when he commands anything contrary to the divine law, as we read in Gratian... Neither is a monk to obey his abbot when he commands anything contrary to the rule, according to the well-known letter of St. Bernard to the monk Adam. A blind obedience excludes the prudence of the flesh, *not the prudence of the spirit*, as shown at length by Suarez."[21]

Since man is by nature a rational being, he should not act irrationally (contrary to his nature) through a false notion of obedience. In the famous twelfth century Dialogue between a Cluniac and a Cistercian, we read that irrational service is not pleasing to God:

> "We must heed our superiors with complete obedience, even though they lead improper lives, so long as they rule over us and instruct us in accordance with the authority of divine law. If, however, they are so completely perverted towards moral ruin that they do not follow the authority of divine law in ruling over their subjects, but follow instead their own willful impulses and fancies, then let us, as scandalized and displeased subjects heedful of the dictates of divine law, flee from them as we would from blind leaders, lest together with them we fall into the pit of eternal damnation... Irrational service is not acceptable to God, as the Apostle tells us in commanding 'reasonable service' (Rom. 12:1)."[22]

Obedience to a sinful command will not excuse on judgment day. In a letter to Pope Gregory XI, St. Catherine of Siena wrote:

> "Alas, Alas, my most sweet Father...those who obey [evil pastors] fall into disorder and iniquity. Alas, I say this with sorrow. How dangerous is the consuming road of self-love [on the part of a pastor], not only because it destroys his own soul, *but also because it leads so many others to Hell.*"[23]

---

[21] Treatise of Benedict XIV, vol. III (London: Thomas Richardson and Son, 1882) pp. 59-60 (emphasis added).
[22] Idung of Prufening, *Cistercians and Cluniacs* (Kalamazoo, Michigan: Cistercian Publications) cited in Coomaraswamy, *The Destruction of the Christian Tradition*, p. 123.
[23] Lettres de Sainte Catherine de Sienne (Paris: Éditions P. Tequi, 1976), Letter I. Cited in *The Destruction of the Christian Tradition*, p. 115 (emphasis added).

The saintly Bishop Grosseteste who, as we will see later, was forced to disobey an unjust command of a Pope, wrote:

> "Those who preside in this most Holy See are most principally among mortals clothed with the person of Christ, and therefore it is necessary that in them especially the works of Christ should shine, and that there should be nothing contrary to Christ's works in them. And for the same reason, just as the Lord Jesus Christ must be obeyed in all things, so also those who preside in this see, insofar as they are clothed with Christ and are as such truly presiding, must be obeyed in all things. But if anyone of them (which God forbid!), should put on the clothing of kingship and the flesh of the world or anything else except Christ, and for love of such things should command anything contrary to Christ's precepts and will, <u>anyone who obeys him in such things manifestly separates himself from Christ and from His Body which is the Church.</u>"[24]

Epikeia

Continuing with the theme of lawful obedience to laws and commands, St. Thomas defines law as an ordinance of reason, for the common good, promulgated by one who has care of the community (that is, one in authority).[25] The purpose of law is to guide man in his actions, so that he will more easily attain the end for which he was created. Due to the Fall, man's intellect has been darkened and his will weakened. Consequently, man often errs in his judgment (defect of the intellect), and chooses what he ought not (defect of the will).

The law is intended to serve as a remedy for these defects. The letter of the law informs the intellect what should be done and what should be avoided, while the sanctions help motivate the will to choose correctly. But, since law is only a general ordinance which does not foresee all possible circumstances, it sometimes happens that a law, good in itself, becomes injurious, and therefore contrary to the intention of the lawgiver. In such circumstances, as St. Thomas teaches, "it is good to set aside the letter of the law and to follow the dictates of justice and the common good."[26]

This exception to the letter of the law is called *epikeia*, or "equity." First proposed by Aristotle and further expounded by St. Thomas,

---

[24] Memorandum 26; ed. Gieben, pp. 362-363; cited in *The Religious Role of The Papacy: Ideals and Realities*, 1150-1300, edited by Christopher Ryan, (Toronto, Ontario, Canada: Pontifical Institute of Medieval Studies, 1989), pp. 165-166 (emphasis added).
[25] ST, I-II, q. 90, a. 4
[26] ST, II-II, q. 120, a. 1.

epikeia is a moral virtue and a subjective part of justice,[27] which can be exercised toward both positive and negative laws.[28] Its purpose is to "defend the common good, the judgment of conscience, the rights of individuals ... from oppression by the abuse of power."[29] It should be noted, however, that one cannot appeal to epikeia to justify violating the natural law, nor will it ever render just an act that is, by its nature, unjust. It is used only when obedience to the letter of the law will be contrary to the intention of the law-giver.[30]

In short, epikeia is good old-fashioned common sense (right reason) applied during extraordinary or unforeseen circumstances. It is a much needed virtue during the present crisis in the Church, when the letter of the law is so often used by the wolves in shepherds' clothing to undermine the faith. In the current ecclesiastical crisis, one need not scruple when necessity requires that epikeia be applied. As St. Thomas taught eight centuries ago: *"Necessitas non habet legem"* ("in the time of necessity there is no law").[31]

We have various examples of epikeia in the Scriptures. For example, Our Lord violated the letter of the law when He healed a man (Mk. 3:1-6) and a woman (Lk. 13:14) on the Sabbath. And in the Gospel of St. Matthew, Jesus defended the Apostles when, being hungry, they violated the letter of the law by picking corn on the Sabbath. When the Pharisees, who were the legal positivists of their day, objected – "thy disciples do that which is not lawful to do on the Sabbath" - Our Lord defended them by pointing to David who himself violated the letter of the law out of necessity (Mt. 12:1-4). Thus, epikeia, which sets aside the positive law for the dictates of the common good (and salvation of souls being the highest good), was practiced and defended by Our Lord Himself.

---

[27] *Cf.* ST, II-II, q. 120, a. 1 and 2.
[28] *Handbook of Moral Theology*, Idem. p. 181.
[29] *Moral Theology*, McHugh, John and Callan, Charles (Wagner, 1958), p. 413.
[30] There is no question that epikeia can be abused, but an abuse does not undermine the licitness of the principle (which, for example, we saw with the Church's teaching on Baptism of Desire). As Fr. Lawrence Riley wrote in his Doctrinal Dissertation, the abuses "might contribute to an attitude that would scorn epikeia as merely a technique to evade the law. It is far from that. Its objective standing as a legitimate institute of Moral Theology is undeniable – its acceptance by all theologians, even the strictest, is amply evidence of that fact." Riley, *The History, Nature and Use of Epikeia in Moral Theology*, (Washington, D.C.: Catholic University of America Press, 1948), p. 138.
[31] ST, I-II, q. 96, a. 6.

A Pope Who Trys to Destroy the Church

Many theologians have speculated about the hypothesis of a Pope who sought to destroy the Church. They unanimously teach that if such an occasion were to occur, the Pope would have to be steadfastly resisted. Cajetan, for example, while rightly defending the thesis that no one has authority over a Pope, nevertheless explains that no authority is needed to resist an aggressor. He said:

"Although it is permissible for anyone to repel force from himself or his neighbor, with a force according to the standard of blameless response, nevertheless, it is not permissible for [just] anyone to punish him for resorting to force. Similarly, although anyone licitly could kill a pope who attacked him, while defending himself [from the attack], nevertheless, no one is permitted to punish a pope for homicide by the death penalty."[32]

Then, applying this to a Pope who would attempt to destroy the Church, he wrote:

"Therefore, you must resist, to his face, a pope who is openly tearing the Church apart, for example, by refusing to confer ecclesiastical benefices except for money, or in exchange for services. ... a case of simony, even committed by a pope, must be denounced."[33]

Cajetan's instructions reflect the common doctrine of the Church's theologians, who all teach that Catholics can *lawfully* resist an evil Pope, who seeks to destroy the Church, without having to commit the *unlawful* act of "judgment by usurpation," that is, declaring the Pope is no longer the Pope.

During the same period, another Dominican theologian, Sylvester Prieras, O.P. (d. 1523) also addressed the necessity to resist an evil Pope who sought to destroy the Church. He asked, "What should be done in cases where the pope destroys the Church by his evil actions?" He responded:

"He would certainly sin; he should neither be permitted to act in such fashion, nor should he be obeyed in what was evil; but he should be resisted with a courteous reprehension. Consequently, if

---

[32] Cajetan, Thomas de Vio – *De Comparatione Auctoritatis Papae et Concilii*, English Translation in *Conciliarism & Papalism*, p. 122.
[33] Ibid.

he wished to give away the whole treasure of the Church or the patrimony of Saint Peter to his relatives, <u>if he wanted to destroy the Church</u> or the like, he should not be permitted to act in that fashion, but one would be obliged to resist him. <u>The reason for this is that he does not have the power to destroy; therefore, if there is evidence that he is doing it, it is licit to resist him.</u> The result of all this is that if the Pope destroys the Church by his orders and acts, he can be resisted and the execution of his mandates prevented. The right of <u>open resistance</u> to prelates' abuse of authority stems also from natural law (...)

Second proof of the thesis. By Natural Law it is licit to repel violence with violence. Now then, with such orders and dispensations the Pope exerts violence, since he acts against the Law, as we have proven. Therefore, it is licit to resist him. <u>As Cajetan observes, we do not affirm all this in the sense that someone could have competence to judge the Pope or have authority over him, but meaning that it is licit to defend oneself.</u> Indeed, anyone has the right to resist an unjust act, to try to prevent it and to defend himself."[34]

After discussing at length the supreme authority of the Pope, Van Noort wrote:

"Finally, from the doctrine outlined above, one should not leap to the absurd conclusion that all things are licit to the pope; or that he may turn things topsy-turvy in the Church at mere whim. Possession of power is one thing; a rightful use of power quite another. The supreme pontiff has received his power for the sake of building up the Church, not tearing it down. In exercising his supreme power he is, by divine law, strictly bound by the laws of justice, equity, and prudence... It is possible, of course, as in all affairs governed by men, for abuses to creep in and for aberrations to occur."[35]

In his classical work, *Moral and Dogmatic Theology* (1859), Archbishop Francis Kenrick said the Pope's "power was given for edification, not for destruction,"and then added: "If he uses it [as he

---

[34] *Dialogus de Potestate Papae*, cited by Vitoria, Francisco de – *Obras de Francisco de Vitoria* (Madrid: B.A.C., 1960), pp. 486-487. Also see http://www.roman catholicism.org/duty-resist.html.
[35] Van Noort, *Christ's Church*, p. 283.

ought] from the love of dominion (*quod absit*) scarcely will he meet with obedient populations."[36]

It is important to note that resisting a Pope does not mean judging a Pope, who has no judge but God. In responding to several arguments attempting to show that a king or council is superior to the Pope, St. Bellarmine explains that a Pope who destroys the Church can be publicly resisted, but he cannot be judged, punished or deposed for such a crime. He wrote:

> "I respond: firstly ... no authority is required to resist an invader and defend oneself ... rather authority is required to judge and punish. Therefore, just as it would be lawful to resist a Pontiff invading a body, so it is lawful to resist him invading souls or disturbing a state, <u>and much more if he should endeavor to destroy the Church. I say, it is lawful to resist him, by not doing what he commands, and by blocking him, lest he should carry out his will; still, it is not lawful to judge or punish or even depose him, because he is nothing other than a superior.</u> See Cajetan[37] on this matter, and John de Turrecremata.[38]"[39]

We note that the above citation from Bellarmine about not judging the Pope does not pertain to a Pope who is teaching heresy. As we saw in Chapters 8 and 9, Bellarmine clearly teaches, along with Cajetan and others, that a Council could in fact "judge" a Pope who fell into heresy (who would then be deposed by God).[40] Indeed, Bellarmine says that "heresy" is "the only reason where it is lawful for inferiors to *judge* superiors,"[41] and this is why he says "a heretical Pope can be judged."[42]

Formal and Material Separation

As we saw in Chapter 8 and other chapters, the Fourth Council of Constantinople forbids anyone to separate from their Patriarch, based upon the alleged knowledge of a crime, before the matter has been

---

[36] Theol. Moral, p. 158; cited in: Newman, John Henry, A *Letter Addressed to His Grace, The Duke of Norfolk*, p. 53.
[37] *Tractatus de auctoritate Papae et Concilii*, ch. 27.
[38] *Loc cit*, bk 2, ch. 106.
[39] *De Romano Pontifice*, bk. 2, ch. 29, seventh reply (translation by Ryan Grant).
[40] We also explained in Chapter 9 how the judgment of heresy would not require an inappropriate judgment of the person of the Pope, but rather the materially heretical proposition.
[41] *De Romano Pontifice*, bk. 2 ch. 30, translation by Ryan Grant (emphasis added).
[42] Ibid.

settled by a synod. But it is important to make a distinction between a *material* separation and a *formal* separation. A *formal separation* would occur if a subject rejected his lawful superior and declared that the superior has no authority over him. A *material separation* occurs when a legitimate authority must be avoided for reasons of necessity. Such a separation is due to extraordinary circumstances, such as the need to protect oneself from danger. A wife and children, for example, can materially separate from an abusive husband if their safety is at stake, even though the husband has authority over them. Such a material separation does not require that the wife and children reject the husband's authority, as such, nor does it mean the wife has *formally* separated from the husband (i.e., by divorce).

Similarly, a person would be justified in separating from a prelate or even the Pope if he posed a physical threat. In this case, a material separation would be justified as a matter of self-defense, according to the natural law. The same principle holds true if a prelate or Pope poses a spiritual danger. In such a case, a material separation may not only be justified, but may be absolutely *necessary* (since our spiritual welfare is more important than our physical welfare). Such a material separation can occur without requiring a formal separation, as in the case of the wife and the abusive husband.

As applied here, to the extent that the Modernist prelates of our day (including the Pope) have posed a spiritual danger to the faithful (e.g., through ecumenism, liturgical abuses, novel doctrines, etc.), Catholics are justified and, at times, even compelled to materially separate from them *to avoid the danger*, while not rejecting their authority. On the other hand, Sedevacantists have *formally* separated from the conciliar hierarchy (the Pope and bishops) because they do not recognize them as holding valid offices in the Church, and thus reject their authority as such. Because their rejection of lawful authority is based upon their own private judgment and not the judgment of the Church, Sedevacantists embrace schism and come under the *anathema* of the Fourth Council of Constantinople.

Resisting the Exercise of Authority

From what we have seen, it should be clear that refusing obedience to a particular command of a lawful superior, or attempting to hinder him from harming the Church, does not require that we reject their authority to rule as such. St. Thomas makes the important distinction between resisting a superior in the *exercise* of his authority, and denying his authority to rule.[43] In his *Commentary on the Book of Galatians*, he wrote the following about St. Paul, who continued to "recognize" St. Peter as Pope, yet "resisted" him to his face. St. Thomas noted:

> "[T]he Apostle opposed Peter in the <u>exercise of authority</u>, not in his <u>authority of ruling</u>. Therefore, from the foregoing we have an example: for prelates, an example of humility, that they not disdain corrections from those who are lower and subject to them; while subjects have an example of zeal and freedom, so they will not fear to correct their prelates, particularly if their crime is public and verges upon danger to the multitude...
>
> The occasion of the rebuke was not slight, but just and useful, namely, <u>the danger to the Gospel teaching</u>. (...) The manner of the rebuke was fitting, i.e., public and plain. For this reason, St. Paul writes: '*I spoke to Cephas*,' that is, Peter, '*before everyone*,' since the simulation practiced by St. Peter was fraught with danger to everyone. This is to be understood of public sins and not of private ones, in which the procedures of fraternal charity ought to be observed."[44]

Using this historical example, St. Thomas indicates that the grounds for resisting a Pope's exercise of authority must be to prevent a danger to the faith ("the danger to the Gospel teaching"), which is necessarily harmful to souls. In such case, the Pope must not only be resisted, but if the danger is a public matter, he can and should be rebuked, even publicly. Commenting on the same event in the *Summa Theologica*, St. Thomas again noted that the public rebuke of St. Paul was justified:

> "<u>There being an imminent danger for the Faith, prelates must be questioned, even publicly, by their subjects</u>. Thus, St. Paul, who was a subject of St. Peter, <u>questioned him publicly on account of an imminent danger of scandal in a matter of Faith</u>. And, as the Glossa of St. Augustine puts it (Ad Galatas 2.14), 'St. Peter himself gave the example to those who govern so that if sometimes they stray from the right way, they will not reject a correction as unworthy even if it comes from their subjects. '"[45]

---

[43] This distinction, in fact, is the key difference between Traditional Catholics (who recognize the authority of the Pope to rule but resist his abuses of that authority in light of Tradition) and Sedevacantists (who deny the Pope's authority to rule). It is the difference between licit resistance and schism.

[44] *Commentary on St. Paul's Epistle to the Galatians*, 2, 11-14, lec. III (emphasis added).

[45] ST, II-II, q. 33, a. 4 (emphasis added).

The illustrious exegete, Cornelius a Lapide, also commented on the public rebuke. In his Commentary on Galatians, he said the rebuke of St. Paul was public "in order that the public scandal caused by him might he removed by a public rebuke." Then, a little later, he added:

> "For superiors may, in the interests of truth, be corrected by their inferiors. Augustine (Ep. xix.), Cyprian, Gregory, and St. Thomas lay down this proposition in maintaining also that Peter, as the superior, was corrected by his inferior. The inference from what they say is that Paul was equal to the other Apostles, inferior to Peter, and hence they all were Peter's inferiors; they were the heads of the whole Church, and Peter was their chief. Gregory (Hom. 18 in Ezech.) says: 'Peter kept silence, that the first in dignity might be first in humility;' and Augustine says the same (Ep. xix. ad Hieron.): 'Peter gave to those who should follow him a rare and holy example of humility under correction by inferiors, as Paul did of bold resistance in defense of truth to subordinates against their superiors, charity being always preserved.'"[46]

It is not a coincidence that God inspired St. Paul to record this event in Scripture. No doubt, God wanted it to be known that it is licit, and even necessary, to publicly resist a Pope whose *public* actions endanger the faith.

Correcting one who errs is an act of charity, provided, of course, the rules of charity be followed. St. Thomas explains that this act of charity should also be extended to prelates. In his *Comments on the Sentences of Peter Lombard*, he wrote:

> "Fraternal correction, being a spiritual alms, is a work of mercy. But mercy is due mainly to the Prelate since he runs the greatest danger. Hence St. Augustine says in Regula (n. 11, PL 32, 1384): 'Have pity not only on yourselves, but on them as well,' that is, on the Prelates 'among you who run a danger as high as the position they occupy.' Therefore, fraternal correction extends also to Prelates.
>
> Furthermore, Ecclus. 17:12, says that God 'gave to every one of them commandment concerning his neighbor.' Now, a Prelate is our neighbor. Therefore, we must correct him when he sins. ... Some say that fraternal correction does not extend to the Prelates, either because man should not raise his voice against Heaven, or because the Prelates are easily scandalized if corrected by their subjects. However, this does not happen, since when they sin, <u>the Prelates do not represent Heaven and, therefore, must be corrected.</u>

---

[46] Lapide, *Commentaria in Scripturam Sacram* (Vivès, Parisiis, 1876), ad Gal. 2, II.

And those who correct them charitably do not raise their voices against them, but in their favor, since the admonishment is for their own sake. ... For this reason ... the precept of fraternal correction extends also to the Prelates, so that they may be corrected by their subjects."[47]

Bishop Robert Grosseteste

One example of a prelate resisting a Pope in the exercise of his authority, while continuing to recognize him as Pope, is found in the life of the saintly Bishop Robert Grosseteste (d. 1253), a doctor of theology at Oxford. After reluctantly accepting the office of Bishop of Lincoln, Pope Innocent IV asked Grosseteste to appoint the Pope's nephew, Frederick de Laragna (an absentee priest), to one of the prebends of his diocese. The appointment would have enabled the Pope's nephew to receive an income from his diocese while living in Rome. Although Bishop Grosseteste was described as "probably the most fervent and thorough going papalist among medieval English writers,"[48] seeing the command as a clear abuse of papal authority, he replied as follows:

"It is well known to your wisdom, that I am ready to obey Apostolical commands with filial affection, and with all devotion and reverence; but to those things which are opposed to Apostolical commands, in my zeal for the honour of my parent, I am also opposed. By Apostolical commands are meant those which are agreeable to the teaching of the Apostles and of Christ Himself, the Lord and Master of the Apostles, whose type and representation is specially borne in the ecclesiastical hierarchy by the Pope. The letter above mentioned is not consonant with Apostolical sanctity, but on the contrary utterly at variance and at discord with it."[49]

He then proceeded to argue, first, that the particular command would disturb and confuse the purity of the Christian religion, and then added:

---

[47] IV *Sententiarum*, d. 19, q. 2, a. 2, cited in John Vennari's "Resisting Wayward Prelates," *Catholic Family News*, 1998 (emphasis added).
[48] Ryan, Christopher, *The Religious Role of The Papacy: Ideals and Realities*, 1150-1300, (Toronto, Ontario Canada: Pontifical Institute of Mediaeval Studies, 1989), pp. 161-162.
[49] Stevenson, Francis Seymour, *Robert Grosseteste, Bishop of Lincoln; a contribution to the religious, political and intellectual history of the thirteenth century* (London: MacMillan and Co., Limited, 1899), p. 310.

"It is not possible, therefore, that the apostolic See, to which has been handed down from Christ Himself power for edification and not for destruction, can issue a precept so hateful and so injurious to the human race as this; for to do so would constitute a falling off, a corruption and abuse of its most holy and plenary power. No one who is subject and faithful to the said See in immaculate and sincere obedience ... can obey commands or precepts such as this, even if it emanated from the highest order of angels; but he must of necessity, and with his whole strength, contradict and rebel against them."[50]

Grosseteste went on to say that it is due to his *obedience* to Christ, and his fidelity to the Church and to the Apostolic See, that he refused to obey the command of the Pope. He argued that the precept was contrary to the unity and sanctity of the Church, as well as the spirit of Christ and the good of souls. He argued that obeying the precept would tend to the destruction, not the edification, of the Church. He wrote:

"It is out of filial reverence and obedience that I disobey, resist, and rebel. To sum up the holiness of the Apostolic See can only tend to edification, and not to destruction; for the plenitude of its power consists in being able to do all things for edification. These provisions, however, as they are called, are not for edification, but for manifest destruction. They are not, therefore, within the power of the Apostolic See: they owe their inspiration to 'flesh and blood' which 'shall not inherit the kingdom of God,' and not to the Father of our Lord Jesus Christ who is in heaven."[51]

When Pope Innocent IV received Grosseteste's reply, he became furious. He said: "Who is this raving old man, this deaf and foolish dotard, who in his audacity and temerity judges my actions?"[52] But the prelates who were present (Cardinal Egidius and Giles de Torres, Archbishop of Toledo) had the courage to side with the Bishop. They said: "We cannot condemn him: he is a Catholic, yea, and most holy, even stricter in his religious observances than we are, and, indeed, he is believed to have no equal [in sanctity], still less a superior, among all prelates. This is known to the whole clergy of France and of England, and our opposition to him would be of no avail. The truth of such a letter, which has by this time, perhaps, become known to many, who

---

[50] Ibid., p. 310.
[51] Ibid., pp. 310-311.
[52] Ibid., p. 313.

have the power of stirring up many against us; for he is held a great philosopher, fully learned ... a zealous champion of justice, a reader of theology in the schools, a preacher to the people, and a persecutor of simoniacal offenders."[53] It is recorded that all of the others who were present agreed and took the Bishop's side, which is quite remarkable given that they were in the presence of the Pope.

The historian, Francis Stevenson, noted that Bishop Grosseteste's letter to the Pope was not an attack on the *authority* of the Pope, but only on an abuse of the *exercise* of his authority. In his own words::

> "It will be observed that the letter is an attack, not upon the authority of the Papal See, to which, indeed, Grosseteste repeatedly expresses his devotion, but upon specific abuses and corruptions connected with its exercise. The Bishop's desire is to purify and strengthen the Church, by eliminating from it all causes of offense, and occasions for falling. ... His method of controversy is, it may be noted, the same as it was in the days when he resisted the King's appointment of abbots as itinerant justices; he begins, that is to say, by citing the exact text, in the one case, of the royal mandate to the Abbot of Eamsey, and, in the other case, of the Pope's letter to the Archdeacon of Canterbury and Master Innocent, and from these particular instances he deduces, on the strength mainly of arguments derived from Scripture, conclusions applicable, in the former instance, to the general question of the invasion of the liberties of the Church by secular interference, and, in the latter, to the general question of the use and abuse of Papal Provisions..."[54]

Here we have an example of a saintly prelate disobeying the unjust command of a Pope. What we can learn from this is that in our day, when the Faith is being undermined continuously by prelates (including the current Pope), the faithful are certainly justified in resisting them in the *exercise* of their authority without, however, having to deny their authority to rule by declaring them deposed. Our Lord Himself warned us to beware of wolves in sheep's clothing, telling us that "if the blind lead the blind, both will fall into the pit" (Mt. 15:14). And the blind guides he was referring were the religious leaders of his day (Mt. 23:15-17; 23-24). But neither Our Lord, nor even the Apostles, declared that the religious leaders had lost their office. In fact, in the very same chapter of St. Matthew's Gospel, in which Our Lord declared the Pharisees to be hypocrites and blind guides (Mt.

---

[53] Ibid.
[54] Ibid., pp. 311-312 (emphasis added).

23:13-16), he acknowledged that they lawfully sat in the Chair of Moses (Mt. 23:1-2).

Refusing Assent to Erroneous Teachings

We have seen that obedience to particular commands (both positive and negative) and to general laws does not always oblige; that a Pope can and should be resisted if he seeks to destroy the Church; and that resisting a person in the *exercise* of his authority does not require that we reject his authority, as such (i.e., by claiming he has lost his office).

But what about the requirement of giving religious assent to the *teachings* of prelates, even Popes, when such teaching is clearly contrary to what the Church has consistently taught? Is it forbidden for the faithful to refuse to listen to such Popes, and to resist their novel *doctrines*, as Fr. Cekada and his Sedevacantist colleagues suggest? We have seen that we can resist unjust laws and commands, but what about resisting erroneous *teachings*? For example, what if a Pope were to teach publicly that abortion is permissible. Would Catholics have an obligation to accept this teaching, or would it be licit to reject it? If a Pope were to make a public statement (as did Pope Francis) suggesting that the souls of the damned are annihilated (which would mean there is no hell), are Catholics simply required to abandon what the Church has consistently taught about hell and embrace the novelty that is contrary to Tradition? Would that be reasonable?[55] To ask the question is to answer it.

Nevertheless, Fr. Cekada claims that Catholics can only resist a Pope's evil *commands* but not his evil *doctrines* and *laws*. To that end, Cekada accuses Traditional Catholics of "mindlessly recycling" a quotation from Bellarmine, who said "I say, it is lawful to resist him [the Pope], by not doing what he commands,"[56] to justify the recognize and resist position. Fr. Cekada claims we have failed to understand the true meaning of Bellarmine's quote, which sanctions resistance to evil

---

[55] As we've seen from the teaching of Popes Innocent III and Adrian VI, and the cases of Popes Honorius and John XXII, Popes *can* teach heresy (certainly a false doctrine that is later declared to be heresy) to the Church. We have also seen from Popes Vigilius and Leo IX as well as St. Thomas that heresy ("the gates of hell") is the only thing that could theoretically destroy the Church (but which Christ prevents through the gift of infallibility). Thus, we should not think it impossible for a true Pope to teach heresy, knowing both that it is not and never will be binding upon the Church ("the gates of hell shall not prevail") and our obligation to reject it ("We ought to obey God rather than man"), while still recognizing the Pope's authority ("who sitteth on the Chair of Peter").
[56] *De Romano Pontifice*, bk. 2, ch. 29.

commands, but not to evil doctrines and laws (as if this is the only citation used to support the Recognize and Resist position!).[57] Fr. Cekada's focus on this single quotation from Bellarmine in his writings is more smoke and mirrors. First, since Bellarmine teaches that individual Catholics cannot depose heretical bishops (or declare them deposed, which amounts to the same thing) and that a Pope can be judged by the Church for heresy – two teachings of Bellarmine that Fr. Cekada *denies* – Cekada is clearly not the best person to explain the "true meaning" of Bellarmine's teachings.

Second, as we will see below, Popes Adrian II and Paul IV expressly teach that a Pope can and must be resisted when he "deviates from the faith" or is "accused of heresy." Thus, the teaching that it is licit to resist evil Popes is not limited to their "evil commands" as Cekada contends, but encompasses *any* papal departures from the Faith (we also saw Torquemada condone resisting a Pope who contradicted "Scripture, the articles of faith, or the truth of the Sacraments"). Third, while Bellarmine (in the quotation cited by Cekada) uses the term "command" and not teaching, the distinction is irrelevant since some teachings are *practical* truths, not just speculative truths. When it is a question of a practical truth, does Fr. Cekada really believe it is licit to resist the teaching and command of a Pope *in practice*, as long as one accepts the teaching itself? For example, if a Pope were to teach that it is permissible for divorced and civilly "remarried" Catholics to receive Holy Communion, and then commanded priests to distribute Communion to such people, would Fr. Cekada claim it is licit for a priest to resist the command, but not licit to reject the teaching? Or again, would Fr. Cekada hold that it is licit for one to refuse to take part in ecumenical practices as long as they accept the teaching of ecumenism (which is not at all clearly defined), upon which the practice is based? Such a notion is absurd and contrary to the practice of the saints.

History provides us with a clear example of prelates (including three saints and a future Pope) resisting the teaching of a Pope which had a practical application. And, in this case, the practical aspect (the discipline) was rejected as being "a declaration of formal heresy."[58] The Pope was Paschal II and the issue at hand was lay investitures (i.e., who has the authority to appoint the clergy – the Emperor or the Church?). Pope Gregory VII, Paschal's immediate predecessor, had

---

[57] See, for example, Cekada, "The Bellarmine 'Resistance' Quote: Another Traditionalist Myth," http://www.traditionalmass.org/articles/article.php?id =67&catname=10.
[58] Mann, Horace, *Lives of the Pope*, vol. VIII (London: K. Paul, Trench, Trübner, & Co., ltd, 1902), p. 62.

condemned lay investiture and excommunicated the Emperor, Henry IV, over the matter. When Pope Gregory and Henry IV died, the newly-elected Paschal II, under duress, entered into an agreement with Henry V (the previous Emperor's son) in which he conceded to him the right of investiture. This provoked the outrage of both the hierarchy and laity. In fact, "Paschal was denounced by many as if he were a heretic."[59]

Three men who would later be canonized (Bruno of Cologne, Hugh of Grenoble, and Godfrey of Amiens), as well as the future Pope Callistus II, all demanded that Pope Paschal renounce the agreement. They didn't simply resist the practical matter, but resisted the agreement itself. Because they considered the matter so serious, they informed the Pope that if he refused to renounce the agreement "we will be obliged to withdraw our allegiance from you."[60] In the end, the Pope admitted he was wrong. "I confess that I failed," declared the repentant Pope, "and ask you to pray to God to pardon me."[61] In response, St. Bruno said:

> "God be praised! For behold that it is the Pope himself, who condemned this pretended privilege (of investiture by the temporal power), which is heretical."[62]

Here we see faithful Catholics (including saints and a future Pope) *rejecting* a disciplinary teaching of a Pope (a teaching with a practical application) as being *heretical*. They did not accept the teaching, as well as resisted the practice.

As we saw in Chapter 13, the *religious assent* that is owed to non-infallible teachings of a Pope is not an act of faith, but a lesser act of obedience. As with all acts of obedience, religious assent is not unconditional, but permits of exceptions. And an exception would certainly be warranted (here, a *refusal* of religious assent) if a non-infallible teaching of a Pope were directly contrary to an infallible teaching of one or more of his predecessors, or even if it were at variance with what the Church has consistently taught.

The anti-Modernist Jesuit, Christian Pesch (d. 1925), whom we've quoted before, explains that the religious assent owed to non-infallible

---

[59] Ibid.
[60] Coomaraswamy, *The Destruction of the Christian Tradition*, p. 125.
[61] Ibid.
[62] Hefele, Charles-Joseph – LECLERCQ, Dom H. – *Histoire des Conciles* (Paris: Letouzey, 1912), vol. V, pt. 1, p. 555.

teachings of a Pope can be withheld when a *sufficient motive* for doubt arises:

> "(...) one must assent to the decrees of the Roman congregations, as long as it does not become positively sure that they have erred. Since the Congregations, *per se*, do not furnish an absolutely certain argument in favor of a given doctrine, one may or even must investigate the reasons for that doctrine. And thus, either it will come to pass that such a doctrine will be gradually accepted in the whole Church, attaining in this way the condition of infallibility, or it will happen that the error is little by little detected. For, since the religious assent referred to is not based on a metaphysical certainty, but only a moral and general one, it does not exclude all suspicion of error. For this reason, as soon as there arises sufficient motives for doubt, the assent will be prudently suspended: nevertheless, as long as such motives for doubt do not arise, the authority of the Congregations is sufficient to oblige one to assent. The same principles apply without difficulty to the declarations which the Supreme Pontiff emits without involving his supreme [infallible] authority, as well as the decisions of the other ecclesiastical superiors who are not infallible."[63]

Franz Diekamp also explains that the *obedience* (religious assent of mind and will) owed to the non-infallible acts of the Papal Magisterium permits of exceptions:

> "These non-infallible acts of the Magisterium of the Roman Pontiff do not oblige one to believe, and do not postulate an absolute and definitive subjection. But it behooves one to adhere with a religious and internal assent to such decisions, since they constitute acts of the supreme Magisterium of the Church, and are founded upon solid natural and supernatural reasons. The obligation to adhere to them can only begin to terminate in case, and this only occurs very rarely, a man fit to judge such a question, after a repeated and very diligent analysis of all the arguments, arrives at the conviction that an error has been introduced into the decision."[64]

Merkelbach teaches the same in his highly respected work, *Summa Theologiae Moralis*:

---

[63] Pesch, *Praelectiones Dogmaticae.*, vol. I, (Freiburg: Herder & Herder, 1898), pp. 314-315 (emphasis added).

[64] Diekamp, *Theologiae Dogmaticae Manual*, vol. I (Desclee, Parisiis – Tornaci-Romae, 1933), p. 72 (emphasis added).

"When the Church does not teach with her infallible authority, the doctrine proposed is not, as such, unreformable; for this reason, if *per accidens*, in a hypothesis which is however very rare, after a very careful examination of the matter, it appears to someone that there exist very grave reasons contrary to the doctrine thus proposed, it will be licit, without falling into temerity, to suspend internal assent (…)"[65]

Now, the Sedevacantists themselves concede that there are "sufficient motives" and "grave reasons" to believe that "error has been introduced into" certain teachings of the post-conciliar Popes, which deviate from what the Church has traditionally taught (religious liberty, ecumenism, collegiality, etc.). Where their reaction differs from the reaction of Traditional Catholics (not to mention the saints of the Church) is that they don't merely resist the novel teachings, which they could easily justify by the writings of the Church's theologians. No, they go further by declaring, on their own authority, that those who have "introduced" these "errors" have lost their office, and then separate from them. As we've seen, this "judgment by usurpation" is rejected by the entire Catholic tradition, and is explicitly condemned by the Fourth Council of Constantinople, as we have seen in previous chapters.

The duty to resist novel teachings and practices (even those of a Pope) has been the constant teaching of the Church's theologians, and a practice that has occurred throughout the Church's history (each and every time a Pope has deviated from the Faith, he has been resisted). In fact, St. Bellarmine cites *Divine law* (Jn. 10, Mt. 7, Gal. 1) to show that heretical bishops should not be listened to by the people (they are "resisted"). He also notes, however, that according to tradition, heretical bishops can only be deposed by the proper authorities (they are "recognized"). This shows that one can refuse to listen to a heretical bishop (and even explicitly reject his erroneous teachings) without, however, having to maintain that he has lost his office. In other words, Bellarmine instructs us to *recognize* and *resist* heretical prelates, and he bases his instruction on revealed truth.

Once again, as we saw in Chapter 10, Bellarmine says:

"We must point out, besides, that the faithful can certainly distinguish a true prophet (teacher) from a false one, by the rule that we have laid down, but for all that, if the pastor is a bishop, they

---

[65] Merkelbach, *Summa Theologiae Moralis*, Vol 1. (Desclee, Parisiis, 1931), p. 601 (emphasis added).

cannot depose him and put another in his place [recognize]. For Our Lord and the Apostles only lay down that false prophets are not to be listened to by the people [resist], and not that they depose them [recognize]. And it is certain that the practice of the Church has always been that heretical bishops be deposed by bishop's councils, or by the Sovereign Pontiff."[66]

If a bishop is found teaching strange, novel, or apparently heretical doctrines, he should not be listened to. He should be ignored. Listening to such a one is a danger to one's faith, and therefore an occasion of sin. Since we are required to avoid occasions of sin, we are justified in not listening to bishops who teach errors, or even heresies. The same holds true for a Pope who deviates from the Faith, which is possible as long as he is not defining a doctrine to be held by the universal Church, since it is only then that the charism of infallibility will prevent him from erring. As we have seen, when not defining a doctrine, Popes can teach, and indeed have taught, error. In such cases, which have become too common in the conciliar crisis, these Popes can and must be resisted.

In addition to the theologians we have cited, we also have the authority of a papal Bull which explicitly teaches that a Pope who deviates from the Faith can be resisted. The following is taken from the Bull of Paul IV, *Cum Ex Apostolatus Officio*:

"In assessing Our duty and the situation now prevailing, We have been weighed upon by the thought that a matter of this kind is so grave and so dangerous [to the Faith] that the Roman Pontiff, who is the representative upon earth of God and our God and Lord Jesus Christ, who holds the fullness of power over peoples and kingdoms, who may judge all and be judged by none in this world, may nonetheless be contradicted if he be found to have deviated from the Faith."[67]

Notice, Pope Paul IV does not say a *former* Pope (who lost his office due to heresy) can be contradicted if he deviates from the Faith. No, he says "the Roman Pontiff, who is the representative upon earth of God ... may nonetheless be contradicted if he be found to have deviated from the Faith." The notion that Catholics cannot *recognize* and *resist* a Pope who deviates from the Faith is entirely contrary to Tradition, and a novelty of the Sedevacantists' own making, just like their novel

---

[66] *De Membris Ecclesiae*, Lib. I *De Clericis*, cap. 7. (Opera Omnia; Paris: Vivès, 1870) pp 428-429.
[67] Pope Paul IV, *Cum Ex Apostolatus Officio*, February 15, 1559 (emphasis added).

solution that Catholics in the street can publicly declare that a Pope has lost his office, simply because they *personally believe* he is a heretic. These ideas are anything but Catholic.

Needless to say, the "deviations" from the Faith that we must reject include *all* errors against the Faith, and most especially heresies, which are the greatest deviations from the Faith. Pope Adrian II (d. 872) clearly teaches this principle when he wrote:

> "We read that the Roman Pontiff has always possessed authority to pass judgment on the heads of all the Churches (i.e., the patriarchs and bishops), but nowhere do we read that he has been the subject of judgment by others. It is true that Honorius was posthumously anathematised by the Eastern churches, <u>but it must be borne in mind that he had been accused of **heresy**, the only offense which renders lawful the **resistance** of subordinates to their superiors, and their rejection of the latter's pernicious teachings</u>. "[68]

Here we have a Pope who specifically uses the word "resistance" in the context of opposing "heresy," which means resistance is not limited to papal commands or even papal laws. This also means Traditional Catholics don't merely rely upon the single quote from St. Bellarmine to support the recognize and resist position as Fr. Cekada suggests, but rather the teaching of two Popes and numerous other theologians, not to mention common sense – a natural virtue that is lacking among the Sedevacantists.

Primary and Secondary Rule of Faith

To further assist our understanding of why it is lawful and necessary to resist papal errors and heresies against Church doctrine and morals, it is important to understand the proper distinction between the rules of faith. St. Thomas explains why it is that we must resist the preaching of a prelate when it is contrary to the Faith, by distinguishing between the primary and the secondary rule of faith. The word rule (Latin: *regula*; Greek: *kanon*) means a standard by which something is measured. The primary rule of faith is the Deposit of Faith (revelation contained in Scripture and Tradition); the secondary rule of faith is the Magisterium, who is to teach and explain what is contained

---

[68] Adrian II, alloc, III, lecta in conc. VIII, "et. 7, cited by, Billot, – *Tractatus de Ecclesia Christi* (Rome: Gregoriana, 1921), vol. I, p. 611; see also: Hefele, Charles-Joseph – LECLERCQ, Dom H. – *Histoire des Conciles* (Paris: Letouzey, 1912), vol. V, pp. 471-472 (emphasis added).

in the revealed Deposit. St. Thomas explains that if the secondary rule deviates from the primary rule, it is not to be followed. He says:

> "A man should submit to the lower authority in so far as the latter observes the order of the higher authority. If the lower authority departs from the order of the higher, we ought not to submit to it…"[69]

St. Thomas also explains how the faithful are able to discern such a deviation. He notes that the *habit* of faith (the supernatural virtue of faith) gives the faithful an inclination contrary to such errors. This explains how those with the faith are able to discern when a prelate is teaching errors (even if they don't know exactly how to refute them). It also explains why "Catholics" on the Left (who have lost the Faith) are utterly blind to such a reality. In his commentary on the Sentences of Peter Lombard, St. Thomas wrote:

> "Because a man ought to obey a lower power in those things only which are not opposed to the higher power; so even a man ought to adapt himself to the rule in all things according to its mode; on the other hand, a man ought to adapt himself to the secondary rule in those things which are not at variance with the primary rule: because in those matters in which it is at variance, it is not a rule: On that account, one is not to give assent to the preaching of a prelate which is contrary to the faith since in this it is discordant with the primary rule. Nor through ignorance is a subject excused from the whole: since the habit of faith causes an inclination to the contrary, since it teaches necessarily of all things that pertain to salvation."[70]

In another place, St. Thomas also says "we believe the successors of the apostles," that is, the secondary rule, *"only in so far as they tell us those things which the apostles and prophets have left in their writings,"*[71] which is the primary rule. If the secondary rule (Pope; bishops; Magisterium) deviates from the primary rule (Deposit of Faith), the secondary rule must not be followed. And if, during a time of crisis, God permits the secondary rule to obscure the primary rule through ambiguous and/or contradictory teachings, prudence dictates that the faithful look to the past, when the secondary rule taught the primary

---

[69] ST, II-II q. 69, a. 3, ad. 1.
[70] Commento Sent. P. Lombardo, vol. 6, (Bologna: PDUL - Edizioni Studio Domenicano, 2000), p. 198 (translated by Ryan Grant).
[71] St. Thomas, *De Veritate*, q. 14, a. 10 (emphasis added). http://www.dhspriory.org/thomas/QDdeVer14.htm#9.

rule with clarity. It is interesting to note that Fr. Culleton, in his book *The Prophets and Our Times* (1941), stated that the chastisement will be brought about due to the Magisterium (the secondary rule) failing "to preach God's word" (the primary rule).[72]

In Chapter 8, we considered the historical example of John XXII, who publicly professed an error (later condemned as a heresy) contrary to Tradition. This error was resisted by a large portion of the Church, even though the Pope attempted to impose it upon the Church (but without using his full authority). In the end, the Pope conceded that he was wrong and renounced the error on his deathbed. Those who resisted him were proven correct, and those who defended the Pope were forced to renounce their error. The victory was with the resistors, not with those who blindly followed the teaching of the Pope. The matter was settled definitively by John XXII's immediately successor, who quickly condemned the teaching of John XXII as being heretical. This historical example proves that a Pope can err in teaching the Faith, and that Catholics can and must *resist* such a Pope *and his erroneous teachings*, while continuing to *recognize* him as holding the papal office.

Hold to Tradition

In St. Paul's second letter to the Thessalonians, he discusses the great apostasy that will precede the rise of the antichrist. He notes that because men of that day will lack love for the truth, God will punish them by sending them "the operation of error to believe lying: That all may be judged who have not believed the truth" (2Thess. 2:10). St. Paul then gives the Thessalonians the antidote, so to speak, that will enable them to avoid being led astray. What is the antidote? It is holding fast to Scripture and Tradition – that is, the Deposit of Faith (the *primary* rule of Faith). He said: "therefore, brethren, stand fast, and hold to the traditions which you have learned, whether by word or by our epistle" (v.14).

Notice that St. Paul doesn't tell the faithful to hold fast to the secondary rule, which could be corrupted by "the operation of error." Rather, he tells them to hold to the primary rule, which they "have learned" from the Apostles and their successors, that is, what has always been believed and taught by the Church. Indeed, holding to Tradition has been the antidote to all of the doctrinal crises in the Church, and will surely be the solution to the current crisis.

---

[72] Culleton, *The Prophets and Our Times* (Rockford, Illinois: TAN Books and Publishers, Inc., 1974), p. 76.

Following the divine injunction of St. Paul, St. Vincent of Lerins wrote, four centuries later:

> "Now in the Catholic Church itself we take the greatest care to hold that which has been believed everwhere, always, and by all. That is truly and properly 'Catholic,' as is shown by the very force and meaning of the word, which comprehends everything almost universally. We shall hold to this rule if we follow universality, antiquity, and consent. We shall follow universality if we acknowledge that one Faith to be true which the whole Church throughout the world confesses; antiquity, if we in no wise depart from those interpretations which it is clear that our ancestors and fathers proclaimed; consent, if in antiquity itself we keep and follow the definitions and opinions of all, or certainly nearly all, bishops and doctors alike." [73]

Then, he asked what Catholics should do if the entire Church was infected by a "novel contagion" - a condition that accurately describes the state of the post-Vatican II Church. St. Vincent explained that if such were to occur, the safe path is not to depose by private judgment those responsible for the contagion, but rather to "cleave to antiquity" (Tradition). He wrote:

> "What then will the Catholic Christian do, if a small part of the Church has cut itself off from the communion of the universal Faith? The answer is sure. He will prefer the healthiness of the whole body to the morbid and corrupt limb. But what if some novel contagion tries to infect the whole Church, and not merely a tiny part of it? Then he will take care to cleave to antiquity (tradition), which can never be led astray by any lying novelty." [74]

Those who hold fast to antiquity, as taught by St. Vincent of Lerins, will be preserved from "the operation of error," even if it comes from the bishops and the Pope himself. They will know that Catholics can recognize their authority, while resisting them in the exercise of authority (Gal. 1:8-10). They will know that obedience to particular commands should be refused when the command itself is sinful (Pope Leo XIII; Bellarmine), or contrary to good customs (Suarez), and they will know that obedience to general laws can be set aside in extraordinary circumstances (Epikeia, Mt. 12:1-4; St. Thomas). By

---

[73] *The Commonitorium of Vincent of Lerins*, taken from: Bettenson, H, Documents of the Christian Church, 2nd ed. (Oxford, London, Glasgow: Oxford University Press, 1963), pp. 84-85.

[74] Ibid.

holding to Tradition, they will also know that a Pope who deviates from the Faith, and even teaches heresy, can be contradicted (Innocent III; Adrian VI), without having to declare that he has ceased to be Pope (Adrian II; Paul IV). They will also know that formally separating from one's Patriarch based upon the alleged knowledge of a crime, before the matter has been decided by a Synod, is absolutely forbidden (Fourth Council of Constantinople).

In order to maintain the straight and narrow path during the present crisis, and prevent being tossed out of the Church to the Right or Left, we simply need to follow the teaching of St. Paul by standing fast and holding to Tradition (2Thess. 2:14) which, as St. Vincent of Lerins said, "can never be led astray by any lying novelty." We are also reminded of the famous words of the great Dominican bishop and theologian at the Council of Trent, Melchior Cano, who said:

> "Peter has no need of our lies or flattery. Those who blindly and indiscriminately defend every decision of the Supreme Pontiff are the very ones who do most to undermine the authority of the Holy See - they destroy instead of strengthening its foundations."[75]

---

[75] Quoted in Weigel, George, *Witness to Hope* (New York: Harper Collins, 1999), p. 15.

Chapter 21

~ The Bitter Fruits of Sedevacantism ~

We complete our study by examining the unfortunate, bitter fruits that issue from the tree of Sedevacantism. Our Lord provides us with the criterion by which we can judge a good tree from an evil tree; a true prophet from a false prophet. In the Gospel of St. Matthew, Our Lord warned us to beware of false prophets, who come to us under deceptive appearances (looking like sheep but are actually vicious wolves). He explained that these will be known *by their fruits*:

> "Beware of false prophets, who come to you in the clothing of sheep, but inwardly they are ravening wolves. By their fruits you shall know them. … every good tree bringeth forth good fruit, and the evil tree bringeth forth evil fruit. A good tree cannot bring forth evil fruit, neither can an evil tree bring forth good fruit. … Wherefore by their fruits you shall know them." (Mt. 7:15-20)

The evil fruits of the Sedevacantist tree are one of the clearest signs of its diabolical character - infighting, division, deception, detraction, condemnations, name-calling and other uncharitable and even inhumane behavior seem not to be the exception in Sedevacantism, but the rule. In this final chapter, in light of Our Lord's directive, we believe it is important to examine some of these rotten fruits, by which we "shall know" the false prophets of the Sedevacantist sect.

Sedevacantists Admit of Their Own Evil Fruits

Right off the bat, what is most telling, is that Sedevacantists *themselves* admit that their movement is plagued by evil and bitter fruits. This fact is so pervasive that it is conceded and complained about even by the most public defenders of the sect. For example, a recent article appeared in the Sedevacantist publication *Reign of Mary* in which the author, Sedevacantist Mario Derksen, explained that the reason some do not embrace the Sedevacantist position is due to the rotten fruits found among its members. He wrote:

> "All too often we hear from people seeking to be traditional Catholics that what keeps them from becoming Sedevacantists is the problem of 'disunity' among them. From disputes about which

Holy Week rites to follow, to contemporary bioethical problems, to the question of whether one may ever assist at non-Sedevacantist Masses, the disagreements among those who do not recognize the papal claimants after Pope Pius XII as legitimate seem too numerous or too daunting for many people's comfort."[1]

Mr. Derksen's explanation is that these divisions are due to the fact that there is not a Pope. He said, "the absence of a Pope means that the principle of unity is temporarily prevented from bringing about the unity of the flock on those matters about which we currently legitimately dispute and disagree."[2] Derksen's explanation, however, does not correspond to reality.

First, as this book has demonstrated, it's not that we don't have a Pope, but rather that the Sedevacantists refuse to recognize that there *is* a Pope. Second, the presence or absence of a Pope does not eliminate "those matters about which [they] currently legitimately dispute and disagree," because "those matters" include precisely how and when a Pope loses his office for heresy. As we saw in this book, the Sedevacantists have very divisive opinions on these matters, and those disagreements would exist irrespective of whether we have a Pope or not.

But as the Sedevacantist, John Lane, noted in his response to Mr. Derksen's article, the problem is not only one of disunity and infighting amongst various Sedevacantist factions, but true *spiritual disorder* in the lives of those who embrace the position. Mr. Lane wrote:

> "...people who get interested in Sedevacantism become <u>unstable in their spiritual lives</u>, confused about what matters and what doesn't, forget their own incompetence in what are often very technically challenging areas of law and doctrine, *often* destabilize others in their parish, and *very often* more broadly disturb the peace of the parish. <u>I've observed all of this myself, and so often that I can't answer it. It's true.</u>"[3]

John Lane admits he has no answer for the spiritual disorders he finds in those who embrace Sedevacantism. He went on to say one might be able to blame the *divisions* on there being no Pope (since the Pope is the principle of unity), but he then noted that this argument

---

[1] Derksen, Mario, "When The Papacy is Struck: The Papacy and Sedevacantist Disunity," *Reign of Mary,* Issue No. 155, Summer 2014.
[2] Ibid.
[3] http://www.sedevacantist.com/viewtopic.php?f=2&t=1771 (emphasis added).

"says nothing whatsoever about why Sedevacantism is *so often concommitant with spiritual maladies.*" [4]

Former Sedevacantist Laszlo Szijarto also refers to the spiritual maladies within the movement, which he himself experienced as a member of the sect. He notes that it was so pervasive that he did not know a single Sedevacantist who did not have spiritual disorders:

> "I myself had once been a Sedevacantist. Only in retrospect can I honestly see the great bitterness and lack of charity that this led to on my part. I have found nothing but spiritual disorder – to one extent or another – in all the Sedevacantists I have ever met (myself included and foremost among them). It would be best to leave out the numerous downfalls – in scandalous fashion – of bitter Sedevacantists." [5]

The obvious answer for these spiritual disorders is that Sedevacantism is an evil tree; and being an evil tree it naturally produces evil fruits, just as Our Lord explained. The evil fruits of Sedevacantism are exactly what one would expect to find. After all, the members of the Sedevacantist sect have effectively embraced the Protestant heresy of the invisible Church, both in their erroneous belief that the sin of heresy severs one from the Church (thus rendering the Church invisible) and that the Church is found in "the hearts and minds of true believers" (again, rendering the Church invisible, with a Pope and hierarchy that are nowhere to be found).

Further, Sedevacantists are among the most fervent persecutors of Christ and his suffering Church. Many of these people spend their lives ridiculing the Church and shining the light on all of its wounds, not in order to expose the wounds so they can be dressed and healed, but in order to discredit the Church and those who remain in it. It is no surprise that those who spend their lives attacking the Mystical Body of Christ when it is suffering its greatest trial, are permitted by God to fall into the gravest of spiritual disorders. As St. Paul says, those who have received the rain of grace, yet "bringeth forth thorns and briers" are "reprobate, and very near unto a curse, whose end is to be burnt" (Heb. 6:8). Let us now look at some of these "thorns" and "briers" from the evil tree of Sedevacantism.

---

[4] Ibid. (emphasis added).
[5] Szijarto, Laszlo, "Pope Sifting - Difficulties with Sedevacantism," the *Angelus* magazine, October 1995 (emphasis added).

Sedevacantists Condemn Each Other

The Sedevacantist sects are notorious for infighting, division and personal attacks launched against one another. The Dimond brothers (who claim to be religious brothers of the Order of St. Benedict, but are not recognized as such by a single Benedictine monastery in the world) are notorious for their insulting, disparaging and abusive language, and often condemn their fellow Sedevacantists to eternal hell-fire, as well as those who follow them.[6]

For example, they condemn the Sedevacantist preacher, Gerry Matatics, for believing in the Church's doctrine on Baptism of Desire, proclaiming him to be a "Christ-denier" and a "heretic of bad will." On their website, they declare: "Gerry Matatics is completely self-condemned. His hypocrisy is mind-boggling and demonic. Those who support the heretic Gerry Matatics can expect to be damned."[7] According to Pete and Mike Dimond, those who even "support" Mr. Matatics will burn in hell. Evidently, the Dimond brothers' false prophecy that John Paul II was "the final antichrist" has not stopped them from continuing to prophesy about the eternal fate of others.

In responding to the allegations of the Dimond brothers, Mr. Matatics posted this on his website:

> "The Dimond brothers, be it noted, have, among their other demonstrable errors - such as having declared John Paul II (while he was still alive) to be 'the final Antichrist'(!) - persisted, even after I have corrected them, in libelously misrepresenting me as having 'sold out' to those who teach the liberal view that one can be saved in other religions, which is a damnable lie...Their outrageous and mortally sinful calumny that I am a supporter of this heresy nevertheless remains prominently featured in the 'Beware (groups and individuals who teach heresy)' section of their website."[8]

It is not just Gerry Matatics whom the Dimond brothers condemn. About their fellow Sedevacantist, John Lane, they publicly announce: "Lane is not a Catholic, period. ... Lane has no faith. ... Lane is almost

---

[6] The Dimond brothers have also been accused of editing out recorded material that hurts their position, from the numerous telephone debates they record while engaging their opponents, before posting the debate on their website and claiming victory. Perhaps this is why they do not engage in live, public, video-recorded, unedited, face-to-face debates with a moderator at neutral locations, which is the professional way in which debates take place.

[7] http://www.mostholyfamilymonastery.com/catholicchurch/gerrymatatics/.

[8] https://www.gerrymatatics.org/GRIsGerrySede.html.

as bad as Bergoglio [Pope Francis] ... Lane is an apostate,"[9] and even "a totally wicked apostate."[10] Peter Dimond refers to another Sedevacantist, Tom Droleskey, as "a disgusting heretic,"[11] and "an obstinate and bad willed heretic."[12] About another Sedevacantist, John Daly, they say: "Daly is truly a blinded heretic, a false pedant...a bad-willed heretic."[13] They also declare the Sedevacantist priest, Fr. Martin Stepanich (RIP) to be "a complete heretic...an abominable heretic" and "a faithless heretic."[14] They describe Fr. Anthony Cekada as "a complete heretic"[15] and they do the same with Sedevacantist bishops Donald Sanborn and Robert McKenna.[16] And all these compliments are for their fellow Sedevacantists!

About Gerry Matatics, Tom Drolesky and all the rest of those "traditionalists" who believe in the Church's teaching on Baptism of Desire, Peter Dimond wrote: "That crowd is accurately described as the scum of the Earth. They are abominable."[17] Of course, if the Dimond brothers' assessment were accurate, then that would also make St. Augustine, St. Thomas Aquinas, St. Pius V, Urban V, Innocent VI, Leo XIII, St. Pius X, Benedict XV, Pius XI, Pope Pius XII and countless other saints "the scum of the Earth" as well. Clearly, these are not just bitter fruits, but wicked and truly demonic fruits.

In an exchange with Catholic traditionalist Ryan Grant (who is not a Sedevacantist), the Dimond brothers, who could not respond to the cogent rebuttals that Mr. Grant levied against their inane argumentation, decided to terminate the exchange with the following good-bye: "I'm done talking with you moronic, blind, brute, schismatic, heretical, modernist, neanderthal false 'traditionalists,' so if you want don't even post my reply, because this is the last email that I send to you. Don't even bother in responding to this email. I won't keep wasting my time with neanderthals like you."[18] That's honoring Mr. Grant with a whopping *eight* descriptive adjectives in a single

---

[9] See http://www.mostholyfamilymonastery.com/catholicchurch/john-lanes-astounding-heresy/# .VddMrq2FPmQ.
[10] http://www.mostholyfamilymonastery.com/John_Daly.php.
[11] See http://www.mostholyfamilymonastery.com/catholicchurch/gerry-matatics/#.VCDIK2FPmQ.
[12] See http://www.mostholyfamilymonastery.com/catholicchurch/dr-tomdrolesky/#.VfCDsq2FPmQ.
[13] See http://www.mostholyfamilymonastery.com/John_Daly.php.
[14] See http://www.mostholyfamilymonastery.com/e_archive1.php.
[15] See http://www.mostholyfamilymonastery.com/refuting_NFP.php.
[16] See http://www.mostholyfamilymonastery.com/catholicchurch/bishop-donald-sanborn/#.Vddf_a2FPmQ.
[17] See http://www.mostholyfamilymonastery.com/catholicchurch/gerrymatatics.
[18] Ibid.

sentence! What bitter fruits from the Dimond brothers, who write such immature and abrasive invective against Catholics with apparently no shame.

The Sedevacantist website, *Today's Catholic World*, uses similar abrasive language in its editorial approach. In criticizing Traditional Catholics who have correctly noted the defunct legal nature of *Cum Ex Apostolatus* (which many Sedevacantists have *also* admitted), the website responded as follows:

> "Very Useful Idiots - The absolutely intellectually dishonest Phony Opposition false traditionalist groups, such as: the priestless SSPX, Una Voce, John Vennari's "Catholic" Family News, Michael Matt's (truly lost) Remnant etc., by willfully refusing to accept the Church's Ex Cathedra (Infallible) teaching of Cum ex Apostolatus Officio which unmistakenly [sic] condemns imposters like Ratzinger a.k.a Anti-Pope Benedict XVI ..."[19]

Here we have another barrage of disparaging adjectives in a single sentence to marginalize, insult and detract from Traditional Catholics. What does this tell you about the spiritual, much less intellectual, standards of these Sedevacantists?

Peter Dimond referred to the Sedevacantist blogger, Steve Speray, as "a heretic and a liar." He declared that Mr. Speray's writings are "filled with blatant errors, omissions, outrageous lies, and false arguments. I could literally write a book proving it."[20] Mr. Speray responded on his website by saying: "The Dimonds are jealous because they're not the only ones out there promoting Sedevacantism,"[21] and accuses them of being "blinded with pride" and "antichrists of the highest level."[22]

Sedevacantist Richard Ibranyi accuses fellow Sedevacantist John Lane of being "foolish, dishonest, and deceptive." He says, "My duty as a Catholic ... obliges me to condemn you as a non-Catholic heretic and schismatic. You, sir, are an abomination in the eyes of God and are under His severe wrath, along with anyone associated with you in religious matters in anyway."[23] He then informs Mr. Lane: "All of your other specific heresies that are condemned by the Catholic Church are found on my website. I will not spend much time with you, as our

---

[19] http://www.todayscatholicworld.com/jan09tcw.htm.
[20] Ibid.
[21] https://www.stevensperay.wordpress.com/2013/07/20/brother-peterdimondslatest.
[22] Ibid.
[23] Ibranyi, Richard, "Against John Lane," December 2009, http://www.johnthebaptist.us /jbw_english/documents/refutations/rjmi/rr10_ag_john_lane.pdf.

Lord said, 'Do not cast your pearls to swine' (Mt. 7:6)."[24] He then accuses Mr. Lane of taking Bellarmine out of context (which, we must say, is something that we ourselves have observed), and further accuses him of twisting the Scriptures. "John, like the Protestant that you are," wrote Mr. Ibranyi, "you have quoted St. Robert out of context and ignore his other writings on this topic... John, you interpret Holy Scripture like a Protestant. You twist it to suit your heresy ... your sin of pride and rebellion have [sic] blinded you, and thus caused you to lose common sense ... you, John Lane, are not Catholic."[25]

And then we have the response of Peter Dimond to a fellow Sedevacantist who criticizes him for attending Mass at a Church in union with Pope Francis. In response, Dimond went on an absolute tirade. He wrote:

> "You are a wicked, lying heretic. You are liar and a fraud... Stop wasting our time you disgraceful heretic, headed for everlasting damnation in the bowels of hell... We are sick of you... You lying hypocrite phony... Servant of satan... You know nothing about the Catholic faith... Don't waste our time anymore, you schismatic, clueless, demonic, loser headed for Hell... By the way, you wouldn't call me a sissy to my face, you punk..."[26]

Clearly, none of this inflammatory rhetoric, quarreling, and dissension is from God, but from the flesh, as St. Paul explains: "Now the works of the flesh are manifest, which are ... enmities, contentions, emulations, wraths, quarrels, dissensions, sects ... revellings, and such like. Of the which I foretell you, as I have foretold to you, that they who do such things shall not obtain the kingdom of God" (Gal. 5:19-21).

It is not only the individual Sedevacantists who continuously attack one another. The various Sedevacantist sects issue sanctions and reprisals *against their own membership* for affiliating with the wrong branch of Sedevacantism. For example, the Sedevacantist sect of the Society of St. Pius V or S.S.P.V. (founded by priests who left the S.S.P.X.) has declared to their parishioners that if they assist at Masses offered by the C.M.R.I. (another Sedevacantist sect), they are committing mortal sin. The C.M.R.I. has returned the favor, by declaring that S.S.P.V. Masses are likewise prohibited and requiring their parishioners to disavow any affiliation with them. As Superior of

---

[24] Ibid.
[25] Ibid.
[26] http://www.catholic-saints.net/heretics/most-holy-family-monastery-exposed.php.

the S.S.P.V., Clarence Kelly even fined families $500 a year for attending Masses at Dolan and Cekada's parish, St. Gertrude the Great.

Then we have the Sedevacantist, Gerry Matatics, who publicly preaches that the clergy of *both* the S.S.P.V. and C.M.R.I. (and all other Sedevacantist priests) are "unauthorized shepherds," whose sacraments cannot be received, while the Dimond brothers publicly state that Matatics is a heretic and that both the S.S.P.V. and C.M.R.I. are heretical sects because they all hold to the Church's doctrine on Baptism of Desire and invincible ignorance. Whew!

All of this bitter infighting and division is what occurred with Luther and his followers when they split from the Church and began to rely upon their private judgment to decide matters of faith. Luther himself complained about this, when he wrote:

> "Noblemen, townsmen, peasants, all classes understand the Evangelium better than I or St. Paul. They are now wise and think themselves more learned than all the ministers.[27] ... This one will not hear of Baptism, that one denies the Sacraments, another puts a world between this and the last day: some teach that Christ is not God, some say this, some say that: there are about as many sects and creeds as there are heads. No Yokel is so rude, but when he has dreams and fancies, he thinks himself inspired by the Holy Ghost and must be a prophet.[28] ... There is no smearer but whenever he has heard a sermon or can read a chapter in German, makes a doctor of himself, and crowns his ass, convincing himself that he knows everything better than all who teach him...[29] ... When we have heard or learned a few things about Holy Scripture, we think we are already doctors and have swallowed the Holy Ghost, feathers and all.[30] ... How many doctors have I made by preaching and writing? Now they say, 'Be off with you. Go off with you. Go to the devil.' Thus it must be. When we preach they laugh. ...when we get angry and threaten them, they mock us, snap their fingers at us and laugh in their sleeves."[31]

Finally, Luther prophesied how this confusion stemming from his doctrine of private judgment would end:

---

[27] Walch XIV, 1360 (p. 214).
[28] De Wette III, 61 (p.214).
[29] Walch V.1652
[30] Walch V.472
[31] Walch VII.2310

"There will be the greatest confusion. Nobody will allow himself to be led by another man's doctrine or authority. Everybody will be his own rabbi: hence the greatest scandals."[32]

It is no surprise to see how the same root error - private judgment - has produced the same bitter fruits issuing from the tree of Sedevacantism: individual Catholics in the pew – "townsmen, peasants" - who imagine themselves to be "more learned than all the ministers," who have "dreams and fancies," imagining themselves to be "inspired by the Holy Ghost" and claim even to be "a prophet" (we will see a little later how one of these Sedevacantists actually believes he is one of the two Witnesses (prophets) spoken of in Apocalypse, chapter 11). Of course, most of these individuals have been led astray by the "ministers" of the Sedevacantist sect (priests and bishops), who likewise imagine themselves to be more learned that the Church's greatest theologians who addressed the question of a heretical Pope (not to mention the council Fathers of Constantinople IV). What is clear for those with eyes to see is that this Protestantism of private judgment has produced the same rotten fruits within Sedevacantism as it did among the unfortunate followers of Martin Luther.

Sedevacantists Condemn Other Sedevacantists
For Attending *"Una Cum"* Masses

Some Sedevacantists also condemn their fellow Sedevacantists for attending a Mass in which the currently recognized Pope's name is included in the canon (in other words, a true Catholic Mass). Sedevacantists call such Masses *"una cum"* Masses, from the Latin phrase prayed by the priest which mentions the name of the reigning Pope: "*una cum* famulo tuo Papa nostro N. ("together with Thy servant N., our Pope"). These "compromisers" are declared to be "public heretics" by their fellow Sedevacantists for worshiping in union with a "heretic Pope," simply because the priest prays for him during the Mass. Such compromisers would include John Lane, who assists at Masses of the S.S.P.X., and the Dimond brothers, who assist at Eastern rite Masses in union with the "Vatican II Church."

We have seen that the Fourth Council of Constantinople has condemned those who adhere to the Sedevacantist thesis, that is, who "separates himself from communion with his own Patriarch" before a

---

[32] Lauterb. 91. All of these citations from Luther were taken from Father Patrick O'Hare's book, *The Facts About Luther* (Frederick Pustet & Co, New York, Cincinnati, 1916), pp. 213-215.

judgment by the Church. Sedevacantists should note well that this condemnation also logically extends to those who act upon their separation by omitting their bishop's name from liturgical rites, including the Mass, before a judgment of the Church, which is exactly the practice of Sedevacantist chapels. The council clearly teaches that "he must not refuse to include his patriarch's name during the divine mysteries or offices," before a judgment by a synod, lest he be "excluded from all communion" [i.e. excommunicated] with the Church.

Fr. Cekada and Bishop Sanborn are among the most public in "defying this holy synod" (in the words of Constantinople IV), by declaring it forbidden to attend the Traditional Mass at a chapel in which the name of the Pope is mentioned in the canon (translation: "you have to assist and financially contribute at *our* Masses, *not theirs*"). Bishop Sanborn declares attendance at such a Mass to be "contrary to the First Commandment" and even "an act of false worship." "Ultimately," wrote the bishop, "it boils down to the principle of offering false worship to God, and an act of false worship."[33] One can only imagine how Sanborn browbeats his flock with such nonsense.

According to Sanborn, Fr. Cekada has written the "definitive article" on this issue.[34] In his article, Fr. Cekada says those who attended a Mass in which the name of Benedict XVI (the Pope at the time) is uttered, "participate in sin," "implicitly profess a false religion," are in "communion with heretics," "condone a violation of Church law," commit "the sin of schism," and "offer an occasion for the sin of scandal." That is quite a hefty list of sins. Cekada's list of sins applies equally to those who attend Masses offered by priests of the S.S.P.X., and even independent priests, who *publicly resist* the modern errors and the new orientation of the Church.

Fr. Cekada claims that Sedevacantists who have no other Mass available, and therefore attend Mass celebrated by a non-Sedevacantist priest (even though they interiorly object when the priest silently names the Pope in the canon) *will derive no sacramental grace*, nor will they fulfill their Sunday obligation. Where then to go? To his parish, St. Gertrude the Great, of course. How does Cekada make this claim? He says that refusing to say the name of the Pope along with the priest during the canon (even in silent, mental prayer) is a failure to "actively

---

[33] Sanborn, "Can We go To The Una Cum Mass In A Pinch?," June 11, 2014. http://www.mostholytrinityseminary.org/bishopsblog.html.

[34] Cekada, "The Grain of Incense: Sedevacantists and Una Cum Masses," http://www.traditionalmass.org/images/articles/SedesUnCum.pdf.

participate" in the Mass. According to Fr. Cekada, participation is all or nothing. From the "definitive article":

> "THE PRIEST at an *una cum* Mass, of course, is the one who utters the objectionable phrase. Couldn't the man in the pew who objects to it simply 'withhold his consent' from that part of the Canon, but still assist at the Mass otherwise in order to fulfill his obligation or obtain sacramental graces?
>
> Well, no. To fulfill your Sunday obligation or obtain sacramental graces at Mass requires active assistance or participation. This is an all-or-nothing proposition. You either actively assist or you don't."[35]

Of course, the entire foundation of Fr. Cekada's "definitive article" (which has led many souls to stop attending Mass altogether) is based upon the same erroneous premise that the conciliar Popes' "sin of heresy" (judged and declared by Fr. Cekada) has severed them from the Church. Because of their "public sin," Fr. Cekada claims they are no longer members of the Church. And, because they are no longer members of the Church, he explains, they certainly cannot be named in the canon as Popes, even if this means we are simply praying *for* them and not *with* them (since the prayers of the canon are only for the members of the Church).

For example, Richard Ibranyi wrote the following publicly to John Lane, who attends a Mass in which the Pope is named in the canon: "You [John] are praying in communion with notorious heretics and schismatics. In this you are guilty of all their crimes by way of association. ... Would you have us believe you can close your eyes and ears when the 'Te Igitur' (one with John Paul II - una cum) is prayed and in so doing escape guilt? Would you have us pretend that God does not see you?"[36]

As we mentioned, this has led many Sedevacantists to avoid the sacraments altogether. For example, we saw that in lieu of going to the Traditional Mass and sacramental confession, Gerry Matatics requires his family to stay at home on Sundays ("home-aloners") and follow his lead in prayer. Matatics also evidently believes he can summon the grace for acts of perfect contrition at will (he admits this in his talks) to forgive his mortal sins. While we do not accuse Mr. Matatics of

---

[35] Cekada, "Should I Assist at a Mass That Names Benedict XVI in the Canon?," http://www.traditionalmass.org/images /articles/B16 inCanon.pdf.

[36] Ibranyi, "Against John Lane," December 2009. http://www.john thebaptist.us/jbw_en glish/documents/refutations/rjmi/rr10_ag_john_lane.pdf.

subjective guilt for his extreme positions (as he does with the conciliar Popes), our Catholic hearts are moved for his children and all the other innocent victims of Sedevacantism who are now being deprived of the sacraments. This is yet another most bitter and evil fruit of the sect.

False Mysticism and Conclavism

Such infighting, cross-condemnations, and utter confusion among Sedevacantist groups have led to the splintering of the movement into various individual sects (just like in Protestantism). Some of these sects have gone on to elect their own "Popes" (these Sedevacantists are called "Conclavists"). Other sects have decided to follow certain men who claim to have been crowned the true Pope by Heaven itself. These phenomena further underscore the cultish nature of the movement.

For example, Fr. Michael Collin (d. 1974) - an early forerunner of the Sedevacantist movement - declared that he was mystically crowned Pope by God the Father on October 7, 1950, during the reign of Pius XII, and took the name Clement XV. His successor was Gaston Tremblay (d. 1998), a former Canadian politician and Mayor in Quebec, who claimed that Jesus Himself named him Pope on June 24, 1968. He took the name Gregory XVII. Clemente Dominguez y Gomez (d. 2005), a Spaniard who was associated with the Palmar de Troya movement, also claimed that Christ granted him the papacy on August 6, 1978, after the death of Paul VI. He also took the name Gregory XVII.

Next, we have American Reinaldus Michael Benjamins, who claims to have been crowned the Pope by angels in 1983 and took the name Gregory XIX. Francis Konrad Schuckardt (d. 2006), an independent American bishop, claims to have received the papal tiara from Our Lady of Guadalupe during the reign of John Paul II. He took the name Hadrian VII. Fr. Valeriano Vestini, an Italian priest of the Caphuchin order, claims to have received the papacy from God in 1990. Then there is Chester Olszewski of Pennsylvania, who claimed he was both Pope (appointed by God in 1980) and savior of the world. He took the name Peter II. There is also the Frenchman and former auto mechanic Maurice Archieri, who claims he was mystically given the papacy in 1995 by the Holy Ghost. He also took the name Peter II. There are still other antipopes who took the name Peter II, such as Peter Henry Bubois of Canada, Aime Baudet of Brussels, and Julius Tischler of Germany. Other mystical claimants include Italian Gino Frediani (Emmanuel, 1973-1984), Spaniards Manuel Alonso Corral (Peter II, 2005-2011) and Sergio Maria Ginés Jesús Hernández y Martinez

(Gregory XVIII since 2011), and American Mesagarde Zion Vollball-Moon of Indianapolis (John Paul III since 2015).

Other antipopes elected by "Conclaves" include Mirko Fabris (d. 2012), a stand-up comedian from Croatia, who was elected in 1978 and took the name Krav (which was his stage name); South African Fr. Victor Von Pentz, who was elected in 1994 by conclavists in Britain and took the name Linus II; and, Timothy Blasio Ahitler (d. 1998) who was elected in Africa in 1991. We previously mentioned seminary drop-out David Bawden of Kansas, who had his mom and dad elect him as Pope Michael I on July 16, 1990. In 1998, Fr. Lucian Pulvermacher (d. 2009), a Capuchin priest, was elected by a larger "Conclave" of between 50 and 100 people, although most of them phoned in their votes to the wood house in Montana where the votes were being tallied. He took the name of Pius XIII. On March 24, 2006, a group of irregular bishops elected Argentine Oscar Michaelli (d. 2007) as Leo XIV. He was succeeded by Juan Bautista Bonetti, who took the name Innocent XIV and resigned in 2007, and was succeed by Alejandro Tomás Greico, who took the name Alexander IX. All kidding aside, some might be tempted to call these the "bitter nuts" (rather than fruits) of Sedevacantism.[37]

The Sedevacantist author, Richard Ibranyi (who teaches that all the Popes since 1130 A.D. have been antipopes) also claims to have received divine revelations. In fact, he actually claims to be "one of the witnesses mentioned in the book of the Apocalypse, Chapter 11." He said "I believe this to be true, based upon many confirmations from God."[38] The self-proclaimed witness of the Apocalypse then declares that those who refuse to associate with him are "guilty of a mortal sin akin to schism."

> "Those who do not want to be associated with me because I claim to be one of the witnesses, in spite of the fact that I am Catholic in word and deed, are guilty of a mortal sin akin to schism."[39]

Although the Dimond brothers have also claimed to have prophetic insights, (such as their declaration that John Paul II was "the final antichrist"), they refuse to associate with Mr. Ibranyi.

---

[37] For more detail, see the website http://www.geocities.ws/orthopapism/robertfhess.html which was compiled by Sedevacantists who reject the conclavist movement within the Sedevacantist sect. See also http://www.angelfire.com/weird2/obscure2/anti-pope.htm and https://www.en.wikipedia.org/wiki/Conclavism.
[38] Ibranyi, "On RJMI," March, 2005.
[39] Ibid.

Interestingly, Ibranyi is a former member of the Dimond brothers' monastery, but was kicked out of their compound for being a Sedevacantist. You read that correctly. Kicked out for being a Sedevacantist! You see, Michael Dimond did not become a Sedevacantist until a year after Mr. Ibranyi's eviction. Today, even though the Dimond brothers now share the Sedevacantist position with him, Mr. Ibranyi declares them to be "apostates and heretics." He wrote:

> "From the time I held the sedevacante position until my expulsion from the monastery, I smuggled the sedevacante teachings out to others by mail. Michael caught some of these mailings before they went out and removed the sedevacante teachings from them.
> A year or more after my departure, Michael changed his belief and held the sedevacante position; but he never admitted that he had expelled me for the real reason mentioned in this letter. Simply put, Michael was wrong and I was right, as even now I am right for denouncing the Dimonds as apostates and heretics, as is evident for all of good will to see."[40]

These are the kinds of evil fruits produced by the evil tree of Sedevacantism. From delusions and deceptions to divisions, detraction and mutual condemnations, the Sedevacantist sect is a poisoned tree, bringing forth nothing but "thorns and briers… whose end is to be burnt" (Heb. 6:8). From this we can see why the Sedevacantist, John Lane, said that "people who get interested in Sedevacantism become unstable in their spiritual lives, confused about what matters and what doesn't, forget their own incompetence in what are often very technically challenging areas of law and doctrine, *often* destabilize others in their parish, and *very often* more broadly disturb the peace of the parish."[41] While Lane concedes that "the sedevacantist solution is wrong" if there are no bishops left with ordinary jurisdiction, he and his colleagues should also recognize that the "Sedevacantist solution" is from the devil and not God, based upon the rotten and wicked fruits it has produced.

---

[40] Ibranyi, Richard, 'On RJMI,' March, 2005.
[41] http://www.sedevacantist.com/viewtopic.php?f=2&t=1771.

The Art of Deception and Detraction

As we have objectively demonstrated throughout the book, Sedevacantists also engage in much editorial deception in their writings and talks in order to "prove" the "veracity" of their thesis. They selectively cut and paste partial quotes from one author, or wrench out of context the quotes of another, or claim that an opponent's research sources, which refute their argument, are dubious or even fabricated - no doubt betting that no one will check their research. We do not mean to say that all Sedevacantists willfully engage in these dishonest tactics. But it suffices to note that the *most published* Sedevacantists – that is, those who purport to represent the movement through their public writings – consistently behave in ways that completely undermine their own credibility, and this also reveals the diabolical spirit that permeates their sect.

For example, in attempting to "prove" his novel "sin of heresy causes the loss of ecclesiastical office" theory, we saw how Fr. Cekada deliberately quoted a sentence fragment from Cardinal Billot which says a heretical Pope "is cast outside the Body of the Church," even though the full quote reveals Billot was referring to the *crime* (not sin) of "notorious heresy," which Cekada must have known by having read the whole quote. We also saw how Sedevacantist Jerry Ming parroted Cekada's argument verbatim in his own article. We saw how Cekada similarly omitted key words from his oral recitation of the Wernz-Vidal quotation on declaratory sentences, which shows the commentary is referring to the declaration of the *crime* of heresy (which results in the loss of office) and not a declaration of *illegitimacy* (which clears title to an office that was already lost). Cekada has consistently used this technique when quoting many other theologians (Beste, Coronata, Iragui, Vermeersch, etc.) in his various articles and videos, attempting to pull the wool over the eyes of his followers by arguing that the "sin" of heresy severs one from the Church, even though – when you look up the actual quotations and context – all the theologians are referring to the *crime* of "notorious" and "openly divulged" heresy. We also saw how Sedevacantists' often remove Bellarmine's qualification "in my judgment..." from his quotation critiquing the Fourth Opinion, to give it the appearance that Bellarmine's subjective opinion is a statement of fact.

We further saw how Fr. Cekada deliberately removed quotations addressing the Church's prudential judgment of universal disciplines from the material he cited, while addressing the infallibility of the doctrinal judgment alone, to make it appear that all aspects of the

Church's disciplines are infallible.[42] The Sedevacantist bishop, Mark Pivarunas, used the same dishonest tactic in his own article on disciplinary infallibility, and in so doing didn't even include an ellipsis indicating that something had been removed. We also saw Fr. Cekada's sleight of hand technique used to justify his theory that the new rite of episcopal consecration is invalid when he compared apples (the Coptic Preface) and oranges (the form of Paul VI's new rite) and then argued that because the apples and oranges "are not equivalent," it confirms that the new rite is invalid.

We also saw how John Daly removed multiple references to the "universality throughout time" (diachronic universality) element of the infallible Ordinary and Universal Magisterium, when he quoted from Pius IX's *Tuas Libenter*. No question he did this to justify his novel theory that "universality in space" (synchronic universality) was all that is required for infallibility of the OUM. We also saw how the Sedevacantist blogger, Steve Speray, failed to verify Mr. Daly's partial quote, and ended up parroting Daly's error verbatim in his own internet article (very common amongst Sedevacantists). Of course, in all the articles and blogs of these self-promoting internet writers (Cekada, Dolan, Sanborn, Lane, Daly, the Dimonds, Speray, Ibranyi, Drolesky, etc.), one will *never* find a reference to the teaching of the Fourth Council of Constantinople, or Bellarmine's *De Membris Ecclesiae*, which explicitly *condemn* the Sedevacantist thesis.

We also learned how Sedevacantists make false allegations of inauthenticity against writings which undermine their position. For example, we saw how John Lane falsely accused Fr. Boulet of being "deceived by fraudulent quotes which he has *carelessly* lifted from some place unknown," when Fr. Boulet quoted Pope Adrian VI, who taught that many Popes were heretics, including John XXII. Lane made his false allegation because the quote represents a problem for his novel theory that a heretic Pope automatically loses his office, even while he is being recognized by the Church as Pope. In his typical

---

[42] It is interesting to note that Fr. Cekada uses an abbreviated format when writing about Sedevacantism (he cuts and pastes partial quotes, uses bullet points, creates summaries, etc.), all so that the material looks quite simple and straightforward (and his readers don't have do any further work). But this approach does not reflect the true complexity of the material, as this book demonstrates. Cekada's style is also much different from the approach he used in his book *Work of Human Hands*, which is a thoroughly researched and detailed presentation of the topic of the New Mass. One can only suspect that Fr. Cekada uses this simplistic and generalized approach for his internet articles on Sedevacantism to mask the deficiencies and weaknesses of his positions, which are discovered by a more thorough and honest analysis of the applicable material.

haughty and demeaning manner, Lane later referred to those who've cited the quotation from Pope Adrian as being "complete charlatans without the slightest affection for the moral law or truth itself." Now that we have provided (in Chapter 8) the original Latin version of Pope Adrian's quotation from two centuries before Mr. Lane claims it was "invented," we will see if he offers a public apology to Fr. Boulet and the others for his public detraction. We also saw how Lane recklessly cast doubt upon the authenticity of Constantinople III's condemnation of Pope Honorius, by implying that Pope St. Leo II didn't understand the council that he himself ratified - once again, because it undermines his Sedevacantist thesis.

It is unfortunate that Sedevacantists are allowed to publish such trash on their websites and in their articles, which is generally swallowed whole by their simple-minded flocks (just like their erroneous theories), without any challenge, inquiry or investigation. For many Sedevacantists, if you can't refute the arguments of your opponents, you must attempt to destroy their credibility, so that your followers won't take them seriously. That is the smear tactic of John Lane and many of his colleagues.

Novel Theories and Contradictions

In our study, we also discovered how Sedevacantists are often forced to create novel theories which have no basis in Church teaching to defend their thesis. Of course, the most novel theory of them all is the Sedevacantist thesis itself, which is based upon the erroneous notion that individual Catholics can depose reigning Popes (or declare them deposed) and thereby separate from them by an act of private judgment. Once the separation occurs, they are then moved to invent other novel theories to justify their action, which only confirms the saying that schism quickly leads to heresy. Just as Catholic truth builds upon truth, so too error breeds more error.

We saw how Fr. Cekada and others claim that the sin of heresy (a matter of the internal forum) severs one from the Body of the Church (a matter of the external forum) and how this false theory permeates the rest of their arguments. Unable to answer his opponents' objections (who have proven that the conciliar Popes have not fallen from office under his "sin of heresy" theory), we saw how Cekada now claims Sedevacantists have a "new" argument (that the conciliar Popes have not been true Popes because they had committed the sin of heresy *before* their elections), even though this "new" argument is nothing more than a different application of the "old" argument, namely, that individual Catholics by private judgment can determine for themselves who is a "true" member of the hierarchy and who is not. We also saw how Sedevacantists repeatedly confuse heresy with lessor theological errors and "hereticizing," and ignore cases in history where Popes (e.g., Pius IX) and saints (e.g., Bellarmine) remained in communion with those clerics (e.g., Archbishop Darboy, Michel de Bay) who pertinaciously[43] professed heresies in public, in the absence of the Church's definitive judgment of the individual.

We saw how Sedevacantists presume the subjective element of pertinacity based solely upon what they personally believe is a materially heretical statement (the objective element), when, in fact, pertinacity is established for clerics through ecclesiastical warnings by those in authority, and not simply by private judgment. We saw how they misunderstand that the nature of heresy severs one from the Body of the Church because it does not require an *additional* ecclesiastical penalty to do so, and not because the Church is precluded from making the judgment, which it must do in the case of a cleric (a judgment that Sedevacantists make by "usurpation," in the words of St. Thomas).

We also saw how Bishop Sanborn created the novel theory that universal and peaceful acceptance of a Pope confirms only the validity of his election, and not that he has received papal jurisdiction, even though just the *opposite* is true: universal and peaceful acceptance guarantees we have a valid Pope, to whom Christ has directly granted jurisdiction, even if there were defects in his election (thus, it does not simply guarantee that an election was valid).

We saw how Fr. Cekada created his own bizarre "doctrine" about univocal signification for sacramental validity, arguing that the way in which words are used in heretical sects – and not the way in which the *Church* uses and understands them – affects the validity of Catholic sacraments. We saw how Cekada created a theory that a liturgical law promulgated by a Pope (i.e., Pius XII) can be set aside by the private judgment of individual Catholics if they personally believe the law lacks "stability," and has become "harmful in hindsight." We also saw how Cekada claims that liturgical laws (of Paul VI) are *legally promulgated* by virtue of one's private interpretation of the Pope's will alone (his "hopes" and "wishes"), and not by the Church's established legal process. We saw how Cekada tried to use canon 151 to claim that when the theologians use the term "declaration," they are referring to a declaration of vacancy (of office) and not the initial fact that *causes* the

---

[43] Msgr. Darboy continued to hold his error even after being warned privately by the Pope, and de Bay continued to profess his heresies after they were formally condemned by the Church.

vacancy, even though the theologians are *unanimous* in holding that the Church's determination of the crime must precede the loss of office (and any subsequent declaration thereof). We further saw how Cekada's objections to the Recognize and Resist position equate to allowing one to resist a Pope's teaching in practice but not the teaching itself. We also saw how Steve Speray argued that altar boys "represent Christ" (acting *in persona Christi*) to "prove" that altar girls violate the Church's disciplinary infallibility. We even saw Speray claim that "a pope doesn't need to be a heretic at all to lose office" for heresy!

We saw how Lane engages in the fallacy of shifting the Burden of Proof to support his "Bishop in the Woods" theory. We saw how Gerry Matatics preaches the novel doctrine that God will impute the alleged heresies of the conciliar Popes to the souls of those who die in union with them (by "crediting to your account the faith of these men"). We saw how Lane, Cekada, the Dimond brothers and many other Sedevacantists falsely claim that Bellarmine and Suarez held different positions on the question of a heretical Pope. They then denigrate Suarez and claim that Bellarmine's opinion must prevail since he is a Doctor of the Church – when, in fact, they have completely misunderstood Bellarmine's position! We also saw how virtually all Sedevacantists subscribe in one way or another to the error of Monolithic Infallibility.

We saw how John Daly created the theory that Vatican II (which defined no doctrines at all) should have been infallible by virtue of the Ordinary and Universal Magisterium, simply because it was a gathering of the world's bishops with the Pope in time, notwithstanding the fact that the novelties of the council were not 1) *definitively proposed* as 2) divinely *revealed truths* – two requirements that must be met for infallibility to apply to the OUM (and the Extraordinary Magisterium). In fact, Daly further implied that *all* the teachings of Vatican II should have been covered by the Church's infallibility, even though not *all* the teachings of ecumenical councils that *do* define dogmas are protected by infallibility, but only the actual definitions themselves. Daly's efforts attempt to "redefine" the infallibility of the OUM to mean anything that is taught non-definitively at a given moment in time, rather than what has been handed down through the ages.

As Sedevacantists concoct their novel theories to defend the indefensible, we also saw how their own argumentation often leads them to directly contradict themselves, even within their own articles. For example, we saw how Steve Speray in his internet article claimed that a heretic Pope is automatically excommunicated under canon 2314,

§1 of the 1917 Code and then, two paragraphs later, said Popes are not subject to canon 2314, §1 or any canon law.

We similarly saw how Gregorius argued that the conciliar Popes lost their office *ipso facto*, according to canon 188, §4, yet, in the same article, said the Pope is not subject to canon law. We also saw how Gregorius claims the loss of papal office is solely a "question of fact, not law" even though he also appeals to canon law and legal arguments (pertaining to law) to make his case. We saw how Fr. Cekada claims one cannot reject the liturgical laws of a valid Pope (and thus he rejects the reforms of Paul VI), even though he himself rejects the liturgical reforms of Pius XII and yet accepts him as a valid Pope (absurdly claiming that Pius XII's reforms *became* evil under Paul VI). We saw how Fr. Cekada and Bishop Sanborn concede that private individuals (even religious societies like the S.S.P.X.) cannot resolve speculative questions of theology and law, while they themselves do just the opposite in their dogmatic defense of the Sedevacantist thesis. We also saw how Cekada falsely accuses Traditional Catholics of having a heretical view of the papacy, while he (along with Matatics, Sanborn and others) essentially holds to the heresy of an invisible and defectible Church, at least in practice, since Cekada cannot tell us where the Pope and episcopacy exist today, and claims that the visible society morphed into a New Church.

We saw how Gerry Matatics accused Archbishop Lefebvre of being "grossly liberal" and perhaps even a "heretic" for holding that non-Catholics can be saved *in* their false religions but not *by* them. Yet, in the same talk, Matatics admits that *Novus Ordo* Catholics can also be saved in their religion, even though Matatics holds the *Novus Ordo* to be a false religion. In fact, Bishop Sanborn claims that those in the *Novus Ordo* are "legally Catholics," even though he also claims that they (especially the *Novus Ordo* Popes) are not members of the Catholic Church, but of a false religion.[44] How the bishop can imagine that a person can be a legal Catholic, yet not a member of the Church, is anyone's guess. We also saw how Matatics excused John XXII from being classified as a public heretic because he did not "impose" his heresy upon the Church as a matter of faith, and yet, at the same time, he claims Paul VI was a public heretic for ratifying Vatican II, even though Paul VI did not "impose" the novelties of Vatican II upon the Church as a matter of faith. We further saw Matatics deny that the Church ever had women deacons since, as he claims, it is against

---

[44] Sanborn, "Explanation Of The Thesis Of Bishop Guérard Des Lauriers," June 29, 2002.

"Divine law," when, in fact, the Church *did* have women serving as "deaconesses" for centuries.

We saw how the Dimond brothers argued that Luther (who they admit was an "obvious heretic") did not have to be avoided until the Church declared his heresy, while the conciliar Popes *must* be avoided *without* a declaration of heresy from the Church, because they are "heretical antipopes" by their private judgment. The Dimond brothers further contradict themselves when they cite Magisterial documents, such as *Mortalium Animos*, which says "... this Apostolic See has never allowed its subjects to take part in the assemblies of non-Catholics...," while they themselves attend Mass at an Eastern rite church in communion with Pope Francis and the *"Novus Ordo,"* which they declare to be a non-Catholic religion. We also saw how Bishop Dan Dolan argued that whether he is a true priest (validly ordained) is a question of fact that *must be resolved by the Church*, while he holds a completely different standard for the Vicars of Christ (i.e., he treats the question of fact about whether they are true Popes as a matter of private judgment). We further saw how Sedevacantists accuse Traditional Catholics of "sifting the Magisterium" by reading and judging the modern documents in the light of Tradition, when they themselves do the exact same thing, although they go further by "sifting Popes" as well. Many other examples could be provided, but the point has been made: Sedevacantists are guilty of creating novel and contradictory theories to defend what cannot be defended. An error in the beginning is an error in the end.

Sarcasm, Ridicule and Condemnations

Because the Sedevacantists have already condemned the conciliar Popes as heretics, it should be no surprise that they ridicule and condemn anyone who is an obstacle to their position. This is another very bitter fruit of Sedevacantism. Setting aside the many condemnations that Sedevacantists have publicly hurled against the authors of this book and other traditional Catholic writers, we saw how Sedevacantists also denigrate the Church's most reputable theologians and accuse them of error and even heresy when their writings do not support the Sedevacantist thesis.

For example, we saw how Fr. Cekada denigrated Suarez by saying he "lost most debates," and was the only theologian to hold that a council must oversee the deposition of a heretical Pope (two complete falsehoods). We saw how John Lane pretended that the axiom "the First See is judged by no one" was first issued by Vatican I in a fruitless attempt to discredit Suarez, even though the axiom dates back to the early Church and was cited by Suarez himself. Mr. Lane even went so far as to accuse Suarez of heresy, since he believed Suarez's opinion would require a "judgment" of a heretical Pope; yet, as we saw, Lane's favorite theologian, Bellarmine, explicitly taught that "a heretical Pope can be judged..."

Of course, Sedevacantists condemn more modern theologians as well. For example, the Dimond brothers publicly condemn Ronald Knox and Msgr. Van Noort as being heretics. On their website, they say: "Heretics such as Knox, Van Noort and the editors of his work were simply devoid of the Catholic and apostolic faith."[45] They also declare that the 1949 Letter of the Holy Office, *Suprema Haec Sacra*, which was approved by Pius XII and condemned the errors of the Feeneyites, to be heretical. They wrote: "Suprema haec sacra is neither authoritative nor infallible, but heretical and false."[46] Why do they reject it? Because Mike and Pete Dimond have embraced the very heresy that the Holy Office condemned in the letter. This shows that they are not only separated from the post-Vatican II Church, but are separated doctrinally from the Church prior to Vatican II as well. And what is their basis for rejecting this Magisterial teaching? Private judgement, of course.

They also declare Msgr. Fenton, one of the most anti-modernist authors in America prior to Vatican II, and who edited the *American Ecclesiastical Review* for nearly 20 years, of being "a dogma denier" – that is, a heretic. Pete Dimond says: "Thus, Msgr. Joseph Clifford Fenton was not a 'wonderful theologian'; he was a dogma denier and a dogma corrupter. In fact, he is all the more dangerous because his heretical ideas are given the semblance of doctrinal fidelity."[47] They even refer to Cardinal Ottaviani, who was in charge of the Holy Office under Pius XII, as "the heretic Cardinal Ottaviani."[48] Richard Ibranyi, however, takes the cake. The self-proclaimed witness of the Apocalypse not only condemns all modern theologians as heretics and apostates, but also every single Pope since Innocent II in 1130, and every single Church theologian and canon lawyer since 1250. Ibranyi's condemnation, then, includes the Universal Doctor of the Church, St. Thomas Aquinas, and the rest of the Doctors who meet Ibranyi's

---

[45] See http://www.mostholyfamilymonastery.com/catholicchurch/revealing-heresies-msgr-van-noorts-dogmatic-theology-manual/#.Vdc77q2FPmR.

[46] See http://www.mostholyfamilymonastery.com/catholicchurch/msgr-fenton-joseph-clifford-book/#.Vdc9ka2FPmQ.

[47] Ibid.

[48] http://www.mostholyfamilymonastery.com/refuting_NFP.php.

criteria, including the well-known Sts. Bonaventure, Albert the Great, John of the Cross, Robert Bellarmine, Francis de Sales, and Alphonse Liguori, among others.

Perhaps what is most revealing is the juvenile, *ad hominem* argumentation that the most published Sedevacantists consistently use to undermine their opponents and tarnish their reputation and credibility. Fr. Cekada is a master of these rhetorical tactics; and, because he is a priest, it makes his behavior all the more unfortunate. For example, in responding to an article written by John Salza, we saw that Fr. Cekada actually lowered himself to make fun of Salza's Italian surname by titling his internet article "Salza on Sedevacantism: Same Old Fare," displaying a picture of the salsa condiment on the web page, and referring to the author's arguments as "a dash of Salza." Cekada engages in such tactics to keep his readers entertained while camouflaging the weakness of his own case (here, his inability to rebut Salza's argument that the crime of heresy, not the sin of heresy, leads to the loss of ecclesiastical office). At a minimum, one can only hope that Fr. Cekada comes to realize the dignity of the priesthood that he publicly represents, and begins to act in a manner more worthy of such a high calling.

Also, after Mr. Salza gave an interview on papal infallibility for the *Voice of Catholic Radio* on March 30, 2014, the Sedevacantists at NovusOrdoWatch (who, as we saw, masquerade behind phony pen-names) revealed their own juvenility by publishing an article feigning a rebuttal of Salza's presentation which they called "Comedy Hour with John Salza," and posted a graphic of Salza's face with a clown's nose on the webpage. Catholic writer Paul Folbrecht, offended by such childish assaults on a fellow Catholic (not to mention their amateurish scholarship), wrote an extensive rebuttal to the NovusOrdoWatch piece, revealing the many errors, omissions and misrepresentations it contains (and, like Salza's extensive rebuttal of "Gregorius" at NovusOrdoWatch, currently remains unanswered).[49]

Fr. Cekada also released a juvenile video on Sedevacantism called "Stuck in a Rut" which he dresses up with humorous caricatures and comical satire to address the most serious and weighty topic of when and how the Vicar of Christ loses his office for heresy. In one scene, Cekada superimposed the heads of Christopher Ferrara, Brian McCall, John Salza and Robert Siscoe upon the bodies of the auditors (judges) of the Apostolic Tribunal of the Roman Rota, who are seated next to Pope Francis, and called the depiction the "Vatican Legal Dream

---

[49] See Folbrecht, http://www.acatholicthinker.net/a-response-to-novus-ordo-watch.

Team" (these four men – three of whom are lawyers - have written articles demonstrating that a legal process is required by the Church's greatest theologians to depose a heretical Pope). Evidently, since Cekada cannot rebut the arguments of these four writers (which reflects the unanimous teaching of the Church's theologians), he has decided to make fun of them instead (which also speaks to the low intellectual standards of Cekada's audience). Such *ad hominem* attacks are commonly recognized as the effeminate response of those who are unable to offer a cogent intellectual rebuttal to an argument.

The Dimond brothers also have a common practice of publicly condemning Catholics who have just departed this life. For example, just after Michael Davies went to his eternal reward, the Dimond brothers posted an article titled: "Michael Davies, defender of the Faith or faithless heretic?" after which, needless to say, they concluded that "Michael Davies was not a defender of the Faith, but a faithless heretic."[50]

After the recent and shocking death of the Fatima priest, Fr. Nicholas Gruner, the Dimond brothers posted an article titled "'Fr.' Nicholas Gruner Dies Of A Heart Attack – What Catholics Should Think Of Him."[51] Their article claims to give "the truth about 'Fr.' Nicholas Gruner that you won't hear almost anywhere else" (even though neither Pete nor Mike Dimond ever personally spoke with or met Fr. Gruner). They nevertheless declared him to be "an obstinate heretic and a major false prophet."[52]

They also accused him of being "a major false teacher the Devil used to deceive conservative-minded people" and "an instrument of Satan who led many people to Hell." They concluded by saying: "Since he died as a heretic and a wicked man, no true Catholic can pray for Gruner or say 'Rest in Peace' in his regard."[53] Such unthinkable cheap shots (not to mention grievous lies) taken at the faithful departed, especially a gentle priestly soul like Fr. Nicholas Gruner, startle the Catholic conscience and only reveal the morbid state of the Dimonds' own souls. Their behavior makes that of the modern pagans appear exemplary.

---

[50] http://www.mostholyfamilymonastery.com/Michael_Davies_defender_or_heretic.php.

[51] http://www.mostholyfamilymonastery.com/catholicchurch/fr-nicholas-gruner-dies-of-a-heart-attack/#.Vdc5m62FPmQ.

[52] Ibid.

[53] Ibid.

Conclusion

We believe it was important to complete our study by exposing some of the evil fruits of Sedevacantism, since this is the criterion by which Our Lord said we "shall know" the false prophets and false teachers of our day. Our coverage of this material, however, was not intended to characterize *all* Sedevacantists as false prophets and bitter souls. Assuredly, there are some Sedevacantists who are in good faith, but have been caught in the Sedevacantist web of deception. Because of the crisis in the Church, and the cultish and overbearing techniques of the Sedevacantist sect, it is understandable how this could happen.

Many Sedevacantists will be quick to respond by pointing out the bad fruits of the post-conciliar Church. These authors, of course, acknowledge that the Vatican II revolution within the Church has indeed produced some bad fruits. This is to be expected while the Church suffers her Mystical Passion. As we've explained, just as Christ suffered in His Body at the hands of the Old Covenant leaders, so the Mystical Body of Christ has been disfigured at the hands of the conciliar Popes. And just as many lost faith in Christ during His Passion (unable to see His Divinity hidden beneath His wounds), so Sedevacantists have lost faith *in the Church*, with her divine nature currently obscured by the wounds of her own Passion.

Rather than suffer with Christ and His Church, and work to bring about the restoration of Tradition, Sedevacantists have departed from the Church, even becoming amongst the Church's most outspoken enemies. For them, this is the easy way out; for no longer do they have the difficulty of explaining the errors and ambiguities of the council, or the abuses found in the New Mass, or the latest act of sacrilegious worship at the Vatican. Their simple solution is to say the Pope is not the Pope and the Church is not the Church.

But, as we explained in the Preface, their apparent difficulty is borne from their false Major Premise, that whatever comes from a true Pope must be true and good, because "the Pope is infallible." As we've seen, the Major Premise is faulty and incomplete, since the Pope is infallible only when he meets some very specific conditions. When he does not meet these conditions, the Pope *can* allow error and evil to afflict the Mystical Body - just as God allowed the Passion of Christ, and just as He has allowed errors and evils to afflict the Church during other times of crisis (as in the cases of Popes Liberius, Honorius, John XXII - and, now, the conciliar Popes).

It is also clear to us that the rotten fruits are qualitatively *worse* within Sedevacantism than among those Traditional Catholics who have remained within the Church, since Sedevacantists suffer dark, spiritual disorders (which they themselves admit) which are *directly attributable* to their affiliation with the sect (not to mention their objectively worse condition of being separated from the Church, and the ordinary means of grace). And these rotten fruits cannot be attributed simply to the sect attracting unbalanced souls. The authors of this book, along with many others, have personally witnessed individuals (priests and laymen) who, after embracing the sect, undergo what appears to be a personality transformation for the worse. From kind and humble, they become bitter, obnoxious and proud. It is a strange phenomenon, but one that seems consistent with what Martin Luther complained about in his followers.

These disorders, combined with a loss of faith in the Church, ultimately lead to a loss of hope and despair, which St. Thomas says is "the origin of other sins" and "a most grievous sin" in itself.[54] St. Thomas also says that "despair is born of sloth," which explains why those who are looking for easy answers and for a simple solution to explain the present crisis often fall into the error of Sedevacantism.[55] Indeed, looking for a simple way to rationalize the current crisis, many Sedevacantists have actually despaired in the process, which is the consequence of rejecting the Church of Jesus Christ. They fall into despair by believing that the visible society of the Church has defected, and seeing no way for the Church to get a new Pope, except through a divine intervention from Heaven.

Unfortunately, the overwhelming majority of those who go down the road of Sedevacantism do not return to the Church. While Protestant conversions to the Church happen daily (since most of these people did not leave the Church, but grew up in a non-Catholic sect), when is the last time you heard of a Sedevacantist renouncing his error and returning to "the Vatican II Church"? It is much rarer. As with other religious cults, members remain "stuck in the rut" (to use Fr. Cekada's terminology) of Sedevacantism, due to family relationships, peer pressure, fear, intellectual pride, mind control, threats, domineering pastors, and other such reasons which are inherent in all cults.

Those who are particularly hardened in their position are the Sedevacantist apologists, who have publicly sold out for the position, and would "lose face" before their followers and benefactors if they converted. This is especially the case for those who make a living by promoting Sedevacantism, such as the Dimond brothers, as well as Fr.

---

[54] ST, II-II, q. 20, a. 1 and 3.
[55] ST, II-II, q. 20, a. 4.

Cekada and Bishop Dolan (not to mention all the clergy of the S.S.P.V. and C.M.R.I., and similar groups). This is yet another evil fruit of the Sedevacantist tree.

While the Church after Vatican II has produced good and bad fruits, they have *both* grown together *within* the field of the Church. The devil sows the cockle in an effort to root up the wheat, and yet God, to test and purify our faith, "suffers both to grow until the harvest" (Mt. 13:30). The devil is the author of Sedevacantism; for while Christ wills these souls to remain in the Church until harvest, the devil leads them out of the battlefield of the Church, and into his kingdom of false comforts and security, and, ultimately, into spiritual disorder and suffering, which explains why, to use the words of John Lane, "Sedevacantism is *so often concommitant with spiritual maladies.*" These souls have not only lost faith in the Church, but in God Himself, who remains in charge of the Church, and whose ways are not our ways. Indeed, as Fr. O'Reilly reminded us, we are never to presume the limits of what God wills to permit His Church to suffer. The promise is not that the Church will not undergo tremendous trials, but rather that "the gates of hell shall not prevail against it."

Like Our Lady and St. John the Apostle, we must stand at the foot of the cross of our suffering Church, and resist those who afflict her, even if it's the Pope; remembering that the Pope is not Jesus Christ, but only His Vicar, and it is possible for him to depart from Christ and lead souls astray (as we saw, for example, with John XXII) when he does not bind or loose. As Catholics, we are able to discern tradition from novelty, good from evil, light from darkness, wheat from cockle – all by the light of faith. This is why St. Paul admonished us to "hold fast to tradition" (2Thess. 2:14), and why the Council of Trent said that by the dogmatic teachings of the Church, "all, making use of the rule of faith, with the assistance of Christ, may be able to recognize more easily the Catholic truth in the midst of the darkness of so many errors." [56]

We conclude this book by returning to what we discussed in Chapter 1, namely, that the explanation for the current crisis is not that we have no Pope, or that the Church morphed into a New Church. Rather, the explanation is that God is permitting His Church – the Mystical Body of Christ - to undergo a Passion similar to what Christ Himself – the Head of the Church – experienced. Just before Our Lord's Passion, He warned his Apostles: "All you shall be scandalized in me this night. For it is written: I will strike the shepherd, and the sheep of the flock shall be dispersed" (Mt. 26:31). This prophecy proved true, for

---

[56] Pope Pius IV, *Council of Trent*, Sess. 13, Chap. 4 (emphasis added).

the Passion of Christ was so devastating that the Apostles themselves –
three of whom had just witnessed the Transfiguration - lost their faith
in Christ. Today, as the Mystical Body of Christ is following Christ
through a similar Passion, it should be no surprise that many
scandalized souls are losing their faith in the Church, *and this for the
same reason*: God has struck the shepherds (especially the Vatican II
Popes), and thus many sheep of the flock (Sedevacantists) have left the
fold.

The Passion of Our Lord not only caused the Apostles to lose faith
in Christ, but also resulted in later heresies concerning the nature of
Christ. These heresies were borne from the erroneous notion that God
Incarnate could not suffer such things, just as the Sedevacantists
believe it is "impossible" for the Church to suffer its Passion. This error
resulted in two opposite heresies: one which maintained that Christ
was not God (Arianism); the other which held that Christ's human
nature, and therefore His human sufferings, were merely an illusion
(Docetism). But the mystery of the divine suffering of Christ was real.
Christ, who suffered such things, was truly a Divine Person and He
possessed a real human nature. His human nature (body and soul),
hypostatically united to the Word of God, truly suffered an
excruciating Passion and death. On Calvary all appeared lost, but we
now know that Our Lord's Passion and death was followed by His
glorious resurrection, which resulted in a restoration of the spiritual
order.

Not only is the Church today following our Lord through His
Passion, but if we consider the mystery at a deeper level, we can even
discern a mystical death taking place. How can the Church experience
death? Death occurs when the body separates from the soul. Now, for
those with eyes to see, it is clear that the Church is enduring precisely
this mystical form of death, as the Body of the Church (the visible
social unit) is separating from the Soul (the Holy Ghost). This occurs as
more and more members of the visible Church lose their interior virtue
of faith, thereby severing themselves from the Soul of the Church. But
just as Our Lord's body remained the true Body of Christ -
hypostatically united to the Word of God - even after it experienced the
separation from His soul following His death on the Cross, so too the
Church today remains the true Mystical Body of Jesus Christ, even as it
experiences the separation of its body and soul during its mystical
Passion. But this Passion and mystical death of the Church will be
followed by a resurrection of the Mystical Body, which will restore the
temporal order (just as the Passion of Christ restored the spiritual
order). This "restoration of all things in Christ" (which was the motto

of St. Pius X) will follow the papal Consecration of Russia to the Immaculate Heart of Mary, and bring about the long-prophesied Age of Peace. In the meantime, let us fulfill God's will as we commend ourselves to the care of His Most Sorrowful Mother, by remaining faithful to Christ and His Church, deviating neither to the Left, nor to the Right.

O Virgin Mary, Conqueror of All Heresies, pray for us.

St. Michael the Archangel, pray for us.

Sts. Peter and Paul, pray for us.

St. Thomas Aquinas, pray for us.

St. Robert Bellarmine, pray for us.

St. Pius V, pray for us.

St. Pius X, pray for us.

Appendix Chart -
Theological Opinions on Loss of Office for a Heretical Pope
(See Chapters 9-11)

Proposition/Opinion	Bellarmine	Suarez	Cajetan	John of St. Thomas
Warnings necessary?	**Yes**[1]	**Yes**[2]	**Yes**[3]	**Yes**[4]
Church establishes the crime?	**Yes**[5]	**Yes**[6]	**Yes**[7]	**Yes**[8]
Declaratory sentence of the crime?	**Probable**[9]	**Yes**[10]	**Yes**[11]	**Yes**[12]
Pope loses his office *ipso facto* after crime established: (Pope separates from Church)?	**Yes**[13]	**Yes**[14]	**No**	**No**
Pope loses his office upon *Vitandus* – "must be avoided" – declaration: (Church separates from Pope)?	**No**	**No**	**Yes**[15]	**Yes**[16]
Human punishment?	**Yes**[17]	**Yes**[18]	**Yes**	**Yes**

---

[1] "A heretic is to be avoided after two warnings" (*De Romano Pontifice*, bk. 2, ch. 30).

[2] "It also seems to be the true opinion… that the [heretic] Pope must be admonished… 'A heretic, after the first and second warning is avoided.'" (*De Fide, disp.* X, sect. VI, n. 11).

[3] "After two admonitions." (*De Comparatione Auct.*, pp. 102-103).

[4] After "the first and second correction." (*Cursus Theologici*, p. 133).

[5] The Church can judge a heretical Pope - Third Opinion. (See *De Romano Pontifice*, bk. 2, ch. 30). Proper authorities must depose. (See *De Membris Ecclesiae*, pp. 428-429).

[6] The Church "declares him a heretic." (*De Fide, Disp.* 10, Sect 6, n. 10, p. 317).

[7] The Church "judges as incorrigible." (*De Comparatione Auct.*, pp. 102-103).

[8] "…with the Church's authority." (*Cursus Theologici*, p. 139).

[9] Although, Bellarmine does not directly address it in *De Romano Pontifice*, John of St. Thomas confirmed that he required a declaration, and Suarez said it was the "common opinion" in his day. Further, Cardinal Journet stated that Bellarmine and Suarez held the same opinion.

[10] The Church "would declare him a heretic … he would then *ipso facto* and immediately be deposed by Christ." (*De Fide*, Disp. 10, Sect. 6, n. 10, p. 317).

[11] "…judged to deserve expulsion as incorrigible." (*De Comparatione Auct.*, pp. 102-103).

[12] "The pontiff cannot be deposed and lose the pontificate except if two conditions are fulfilled … that the heresy is … *public* and *legally notorious* [declared]" (*Cursus Theologici*).

[13] "…automatically ceases to be a member of the Church." (*De Romano Pont.*, bk. 2, ch. 30).

[14] "…*ipso facto* he is immediately deposed by Christ." (*De Fide, Disp.* 10, Sec. 6, n. 10, p. 317).

[15] In the case of heresy, the Church separates from the Pope. (*De Compar. Auct.*, p. 84).

[16] Church plays ministerial role in issuing *Vitandus* declaration. (*Cursus Theologici*, p.139).

[17] "…can be judged and punished by the Church" (*De Romano Pontifice*, bk. 2, ch. 30).

[18] "…would be able to be punished." (*De Fide*, Disp. 10, Sect 6, n. 10, p. 318).

Bibliography of Selected References

Aquinas, St. Thomas – *Summa Theologica* - Translated by Fathers of the English Dominican Province. New York: Benziger Brothers, Inc., 1947.

Aquinas, St. Thomas – *Super Epistolam ad Galatas Lectura* – in *Super Epistolas s. Pauli Lectura*. Marietti, Taurini-Romae, Vol. I, 1953.

Augustine, St. - *City of God* - Edinburgh: T&T Clark, Vol. I, 1888.

Augustine, Charles - *A Commentary of Canon Law* - Vol. VIII, bk. 4, St. Louis: Herder Book Co, 1918.

Ayrinhac, Henry - *Penal Legislation in the New Code of Canon Law* - New York, Cincinnati, Chicago: Benzinger Bros., 1920.

Ballerini, Pietro – *De Potestate Ecclesiastica Summorum Pontificum et Conciliorum Generalium* - 1st. ed. Rome, De Prop. Fidei, Romae, 1850.

Baltimore Catechism No. 3, 3rd ed. - Colorado Springs, Colorado: The Seraphim Company Inc., 1995.

Beal, John; Coriden, James; Green, Thomas - *A New Commentary on the Code of Canon Law* - New York: Paulist Press, 2000.

Bellarmine, St. Robert – *De Ecclesia Militante* – Opera Omnia, Battezzati, Mediolani, Vol. II, 1858.

Bellarmine, St. Robert – *De Membris Ecclesiae* - bk. I, *De Clericis*, Opera Omnia, Paris, Vivès, 1870.

Bellarmine, St. Robert – *De Romano Pontifice* – Opera Omnia, Battezzati, Mediolani, Vol. I, 1857.

Berry, Sylvester – *The Church of Christ* - Eugene, Oregon: Wipf and Stock Publishers, 2009, previously published by Mount Saint Mary's Seminary, 1955.

Bettenson, H. - *Documents of the Christian Church* - Oxford, London, Glasgow: Oxford University Press, 2nd ed, 1963.

685

Billot, Louis – *De Ecclesiae Sacramentis* – Typ. Pont. Inst. Pii IX, Romae, tom. I, 1914.

Billot, Louis – *Tractatus de Ecclesia Christi* – Gregoriana, Roma, 1921, tom. I.

Bligh, John - *Ordination to the Priesthood* - New York: Sheed and Ward, 1956.

Bouix, Dominique – *Tractatus de Iure Liturgico* – Ruffet, Parisiis, 1873.

Bouix, Dominique – *Tractatus de Papa* – Lecoffre, Parisiis-Lugduni, tom. II, 1869.

Bruno of Signi, St. – Letter to Paschal II – PL 163, 463.

Burns, J. H.; Izbicki, Thomas - *Conciliarism & Papalism* - New York: Cambridge University Press, 1997.

Butler, Cuthbert - *The Vatican Council, 1869-1870* - London: Collin and Harvill Press, 1962.

Cabié, Robert - *The Church at Prayers: The Sacraments*, Vol. III - Collegevile, Minnesota: Liturgical Press, 1988.

Cajetan, Thomas de Vio – Commentary on the "Summa Theologica" II - II – in *Sancti Thomae Aquinatis (...)* Opera Omnia, editio leonina, Polyglotta, Romae, 1895.

Cajetan, Thomas de Vio – *De Comparatione Auctoritatis Papae et Concilii*, English Translation in *Conciliarism & Papalism*, by Burns & Izbicki, New York: Cambridge University Press, 1997.

Callan, Charles - *Illustrations for Sermons and Instructions* - New York: Joseph Wagner, 1916.

Catechism of the Council of Trent - Rockford, Illinois: TAN Books and Publishers, Inc., 1982.

Catechism of the Council of Trent - South Bend, Indiana: Marian Publications, Third Printing, 1976.

Catechism of St. Pius X – Australia: Instauratio Press, 1993.

Catholic Encyclopedia – New York: Encyclopedia Press, 1913.

Cekada, Anthony - *Work of Human Hands* - West Chester, Ohio: Philothea Press, 2010.

Chapman, John - *The Condemnation of Pope Honorius* – London: Catholic Truth Society, 1907.

Code of Canon Law: Latin-English Edition – Canon Law Society of America (1st edition), 1983.

Coomaraswamy, Rama - *The Destruction of the Christian Tradition* - Bloomington, Indiana: World Wisdom, Inc., 2006.

Coronata, Mattheus Conte a - *Institutiones Iuris Canonici*, Rome: Marietti, 1950.

Coronata, Mattheus Conte a – *Tractatus Postumus* (Liège, 1677), Tract I, Chapter XXI, translated by Br. Alexis Bugnolo.

Correa de Oliveira, Plinio – *Baldeacao Ideologica Inadvertida e Dialogo* - Vera Cruz, Sao Paulo, 4th ed., 1966.

Council of Constantinople III (VI Ecumenical) - Session XIII: Condemnation of the Monothelites and of Pope Honorius I – Denz. – Sch. 550-552.

Council of Florence (XVII Ecumenical) - *Decretum pro Armeniis*, Denz. – Sch. 1310-1328.

Council of Trent - Session XXII: Decree on the Most Holy Sacrifice of the Mass – Denz. – Sch. 1738-1759.

Council of Trent - Session XXIII: Doctrine on the Sacrament of Orders – Denz. – Sch. 1763-1778; Denz, - Umb. 956a-968.

Council of Trent - Session XXV: Decree on the Invocation, Veneration and Relics of the Saints, and on Sacred Images – Denz. – Sch. 1821-1825; Denz. – Umb.984-988.

Council of Vatican I - See: Vatican Council I.

Cox, Thomas E. - *The Pillar and Ground of Truth, a Series of Lenten Lectures on the True Church, Its Marks and Attributes* – Chicago: J. S. Hyland and Co., 1900.

Culleton, Gerald - *The Prophets and Our Times* - Rockford, Illinois: TAN Books and Publishers, Inc., 1974.

Davies, Michael - *Apologia Pro Marcel Lefebvre* - Kansas City, Missouri: Angelus Press, 1999.

Davies, Michael – *Pope John's Council* - Kansas City, Missouri: Angelus Press, 1992.

Davies, Michael – *Pope Paul's New Mass* - Kansas City, Missouri: Angelus Press, 1980; second printing, 1988.

De La Rocque, Patrick – *Pope John Paul II: Doubts About a Beatification* – Kansas City, Missouri: Angelus Press, 2012.

De Lugo, Francis – *Tractatus de Eucharistia*, in *Disputationes Scholasticae et Morales* – Vivès, Parisiis, tom. IV, 1869.

De Sales, St. Francis - *The Catholic Controversy* - Charlotte, North Carolina: TAN Books & Publishers, Inc., 1986.

De Sales, St. Francis - *The True Spiritual Conferences of St. Francis de Sales* - London: Richardson and Son, 1862.

Dear Newlyweds, Kansas City, Missouri: Sarto House, 2001.

Denzinger, Henry; Schoenmetzer, Adolf – *Enchiridion Symbolorum* – Freiburg: Herder, 1965.

Denzinger, Henry – *The Sources of Catholic Dogma* - Translated by Roy J. Deferrari; London: Herder, 1957.

Devine, Arthur - *The Creed Explained, an Exposition of Catholic Doctrine* - 2nd ed., New York, Cincinnati, Chicago: Benzinger Bros., 1897.

Diekamp, Franz; Hoffmann, Adolf M. - *Theologiae Dogmaticae Manuale* – Desclee, Parisiis – Tornaci-Romae, Vol. I, 1933: vol. II, 1933; Vol. IV, 1934.

Dimond, Michael and Peter - *The Truth About What Really Happened to the Catholic Church After Vatican II* - New York: Most Holy Family Monastery, 2007.

Dupont, Yves - *Catholic Prophecy: The Coming Chastisement* - Rockford, Illinois: Tan Books and Publishers, 1970, 1973.

Emerton, Ephraim - *The Correspondence of Pope Gregory VII* - New York; Oxford: Columbia University Press, 1932.

Fenton, Joseph - *The Catholic Church and Salvation* - New York: Seminary Press, Round Top, 2006.

Fessler, Joseph - *The True and False Infallibility of the Popes* - New York: The Catholic Publication Society, 1875.

Fortescue, Adrian – *The Greek Fathers, Their Lives and Writings* - San Francisco: Ignatius Press, 2007.

Fortescue, Adrian - *The Mass — A Study of the Roman Liturgy* - London: Longmans, Green & Co., 1950.

Gamber, Klaus - *The Reform of the Roman Liturgy: Its Problems and Background* - Fort Collins, Colorado: Roman Catholic Books, 1993.

Garrigou-Lagrange, Reginald - *The Theological Virtues: I On Faith* - St. Louis & London: Herder Book Co, 1964, originally published by Torino, Italy: Robert Berruti & Co., 1949.

Gaudron, Matthias - *The Catechism of the Crisis in the Church* - Kansas City, Missouri: Angelus Press, 2010.

Gibson, Edmund - *A Preservative Against Popery* - Vol. I, London, 1738.

Gratian - *Decretum* – in *Corpus Iuris Canonici* – Leipzig, 1879.

Gury, Jean-Pierre - *Compendium Theologiae Moralis* – Civiltà Catt., Romae; Marietti, Taurini; tom. I, 1866.

Heenan, John - *Council and Clergy* - London, G. Chapman, 1966.

Hermann, R. P. - *Theologiæ Dogmaticæ Institutiones* – Rome: Pacis Philippi Cuggiani, 1897.

Hervé, J. M. – *Manuale Theologiae Dogmaticae* – Berche et Pagis, Parisiis, vol. I, 1952; vol. III, 1953.

Higden, Ranulf - *Polychronicon Ranulphi Higden Monachi Cestrensis* - vol. 5, London: Longman, 1865.

Horner, George, - *The Statues of the Apostles or Canones Ecclesiastici* – London: Williams & Norgate, 1904.

Innocent III - *Between God and Man: Sermons of Pope Innocent III* - Catholic University of America Press, 2004.

Iragui, Sirapino de - *Manuale Theologiae Dogmaticae* - Madrid: Ediciones Studium, 1959.

Jerome, St. – *Expos. in Epist. ad Titum* - c. III, v. 11 – PL 26, 598, apud Congar, article "Schisme."

John of St. Thomas - *Cursus Theologici* II-II, *De Auctoritate Summi Pontificis*, Disp. VIII, Art. III., 1663.

Journet, Charles – *The Church of the Word Incarnate* - London and New York: Sheed and Ward, 1955.

Jurgens, William A – *The Faith of the Early Fathers* - vol. 2, Collegeville, Minnesota: Liturgical Press, 1979.

Kramer, Paul – *The Suicide of Altering the Faith in the Liturgy* - Terryville, Connecticut: The Missionary Association, 2006.

Koch, Anton - *Handbook of Moral Theology* - London: B. Herder Book Co, 1918.

Lapide, Cornelius a – *Commentaria in Scripturam Sacram* – Vivès, Parisiis, im Mat., tomus XV, 1877; ad Gel., tom. XVIII, 1876.

Laymann, Paul – *Theologia Moralis* – Maldura, Venetiis, 1700.

Lefebvre, Marcel – *Open Letter to Confused Catholics* - Kansas City, Missouri: Angelus Press, 1992.

Liguori, St. Alphonsus - *The History of Heresies, and Their Refutation* - vol. I, Dublin: Published by James Duffy, Wellington Qua, 1847.

Liguori, St. Alponsus – *Oeuvres Dogmatiques*, trad. Vidal-Delalle-Bousquet – Parent-Desbarres, Paris, 1836.

Liguori, St. Alphonsus – *Verita della Fede – Opera de S. Alfonso Maria de Liguori*, Marietti, Torino, 1887, vol. VIII.

Logan, Donald, *Excommunication and the Secular Arm in Medieval England: A Study in Legal Procedure From the Thirteenth to the Sixteenth Century* - Pontifical Institute of Medieval Studies, 1968.

Lyons, Daniel - *Christianity and Infallibility* - New York: Longmans, Green & Co, 1892.

Mann, Horace, *Lives of the Pope* – London: K. Paul, Trench, Trübner, & Co., ltd, Vol. VIII, 1902.

Mansi, Giovanni - *Sacrorum Conciliorum nova collectio amplissima* - Venice, 1771, vol. 16, col. 126.

Mazzella, C. - *De Religione et Ecclesia* - Sixth Edition, Prati: Giachetti, filii et soc., 1905.

Merkelbach, Benedict – *Summa Theologiae Moralis* – Desclée, Parisiis, tom. I, 1931.

McHugh, John; Callan, Charles - *Moral Theology* – New York: J. Wagner, 1958.

Nau, Dom Paul – *Pope or Church? The Infallibility of the Church's Ordinary Magisterium* - Kansas City, Missouri: Angelus Press, 1998.

Newman, John Henry - *A Letter Addressed to His Grace, The Duke of Norfolk* - London: Pickering and Co., 1875.

Newman, John Henry - *Arians of the 4th Century* - London: Pickering and Co., 1883.

O'Brien, Darcy - *The Hidden Pope* - New York: Daybreak Books, 1998.

O'Connor, James - *The Gift of Infallibility* - San Francisco: Ignatius Press, 1986.

O'Hare, Patrick - *The Facts About Luther* - New York, Cincinnati: Frederick Pustet & Co., 1916.

O'Reilly, Edmund - *The Relations of the Church to Society – Theological Essays* - London: John Hodges, 1892.

Parsons, Reuben - *Studies in Church History* - Vol. II, Philadelphia: John Joseph McVey, 1900.

Penido, M. Teixeira-Leite – *O Misterio dos Sacramentos* – Vozes, Petropolis, 1961.

Pesch, Christian – *Compendium Theologiae Dogmaticae* – Herder, Friburgi Brisgoviae, tomus I, 1921.

Pesch, Christian – *Praelectiones Dogmaticae* – Herder, Friburgi Brisgoviae, tom. I, 1898; tom. VI. 1900; tom. IX, 1899.

Pighi, Albert – *Hierarchiae Ecclesiasticae Assertio* – bk. IV, c. VIII, Vol. CXXXI ff., Cologne, 1538, apud Dublanchy, article "Infaillibilité du Pape," D. T. C., vol. 1715.

Ratzinger, Joseph - *Introduction to Christianity* - San Francisco: Ignatius Press, 2004.

Ratzinger, Joseph - *Principles of Catholic Theology* - San Francisco: Ignatius Press, 1987.

Ratzinger, Joseph - *Theological Highlights of Vatican II* - New York: Paulist Press, 1966.

Riley, Lawrence - *The History, Nature and Use of Epikeia in Moral Theology* - Washington, D.C.: Catholic University of America Press, 1948.

Roberts, Marshall - *Catechism of Pope St. Pius X* - Winchester, Virginia: St. Michael Press, 2010.

Ryan, Christopher, *The Religious Role of The Papacy: Ideals and Realities, 1150-1300* - Toronto, Ontario Canada: Pontifical Institute of Mediaeval Studies, 1989.

Sale, George; Psalmanazar, George; Bower, Archibald; Shelvocke, George; Campbell, John; Swinton, John - *An Universal History: From The Earliest Accounts To The Present Time*, Vol. XXV, London: Miller, John Rivington, S. Crowder, 1761.

Salaverri, Joachim – *De Ecclesia Christi* – in *Sacrae Theologiae Summa* B.A.C., Matriti, vol. I, 1958.

Salza, John – *A Catechism on Fatima – and the Related Crisis in the Church* - North Prairie, Wisconsin: John Salza Productions, 2015.

Salza, John – *The Biblical Basis for the Papacy* - Huntington, Indiana: Our Sunday Visitor, 2007.

Salza, John - *The Mystery of Predestination – According to Scripture, the Church and St. Thomas Aquinas* - Charlotte, North Carolina: TAN Books and Publishers, Inc., 2010.

Schaff, Philip - *A Select Library of the Nicene and Post-Nicene Fathers of the Christian Church* – Vol. I, New York: Charles Scribner and Son's, 1907.

Schmitt, Edm. J. P. - *Dismas, The Good Thief* - 2nd ed., Cincinnati, Ohio: Rosenthal & Co., 1892.

Silveira, Arnaldo Vidigal Xavier da – *Part II, Theological Hypothesis of a Heretic Pope* – Translated by John Russell Spann, http://www.traditioninaction.org/Questions/WebSources/B_612_AX-English.pdf.

Smith, Sebastian - *Elements of Ecclesiastical Law* - New York: Benzinger Brothers, 1881.

Soto, Domingo – *Commentarium Fratris Dominici Soto Segobiensis (…) in Quartum Sententiarum* – Salmanticae, 1561.

Speray, Steven - *Papal Anomalies and Their Implications* - Second ed., Versailles, Kentucky: Confiteor, 2011.

Straub, Antonius – *De Ecclesia Christi* – Pustet, Oeniponte, vol. II, 1912.

Stevenson, Francis Seymour - *Robert Grosseteste, Bishop of Lincoln; a contribution to the religious, political and intellectual history of the thirteenth century* - London: MacMillan and Co., Limited, 1899.

Suarez, Francisco – *De Caritate* – *Opera Omnia*, Vivès, Parisiis, tom. XII, 1858.

Suarez, Francisco – *De Fide* – *Opera Omnia*, Vivès, Parisiis, tom. XII, 1858.

Sylvain, Charles - *The Life of Rev. Father Hermann, In Religion Augustin-Marie of the Most Holy Sacrament, Discalced Carmelite* – Paris, Oudin, 1883.

Sylvius, Francisco – *Commentarium in Totam II-II S. Thomae Aquinatis* – Verdussen, Antuerpiae, 1697.

Tanquerey, Adolphe - *A Manual of Dogmatic Theology* - Vol. II, New York; Tournai; Paris; Rome: Desclee Company, 1959.

The 1917 Pio-Benedictine Code of Canon Law – Edward N. Peters, Curator, San Francisco: Ignatius Press, 2001.

The Canons and Decrees of the Sacred Oecumenical Council of Trent - Edited and translated by J. Waterworth, London: Dolman, 1848.

The Companion to the Catechism of the Catholic Church - San Francisco, California: Ignatius Press, 1995.

The Popes Against Modern Errors - 16 Papal Encyclicals, Rockford, Illinois: TAN Books and Publishers, Inc., 1999.

The Seven Ecumenical Councils of the Church – Vol. XIV, Henry Percival ed., Oxford: James Parker and Company, 1900.

Tierney, Brian - *The Crisis of Church and State* - Englewood Cliffs, New Jersey: Prentice-Hall, 1964.

Torquemada, Juan de – *Summa de Ecclesia* – Tramezinus, Venetiis, 1561.

Treatise of Benedict XIV, Vol. III, London: Thomas Richardson and Son, 1882.

Turberville, Henry - *An Abridgment of the Christian Doctrine* - NewYork: Excelsior Catholic Publishing House, 1833.

Van der Veer, Peter - *Conversion to Modernities: The Globalization of Christianity* - London: Routledge, 1996.

Van Noort, Gerard - *Christ's Church* - Westminster, Maryland: Newman Press, 1961.

Van Noort, Gerard - *The Sources of Revelation* - Westminster, Maryland: Newman Press, 1961.

Van Ott, Ludwig - *Fundamentals of Catholic Dogma* - Fourth Edition, May 1960, Rockford, Illinois: TAN Books and Publishers, 1974.

Vasquez, Gabriel – *De Eucharistia – Commentariorum ac Disputationum in Tertiam Partem Sancti Thomae Tomus Tartinua* – Pillehote, Lugduni, 1620.

Vatican Council I – Dogmatic Constitution *Dei Filius* on the Catholic Faith – Denz.-Sch. 3000-3045.

Vatican Council I – Dogmatic Constitution *Pastor Aeternus* on the Church – Denz.-Sch. 3050-3075.

Vatican Council II - Documents of Vatican II - edited by Walter M. Abbot, New York: American Press, 1966.

Vermeersch, Arthur; Creusen, Ios. – *Epitome Iuris Canonici* – Dessain, Mechliniae-Romae, tom. I, 1949; tom. II, 1940; tom. III, 1946.

Vigue, Paul – *Ecclesia* - edited by Agrain; Paris: Bloud et Gay, 1933.

Vincent of Lerins, St. - *The Commonitorium of Vincent of Lerins*, taken from Bettenson, Henry, Documents of the Christian Church – second edition, Oxford; London; Glasgow: Oxford University Press, 1963.

Vitoria, Francisco de – *Obras de Francisco de Vitoria* – Madrid: B.A.C., 1960.

Von Döllinger, Johann Joseph Ignaz - *The Pope and the Council* – London; Oxford; Cambridge: Rivingtons, 1869.

Von Hefele, Charles - *A History of the Councils of the Church, from the Original Documents* - vol. V, Edinburgh: T&T Clark, 1896.

Walsh, William Thomas - *The Saints in Action* - New York: Hanover, 1961.

Wathen, James - *The Great Sacrilege* - Rockford, Illinois: TAN Books and Publishers, 1971.

Weigel, George - *Witness to Hope* - New York: Harper Collins, 1999.

Wernz, F.; Vidal, P. – *Ius Canonicum* – Gregoriana, Romae, tom. I, 1938; tom. II, 1923.

Wilhelm, Joseph; Scannell, Thomas - *A Manual of Catholic Theology* - Vol. I, 3rd ed., New York; Cincinnati; Chicago: Benzinger Brothers, 1906.

Wilks, G.A.F. - *The Popes: An Historical Study, from Linus to Pius IX* - London: Francis and John Rivington, St. Paul's Churchyard and Waterloo Place, 1851.

Woodward, Kenneth L. - *Making Saints: How the Catholic Church Determines Who Becomes a Saint, Who Doesn't, and Why* - New York: Simon and Schuster, 1990.

Woywod, Stanislaus - *A Practical Commentary on the Code of Canon Law* - New York: Joseph F. Wagner, 1943.

Zaccaria, Franceso Antonio – *De Usu Librorum Liturgicorum in Rebus Theologicis* – in *Theologiae Cursus Completus*, Migne, Parisiis, tom. V., 1860 cols. 207-310.

Zalba, Marcellino – *Theologiae Moralis Compendium* – 2 vols., Matriti: B.A.C., 1958.

Selected Articles by the Authors

Salza, John - "Can Vatican II's Teaching on Religious Liberty Be Reconciled with Tradition?" - *The Remnant* newspaper, November 15, 2009.

"John Salza vs. Father Brian Harrison on Religious Liberty" - *The Remnant* newspaper, March 31, 2010; April 20, 2010; April 30, 2010; and May 15, 2010).

Salza, John – "The Errors of Sedevacantism and Ecclesiastical Law" – *The Remnant* newspaper, June 2010.

"John Salza Responds to the Lies, Errors and Hypocrisy of Sedevacantist Peter Dimond" - http://www.johnsalza.com, 2010.

Salza, John - "Sedevacantism and the Sin of Presumption" - *Catholic Family News*, April 2011.

Salza, John - "The *Novus Ordo* Mass and Divine Law" - *Catholic Family News*, November 2012.

Salza, John – "Freemasonry, Vatican II and 1960" – Rome, May 13, 2011, http://www.johnsalza.com.

Salza, John – "Baptism of Desire: Fact or Fiction?" – *The Remnant* newspaper, July 2013.

Salza, John - "The Implications of the *Novus Ordo* as a New Rite of Mass" - *The Remnant* newspaper, August 2013.

"John Salza vs. Father Harrison on the New Mass" - *The Remnant* newspaper, September 2013.

Salza, John – "Pope Francis, Archbishop Lefebvre and Sedevacantism" – *Catholic Family News*, February 2014.

"John Salza vs. Fr. Brian Harrison on the Canonizations of John XXIII and John Paul II" – *The Remnant* newspaper, July 15, 2014.

Salza, John - "Who is a Member of the Church?" - *The Remnant* newspaper, Three-Part Feature, September-October, 2014.

Salza, John – "Bellarmine Against Suarez? Another Critical Error in the Sedevacantist Thesis" – *The Remnant* newspaper, November 2014.

"John Salza vs. *Novus Ordo* Apologist on Religious Liberty" – http://www.johnsalza.com, 2014.

Salza, John – "The Chair is Empty? Says Who? John Salza Responds to NovusOrdoWatch" – http://www.johnsalza.com, 2014.

"John Salza Responds to Another Sedevacantist," http://www.johnsalza.com, March 2015.

Salza, John - "The Conciliar Church of Freemasonry," Society of St. Pius X Seminary, Winona, Minnesota, March 25, 2015, http://www.johnsalza.com.

Salza, John - "Questioning the Validity of the Canonizations: Against a Fact There is No Argument" - *The Remnant* newspaper, May 15, 2014.

Salza, John - "Apocalypse 12 and the Masonic Infiltration of the Church," *Catholic Family News* conference, May 30, 2015, http://www.johnsalza.com.

Salza, John – "Sedevacantism and Pius XII's Liturgical Reforms" – *The Remnant* newspaper, August 15 and 31, 2015.

Siscoe, Robert – "Modernism: The Synthesis of all Heresies" – *Catholic Family News*, October 2012.

Siscoe, Robert – "Who was Paul VI? A review of Msgr. Villa's Paul VI Beatified?" – *Catholic Family News*, February 2013.

Siscoe, Robert – "A Bishop Dressed in White" – *The Remnant* newspaper" – March 2013.

Siscoe, Robert – "Sedevacantism and the Manifest Heretic" (Parts I through IV) – *The Remnant* newspaper, April - June 2013.

Siscoe, Robert – "The Unholy Trinity of Modern Errors: Naturalism, Rationalism and Modernism" – *Catholic Family News*, June 2013.

Siscoe, Robert – "The Unholy Trinity and the New World Order" – *Catholic Family News*, July 2013.

Siscoe, Robert – "The History of Apostasy and the Third Secret of Fatima" –*The Remnant* newspaper, August 2013.

Siscoe, Robert – "Papal Infallibility and Its Limitations" – *The Remnant* newspaper, October 2013.

Siscoe, Robert – "Is the Old Covenant still Valid?" – *The Remnant* newspaper – December 2013.

Siscoe, Robert – "Bellarmine and Suarez on The Question of a Heretical Pope" – *Catholic Family News*, April 2014.

Siscoe, Robert – "Was Vatican II Infallible? Part I" – *Catholic Family News*, June 2014.

Siscoe, Robert – "Was Vatican II Infallible? Part II" – *Catholic Family News*, July 2014.

Siscoe, Robert – "In a Papal Diarchy, Which Half is Infallible?" – *The Remnant* newspaper, July 2014.

Siscoe, Robert – "Can the Church Depose a Heretical Pope?" – *The Remnant* newspaper, November 2014.

Siscoe, Robert – "Can We Recognize and Resist?" – *Catholic Family News*, January 2015.

Siscoe, Robert – "Answering a Sedevacantist Critic" – *The Remnant* newspaper, March 2015.

Siscoe, Robert – "Deposing a Pope," Part I – *Catholic Family News*, July 2015.

Siscoe, Robert – "Deposing a Pope," Part II – *Catholic Family News*, August 2015.

Index of
Selected Persons and Topics

True or False Pope?

Infallibility
  -conciliar, 409-416
  -disciplinary, 461-470
  -general, 31
  -"Monolithic," 416-421, 460, 478, 481, 671
  -objects of, 201-202, 379-381, 446-449, 469-475
  -Ordinary and Universal Magisterium, 409, 435-446
  -papal, 3-4, 198-205, 224-227

Innocent III, Pope, 123-124, 191-195, 198, 239, 263, 264, 333-334, 561, 651

Invincible ignorance, 102, 116-118, 142

Interregnums, 22, 67, 386-387

J

John XXII, 193, 206-213

John XXIII, 1, 31, 36-37, 41-42, 59, 68, 208, 372-373, 432, 479, 529

John Paul II
  -canonization of, 529-532
  -changed canonization process, 525-528
  -interreligious worship, 10-11, 163
  -novel teachings, 185-186

John of St. Thomas
  -answers objections of Bellarmine and Suarez, 365-368
  -Bellarmine and Suarez had

same opinion, 273-274
  -Church must declare papal heresy, 156-158, 240-243, 245-249, 265, 273, 299, 336, 338, 345-346
  -explanation of how heretical Pope loses office, 351-356, 358-359
  -opinion same as Cajetan, 345, 358-359

Journet, Cardinal Charles 58, 274-277, 302, 352, 364, 385, 438, 467-468, 470, 472-474

Jurisdiction
  -general, 60-68
  -bishops receive from Pope, 65
  -ordinary will always exist, 66-68
  -supplied, 74-75
  -loss of faith no effect on, 144-145

K

Kelly, Bishop Clarence, 8, 612-616, 618, 660

L

Lane, John
  -accuses Suarez of heresy, 301
  -admits Paul VI did not promulgate New Mass, 504, 506-507
  -admits Sedevacantism is possibly wrong, 70
  -admits spiritual disorders within Sedevacantism, 210, 654-655
  -assumes pertinacity based

706